NATURAL SELECTION

AND

SOCIAL BEHAVIOR

NATURAL SELECTION
AND
SOCIAL BEHAVIOR

Recent Research and New Theory

Edited by

RICHARD D. ALEXANDER AND DONALD W. TINKLE

University of Michigan
Ann Arbor

CHIRON  PRESS

INCORPORATED

New York & Concord

Distributed Outside North America
by
BLACKWELL SCIENTIFIC PUBLICATIONS
Oxford   London   Edinburgh   Melbourne

Sales: Chiron Press, Incorporated
            Publishers Storage & Shipping Corp.
            2352 Main Street
            Concord, Massachusetts 01742

Editorial: Chiron Press, Incorporated
            24 West 96th Street
            New York, New York 10025

Distributed throughout the World excluding North America by:
            Blackwell Scientific Publications
            Osney Mead, Oxford OX2 OEL
            8 John Street, London WC1N 2ES
            9 Forrest Road, Edinburgh EH1 2QH
            214 Berkeley Street, Carlton, Victoria 3053, Australia

Library of Congress Catalogue Card Number 80-65758

ISBN 0-913462-08-X   Blackwell ISBN 0-632-00624-2

First Printing

This volume is dedicated to George C. Williams, whose pioneering efforts to return our attention to the crucial question of what are the units of selection and whose ideas regarding that crucial question, applied to such areas of research as senescence, sterile castes in the social insects, reproductive effort, sexuality, sex ratios, among many others, in large part fostered the revolution responsible for the research presented here.

In Memorium Donald W. Tinkle, 1930–1980

I

Donald W. Tinkle passed away on February 21, 1980. Without his efforts this volume would not have appeared. He was largely responsible for the symposium from which it derived, and he read and criticized carefully all of the chapters. As the authors themselves know, his unusual intelligence and perspicacity are reflected in the structure of many arguments throughout the book. His excellence in field research, teaching, and administration also affected in more direct ways, and sometimes profoundly, the lives of most of the authors represented here.

RDA

II

Our acquaintance with Donald Tinkle was unhappily brief and all too slight. We knew, of course, that he was a distinguished biologist, with a broad knowledge of evolution and an outstanding ability to devise experimental measurements of ecological theory. We also knew his reputation for being a gifted and imaginative administrator and a superb teacher. Our lasting impressions of him are his keen perception and intelligence and his open and generous spirit.

Since his death, we have talked about him with several of his students and friends. From knowledge of him far greater than ours, they bear multiple witness to these qualities. As a scientist, Donald Tinkle was highly productive, publishing some eighty papers and leaving more than a dozen manuscripts. He had a reverence for the classics and an understanding of what was important historically. In his thirties and forties, he displayed a willingness to go on learning new techniques and the capacity to master them. He was a well-rounded critic of both science and writing, and though unyielding, his criticism was inevitably friendly and constructive.

The quality of friendliness particularly impressed his students, to whom his door was always open. He seems to have given them the impression that he was learning from them, that he was their guide but they were his equals. He was absolutely lacking in pettiness and was absolutely fair. It all seems to have worked. One cannot fail to be struck by the excellence of his students. They may be his most remarkable legacy.

The Publisher

Contents

Part Seven   HUMANS

Introduction

This volume results from a symposium held at The University of Michigan, Ann Arbor, in October of 1978 and sponsored by the National Science Foundation. The papers included were, for the most part, presented at the symposium, though a few additional ones were requested for the publication.

The occasion for the symposium was the fiftieth anniversary of the University of Michigan Museum of Zoology in its present structure. It seemed to us that no better commemoration could be planned than a general discussion of the questions raised by the revolution in evolutionary biology that has occurred during the past two decades. The part of that revolution currently attracting the most attention concerns the evolutionary basis of social behavior in all parts of the animal kingdom—hence the title of the symposium and of this volume.

Museums have always played a special role in the nurture of evolutionary biology, and so it is not surprising that most of the participants in this symposium are now, or have been in the past, associated with such institutions. We are pleased that about half of the contributing authors have direct connections to the University of Michigan Museum of Zoology.

In planning the symposium we were particularly interested in including field studies designed to test significant predictions from recent new theory about the evolution of social behavior. As the list of authors demonstrates, such studies—as well as important theoretical contributions—are often the work of young investigators.

We believe that the papers included here represent most of the topics that have sparked the recent interest in behavioral evolution. Read in sequence, the papers provide an excellent overview of current research and theory. Differences of opinion and approach are obvious and are often provocative and stimulating. We have not tried to eliminate such differences, feeling instead that each paper should stand on its own merits. We also believe that this is the first major volume of original papers devoted almost wholly to research stimulated principally by George C. Williams and William D. Hamilton, who stressed two main ideas: first, it is valuable to identify the level (gene, individual, population, species) at which natural selection acts most consistently and powerfully and, second, natural selection can favor contributions to genetic reproduction not only through descendant but also through nondescendant relatives. The importance of these two ideas is apparent throughout the volume.

The organization of the volume is partly taxonomic and partly by subject. We thought it appropriate to begin with the social insects, for their sterile castes have, since Darwin, been a focal point in the understanding of natural selection. What, after all, could be more challenging to a theory of evolution based on differential reproduction than explaining the existence of individuals that normally produce no offspring of their own? The currently intensive study of cooperative breeding in birds, represented here by several investigations, involves obvious parallels, because helpers sometimes die without producing offspring; however, the conclusions reached in studies of social insects and cooperatively breeding birds often diverge intriguingly. Nevertheless, in both cases the emerging picture suggests that two crucial variables are genetic relatedness and fluctuations in the availability of breeding habitat.

Nearly all of the investigators in this symposium, including those interested in caste systems and cooperative breeding, have sought to measure the reproductive success of individuals in systems of sexual competition and parental care. Data on this long-neglected problem are presented for insects, fish, frogs, lizards, birds, and mammals, including humans.

Sexuality can be viewed as involving a kind of proto-social cooperative behavior. Among prominent questions in evolutionary biology at present, the evolutionary *raison d'etre* of sexuality is fairly described as the most difficult. It is fitting, therefore, that this volume should include two papers with promising new ideas on this question.

Finally, we are particularly pleased with the section on human sociality, for it shows clearly that the theory of natural selection, which has for so long guided research at all levels of inquiry in biology, has significant implications for the study of human behavior and social systems as well.

I

Eusocialty in Insects

Intragroup Selection and the Evolution of Insect Societies

Mary Jane West-Eberhard

Theories of insect sociality have recently become very complicated and rather narrowly focused on the problem of worker altruism or helping behavior. Current discussions often seem overly preoccupied with theoretical fine points and with the debate over whether insect societies are despotic matriarchies, families united by kin selection and (when hymenopteran) the genetic strictures of haplodiploidy, or tense communes of selfish mutualists. As a result, students of social insects are sometimes distracted from the broader picture. So I shall begin by reconsidering the idea that led to the present burst of interest in social phenomena—lest it be lost in specialized controversies that, like the bickering in a love affair gone sour, tend to make us forget what the excitement was about in the first place.

The insight that has transformed present-day evolutionary analyses of sociality is a simple extension or rethinking of how natural selection applies to interacting individuals. It states that an important influence on social behavior, whether antagonistic or collaborative, is the degree to which interacting individuals are likely to carry copies of the same genetic alleles (Hamilton, 1964). The idea can be summarized by two related principles.

The first concerns *genetic similarity and social collaboration*. It says that gene frequencies can be affected not only by differential *direct* reproduction (production of offspring) but also by *indirect* effects (Fisher, 1930) such as helping offspring or other relatives. For traits affecting indirect reproduction to evolve, a sufficient proportion of the affected (helped) individuals must be co-carriers of the genetic allele(s) for helping borne by the helping individual (Hamilton, 1964). Such selection could well be called "co-carrier" selection. Because relatives are the genetic co-carriers most obviously associated in nature, it is usually called "kin" selection (Maynard Smith, 1964), even though alleles may be co-carried for reasons other than close genealogical connections (see Hamilton, 1975, p. 141).

The second principle involves *genetic dissimilarity and social competition*. It states that as long as individuals (i.e., members of a group) are genetically different they are expected to compete and express conflicts of interest under natural selection. Therefore group selection arguments that regard the social group as a single unit of selection will sometimes be misleading because of heterogeneities, even within highly integrated colonies, or families (see Williams, 1966). Individuals of such groups may show a high degree of "community of interests" (sensu Alexander and Borgia, 1978) because of genetic kinship, manipulation, and mutual benefits, but individualistic behavior and the means of suppressing it should continue to evolve as long as intragroup genetic heterogeneity persists. Illustrative examples in highly social insects are given below.

In keeping with these two principles I shall examine some special consequences of intragroup competition for the organization and evolution of insect societies. I will use particular examples from field studies of tropical social wasps to make the following general points.

1. As organisms come to depend on life (or competition) in *groups,* the reproductive success of individuals depends increasingly on their ability to win in *social* competition rather than on their ability to confront other aspects of the environment. Social interactions become a kind of screening process determining reproductive success.
2. When group life or competition (e.g., in mating aggregations) is obligatory or highly advantageous—that is, individuals cannot go off and become ''winners'' independent of the group—competition within the group may severely limit the access of some individuals to essential resources, producing ''winners'' and ''losers'' within the group.
3. Alternative strategies may then evolve that enable ''losers'' to salvage at least some reproductive success.
4. Even after a facultative alternative has developed, the original pattern is likely to remain the more productive one, and how readily a costly or irreversible secondary alternative is adopted will depend on the extent to which an individual can expect to win by adopting the primary pattern in the future.

In particular, I will argue that worker behavior in social insects has evolved as an alternative reproductive strategy, and that the worker–queen functional dimorphism is thus basically similar to other kinds of facultative alternative reproductive strategies under strong intraspecific competition.

WORKER BEHAVIOR AS A SECONDARY REPRODUCTIVE ALTERNATIVE

Social competition begins in the social insects with the advent of group living, whatever its selective basis (in primitively social wasps group living seems often to be associated with the advantage of re-using nests; other possible bases are discussed by Lin and Michener, 1972, and Alexander, 1974). In some nest sharing, casteless species, such as the sphecid wasp, *Trigonopsis cameroni* (Eberhard, 1974), each female provisions her own cells as would a solitary individual while tolerating the activities of others in close proximity and only occasionally competing for an empty cell. In other species (reviewed in West-Eberhard, 1978b) competition among nestmates results in at least temporary reproductive dominance with one or a few females gaining exclusive control of the nest.

In socially unspecialized group-living forms like *Zethus miniatus,* a eumenid wasp I have observed in Colombia, a female who loses out in competition for a cell either builds another on the same nest or leaves the group to found a nest of her own. However, most eusocial (worker-containing) forms have two characteristics that severely limit the reproductive options of defeated individuals: group life is obligatory (solitary production of sexual offspring is unknown or rare), and reproduction within groups is dominated by one or a few aggressive individuals whose activities curtail or completely suppress reproduction by others. Thus, a female defeated in the attempt to control a cell is not only unable to leave the nest and reproduce independently, but her reproduction on the nest is not tolerated.

In a few species (e.g., in the genus *Polistes*) defeated or subordinate females lurk at the margins of the nest or move from nest to nest, apparently attempting to usurp the positions of dominant females (West-Eberhard, 1969; Gamboa, 1978). However, for reasons discussed elsewhere (West-Eberhard, 1978b), most insects in which group life is obligatory or highly advantageous live in family groups. Individuals living among relatives have an added reproductive option: If the benefit/cost ratio is sufficiently high (see Hamilton, 1964; West-Eberhard, 1975), they may reproduce indirectly by contributing to the direct reproductive success of nestmates. Thus, helping a relative can be viewed as one of the alternatives available to worker females losing out in social competition for available cells. Helping relatives is a way of salvaging some reproductive success in a situation where alternatives involving direct reproduction are closed or relatively unprofitable.

The queen–worker dimorphism in social insects is therefore fundamentally similar to other facultative polymorphisms. Such polymorphisms include the "high-low" (or major-minor) dimorphisms of horned beetles (Eberhard, ms., demonstrates their facultative and competitive nature); the divergent behavioral strategies common in male-male competition for mates [e.g., in beetles (Eberhard, ms.,); bullfrogs (Emlen, 1976; Howard, this volume); solitary bees (Alcock et al., 1977); fish (Robertson and Warner, 1978); elephant seals (Le-Beouf, 1974); and lekking birds Hogan-Warburg, 1966]; solitary vs. gregarious (migratory) phases in locusts (see Wynne-Edwards, 1962); and asexual vs. sexual reproduction in certain plants and animals, e.g., strawberries and corals (Williams, 1975). All of these phenomena show the following characteristics:

1. Strong local intraspecific competition for some resource (e.g., brood cells, mates, food, or growing space) essential to reproduction.
2. Greater success of some individuals (e.g., larger, more established, or more aggressive ones) at securing the resource via some pre-empting behavior pattern (e.g., fighting).
3. Adoption of an alternative behavior pattern by individuals relatively unsuccessful at the original pattern, enabling them to reproduce by another means (e.g., helping, sneaking copulations, or invading a new region).
4. Facultative (conditional) rather than genetic differentiation of morphs or strategies.

THE EVOLUTION OF A REPRODUCTIVE "DIVISION OF LABOR" AS A PRODUCT OF SOCIAL COMPETITION

The winner and loser classes emerging under strong intra-group competition could originally be based on the variation (e.g., in size or aggressiveness) expected in any population of solitary organisms. However once group life becomes highly advantageous or obligate, with differential reproductive success dependent on the outcome of social interactions, the characters determining social success become a special focus of natural selection and a specialization of the winner "morph." In the case of the social insects, these winner morphs are the queens.

One favorable characteristic of a good alternative behavior pattern is that it be something that is *not* done well by winners or is precluded by their specialization in the primary pattern. That is, selection might be expected to create an "opposite" (mutually exclusive, or "interfering"—see Ghiselin, 1974) alternative specialization allowing the original losers to compete in a way in which they are better equipped to win (see Hamilton, 1978; West-Eberhard, 1979). If increasing specialization in one alternative leads to decreasing ability to perform the other, the two morphs are complementary. If they are performing tasks essential for reproduction they may become mutually dependent.

The queen–worker functional dichotomy in the social insects is opposite and complementary in this way, and the opposite nature of queen and worker specializations must have facilitated their evolution. Being an effective queen entails being present on the nest, which both prevents egg laying by competitors and conserves energy and fat reserves for egg production. Foraging, on the other hand, requires leaving the nest, diversion of energy from egg-production to locomotion, and increased mortality. The hungry brood of an egg layer who is preoccupied with defending her position against usurpers (see Gamboa, 1978) creates an opportunity for indirect reproduction (via helping) by her relatives. Thus, although queen–worker specialization can originate as and may ultimately produce a "cooperative" division of labor (sensu Ghiselin, 1974), it can be fundamentally "competitive" in origin—just as is the division of labor arising in capitalistic human societies through product diversification under competition.

The basic "division of labor" between the sexes—between large, nutritive female gametes and small, motile male ones—likewise involved opposite, complementary, mutually dependent morphs. And, like the division of labor in social insects, it can be viewed as having originated via competition and disruptive selection within a variable isogametic population, leading to gamete dimorphism (see Parker et al., 1972). The evolutionary causes and consequences of division of labor are further discussed in West-Eberhard, 1979.

COMPETITION FOR REPRODUCTIVE PRIORITY IN *METAPOLYBIA* AND *SYNOECA*: THE SIGNIFICANCE OF SOCIAL RITUALS AND DISPLAYS

As already mentioned, once social interactions become critical determinants of individual reproductive success, these interactions become a special focus of natural selection. As a result social behavior may become elaborate and complex or even "extravagant," as do male morphology and display under sexual selection (Fisher, 1930; Thompson, ms.; West-Eberhard, 1979).

Behavior observed in two neotropical polybiine wasps, *Metapolybia aztecoides* Richards and *Synoeca surinama* (L.) (Vespidae, Polistinae, Polybiini) illustrates the functioning and elaboration of fitness-determining interactions in social insects. These species represent closely related genera (Richards, 1978) in which multi-queen groups are common. My observations indicate that their biologies are so similar in the respects discussed here that they can be considered together.

Both *Metapolybia* and *Synoeca* found nests in swarms containing numerous workers and (usually) several queens (as many as 35 in *Metapolybia*), only one of which eventually becomes the sole egg layer on the nest in the populations observed (see West-Eberhard, 1973, 1978b). Thus intra-group competition is very strong, and the stakes are high; the winner (which in older colonies may be a small group of persistent queens) gains the entire nest and worker staff; defeated females are completely excluded from direct reproduction, because in these species females are not known to reproduce outside of groups.

The reduction in queen number in a newly founded colony of *M. aztecoides* is described by West-Eberhard (1978a). Over a period of six months 30 queens were eliminated, mainly during two episodes of strong social competition. These periods were characterized by an increased frequency of certain displays such as "bending" by queens, and the "queen dance" performed by workers (West-Eberhard, 1978a). Bending behavior seems to function as a threat in both species. Queens direct it at approaching individuals and perform it more vigorously near other queens, sometimes with aggressive jerking and shoving. The workers' queen dance, performed when they encounter queens walking on the comb, appears to represent arrested or inhibited aggressiveness. During episodes of queen elimination this worker display intensifies until it becomes an attack and results in the elimination of queens that fail to respond aggressively, apparently functioning as a test of dominance.

Egg-guarding behavior is another pattern associated with reproductive competition in a variety of social wasps, including *Polistes fuscatus* (West-Eberhard, 1969), *Protopolybia pumila* (Naumann, 1970), *Polybia occidentalis,* and *Metapolybia azteca* (Forsyth, 1978) as well as *M. aztecoides* and *S. surinama*. Figure 1–1 shows the increasing length of time newly laid eggs are guarded as competition gets stronger in a colony of *M. aztecoides*: As the colony gets older, the number of competing queens goes down, but those present have increasingly developed ovaries and are increasingly aggressive toward each other. In effect, available egg-laying space is decreased for each female by the increased capacity of her competitors to monopolize it. Correspondingly, the egg-guarding vigil becomes more and more prolonged (see also Forsyth, 1978, on *M. azteca*). When there is a large emergence of young, unsuppressed females on a nest with developing competing queens, competition is most severe, and the egg-guarding vigil near a single newly laid egg can last as long as three hours. On the other hand, in single-queen colonies, aggressive competitors with developing ovaries and the egg-guarding vigil are both absent.

In wasp species with the egg-guarding vigil, overt fighting among competitors is rare (see West-Eberhard, 1969). During this vigil the "guarding" queens do not attack approachers, but unguarded newly-laid eggs are occasionally eaten by other females. As escalated bending behavior and the queen dance indicate, queens are potentially hyperaggressive females and are recognized as such by nestmates. Evidently the threat of their presence near a newly laid egg suffices to protect it.

These observations indicate that bending and egg-guarding in social wasps are functionally analogous to the displays and plumage of lekking male birds (see Selander, 1974; Armstrong, 1965; and Wynne-Edwards, 1962, for many examples) that compete socially for mates. In mating leks, as in the wasp colonies described here, social competition is very strong, with one or a few individuals responsible for most of the successful reproduction. The specialized displays are part of the screening process in high-stakes competition separating the major from the minor (or non-) reproductives. In social insects (West-Eberhard, 1977), as in birds and fish (see Hinde, 1966), ritualized dominance and threat come to replace direct combat among hyperaggressive competitors. The resultant interactions incorporate both approach and avoidance, with aggressiveness countered by selection to avoid costly encounters during peak reproductive activity, when such expenditures would be particularly detrimental to contestants. Avoidance of nestmates is characteristic among polybiine queens in multi-queen colonies. In the oviposition rituals of some species (e.g., *Leipomeles dorsata,* pers. obs.), competing queens seem to avoid one another by ovipositing one at a time on empty new combs; and in *Polybia scrobalis* (pers. obs.) queens oviposit at night when workers are relatively inactive. In both of these species, as in *Metapolybia* spp. and *Synoeca* spp., queens typically sit immobile at the margins of combs and when walking do so with a peculiar slowness that contrasts with the quick and interactive movements of the workers.

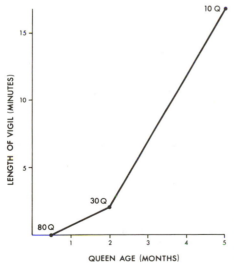

Figure 1–1.   Duration of post-oviposition vigil and age of queens in a colony of *Metapolybia aztecoides*. Numeral above each point indicates number of queens present.

CASTE FLEXIBILITY IN *SYNOECA* AND *METAPOLYBIA*: A GENERAL MODEL OF ROLE DETERMINATION BASED ON INCLUSIVE REPRODUCTIVE VALUE

Social competition is particularly dramatic in the swarming polybiine wasps because these are specialized social insects with relatively large colonies (a high payoff for winning), yet castes are flexible and determined by contests among adults rather than by manipulations of larvae.

The ultimate selective basis for the caste flexibility of tropical polybiines is apparently predation. Predation on colonies is frequent (Forsyth, 1978) and devastating, causing wasps to abandon nest and brood and abscond to a new site, so that the long process of rearing replacement workers and, subsequently, sexual offspring is sometimes reinitiated repeatedly before the cycle is completed (see West-Eberhard, 1978a). The caste flexibility of these wasps enables individuals to respond to the erratically fluctuating reproductive opportunities and colony maintenance crises associated with the repeatedly truncated reproductive cycle. Perhaps significantly, the most marked (least flexible) morphological castes in the Polybiini are present in species such as *Stelopolybia areata* (Jeanne and Fagen, 1974), that have very large colonies. Large colonies are presumably better defended and better able to sustain a worker population even if repeatedly forced to abscond.

In *Metapolybia* and *Synoeca* all newly emerged females are potential queens (West-Eberhard, 1978a). Whether a given female becomes a queen or a worker depends on her situation relative to others. If there is a queen or group of queens present during her first days of adult life she first enters an idle period, during which she is occasionally attacked and actively dominated by the queen(s). Then, at the age of 6–10 days, she begins to build and care for the brood, and at 10–15 days she begins to forage (West-Eberhard, 1978a; Forsyth, 1978). If the colony happens to become queenless during the initial idle period young non-worker females become queens (see West-Eberhard, 1978a, and Figure 1–2).

Young queens present in a swarm or in a group of replacement queens become increasingly aggressive and competitive as they grow older. Eventually all but one (in small colonies) or a few (in large colonies) leave in swarms or become workers (West-Eberhard, 1978a). As in the case of newly emerged females, defeated queens usually pass through a period of idleness and take up nest building and brood attendance before foraging. Al-

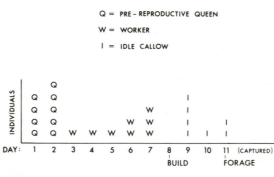

Figure 1–2.   Emergence time and role when captured of females produced in a queenless colony of *Synoeca surinama*. The queen that laid the eggs producing these females was removed four days before they began to emerge. Each letter represents one individual. Building by an offspring female was first observed on day 8 (day 1 being day of emergence of first offspring females). Foraging was first observed on day 11. "Pre-reproductive queens" performed the bending display and were danced to by workers (see text). "Workers" foraged or added pulp to the nest.

though I have seen idle *Metapolybia* females perform nest duties briefly and then resume queenlike behavior, I have never seen a forager later become a queen.

The changes in social role observed in *M. aztecoides* and *S. surinama* are summarized in Figure 1–3. Figure 1–4 shows a hypothetical scheme to explain the movement toward "indirect" reproduction and ultimately irreversible worker behavior (foraging) by a defeated swarm queen. According to this scheme a female begins to work only when the cost of aid, in terms of her own future direct reproductive success (RS), drops below the benefit (the augmented RS of aided queens devalued by their relatedness to the helper). Among other factors, the cost of aid is directly proportional to the female's probability of reproduction. This probability rises as long as the individual is an egg-layer with an increasingly developed ovary but drops off sharply when she is defeated in social competition (setting the point of downward inflection of the cost curve in Figure 1–4). The cost of helping a defeated queen does not drop immediately to zero because there must remain some probability of reproduction should the dominant queen(s) die. Meanwhile, the benefit of working rises with the increasing shortage of workers in the newly founded colony (see Figure 1–5)

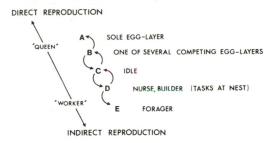

Figure 1–3.   Behavioral changes observed in *Metapolybia aztecoides* and *Synoeca surinama*.

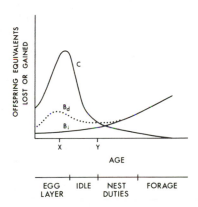

Figure 1–4.   Hypothesized cost/benefit explanation for changes in the behavior of a defeated swarm queen. The line below graph represents the behavioral role changes typically undergone by a *Metapolybia* or *Synoeca* queen defeated at age x (the sequence shown is invariable but the length of time spent in each role is highly variable). The cost curve (C) reflects the changes in inclusive reproductive value that would presumably be experienced by such a female (see text). The indirect benefit (B_i) or payoff for performing aid increases gradually as the brood grows and swarm workers die off. The dotted line (B_d) represents the level to which the benefit for aid is raised as a result of the individual's own probability of direct reproduction in the aided colony. This value (B_d), like the cost of aid, reflects reproductive value. Low cost aid (nest duties) begin when $B_i + B_d > C$.

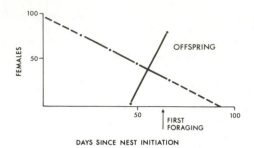

Figure 1–5.   Size of worker population in a newly founded colony of *Synoeca surinama* (Hacienda Mozambique, Meta, Colombia). The declining line represents workers present in the founding swarm (dashed portion extrapolated). The ascending line represents offspring workers, whose foraging began on the day indicated by the arrow. Dots are data points taken between 21 June 1978 (three weeks after the newly initiated nest was discovered) and 7 August 1978 (when it was destroyed by a predator). This colony was observed daily and all wasps marked for individual indentification with color paints. Offspring adults began to emerge on 17 July and began to forage on 3 August (arrow).

(rationale in West-Eberhard, 1975a, pp. 8–11). When the two curves cross, the female should begin to work, at first performing ''low-risk'' (nest) duties, and later (when the benefit/cost margin is greater) taking up the ''high-cost'' (high energetic cost, high mortality) activity of foraging. Ghiselin (1974, p. 235), discussing the same task change with age in honeybees, makes a superficially similar argument with reference to the best interests of the colony: ''In order to get the most out of each individual, it is best to employ the younger members at 'safe' tasks and only expose them to danger when they are soon to die anyway.'' I consider an explanation in terms of individual reproductive value likely to be more accurate.

As long as an individual has some probability of direct reproduction, the payoff for worker behavior has two components, one indirect (benefit to relatives) and the other direct—the contribution made to her own direct RS in the event that she lays eggs in the future (Figure 1–4, and Lin and Michener, 1972). The cost of aid is likewise twofold. By expending energy and resources and risking death as a worker, a female reduces her future chances of both direct and indirect reproduction.

There is a ready-made way to estimate future reproductive probability, namely, by consulting a curve of reproductive value (Fisher, 1930). Although such curves have never been obtained for any social wasp species, they are obtainable by measuring the rates of death and reproduction of a large population of individuals. Although Fisher (1930, 1958, p. 27) pointed out that there would be ''indirect effects'' on reproductive value in organisms having parental care, ''most strikingly of all in the services of neuter insects to their queen,'' he considered that such effects would usually be ''unimportant compared to the effects of personal reproduction'' and therefore did not further consider them. However, in the case of the kinds of behavioral changes being discussed here, the ''indirect effects'' may be of even greater importance than direct effects.

If the cost of aid is measured in terms of its effect on survivorship, then it seems clear that the effective cost of a given act or role is greater for individuals representing high values on the curve of inclusive (direct plus indirect) reproductive value than for females representing lower values. That is, the reduction in future RS (cost) is greater for a given act in individuals representing high reproductive values. Thus the cost of aid is proportional to *inclusive* reproductive value.

Individual wasps do indeed seem to take future reproductive probabilities (reproductive value) into account when switching from idleness to worker behavior. As already mentioned, newly emerged *Metapolybia* females of queenless colonies (a class of individuals with high reproductive value) refrain from working and eventually lay eggs (West-Eberhard, 1978a), whereas those immediately dominated (and therefore of a class having lower reproductive value) begin working within a few days of emergence. The details of this difference were observed in a small queenless colony of *Synoeca surinama* (Figure 1–2). The first three female offspring were idle and aggressive (queenlike) and were treated as queens (danced to) by nestmates. Females emerging just two days later and thereafter were dominated by these early-emerged females and some began working at the age of six days. Observations of another newly founded colony revealed that certain females remained idle (although not laying eggs or treated as queens) until near the end of the pre-emergence period when they finally began to work. These idle females were unusual in becoming aggressive and vigilant near empty cells, and they sometimes inspected and "guarded" newly laid eggs ofter oviposition by the queen. One such female laid an egg soon after the nest was initiated. Dissection of such females revealed that they were mated and had previously developed but now degenerated ovaries (described in West-Eberhard, 1975b). That is, they were probably defeated queens behaving as "hopeful" reproductives and therefore refraining from work for several weeks, during which time they neither oviposited nor were treated as queens.

Colonies at the end of the pre-emergence period are sometimes maintained entirely by the labor of defeated queens (West-Eberhard, 1978a). Because working and the high mortality associated with foraging (West-Eberhard, 1978a, Forsyth, 1978) are deferred until a relatively late age in such females, they serve as a reserve worker force when the supply of workers declines precariously prior to the emergence of offspring females on newly founded nests (Figure 1–5). Comparing the hypothetical reproductive value curves of ordinary workers (females who spent their early adulthood in queen-containing colonies) and defeated queens (Figure 1–6) offers an individual-level explanation for the functioning of defeated queens as reserve workers.

In conclusion, individual females in highly social polybiine wasp colonies behave as if consulting a curve of reproductive value to determine the cost of queenlike, idle, or high-

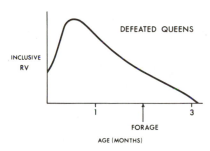

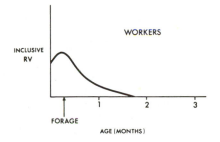

Figure 1–6.   Comparative inclusive reproductive values of workers and defeated queens (hypothetical, based on observations described in text).

vs. low-risk worker behavior. Part of the benefit of helping behavior by a female of relatively high direct reproductive value derives from investment in a colony that has a certain probability of serving as a resource for her own direct reproduction in the future.

Other authors (Emlen, 1970; West-Eberhard, 1975; and Hrdy and Hrdy, 1976) have discussed the likelihood that the disposition to perform costly social aid increases with age and decreased reproductive value (see especially Hrdy and Hrdy, 1976). Future studies should demonstrate the general importance of inclusive reproductive value as a determinant of the cost (and, hence, likelihood) of social aid, regardless of its selective basis (whether kin directed, imposed, or mutualistic). Many features of social organization based on individual differences in behavior may prove explicable by finer analyses of differing probabilities of future reproduction.

RELATION OF THIS "SYNTHETIC INDIVIDUAL-SELECTION" MODEL TO THEORIES OF WORKER ALTRUISM

Three major theories of worker altruism in the literature on social insects are consistent with the principles of natural selection applied to social organisms as outlined here: the parental manipulation hypothesis (Alexander, 1974); the kin selection hypothesis (Hamilton, 1964), of which the haplodiploidy model (Hamilton, 1964) is a specialized subset (see West-Eberhard, 1975, 1978b); and the mutualism hypothesis (Lin and Michener, 1972; West-Eberhard, 1978a).

The approach illustrated in Figure 1–4 shows the relationship of these hypotheses as parts of a more comprehensive scheme—one reflecting ontogenetic changes in the reproductive value of individuals under social competition. The indirect and direct components of the benefit from working (Figure 1–4) correspond, respectively, to a payoff via the consequently augmented RS of relatives (the "kinship component" of inclusive fitness, West-Eberhard, 1975); and to a payoff via augmented personal RS (the "classical" component of inclusive fitness). This latter "direct" benefit of worker behavior is the basis for the contention (Lin and Michener, 1972) that classical individual selection can account for helping without kin selection (without an indirect payoff). This is the "mutualism" hypothesis— the idea that behavior primarily beneficial in terms of production or care of the performer's own zygotes may incidentally benefit others. The incidental aid to nearby individuals makes cooperation mutually profitable.

Parental (or worker) manipulation of the brood—in social insects often simply the underfeeding of some larvae—creates a class of individuals with low direct reproductive value. For such individuals the cost of aid is low from the time they emerge as adults (in termites workers do not even mature sexually), and the threshold benefit/cost ratio for profitable indirect reproduction is passed early. They are forced into a reproductive category (handicapped loser) for which indirect reproduction is the most profitable alternative. From this perspective it is clear that kin selection can be an auxiliary to parental manipulation; kin selection may usually explain the conformity of manipulated offspring to the helper role.

INDIVIDUAL SELECTION AND THE GOOD OF THE GROUP

Despite the logical force of arguments against group (or colony) selection (e.g., Williams 1966) and the invention of tidy explanations for collaboration in individual terms (e.g., Hamilton, 1964; Lin and Michener, 1972; and Alexander, 1974), the supraorganism (colony-level selection) still haunts evolutionary discussions of insect sociality. Wilson (1968, p. 41) maintains that "colony selection in the advanced social insects does appear to be the one example of group selection that can be accepted unequivocally." He has proposed a colony optimization "ergonomic" theory of caste (Wilson, 1968, 1971, 1975; Oster and Wilson, 1978) that, while addressing ecological questions often neglected in depictions of insect societies derived from models of worker altruism, tends to overlook intragroup conflict affecting social roles and the rates at which tasks are performed. Conversely, individual selectionists err in acting as if colony-level selection does not occur when it so obviously does: colonies, like species in geological time, differentially multiply and differentially persist or become extinct (see Leigh, 1977), and this must affect the rate of selection and extinction of alleles (see Maynard Smith, 1976, Wade, 1978).

I believe that some of the confusion on this point stems from a misleading either-or attitude regarding levels of selection (see Simpson, 1977) as well as a misunderstanding of critiques of simplistic group-selection models (those that ignore the effects of individual selection within groups). It is now well established (Williams, 1966) that group selection cannot account for the spread of individually harmful alleles except under special circumstances (for a concise summary of the reasons see Wilson, 1975, pp. 107–117). However, this is not the same as saying that group selection does not operate under ordinary circumstances (e.g., when the interests of group members regarding a particular character are synonymous or when the rate of fixation or the persistence of a character established primarily by individual selection is altered by higher-level effects).

As Maynard Smith (1976) points out, the question is quantitative, not qualitative. Group selection will have an evolutionary effect, but it will usually be smaller or slower than that of individual-level selection. As a general rule (this rule fails under such special circumstances as when the effect of selection at one level is very much greater than that at the other), it may help to consider the two levels of selection as consecutive tests of alleles and admit that the long-term persistence of an allele requires successfully passing both tests (see also Grant, 1978, p. 386). Individually harmful alleles may be quickly eliminated in competition among individuals and therefore not significantly tested at the group level. On the other hand, individually favorable alleles detrimental to the group or species can eventually be eliminated via either reduced survival or productivity of groups possessing them. (Ironically, weakly group-detrimental traits seem more likely to lead to species extinction than very strongly group-detrimental traits, because the latter are more likely to be eliminated via group extinction before "infecting" the entire population or species.) Thus Wade (1978) and Grant (1978) are correct to assert that the group should not be summarily dismissed as a commonly important unit of selection. But they are somewhat unfair to label Williams' (1966) advocacy of a lower-levels-of-selection approach simply an appeal to parsimony, because (as Williams took pains to show) lower- (especially, genic-) level interpretations have a greater probability of accuracy in most situations.

The good of the group has a special significance for organisms like most social insects in which life and reproduction in groups is obligatory. In such species the immediate good of the group must often be synonymous with that of the individual for whom the group is an indispensable resource. Kinship, manipulation, and mutualistic interdependence may cause convergence of interests among group members (West-Eberhard, 1979), leading to the "emergence" of the group as an integrated unit of selection (Alexander and Borgia, 1978). All gradations in the relative importance of group selection vs. intragroup competition must exist among social insect species, and commonality of interests must affect some characters (foraging efficiency, nest architecture) more than others (egg laying precedence and individual differences in task performance). It could therefore be argued that the individualistic interpretations given throughout this paper are fine for the social wasps, in which multi-queen colonies and intracolony reproductive competition are common; but that this approach can be safely replaced with the colony–unit model when dealing with more highly integrated "supraorganismic" colonies such as those of monogynous ants and bees and the termites.

In some species and for some characters, this may be true: *If* the workers of family groups are completely and irreversibly sterile, or the colony is completely inbred (clonal), the worker's interests are indeed perfectly synonymous with those of the colony or queen(s). So, although the primary reproductive division of labor between queens and workers may often be a product of intra-group competition, the morphological caste differences among workers in highly specialized social species (in which intragroup competition is rare or ineffective) have probably evolved via benefits to the colony or queen (see West-Eberhard, 1979). The same is probably true for the evolution of increased work efficiency by workers with no hope of laying eggs. However, even in specialized social species an exclusively colony-level analysis can be as misleading as a narrowly individualistic one. One reason, already discussed, has to do with the ubiquity of intracolony genetic heterogeneity in social insects, in which inbreeding in apparently rare (see Hamilton, 1972; Lin and Michener, 1972). A second, equally compelling reason has to do with their evolutionary history. All social insects have evolved from solitary ancestors via a long history in which the development of reproductive dominance by one or a few individuals is a major theme. It would be inconceivable if this history of intragroup competition and its suppression had not left important and peculiar marks on the organization of the most developed insect societies—which is the same as saying that these societies can only be understood in the light of this history.

Many illustrations of this point could be drawn from the literature on caste determination, egg laying rituals, worker reproductive systems, etc. To cite just one example, "queen control" or the suppression of reproduction by nestmates in the honeybee (*Apis mellifera*) is mediated by numerous pheromones, none of which is completely effective by itself (reviewed in Michener, 1974). Velthuis (1976, p. 433) lists ten "known and postulated" pheromones of the queen affecting the behavior of workers. Four of them are known to lead to inhibition of ovary development in workers, and some affect behavior of the workers toward the queen, for example, causing "retinue behavior," which Velthuis interprets as arrested approach behavior. Velthuis (1976) also discusses worker–queen reproductive conflict in highly evolved bees (stingless bees and honeybees), giving evidence that the complex oviposition process in stingless bees is a ritualized dominance contest; his outline of increasing complexity and ritualization in the evolution of queen control in bees also applies as well to the social wasps (West-Eberhard, 1977).

The complexity of queen control mechanisms can be interpreted as a response to the development of large colonies and the advantage to a queen of "a warning system to extend her influence beyond the reach of her mandibles and sting" (Velthuis, 1978, p. 447). However, an additional factor may be involved in view of the apparent readiness of workers to lay eggs in the event of the absence or weakness of the queen (Velthuis, 1976), namely, consistent selection on workers to escape suppression. The evolution of queen control may have involved a succession of escapes by workers and mechanisms to counter this by queens. This might explain both the multiplicity of queen control substances and the fact that each is only partially effective. And it may help explain the complex sequence of maneuvering preceding oviposition in stingless bees that includes provisioning and *oviposition* by excited and sometimes aggressive workers. The worker-laid eggs of these bees and some ants, traditionally called "trophic eggs" (a term tacitly implying worker donorism), might sometimes function to maintain active ovaries for egg-production should the queen become senile or weak. In some ants and bees the workers laying "trophic" eggs produce reproductive eggs in queenless colonies (Brian and Rigby, 1978).

The advantage of direct reproduction by workers can be appreciated by considering the enormous payoff, as compared to a lifetime of working, for laying a single male-producing egg. Data on the colony composition and productivity of Africanized honeybees—descendants of *Apis mellifera scutellata,* formerly *adansonii,* following their introduction into South America—show that the average inclusive fitness or (in this case) indirect reproductive success of workers is only 0.04 offspring equivalents, compared to 1.0 for a worker producing just one son (data from Winston 1978, and pers. comm.; calculations in the Appendix). That is, the genetic contribution of even the poorest unmated egg layer is potentially (if her offspring matures) 25 times greater than that of the average worker, and individual-level selection for oviposition is very strong. Furthermore, selection for perfect suppression by queens is always countered by very strong selection on both workers and queens to allow for queen replacement following swarming or when the queen dies. (However, it should not be supposed that laying by workers has evolved as a means of colony maintenance when the queen dies, because the unmated workers can produce only drones; replacement queens are especially reared large females that mate and lay both male- and female-producing eggs—see Michener, 1974.)

We can only conclude that even in the most specialized "supraorganismic" social insects, selection is still operating at the individual level. Phenomena like worker oviposition (see Lin and Michener, 1972), ovary-developed morphological "intermediates" (Richards and Richards, 1951), and egg laying rituals are traditionally glossed over in studies of highly integrated colonies. But they are worthy of renewed attention because they are symptomatic of intragroup competition likely to be fundamental to larger patterns of behavior and social organization.

ACKNOWLEDGEMENTS

Dr. Nicholas A. Thompson (Department of Psychology, Clark University) first drew my attention to similarities between the results of sexual selection and other kinds of social competition. The Dixon Stroud family and Dr. Luis Arango generously provided facilities and living quarters during four months of fieldwork at Hacienda Mozambique, Meta, Colombia. The Scholarly Studies Program of the Smithsonian Institution supported fieldwork and preparation of the manuscript. For thoughtfully reading and commenting on the penultimate version I thank R. D. Alexander, E. Curio, R. Dawkins, W. G. Eberhard, H. E. Evans, A. B. Forsyth, G. Gamboa, D. Gwynne, W. D. Hamilton, R. L. Jeanne, E. G. Leigh, Jr., C. D. Michener, N. A. Thompson, and M. L. Winston.

APPENDIX: Estimation of the Average Inclusive Fitness of Non-laying Workers of the Africanized Honeybee

Dr. Mark L. Winston (pers. comm.; see Winston, 1978) kindly provided the following data on production of adult brood by colonies of the Africanized honeybee (descended from the imported South African honeybee *Apis mellifera scutellata,* formerly called *adansonii*) in French Guiana:

Workers produced per swarming cycle (a) = 41,691 (S.E. = 2281)

Queen-containing swarms produced per cycle (b) = 2.8

Males per swarming cycle (c) = 903 (S.E. = 8.4)

My calculations are as follows (for a detailed discussion of their rationale see West-Eberhard, 1975): The average relatedness (fractional identity by descent) of a worker and the males of the brood in these monogynous matrifilial colonies is $1/4$, or 0.5 times the relatedness a worker would have with her own offspring ($r = 1/2$). Therefore, the value in offspring equivalents of the average worker's contribution to the male brood of her mother (d) is 0.5c/a or 0.01 offspring equivalents.

The maximum average relatedness (that which obtains if queens mate only once) of a worker and the females of the brood is $3/4$, or 1.5 times the relatedness she would have with her own offspring, making the value of the average worker's contribution to the female reproductive brood (e) 1.5b/a or 0.0001 offspring equivalents

The average worker's inclusive fitness is d + e or 0.0101 offspring equivalents.

REFERENCES

Alcock, J., C.E. Jones, and S.L. Buchmann. 1977. Male mating strategies in the bee *Centris pallidus* Fox (Hymenoptera: Anthophoridae). *Amer. Nat.* 111:145–155.

Alexander, R. D. 1974. The evolution of social behavior. *Ann. Rev. Ecol. Syst.*, 4:325–383.

_____and G. Borgia. 1978. Group selection, altruism, and the levels of organization of life. *Ann. Rev. Ecol. Syst.* 9:449–74.

Armstrong, E. A. 1965. *Bird Display and Behaviour*. Dover, N.Y., 431 pp..

Brian, M. V., and C. Rigby. 1978. The trophic eggs of *Myrmica rubra* L. *Insectes Sociaux* 25(1):89–110.

Eberhard, W. G. 1974. The natural history and behaviour of *Trigonopsis cameronii* Kohl (Sphecidae). *Trans. Roy. Ent. Soc.* London 125(3):295–328.

_____. 1980. Horned beetles. *Sci. Amer.* 242(3):166–182.

Emlen, J. M. 1970. Age specificity and ecological theory. *Ecology* 51(4):588–601.

Emlen, S. T. 1976. Lek organization and mating strategies in the bullfrog. *Behav. Ecol. and Sociobiol.* 1:283–313.

Fisher, R. A. 1930 (1958). *The Genetical Theory of Natural Selection*. Dover, N.Y. xiv + 291 pp..

Forsyth, A. B. 1978. Studies on the behavioral ecology of polygynous social wasps. Ph.D. Thesis, Harvard University, 226 pp..

Gamboa, G. J. 1978. Intraspecific defense: Advantage of social cooperation among paper wasp foundresses. *Science* 199:1463–1465.

Ghiselin, M. T. 1974. *The Economy of Nature and the Evolution of Sex*. University of California Press, Los Angeles, xii + 346 pp.

Grant, V. 1978. Kin selection: a critique, *Biol. Zbl.* 97:385–392.

Hamilton, W. D. 1964. The genetical evolution of social behaviour. I, II. *J. Theor. Biol.* 7:1–16; 17–52.

_____. 1972. Altruism and related phenomena, mainly in the social insects. *Ann. Rev. Ecol. Syst.*, 3:193–232.

_____. 1975. Innate social aptitudes of man: an approach from evolutionary genetics. in *Biosocial Anthropology*, R. Fox, ed., Malaby Press, N.Y., pp. 133–155.

_____. 1978. Evolution and diversity under bark. In: *Diversity of Insect Faunas*. L.A. Mound and N. Waloff, eds., Blackwell Sci. Pub., Oxford, pp. 154-175.

Hinde, A. 1970. *Animal Behaviour*. McGraw-Hill, N.Y. xvi + 876 pp.

Hogan-Warburg, A. J. 1966. Social behavior of the ruff, *Philomachus pugnax* (L.). *Ardea* 54:109–229.

Howard, R. 1981. Male age-size distribution and male mating success in bull-frogs. (this volume).

Hrdy, S. B., and D. B. Hrdy. 1976. Hierarchical relations among female Hanuman Langurs (Primates: Colobinae, *Presbytis entellus*). *Science* 193:913–915.

Jeanne, R. L., and R. Fagen. 1974. Polymorphism in *Stelopolybia areata* (Hymenoptera, Vespidae). *Psyche* 81(1):155–166.

Leigh, E. G., Jr., 1977. How does selection reconcile individual advantage with the good of the group? *Proc. Nat. Acad. Sci.* 74(10):4542–4546.

Lin, N., and C. D. Michener. 1972. Evolution of sociality in insects. *Quart. Rev. Biol.* 47(2):131–159.

Maynard Smith, J. 1964. Kin selection and group selection. *Nature* 201:1145–1147.

_____. 1976. Group selection. *Quart. Rev. Biol.* 51:277–283.

Michener, C. D. 1974. *The Social Behavior of the Bees*. Harvard Univ. Press, Cambridge, Mass. xii + 404 pp.

Naumann, M. 1970. The nesting behavior of *Protopolybia pumila* in Panama (Hymenoptera, Vespidae). Ph.D. Thesis, Univ. Kansas.

Oster, G. and E. O. Wilson, 1978. *Caste and the Ecology of the Social Insects*. Princeton Univ. Press, Princeton, N.J.

Parker, G. A., R. R. Baker, V. G. F. Smith. 1972. The origin and evolution of gamete dimorphism and the male–female phenomenon. *J. Theoret. Biol.*, 36:529–553.

Richards, O. W. 1978. *The Social Wasps of the Americas*. British Museum (Natural History), London, vii + 580 pp.

_____, and M. J. Richards. 1951. Observations on the social wasps of South America (Hymenoptera, Vespidae). *Trans. Roy. Ent. Soc.* London 102:1–167.

Robertson, D. R., and R. R. Warner. 1978. Sexual patterns in the Labroid Fishes of the Western Caribbean, II: The Parrotfishes (Scaridae). *Smithsonian Contr. Zool.* No. 255, iii + 26 pp.

Selander, R. K. 1972. Sexual selection and dimorphism in birds. in *Sexual Selection and the Descent of Man* 1871–1971. B. Campbell, ed., Aldine, Chicago, pp. 180–230.

Simpson, G. G. 1977. An adversary view of sociobiology. *Science* 195 (4280):773–774.

Thompson, N. S. ms. Toward a non-tautological theory of evolution: a working paper. (Psychology, Clark University).

Velthuis, H. H. W. 1976. Egg laying, aggression and dominance in bees. *Proc. XV Int. Congress Entomol.* pp. 436–449.

Wade, M. J. 1978. A critical review of the models of group selection. *Quart. Rev. Biol.* 53(2):101–114.

West-Eberhard, M. J. 1969. The social biology of polistine wasps. *Misc. Publ. Mus. Zool. Univ. Mich.* No. 140:1–101.

———. 1973. Monogyny in "polygynous" social wasps. *Proc. VII Congress Int. Union for the Study of Social Insects,* London, pp. 396–403.

———. 1975a. The evolution of social behavior by kin selection. *Quart. Rev. Biol.* 50(1):1–33.

———. 1975b. Estudios de las avispas sociales (Hymenoptera, Vespidae) del Valle del Cauca. I. Objetivos, métodos, y notas para facilitar la identificación de especies comunes. *Cespedesia* 4(16):245–267.

———. 1977. The establishment of the dominance of the queen in social wasp colonies. *Proc. VIII Cong. Int. Union for the Study of Social Insects,* Wageningen, Holland, pp. 223–227.

———. 1978a. Temporary queens in Metapolybia wasps: non-reproductive helpers without altruism? *Science* 200(4340):441–443.

———. 1978b. Polygyny and the evolution of social behavior in wasps. *J. Kansas Ent. Soc.* 51(4):832–856.

———. 1979. Sexual selection, social competition, and evolution. *Proc. Amer. Phil. Soc.* I, II, III: 222–234.

Williams, G. C. 1966. *Adaptation and Natural Selection.* Princeton Univ. Press, Princeton, N.J. x + 307 pp.

———. 1975. *Sex and Evolution.* Princeton Univ. Press, Princeton, N.J. x + 200 pp.

Wilson, E. O. 1968. The ergonomics of caste in the social insects. *Amer. Nat.* 102:41–66.

———. 1971. *The Insect Societies.* Belknap Press, Cambridge, Mass. x + 548 pp.

———. 1975. *Sociobiology.* Belknap Press, Cambridge, Mass. ix + 697 pp.

Winston, M. L. 1978. Intra-colony demography and reproductive rate of the Africanized honeybee in South America. *Behav. Ecol. and Sociobiology* IV: 279–292.

Wynne-Edwards, V. C. 1962. *Animal Dispersion in Relation to Social Behaviour.* Oliver and Boyd, Edinburgh. xi + 653 pp.

2.

Individual Strategies of Inclusive-Fitness-Maximizing in *Polistes fuscatus* Foundresses

Katharine M. Noonan

INTRODUCTION

Evolutionary theory argues increasingly that natural selection acts most powerfully at the individual level or at subgenomic levels (Williams, 1966, 1973; Hamilton, 1964a, b 1972, 1975; Alexander, 1972, 1974a, b; Lewontin, 1970; Ghiselin, 1974; Alexander and Borgia, 1978). The development in social insects of sterile helpers and individuals that, although fertile, devote their reproductive efforts to rearing the offspring of others therefore continues to challenge the general theory (Darwin, 1859; Sturtevant, 1938; Hamilton, 1972). In many social bees and wasps, fertile females cooperate in the early stages of colony-founding, so that some appear to sacrifice opportunities to found nests of their own to help reproductive competitors (Wilson, 1971; Evans and Eberhard, 1970; Michener, 1974). Foundresses of the social paper wasp, *Polistes fuscatus,* frequently cooperate in colony-founding and in rearing both workers and reproductives. Within a foundress group, one female (the queen) dominates the others and lays most of the eggs, while her subordinates take up the risky tasks of foraging for food and building materials without apparent direct reproductive gain. Why they do so is the subject of this paper.

The concept of inclusive fitness (Hamilton, 1964a, b) provided a key breakthrough in understanding helping behavior as an evolutionary product of reproductive competition among individuals. Hamilton argued that traits are selected not only for their effects on the individual's own offspring production but also for their effects on the reproduction of genetic relatives that share predictable fractions of the individual's genes by descent from common ancestors. He therefore divided fitness into two components: a classical (or direct) fitness component[1] realized through offspring and an inclusive (or indirect) fitness component realized through effects on other genetic relatives. Natural selection tends to maximize the sum of the two components, the individual's total genetic contribution to future generations. So, reproductive strategies should evolve to emphasize direct or indirect components according to the likelihood of genetic pay-off by each, and variations in individual strategies should reflect individual differences in expectation of success by direct and indirect avenues (Hamilton, 1964a, b; Alexander, 1974a, b; West-Eberhard, 1975, this volume).

Polistes fuscatus foundresses follow three distinct reproductive strategies or alternative reproductive behaviors: (1) founding colonies alone as single-foundresses, (2) founding colonies as queens of multiple-foundress groups, and (3) adopting subordinate roles in multiple-foundress groups. In this paper, I test predictions from the inclusive fitness model, first, to examine possible genetic pay-offs for helping by subordinate foundresses, and, second, to try to explain differences in individual strategies.

[1]I refer to the neighbor-modulated classical fitness (a*) of Hamilton (1964a:3) that comprises the effect of the individual's genotype plus effects of its social environment on its offspring production.

MATERIALS AND METHODS

Animals and Study Sites

The subject of this research is the common brown paper wasp of the northeastern United States, *Polistes fuscatus fuscatus* (Fabricius) (Hymenoptera: Vespidae). Details of its taxonomy and distribution may be found in Richards (1978), its natural history and social biology in Owen (1962), West-Eberhard (1967a, b, 1969), and Noonan (1979). It is a medium-sized wasp (foundresses average 1.36 centimeters in winglength, tip to tegulum) dark brown, black, and yellow in color. The females build single-combed, unenveloped nests of paper made from fiber that they scrape with their mandibles from weathered boards and sticks. The nests hang by short pedicels from horizontal supports, with cells opening downward and roughly parallel to the ground. Offspring are reared one to a cell and fed on arthropod prey (mainly caterpillars) brought to the nest and chewed to a pulp by the adults. The species has adapted very successfully to nesting in the eaves of houses and other buildings. It was in such places that I conducted my study (see Noonan, 1979, for precise locations of the study sites). Natural nesting sites are under rocks, in treeholes, and under the leaves of bushes.

Colonies are annual, and the behavior and life histories of individuals are geared to the seasonal cycle. In the spring, mated females emerge from hibernation sites in cracks and crevices and return to their natal nests before dispersing to found new ones. Old nests are seldom reused (Starr, 1978; Noonan, 1979). Both single-foundresses and multiple-foundress groups begin rearing a brood of true workers that matures in about 45 days (West-Eberhard, 1969). Within multiple-foundress units the dominant queen inhibits the reproduction of her subordinates by eating their eggs and forcing them into riskier and energetically more expensive occupations (West-Eberhard, 1969; Noonan, 1979). Their ovaries regress during this period, but if the queen is lost or removed experimentally, one of them assumes her place and functions as a normal queen (West-Eberhard, 1969; Noonan, 1979).

At about the time that workers mature, queens and single-foundresses begin to lay eggs that will develop into males and potential foundress females. The transition is abrupt (West-Eberhard, 1969; Noonan, 1979), allowing one to define the period during which reproductives are produced. The differential contribution of foundresses to the reproductive brood determines their direct genetic contribution to the next generation, because only these offspring and not workers transmit their genes directly. Males and potential foundress females mature in late summer and fall and leave their natal nests to mate. The females then hibernate, beginning the cycle again. The old foundresses do not survive the winter to have a second season.

Methods of Marking, Measuring, and Transfer

This report is based on field observations of individually-marked foundresses at their nests (approximately 400 hours of observation of undisturbed colonies) in 1974–1977. I marked the wasps with Testor's enamel on the thorax and occasionally by accident on the wings, head, or abdomen. The marks did not seem to impair their normal activities unless applied directly to joints (such accidents were rare) and remained recognizable in most cases without retouching for several months. I marked potential foundresses emerging as adults on colonies in the late summer and fall by colony only, using a color code. I found no equivocal colony marks on overwintered foundresses. In the spring, I recaptured foundresses and marked them individually with small spots of enamel superimposed on the colony marks if there were any. In 1974 and 1975, I removed wasps from their nests for marking with a stick or forceps and returned them as gently as possible after marking. In 1976, I marked all potential foundresses while they were on their nests by daubing them with paint on the end of a straw. Foreign wasps were not allowed on nests, so I could be confident that the individuals marked on nests according to these procedures were reared on those nests.

I measured the winglengths of the wasps (tip to tegulum) using Helios dial calipers with needle points. This measure has been shown to correlate with total body length (West-Eberhard, 1967a, 1969).

Patterns of Foundress Associations

During the first weeks of colony-founding, foundresses shift frequently from nest to nest, fighting intensely for possession of nest-starts and dominance within groups (West-Eberhard, 1967a, b, 1969; Noonan, 1979). By the first week in June, however, in all three years of my study, most individuals were consistent residents of one nest, and dominance within social groups had stabilized. According to their behavior at this time, I classified individuals as single-foundresses, queens of multiple-foundress associations, or subordinate cofoundresses in multiple-foundress associations. In 1975 and 1976, I classified individuals on the basis of many hours of observation of the foundresses at their nests. In 1977, I associated foundresses with particular nests if they were observed on that nest and on no other during periodic censusing after June 1 or on several occasions before June 1.

Measuring Colony Productivity

To estimate the productivity of colonies in terms of reproductives reared, and my efficiency in marking the reproductives, I kept nest-map records of pupae and their emergence as adults on all nests from about August 1 through September 30 when reproductives were maturing. During this period, I marked from 50 per cent to 100 per cent of individuals emerging as adults as indicated by the numbers of vacated cells which had contained pupae. For convenience, I will refer to females reared on the same parental nest as sisters, although they may be full or half-sisters depending on whether their mother mated singly or multiply, and, if the parent colony had more than one laying foundress, some may be more distantly related. I estimated the sizes of sister groups in the foundress population the following spring, including the expected numbers of unmarked individuals, by assuming that marked and unmarked individuals were equally likely to survive the winter.

Behavioral Observations and Manipulations

I watched colonies regularly for periods of usually 1 to 2 hours a day (in some cases, I could watch 2 closely-spaced colonies simultaneously). I recorded the frequency and duration of various activities carried out by individuals, including: egg laying, egg eating, sitting, fighting, foraging, building, and tending brood. In addition to observing the behavior of unmanipulated individuals, I devised an experiment to test the tolerance of spring foundresses to non-nestmates placed on their nests depending on whether they were sisters or nonsisters. The experiment was carried out on cool spring days (60° – 70°F.) in late May and early June, 1975 and 1976. In each trial, a foundress was removed from her nest and transferred on the end of a stick to the nest of a sister or a nonsister (on the nest at the time of the trial). She was counted as accepted if she remained on the nest for 15 minutes (an arbitrary criterion). I rated the most intense aggressive interaction between the test wasp and residents on a I–IV scale as follows: I — no response, or light tapping with the antennae (characteristic of interactions among nestmates), II — nipping, biting, and chasing, III — grappling and buzz-fighting, and IV — falling fights in which grappling wasps lose their footing and fall to the ground (this is sometimes accompanied by jabbing with the sting). I presented residents with test wasps no more than twice a day, once in the morning and once in the afternoon. I used individuals as test wasps no more than twice in a morning or afternoon, each trial separated by at least 30 minutes.

Inclusive Fitness Estimates

I estimated the direct and indirect components of inclusive fitness in offspring equivalents (West-Eberhard, 1975) for single-foundresses, queens of multiple-foundress associations, and their subordinate cofoundresses. Only reproductive offspring (not workers) were counted.

I considered the inclusive fitnesses of single-foundresses to be the amount of direct reproductive success (DRS) they realized. This estimate somewhat arbitrarily ignored possible indirect effects on their inclusive fitnesses of refusing to aid relatives or to accept aid. (West-Eberhard, 1969). However, such effects were considered in my estimates of the relative inclusive fitnesses of cooperating foundresses and, hence, in my comparisons of single-founding and cooperative strategies (see below). Circumstances in which single-foundresses disappeared but their worker daughters succeeded in rearing their grandsons were sufficiently rare that they could be disregarded (3 per cent of 72 single-foundress colonies in 1976). Therefore, I estimated the inclusive fitnesses of single-foundresses to be the average productivity in terms of reproductives of single-foundress colonies.

The inclusive fitnesses of cooperating queens and subordinate cofoundresses were considered to have both direct and indirect components. I estimated the following parameters of the direct component (DRS) for the individuals in different-sized groups:

(1) 1_{Q_N} and 1_{S_N} — the survivorship of queens and subordinates, respectively, from colony initiation to the time when reproductives were produced in an N-foundress group.

(2) P_N — the productivity in terms of reproductives of N-foundress colonies that were active at the time when reproductives were being produced.

(3) m_{Q_N} and m_{S_N} — the proportions of eggs contributed to the reproductive brood per queen and per subordinate surviving to the time when reproductives were produced in N-foundress colonies.

The product of m_N and P_N was thus an estimate of the fecundity of foundresses that survived to the time when reproductives were produced. Multiplied together, the three parameters yielded estimates of DRS for queens and subordinates in colonies with from 2 to 9 foundresses:

$$DRS_{Q_N} = 1_{Q_N} m_{Q_N} P_N \quad \text{for queens and}$$

$$DRS_{S_N} = 1_{S_N} m_{S_N} P_N \quad \text{for subordinate cofoundresses.}$$

Estimating 1_Q and 1_S: I estimated the survivorship of queens and subordinates in 2- to 9-foundress groups by periodically censusing colonies with marked foundresses of known status. Colonies were censused on cool days and in the evening when foragers were most likely to be at the nest. A special effort was made to census colonies at the beginning of the reproductive-producing period.

Estimating m_{Q_N} and m_{S_N}: I estimated the proportional contributions to P_N of queens (m_{Q_N}) and individual subordinates (m_{S_N}) by making extensive observations of foundresses at their nests during the reproductive-producing period (180 hours in July and 80 hours in August). I determined the average proportions of eggs (corrected for eggs eaten by nestmates) contributed per queen and per subordinate to the reproductive brood by regularly observing the oviposition behavior of undisturbed, marked individuals (14 queens and 36 subordinates in 14 colonies). In *Polistes fuscatus,* egg eating usually occurs within a half-hour of laying

(West-Eberhard, 1969; Noonan, 1979). I observed colonies long enough after ovipositions to be relatively sure that eggs remaining at the end of watches were not eaten subsequently. However, because the eggs of subordinates are eaten more often than those of queens (West-Eberhard, 1969; Noonan, 1979), egg eating after watches terminated would cause my estimates of subordinate direct reproduction to be high.

I estimated the probability per subordinate of taking over or inheriting the nest from its original queen by observing regularly the attendance and dominance relationships of the 14 queens and 36 subordinate cofoundresses. I also continued to census colonies and to search for new colonies established at mid-season to estimate the likelihood of direct reproduction by foundresses leaving the original colony and joining another, or else founding a new colony during the reproductive-producing period. I combined the probabilities of direct reproduction above, weighted by their frequencies of occurrence among the subordinates, into an average value of m_N per subordinate cofoundress. I estimated m_Q for queens in associations of N foundresses as $1-(N-1)1_s m_s$, or 1 minus the proportion of eggs contributed by the $N-1$ subordinate cofoundresses present during the reproductive-producing period.

I used the method of Metcalf and Whitt (1977b) modified to fit the form of the data to estimate the inclusive fitnesses of queens and subordinates in multiple-foundress colonies relative to that of single-foundresses. First, I computed the net effect of cooperation on the transmission of a foundress (F)'s genes as the ratio of her genes transmitted directly and indirectly by her and her associates (A_{1-N}) in the multiple-foundress group to those that would have been transmitted by her and her associates had they founded colonies separately. The formula I used was as follows:

$$\text{Relative Inclusive Fitness} = \frac{DRS_F \text{ in association} + \sum_{A=1}^{N-1} r_{F-A} \, DRS_A \text{ in association}}{DRS_F \text{ as single foundress} + \sum_{A=1}^{N-1} r_{F-A} \, DRS_A \text{ as single foundresses}}$$

where F is the foundress whose fitness is being calculated, $A_{1-(N-1)}$ are her associates in a multiple-foundress colony with N foundresses, and r_{F-A} is the degree of genetic relatedness between F and associate A (assumed to be the same between all cofoundresses in the calculations).

I multiplied the relative inclusive fitnesses obtained by the above formula by the average direct reproduction of single-foundresses to get inclusive fitnesses in comparable units of offspring equivalents (West-Eberhard, 1975). I subtracted the direct reproduction of queens and subordinate foundresses from their overall inclusive fitnesses to estimate an indirect component of their inclusive fitnesses, i.e., *the adjustment of direct reproductive success in offspring equivalents that must be made because of effects on genetic relatives*.

I used three hypothetical values of r_{F-A} ($3/4$, $3/8$, and $1/4$) to calculate a range of probable inclusive fitnesses. Data published by Metcalf and Whitt (1977a) indicate that *Polistes metricus* females usually mate twice and use sperm from the two inseminations in a ratio of 9:1. If the same is true of *P. fuscatus* females, then most females reared on the same nest will be full sisters related by $3/4$, and a few will be half-sisters (with different fathers) related by $1/4$. If two females are offspring of different mothers that were cofoundresses, it is most likely that they will be full cousins related by $3/8$ (that is, daughters of full sisters). The average value of r_{F-A} depends upon the frequencies of these different situations, and the abilities of individuals to discriminate and select among them in forming associations.

Statistical Procedures

I used several non-parametric statistical procedures to analyse the data: Chi^2 test for independence (Chi^2; Siegal, 1956), Mann-Whitney U test (U; Conover, 1971), Fisher's exact probability test (Siegal, 1956), G test (G; Sokal and Rohlf, 1969) and Spearman's rank correlation (r_s; Conover, 1971). I also used t-tests (t; Remington and Schork, 1970).

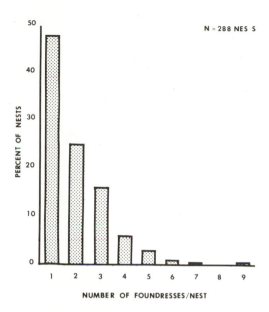

N = 288 NES S

Figure 2–1.   The frequency distribution of the numbers of foundresses on nests in late May and early June 1974–1977. Data from seven localities within a 5-mile radius of the University of Michigan Botanical Gardens were combined (see Noonan, 1979, for precise locations).

RELATEDNESS AMONG COFOUNDRESSES

Substantial proportions of foundresses adopted each of the three strategies (becoming single-foundresses, or queens or subordinates in multiple-foundress associations). Figure 2–1 shows the frequencies of colonies with different numbers of foundresses in late May and early June 1974–1977. Of 288 colonies censused, 52 per cent were attended by multiple-foundresses, accounting for 76 per cent of all foundresses ($N = 578$). Thus, 49.8 per cent of overwintered wasps settling on nests assumed subordinate positions in groups rather than founding colonies of their own, and 26.1 per cent were dominant queens in multiple-foundress groups, and 24.1 per cent were single-foundresses.

If effects on genetic relatives figure importantly in foundress reproductive strategies, then cofoundresses should most often be sisters. Evidence from association of marked nest progeny in several Polistine wasp species suggests that they usually are: *Polistes fuscatus* (West-Eberhard, 1969; Noonan, 1979; Klahn, 1979), *Polistes canadensis* (West-Eberhard, 1969), *P. gallicus* (Heldmann, 1936), *P. annularis* (Rau, 1940; Strassmann, 1979), *P. metricus* (Metcalf and Whitt, using genetic markers, 1977a), *Mischocyttarus drewseni* (Jeanne, 1971) and *M. mexicanus* (Litte, 1977). In West-Eberhard's study of *Polistes fuscatus*, 14 of 18 marked progeny of a single parental nest associated only with sisters. Since foundresses return to their natal eaves to nest, it was not clear whether sister-groupings resulted from active selection by the wasps or incidentally from sluggish dispersal. If helping sisters contributes importantly to subordinate inclusive fitness, I would expect them to have evolved mechanisms preventing the misdirection or parasitism of that help by unrelated wasps. I looked for evidence of this in the spatial arrangement of sister-groups from different parental nests and in the behavior of individuals toward sisters and nonsisters when both were founding colonies in the same locality.

Table 2–1.   Association patterns of marked sisters, 1975–1977.

Parental Nest	Potential Foundresses Marked	% Returned the Next Year	Single Foundresses	FOUNDRESS ASSOCIATIONS:			
				Exclusively Sisters	Sisters and Unmarked Wasps	With Unmarked Wasps Only	With Non-Sisters
1974:							
M-1	33 (77%)	12%	1	—	3	—	—
M-2	15 (75%)	20%	1	2	—	—	—
M-3	15 (100%)	13%	1	—	—	1	—
O-1	21 (60%)	28%	1	—	—	2	3
O-3	35 (75%)	31%	1	2	7	—	1
SUBTOTAL N = 26 foundresses			5	4	10	3	4
1975:							
B-30	136 (84%)	11%	2	7	—	1	2
B-20	94 (65%)	11%	2	2	—	—	3
B-22	55 (87%)	9%	1	—	2	—	1
B-16	86 (60%)	7%	2	—	—	—	—
B-5	15 (100%)	13%	2	—	—	—	—
O-13	13 (100%)	15%	1	—	—	—	—
O-16	15 (100%)	13%	2	—	—	—	—
O-19	42 (75%)	18%	1	—	2	—	—
O-22	25 (100%)	24%	—	4	2	—	—
M*-1	53 (86%)	21%	—	—	6	2	—
M-2	19 (84%)	10%	2	—	—	—	—
M-P	6 (74%)	16%	1	—	—	—	—
M-8	5 (100%)	20%	1	—	—	—	—
Z-6	20 (60%)	10%	—	2	—	—	—
Z-6F	26 (68%)	0%	—	—	—	—	—
Z-2	19 (100%)	4%	1	—	—	—	—
Z-5	2 (67%)	50%	1	—	—	—	—
SUBTOTAL N = 53 foundresses			19	17	10	1	6

1976:

O-A	35 (100%)	20%	—	7	—	—	—
O-B	80 (80%)	15%	1	12	5	—	—
O-C	82 (88%)	14%	—	6	1	—	—
O-D	40 (86%)	18%	—	6	—	—	—
O-E	15 (76%)	20%	—	—	—	3	—
B-A	81 (100%)	3%	—	2	—	—	—
B-B	130 (75%)	12%	2	13	—	—	—
B-C	59 (86%)	9%	—	5	—	—	—
B-D	72 (70%)	3%	—	2	—	—	—
B-E	44 (83%)	9%	—	4	—	—	—
SUBTOTAL N = 68 foundresses			3	57	6	3	0
GRAND TOTAL: N = 148 foundresses			27 (19%)	78 (52%)	26 (17%)	7 (5%)	10 (7%)

Association Patterns of Marked Foundresses

I repeated West-Eberhard's (1969) observations, marking progeny from several parental nests in each locality. Of 1,268 potential foundresses marked at four localities from 1974–1976, 148 (or 11.6 per cent) returned to found colonies the following spring (1975–1977). No marked wasps were found outside their home localities although nearby wasp-inhabited sites were searched periodically. Table 2–1 summarizes the association patterns of sisters and nonsisters with respect to one another. Of marked foundresses, 52 per cent associated only with sisters, 17 per cent with sisters and a few unmarked wasps, 5 per cent with unmarked wasps only, and 7 per cent with marked nonsisters. For 27 of the 31 families (progeny of one parental nest), the associating unmarked wasps could have been individuals missed during the marking in the previous season.

Significantly, the mixing of sisters and nonsisters occurred only after seasons in which I marked potential foundresses by removing them from nests. In 1976, I marked all potential foundresses directly on their nests, and in 1977, although the number of marked returning foundresses (68) was higher than in any previous year, there was no mixing of sisters and nonsisters. This suggests that females learn or imprint on some aspect of the parental colonies before leaving them in the fall, and that this functions in the assortment of sisters in the spring.

The composition of foundress groups diverged considerably from what one would expect on the basis of population viscosity alone. Although foundresses tended to settle near their natal nest sites (56 per cent of individuals directly on it, and an additional 20 per cent within five feet of it), offspring of different nests mingled extensively in a locality without cofounding. Sibling groups established new nests up to 72 feet from their parental nest site and in places that were, for a human at least, hard to find. Thus, foundresses seem to rely on more than proximity to their natal nests to discriminate sisters from nonsisters (but see Klahn, 1979, for a different conclusion). Returning to the natal nest may function in uniting siblings dispersed during hibernation, however, and in selecting a good nest site (West-Eberhard, 1969; Metcalf and Whitt, 1977b).

Differences in Behavior Toward Sisters and Nonsisters

As described above, I tested the responses of foundresses to unassociated sisters and nonsisters placed on their nests. Figure 2–2a shows the results: 67 per cent of 49 sisters were accepted on nests, but only 9 per cent of 69 nonsisters (G = 44.13, $p <.0001$). Members of different families consistently biased their acceptances in favor of sisters, significantly so in cases where the sample size was large enough to permit a statistical test (Chi^2 tests).

Although the range of aggressive responses to sisters and nonsisters was the same (Figure 2–2b), the distribution over the four levels of intensity differed (Chi^2 = 29.89; $p <.001$). Sisters received proportionally more of the mildest (level I) response (40 per cent vs. 7 per cent; Chi^2 = 18.62, $p <.001$). Sisters and nonsisters did not differ, however, in the proportion of the two most intense responses received (40 per cent and 26 per cent, respectively; Chi^2 = 2.3, NS). For level II and level III responses, the acceptance rate was higher for sisters than for nonsisters (Fisher's exact probability = .028 and .003, respectively). This experiment mimicked natural encounters between unmanipulated marked foundresses. On 13 occasions, unassociated sisters were allowed to sit on and inspect nests, but on at least 16 occasions, nonsisters were driven off when they attempted to land.

Costs of choosing sisters as associates also support the view that sibling groups are products of selection and not incidental effects of limited dispersal. The behaviors involved would soon disappear if they did not have compensating genetic advantages. Foundresses spent both time and energy guarding their newly-started nests against intruding conspecifics. During the first two weeks in May 1975, when foundresses were initiating nests, fights occurred at a rate of .67/nest/hour (46.5 nest-hours of observation on 19 nests). My

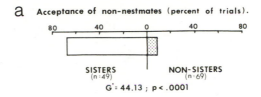

a Acceptance of non-nestmates (percent of trials).

SISTERS
(n = 49)

NON-SISTERS
(n = 69)

G' = 44.13 ; p < .0001

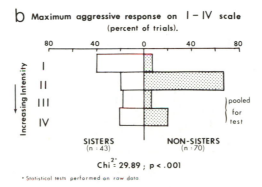

b Maximum aggressive response on I – IV scale
(percent of trials).

Increasing Intensity

I
II
III
IV

}pooled
for
test

SISTERS
(n = 43)

NON-SISTERS
(n = 70)

Chi^{2*} = 29.89 ; p < .001

* Statistical tests performed on raw data

TREATMENT OF   SISTERS   &   NON-SISTERS

Figure 2–2a.   The response of spring foundresses to nonassociates put on their nests. Sister and nonsister intruders were used. The criterion for acceptance of an intruder was its remaining on the recipient nest for at least 15 minutes. 2–2b. The distributions of maximum aggressive responses of intruders and resident foundresses, for sister and nonsister intruders.

field assistants and I observed 3 deaths following fights. In each case, the victim showed no external damage, but was unable to walk or fly, suggesting that it had been stung. Although fighting may serve in part to prevent nest usurpation by sisters and nonsisters alike (Gamboa, 1978; Gibo, 1978; Noonan, 1979), evidence suggests that nonsisters are repelled more often than sisters: 40 per cent of fights occurred between residents and foundresses from other nests, while 25 per cent occurred between residents and individuals that later associated with them, and 35 per cent occurred between residents and unidentified wasps.

ESTIMATES OF INCLUSIVE FITNESS

The different treatment of sisters and nonsisters indicates that effects on genetic relatives have been important in the evolutionary background of subordinate behavior. But do subordinates gain enough indirectly by helping sister queens to compensate foregoing direct reproduction on their own, or do they somehow increase their probability of reproducing directly by joining a dominant sister and realize an indirect bonus in fitness through mutualistic benefits to her? Subordinates could even pursue a mixed strategy in which combined direct and indirect components of fitness in offspring equivalents surpassed what they could expect to produce as single-foundresses although neither component did so

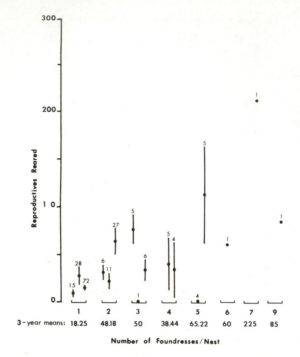

Figure 2–3.   Productivity of nests with different numbers of foundresses in terms of reproductives reared. Data from 1974, 1975, and 1976 are shown separately. Lines indicate standard errors. The numbers above the bars indicate the sample sizes. The mean productivities for all three years combined is shown below the horizontal axis.

alone. To investigate these possibilities, I estimated the average inclusive fitness for subordinate foundresses and compared it with that of single-foundresses and queens of multiple-foundress colonies.

Success of Single- and Multiple-foundress Colonies

Figure 2–3 shows the mean success in reproductive offspring reared by year for 192 colonies with different numbers of foundresses in three different years (1974–1977). Success varied considerably among and within localities in any given year as well as among years (Noonan, 1979). Colony success correlated significantly with the number of foundresses in early June ($r_s = 0.37$, $p < .01$), as did success per individual foundress ($r_s = 0.16$, $p < .05$). These correlations result mainly from the difference in success between single- and multiple-foundress nests. There was no relationship between success and foundress number among multiple-foundress nests only ($r_s = 0.07$, $NS; n = 77$). The success of multiple-foundress nests relative to single-foundress nests resulted mainly from a difference in the likelihood that the two kinds of colonies would produce any reproductives at all (Chi^2 = 19.07, $p < .01$, 1976 data only). There was a significant relationship, however, between foundress number and success when only nests that produced reproductives were considered ($r_s = 0.38$, $p < .01$). Successful two-foundress nests were significantly more productive than successful single-foundress nests (U test; $p < .005$), but successful nests with more than two foundresses were not. Thus, subordinate cofoundresses increased both the likelihood that a colony would produce reproductives and the numbers of reproductives produced if successful.

I combined data from all three years to calculate P_N, the productivity in terms of reproductives of colonies that were active at the time when reproductives were being produced. The values of P_N thus obtained, which I used in calculating the inclusive fitnesses of queens and subordinates in multiple-foundress colonies, are shown in Table 2–2.

Direct Reproduction by Queens and Subordinates in Multiple-foundress Colonies

Survivorship (1_Q and 1_s), fecundity ($P_N m_Q$ and $P_N m_s$), and total direct reproductive success (DRS) estimates for queens and their subordinate cofoundresses in different-sized associations are summarized in Table 2. Although queens and their subordinates differed significantly in survivorship from colony-initiation to the reproductive-producing period (90 per cent of 40 queens versus 68 per cent of 79 subordinates in 1976; $Chi^2 = 7.29$, $p < .01$), they did not differ significantly in survivorship during that period (82 per cent of 17 queens versus 79 per cent of 34 subordinates in 1976; $Chi^2 = 0.95$, NS). Both queens and subordinates had higher survivorship to the period when reproductives were produced than did single-foundresses (53 per cent of 55 single-foundresses; Chi^2 tests, $p < .001$, and $.05 < p < .10$, respectively).

Table 2–3 shows the egg contributions of 14 queens and 36 subordinates in 14 multiple-foundress colonies during 180 hours of observation in July: 159 eggs were laid, 60 per cent by queens and 40 per cent by subordinates. About one third of all subordinate eggs were eaten by the queen or other subordinates. This reduced the net contribution of eggs by subordinate cofoundresses to 33 per cent or 13 per cent per individual subordinate and raised the queen's to 67 per cent. The fractional contribution per subordinate varied little with association size (Noonan, 1979), but the absolute contribution did (3–26 eggs/ subordinate) depending on the expected success of the multiple-foundress colony (P_N).

None of the 36 subordinate cofoundresses inherited a nest from an original queen, but one apparently took over. C, the dominant on M*-1 in 1975, fell in rank precipitously at the end of June and was attacked by all of her former subordinates (including 2 marked sisters). On July 4th and 5th, she spent hardly any time on the nest and was thrown off twice by the lowest-ranking subordinate. I dissected her on July 5th. Her ovaries were greatly expanded as is characteristic of queens in mid-season and had no visible abnormalities. After C's death, the next-dominant foundress became queen, dominating the remaining two subordinates and eating many of their eggs. Thus, I estimated the probability of taking over per subordinate as 1 in 36 (2.8 per cent) for subordinates surviving to the period when reproductives are produced (approximately July 1). I considered the probability of a superseding subordinate herself being superseded as small enough to be disregarded.

Neither queens nor subordinates left their original colonies in mid-season to found new ones elsewhere except when moving en masse to rebuild nests destroyed by predators (a circumstance I treated as an extension of the original colony; Noonan, 1979). In addition, new colonies attended by unmarked individuals at mid-season were extremely rare and unsuccessful in producing offspring. This avenue of direct reproduction for queens and subordinates was therefore considered negligible. Thus, m_s per subordinate cofoundress was:

$$m_s = .97 (.13) + .03 (.67) = .14$$

m_Q was calculated for queens in different-sized associations according to the formula given in the *Inclusive Fitness Estimates* Section (above). The results are shown in Table 2–2.

The estimated values of direct reproductive success for single-foundresses and for queens and subordinate cofoundresses in multiple-foundress colonies are compared in Fig-

Table 2–2.   Survivorship, fecundity, and total direct reproductive success (DRS) of single-foundresses, and queens and their subordinate cofoundresses in 2- to 9-foundress associations. m_S per subordinate was estimated to be .14. m_Q for queens in 2- to 9-foundress associations was calculated according to the formula, $1 - (N-1)l_S m_S$. The number of colonies on which the survivorship estimates were based is shown in parentheses below l_Q.

		Association Size							
	1	2	3	4	5	6	7	9
P_N:	34.5	54.5	54.5	57.7	117.5	60	225	85
(number of colonies)	(61)	(33)	(11)	(6)	(1)	(1)	(1)	(1)
Queens:								
Survivorship (l_Q)	.53	.90	.80	.63	.50	1.0	1.0	1.0
	(100)	(29)	(20)	(14)	(4)	(3)	(1)	(1)
m_{QN}		.91	.82	.81	.78	.63	.30	.16
Fecundity ($P_N m_Q$)	—	49.8	44.9	46.8	91.8	37.7	68.1	13.6
Total DRS_Q (offspring)	18.25	46.4	35.9	29.5	45.9	37.7	68.1	13.6
Subordinates:								
Survivorship (l_S)		.61	.63	.45	.39	.53	.83	.75
Fecundity ($P_N m_S$)		7.6	7.6	8.0	16.4	8.4	31.5	11.9
Total DRS_S		4.6	4.8	3.6	6.4	4.4	26.1	8.9

Table 2–3.   Egg laying and egg eating by queens and subordinate cofoundresses on multiple-foundress nests in July.

Nest	# Hrs. Obs'd.	# Foundresses	Queen Eggs (# Eaten)	Subordinate Eggs (# Eaten)	Remaining Sub. Eggs
1975:					
M*-1	27	5	23 (2)	25 (7)	18
O-1/19	14.5	3	0	1 (0)	1
B-6F	15	6	3 (0)	3 (1)	2
B-02	4.5	2	2 (0)	1 (0)	1
R-1	19	5	2 (0)	3 (0)	3
1976:					
M-30	20	5	14 (0)	11 (5)	6
M-28	8	2	1 (0)	0	—
M-42	8	2	1 (0)	0	—
B-1	16	2	8 (0)	0	—
O-36	16	2	10 (0)	1?(0)	1?
O-51	7	3	0	0	—
Bu-P	10	5	3 (0)	0	—
O-35	5	3	0	0	—
1977:					
A-9B	10	5	28 (0)	19 (6)	13
TOTAL	180	50	95 (2)	64 (19)	45
		(14Q,36S)	(67%)		(33%)
% egg contribution:			Queens: 67%	Individual Subordinates 13%	

ure 2–4 (black portions of bars). Subordinates in all colonies combined averaged a direct reproductive success of 5.2 offspring. If the average direct reproduction of single-foundresses (18.25 offspring) is taken as an estimate of a subordinate's expected success if she founded a colony alone, these data suggest that subordinates do not reproduce enough directly for the strategy to pay if this were their only reproductive contribution.

Indirect Reproduction by Subordinates

The indirect components of subordinate inclusive fitnesses for each of the three probable degrees of relatedness between queen and subordinate ($3/4$, $3/8$, and $1/4$) are shown in Figure 2–4. Indirect reproduction achieved by a full sister ($r = 3/4$) varied for colonies with different numbers of foundresses. For all 150 subordinates on 192 nests, it averaged 10.7 offspring equivalents, less than the average direct reproduction of single-foundresses. Together with direct reproduction, the average inclusive fitness of a subordinate was 15.9 offspring equivalents, again slightly less than the 18.25 realized by single-foundresses.

However, a strong annual effect contributes to the relatively low success of subordinates in the three-year sample. In 1975, multiple-foundress nests actually did worse than single-foundress nests (22.6 versus 27.9 reproductives). Possible causes of this were heavy predation on multiple-foundress nests and a high frequency of single-founding in one very productive locality (although single-founding in 1975 was no more frequent than in other years). In both 1974 and 1976, by contrast, multiple-foundress nests produced enough reproductives compared to single-foundress nests for subordinates to gain in inclusive fitness by joining multiple-foundress groups if they were full sisters of the colony queen. Overall, subordinates did better than or equalled single-foundresses in inclusive fitness if they were related by only $3/8$ and not significantly worse if related by only $1/4$ (Table 2–4).

Table 2–4.   The inclusive fitnesses of single-foundresses and the average subordinate cofoundress in 1974 and 1975. Direct and indirect components are shown for subordinates for different hypothetical degrees of relatedness between them and the queen.

	(N)	Direct	Indirect	Total
1974: Single foundresses	(15)	13.1	—	13.1
Average subordinate	(11)			
$r = {}^3/_4$		5.1	11.9	17.0
$r = {}^3/_8$		5.1	8.5	13.6
$r = {}^1/_4$		5.1	6.5	11.6
1976: Single foundresses	(72)	15.6	—	15.6
Average subordinate	(85)			
$r = {}^3/_4$		5.7	13.2	18.9
$r = {}^3/_8$		5.7	9.5	15.2
$r = {}^1/_4$		5.7	7.8	13.5

Individual Differences and Strategy

Females that become subordinate foundresses are probably less likely to succeed alone than females that actually found nests singly. Subordinate cofoundresses were generally smaller than single-foundresses (U test, $n = 55, 27$) and association queens (U test; $p <.01$, $n = 55, 26$), and this was especially true within sibling groups (Figure 2–5). Turillazzi and Pardi (1977) report the same relationship between size and dominance among cofoundresses in *Polistes gallicus*. I hypothesized that small wasps were less likely to succeed as single-foundresses than larger ones. In 1975, the size of single-foundress nests at mid-season just before workers matured correlated positively with foundress size (estimated by wing length) at three localities ($r_s = 0.62, p <.01$). However, a larger sample of single-foundress nests in 1976 failed to show a significant relationship between nest size and foundress size (Noonan, 1979).

The estimated inclusive fitnesses of subordinate foundresses suggest that the subordinate strategy pays off to individuals mainly through help conferred on sister queens. Subordinates reproduced nearly as much as single-foundresses and in two of the three years outreproduced them (if they were full sisters of the queen and other associates). However, their direct reproduction was consistently and substantially less than that of single-foundresses. If subordinates are less likely to succeed alone than single foundresses, then the advantage to them of indirect as opposed to direct reproductive effort has been underestimated in my analysis. If their likelihood of success alone were low enough, founding a colony jointly with even an unrelated dominant might prove a better strategy of direct reproduction (Gibo, 1974; West-Eberhard, 1975; Klahn, 1979).

Availability of Sisters and Foundress Strategy

A critical question relating to the relative importance of direct and indirect reproduction in subordinates' strategies is: What does a female do if she arrives at nesting sites in the spring and finds no sisters? I investigated the effect of size of sibling groups on the frequency of single-founding in 31 families during the three seasons (1975–1977). Single-foundresses had significantly fewer sisters than associating foundresses (6.8 versus 10.5, U, $p <.01$; $n = 26, 115$). Figure 2–6 shows the proportion of siblings founding colonies alone as a function of the size of the sibship. None of the wasps with no sisters joined an association or was joined by other wasps although other foundresses nested nearby. Foundresses from very small sibships tended to found colonies alone as well. This suggests that joining is not advantageous to individuals unless there are sisters available for helping and thereby deriving indirect fitness.

COMPETITION AMONG COFOUNDRESSES

Although subordinate foundresses appear to gain by helping their sister queens as opposed to founding colonies alone, they should gain more as queens than as helpers (Figure 2–4). In addition, as the season progresses, the costs and benefits of giving further help versus contending for direct reproduction change. Especially after the emergence of true workers, the continuing help of subordinates becomes less critical to the queen's reproductive success (Noonan, 1979). I predicted that subordinates should behave in a more directly selfish fashion once workers were reared and the eggs producing reproductives were being laid. Specifically, I expected an increase in the proportion of time they spent at the nest, a decrease in foraging rate, and increases in egg laying, and aggressive behavior among cofoundresses.

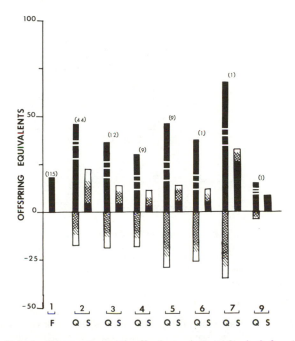

Figure 2–4.   Inclusive fitness estimates (in offspring equivalents) for single foundresses, queens of multiple-foundress associations, and subordinate cofoundresses. Direct reproduction is indicated by black bars. The indirect component of inclusive fitness—that is, fitness in offspring equivalents gained or lost because of effects on the reproduction of genetic relatives is indicated by cross-hatched, hatched, and clear portions of bars. Cross-hatched portions indicate the effect of association if the individual is related to its cofoundresses by ¼; hatched portions indicate the effect in addition to the cross-hatched portion if the individual is related to its cofoundresses by ⅜; and, clear portions indicate the effect in addition to the above if the individual is related to its cofoundresses by ¾. The inclusive fitnesses of multiple-foundress association queens are less than their total direct reproduction because of negative effects on the reproduction of their cofoundresses. Their net inclusive fitnesses are therefore indicated by white lines cutting across the black bars that denote their direct reproduction. The highest white line indicates the inclusive fitness realized by queens related to their subordinates by ¼, the next highest line that realized by queens related to their subordinates by ⅜, and the lowest line that of queens related to their subordinates by ¾. The numbers in parentheses above the bars indicate sample size (numbers of colonies).

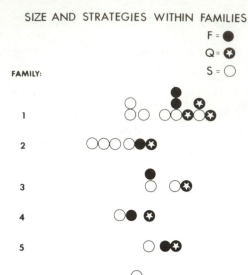

SIZE AND STRATEGIES WITHIN FAMILIES

F = ●
Q = ✪
S = ○

FAMILY:

WING LENGTH IN CM.

Figure 2–5.   Reproductive strategies of sisters (foundresses reared on the same parental nest) as a function of body size (winglength in centimeters). Sisters from each family are shown on a separate histogram with respect to winglength (Families 1–8). Solid dots indicate single foundresses. Dots with starred centers indicate queens of multiple-foundress associations. Open circles indicate subordinate cofoundresses. (The associations of individuals in new colonies are not indicated).

Testing these predictions about changes in individual behavior was complicated by the high mortality of subordinate foundresses before production of reproductive offspring. Only 16 (38 percent) of 42 subordinate foundresses observed in June survived until July. To increase my sample, I began watching 17 additional subordinate foundresses at the beginning of July at nests not watched earlier in the season. However, neither these individuals nor the 16 original foundresses that survived the whole season are likely to be an unbiased sample of all subordinate foundresses with respect to their behavior. Survival probably correlates with exactly those behaviors I wished to investigate. Therefore, inferences about behavior changes in individuals from the mean values for all individuals watched could be misleading. For example, subordinate foundresses might consist of two types: one that worked hard and suffered a high mortality as a result and one that worked hardly at all and so survived to compete directly with the foundress queen for direct reproduction in July. If I pooled the behavior frequencies of both types, I might conclude that subordinate altruism early in the season shifted to selfishness later, when in fact the selfish individuals in July had never shown much altruism. To investigate this possibility, I looked for significant

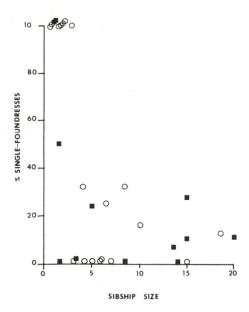

Figure 2–6.   Percentage of foundresses establishing colonies alone (single-foundresses) as a function of sibship size (numbers of sisters in the foundress population). Each point represents one sibship, the foundresses derived from one parental nest the previous season ($n = 31$). Solid squares indicate the progeny of multiple-foundress colonies. Open circles indicate the progeny of single-foundress colonies.

differences between the behavior of individuals observed in both months and those observed only in June or July. Significantly more altruistic behaviors in the June-only foundresses and significantly less in the July-only foundresses would suggest that differences in the overall sample, if any, resulted from heterogeneity in the behavior of individuals sampled at the two times rather than a change over time in individual behavior. I used t-tests, which are more likely to detect differences than analogous non-parametric tests. Only one behavior (loads brought to the nest in June) differed at the .05 level of significance between the two samples (Noonan, 1979). June-only subordinates brought fewer loads to the nest than did the 16 surviving subordinates, contrary to my prediction that foraging should decrease from June to July. I therefore included the behavior records of all foundresses from both samples in my analysis.

Variation among individuals presents an additional problem in interpreting the results as a shift in behavior over the season. Mean differences might reflect the dramatic shifts in behavior of a few individuals, while most did not change or made less significant shifts in either direction. To investigate this possibility, I made pairwise t-tests for differences in behavior in June versus July for the foundresses present in both months. In addition, I considered the proportion of individuals in the sample that shifted their behavior in the direction of the shift in means.

Figure 2–7 shows the results for the entire sample of subordinates observed in June, July, or in both months. Time spent at the nest increased from 52 per cent in June to 62 per cent in July (U test; $p <.04$, $n=42, 33$). Foraging of solid loads decreased from 0.65 to 0.26 loads per hour (U test; $p <.001$, $n = 42, 33$). Egg laying did not increase significantly (0.05 eggs per hour in June compared to 0.13 eggs per hour in July; U test). Attacks (antenna-tapping, biting, chewing, and chasing) received from cofoundresses (2.02/hour

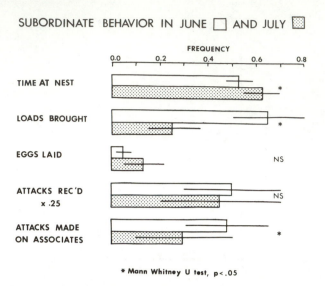

Figure 2–7.   Comparisons of the frequencies of behaviors of subordinate cofoundresses in June and July (based on 217 hours of observation in June and 174 hours of observation in July).

in June and 1.77/hour in July) and attacks made on cofoundresses (.48/hour in June and .30/hour in July) did not change significantly (U tests). Thus foundresses in July were more directly selfish in that they spent more time at the nest and foraged less. However, there was no evidence that aggression among cofoundresses increased.

The mean values and direction of changes from June to July for the subordinates observed in both months and the pooled sample agreed closely. However, in pairwise t-tests of the former sample, only egg laying (p < .17), loads foraged/hour (p < .005) and attacks received (p < .08) approached or reached significance. Six of the sixteen individuals increased time spent at the nest from June to July, nine decreased it, and one did not change. Twelve decreased their foraging rates, and four increased them. Egg laying increased for six, declined for three, and stayed the same for seven. However, it increased for six of the nine subordinates that laid at least one egg during the two months. Twelve foundresses received fewer attacks in July than June, and four received more. Finally, eight individuals attacked other foundresses less frequently in July than in June, two more frequently, and six at the same rate. These data indicate that there is considerable variability among individuals in behavior over the season and that factors other than the one investigated significantly influence individual behavior patterns. However, the observed trends have some general significance.

Production of reproductive offspring begins at slightly different times in different colonies. One can estimate its onset in specific cases by counting back from the date of appearance of the first adult male the 45.5 days average development time from egg to adult (West-Eberhard, 1969). To increase the precision of the tests of my predictions about aggression, I determined the approximate date of the first reproductive egg for the 10 colonies in which the 16 subordinates of my June–July sample were residents. I then compared the aggression rates among cofoundresses before and after that date. In this analysis, neither the number of attacks received by subordinates (1.95/hour before reproductive offspring were produced and 1.80 after) nor the number of attacks made by subordinates (.31/hour before and .38/hour after) increased during the period when reproductives were produced (t-tests). Finally, I plotted the weekly rates of aggression by queens toward subordinates (attacks/subordinate/hour) and of subordinates toward cofoundresses (attacks/cofoundress/hour) as a function of time during June and July. Figures 2–8 and 2–9 show that the onset of production of reproductive offspring was marked by an increase in aggression by queens toward subordinates and an increase in aggressiveness by subordinates. Subordinates increased their frequency of attacking both the queen and fellow subordinates at this time.

I interpret the shifts in subordinate behavior as an increasing emphasis over the season on direct versus indirect reproduction. Alternatively, they might reflect the decreased activity of senile individuals. (This would not explain the increases in egg laying or aggressiveness, but these changes were not significant.) The rate of foraging (helping) in June did not correlate significantly with decreases in helping in July as might be expected if the shifts in behavior were owing largely to senescence. Rather, the directions of the correlations were generally opposite to what would be expected under that hypothesis: time spent at the nest ($r_s = -.40$, $p < .11$), attacks made ($r_s = -.36$, $p < .19$), foraging in July ($r_s = +.36$, $p < .19$), and eggs laid ($r_s = -.59$, $p < .01$).

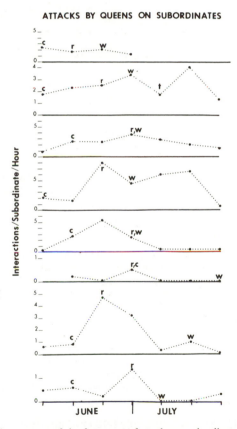

ATTACKS BY QUEENS ON SUBORDINATES

Interactions/Subordinate/Hour

JUNE   JULY

Figure 2–8.   Weekly averages of the frequency of attacks on subordinates (attacks/subordinate/hour) by 8 queens of multiple-foundress associations in June and July. "c" indicates the date of appearance of the first worker-pupa, "w" the emergence of the first adult worker, and "r" the estimated onset of the production of reproductives. "t" marks the date of takeover by a subordinate cofoundress.

ATTACKS BY SUBORDINATES ON COFOUNDRESSES

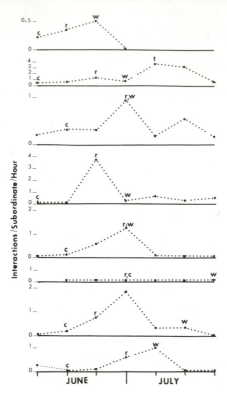

Figure 2–9.   Weekly averages of the frequency of attacks on nestmates (attacks/subordinate/hour) by 18 subordinate foundresses in 8 multiple-foundress associations in June and July.

DISCUSSION

Polistes fuscatus foundresses cooperate almost exclusively with sisters (Table 2–1), and employ directly selfish and helping strategies in proportion to the likelihood of direct and indirect reproductive gain (Table 2–4, Figures 2–4 – 2–9). Their social behavior thus fits the predictions of the general inclusive fitness model (Hamilton, 1964a,b, 1972; Alexander, 1974a; West-Eberhard, 1975). It also pertains to some more specific questions: (1) What is the role of population viscosity in the evolution of foundress cooperation? (2) What is the relative importance of direct (mutualistic) and indirect (nepotistic) gains in the evolution of subordinate behavior? (3) Why do foundress groups vary in size so widely? (4) Why is single-founding maintained if subordinate behavior is advantageous to individual inclusive fitness?, and (5) How is the conflict of reproductive interests between queens and their foundress daughters over the gain-threshold for advantageous cofounding resolved? I will discuss these questions here.

Population Viscosity and Helping Behavior

Hamilton (1964a,b, 1972, 1975) and others have argued that sluggish dispersal might concentrate relatives and raise their average relatedness through inbreeding to a level favoring general altruism and reduced competition locally. However, groups of cooperating relatives formed in this way would be susceptible to parasitism by selfish migrants and also by individuals within groups that were capable of discriminating between nearer and more distant relatives in giving help. Selection should rapidly favor the evolution of mechanisms besides proximity to identify appropriate recipients of help.

Polistes fuscatus foundresses were viscous among and within localities. So far as I could determine, they did not found nests outside their home localities, and within them they tended to nest near their parental nest sites. They probably did not inbreed closely (Noonan, 1978; Metcalf and Whitt, 1977a). However, helping was not indiscriminate within localities. It was confined almost exclusively to former nestmates. This indicates that if helping originated as an indiscriminate behavior, it was replaced by another means of identifying appropriate cofoundresses. Barrows et al. (1975) and Kukuk et al. (1977) present evidence that primitively social bees (*Lassioglossum zephyrum*) that form foundress associations also accept sisters more readily than nonsisters when they are placed in their nests. That potential foundresses in *Polistes fuscatus* can be disoriented with respect to sisters and nonsisters by disturbing them at their parental nests soon after they mature suggests that important cues for sister recognition are learned at the parental nest before they leave to hibernate. Similarly, foundresses in *Lassioglossum zephyrum*, which normally mature together in their parental nests, readily nest with nonsisters if groups of unrelated pupae are allowed to mature together in artificial nests in the laboratory (Kukuk et al., 1977).

Alexander and Borgia (1978) have argued that nepotism evolves usually as an extension of behaviors originating in parent-offspring interactions rather than as indiscriminate altruism toward highly related neighbors in viscous populations, and Hamilton (1964a) derived the inclusive fitness model theoretically as an extension of the altruism common in parent–offspring interactions. The confinement of cooperation in *Polistes fuscatus* to individuals reared on the same parental nest agrees with this interpretation although it could result by a more complicated route from the refinement of generalized cooperation.

The Relative Importance of Direct and Indirect Gains in the Evolution of Subordinate Behavior

Three models have been proposed to explain apparently altruistic behavior by selection among individuals. They are: (1) kin selection (Hamilton, 1964a,b, 1972); (2) reciprocal altruism (Trivers, 1971), or mutualism (Lin and Michener, 1972); and (3) parental manipulation of offspring (Alexander, 1972, 1974a,b). The selective forces involved in each are not mutually exclusive, and all fit into the general theory of inclusive-fitness-maximizing (Hamilton, 1972; Alexander, 1972, 1974a,b; West-Eberhard, 1975; Trivers, 1974). Yet, it is important to ask what their relative importance is in the background of specific cases.

In *Polistes fuscatus* foundresses, the restriction of helping to former nestmates and the absence of co-founding if nestmates are not available together indicate that presently subordinate behavior is being maintained primarily by kin selection rather than mutualism or direct gain. The estimated values of direct and indirect components of subordinate inclusive fitness (Figure 2–4, Table 2–4) support this conclusion as well although the high variance in success of single- and multiple-foundress nests provides a less powerful indication than the behavioral evidence. This does not require, however, that helping originated through kin selection. It could have begun as cooperation of individuals without regard to relatedness, each increasing her direct reproduction by founding a nest jointly with the other(s). In such a system, individuals that associated with sisters would have an advantage over ones that did not, initially through effects on their sisters' reproductive success, and later (in addition) through a reduced likelihood of cheating (Trivers, 1971; Alexander, 1974a; Alexander and Borgia, 1978). This would select for the ability to discriminate and restrict associates to sisters. It seems more likely, however, that foundress cooperation evolved by extension of the highly developed patterns of helping and association in the matrifilial colony (Hamilton, 1972; Alexander, 1974a,b, 1978; Alexander and Borgia, 1978).

Once sister cooperation was established, individuals, as a result of intracolony competition, may have adjusted their reproductive efforts between direct and indirect striving to maximize inclusive fitness, leading to the divergence of emphasis now seen between queens and subordinates (West-Eberhard, 1967a,b, this volume). Variations in social behavior among individuals and over individual lifetimes suggest that *Polistes fuscatus* foundresses respond to shifting opportunities to reproduce directly and indirectly. The rigors of overwintering plus unpredictable conditions during the vulnerable early stages of colony founding in the temperate zone undoubtedly promote a high degree of flexibility in reproductive strategies.

Inclusive Fitness and Variation in Foundress Group Sizes

Queens of multiple-foundress colonies outreproduced both subordinates and single-foundresses, averaging 22.6 offspring equivalents (if related to their cofoundresses by $3/4$) compared to 15.9 for subordinate cofoundresses and 18.25 for single-foundresses (Figure 2–4). In foundress groups of 3 or more, however, queens related to their cofoundresses by $3/4$ realized fewer offspring equivalents than single-foundresses, even though their direct reproduction was higher (Figure 2–4). This paradox illustrates Hamilton's (1964a,b) argument that harm done to a genetic relative's inclusive fitness may select for the refusal of help even though the recipient increases its direct reproduction. The inclusive fitnesses of queens in large associations fall below that of single-foundresses because their subordinates promote fewer copies of the *queen*'s genes by helping than they would by founding colonies separately. Potential subordinates should be selected even more strongly to avoid helping in such circumstances.

The inclusive fitnesses of subordinate cofoundresses also correlate negatively with foundress association size (Figure 2–4). These data therefore raise the question: Why do groups or more than two foundresses ever form? Subordinate inclusive fitnesses were calculated under the assumption that subordinates were as likely to succeed alone as actual single foundresses. If their likelihood of success alone is lower and if large associations attract the subordinates least likely to succeed alone, then the discrepancy between larger foundress associations and inclusive-fitness-maximizing may be reduced or disappear. The lower indirect gain by subordinates in larger associations may be compensated by an increase in direct reproduction undetected in this study. Subordinates may shift to a more directly competitive strategy if helping, in terms of additional offspring reared by the colony queen, reaches a point of diminishing returns with association size or if the success of the colony depends less on the efforts of any individual subordinate. Finally, some subordinates, hopelessly outcompeted by more dominant cofoundresses in the larger groups (West-Eberhard, this volume), may adopt pure helping strategies, freeing others to contend more seriously with the colony queen for direct reproduction (Noonan, 1979; Gamboa et al., 1978, for *P. metricus*).

Fighting in the early stages of colony founding may allow potential subordinates to test the quality of queens and the intensity of competition for nest sites—two factors that may influence the advantages of cooperation to individuals (West-Eberhard, 1967a,b, 1969; Gamboa, 1978; Noonan, 1979). It may also allow potential queens of associations to test the quality of potential subordinates. Queens tended to accept smaller siblings as subordinates rather than larger ones (Figure 2–5). If size is positively correlated with success of single-foundresses, then the queens select as subordinates individuals that are least likely to

succeed alone. In addition, small helpers probably pose less of a threat to the queen's reproductive dominance. Large associations were formed most often by siblings at their parental
nest site, and nests were built in the same places year after year (Noonan, 1979; Klahn,
1979). This suggests that nest sites vary in quality and that siblings may cooperate to defend
a proven site (the one that produced them) against unrelated usurpers (Gamboa, 1978;
Noonan, 1979). Nests built on the parental nest site, however, were not more productive
than nests built elsewhere (Noonan, unpubl.; but see Metcalf and Whitt, 1977b).

Parent-offspring Conflict and Foundress Cooperation

The reproductive interests of colony queens and their foundress daughters conflict
over the gain-threshold for advantageous cooperation among sisters (Alexander, 1972,
1974a,b; Trivers, 1974; Metcalf and Whitt, 1977b; Gibo, 1978). Queens prefer their daughters to cooperate if by doing so they increase the numbers of their grandchildren. For example, a two-foundress colony must be at least twice as successful as a single-foundress
colony for a queen to gain by her daughters' cooperation. But, for her daughter to gain by
founding a nest jointly with a dominant sister (assuming $r = {}^{3}/_{4}$ and the sister does all the
direct reproducing) the nest must be at least 2.33 times as successful as a single-foundress
nest (West-Eberhard, 1967a,b).

Estimates of subordinate inclusive fitness (Figure 2–4, Table 2–4) indicate that subordinates often reproduce enough indirectly for the strategy to pay off (for the subordinate
herself) in comparison with founding a colony alone (Table 4). Because the queen's threshold is even lower than her foundress daughter's, queens should therefore be selected to manipulate more of their daughters into founding colonies jointly. Does the persistence of a
high proportion of single-foundresses (24.1 per cent) indicate a failure of the queen's power
to manipulate her daughters' behavior so as to maximize her own inclusive fitness? Metcalf
and Whitt (1977b) argue that it does from similar data on the success of single- and multiple-
foundress nests in *Polistes metricus*.

For several reasons, however, the present evidence does not support this conclusion.
First, in some circumstances, the queen and her potentially subordinate foundress daughter
prefer single-founding. Thus, if there are no sisters for the foundress to join, her interests
coincide with her mother's in preferring to found a colony alone, no matter how successful
multiple-foundress colonies are (unless the foundress can identify more distant relatives
with $r > \bar{r}$, and multiple-foundress colonies are sufficiently successful). Similarly, if an individual is likely to be much more successful than the average single-foundress, her mother
might also prefer her to found a colony alone, even though the average single-foundress
nest was not sufficiently successful. The high variance in success of single-foundress nests
(Figure 2–3) suggests that this might frequently be the case. To test the hypothesis that the
reproductive interests of queens were not met by the single-founding tendencies of their
daughters one would have to know what proportions of foundresses fit the above descriptions as well as what proportion did not. This information is not yet available for either
Polistes fuscatus or *P. metricus*.

Second, it may be misleading to test quantitative predictions that are so similar by
using means of data as highly variable as the success of nests with different numbers of
foundresses. If the confidence interval around the mean includes both predictions, it is
pointless to argue that it is nearer one or the other. For two-foundress nests in the present
study, both kin selection and parental manipulation predictions were within the 95 per cent
confidence limits of the mean for two of the three years (1974 and 1976), and both were
above them in one (1975). Finally, the high variance in the success of nests means that sampling error could be significant, both in the form of censusing bias and in the form of random variation mistakes made by the wasps, especially in view of the small samples
available in each locality.

Alexander (1974a) and Trivers (1974) hypothesized that queens might gain by molding some of their potential foundress daughters into helpers for the others, lowering the inclusive fitnesses of some to maximize the number of grandchildren produced by the brood as a whole. Such manipulation would be costly if the severity of winters and the availability of nest sites were unpredictable from one season to the next as is likely in *P. fuscatus*. In addition, the high variance in success of nests and the variability in individual behavior suggest that selection is strong for individuals to be able to predict within a season the likely success of different strategies or alternative behaviors open to them and respond accordingly. If flexibility is at a premium, queens may gain more by permitting their daughters a wide range of flexibility in behavior even at the expense of some selfish tendencies than by molding them into obligate helpers or direct reproducers.

The Maintenance of Subordinate and Single-foundress Strategies

If subordinate cofoundresses consistently outreproduced single-foundresses, one would expect that tendencies for foundresses to establish colonies alone would soon disappear. There is no evidence that this is occurring in the study populations (Owen, 1962; West-Eberhard, 1967a, 1969; Noonan, 1979). Why does single-colony founding persist? Data on the success of nests with different numbers of foundresses in 1975 indicate that in some years, single-foundresses do better than some multiple-foundress colony queens as well as most subordinates. Variation in selection between years with some unpredictability of the relative success of single-foundresses and subordinates would maintain both strategies. The frequency of single-foundress colonies did not change over the three years of the study for all localities combined but fluctuated widely among localities and within localities from year to year (Noonan, 1979), as might be expected if foundresses are tracking different probabilities of success in different circumstances. In addition, as discussed above, single founding may be a more reproductive strategy for some individuals with no sister to join or with predictably high probabilities of success alone (e.g., larger foundresses; Figure 2–5) than joining a multiple-foundress colony as a subordinate in a population in which subordinates, on average, outreproduce single-foundresses. Both strategies could persist if such variation existed and could be capitalized upon by individual foundresses.

SUMMARY

Foundresses of the social paper wasp, *Polistes fuscatus,* adopt three different reproductive strategies: (1) founding a colony alone, (2) joining a multiple-foundress group as a dominant queen, and (3) becoming a subordinate foundress in a multiple-foundress group. Individuals seem to adjust their reproductive behavior according to factors important to inclusive-fitness-maximizing: the availability of sisters, the likelihood of their success as single-foundresses, and changing costs and benefits of giving further help rather than striving to reproduce directly. Although subordinate cofoundresses do raise some offspring of their own on multiple-foundress nests, they probably do not raise enough to make joining a multiple-foundress group advantageous unless there are sisters available for helping and thereby deriving indirect fitness.

ACKNOWLEDGEMENTS

For assistance in the field, I thank Mark Cochran, Carol Hartley Comacho, Joanne Ehret, Paul Etzler, Laura Frey, Bob Noonan, Deborah Trowbridge, Cindy Rosen, Steve

Weber, and Polly Yocum Fairchild. Richard D. Alexander, William D. Hamilton, Jeff E. Klahn, Bobbi S. Low, Thomas E. Moore, and Donald W. Tinkle provided valuable criticisms of the manuscript or parts of it. I am indebted to Dr. Hamilton and to Dr. Mary Jane West-Eberhard for insights concerning inclusive fitness. Finally, I am expecially grateful to my doctoral chairman, Richard D. Alexander, for his advice and encouragement throughout this research.

REFERENCES

Alexander, R. D. 1972. Reproductive competition and the evolution of sociality. *Am. Zool.* 12:648–649 (abstr.).

Alexander, R. D. 1974a. The evolution of social behavior. *Ann. Rev. Ecol. Syst.* 5:325–383.

———1974b. Evolution of sterile castes in the social insects: Kin selection or parental manipulation? *Fla. Ent.* 57:32.

———, and G. Borgia. 1978. Group selection, altruism and the levels of organization of life. *Ann. Rev. Ecol. Syst.* 9:449–474.

Barrows, E.M., W.D. Bell, and C.D. Michener. 1975. Individual odor differences and their social functions in insects. *PNAS* (Wash.) 72:2824–2828.

Conover, W. D. 1971. *Practical Nonparametric Statistics.* Wiley, New York.

Darwin, C. D. 1859. *The Origin of Species and the Descent of Man.* A Modern Library, New York.

Evans, H. E., and M. J. West-Eberhard. 1970. *The Wasps.* University of Michigan Press, Ann Arbor.

Gamboa, G. J. 1978. Intraspecific defense: Advantage of social cooperation among paper wasp foundresses. *Science* 199:1463–1465.

———, B. D. Heacock, and S. Wittjer. 1978. Division of labor and subordinate longevity in foundress associations of the paper wasp, *Polistes metricus* (Hymenoptera: Vespidae). *J. Kans. Ent. Soc.* 51:343–352.

Ghiselin, M. T. 1974. *The Economy of Nature and the Evolution of Sex.* Berkeley: University of Calif. Press xii + 346 pp.

Gibo, D. L. 1974. A laboratory study on the selective advantage of foundress associations in *Polistes fuscatus. Can. Ent.* 106: 101–106.

——— 1978. The selective advantage of foundress associations in *Polistes fuscatus* (Hymenoptera: Vespidae): A field study of the effects of predation on productivity. *Can. Ent.* 110: 519–540.

Hamilton, W. D. 1964a. The genetical evolution of social behavior. I *J. Theor. Biol.* 7:1–16.

——— 1964b. The genetical evolution of social behavior. II *J. Theor. Biol.* 7:17–52.

——— 1972. Altruism and related phenomena, mainly in social insects. *Ann. Rev. Ecol. Syst.* 3:193–232.

——— 1975. Innate social aptitudes of man: An approach from evolutionary genetics. In R. Fox (ed.) *Biosocial Anthropology.* Wiley, New York. p. 133.

Heldmann, G. 1936. Über die Entwicklung der Polygynen Wabe von *Polistes gallica* L. *Arb. Physiol. Angeu. Ent.,* Berlin 3:257–259.

Jeanne, R. L. 1972. Social biology of the neotropical wasp, *Mischocyttarus drewseni. Bull. Mus. Compar. Zool.,* Harvard University. 144:63–150.

Klahn, J. E. 1979. Philopatric and non-philopatric foundress associations in the social wasp *Polistes fuscatus. Beh. Ecol. Sociobiol.* 5:417–424.

Kukuk, P. F., M. D. Breed, A. Sobti, and W. J. Bell. 1977. The contributions of kinship and conditioning to nest recognition and colony member recognition in a primitively eusocial bee, *Lassioglossum zephyrum* (Hymenoptera: Halictidae). *Beh. Ecol. Sociobiol.* 2: 319–328.

Lewontin, R. C. 1970. The units of selection. *Ann. Rev. Ecol. Syst.* I:1–18.

Lin, N., and C. D. Michener. 1972. Evolution of sociality in insects. *Quart. Rev. Biol.* 47:131–159.

Litte, M. 1977. Behavioral ecology of the social wasp, *Mischocyttarus mexicanus. Beh. Ecol. Sociobiol.* 2:229–246.

Metcalf, R. A., and Whitt, G. S. 1977a. Intra-nest relatedness in the social wasp, *Polistes metricus. Behav. Ecol. Sociobiol.* 2:339–351.

——— 1977b. Relative inclusive fitness in the social wasp, *Polistes metricus. Behav. Ecol. Sociobiol.* 2:353–360.

Michener, C. D. 1974. *The Social Bees. A Comparative Study.* Belknap, Harvard Univ. Press. Cambridge, Mass. xii+ 404 pp.

Noonan, K. M. 1978. The sex ratio of parental investment in the social wasp, *Polistes fuscatus*. *Science* 199:1354–1356.

———. 1979. Individual strategies of inclusive-fitness-maximizing in foundresses of the social wasp, *Polistes fuscatus* (Hymenoptera: Vespidae). Ph. D. dissertation, The University of Michigan.

Owen, J. 1962. The behavior of a social wasp, *Polistes fuscatus* (Vespidae) at the nest, with special reference to the differences between individuals. Ph. D. dissertation, The University of Michigan, 156 pp.

Rau, P. 1940. Cooperative nest-founding in the wasp, *Polistes annularis* Linnaeus. *Ann. Ent. Soc. Amer.* 33:617–620.

Remington, R. D., and M. A. Schork. 1970. *Statistics with Applications to the Biological and Health Sciences*. Prentice-Hall, N.J. xii + 418 pp.

Richards, O. W. 1978. The social wasps of the Americas, excluding the Vespinae. *Br. Mus. Nat. Hist.* vii + 580 pp.

Siegal, S. 1956. *Nonparametric Statistics for the Behavioral Sciences*. McGraw-Hill. 312 pp.

Sokal, R. R., and R. J. Rohlf. 1969. *Biometry*. W. H. Freeman and Co. 776 pp.

Starr, C. K. 1978. Nest re-utilization in North American *Polistes* (Hymenoptera: Vespidae). Two possible selective factors. *J. Kans. Ent. Soc.* 51:394–397.

Strassmann, J. E. 1979. Honey caches help female paper wasps *(Polistes annularis)* survive Texas winters. *Science* 204:207–209.

Sturtevant, A. H. 1938. Essay on evolution II. On the effect of selection on social insects. *Quart. Rev. Biol.* 13:74–76.

Trivers, R. L. 1971. The evolution of reciprocal altruism. *Quart. Rev. Biol.* 46:35–57.

———. 1974. Parent–offspring conflict. *Amer. Zool.* 14:249–264.

Turillazzi, S., and L. Pardi. 1977. Body size and hierarchy in polygynic nests of *Polistes gallicus* (L.) (Hymenoptera: Vespidae). *Monitore Zool. Ital. N. S.* 11:101–112.

West-Eberhard, M. J. 1967a. The social biology of polistine wasps. Ph. D. dissertation, The University of Michigan.

———. 1967b. Foundress associations in polistine wasps: dominance hierarchies and the evolution of social behavior. *Science* 157:1584–1585.

———. 1969. The social biology of polistine wasps. *Misc. Publ. Mus. Zool.*, U. of M. No. 140, 101 pp.

———. 1975. The evolution of social behavior by kin selection. *Quart. Rev. Biol.* 50:1–34.

———. 1981. Intra-group selection and the evolution of insect societies (this volume).

Williams, G. C. 1966. *Adaptation and Natural Selection: A Critique of Some Current Evolutionary Thought*. Princeton Univ. Press, x + 307 pp.

———, (ed.). 1973. *Group Selection*. Aldine Atherton. 210 pp.

Wilson, E. O. 1971. *The Insect Societies*. Harvard Univ. Press. x + 548 pp.

3

Kin Selection and Satellite Nests in *Polistes exclamans*

Joan E. Strassmann

Williams and Williams (1957) developed a mathematical model to demonstrate how sterile castes can evolve by natural selection. If sterile individuals raise exclusively sibs under conditions of competition between sibships, they can perpetuate the genes they carry without direct reproduction. This concept, also suggested by Fisher (1930), was expanded by Hamilton (1964a,b). He showed mathematically how help given to a relative that increased its numbers or quality of offspring as a result of aid received could be explained if the magnitude of the increase were high enough to make up for a decrease in numbers and quality of the benefactor's own offspring. Hamilton termed his calculation of reproductive success that included benefits to relatives as well as direct reproduction "inclusive fitness." Kin selection potentially can explain any form of aid to relatives, from the extreme case of sterile castes to occasional aid to a needy, fecund relative (see Hamilton, 1972; Alexander, 1974; West-Eberhard, 1975; Wilson, 1975). Alexander (1974) proposed that, in the case of conflicts of interest between parents and their offspring, selection working on the parent is most potent and that offspring under parental care cannot evolve to do anything that will lead to a reduced number of grandchildren for its parent. West-Eberhard (1975) referred to altruism forced upon another individual as "imposed altruism." Dawkins (1976), Blick (1977), and Parker and McNair (1978) have shown that Alexander's argument was partly wrong because genes that in an offspring serve the offspring's interests against the parent's interests can spread so long as the parent cannot counteract their effects phenotypically by its power advantage. The actual extent of the parental power advantage has never been quantified, but the threshold for aid to sibs is lower under the assumptions of a theory of parental power advantage than under those of kin selection alone (Alexander, 1974; West-Eberhard, 1975; Charlesworth, 1978).

Studies on social organisms (see the papers in this volume) indicate the following: (1) there are times when some individuals aid others in a social group; (2) the more closely related the individual is to the benefactor, the more aid it is likely to receive; (3) in some cases individuals entirely forego reproduction to help close relatives reproduce. Such results support Hamilton's theory of inclusive fitness even if precise measures of the cost and benefit of aid are not achieved.

Quantification of kin selection beyond these general results is very difficult. The situation may be clearest in the primitively eusocial insects (see also Noonan, this volume). Some fertile or potentially fertile individuals routinely use their entire reproductive efforts to aid the reproduction of relatives. What would the reproductive success of such individuals have been if they had themselves produced offspring? An indirect measure can be gained by comparing individuals following different strategies. The ideal study should meet three criteria: (1) genetic relatedness between individuals is known; (2) individuals follow alternative choices as to whom they raise; (3) individuals possess similar potential reproductive success before the choice between strategies is made.

Here I report an experimental test of kin selection using a newly discovered nesting cycle found in Texas populations of the paper wasp, *Polistes exclamans* Viereck. In this species the three conditions just presented are very nearly met. *P. exclamans* exhibits two colony cycle modifications that correlate with factors attributable to the long Texas summers, specifically, increased vulnerability to predators and parasitoids over time (see Strassmann, in prep).

First, unlike the northern congeneric form, *P. fuscatus* (see West-Eberhard, 1969; Noonan, this volume), males are produced in the early spring along with the first brood of workers, providing workers with the opportunity to mate and start their own nests. Second, workers and queens sometimes leave their original nest and initiate new nests nearby (10 cm–10 m away, $\bar{x} = 3.4$ m). I have called such new nests *satellite nests*. The original nest is then called the *main nest* to distinguish it from an *independent nest* without satellites. Once a satellite has been formed, its queen is dependent on help from workers on the main nest to feed larvae and care for the nest. If workers do not join, the satellite fails.

When a satellite nest is initiated, workers on the main nest have a choice of raising larvae on the satellite or raising larvae on the main nest. The alternative that workers choose was investigated to determine if they choose in a way that maximizes their inclusive fitness. In this case inclusive fitness is maximized at the greatest value of Nr where N is the number of larvae that can be raised by a worker on one given nest and r is the individual's relatedness to those larvae. N has two components. First, on smaller nests a worker may be able to raise more larvae because of less overlap of effort (i.e., central cells may receive much more food than peripheral cells when the nest is too large). Second, the larvae on a second nest may have a greater chance of avoiding predators and parasitoids so that an equivalent effort by a worker can result in more larvae reaching adulthood. Relatedness of workers to the larvae they raise as measured in genes identical by descent is calculated by knowing genealogical connections; it is affected by the number of times the queen mates and by the degree of inbreeding, which were not measured. N and r can be measured for (1) the original queen, (2) the worker or queen who starts the satellite, and (3) the worker who joins the satellite. Nr values can be determined between a main nest and its satellites and compared for those individuals initiating satellites, original queens, and workers joining satellites to determine if all or any of the above individuals increase their inclusive fitness by joining satellites.

Table 3–1 presents values of relatedness from the point of view of (1) the queen, (2) a worker initiating a satellite, and (3) a worker joining a satellite. Males produced in the first brood usually constitute less than 5 per cent of all larvae, are produced by only about a third of all nests, and, hence, can be omitted with little effect. (However a male produced by a nest that subsequently failed before producing other reproductives may be very important.) Although Metcalf and Whitt (1977) demonstrated that *P. metricus* females often mate twice, the sperm of one male fathers 90 per cent of all offspring; therefore the assumption of one mating is probably not unreasonable. As long as the original queen is alive and the nest contains fewer than about 30 females, there is only one queen on the nest. Since workers are equally related to offspring of their different sisters, sister queens with sister workers may be treated as one queen at the time satellites are formed. In column C, Table 1 gives values for how many more larvae a satellite must produce as compared to a main nest if joining a satellite is to increase the inclusive fitnesses of the individuals involved. While the queen is still alive, and laying eggs on the main nest, a daughter-initiated satellite must be able to produce more than twice as many larvae per worker, if joining a satellite nest is to increase the inclusive fitnesses of either the original queen (line 4) or the non-ovipositing workers who join the satellite (line 10). A worker who initiates a satellite and serves as its queen while her mother lays eggs on the main nest need produce only $3/2$ times as many larvae per worker on the satellite (line 6). If the original queen initiates the satellite, she only needs to

Table 3–1.   Relatedness of an individual to larvae on the main nest and the satellite nest for all possible egg layers is presented from the standpoint of (1) the queen, (2) the daughter who initiated the satellite, and (3) the daughter who joined the satellite. Relatedness is calculated by assuming there are no male larvae; the queen mates only once and there is only one queen per nest. In column C are presented values for the number of times more larvae the satellite must produce for the individual whose standpoint is considered to leave the main nest and join the satellite, maximizing Nr, and inclusive fitness. These values in column C are equal to the ratio of column A over column B.

Line Number	Egg layer		Individual's relatedness to larvae on nest		Number of times more larvae satellite must produce
	Main	Satellite	Main	Satellite	
			A	B	C
Queen's standpoint					
1.	Queen	Queen	$1/2$	$1/2$	1
2.	Daughter	Daughter	$1/4$	$1/4$	1
3.	Daughter	Queen	$1/4$	$1/2$	$1/2$
4.	Queen	Daughter	$1/2$	$1/4$	2
Standpoint of daughter that is egg layer (referred to as ELD in lines 5–8)					
5.	Sister	ELD	$3/8$	$1/2$	$3/4$
6.	Queen	ELD	$3/4$	$1/2$	$3/2$
7.	ELD	Queen	$1/2$	$3/4$	$2/3$
8.	ELD	Sister	$1/2$	$3/8$	$4/3$
Non-reproductive daughter's standpoint					
9.	Queen	Queen	$3/4$	$3/4$	1
10.	Queen	Sister	$3/4$	$3/8$	2
11.	Sister	Sister	$3/8$	$3/8$	1
12.	Sister	Queen	$3/8$	$3/4$	$1/2$

produce more larvae per worker than on the main nest to serve everyone's interests better (line 1 and 9). When the queen is dead, a worker joining a satellite that produces more larvae per worker than the main nest will increase the inclusive fitness of a satellite joiner and the satellite's queen (lines 5 and 11). A satellite need only produce $3/4$ times as many larvae per worker as are produced on the main nest for a worker on the main nest to increase her inclusive fitness by initiating and ovipositing on a satellite after the queen is dead (line 5). If satellite initiators and joiners are maximizing their inclusive fitnesses, and satellites do not normally produce more than twice as many larvae per worker as can be produced on the main nest, we can predict the following under the hypothesis of kin selection.

1.   When the queen is alive, she will initiate most satellites.
2.   When the queen is dead, at least as many satellites will be initiated by workers as were previously begun by queens.
3.   All else being equal, more workers will join a queen satellite than will join a worker satellite while the queen is alive. After her death workers will freely join worker satellites.

These predictions were tested by observing circumstances of natural satellite formation from 1976–1978 in Austin, Texas, and by performing experiments of worker choice between the main nest and the satellite nest when all workers on the satellite were removed. Workers chose between (1) queen satellites and (2) worker satellites with (a) living queens and (b) dead queens. Then main nests were knocked down to determine if all workers would then go to satellites. Finally all workers and queens were collected and dissected to affirm that the identified queen was a sole ovipositor and to determine if workers joining satellites were different in age or ovarian condition from workers not joining satellites.

METHODS

This study was carried out at Brackenridge Field Laboratory (BFL) of The University of Texas at Austin. BFL consists of 80 acres of fields and forests on the Colorado River in Austin, Texas, and an associated laboratory. Artificial ponds throughout the property provide water and contribute to the abundance of wasps and their nests in the area.

Naturally occurring nests of *P. exclamans* were found in bushes and wooden structures in the fields of BFL and followed until each nest's demise in the years 1976, 1977, and 1978. When a nest was found, it was assigned a number, its precise location and position were noted, and all individuals were marked with dots of Testor's PLA enamel, applied with a cotton-wrapped insect pin in a number code from 1 to 63. Individual numbers were obtained by delineating 6 positions on the wings: base, middle, and tip for each wing. Each position had a value: 1, 2, 4, 8, 16, and 32. Combinations of marks yielded every number from 1 to 63; when 63 wasps on one nest were marked, a new color was used. Many-spot numbers were usually omitted (e.g., 31, which requires every spot painted except the 32). In 1977 and 1978 individuals were marked between midnight and sunrise when all wasps were on the nest and quiet enough for accurate marking. In 1976 daytime marking yielded less readable marks.

After the wasps were marked, each nest was watched for several hours to determine the identity of the queen. When a nest was watched all behaviors performed by all individuals were recorded in an abbreviated code. On large nests a tape recorder was sometimes used, and data were subsequently transcribed. These data were computer-stored for analysis. The queen was identified by observing her perform all of the following behaviors: (1) egg laying, (2) initiation of new cells, (3) abdomen shaking (also called tail-wagging), (4) frequent antennation of cells containing eggs, (5) chewing and biting other individuals but never being the victim of these attacks, and (6) never foraging for caterpillars. All nests in these experiments possessed easily identifiable queens; this was not always the case on nests later in the season, however (Strassmann, in prep.).

Each nest was observed for a short time at least once a week to determine whether or not the queen was still present and acting as a queen does (as defined in the previous paragraph). During all experiments each nest was observed briefly every day. Whenever any disturbance of the nest occurred, (such as its destruction, disappearance of its queen, or initiation of a new nest) that nest was then observed intensively until behavior stabilized. Thus the role of each individual in the changeover was ascertained. To facilitate identification of egg layers, empty cells were sometimes created by removing an egg from a cell with forceps or by destroying it with a pin.

Brood development and parasitism were determined by counting number of cells, eggs, larvae, pupae (cells where larvae had spun their silken cap prior to pupation), cells where an adult had emerged, and evidence of parasitoids. A headlamp was usually used to illuminate cell contents and sometimes a dentist's mirror or a car mechanic's mirror facilitated seeing into the cells. The three parasitoids present in this population, a pyralid moth, *Chalcoela iphitalis,* a chalcid wasp, *Elasmus polistis,* and an ichneumonid wasp, *Pachysomoides stupidus,* all leave evidence of their pupae in the nest. *C. iphitalis* leaves characteristic webbing in the cells (Rau, 1941). A cell that has been infested with *E. polistis* has a characteristic brown flat bottom, made of meconium from the wasp larva, a few millimeters above the cell floor, on top of the exuviae from early molts of the chalcid immatures. *P. stupidus* leaves a pale yellow longitudinally divided papery material in the cells in which its larvae pupate (Nelson, 1968, and personal observation). Voucher specimens of all wasps and parasitoids were deposited in the University of Texas Insect Collection.

Nests were checked daily to see if they had been knocked down by nest predators. Wasps on each nest were marked twice a week. At that time a ''rollcall'' of marked individuals was taken and any unmarked individuals that had emerged since the last visit were marked. Exact counts of cell contents were usually made biweekly.

Satellite nests were discovered by several methods. First, the bushes and buildings within 10 meters of each nest were searched during each daylight visit to the nest in an attempt to discover satellites. Second, about once a week, individuals leaving the nest were followed to see if they were going to a satellite that was too well-hidden to discover otherwise. When a new nest was discovered in the vicinity of one or more other nests, its relation to those nests was evaluated by transfers of wasps. Transfers were either forced (moved from main to satellite or vice versa by picking them up with forceps and transferring them) or voluntary (noted by marking wasps on the main nest and observing whether they appeared on the suspected satellite). After a forced transfer, the female either stayed on the new nest and antennated and was antennated by wasps on the new nest, or she fell to the ground fighting with one of the resident wasps on the new nest. In about thirty transfers of known non-relatives, the transferred wasp was invariably attacked. Transfers were made to the new nest from the original nest and vice versa to provide a double check on the results.

Experiments were performed on nests whose contents and individuals were documented as described here. They were performed between 21 May and 25 June, 1978, on nests of similar developmental stages whose satellites contained eggs, larvae, and pupae but no emergences. Each experiment was performed on the same date for all replicates. Subsequent to the experiments all but five nests were collected. All females were dissected to determine ovarian development and age and then frozen in an ultracold freezer for future work. During the experiments, nests were observed briefly each day. The first experiment consisted of removing five eggs from the main nest and five eggs from the satellite to determine which eggs the queen replaces first. In the second experiment, workers were removed from their satellites about half an hour before sunrise, a time at which only females most firmly allied with the satellite are on them. This excludes daytime visitors to the satellite. Females were removed with forceps, one by one, until the satellite queen was left alone on the satellite. Worker removal was performed on 9 June 1978. The nest was subsequently observed to note how many workers from the main nest now joined the satellite. In the third experiment 11 days later all individuals on the satellite were collected at night, then, at dawn, the main nest was knocked down. Identification numbers of wasps near the site of the nest that had been knocked down were noted as were wasps that now joined the satellites that all had been left intact. When it was clear which females joined the satellite and which initiated new nests, all females were collected, noting what nest they were on, satellite or a newly constructed nest, and they were dissected.

Females were dissected to determine their age class, whether they had mated, and their degree of ovarian development. Dissections were performed as described by West-Eberhard (1975). When the abdomen is extended, age can be determined by degree of sclerotization of the sternal cuticle normally covered by the overlapping segment (West-Eberhard, 1975). Five distinct degrees of sclerotization were recognized; these were approximately equated with age in days by comparison with the sternal cuticle of females of known age. Insemination was determined by presence of sperm in the spermatheca. Oocytes per ovariole were counted. Nurse cell clumps were distinguished from oocytes in the region of the ovariole where they are easy to confuse by using a key prepared from Feulgen-stained ovaries (Dunlap-Pianka and Strassmann, unpublished). Presence of yolk was determined by visual inspection for opacity. Presence of resorbing oocytes was noted.

RESULTS

Naturally Occurring Satellite Nests

In the three populations of nests examined, from 16 per cent to 39 per cent of all nests formed satellites (9 of 57 nests in 1977, 17 of 44 nests in 1978; see Strassmann, in press for a more detailed account of satellite nests and their characteristics). Of the nests with satellites, 11 to 57 per cent formed more than one satellite. No nest formed more than five satellites. Overall, those nests that formed satellites were larger than those that did not in number of workers and numbers of pupae (p <0.001, p <0.01, Mann-Whitney U Test, 1978 queen satellite data). Workers formed satellites in all years. In the dry spring of 1977 no queen satellites were formed. Queen satellites are usually formed in May and early June, when the queen still forages actively for pulp that is used in nest construction. When unfavorable conditions cause a nest to increase slowly in size in the spring, numbers of workers may be low, and queens may not initiate satellites at all. This was probably the case in 1977.

Because there were no queen satellites in 1977, nests with worker satellites were compared to nests without worker satellites in that year for presence of original queen on the main nest. To eliminate variation resulting from number of workers on the nest, a variable known to be important in satellite formation, only nests that had reached the minimum number of workers necessary for satellite formation were compared. Inspection of the mean and range of number or workers on nests with and without satellites the previous year resulted in the selection of 20 workers as the cutoff. Thus, in this analysis, only nests with 20 or more workers were used. In the population of nests in 1977 at BFL, 23 nests possessed 20 or more workers at some point during June or July. Eight of the 23 nests initiated satellites; 7 were from nests whose original queen was dead, and 1 originated from a nest whose queen was still alive. Only 4 nests without satellites that met the number of workers criterion lacked their original queen; the other 11 possessed living queens. This is a highly significant difference indicating that workers are much more likely to initiate satellites when the original queen is dead (Fisher Exact Test, $p = 0.008$, 1-tailed; Table 3–2).

Table 3–2.   Worker satellite nest formation from nests with at least 20 workers compared for presence of original queen.

	Queen alive	Queen dead	Fisher Exact Test
Satellite	1	7	
No satellite	11	4	$p = 0.008$

In 1978 most satellites were initiated during the second half of May and early June. In all, 16 queen satellites and 23 worker satellites were begun. Workers from six nests with queen-initiated satellites began satellites about three weeks after queen satellite initiation. Five nests lacking queens began worker satellites; two nests with queens formed worker satellites. Two nests with queens formed unsuccessful worker satellites that were never joined by other workers. One nest had three worker satellites; another had one queen satellite and four worker satellites. Considering only the first satellite formed by a given nest, only 2 of 17 satellites were initiated by workers when the queen was alive; the rest were initiated by the queen herself. Again considering only the first satellites formed by nests, 5 of 7 worker satellites were formed after the queen had died. When the queen is alive, she tends to initiate satellites; when she is dead, workers do.

As previously demonstrated, satellite nests are produced by main nests that are on the average larger than nests without satellites, indicating that these nests are somehow able to spare some investment in the main nest for the satellite. Larger nests require more wasps to rear the larger numbers of larvae. Nests that form satellites were investigated to determine if they have a higher worker-to-larva ratio than nests without satellites in 1978. It was found that nests with satellites have more workers per larva at about the time satellites were initiated (Komolgorov-Smirnov Test, $p < 0.05$, Figure 3–1). Therefore, workers that join satellites may represent an excess of workers on the main nest.

WORKER AND QUEEN CHOICE BETWEEN THE MAIN AND SATELLITE NESTS

Three experiments were performed on nests with queen or worker satellites to determine (1) which nest a queen preferred to lay eggs on, (2) whether workers showed any preference between satellites started by workers or queens once existing satellite workers were removed, and, finally, (3) whether all workers join the satellite when the main nest was removed (Table 3–3).

(1). For nine nest systems, five eggs were removed from the main nest and five eggs were removed from the queen satellite on 31 May, 1978. At that time the queen spent more time on the satellite than she spent on the main nest, but she visited the main nest several times an hour. At each visit she checked all egg cells, usually walking around the edge of the nest antennating each cell and tail-wagging. She also antennated most workers present on the nest. On all nine nests the queen replaced all five eggs in the satellite in two days or less. On one nest she subsequently replaced the eggs in the main nest also. Evidently, the queen replaces eggs on the satellite more frequently (Fisher Exact Test, $p = 0.0002$; Table 3–4).

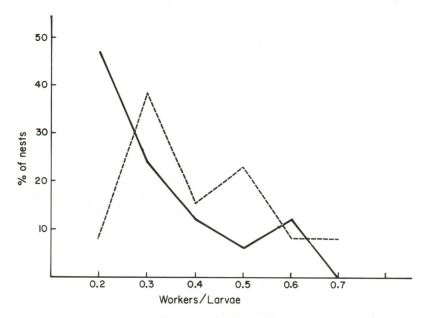

Figure 3–1.   Nests with queen satellites (dashed line) are compared to nests without satellites (solid line) for worker/larvae ratios that are grouped so each value on the x axis represents that value and all intermediate points below it to the next lower value. For example 0.2 workers to larvae contains all nests with more than 0.1 workers to larvae up to and including nests with 0.2 workers to larvae. $N = 17$ for nests without satellites, $N = 13$ for nests with queen satellites.

Table 3–3.   This table represents all nests involved in worker choice experiments, nest type, number of wasps on main and satellite during experiment and results of experiments.

Nest number	Satellite number	Queen alive	Satellite type		Number of females on satellite 6/9	Number of females on main 6/9	Females on main when knocked	Number of satellite joiners 6/17	Join satellite	+ = All join satellite − = Some start new nest
			Queen	Worker						
55	74	+	*		5	12	4	6	+	+
47	56	+	*		2	15	19	3	+	+
11	75	+	*		3	12	10	1	+	+
38	51	+	*		3	16	20	7	+	+
8	23	+	*				9			+
39	41	+	*				25			+
5	61	+	*		3	18	30	4	+	−
7	60	−		*	10	17	17	5	+	−
43	44	+		*	3	10	14	0	−	−
62	78	+		*	1	11	20	0	−	−
54	82	−		*		12	8			+

Table 3–4.   Replacement of eggs by queens when five eggs are removed from main nests and five eggs are removed from queen-initiated satellites.

	Eggs Replaced	Eggs not Replaced	Fisher Exact Test
Main nest	1	8	$p = 0.0002$
Satellite nest	9	0	

(2). All workers that spent the night on a satellite were removed. The satellite was subsequently observed to determine if additional workers would join and spend subsequent nights on the satellite. At this time there are usually a number of workers that visit both the main nest and the satellite (Strassmann and Matlock, in prep.). All workers were removed from eight satellites just before sunrise, leaving the satellite queen alone. Of these eight nests, two were worker satellites initiated by workers while the original queen was still present, five were queen satellites, and one was a worker satellite formed after the original queen had disappeared.

Workers marked on the main nest joined the satellite, replacing the workers that had been removed on all five queen satellites and on the one worker satellite without an original queen. On the two worker satellites initiated while the queen was still on the main nest, no workers joined the satellite after removal of the original satellite workers. This means that workers joined the satellites when their relatedness to satellite larvae was equal to their relatedness to main larvae, i.e., queen alive, queen satellite (lines 1 and 9 in Table 3–1) and queen dead, worker satellite (lines 2 and 11 in Table 3–1). Workers did not join the satellite when they were less related to satellite larvae (queen alive, worker satellite (line 10 in Table

3–1; Fisher Exact Test, $p = 0.036$, Table 3–5). It is possible that workers monitored queen satellites more closely than they monitored worker satellites in this case and therefore were not aware when worker satellites lost their workers; in this case, the monitoring itself follows genetic lines.

(3). In the final experiment, the alternative of raising larvae on the main nest was removed by knocking down the 11 main nests. The wasps responded in two ways: (1) All wasps went to the satellite; (2) A few wasps joined the satellite, and the rest initiated a new nest near the site of the destroyed original nest. On six of the seven queen-initiated satellites, all wasps joined the satellite. In one case a few workers started a new nest at the exact site of the original nest instead of joining the queen-initiated satellite. On three of four worker-initiated satellites, several of the wasps from the main nest started a new nest instead of joining the satellite; in one case all joined the worker-initiated satellite. Although the difference in satellite joining between wasps from nests with queen satellites and wasps from nests with worker satellites is not significant in this experiment, there is a clear trend indicating workers join queen satellites and do not join worker satellites (Fisher Exact Test, $p = 0.088$; Table 3–6).

These three experiments indicate (1) the queen is more likely to replace eggs on the satellite than on the main nest; (2) workers are more likely to join a queen satellite than they are to join a worker satellite while the queen is alive though they will join a worker satellite after the queen is dead; (3) after the main nest is destroyed, workers are more likely to join queen satellites than they are to join worker satellites.

Ovarian Condition of Experimental Females

Immediately after collecting all types of females from satellites, I dissected them to determine approximate age and ovarian condition. Dissected individuals fall into three groups: (1) those originally collected from satellites; (2) those that had joined satellites after

Table 3–5.   Joining of satellites by workers when original workers are removed from the satellite according to whether relatedness of workers to larvae is the same on the satellite as it is on the main nest or if relatedness of workers to larvae is greater on the main nest.

| | Relatedness Is | | |
	Equal	Greater on Main	Fisher Exact Test
Satellite joined by workers	6	0	
			$p = 0.04$
Satellite not joined by workers	0	2	

Table 3–6.   Workers joining satellites or initiating new nests depending on satellite type.

	New Nest Formed	New Nest Not Formed	Fisher Exact Test
Queen satellite	6	1	
Worker satellite	1	3	$p = 0.09$

group 1 had been removed; and (3) those collected at the end of the experiments. Because so few wasps are involved, they are divided into young individuals less than two weeks old and old individuals older than two weeks. Ovaries are classified as (1) developed, (2) intermediate, (3) slightly developed, and (4) undeveloped. A wasp with a developed ovary has at least one fully-developed egg (usually 3–4) and 10 to 20 oocytes per ovariole. Intermediate ovaries contained no fully developed eggs—at least 2 oocytes with yolk per ovariole and 8–10 total oocytes per ovariole. There were no individuals with intermediate ovaries in this sample. Slightly developed ovaries contain 3 to 7 oocytes per ovariole; at least one oocyte contains yolk. Undeveloped ovaries contain 0 to 2 minuscule oocytes per ovariole, neither with yolk.

Age and ovarian development were compared within each sample. All types of satellites are pooled to achieve a sample size that could be analyzed; there did not appear to be any striking differences between worker-initiated and queen-initiated satellites that would preclude lumping.

Females were evenly distributed into young and old within (1) the group that originally was on the satellite, and (2) the group that went to the satellite when the original workers were removed ($N_1 = N_2 = 8$, Mann-Whitney $U = 21; N_1 = N_2 = 6$; Mann-Whitney $U = 15$), (3) the group that was on the satellite after the main nest was knocked down in which there was a significant excess of older females ($N_1 = N_2 = 8$, Mann-Whitney $U = 12.5$, $p < 0.025$). Older females are somewhat less likely to join satellites.

Observation of marked wasps on all nests indicated that there was only one queen per nest. This was substantiated by examination of ovaries. In all cases the queen was the individual previously determined to be queen and therefore had purposely not been collected until the final sample. The eight queens that were dissected had a mean of $13.2 (\pm S.D. 3.2)$ oocytes per ovariole. No females on the nests possessed intermediate ovaries. The 31 females with slightly developed ovaries had a mean of $4.6 (\pm S.D. 1.5)$ oocytes per ovariole. The largest oocyte of each female in this class contained some yolk and was equivalent in size to the fourth to sixth oocyte in line in a queen's ovaries. There were 94 females with entirely undeveloped ovaries possessing two or fewer minuscule oocytes per ovariole.

Number of females with slightly developed ovaries was compared to the number with undeveloped ovaries in each of the three experimental groups of workers. The individuals that originally occupied the satellites and those that first joined the satellites were evenly distributed between those with slightly developed ovaries and those with undeveloped ovaries ($N_1 = N_2 = 8$, Mann-Whitney $U = 27; N_1 = N_2 = 6$, Mann-Whitney $U = 8.5$). The individuals joining the satellites last possessed a preponderance of undeveloped ovaries ($N_1 = N_2 = 8$, Mann-Whitney $U = 9, p = 0.007$).

Ovary development was compared between groups of wasps by pooling the last two groups that were collected because they were collected a couple of days apart and were both made up of individuals on the main nest that did not originally join the satellite. The proportion of individuals with slightly developed ovaries originally on the satellite was compared to that originally on the main nest. There was no significant difference in proportion of females with slightly developed ovaries although there was a trend towards less developed ovaries in wasps on the satellite as compared to those on the original main nests ($N_1 = 7, N_2 = 8$, Mann-Whitney $U = 14.5, p = 0.076$).

DISCUSSION

On nests with original queens, queens usually initiated satellites. From nests without queens, workers initiated satellites in greater numbers than did workers initiating satellites while original queens were alive and present on the main nest. Workers were less likely to join worker-initiated satellites while original queens were still alive and present on the main nest. The behavior of workers and queens as compared with their obvious alternatives maximized the inclusive fitness of both workers and queens. Worker behavior seemed to follow the predictions of a genetical theory of sociality.

The experimental manipulations reported here are similar to natural occurrences to which the wasps may be expected to have evolved an adaptive response. Workers commonly die while foraging, and with the small numbers involved it is not impossible that a satellite could be deprived of all its workers. Nests were knocked down at dawn, the time birds most often knock down nests, so this also represents a natural manipulation.

It is interesting that after the original queen dies or permanently leaves the main nest for a satellite, satellite formation by workers increases, but such satellites are no more numerous than those constructed by the queen while she is present. When the queen is dead and satellites are initiated by workers, satellite joining, non-reproductive workers routinely choose to raise nieces, related to them by $3/8$, and do not leave the nest to raise their own offspring related to them by $1/2$. This suggests strong ecological reasons for subdividing the nest, which causes enough more larvae to be raised to make up for the loss in relatedness. Alexander (1974) and West-Eberhard (1975, 1978) anticipated these results and stated that haplodiploidy may not have been crucial to the evolution of eusociality. An alternative explanation of these results may be that workers are simply unlikely to possess developed ovaries and initiate satellites while the queen is present because she inhibits their ovarian development and dominance. Three observations make this explanation unlikely. First, satellites initiated by workers do not acquire eggs until about five cells are completed over four or five days. This is about the number of days necessary for mature eggs to develop, which suggests that satellites are initiated by females with undeveloped ovaries. Presumably, they are somehow stimulated to start a satellite, mate while foraging (I have never found a mated worker on a nest where another wasp was queen), and then begin building the satellite. Second, more satellites are initiated by workers than are successfully joined by other workers. (There were eight such satellites in 1977, and two in 1978.) Satellites not joined are usually either from small nests that may be unable to support a satellite, or they are initiated by workers from nests still possessing original queens. The queen of a satellite whose mother is still alive must produce $3/2$ times more offspring on the satellite than she could have raised on the main nest to increase her inclusive fitness. A worker who joins that satellite while her mother is still alive is forsaking sisters to raise nieces and therefore must produce two times as many larvae on the satellite to increase her inclusive fitness. The difference in the number of times more larvae the satellite must produce for the *satellite foundress* to increase her fitness $3/2$ times and that necessary for a *satellite joiner* to increase her inclusive fitness two times may result in some workers initiating satellites that are never joined. Finally, worker inhibition by the queen is unlikely because workers occasionally start satellites while the queen is still alive. Kin selection thus appears to be a better explanation than queen dominance of the workers for the genetics of satellite nest initiation and joining (the actual reason satellite nests of any type are advantageous is probably ecological—avoidance of predators or parasitoids; Strassmann in prep.).

It is clear that satellite workers were not about to become ovipositors because they did not have developed or even intermediate ovaries; their sometimes more youthful condition and slightly more developed ovaries do not rule out the possibility that future opportunities for oviposition may be greater on the satellite, for some of the joiners. Therefore a potential increase in direct fitness may accompany satellite joining. However, as a result of high worker mortality and the immediate opportunity to raise relatives other than offspring, the indirect component of inclusive fitness is probably greater than the direct component for workers joining satellites.

In this presentation I have not precisely compared survival of larvae on satellites and main nests. In the years examined here, larvae on satellites are predicted to have survived better than main nest larvae, but the survival probability of satellite larvae should not be more than double that on the main nest. Otherwise more worker satellites from main nests with living queens would be expected according to kin selection. Measuring larvae raised to adulthood per worker on the main nest and the satellite is difficult, requiring a compilation of (1) the efficiency in worker utilization, (2) predator and parasitoid attacks, (3) the cost of initiating a new nest, (4) the probability that in the future there will be enough workers available to maintain both nests, and (5) whether it is more important to have two nests or to replace an old nest with a new nest. The best strategy may vary from year to year. If nest predation is the most important problem, two nests increase the likelihood of some larvae avoiding predators for birds destroy nests without regard to size and seldom discover the main nest and the satellite at once (Strassmann, in prep.). The major parasitoids kill larvae and remain to kill new larvae in the nest—the moth, *Chalcoela iphitalis,* by tunnelling into new cells, and the chalcid, *Elasmis polistis,* by remaining near the nest after adulthood, mating, and laying more eggs in the same nest (Strassmann, in prep.). To avoid either of these pests, moving periodically to a new nest may be effective. However, the severity with which these nest pests attack varies greatly from year to year, and the wasp's response of forming satellites and subsequently either maintaining or abandoning the main nest also varies.

Effects of Multiple Mating

The assumptions used in calculating the inclusive fitness values presented in Table 1 (that no males are produced and that only one female lays eggs in the nest at this time) represent realities in the biology of *P. exclamans* ascertained by measurement. The assumption that females mate only once, however, has been made simply because no data are available on this question, and this seems the most parsimonious assumption. Ultimately, the veracity of this assumption must be determined and the model adjusted if the queen does mate more than once, for this will change predictions concerning a worker's inclusive fitness. It will not affect those concerning the mother. If worker preferences override those of their mother, and larvae from more than one father coexist on a nest, it would be advantageous for a worker to distinguish between full and half sibs and raise only full sibs, leave the nest and raise daughters when no full sibs are present or when they cannot be distinguished from half sibs, or join a full sister on a satellite and raise nieces because even full nieces are more related than half sisters are to the worker (nieces, $r = \frac{3}{8}$; half sisters, $r = \frac{1}{4}$). Workers may join a worker-initiated satellite only if the initiator is a full sister. In these cases certain workers will join a satellite and others will not, according to paternity. There will not be the free movement to satellites reported here for queen satellites. Sibships dividing into the distinctive groups prescribed by this model do not occur when the satellite is initiated by the queen though the lack of workers joining worker-initiated satellites after the workers there have been removed may fit this model. Workers do not seem to initiate their own nests in great numbers to avoid raising half sibs.

Production of Autumn Reproductives

This discussion has concentrated on the relatedness between workers and female larvae because primarily female larvae (except for a few spring males) are present in nests at the time workers usually decide between main nests and satellites. By the time autumn reproductives, both males and females, are reared, satellites and main nests have usually experienced one of the following fates: (1) main and satellite(s) are still extant and possess entirely separate workers and queen(s); (2) the main nest has been abandoned entirely in favor of the satellite(s); (3) either main or satellite nest was destroyed and all or some workers and queen(s) joined the remaining nest (some perhaps also initiating a new nest). (See Strassmann in press for discussion of frequencies of these events.) Only the last of these possibilities results in a brood originating from another nest serving as workers on the nest. Thus the relatedness of workers to immature future reproductives usually involves relatedness on one nest at a time well after satellite nests are formed when the workers from the original nest are dead or a very few are egg layers on the nest (because only by becoming a non-foraging egg layer are they likely to live until reproductives are reared). At this time, however, relatedness questions are no less complicated than they were when main workers went to satellites because of the following factors: (1) These larger nests are more likely to have more than one egg layer; (2) each egg layer may mate more than once; (3) even nests with only one egg layer often lose her, and she is replaced by another egg layer. The impact of all these possibilities on sociality has been discussed in detail by West-Eberhard (1978). Their overall effect is to decrease the relatedness between workers and larvae.

CONCLUSIONS

Three criteria must be met to test kin selection: (1) There must exist knowledge of genetic relatedness among interacting individuals; (2) individuals must follow alternative behavioral choices; and (3) individuals must initially possess similar potential reproductive success. These criteria are largely met in *P. exclamans*. Relatedness is known through the maternal line. The alternatives that have been examined are the choice by workers between raising larvae on the main nest and raising larvae on the satellite when the original queen is alive and when she is dead, whether the satellite is worker initiated or queen initiated. Finally, workers making choices apparently are initially similar in reproductive potential and age. The outcome of the choice made by workers appears to be based on maximizing the workers' general relatedness to the larvae. Apparently, the genetic variations in the situation and not the condition of the wasps determine the outcome of the choice. Thus, the criteria established at the outset are probably met in this experiment, and the results support the theory of inclusive fitness.

Three other studies have compared number of offspring produced by polistine nests according to numbers of foundresses (Gibo, 1978; Metcalf and Whitt, 1977; Noonan, this volume). However, it is unlikely that individuals joining a nest as a subordinate foundress are actually of similar potential reproductive success as those females that initiate their own nest. Therefore, the nests that are compared may not be made up of females of similar original condition. Noonan (this volume) has considered this variable.

ACKNOWLEDGEMENTS

This research has profited greatly from discussions with R. D. Alexander, L. E. Gilbert, W. D. Hamilton, W. H. Mueller, D. Otte, P. W. Sherman, J. T. Smiley, A. R. Templeton, and participants in L. R. Lawlor's Monday noon seminar. I particularly thank J. T. Smiley for extensive assistance with experimental design. I thank R. B. Matlock, D. C. Meyer, and R. R. Thomas for field assistance. I thank my committee members, R. H. Barth, Y. Hiraizumi, D. A. Levin, M. C. Singer, and especially my major professors, L. E. Gilbert and A. R. Templeton, for their helpful comments on an earlier version of this paper that was submitted as part of a dissertation to The University of Texas at Austin. The manuscript was greatly improved by the criticisms of R. D. Alexander, C. D. Michener, W. H. Mueller, J. T. Smiley, G. J. Steck, D. W. Tinkle, and G. C. Williams. I thank N. C. Kays Smiley for preparing the figure. Support was provided by NIH grant 5 T32 GM 07126.

REFERENCES

Alexander, R. D. 1974. The evolution of social behavior. *Ann. Rev. Ecol. Syst.* 5:325–383.

Blick, J. 1977. Selection for traits which lower individual reproduction. *J. Theor. Biol.* 67:597–601.

Charlesworth, B. 1978. Some models of the evolution of altruistic behavior between siblings. *J. Theor. Biol.* 72:297–319.

Dawkins, R. 1976. *The Selfish Gene.* Oxford: Oxford University Press.

Fisher, R. A. 1930. *The Genetical Theory of Natural Selection.* Dover Edition (1958).

Gibo, D. L. 1978. The selective advantage of foundress associations in *Polistes fuscatus* (Hymenoptera:Vespidae): a field study of the effects of predation on productivity. *Can. Ent.* 110:519–540.

Hamilton, W. D. 1964a. The genetical evolution of social behavior. I. *J. Theor. Biol.* 7:1–16.

———. 1964b. The genetical evolution of social behavior. II. *J. Theor. Biol.* 7:17–52.

———. 1972. Altruism and related phenomena, mainly in the social insects. *Ann. Rev. Ecol. Syst.* 3:193–232.

Metcalf, R. A., and G. S. Whitt. 1977. Relative inclusive fitness in the social wasp, *Polistes metricus. Behav. Ecol. Sociobiol.* 2:353–360.

Nelson, J. M. 1968. Parasites and symbionts of nests of *Polistes* wasps. *Ann. Entomol. Soc. Amer.* 61:1528–1539.

Noonan, K. Individual strategies of inclusive fitness maximizing in *Polistes fuscatus* foundresses. (this volume).

Parker, G. A., and M. R. MacNair. 1978. Models of parent–offspring conflict. I. Monogamy. *Anim. Behav.* 26:97–110.

Rau, P. 1941. Observations on certain lepidopterous and hymenopterous parasites of *Polistes* wasps. *Ann. Ent. Soc. Amer.* 34:355–366.

Strassmann, J. E. Evolutionary implications of early male and satellite nest production in *Polistes exclamans* colony cycles. *Behav. Ecol. and Sociobiol.* In press.

West-Eberhard, M. J. 1975. The evolution of social behavior by kin selection. *Quart. Rev. Biol.* 50:1–33.

———. 1975. Estudios de las avispas sociales (Hymenoptera, Vespidae), del Valle del Cauca. I. Objectivos, métodos, y notas para facilitar la identificación de especies communes. *Cespedesia* 4(16), 245–267.

———. 1978. Polygyny and the evolution of social behavior in wasps. *J. Kansas Ent. Soc.* 51(4):832–856.

———. Social biology of polistine wasps. 1969. *Misc. Publ. Mus. Zool.* Univ. Mich. 140:1–101.

Williams, G. C., and D. C. Williams. 1957. Natural selection of individually harmful social adaptations among sibs with special reference to social insects. *Evol.* 11:32–39.

Wilson, E. O. 1975. *Sociobiology: The New Synthesis.* Belknap Press of Harvard Univ.

II

Correlates of Male and Female Reproductive Success in Various Vertebrates

4

Male Age-Size Distribution and Male Mating Success in Bullfrogs

Richard D. Howard

INTRODUCTION

Darwin's (1871) concept of sexual selection provides a basic foundation for understanding the evolution of social behavior in all species. By sexual selection, I mean (a) that members of one sex (usually males) compete more vigorously among themselves to obtain mates than members of the opposite sex and (b) that members of one sex (usually females) are more discriminating about mate quality than members of the other sex. Theoretical extensions of Darwin's seminal works can be found in Fisher (1958), Williams (1966, 1975), Orians (1969), Trivers (1972), Emlen and Oring (1977), and Alexander and Borgia (1979) among others. Sexual selection influences many biological phenomena including amount of parental care, type of mating system, degree of sexual dimorphism, variations in sex ratios, and patterns of mortality and senescence. Data necessary to test theories of sexual selection include the amount of variation in lifetime reproductive success within and between the sexes. Such data are presently unknown for any repeatedly breeding species in nature; however, estimates of yearly variation in reproductive success (as estimated by mating success) are available for a few species (e.g., Downhower and Armitage, 1971; LeBoeuf, 1974; Chagnon, 1974; Howard, 1978a, 1979; Payne, 1979).

In this paper, I present data on variation in yearly mating success within and between the sexes for bullfrogs, *Rana catesbeiana,* for four years, point out how age-size distribution can influence such variation, and discuss how phenotypic plasticity in male mating behaviors can be viewed as an evolutionary response to relatively predictable environmental variations that individuals could encounter during their lifetimes.

Bullfrogs provide a number of advantages for studying reproductive success. Much is known concerning their natural history and mating behavior (e.g., Wright and Wright, 1949; Emlen, 1968a, 1976; Schroeder and Baskett, 1968; Wiewandt, 1969; Collins, 1975, 1979, ms; Howard, 1978a,b, 1979). Also, individual bullfrogs can be readily marked and observed in the field (Emlen, 1968b; Howard, 1978a); and because bullfrogs, like all anurans, fertilize their eggs externally, there is no doubt as to male parentage. Thus, estimates of male reproductive success are as accurate as those of female reproductive success (Howard, 1979). By contrast, assignment of male parentage in species with internal fertilization may be subject to error because females often mate with more than one male.

The necessity of long-term field studies of marked individuals in testing evolutionary hypotheses is becoming increasingly apparent as is evident in other papers in this volume. Long-term studies not only provide more information as to how ontogeny affects individual behavior patterns but also lends insight on how differing environmental conditions affect the generality of predicted relationships for the same population, i.e., are some predictions true only under a limited set of conditions?

STUDY AREA, MATERIALS, AND METHODS

This study was conducted between 1975–1978 at Crane Pond in the Edwin S. George Reserve of the University of Michigan, located 39 kilometers northwest of Ann Arbor, Michigan. The general habitat of the Reserve has been described elsewhere (Rogers, 1942; Cantrall, 1943; Cooper, 1958). Crane Pond is a permanent body of water, approximately 2.14 hectares, that consists of three distinct lobes differing markedly in habitat (see Howard, 1978a).

Marshy areas border the east and west shorelines of Crane Pond; these areas not only serve as overwintering sites but also contain breeding choruses in some years. Water flow is continuous between these areas throughout most of the year. Migration between choruses during the breeding season is almost exclusively limited to females. Movements are monitored with the aid of a one-meter-high hardware cloth fence that completely encloses Crane Pond.

Adult bullfrogs collected along the fence or inside the pond were sexed, measured, and weighed. Three marking methods were employed to insure future identification of individuals in the field: waistbands constructed from surveyor's flagging tape permitted accurate individual recognition at a distance; unique numbers tattooed on the abdomen of each animal provided a semi-permanent means of identification; unique combinations of toes clipped from each individual provided the most permanent system of identification (see Howard, 1978a).

Mating behavior in this chiefly nocturnal species was observed using binoculars and a battery-powered headlamp. Observations were made from a boat and from 6m observation towers constructed from scaffold material that I placed inside the pond near areas of activity. Artificial light usually had no detectable effect on most behaviors (e.g., calling, male–male interactions) but did disturb amplexed pairs. To avoid such disturbances, I identified males and locations of pairs from a distance of at least 15m and did not approach them until egg deposition. During egg deposition, the pair could be approached without disturbance; I then identified females, photographed the amplexed pair, and marked the location of the egg mass with a stake.

Mating success was determined by direct observations of copulations. Using this criterion, I knew parentage of 74 per cent of known egg masses deposited in 1975, 97 per cent of known egg masses in 1976, 95 per cent of known egg masses in 1977, and 93 per cent of known egg masses in 1978. Since a relatively large number of matings were not observed in 1975, I did not calculate estimates of the variance in male and female reproductive success for this year.

In this paper, I adopt the following convention: males smaller than 130mm are referred to as "small", males between 130–140mm are referred to as "intermediate" in size, and males larger than 140mm are referred to as "large." This terminology allows easier comparison between years. It is also important to note that in some years males of intermediate size are actually the largest males observed in that year.

Only interactions between calling males were used in analysis of male–male encounters. This criterion excludes interactions between territorial males and parasitic males. I did not present data on the frequency of encounters during the 1975 breeding season because in this year I only recorded encounters in which both males could be positively identified; in the latter years, I noted all encounters regardless of knowledge of male identity.

Various parametric and non-parametric statistical procedures were used to analyze data: regression, F-tests, analysis of covariance, coefficient of variation, c.v. (Sokal and Rohlf, 1969); and the Wilcoxon-Mann-Whitney U test, and Spearman rank correlation, r_s (Siegal, 1956; Wonnacott and Wonnacott, 1972). Non-parametric tests were used when it was clear that the more stringent assumptions of alternative parametric tests were violated.

RESULTS AND DISCUSSION

Bullfrogs are relatively long-lived iteroparous organisms. In my study area, individuals of each sex may become sexually mature in one year (sometimes two years in females) after metamorphosis, and adults may live for five to eight years (Collins, 1975, ms.; Howard, 1978a). Adults grow continuously during their lifetimes and may reach lengths of more than 168 mm (snout–ischium length) and weights of more than 450g. Bullfrogs are the largest North American frog and require permanent aquatic habitats as breeding sites because tadpoles may take up to two years to complete metamorphosis (e.g., Walker, 1946; Smith, 1950; Seale, 1973, Collins, 1975, 1979).

Mating behavior occurs in June and July in most northern sections of the United States (Wright and Wright, 1949). However, mating activity may not be continuously distributed throughout this time but may occur in two or three distinct periods (Figure 4–1) separated by periods in which mating activity is either dramatically reduced or totally absent. Such quiescent periods correspond to the length of time required for females that have already mated to prepare a second clutch of eggs and for virgin females to complete their initial egg complement. During this time, calling and aggression in males is significantly reduced, thus lowering energetic costs and, perhaps more importantly, risks of predation.

Location of chorusing sites changes during the summer. Two types of relocations were noted: Usually chorusing sites in different mating periods varied; sites utilized later in the

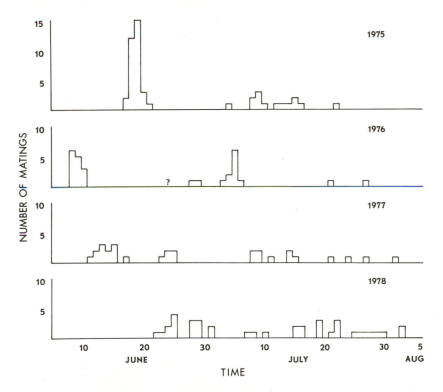

Figure 4–1.   Distribution of matings during the 1975–1978 breeding seasons in Crane Pond. Question mark refers to a possible but unobserved mating. Clearly defined mating periods occurred each year during 1975–1977; however, little or no periodicity was observed in 1978.

breeding season tended to be in progressively cooler areas of the pond and indicate that adults may be avoiding areas that have an increased probability of lethally high water temperatures later in the summer (Howard, 1978a). Within a mating period the chorusing site may shift abruptly within a 24-hour period (Emlen, 1976; Howard, 1978a). Underlying reasons for such rapid relocations are unclear but are sometimes correlated with high leech, *Macrobdella decora,* density (Howard, 1978b) and high snapping turtle, *Chelydra serpentina,* activity. These leeches are significant sources of mortality for developing embryos and are parasites on adults; snapping turtles are the major predator on adult bullfrogs during the mating season in Crane Pond. One result of all relocations is that all lobes of Crane Pond are utilized as breeding habitats during the mating season. Within each lobe, certain areas tend to be preferred year after year (Figure 4–2). Most oviposition sites occur either near the shorelines or on edges of vegetation mats. Criteria that determine suitable egg deposition sites are poorly understood because habitats with similar characteristics to areas used for breeding are often avoided. It is known that water temperature and vegetation structure play a key role in embryo survivorship (Howard, 1978b).

Most mating activities occur at night, i.e., sustained choruses, most male–male encounters, and copulations. However, ephemeral chorusing may occur during the day, particularly when choruses are first forming. Sustained choruses usually begin about 2100 and continue until dawn. Copulations occur during the early morning hours ($\bar{x} = 0318$hr; $SD = 1.37$hr; $N = 102$).

The mating system of bullfrogs can be described as a polygynous, resource-based territoriality. The differential abilities of larger, older males in controlling oviposition sites preferred by females confers increased mating success (Figures 4–3 through 4–6). Female choice is evident: During a chorus, females move silently from male to male, presumably assaying some features of the male's phenotype and/or the quality of the territory he con-

SITES OF EGG MASS DEPOSITION

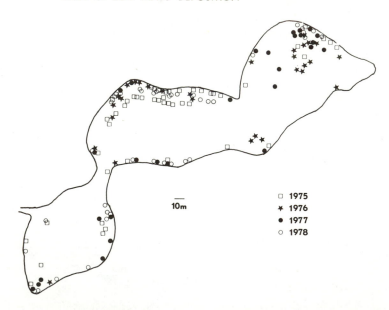

□ 1975
★ 1976
● 1977
○ 1978

10m

Figure 4–2.   Sites of egg mass deposition in Crane Pond during 1975–1978. Matings occurred in each of the three lobes every year, usually in the same general regions.

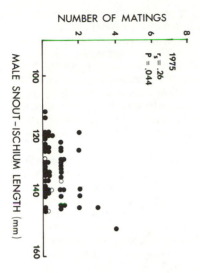

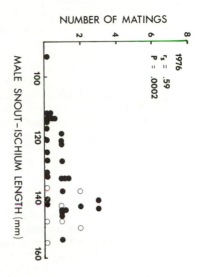

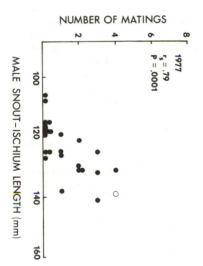

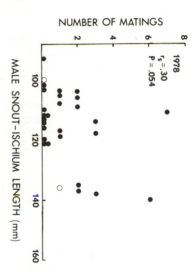

Figure 4–3 through 4–6.   Relationship between mating success and male size during 1975–1978 for the Crane Pond population. Open circles refer to males that were preyed upon during the mating season.

trols. A copulation is typically initiated when a female approaches a calling male. As the female approaches, the male usually continues to call but otherwise remains motionless. The female then swims up to the male and touches him; at this point the male gives a prolonged low-volume vocalization and turns and clasps the female, a behavior known as amplexus. Duration of amplexus in bullfrogs is short ($\bar{x}$ = 52min; SD = 31min; N = 77) compared to available data on other anurans (see Wells, 1977a for a review). Egg deposition usually occurs within 1–2m of the site of amplexus. Data on embryo survivorship suggest that offspring deposited in the territories of larger males suffer significantly less mortality than offspring deposited in the territories of smaller males (R^2 = .37; P = .0012; N = 26) (Howard, 1978a,b). Thus, females that discriminate on the basis of male size and/ or territorial quality have increased reproductive success.

Variation in yearly mating success is significantly greater in males than in females as is expected in a polygynous species (Table 4–1). Thus, the intensity of sexual selection should be greater on males than on females (Trivers, 1972). Such selection may act on a number of male attributes by favoring (a) traits that maximize reproductive success by increasing competitive ability in physical encounters with other males (e.g., large body size), and (b) alternative ways to increase reproductive success in males that are at a disadvantage in physically competing with more dominant males. The latter selection may favor the proliferation of alternative mating behaviors during either a portion (e.g., bullfrogs) or all of a male's life (e.g., red deer, *Cervus elephus*—Darling, 1937; ruffs, *Philomachus pugnax*—Hogan-Warburg, 1966, VanRhijn, 1973; bees, *Centris pallida*—Alcock et al., 1977, and dung flies, *Scatophagia stercoraria*—Borgia, 1979).

In bullfrogs, a male's size relative to other males was an important factor influencing the type of mating behavior utilized, and subsequent mating success. I have observed three patterns of mating behavior in male bullfrogs: territoriality, opportunism, and male parasitism (Howard, 1978a). As described earlier, territoriality consisted of active physical defense of potential oviposition sites and was usually employed by only the larger males in the population. Larger males were involved in significantly more male–male encounters (i.e., fights and threats) than smaller males and won more than 74 per cent (125 of 168) of observed encounters. Smaller males won only 10 per cent (16 of 168) of observed contests. The remaining 16 per cent (27 of 168) of the encounters occurred between males of similar size.

Opportunism refers to ephemeral territoriality in which males call from potential oviposition sites but would not defend such sites. If challenged, opportunistic males will vacate their calling site only to go elsewhere and resume calling. Opportunistic males are usually intermediate in size and such behavior may reduce costs and risks associated with territoriality.

Parasitism entails neither calling nor physical defense of areas but the employment of submissive postures (see also Emlen, 1976) while remaining motionless about 1–2m from large territorial males; parasitic males actively attempt to intercept and mate with females attracted to territorial males. Parasitic males are typically the smallest males in the population and selectively frequent the largest territorial males (Figure 4–7). Despite their seemingly submissive posture, parasitic males are subject to repeated attacks from the territorial males; however, parasitic males are quick to retreat and are rarely captured.

Table 4–1. Variation In Mating Success Within and Between the Sexes for Bullfrogs.

Year	C.V.		S²		N	
	♂	♀	♂	♀	♂	♀
1976	117.56	33.40	0.84	0.16	38	22
1977	122.48	44.17	1.87	0.23	26	26
1978	140.36	30.09	3.15	0.35	29	23

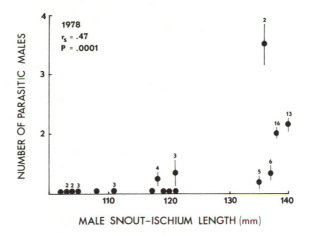

Figure 4–7.   Relationship between number of parasitic males near territorial males and size of territorial males for 1978. Circles refer to means ± SE, $N = 65$. Correlation based on raw data not means. Numbers above circles refer to number of times each territorial male was parasitized during the breeding season. Note that larger territorial males are not only parasitized by more parasitic males than smaller territorial males but they are also parasitized more often. A similar relationship was obtained in 1976 (Howard, 1978a).

Females appear to detect the presence of parasitic males when approaching territorial males. If no parasitic males are near, a female usually swims toward a territorial male in several movements, usually advancing about .5 to 1m each time, then remaining motionless for at least several minutes. If parasitic males are close by, an approaching female will dodge them and dart to the territorial male in one or two quick movements. Females that are attacked by parasitic males while approaching veer away only to advance again in one rapid movement. Females successfully amplexed by parasitic males are usually driven away by the territorial male before egg deposition and must locate a suitable egg deposition site elsewhere. During this time, some females attempt to dislodge the small male amplexed to them but have never been observed to be successful.

Age-size distributions for breeding males and females are given in Figures 4–8 and 4–9 for the four years of this investigation. The amount of variation in size observed during any one year depends on survivorship of older individuals and number and size of newly maturing individuals. Because bullfrogs grow continuously throughout their life, the oldest individuals are usually the largest individuals in the population (Schroeder and Baskett, 1968; Collins, 1975). Survivorship of adults is high relative to earlier stages (Collins, ms.); adult mortality during the breeding season appears to be heavily biased toward larger males and results from increased risks of predation involved in conspicuous territorial defense (Howard, 1978a, in prep.). Mortality during the non-breeding season appears to be independent of sex and includes not only predation but also failure to overwinter. Recruitment each year is relatively low as a result of extremely high larval and juvenile mortality (Collins, ms.). Sources of juvenile mortality include predation by adult bullfrogs (Collins, ms.; pers. observ.) as well as by other predators and abiotic factors.

In all years, females were significantly larger than males on average (see Table 4–2). However, the observed body size dimorphism appears to result from differences between the sexes in adult survivorship and size at sexual maturation rather than from differential growth rates (Howard, in prep.). Large body size provides reproductive advantages to both females (increased clutch volume—Collins, 1975, ms.; Howard, 1978b) and males (increased probability of mating success—Howard, 1978a, this study).

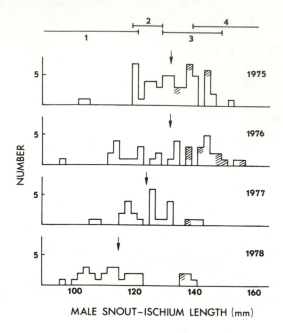

Figure 4–8.   Male size histograms for 1975–1978. Bars above histograms indicate estimated age according to Collins (1975). Shading indicates depredated males.

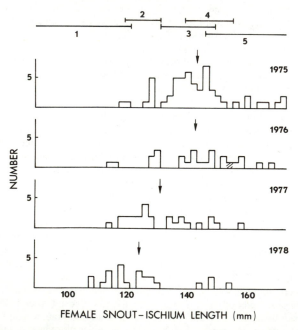

Figure 4–9.   Female size histograms for 1975–1978. Bars above histograms indicate estimated age according to Collins (1975). Shading indicates depredated females.

Table 4–2. Summary statistics on average body size in mm and variance for males and females during 1975–1978. Matrix on right hand side provides a comparison between years for both differences in average body size (Mann-Whitney U statistic, above the diagonal), and variance (F statistic, below the diagonal).

(a) Males:

Year	$\bar{X}$ Size (mm)	S^2	N	Comparisons Between Years (F and U Statistics)			
				1975	1976	1977	1978
1975	132.02	81.41	54		1017.0	380.0**	215.0***
1976	131.77	206.02	39	2.53**		331.0*	207.0***
1977	124.08	77.43	26	1.05	2.66**		190.5**
1978	114.73	147.72	30	1.81*	1.39	1.91*	

(b) Females:

Year	$\bar{X}$ Size (mm)	S^2	N	Comparisons Between Years (F and U Statistics)			
				1975	1976	1977	1978
1975	142.51	143.25	55		670.0	361.5***	193.5***
1976	142.42	184.57	26	1.29		176.5***	97.0***
1977	131.35	153.60	26	1.07	1.20		191.5*
1978	124.22	163.54	23	1.14	1.13	1.06	

*$p < .05$
**$p < .01$
***$p < .001$

Despite the differences in size distribution between the sexes, similar trends occurred for each sex during 1975–1978: Size distributions were not statistically different between 1975 and 1976; however, there was a significant reduction in average body size in 1977 and a further reduction in 1978 (Table 4–2). In the latter two years, the number of large individuals decreased dramatically and the number of newly maturing individuals increased slightly. The relative decline in number of large individuals probably resulted from increased overwintering mortality during the exceptionally harsh winters of 1976 and 1977; larger individuals generally face increased overwintering stress during any prolonged period of low oxygen concentration because of their lower surface to volume ratio.

Different age-size distributions of females need not necessarily affect female mating behavior or mating success as female–female competition is low in most species. However, as male–male competition is usually more intense, different age-size distributions of males can affect such characteristics as amount of time spent in aggressive behavior, type of mating behavior employed, and size-related mating success.

The amount of aggressive behavior observed varied both within and between years (Figure 4–10). Factors affecting such variation include not only the age–size distribution of competing males but also male spatial distribution in a chorus, i.e., the average number of and distance between males. In 1976 and 1977, a roughly circular distribution of chorusing males existed in the early mating periods; in the latter periods, males were aligned in a linear fashion along the shore and vegetation mats. Thus, in the early periods, most territorial males interacted with more neighboring males, and often the average distance between territorial males was less than in the latter periods. As a result, encounters were relatively frequent during early mating periods but were markedly lower in later mating periods.

In 1978, two general size classes of males existed (Figure 4–8): a few relatively large males and many small males. Under these conditions, few male–male encounters were observed regardless of male density. The large territorial males seldom had adjacent territories (sometimes they were in completely different parts of the pond), thus they rarely interacted with each other. The small males that were territorial usually avoided all potential male–male encounters with large males and only occasionally interacted with other small males.

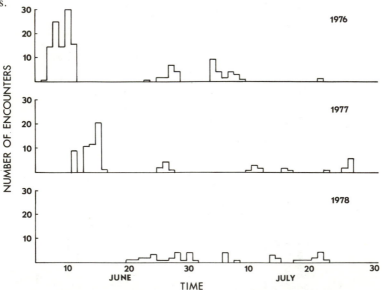

Figure 4–10.   Distribution of male–male aggressive encounters during the breeding season for 1976–1978. Data for 1975 were omitted because many encounters were not recorded (see text).

The relative importance of density and variation in male size in determining the number of male–male encounters observed is difficult to determine (Table 4–3). Increasing density usually increases amount of aggression. The importance of size distribution is supported by the observed reduction in aggression when competing males are more disparate in size. However, amount of aggression does not continue to increase as males become more and more similar in size: In 1977, variance in male size was significantly lower than in 1976 and 1978 (Table 4–2), but the frequency of male–male encounters was not greater than that observed at corresponding densities in 1976 (Figure 4–10; Table 4–3).

Table 4–3. Summary Statistics For Male-Male Encounters.

Year	Average Number of Male-Male Encounters/Night	SD	Number of Nights	Total Number of Encounters
1976	7.94	9.00	17	135
1977	4.93	5.86	15	74
1978	1.55	1.43	29	45

Size-specific male mating behaviors varied with overall male age-size distribution. Opportunistic behaviors observed during 1975 and 1976 were only rarely observed in 1977 and 1978. In the latter years, males of the intermediate size class of previous opportunistic males ($\bar{x} = 135.67$mm; $SD = 8.52$; $N = 43$ for 1976) were either totally absent (1977) or constituted the largest size class (1978) in the population. Small males usually did not employ opportunistic behaviors.

Male parasitism was observed in all years although its prevalence varied both within and between years (Figure 4–11; Table 4–4). Within years, male parasitism was usually most common when small males initially joined the breeding chorus. In 1975 and 1976, small males joined choruses in the later mating periods; they were parasitic at first but most soon established territories of their own. In 1977, small males joined the chorus during the initial mating period, remained parasitic for only a few nights, and then employed territorial behaviors for the remainder of the mating season. In 1978, small males also joined the breeding chorus at the onset of the mating season, but, in contrast to 1977, most of these males remained parasitic for the entire mating season.

Table 4–4.   Summary Statistics For Parasitic Males.

Year	Number Males Parasitic During The Year	Average Per Cent Parasitic Males Each Night	SD	Number Nights
1975	8 (13.8%)	8	0.09	14
1976	16 (43.2%)	22	0.17	17
1977	14 (53.8%)	9	0.09	15
1978	24 (80.0%)	19	0.11	29

Factors that influence whether or not small males become territorial at some point during the mating season are complex and poorly understood. My observations indicate that scarcity of premium oviposition sites is probably not a major cause for retention of parasitic behaviors for the following reasons. First, suitable habitat appears to exist in relative abundance in Crane Pond, and such habitat is often utilized at some point in the season by large males. Second, in 1978, larger males that were parasitized would often vacate their territories (without being displaced) and set up new territories elsewhere; the original sites were never subsequently defended by any of the former parasitic males. Because the territorial males would often return to the original site several days later, I assume that the quality of these areas per se did not decrease. And finally, parasitic males did not take the opportunity to call when territorial males were in amplexus (although nearby territorial males occasionally invaded the territory during this time and began calling).

One factor that may favor the utilization of parasitic behaviors throughout the season is the superior ability of large territorial males to attract females into their territories. The deeper, more resonant calls of large males probably provide a stronger stimulus for females compared to the relatively high-pitched hollow calls of small males. (Whether or not attracted females actually select such large males as mates is probably based on additional criteria as well, e.g., territorial quality.) Thus, it is possible that the probability of stealing a copulation from a large territorial male would exceed the chance that a small male could attract a female in the first place (Howard, 1978a). In 1978, the five males of intermediate or large size were heavily parasitized each night, sometimes by as many as four parasitic males; by contrast, the small territorial males were seldom parasitized (Figure 4–7).

Figure 4–12 summarizes the probability of obtaining at least one mating for males of various sizes from 1975–1978. The underlying age-size distribution had a definite impact on size-specific mating probabilities. An analysis of covariance indicated that the relationship between mating probability and male size was similar in 1975 and 1976 ($F_{2,8} = .33$; $N.S.$). The assumption of equal variances about the regression lines necessary for this analysis was not violated ($F_{4,4} = 1.11$; $N.S.$). These years also had similar age-size distributions. The curves shown in Figure 12 for 1977 and 1978 were fitted by eye rather than by a regression equation and suggest quite a different relationship for mating probabilities than that observed in the previous two years. In 1977, the absence of large males in the population greatly increased the probability of mating success for males of intermediate size. In

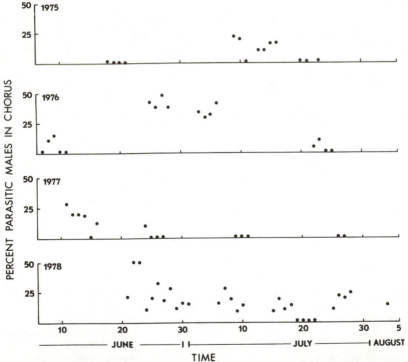

Figure 4–11.   Percentage of parasitic males (number of parasitic males observed /total number of breeding males in a chorus) during the breeding season for 1975–1978. Decline in percentage of parasitic males late in the season reflects the employment of territorial behaviors by formerly parasitic males.

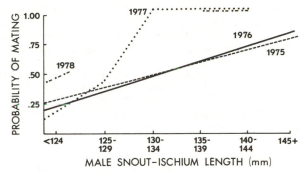

Figure 4–12.   Probability of obtaining at least one mating during the breeding season as a function of male body size for 1975–1978. Curves for 1975 and 1976 are based on a regression equation (Howard, 1978a); curves for 1977 and 1978 were fitted by eye.

1978, the population consisted of five males of intermediate to large size and 25 small males. The few larger males demonstrated their dominance by 100 per cent success in obtaining at least one mating during this year. However, the prediction that such an extreme male age-size distribution would result in larger males obtaining almost every mating was unsupported. Indeed, the relationship between male size and mating success (Figure 4–6) was the weakest of all four years. Success of larger territorial males in copulating with the females that they attracted was reduced by the activity of parasitic males. Success of smaller territorial males was higher than expected: Because these males were rarely parasitized, they had a better chance of copulating with any female that would approach.

Results from 1977 and 1978 indicate that no simple relationship exists between male age-size distributions and size-specific utilization of alternative mating behaviors or subsequent mating success. Variability between years in age-size distribution resulted in a natural experiment while still permitting a meaningful interpretation of yearly mating success. Variation in behavior of smaller males during these years can also be placed in the context of lifetime reproductive success, e.g., will the employment of territoriality while small result in lower growth rates and/or decreased survival such that subsequent reproductive success is jeopardized? One discomforting fact emerges from the data already obtained: Just as estimates of yearly mating success are highly variable between years, estimates of lifetime reproductive success should be highly sensitive to the specific biotic and abiotic conditions that prevail during a study. Thus, any generalities that come from such estimates should be tempered.

CONCLUDING REMARKS

Prerequisites for alternative male mating behaviors in any species should include greater variation in reproductive success in males than in females and substantial variation in male phenotypic attributes affecting such differential reproductive success. Alternative mating behaviors have been reported in several organisms besides bullfrogs including insects (Alcock et al., 1977; Borgia, 1979), fish (Briggs, 1953; Selmer, 1971; Robertson, 1972), other anurans (Fellers, 1975; Wells, 1977b; Perrill et al., 1978), birds (Hogan-Warburg, 1966; VanRhijn, 1973; Wiley, 1974 and references therein; Cronin and Sherman, 1977), and mammals (Darling, 1937; Kummer, 1968; LeBoeuf, 1974). For some species, available evidence indicates that variations in male mating behaviors correspond to genetic differences among males (Hogan-Warburg, 1966; Semler, 1971; VanRhijn, 1973). For other species, different male mating behaviors do not appear to result from genetic *differ-*

ences among males; however, this does not imply the absence of a genetic component, only that no genetic differences are known to exist. All males may possess the genetic information necessary to perform the entire repertoire of mating behaviors that characterize their population or species; however, the specific behaviors employed depend on how a male differs from competing males in crucial phenotypic characteristics (e.g., body size).

Phenotypic variations among males affecting the proliferation of alternative mating behaviors can result from a number of factors including variations in parental ability in providing care during their period of dependency (e.g., see Trivers and Willard, 1973), environmental conditions during development (Alcock et al., 1977; Borgia, 1979), parental manipulation (Alexander, 1974), age relative to competing males (Howard, 1978a; this study), and social status of relatives (e.g., some primates—Koford, 1963; Sade, 1966) as well as genetic differences. Viewed in this manner, alternative mating behaviors might be best considered as a form of phenotypic plasticity in variable competitive environments. Necessary prerequisites for such plasticity to be an evolved response include competitive environments varied frequently during the evolutionary past, some degree of environmental predictability, and/or environmental variations that are short term in nature, i.e., occur within the lifetime of an individual.

For example, in bullfrogs, a male's size relative to other males is influenced by his age and growth rate and the overall age-size distribution of competing males during each breeding season. Even if male age-size distributions never vary significantly between years, a male will experience differing competitive environments as he ages and grows. Present data suggest that variations in age-size distributions among years may also be common in bullfrogs: Intensity of mortality can be highly size-specific during years with significant overwintering stress. Additionally, juvenile recruitment could often vary between years (Collins, ms.). Many of the attributes that are thought to be indicative of species with variable juvenile recruitment (Charnov and Schaffer, 1973; Hirshfield and Tinkle, 1975; Stearns, 1976; Collins, ms.) can be found in bullfrogs: relatively long adult lifetimes, iteroparity, and large clutches with little parental investment. Such variable recruitment could result in definite "year class effects," thus contributing to variability in male age-size distributions through time.

The relative reproductive success of males employing alternative mating behaviors should be influenced by the type of mating behaviors involved, underlying phenotypic basis for the existence of alternative behaviors, and the amount of mate discrimination females exhibit. In bullfrogs, territoriality can confer relatively high mating success upon males provided they can defend suitable oviposition sites and attract females; however, costs of territoriality in terms of energy expenditure and risks of predation also appear to be relatively high. Opportunism and male parasitism should confer lower costs but also lower mating success regardless of male phenotype and abilities. Thus, opportunism and male parasitism should only occur in males whose size relative to other males renders them less effective in physical competition. Smaller males may best increase their lifetime reproductive success by deferring costs and risks of male–male competition in favor of increased growth and/or survival to future breeding seasons. However, if most competing males are also small as in 1977, small males may obtain a reproductive advantage by being territorial.

It seems unlikely that opportunism and male parasitism would have evolved in bullfrogs for any reason other than as possible counterstrategies in smaller males against the physical dominance of large territorial males. For example, unless some territorial males were unusually successful in attracting females, male parasitism would confer little or no reproductive advantage. Ironically, matings by opportunistic and parasitic males incidentally reduce or perhaps even eliminate the relationship between male size and mating success. Thus, in some years, large male size may provide little or no advantage in mating success as occurred in 1978. However, to conclude that large male size is unimportant in the determination of alternative mating behaviors and mating success would obviously be an error. In a similar fashion, alternative mating behaviors employed by smaller or lower-ranking males in other species might obscure any detectable relationship between male size, rank, and mating success. This result may be particularly true if the relative success of alternative mating behaviors becomes less disparate.

ACKNOWLEDGEMENTS

I am indebted to R. D. Alexander, A. G. Kluge, and D. W. Tinkle for their advice during the course of my investigations. I appreciate the field assistance provided by R. D. Alexander, M. Flinn, M. F. Hirshfield, R. B. King, S. Moody, D. W. Tinkle, and T. Wurster. R. D. Alexander, J. P. Collins, M. Gromko, D. W. Tinkle, and R. C. Woodruff provided valuable comments on this manuscript. I thank R. D. Alexander for his insights concerning the evolutionary significance of phenotypic plasticity.

I am grateful to Drs. F. C. Evans and D. W. Tinkle for allowing me to continue my work on bullfrogs at the E. S. George Reserve and for providing accommodations during the course of my study.

I thank my wife, Sharron, for her assistance in preparing this manuscript and for her encouragement.

This work was supported by NSF grant DEB 78-07447, a NSF Doctoral Dissertation under the guidance of R. D. Alexander, Theodore Roosevelt Memorial Fund Grant, Horace H. Rackham School of Graduate Studies Dissertation Grant, University of Michigan Museum of Zoology Grant, E. S. George Reserve Grant, and E. S. George Fellowship.

REFERENCES

Alcock, J., C. E. Jones, and S. L. Buchmann. 1977. Male mating strategies in the bee, *Centris pallida* Fox (Anthophoridae: Hymenoptera). *Amer. Nat.* 111:145–155.

Alexander, R. D. 1974. The evolution of social behavior. *Ann. Rev. Ecol. Syst.* 5:325–383.

Alexander, R. D., and G. Borgia. 1979. On the origin and basis of the male-female phenomenon. In M. F. Blum and N. Blum (ed.), *Sexual Selection and Reproductive Competition in Insects*. Academic Press. N.Y. pp.417–440.

Borgia, G. 1979. Sexual selection and the evolution of mating systems. In M. F. Blum and N. Blum (ed.), *Sexual Selection and Reproductive Competition in Insects*. Academic Press. N.Y. pp. 19–80.

Briggs, J. C. 1953. The behavior and reproduction of salmonid fishes in a small coastal stream. *California Fish. Bull.* 94: 1–62.

Cantrall, I. J. 1943. The ecology of the Orthoptera and Dermaptera of the George Reserve, Michigan. *Misc. Publ. Mus. Zool.* Univ. of Michigan. No. 54. 182p.

Chagnon, N. 1974. *Studying the Yanamamo: Studies in Anthropological Method*. Holt, Rinehart, and Winston. N.Y. 270p.

Charnov, E. L., and W. M. Schaffer. 1973. Life history consequences of natural selection: Cole's result revisited. *Amer. Nat.* 107: 791–793.

Collins, J. P. 1975. A comparative study of the life history strategies in a community of frogs. Ph.D. Dissertation, Univ. of Michigan. 148p.

———. 1979. Intrapopulation variation in the body size at metamorphosis and timing of metamorphosis in the bullfrog. *Ecology* 60:738–749.

———. ms. Variation in juvenile and adult survival in a population of bullfrogs, *Rana catesbeiana*.

Cooper, A. W. 1958. Plant life forms as indicators of microclimate. Ph.D. Dissertation, Univ. of Michigan. 387p.

Cronin, E. W., Jr., and P. W. Sherman. 1977. A resource-based mating system: the orange-rumped honeyguide. *Living Bird* 15: 5–32.

Darling, F. F. 1937. *A Herd of Red Deer*. Doubleday. N.Y. 226p.

Darwin, C. 1871. *Descent of Man and Selection in Relation to Sex*. John Murray, London

Downhower, J. F., and K. B. Armitage. 1971. The yellow-bellied marmot and the evolution of polygamy. *Amer. Nat.* 105: 355–370.

Emlen, S. T. 1968a. Territoriality in the bullfrog, *Rana catesbeiana*. *Copeia* 1968: 240–243.

———. 1968b. A technique for marking anuran amphibians for behavioral studies. *Herpetologica* 24:
172–173.

———. 1976. Lek organization and mating strategies in the bullfrog. *Behavioral Ecology and Sociobiology* 1: 283–313.

Emlen, S. T., and L. W. Oring. 1977. Ecology, sexual selection, and the evolution of mating systems.
Science 197: 215–223.

Fellers, G. M. 1975. Behavioral interactions in North American treefrogs (Hylidae). *Chesapeake Sci.*
16: 218–219.

Fisher, R. A. 1958. *The Genetical Theory of Natural Selection*. 2nd Edit. Dover Publ. N.Y. 291p.

Hirshfield, M. F., and D. W. Tinkle. 1975. Natural selection and the evolution of reproductive effort.
Proc. Nat. Acad. Sci. 72 (6): 2227–2231.

Hogan-Warburg, A. J. 1966. Social behavior of the ruff, *Philomachus pugnax* (L.). *Ardea* 54:
109–229.

Howard, R. D. 1978a. The evolution of mating strategies in bullfrogs. *Rana catesbeiana*. *Evolution*.
32:850–871.

———. 1978b. The influence of male-defended oviposition sites on early embryo mortality in bullfrogs. *Ecology* 59: 789–798.

———. 1979. Estimating reproductive success in natural populations. *Amer. Nat.* 114:221–231.

Koford, C. B. 1963. Ranks of mothers and sons in bands of Rhesus monkeys. *Science* 141: 356–357.

Krummer, H. 1968. Two variations in the social organization of baboons. pp. 293–312. In P. C. Jay
(ed.), *Primates, Studies in Adaptation and Variability*. Holt, Rinehart, and Winston. N.Y.

LeBoeuf, B. J. 1974. Male–male competition and reproductive success in elephant seals. *Amer. Zool.*
14 (1): 163–176.

Orians, G. H. 1969. On the evolution of mating systems in birds and mammals. *Amer. Nat.* 103:
589–603.

Payne, R. B. 1979. Sexual selection and intersexual differences in variance of breeding success. *Amer.
Nat.* 114:447–452.

Perrill, S. A., H. C. Gerhardt, and R. Daniel. 1978. Sexual parasitism in the green treefrog *(Hyla
cinerea)*. *Science* 200: 1179–1180.

Robertson, D. R. 1972. Social control of sex reversal in a coral reef fish. *Science* 177: 1007–1009.

Rogers, J. S. 1942. The craneflies (Tipulidae) of the George Reserve, Michigan. *Misc. Publ. Mus.
Zool.* Univ. of Michigan. No. 53. 128p.

Sade, D. S. 1966. Determinants of dominance in a group of free ranging Rhesus monkeys. In S. Altmann (ed.) *Social Communication among Primates*. Univ. of Chicago Press. Chicago.

Schroeder, E. E., and T. S. Baskett. 1968. Age estimation, growth rate, and population structure in
Missouri bullfrogs. *Copeia* 1968: 583–592.

Seale, D. 1973. Impact of amphibian larval populations on an aquatic community. Ph.D. Dissertation.
Washington Univ. 167p.

Semler, D. E. 1971. Some aspects of adaptation in a polymorphism for breeding colours in the three-
spined stickleback *(Gasterosteus aculeatus)*. *J. Zool. Lond.* 165: 291–302.

Siegal, S. 1956. *Nonparametric Statistics for the Behavioral Sciences*. McGraw-Hill. N.Y. 312p.

Smith, H. M. 1950. Handbook of amphibians and reptiles of Kansas. *Misc. Publ. Univ. of Kansas
Mus. Nat. Hist.* No. 2. 336p.

Sokal, R. R., and F. J. Rohlf. 1969. *Biometry*. W. H. Freeman and Co. San Francisco. 776p.

Stearns, S. C. 1976. Life-history tactics: a review of the ideas. *Quart. Rev. Biol.* 51: 3–47.

Trivers, R. L. 1972. Parental investment and sexual selection. pp.136–179. In B. Campbell (ed.), *Sexual Selection and the Descent of Man* (1871–1971). Aldine Press. Chicago.

Trivers, R. L., and D. E. Willard. 1973. Natural selection and parental ability to vary the sex ratio of
offspring. *Science* 179: 190–192.

VanRhijn, J. G. 1973. Behavioral dimorphism in male ruffs, *Philomachus pugnax* (L.). *Behaviour*
47:10–229.

Walker, C. F. 1946. The amphibians of Ohio. Part 1. The frogs and toads. *Ohio St. Mus. Sci. Bull.* 1:
1–109.

Wells, K. D. 1977a. The social behaviour of anuran amphibians. *Animal Behaviour* 25: 666–693.

———. 1977b. Territoriality and male mating success in the green frog *(Rana clamitans)*. *Ecology* 58:
750–762.

Wiewandt, T. A. 1969. Vocalization, aggressive behavior, and territoriality in the bullfrog, *Rana cates-beiana*. *Copeia* 1969: 276–285.

Wiley, R. H. 1974. Evolution of social organization and life history patterns among grouse. *Quart. Rev. Biol.* 49: 201–227.

Williams, G. C. 1966. *Adaptation and Natural Selection, A Critique of Some Current Evolutionary Thought*. Princeton Univ. Press. Princeton, N.J. 307p.

_____. 1975. *Sex and Evolution*. Princeton Monographs No. 8. Princeton, N.J. 200p.

Wonnacott, T. H., and R. J. Wonnacott. 1972. *Introductory Statistics for Business and Economics*. John Wiley and Sons. N.Y. 622p.

Wright, A. H., and A. A. Wright. 1949. *Handbook of Frogs and Toads of the United States and Canada*. Comstock Publ. Co. Ithaca, N.Y. 640p.

5.

The Timing of Reproduction and Its Behavioral Consequences for Mottled Sculpins, *Cottus bairdi*

Jerry F. Downhower and Luther Brown

Among fishes timing of reproduction may coincide with physical and biological events that determine the subsequent survival of progeny. Whether these are predictable events [e.g., tidal cycles (Clark, 1925)], temperature and photoperiod events (e.g., Wootten, 1976), seasonal flooding (Lowe-McConnell, 1975), or biological events such as ephemeral availability of larval food (May, 1974; Cushing, 1974; Jones and Hall, 1974), the reproductive success of individuals is influenced by when they breed relative to those events. For example, survival of larval anchovies (*Engraulis mordax*) is determined by the availability of specific densities of phytoplankton of specific sizes and particular species composition. These conditions are transient in nature and delays in reproduction may have drastic effects on larval survival (Lasker, 1975).

Timing of reproduction has important effects in other vertebrates as well. Early breeders frequently have higher reproductive success than late breeders (birds: Emlen and Deming, 1975; amphibians: Emlen, 1977; mammals: Armitage and Downhower, 1974).

Further, the importance of timing of reproduction has been linked to the evolution of sexual dimorphism (Downhower, 1976), because the ability of an individual to respond to environmental changes and hence "time" its reproduction is determined in part by body size.

The relationship between timing of reproduction and the social organization of a species remains to be explored. However, if mating systems are largely determined by preferences of females (female choice) for males who occupy sites of differént quality (Orians, 1969; Wittenberger, 1976; Emlen and Oring, 1977) or males of different quality (Wiley, 1974) or by differential patterns of parental investment (Trivers, 1972; Dawkins and Carlisle, 1976), then alterations in reproductive success associated with when a female breeds are likely to influence the kinds of choices that females are able to make. The only study that has attempted to include the effect of timing of reproduction on female choice is that of Pleszczynska (1978), whose analysis of mate preferences of lark buntings (*Calamospiza melanocorys*) indicated that the reproductive success of a female who mated with an already mated male was no different from that of a female who mated with a bachelor male at the same time. The crucial point is that female reproductive success varied seasonally, and why a female would choose to mate with a particular male could only be understood when seasonal differences in reproduction were taken into account. Since most of the animals studied by biologists breed seasonally, we believe that the influences of timing of reproduction are general and that they are likely to play an important role in the evolution of mating systems (Brown and Downhower, in prep.).

In this paper we review the breeding biology of a polygynous freshwater fish—the mottled sculpin, *Cottus bairdi*, describe the characteristics that influence how a female chooses a mate, define those factors that limit the opportunity for females to maximize certain aspects of their mate preferences, and examine how those factors would modify other aspects of the behavior of both females and males. What we suggest is that when a female sculpin spawns is likely to be as important as where she spawns or with whom she spawns. As a consequence, the advantages of increased selectivity among potential mates or breeding sites are compromised by patterns of reproductive success associated with the timing of reproduction. Such compromises must occur because increased selectivity on the part of females will require more time to locate and compare mates or sites.

Breeding Biology

In early spring male mottled sculpins take up residence in cavities under rocks or other stream bed rubble (Smith, 1922; Hann, 1927; Bailey, 1952; Ludwig and Norden, 1969). Males modify such sites only slightly and show no obvious adaptations for excavation of breeding sites. Thus, the distribution and nature of available sites are determined by factors over which the fish have little control. If a site is large enough, two or more males may subdivide it (personal observation). Males defend these sites against other males, but defense is limited to the spawning site and does not include any of the surrounding stream bed (Downhower and Brown, 1979a).

How females locate males is not known, but females must visit more than one male before spawning (Downhower and Brown, 1979a). When a female spawns, she deposits her egg mass on the ceiling of the male's spawning site. This egg mass represents her entire reproductive output for that year (Smith, 1922; Hann, 1927; Bailey, 1952; Savage, 1963; Ludwig and Norden, 1969). After spawning the female departs or is driven out (Savage, 1963), and the male remains at the site. Certain males may spawn with as many as 13 females in a single season (Downhower and Brown, 1979b). After spawning, the male remains with the eggs until they hatch and most males remain with the fry for from two to four additional weeks.

Female Choice: Male Size and Site Quality

Female sculpins might base their choice of mates on attributes of the breeding site (Orians, 1969; Wittenberger, 1976), attributes of the male (Wiley, 1974), or some combination of these factors. Site attributes may be important because the eggs and fry remain at the site for prolonged periods of time. The size or area of a site might be an important indicator of site quality. Eggs require an incubation period of a month, and fry require nearly two weeks to absorb their yolk sacs (Bailey, 1952). Thus, the fate of eggs and fry is closely associated with a specific site for nearly six weeks. Male characteristics may also be important as males remain with the eggs and fry (Simon and Brown, 1943; Bailey, 1952). Male size seemed a reasonable measure of male "quality" because courtship displays of this species involve behaviors such as gaping, spreading, and fanning of the pectoral fins, and in certain instances the male takes the female's head into his mouth (Morris, 1955 and pers. obs.), all behaviors that would indicate the size of the male. In addition, males defend the eggs against predators (Downhower and Yost, 1977), and large size may facilitate such defense.

Because sculpins accept a variety of materials as suitable spawning sites (e.g., Hann, 1927), we placed different-sized slate tiles in our study stream (a 200m stretch of Anderson Creek in the Mad River drainage of Ohio) in order to manipulate site quality. In 1975, 75 tiles of each of three sizes were placed in the stream; 50 tiles of each of 6 sizes were placed in the stream in 1976; and in 1977, 300 tiles of one size were placed in the stream. In each year the tiles were placed in the stream just prior to the onset of spawning. The tiles were sampled at regular intervals throughout the breeding season. When a tile was sampled, the fish present under it were collected, sexed, measured, and returned to the tile (Downhower and Brown, 1977).

Because each egg mass differed from others in color, size, and shape, it was a simple matter to determine the number of females that had spawned with a male by counting the number of egg masses that were being guarded. The egg masses at each breeding site were photographed when the tile was sampled, and, thus, it was possible to determine the fate of each egg mass in the study area.

The slate tiles did not attract a population of males that was different from those at natural sites (Brown, 1978; Downhower and Brown, 1979b), nor was the reproductive success of males at those sites different from that of males at natural sites (Figure 5–1). Thus, the use of slate tiles provided a means to manipulate site quality and did not produce any obvious distortion of the reproductive biology of this species.

In 1977 when tiles of one size were placed in the stream, the reproductive success of males occupying those sites was no different from that of males occupying natural sites in

Table 5–1.   Analysis of Covariance for male size and tile size. Maximum number of egg masses present at each site was used to estimate the number of spawnings per male. Sites at which loss of an egg mass could be attributed to our activities were excluded. Regression coefficients were similar for all six tile size classes ($F = 2.07$, $d.f. = 5, 373$, $P < .05$). From Downhower and Brown (1979b).

Ancova Table

Dependent Variable: Matings per male

Source	d.f.	S.S.	M.S.	F.	R²
Model	6	278.8	46.46	12.26	.163
Error	378	1432.2	3.79	($P < .0001$)	
Corrected Total	384	1711.0			
Partial S.S. Source					
Tile Size	5	28.03		1.48 ($P < .20$)	
Male Size	1	154.23		40.71 ($P < .0001$)	

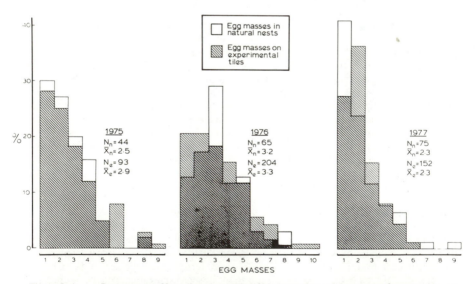

Figure 5–1.   Percentages of breeding sites with different numbers of egg masses for natural breeding sites and experimental breeding sites in each year of the study. The subscript n refers to natural sites; the subscript e refers to experimental sites. N refers to sample size and $\bar{X}$ indicates the average number of egg masses at each site (From Downhower and Brown, 1979b).

that year (Figure 5–1). As experimental sites were identical and natural sites must have been variable, the size of a site or differences in the sizes of sites do not appear to influence female mating preferences.

In seeming contrast to that conclusion, male reproductive success was correlated with the area of sites in both 1975 and 1976 when sites of different sizes were seeded in the study area (Figure 5–2). Males that occupied larger sites spawned with more females than did males occupying smaller sites; however, larger males tended to occupy the larger tiles and smaller males occupied smaller tiles. An analysis of covariance where male size was the co-variate and tile size was the treatment variable revealed that male size was the important variable and tile size did not account for a significant portion of male reproductive success (Table 5–1). Thus the correlation between tile size and male reproductive success was a reflection of choices of breeding sites made by males and did not indicate the nature of female mating preferences (Downhower and Brown, 1979b).

It seems fair to infer that females should make choices among attributes whose varia-

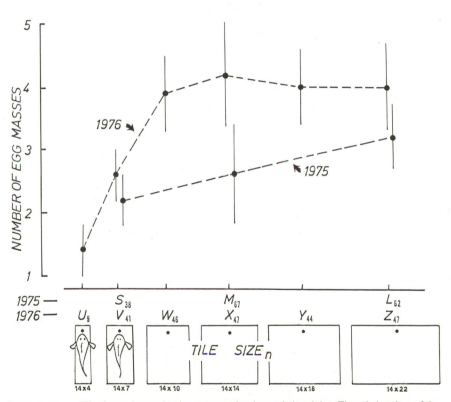

Figure 5–2.   Tile size and reproductive success of male mottled sculpins. The relative sizes of the tiles are illustrated along the abcissa as is the size of an "average male." Sample sizes are subscripted to the letter designating each tile size. Means are bounded by 2 standard errors. Dimensions of the tile are given in cm (From Downhower and Brown, 1979b).

bility has a direct influence on her reproductive success (that is, hatching success*). Thus, to expect females to discriminate among sites on the basis of the size of the site is equivalent to expecting survivorship of eggs or fry to be different at different sites. It was not (Table 5–2). However, hatching success did increase with male size, and females that chose larger males seemed to improve the hatching success of their eggs (Figure 5–3). Hatching success increased by about 10 per cent per cm. of increase in male length. If a female mated with a male who was larger than 95 per cent of all other breeding males, then she might increase her reproductive success by as much as 22 per cent over that of a female who spawned with an average male (standard deviation for breeding males in 1976: 5.7mm).

In mottled sculpins male size and tile size were correlated with male reproductive success. Males that were larger occupied sites of higher quality. Such correlations are probably common in vertebrate mating systems (Downhower and Brown, 1979b) but seem to be

Table 5–2.   Hatching success of egg masses and tile size. An egg mass was considered to have failed to hatch when all of the eggs had disappeared (From Downhower and Brown, 1979b).

| | | Tile Size | | |
	U & V	W	X	Y	Z
Proportion Hatching	0.69	0.73	0.68	0.69	0.58
Total Number of Egg Masses	96	163	182	165	167

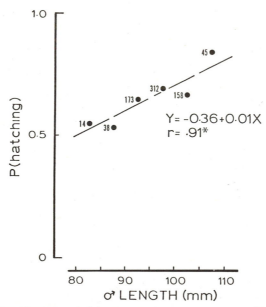

Figure 5–3.   Hatching success and male size. The number of egg masses in each sample is indicated in the figure (From Downhower and Brown, 1979b).

* Hatching success was calculated as the numbers of egg masses from which one or more eggs hatched divided by the total number of egg masses deposited.

rarely sorted out. For example, Carey and Noland (1978) provide data that bigamous male indigo buntings (*Passerina cyanea*) are older and occupy better territories than monogamous males. However, the contributions of males and the sites they occupy to female reproductive success were not separated.

Simulation Studies

As a result of these field experiments, one of us (L. B.) attempted to model some of the ways in which females might choose their mates (Brown, 1978). The models assumed that females have no way of determining the spatial distribution of either breeding sites or males. Females were presumed to move from nearest neighbor to nearest neighbor, and comparisons among potential mates or sites were presumed to be relative (see Mitchell, 1975).

To date, five models have been evaluated (Brown, 1978, and in prep.). They include a random model (random spawning differed from a Poisson distribution because tiles differed in both size and likelihood of occupancy), a model based on size of males, one based on tile size, and two that presumed interactions between male size and tile size. Only the male size model accurately predicted the observed patterns of spawning success of males (Figure 5–4).

The size model assumed that females only compared two males and spawned the larger. A choice based on a sample size of two is the simplest comparison that a female could make. The algorithm of the size model was as follows. The distribution of nearest neighbors and the sizes of males under each tile were stored in the computer. A "female" was presumed to be ready to spawn at some place in our study area. That place was determined by a random draw among all sites. If that site was occupied by a male, his size was recorded and the nearest neighbor of that tile was censused. If that tile was occupied and if that male were larger than the previous male, a spawning was recorded for the second male. If the second male was smaller, his size replaced the size of the first male, and the nearest neighbor of that tile was censused. If that tile was unoccupied, the model searched from nearest neighbor to nearest neighbor until two tiles were located such that the second tile was occupied by a male who was larger than the male occupying the first tile. A spawning was then recorded for the second or larger male.

The size model elegantly mimicked the number of spawnings per male that were observed during the 1976 breeding season (Figure 5–4). Of the 40 comparisons that we could make, predictions of the male size model differed from the observed patterns in only 8 cases. All but one of the errors occurred in the last three sample periods of the spawning season; a period in which less than 10 per cent of the females remained to spawn. The model suggested that the spatial distribution of males had an important effect on the outcome of female mate preferences. For although male size accounted for about 10 per cent to 15 per cent of the variation in male reproductive success (Table 5–1), a simple model in which male size was the essential determinant of female spawning patterns described the observed patterns almost exactly.

The model also suggested that females made relatively unsophisticated comparisons among males. More precisely, if a female spawned with the first male she encountered, then the probability is .5 that the male was of larger than average size. If she chose the larger of two males, then the probability that the male she spawned with was larger than average was about .70. If she chose the largest of three males, the probability that her mate was larger than average was about .85 (Brown, 1978). Thus, a female that chose among more males would increase her reproductive success. Yet choices between two males adequately described the observed patterns of spawning in our populations and choices among three males did not (Brown, 1978). Females were less selective than they might have been, and the reason was not immediately obvious.

The Timing of Reproduction

The freedom of a female sculpin to choose among many males appears to be limited by the effect that timing of reproduction has on the subsequent survival of her eggs. Egg masses deposited at different times during the breeding season had different probabilities of survival. Early egg masses had higher survival than later ones (Table 5–3). However, the decline in survivorship of egg masses was not only a seasonal effect, the timing of reproduction was also a matter of a female's position in the temporal sequence of all females that spawned with a particular male.

When a female sculpin courted by an unmated male spawned with him, her egg mass may have been the only egg mass he fertilized, or it may have been the first in a series. If a

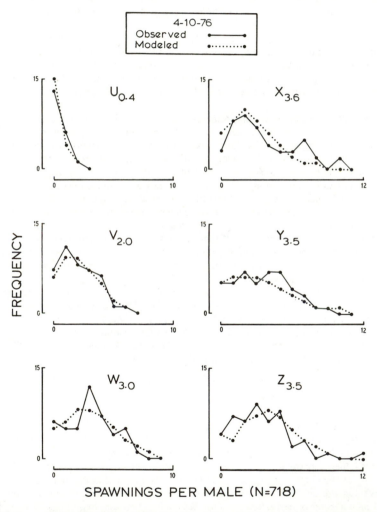

Figure 5–4.   Observed and expected frequencies of spawnings per male for each of six tile sizes and as generated by a computer model that assigned spawnings to males on the basis of male size. Tile sizes are as shown in Figure 5–2, and the average number of spawnings per male is indicated as a subscript (From Brown, 1978).

female spawned with a male that had previously mated, her egg mass may have been the last egg mass that he fertilized, or it may have been one intermediate in a series. The survivorship of egg masses in each of these categories differed (Table 5–3). If a female's eggs were the only eggs fertilized by a male, then survivorship was about 35 per cent. If her eggs were the last egg mass in a series, then the survival of those eggs was about 55 per cent. Survival of first and middle egg masses was similar—about 75 per cent. Analysis of these data indicates that both sequence (first, middle, last, and only) and season influence survivorship (distribution-free two-way layout, $S = 8.63$, treatments $= 4$, groups $= 4, P = <.02$—Hollander and Wolfe, 1973). Egg masses in all categories had higher survival in mid-breeding season than they did at other times. However, there was no significant variation within classes over time. Indeed, if the average survival of single- and multiple-egg masses is calculated from the average survivorship of first, middle, last, and only egg masses, the expected survivorship is almost exactly what is observed (Figure 5–5). Thus, the position of a female in a series of females with which a male will spawn plays a crucial role in the survival of her eggs.

Females that bred at different times during the spawning seasons had different probabilities of being first, middle, or last in a sequence as well as being the only female with which a male spawned (Figure 5–6). If a female spawned with a bachelor, the likelihood that she would be the *only* female to do so was independent of season and was about one chance in ten. By contrast, the likelihood that a female would be the last to spawn with an already mated male rose during the spawning season and the likelihood of being first or middle declined. Since the likelihood of being the only female to mate with a bachelor was independent of season, the decreased average survivorship on a seasonal basis is also independent of matings in which a male only mated with one female. The seasonal decrease in average survival is caused by the increase in the proportion of spawnings that are the last of a series.

The probability that a female will be the last to spawn with a male might be influenced by several factors. First, female sculpins spawn only once in a season, and because there are a finite number of them spawning in any area, it is inevitable that late spawners are more likely to be last: No other females are around to spawn. Second, a female may be more likely to be last because the male accepts a limited number of mates or the area available for

Table 5–3.   Hatching success of egg masses deposited on different dates during the 1976 spawning season. Sample sizes are given in parentheses. The total number of egg masses recorded on each date exceeded the total for egg masses assigned to each category on each day. This is because it was not always possible to assign a position to each egg mass.

| | | DATE | | | Overall | |
Position	3/28–4/2	4/7	4/10	4/13*	Success	X^2 (3 df)
First in Series	.76 (92)	.79 (33)	.65 (26)	.58 (12)	.74 (120)	3.40 n.s.
Middle in Series	.79 (72)	.80 (146)	.71 (110)	.64 (22)	.77 (350)	5.94 n.s.
Last in Series	.50 (12)	.77 (30)	.55 (66)	.45 (55)	.55 (163)	5.57 n.s.
Solitary Egg Masses	.33 (18)	.38 (8)	.36 (11)	.36 (11)	.35 (48)	.00 (3) n.s.
Overall Survivorship	.71 (204)	.78 (221)	.64 (220)	.50 (100)	.68 (745)	29.89 $P<.001$

* includes samples taken on 4/17, 4/20, and 4/24

egg deposition is limited. Thus, certain males or certain sites become unlikely places for further spawning. The second consideration may be evaluated by calculating the probability that a male guarding a certain number of egg masses is likely to obtain an additional spawning. If there is a threshold at which males or sites become satiated, then the probability of a male spawning with more than that number of females should be much lower than the probability that he would spawn with fewer than that number.

The relative proportions of males that took up residence under our experimental tiles in 1976 and spawned with one or more females is illustrated in Figure 5–7. Of the 252 males who were in residence, 199 spawned with one or more females. Thus, our best estimate of the probability that a male will spawn with at least one female is 199/252 or 0.79. If the probability that a female will spawn with a male is independent of the past success of a male, then the probability that a male will obtain the nth spawning is the nth root of the proportion of males who obtained n or more spawnings. That relationship is shown as the upper line in Figure 5–7. The relationship is a linear one, and on the average the probability that a male will obtain an additional spawning decreases by 0.01 per additional female.

Calculation of the probability of obtaining another egg mass in the manner just described results in an averaging of probabilities over several egg masses. That is, if there is a point at which males are unlikely to obtain additional spawnings, then calculating the nth root of product of those probabilities that culminate in that probability simply spreads that change over the probabilities of obtaining all previous spawnings. A more sensitive evaluation is the second line shown in Figure 5–7. Here the probability of obtaining exactly one more egg mass is calculated by dividing the probability of obtaining n egg masses by the probability of obtaining $n-1$ egg masses. Again the relationship is linear, and the probability of obtaining an additional egg mass declines more steeply at about 0.02 per additional spawning. Both measures indicate that there is no threshold beyond which a male becomes

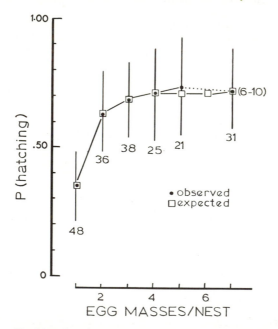

Figure 5–5.   Hatching success of individual egg masses as a function of the number of egg masses being guarded by a male. Expected values were generated from the survival data on first, middle, last, and solitary egg masses (Table 5–3). Each observed value is bounded by 95 per cent confidence limits. Subscripts indicate the number of breeding sites. Sites with more than six egg masses were pooled.

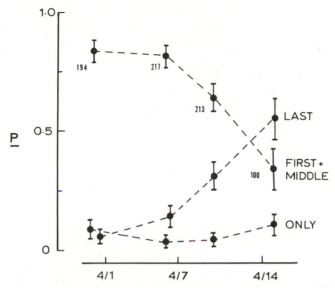

Figure 5–6.   The proportions of egg masses deposited in each sample interval that fell in to each of four categories: the only egg mass deposited with a male; the first and middle egg masses in a series deposited with a male; and the last egg mass deposited at a site. The total number of egg masses deposited in each interval is given as a subscript to the first and middle egg mass curve. Each proportion is bounded by 95 per cent confidence intervals. Samples for 4/17, 4/24, and 4/27 are pooled. The data are from the 1976 breeding season.

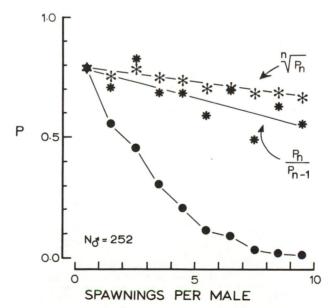

Figure 5–7.   The relative frequencies of breeding sites with differing number of egg masses in the 1976 breeding season (dots). The upper lines in the figure (indicated by asterisks) indicate the probability that a male with n egg masses will gain an addition spawning.

extraordinarily unlikely to obtain an additional mating. Nor do males become more attractive to females once they have obtained a first spawning as has been suggested for species of fishes where a female produces several clutches of eggs each year (Rohwer, 1978). Thus, the probability that a female will be the last to spawn with a male is primarily determined by the number of females that remain to spawn.

In order to minimize the likelihood of being last, we might infer that females should somehow assess the number of other females who will spawn. This seems unlikely for several reasons. First, the number of females spawning in the study area has varied by nearly a factor of 5 over different years. Second, the computer simulations of female choice patterns suggest that females make rather limited choices among males, and it seems inconsistent, therefore, to presume that females sample more exhaustively with regard to competitors (other females) than they do with regard to mates. Third, collection of information regarding when to spawn involves time, and delays in spawning increase the likelihood that a female will be the last to spawn with a male. We suggest then that the most probable tactic that would reduce the likelihood of being last is to spawn early.

In all years of this study the temporal pattern of spawnings did not follow a normal distribution (Figure 5–8). Rather the distributions are leptokurtic and skewed to the right indicating that spawnings are highly synchronous. Synchronous spawning results from several factors, all of which can be viewed as complementary. First, synchronous spawning will result from the selective advantage conferred from not being last. Once environmental conditions (temperature and photoperiod, e.g., Wootten, 1976) are appropriate for spawning, a female that spawns first will minimize the likelihood of being last. Second, there may be restricted periods during which oviposition will be successful; that is, there may be environmental variables that limit the breeding season. Surely such limitations exist for sculpins, but analysis of seasonal and sequential patterns of oviposition suggests that sequence is at least as important as season in determining survivorship of sculpin eggs. Third, the ability of males to care for eggs and fry may be limited because a male who obtains all of his spawnings over a long period of time is not able to remain with the eggs or fry long enough to insure their survival. Indeed the male may nourish himself while guarding the

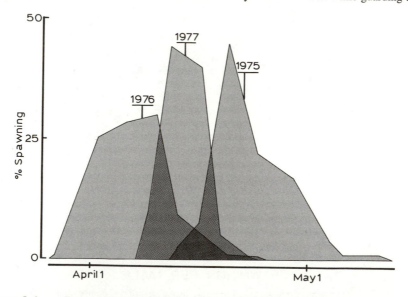

Figure 5–8.   Frequency histograms for spawnings in 1975, 76, and 77. In 1975, 540 females spawned, in 1976, 891 females spawned and in 1977, 430 females spawned.

eggs by cannibalizing some of them. In a number of other species males are known to eat some of the eggs that they guard (reviewed by Rohwer, 1978). In mottled sculpins we have experimentally manipulated patterns of parental care and find that sculpins other than the guarding male are also predators of egg masses (Staples, unpublished data).

Consequences: The Importance of Male Choice

Synchronous spawning has important consequences for male sculpins, because males are frequently confronted with the opportunity to choose among two or more females. For example, on April 31, 1976, 228 of the 300 available sites were occupied by males; of these 127 were cohabiting with at least one gravid female and of those males 24 per cent (30 of 127) shared their site with 2 or more gravid females.

How males and females behaved under the circumstance that a male could choose among females and females could respond to one another was investigated in a simple laboratory experiment. A male was placed in an aquarium and allowed to establish himself under a tile. Twenty-four hours later, two gravid females of different sizes were placed in the tank with the male. After 5 minutes the position of each female (under the tile versus not under the tile) and the behavior of the male (courting or not courting) were recorded. If a male was courting a female, then the size (large or small) of the female was also recorded. After 30 minutes the female who had been courted first was removed from the tank. The fish that remained were displaced from under the tile, and the experiment was allowed to proceed as before with only one female being present. Females of different sizes were chosen to facilitate individual identification and to determine if males would discriminate among females on the basis of size.

At the end of the first 5-minute interval, one or more of the females had moved under the tile with the male in all but nine instances (Table 5–4). Courtship activity was observed in half of the tanks (26 out of 52) where a female could be courted. When only the larger female was present under the tile, she was courted in 9 out of 19 tanks. When only the small

Table 5–4.   Courtship activity and mating preferences of male mottled sculpins. The data in part A of the table were recorded 5 minutes after the experiment was initiated. The data in part B were recorded after 25 minutes.

| | Position of Larger Female: | Under | Under | Out | Out | |
	Position of Smaller Female:	Out	Under	Under	Out	Total
	Larger	9	12	–	–	21
A	Male Courts:					
	Smaller	–	1	4	–	5
	No Courtship Observed	10	13	3	9	35
	Total:	19	26	7	9	61
	Expected Frequencies	21	24	7	9	$X^2 = 0.36$, 3 df, n.s.
	Larger	13	16	–	–	29
B	Male Courts:					
	Smaller	–	4	2	–	6
	No Courtship Observed	4	6	1	9	20
	Total:	17	32*	3	9	61
	Expected Frequencies	21	28	7	5	$X^2 = 6.82$, 3 df, $P<0.10$

* In six instances we were unable to determine which female was being courted by the male.

female was present under the tile, she was courted in 4 out of 7 tanks. However, when both females were present under the tile, courtship was not observed more frequently, but the larger female was courted in 12 out of 13 instances ($X^2 = 9.31, P < .01, 1df$). Initially, larger females were found under the tile more frequently than were small females (74 per cent vs. 54 per cent). However, there is no indication of direct interactions between females of different sizes. The spatial arrangements of females of each size were identical to what would be expected on the basis of the separate probabilities of a female of a particular size being observed under the tile or out in the tank. Prior to the removal of one of the females, the tanks were again censused (Table 4). The proportions of large and small females found under the tiles were nearly identical to those recorded in the initial census (80 per cent and 57 per cent). Again, there is no indication of interactions between females. Although the proportion of males courting females has risen to 79 per cent, males do not appear to discriminate when only one female is present and still show preferences for larger females when the opportunity to choose occurs (16 vs. 4, $X^2 = 7.2, P < 0.01$).

After the removal of the larger female, there was some indication that the behavior of the smaller female shifted. When only a small female was present in the tank ($N = 45$) she was found under the tile 69 per cent of the time. This percentage is not significantly different from that of small females when both females were present ($X^2 = 1.48, P < .05, 1df$), and it is not different from the proportion of times larger females were under a tile ($X^2 = 1.88, P < .05, 1df$). In 71 per cent of the instances where a female was under the tile, she was being courted. This proportion does not differ from that recorded at the end of the first half of the experiment.

Thus the experiment indicates that males discriminate among females on the basis of female size provided they have the opportunity to choose. Synchronous spawning on the part of female sculpins provides that opportunity. That males should choose the larger female was not unexpected (Williams, 1975) because larger females carry more eggs (Ludwig and Norden, 1969; Patten, 1971; Ludwig and Lange, 1975).

If there is an advantage to spawning early, then male choice behavior will insure that it is the larger females that spawn first. Such behavior on the part of males will enhance any additional factors that might lead larger females to spawn first and will be especially effective under conditions of competition among females for spawning sites. In our study populations spawning sequence is clearly size dependent; the larger females spawn first and small females spawn later (Figure 5–9).

Interactions Between Size and Time

Our information on patterns of female choice in mottled sculpins indicate that females show preferences for larger males and that females seem to behave in ways that would tend to minimize the probability of being the last female to spawn with a male. Thus far we have considered how the latter consideration could lead to alterations in the timing of reproduction and to size-related sequences of spawning that are in part mediated by male behavior. Now we wish to consider the consequences of interactions between timing and size.

Female preferences for larger males lead to disparities in the reproductive success of males; certain males do not spawn, whereas others do. As this disparity increases, then females are likely to be confronted with males who have spawned several times and males who have not spawned at all. That is, the preferences of females will accentuate a dichotomy among males into the ''haves and have nots.'' Under these circumstances the choices that females make are influenced by real differences in the likelihood that a male with one egg mass will gain another egg mass and the likelihood that a male with, for example, five egg masses will gain another. Whether or not a female should choose to mate with a bachelor male and provide the first egg mass deposited with him depends on the likelihood that the male will gain an additional egg mass. That probability remains high throughout the breeding season. On the other hand the likelihood that a female will be last increases during the breeding season, and as the number of egg masses per male increases, so does the probability that no additional females will spawn with the male. Thus as the season progresses, bachelors might be expected to become more attractive as mates. Indeed, the proportion of spawnings with bachelors is significantly lower than expected during the first portion of the breeding season and rises during the latter half of the season (Figure 5–10). In addition, we infer that the kinds of choices that females may make early in the spawning season are simpler than those made by females late in the spawning season. This is because females are initially confronted with a selection of bachelor males, and choices will be determined primarily by size. However, as males accumulate spawnings, females are confronted with choices among males of different sizes and different spawning success. The increase in complexity of choices implies that a female who spawns late in the breeding season will require more time to locate males.

How long it takes a female to locate a male can be estimated from information on the sizes of gravid females in the study area and the sizes of spawned females (Figure 5–9). Since large females spawn first, it is possible to estimate the time required for spawning (including search time) as the difference between the dates on which a female of a given size appears among the cohort of gravid females and when females of that size appear among the cohort of spawned females. For simplicity females have been divided into three size classes: small (<70mm), medium (70–74mm), and large (>74mm).

Larger females who spawned early required the least time to select a mate, and the time required increased as the breeding season passed (Figure 5–11). Medium-sized females took more time than did large females but less time than small females. Small females required the most time. Thus, the time required for a female to locate and spawn with a mate increased during the spawning season.

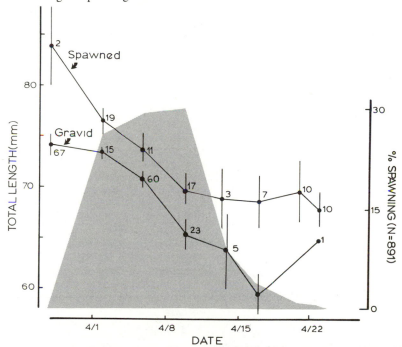

Figure 5–9.   Sizes of gravid and spawned females captured in the Anderson Creek study area in the 1976 breeding season. Each mean is bounded by two standard errors. Sample sizes are subscripted. The shaded area indicates the relative proportions of females spawning in each interval.

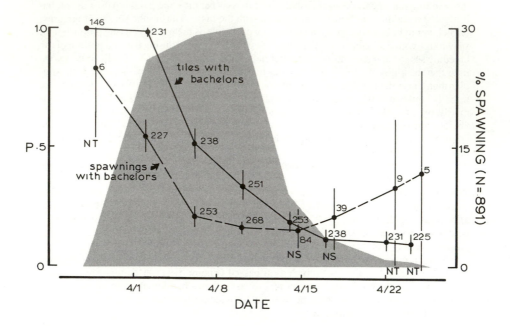

Figure 5–10.   Proportions of females spawning with bachelor males in 1976 and the proportion of all sites occupied by unmated males. Each proportion is bounded by 95 per cent confidence intervals, and sample sizes are subscripted. The shaded area indicates the relative proportion of all females that spawned in each sample interval.

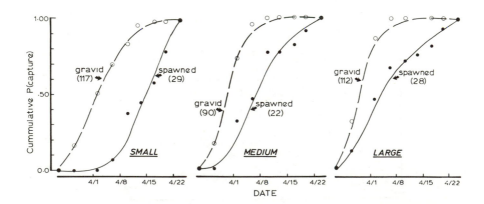

Figure 5–11.   Estimated times required for small (<70 mm), medium (70–74 mm), and large (>74 mm) females to locate and spawn with a male. Estimates were derived from data illustrated in Figure 5–9.

Summary and Implications

The reproductive success of a female mottled sculpin was correlated with the size of the male with whom she spawned and whether or not she was the last female to spawn with that male. Increases in hatching success associated with differences in the sizes of males with which females spawned were modest; about 10 per cent per centimeter of increase in male length. The standard deviation of male length in the 1976 breeding season was 5.7mm; therefore, a female might increase her reproductive success by as much as 22 per cent by choosing to mate with one of the largest available males (as opposed to mating with an average-sized male). By contrast, the hatching success of a female's eggs increased from 55 per cent to 75 per cent if she was not the last female to breed with a particular male. The differences in reproductive success that result from timing of reproduction are as great or greater than those resulting from extraordinary mate preferences of females.

Female mottled sculpins appear to choose to breed with a male after a brief sampling period. Females may base their choice of a preferred mate on an evaluation of as few as two males. Although preference for males of certain qualities is sufficient to account for polygyny in this species, it provides little insight as to the reason for the relatively limited choices that females appear to make. This situation is further surprising because the increase in reproductive success associated with locating ever-larger males appears to be linear (at least over the range of sizes we have sampled). Thus, simple evaluation of the consequences of females preferences among males of varying quality is insufficient to account for the degree of polygyny observed in these populations. However, *when* a female breeds with a male is as important as the size of the male with whom she breeds. In particular, hatching success is extraordinarily low for solitary egg masses and egg masses that are the last to be deposited with a male. Thus, the selective advantages of searching for an ever-larger male are compromised by the costs of being the last or the only female to spawn with a male.

Whether a female was the last to breed with a male is primarily determined by the number of females that have spawned and the number that remain to spawn. It is only slightly influenced by the number of females with which a male had spawned. A simple tactic that would reduce the likelihood that a female would be last to spawn with a male is early spawning. Spawning in this species is highly synchronous, and the distribution of spawnings is skewed to the right, suggesting that the majority of females are spawning as early as possible.

Synchronous spawning, while reducing the likelihood of being last, allows males to exert preferences among females. Because spawning is synchronous among females, males were frequently confronted with choices among two or more gravid females. Males courted larger females in preference to small ones. Thus male choice patterns compromised the breeding tactics of females in a way that is advantageous to large females and disadvantageous to small females. As a consequence, any tendency for larger females to spawn first will be accentuated by male preferences.

The breeding biology of this species thus represents an interaction between the behavior of a female that would increase the hatching success of her eggs and the activities of the male that would tend to increase the number of eggs he fertilizes.

That both variation in male quality and the timing of reproduction influence the reproductive success of a female sculpin is of general importance to theories dealing with the evolution of social systems and the role that sexual selection has played in that process. Our studies of mottled sculpins suggest that female choice should be viewed as a sampling problem. If that is done, then it becomes clear that a female must locate mates and/or breeding sites that would maximize her fitness and avoid situations that would reduce her reproductive success relative to other females (Orians, 1969; Wittenburger, 1976). In particular she should sample as many males or sites as possible without compromising those gains by losses that would be associated with the added search time required for such determinations. It is therefore not surprising that the most exhaustive comparisons among males or sites are those made by females of highly mobile species (e.g., bee eaters, Cronin and Sherman, 1976; bats, Bradbury, 1977) and species in which available mates are restricted to a small area (e.g., lek species—grouse: Robel, 1966; pinnipeds: LeBoeuf, 1974). Finally, we suggest that evaluation of temporal and spatial distribution of available breeding sites and potential mates as well as the variability of the quality of those sites and mates may provide a general framework for the interpretation of the evolution of polygamy, the degree of polygamy, and the diverse relationships between degree of polygamy and female reproductive success (e.g., Holm, 1973; Verner, 1964; Downhower and Armitage, 1971).

REFERENCES

Armitage, K. B., and J. F. Downhower. 1974. Demography of yellow-bellied marmot populations. *Ecol.* 55:1233–1245.

Bailey, J. E. 1952. Life history and ecology of the sculpin *Cottus bairdi punctulatus* in southwest Montana. *Copeia* (4):243–255.

Bradbury, J. W. 1977. Lek mating behavior in the hammerheaded bat. *Z. Tierpsychol.* 45:225–255.

Brown, L. 1978. Polygamy, female choice, and the mottled sculpin, *Cottus bairdi*. Ph.D. thesis, The Ohio State University.

Carey, M., and V. Nolan, Jr. 1975. Polygyny in indigo buntings: a hypothesis tested. *Science* 190:1296–1297.

Clark, F. N. 1925. The life history of *Leuresthes tenuis,* an atherine fish with tide controlled spawning habits. *Fish. Bull.* Calif. Div. Fish and Game, no. 10, 22p.

Cronin, E. W., and P. W. Sherman. 1976. A resource based mating system: the orange-rumped honeyguide. *Living Bird* 1976:5–32.

Cushing, D. H. 1974. The possible density-dependence of larval mortality and adult mortality in fishes. In J. H. S. Blaxter, ed., *The Early Life History of Fishes.* Springer Verlag, New York.

Dawkins, R. and Carlisle, T. R. 1976. Parental investment, mate desertion and a fallacy. *Nature* 262:131–132.

Downhower, J. F. 1976. Darwin's finches and the evolution of sexual dimorphism in body size. *Nature* 263:558–563.

———, and K. B. Armitage. 1971. The yellow-bellied marmot and the evolution of polygamy. *Amer. Natur.* 105:355–370.

———, and L. Brown. 1977. A sampling technique for benthic fish populations. *Copeia* 1977:403–405.

———. 1979a. Seasonal changes in the social organization of a population of mottled sculpins, *Cottus bairdi. Anim. Behav.* In Press.

———. 1979b. Mate preferences of female mottled sculpins, *Cottus bairdi. Nature* In Review.

Downhower, J. F., and R. J. Yost. 1977. The significance of male parental care in the mottled sculpin, *Cottus bairdi. Amer. Zool.* 17(4):936 (Abstract).

Emlen, S. T. 1977. "Double clutching" and its possible significance in the bullfrog. *Copeia* 1977:749–751.

———, and N. J. Demong. 1975. Adaptive significance of synchronized breeding in a colonial bird: a new hypothesis. *Science* 188:1029–1031.

———, and L. W. Oring. 1977. Ecology, sexual selection, and the evolution of mating systems. *Science* 197:215–223.

Hann, H. W. 1927. The history of the germ cells of *Cottus bairdi* Girard. *J. Morph. Physiol.* 43:427–497.

Hollander, M., and D. A. Wolfe. 1973. *Nonparametric Statistical Methods.* John Wiley and Sons, New York.

Holm, C. H. 1973. Breeding sex ratios, territoriality, and reproductive success in the red-winged blackbird (*Agelaius phoeniceus*). *Ecology* 54:356–365.

Jones, R., and W. B. Hall. 1974. Some observations on the population dynamics of the larval stage in the common gadoids. In J. H. S. Blaxter, ed. *The Early Life History of Fishes.* Springer Verlag, New York.

Lasker, R. 1975. Field criteria for survival of anchovy larvae: The relationship between inshore chlorophyll maximum layers and successful first feeding. *Fishery Bull.* 73(3):453–462.

LeBoeuf, B. J. 1974. Male–male competition and reproductive success in elephant seals. *Amer. Zool.* 14:163–176.

Lowe-McConnell, R. H. 1975. *Fish Communities in Tropical Freshwaters.* Longman, New York.

Ludwig, G. M., and E. L. Lange. 1975. The relationship of length, age, and age-length interaction to the fecundity of the northern mottled sculpin, *Cottus b. bairdi. Trans. Amer. Fish. Soc.* 104(1):64–67.

———, and C. R. Norden. 1969. Age, growth, and reproduction of the northern mottled sculpin (*Cottus bairdi bairdi*) in Mt. Vernon Creek, Wisconsin. *Milwaukee Pub. Mus.,* Occ. Pap. No. 2:1–67.

May, R. C. 1974. Larval mortality in marine fishes and the critical period concept. In J. H. S. Blaxter, ed. *The Early Life History of Fishes.* Springer Verlag, New York.

Mitchell, R. 1975. The evolution of oviposition tactics in the bean weevil, *Callosobruchus maculatus* (F.). *Ecology* 56:696–702.

Morris, D. 1955. The reproductive behavior of the river bullhead (*Cottus gobio*) with special reference to the fanning activity. *Behaviour* 7(1):1–32.

Orians, G. H. 1969. On the evolution of mating systems in birds and mammals. *Amer. Natur.* 103:589–603.

Patten, B. G. 1971. Spawning and fecundity of seven species of Northwestern American *Cottus. Amer. Mdl. Natur.* 85(2):493–506.

Pleszczynska, W. K. 1978. Microgeographic prediction of polygyny in the lark bunting. *Science* 201:935–937.

Rohwer, S. 1978. Parent cannibalism of offspring and egg raiding as a courtship strategy. *Am. Natur.* 112:429–440.

Robel, R. J. 1966. Booming territory size and mating success of the greater prairie chicken (*Tympanuchus cupido pinnatus*). *Anim. Behav.* 14:328–331.

Savage, T. 1963. Reproductive behavior in the mottled sculpin, *Cottus bairdi* Girard. *Copeia* 1963:317–325.

Simon, J. R., and R. C. Brown. 1943. Observations on the spawning of the sculpin, *Cottus semiscaber. Copeia* 1943:41–42.

Smith, B. G. 1922. Notes on the nesting habits of *Cottus. Pap. Mich. Acad. Sci., Arts,* Lett. 2:222–224.

Trivers, R. L. 1972. Parental investment and sexual selection. In B. Campbell, ed. *Sexual Selection and the Descent of Man, 1871—1971.* Aldine, Chicago.

Verner, J. 1964. Evolution of polygamy in the long-billed marsh wren. *Evolution* 18:252–261.

Wiley, R. H. 1974. Evolution of social organization and life-history patterns among grouse. *Quart. Rev. Biol.* 49:201–227.

Williams, G. C. 1975. *Sex and Evolution.* Princeton Univ. Press, Princeton.

Wittenberger, J. F. 1976. The ecological factors selecting for polygyny in altricial birds. *Amer. Natur.* 110:779–799.

Wootten, R. J. 1976. *The Biology of Sticklebacks.* Academic Press, New York.

6.

Phenotypic Correlates of Male Reproductive Success in the Lizard, *Sceloporus jarrovi*

Douglas E. Ruby

Differential reproductive success (*RS*) among organisms is the driving force in evolution. The means by which an organism obtains its mates and invests in its offspring have evolved to maximize the parent's genetic contribution to future generations. Consequently, attributes or behaviors that enhance mating success are subject to strong positive selection.

In his theory of sexual selection, Darwin (1871) considered how each sex could optimize its success. He observed that males attempted to court any female while females generally resisted males' efforts. These sexual differences in courtship behavior may best be interpreted as the result of selection upon members of each sex to maximize individual *RS* (Orians, 1969). In most species, the females invest more energy in gametes and have greater confidence in their genetic relationship to the zygote than males. Consequently, females are more careful in their choice of mates and are more likely to invest in their offspring after mating (Trivers, 1972). Because paternity may be uncertain, males frequently gain by mating promiscuously and investing less in each offspring. Females should mate promiscuously only if maximal genetic diversity within clutches was advantageous (Williams, 1975) or several matings were necessary to fertilize all eggs. Because of these differences in investment and certainty of parentage, males should vary more in their *RS* than females. This has been demonstrated or implied in a variety of organisms (Trivers, 1972).

Patterns of parental investment can be modified by ecological factors (Orians, 1969). If both parents can raise more offspring than a single parent, monogamous breeding is predicted. Otherwise, polygyny is favored for reasons given above. Also, variance in the quality of territories, from which necessary resources to raise offspring are obtained, can influence females to select areas rather than to select males. In this case, some territories may be so superior or desirable that the female can gain by sharing the resources of a good territory rather than monopolizing the resources of a poor territory. A male strategy where females select territories for their resources must therefore involve controlling the resources important to females.

In order to understand how behavior or other male attributes contribute to male fitness, it is necessary to quantify male *RS* while measuring simultaneously the desired phenotypic or behavioral patterns. However, determination of *RS* in the field can be difficult and time-consuming. Detailed information about the breeding structure is required, including the copulation frequency of individual males, the probability of females mating more than once, the relationship between copulation and insemination, and the probability of offspring survival as a function of paternal degree of polygyny. Partly because of the detailed information needed, only a few studies have quantitatively tested widely accepted (but untested) hypotheses on the significance of specific phenotypic characters toward achieving male *RS*. Trivers (1972) reviewed a number of characters, including body size (Parker,

1970; Constantz, 1975; Trivers, 1976), age (LeBoeuf, 1972), dominance position in a hierarchy (Hausfater, 1975), territory size (Rand, 1967; Tinkle, 1969) and location within the distribution of competing males (Campanella and Wolf, 1974; Wiley, 1973; Ballard and Robel, 1974). Presumably, each factor enhances either success in the male–male competition for mates and/or provides a cue for female choice of fit males. The few existing studies do not permit generalizations about the nature of the relationship between any attribute and male RS. However, the greater values of a particular trait generally lead to greater male RS.

Male RS has been measured as the number of copulations (Robel, 1966; Ballard and Robel, 1974; LeBoeuf, 1974; Trivers, 1976) or the number of fledglings (Lack, 1954, 1968, and others). In this study I used size-specific fecundity estimates of females mating with particular males to make estimates of potential offspring fathered by specific males. Such estimates incorporate biologically useful information into the measurement of male RS. Males who mate with larger females with potentially larger clutches or litters actually have greater RS than males mating with a smaller female. This difference in male RS is not measured by estimates of harem size or number of copulations. However, both types of mating information are valuable. Some males may obtain the same number of offspring through different numbers of females. For example, one male may mate with a large female bearing ten young, and another may mate with two females each bearing five young. In situations where survivorship is not high between copulation and birth, the second male with two mates may have more surviving offspring because the only mate of the first male may not survive.

Reptiles display a wide range of social patterns (Stamps, 1977) that are generally unappreciated by behaviorists (Wilson, 1975). Varying degrees of territoriality have been described as well as maternal nest guarding, site-specific defense, hierarchical social structures in dense populations, and dispersed spacing in the apparent absence of territoriality. Because breeding structures are very poorly known, the underlying ecological causes and adaptive values of particular social systems cannot be determined at present. Because lizards are particularly suitable for field study and manipulation (Tinkle, 1967), the investigation of behavior in this group of reptiles could be profitable in elucidating the general factors determining social behavior of animals. The present study sought to identify correlates of male reproductive success in the lizard, *Sceloporus jarrovi*. Some direction for future investigations on reptilian social behavior is suggested.

METHODS

The study species, *Sceloporus jarrovi*, is a montane viviparous lizard found in southwestern New Mexico, southeastern Arizona, and Mexico above 1460 m altitude (Stebbins, 1966). Relevant aspects of its annual cycle are shown in Figure 6–1. The species is active year round. From May through October, both sexes are territorial (Simon, 1975; Ruby, 1978) but they aggregate strongly during the rest of the year. Males are more aggressive in territorial defense than females. Male defense is strongest in the fall breeding season (Ruby, 1978). The species mates in September and October, females ovulate in November or December and the young are born in late May or June (Goldberg, 1971; Ruby, 1977). Animals may reach maturity within six months after birth (Ballinger, 1973) but the actual percentage doing so varies yearly (Ruby, 1977).

The study area (0.75 ha) was a small canyon with an oak-juniper association at 1825 m elevation in the Pinaleno Mountains near Safford, Arizona (Graham Co.). Prior to the onset of the breeding season, all individuals were captured, toe-clipped, painted for visual identification, and released. During the 1972–74 seasons, I censused the study area at least once each day, observed and recorded interactions between animals, and followed specific individuals (usually males) for periods of several hours. Probable mating pairs and frequency of

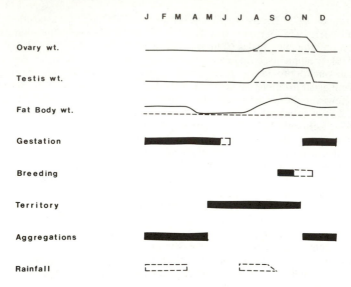

Figure 6–1.   Summary of annual cycle of *Sceloporus jarrovi*. Data taken from Goldberg, 1971; Ballinger, 1973; and Ruby, 1976. Rainfall pattern is schematic for southeastern Arizona. Letters at top represent months, January through December.

courtship between pairs of animals were determined for 55 males, from over 500 manhours of observations during September and October 1972–74.

The breeding season was standardized to an 18-day period that encompassed all adult matings plus 3–5 days preceding the first mating and 1–3 days following the last to permit comparisons between years. This standardization eliminated between-year differences in territory size and activity caused by varying time lengths of courting behavior.

Based on observations of courtships and matings and on the conclusion that females mate only once (Ruby, 1976), I made two estimates of the *RS* of 55 males. The first method (Estimate 1) assigned only those females to a particular male when (1) mating of the pair was observed or (2) the female's territory was exclusively overlapped by that male's territory during the breeding season as defined above. The second method (Estimate 2) attempted to assign all mature (over 54 mm SVL) females to mature males (over 54 mm SVL). The females not already assigned by Estimate 1 were credited to males in Estimate 2 by the following criteria (in order of importance): (1) More than one male overlapped the female's territory, but only one male was observed courting the female; (2) more than one male courted the female but one courted much more frequently than the others; and (3) yearling females were assigned to yearling males when possible. I justify this preferential assignment of yearlings to each other from observations that (1) yearlings avoid older adults, and (2) yearlings may breed after adults complete their breeding in some years (Ruby, 1976). Such a policy also avoids biasing the data in favor of older males.

Following the male–female assignments, I determined the probable litter size of each female (Ballinger, 1973), rounded to the lower whole number (offspring occur as integrals), and totalled the number of potential offspring for each male. Postbreeding mortality of gravid females or their young was ignored in the calculation. The *RS* estimates were then tested for significant relationships with phenotypic characters of each male. Here I consider (1) body size, SVL, in mm, (2) age in years, (3) activity in days sighted during the breeding season, (4) territory size during the breeding season, (5) the number of courtship observations, and (6) the length of domicile by the male at a particular territory location. Aggression and movement (distance traveled per hour) were also measured and included in the data analysis. However, estimates of these two variables were not complete for all males, hence less will be stated about them.

Because male RS can be divided into two classes, those males with zero RS and those with positive RS, I compared the phenotypic characters of these two groups. Simple correlations between each pair of variables and least square linear regressions of phenotypic characters upon male RS were computed for each group and for all males together. Stepwise multiple regression analysis was performed to determine which variables contribute to predicting male RS. In the regression analysis, I used a log transformation on male RS to reduce heteroscedasticity. Negative log values were avoided by adding one to the RS estimate for each male before transformation. Data from all three years were combined because covariance analysis for traits indicated no significant differences in slope or intercept for any particular trait between years.

Factor analysis with varimax rotation was performed using the five complete variables (excluding courtship). All factors with eigenvalues above 1.0 were retained. Multiple regression analysis using factor 1 and all eight variables was performed.

RESULTS

Male *S. jarrovi* are promiscuous breeders, but females mate only once (Ruby 1976). Males defend large, generally nonoverlapping territories that contain females. Nearly all of the male's time during the breeding season is spent searching for females within the territory or interacting across territorial boundaries with other males. Much search behavior appears necessary because females are much less conspicuous than in previous months (Ruby, 1978). Females show strong site fidelity during the year. Males shift their territories during the year in a way consistent with a hypothesis that they are sensitive to the location of females (Ruby, 1978). Courtship is typical of iguanid lizards (as in Carpenter, 1977) but brief. Lizards mate in the open and predatory risks during the breeding season appear low (unpublished data).

Male RS varied widely by either estimate of male RS. In Estimate 2, the number of females per male ranged from zero to eight ($\bar{x} = 1.24 \pm 1.48$) (Table 6–1). Of the total estimated offspring ($N = 521$), the number assigned to any male ranged from zero to 63 ($\bar{x} = 9.47 \pm 12.30$). The maximal male RS of 63 is over four times the female maximum of 15 offspring (Ballinger 1973). Nearly 77 per cent of the total potential offspring were assigned by criteria of either mating or exclusive territorial overlap between pairs. The two courtship criteria accounted for 17 per cent of the offspring and the remaining 6 per cent were offspring of yearlings.

Male attributes were compared for the two groups: males without success and males with success. Based on either estimate, males that presumably mated were significantly (*t*-test, $p < 0.05$) larger, older, and more active (Table 6–2). Frequency of courtship, territory size, and length of domicile were not significantly different.

Correlations between phenotypic characters and the two RS estimates are shown in Table 6–3. Body size and activity were correlated with male RS in either estimate. Although body size, age, and activity were highly intercorrelated (Table 6–4), age did not correlate with Estimate 1 but did correlate with Estimate 2. Estimate 1 poorly measures the success of yearlings because few yearlings are indicated in that estimate. Inclusion of more yearlings in Estimate 2 may explain the difference between the two correlations. The months of territorial residency is also significant only in one estimate of male RS. The correlation between Estimate 1 and courtship frequency is particularly interesting because this variable was not a criterion of Estimate 1.

Table 6–1.   Patterns of reproductive success in male *Sceloporus jarrovi*.

NUMBER OF FEMALES MATED PER MALE

Number of Females	Number of Males Known estimate	Number of Males Probable estimate
0	29	20
1	13	17
2	8	11
3	3	4
4	1	1
5	0	1
6	1	0
7	0	0
8	0	1
	55	55

NUMBER OF OFFSPRING PER MALE

Number of Offspring	Number of Males Known estimate	Number of Males Probable estimate
0	29	20
1–5	2	7
6–10	5	8
11–15	8	7
16–20	6	5
21–30	4	4
31–40	0	3
>40	1	1
	55	55

Least-squares regression analysis indicated that male RS is linearly related to some phenotypic characters. Body size, age, activity, and courtship frequency were significantly correlated ($p<0.05$) with male RS in both the successful group of 35 males and the entire group of 55 males (Table 6–5). R^2 values are higher for equations using only successful males compared to equations using all 55 males. The phenotypic characters explain more of the variance of a given equation when unsuccessful males are excluded. In both groups, age explains less variance than body size. Since males of the same age may differ in body size, females may favor larger animals without regard to age. An effect of such preference should be most noticeable in second-year males where the size variance is greatest. Comparison of RS by second-year males ($N = 17$) above and below the range midpoint of 80 mm SVL did not support this hypothesis (Mann-Whitney U test, $p >0.1$).

Multiple stepwise regression indicated that activity was the best predictor of RS for all males, explaining 44 per cent of the total variation. Age was the second variable added, explaining an additional 8 per cent of the variance. Movement was third, increasing the R^2 by 15 per cent to a total of 67 per cent. Other variables contributed smaller amounts to the regression. However, when stepwise regression was performed on only the 35 males with positive RS, body size was the best variable, explaining 53 per cent of the total variation. The second variable chosen was movement, explaining an additional 38 per cent of the variance for a total R^2 of 0.91.

Factor analysis was performed to see if the measured variables grouped into a more limited number of factors. Two factors had eigenvalues greater than one. Varimax rotation was performed on these factors. Table 6–6 shows the correlations between the five varia-

Table 6–2.   Phenotypes of males according to two estimates of reproductive success. Sample sizes are given parenthetically.

Attribute	Known Mated Mean ± 1 S.D.		Unknown or Zero RS Mean ± 1 S.D.		t-test	Significance
Known estimate:						
SVL (in mm)	83.73 ± 10.59	(26)	65.38 ± 11.22	(29)	6.216	$p < 0.001$
Age (years)	3.07 ± 1.23	(26)	1.52 ± 0.78	(29)	5.664	$p < 0.001$
Activity (days)	13.23 ± 4.62	(26)	7.55 ± 4.41	(29)	4.658	$p < 0.001$
Territory (m^2)	681.04 ± 577.67	(26)	692.79 ± 522.21	(29)	0.079	$p < 0.5$
Months resident	2.68 ± 1.21	(22)	2.21 ± 1.30	(9)	0.939	$p > 0.25$
Courtship frequency	3.00 ± 4.68	(26)	0.60 ± 0.69	(10)	1.600	$p > 0.1$
Probable estimate:						
SVL (in mm)	78.71 ± 13.47	(35)	65.90 ± 11.89	(20)	3.536	$p < 0.001$
Age (years)	2.68 ± 1.35	(35)	1.50 ± 0.69	(20)	3.666	$p < 0.001$
Activity (days)	12.31 ± 4.89	(35)	6.60 ± 3.94	(20)	−4.462	$p < 0.001$
Territory (m^2)	663.77 ± 556.18	(35)	728.30 ± 533.58	(20)	0.419	$p > 0.5$
Months resident	2.60 ± 1.26	(25)	2.33 ± 1.21	(6)	−0.469	$p > 0.5$
Courtship frequency	2.79 ± 4.48	(29)	0.42 ± 0.53	(7)	−1.380	$p > 0.1$

Table 6–3.   Pearson product-moment correlations between phenotypic attributes and two estimates of male reproductive success.

Character	Known Estimate	Probable Estimate
Body size (SVL)	.3903*	.570**
Age	.056	.470**
Activity	.584**	.630**
Territory size	.326	.190
Courtship frequency	.735**	.780**
Months of residency	.368	.400**

* = $p < 0.05$
** = $p < 0.01$

Table 6–4.   Correlations between body size, age, and activity in male *Sceloporus jarrovi*.

Body size	1.000		
Age	0.793**	1.000	
Activity	0.694**	0.439*	1.000
	Body size	Age	Activity

$N = 55$
* = $p < 0.05$
** = $p < 0.01$

Table 6–5.   Least squares regression analysis of the effect of some male phenotypic characters upon the log of male reproductive success.

Variable	Equation	F-Statistic	Significance	R^2
Using all males ($N = 55$):				
Body size	$Y = 0.060X - 2.90$	36.326	0.000	.4066
Age	$Y = 0.646X + 0.129$	31.572	0.000	.3733
Activity	$Y = 0.170X - 0.157$	42.710	0.000	.4462
Territory size	$Y = 0.001X + 1.545$	0.031	–	.0005
Courtship frequency	$Y = 0.149X + 1.846$	11.591	0.0017	.2542
Months residency	$Y = 0.463X + 0.718$	10.210	0.000	.2130
Using only males with positive reproductive success ($N = 35$):				
Body size	$Y = 0.041X - 0.787$	38.759	0.000	.5401
Age	$Y = 0.317X + 1.641$	14.977	0.005	.3124
Activity	$Y = 0.096X + 1.311$	19.974	0.001	.3770
Territory size	$Y = 0.001X + 2.304$	1.497	–	.0434
Courtship frequency	$Y = 0.093X + 2.464$	24.683	0.000	.4775
Months residency	$Y = 0.351X + 1.740$	20.247	0.000	.3882

Table 6–6.   Correlations between varimax rotated factor matrix and five phenotypic variables.

Variable	Factor 1	Factor 2
Body size	0.9324	0.1518
Age	0.9620	−0.068
Activity	0.5925	0.3466
Territory size	−0.0387	0.4433
Months residency	0.4453	0.7492

Table 6–7.   Degree of sexual dimorphism by age class in *Sceloporus jarrovi*.

Age Class	Males N	Males Mean Size ± S.E.	Females N	Females Mean Size ± S.E.	t-test	Significance level
1	9	55.52 ± 3.37 mm	31	51.08 ± 3.43 mm	5.34	$p < 0.001$
2	19	78.35 ± 3.98	15	70.15 ± 3.79	7.16	$p < 0.001$
3	18	86.87 ± 3.76	33	78.48 ± 3.33	5.51	$p < 0.001$
4+	18	90.90 ± 2.64	23	81.12 ± 1.46	9.37	$p < 0.001$

Table 6–8.   Survivorship and breeding success in second-year males.

	Nonoverlapping Males	Overlapping Males	Test
Survival to fall	7/27 (26%)	12/30 (40%)	x^2 test, > 0.1
Positive RS	4/7 (57%)	7/12 (58%)	Mann-Whitney U test, $p > 0.1$

bles and the two factors. Factor 1 is a "maturation" factor including body size, age, and activity, which are intercorrelated (Table 6–4). Months is weakly related to factor 1—a relationship caused by the shorter residency possible for a yearling male. Factor 2 is a "spatial" measure, consisting largely of months residency but weakly related to territory size (and possibly activity). Factor 1 explains 55 per cent of the variation in male *RS*, and factor 2 explains an additional 23 per cent.

If factor 1 is used in a stepwise regression with the measured variables, activity is selected first for the group of all males and factor 1 is selected second. This indicates that the single variable *activity* predicts more of the variance than the factor that combines body size, age, and activity together. If only the group of 35 successful males is considered for the regression analysis, factor 1 is selected first, followed by movement. These results are similar to the stepwise regression analysis performed with the independent variables without factor combinations.

The strong selection for large body size found in my analysis coincides with sexual dimorphism in body size of breeding individuals (Table 6–7). Males of known age are larger than females of known age for each age class (*t*-test, $p<0.01$). In fact, the magnitude of difference increased with age, from 8 per cent to 11 per cent of the average male size for each age class. Sexual dimorphism also occurs in general coloration and the intensity of the blue coloration on the throat and belly patches (Stebbins, 1966). The color differences are enhanced during the breeding season.

Elsewhere (Ruby, 1978), I presented data indicating the greater frequency of male territorial overlap during the spring and summer than during the breeding season when male territorial defense is highly effective. During the three breeding seasons observed, ten second-year males had wide overlap with the territory of a large male, which the smaller males avoided. Overlap also occurs between yearlings and adults, but the animals have some temporal separation of breeding (Ruby, 1976). Submissive behavior by second-year males may be successful if males could mate with females in the dominant's territory while the dominant was temporarily absent, or if survivorship was increased, or if they could take over the dominant's territory when the dominant disappeared. Table 6–8 summarizes survivorship and breeding success of second-year males by degree of territorial overlap, in an effort to measure the relative success of alternate strategies. Overlapping males had 45 per cent or more overlap with another male during one month of the year, but non-overlapping males never exceeded 44 per cent overlap. Survivorship or probability of breeding was not significantly different between the two groups. The groups did not differ in their average number of offspring either, as a result of high success in the non-overlapping group by two males during 1972, when all mature males mated because of highly skewed sex ratios (Ruby, 1976). However, the overlapping males all achieved their *RS* by replacing a missing dominant. Many opportunities for territory takeover occur because of the unpredictable mortality. I never saw a female mate with a subordinate male, and the females appeared to reject such males strongly during courtship activities. Dominant males usually interrupted courtships of subordinates, but the reverse also occurred.

DISCUSSION

Male *RS* varied more in male *S. jarrovi* lizards than in females as predicted for a species lacking paternal investment after copulation. Since males cannot invest further in their offspring, the optimal breeding strategy for males is maximizing the number of copulations. Females are then a scarce resource for males for a few males could monopolize all of the females. Intrasexual competition for mates among males is intense, but the intensity is not quickly perceived by the observer because the competition extends over the four-month period before the breeding season as well as during the breeding season.

Reproductive success in male *S. jarrovi* lizards is related to those phenotypic and behavioral characteristics necessary to obtain and defend a territory. Body size was important in winning encounters (Ruby, 1978), hence its prime importance in determining *RS*. Age and activity were correlated with body size and relate to *RS* in the same way. The varying levels of activity are the result of the ability to defend a territory and not a cause of the success of such defense. My measure of activity quantifies the conspicuousness of the animal to both the observer and to other lizards. Highly conspicuous males must be well-equipped (large, aggressive, alert) to defend their territories, and those less able to defend, such as yearlings and subordinates, will be less noticeable. Similarly, the number of observed courtships will also indicate the conspicuousness of the animal. Subordinates and neighboring males may interrupt the courtship as was observed several times.

Several strategies may be used to obtain the territory necessary for breeding success. The strategy used by a particular animal is determined by considerations of body size and the site chosen. Larger, older animals generally return to a previously used area. Familiarity with an area is apparently important and gives priority of ownership. However, animals picking their territory in May for the first time frequently do not utilize previously used locations but seek new territories. Many of these animals occupy an area that overlaps that of another individual. Aggression levels are not high enough during the summer to prevent such overlap from persisting. Also, mortality during the summer is sufficiently high (about 50 per cent) that mere survival may enable an animal to take over an area. However, the lack of courtship success by subordinates during the breeding season indicates that animals that are not dominant do not breed. Thus, subordinance may be a strategy suitable for obtaining a territory but not for obtaining females if males are without a territory. The extent of the subordinance strategy will depend upon the number of vacant spaces available in the spring and the willingness of males to migrate to new locations.

Interestingly, despite the apparent requirement of a territory for breeding success, territory size did not correlate with male *RS*. The lack of correlation occurs in part because yearlings, which have only poor success compared to adults, have large territories. Removal of yearling data from the analysis did not make the correlation significant. A correlation between territory size and male *RS* may require some regular or even distribution of females. If the relationship between territorial expansion and the number of females within that acquired area is weak, we should not expect strong correlations between territory size and male *RS*. In my observations, several highly successful males had small territories containing several females completely sharing an area. Territory size was also not correlated with body size. Since body size, territory size, and male *RS* are usually related (Trivers, 1972, 1976), it is possible that significant correlations between territory size and *RS*, as found in other species, may be secondary effects of a relationship between body size and territory size.

Male *S. jarrovi* lizards do appear sensitive to the size of their territory. Mean territory size increased during each year (Ruby, 1978), four cases of courtship interference were observed, and nearly 25 per cent of the females were courted by more than one male. Since one function of the territory appears to be restricting access to females, males should attempt to overlap the available females and exclude other males. They are apparently not completely successful in their efforts.

Because males are aggressive toward each other, it is commonly assumed that aggression is related to *RS*. Aggression, as measured by display behavior, was quantified during this study but did not significantly correlate with male *RS* (Ruby, 1976). Fall interactions between males were uniformly high in intensity, and spring interactions were too variable. Many large males appeared to use advantages of large size rather than intense display to discourage intruding males in the spring and summer. Conspicuous display might attract visually hunting predators such as hawks, which would reduce the ultimate success of a highly aggressive strategy. Mortality in the fall, when much display does occur, is very low (unpublished data) as a result of the lower numbers of predators at that time.

The pattern of territorial establishment is different between the sexes (Ruby, 1978) and strongly influences the breeding strategies. Females are relatively sedentary and occupy the same area each year after an initial shift from yearling to adult locations. In contrast, males shift their territories during the year in a way consistent with a hypothesis that they are responsive to female distributions (Ruby, 1978). Because mortality of either sex is high, establishment of permanent territorial boundaries prior to the breeding season may leave a male without females in his territory. Consequently, males before the breeding season attempt to defend areas that are too large for their defense to exclude other males. Several males may persist in an area if they maintain some distance between themselves. A male could then claim an area if other overlapping males disappeared. In the breeding season, the reproductive gain from mating dictates exclusive or restricted access to females, so males tolerate little or no overlap. Defense efforts of males are intensified to achieve the reduced overlap.

The direct appraisal by males of female distributions is possible because males delay territorial establishment. Breeding also occurs after most food-gathering activity is completed for the year (Simon, 1975; Ruby, 1976), so the hoarding of resources important to females may be difficult or impossible for males. Because females choose locations in May, they are apparently more influenced by site qualities than by the male(s) available in the spring (who may not be present in the fall). The temporal separation of food acquisition and breeding behavior is an important influence upon the type of reproductive strategy observed in male *S. jarrovi*. Male control of access to females (Emlen and Oring, 1977) seems more important in determining reproductive success than male control of resources important to females (Orians, 1969) because of the temporal separation of food-gathering and breeding and because of the substantial overlap between males during the food-gathering period.

I did not observe female choice of mates. Females have low levels of activity and visibility during the breeding season (Ruby, 1978). Opportunities for comparing neighboring males occur but were not observed. Only one female ($N = 68$) shifted her territory significantly during the three breeding seasons. Because females are less visible, males must spend much time searching for females. Consequently, measures of activity or movement correlate with male RS. The introduction of movement into the multiple regression, particularly among the successful male group, indicates the physical effort by the male in searching for females does correlate with the reproductive gain.

Since breeding behavior of other lizards is poorly known, precise comparisons with this study cannot be made. Present knowledge indicates that most lizards are polygynous although the degree to which they are is not accurately known. I would suggest three factors that may modify breeding patterns in lizards: predictability of female receptivity, the distribution of females and the resources important to them, and the demographic characteristics of the population. The present study was facilitated by the short breeding period of about two to three weeks. Much of the breeding strategy involved jockeying for position prior to the actual mating period. A prolonged breeding season increases the unpredictability of the time(s) at which females are receptive. Other behavioral strategies may result in greater RS. One change may be in aggression levels. Intraspecific variation in aggression (Vinegar, 1975; Stamps, 1977; Ruby, 1978) suggests that seasonal changes in aggression relate to changes in reproductive gain. If this relationship applies to interspecific comparisons, changes in aggression should occur with increased unpredictability in female receptivity. Changes in aggression may also produce altered patterns of area defense or extent of overlap between territories. Lower aggression should correlate with reduced predictability of female receptivity, because the reproductive gain from high aggression would not be as certainly rewarded while costs from aggressive behavior would increase during a prolonged period. The frequency of subordinance and other alternate strategies should also increase as aggression levels decline.

The effect of female distributions upon male RS needs further clarification. Demonstrations that males alter their positions relative to females (Ruby, 1978) are important in demonstrating the role of territoriality in breeding success. Although male lizards tend to occupy larger territories than females (Turner et al., 1969), such evidence is only circumstantial support for the hypothesis that mates are the limiting resource for males. An alternate explanation for the greater territory size of males may be differential utilization of space or the food resources in the space. Detailed information about animal locations plus carefully planned manipulations of populations in the field would prove helpful in identifying those factors controlling territory size and position.

Lastly, the degree of behavioral flexibility is unknown. We should find great flexibility in the behavioral responses of lizards if demographic characteristics alter the feasibility of alternate strategies. Demographic characters of lizards are known to vary geographically (Pianka, 1970; Tinkle and Ballinger, 1972; Parker and Pianka, 1976) and microgeographically (Ballinger, 1973). The ease with which many different lizard species form hierarchical social systems in the laboratory is well known (Brattstrom, 1974) and an impediment to laboratory study of ''natural'' behavior of lizards. However, the adaptive value of this flexibility has not been interpreted as a useful strategy of individual lizards but as a response to variations in density. Density is a result of other ecological and behavioral factors including, but not limited to, food levels, number of predators, and behavioral tolerance among individuals. We should find behavioral strategies varying from locale to locale, from good habitat to poor habitat (personal observations) and from one region to another. Defining the limitations on the flexibility of behavioral responses and correlating particular suites of behaviors with specific ecological conditions remains an enormous challenge to the field biologist.

ACKNOWLEDGEMENTS

The support of my doctoral chairman, D. W. Tinkle, and my doctoral committee is gratefully acknowledged. This report grew from the simple question posed by Dr. Tinkle— why measure territories? Larry Foote, Laurie Bingham, and Ruth Ann Powell assisted in the field. The support of Mr. Cecil Sims and the U. S. Forest Service was vital to my success. Dr. Gary Fowler (Michigan) and Stephen Welsh and Scott Ray (Xavier) performed essential services in the data analysis. An enormous debt goes to my wife Sally who participated in all aspects of the study. Partial support for this project came from NSF grant GB-39715 to D. W. Tinkle. I dedicate this paper to Helen Early Ruby.

REFERENCES

Ballard, W. B., and R. J. Robel. 1974. Reproductive importance of dominant male Greater Prairie Chickens. *Auk* 91:75–85.
Ballinger, R. E. 1973. Comparative demography of two ovoviviparous iguanid lizards (*Sceloporus jarrovi* and *Sceloporus poinsetti*). *Ecology* 55:269–283.
Brattstrom, B. H. 1974. The evolution of reptilian social behavior. *Amer. Zool.* 14:35–49.
Campanella, P. J., and L. Wolf. 1974. Temporal leks as a mating system in a temperate zone dragonfly (Odonata: Anisoptera) I: *Plathemis lydia*. *Behaviour* 51:49–87.
Carpenter, C. C. 1977. Survey of stereotyped reptilian behavioral patterns. In C. Gans and D. Tinkle (eds.) *Biology of the Reptilia* 7. p. 335–404.
Constantz, G. D. 1975. Behavioral ecology of mating in the Gila topminnow, *Poeciliopsis occidentalis* (Cyprinodontiformes: Poeciliidae). *Ecology* 56:966–973.
Darwin, C. 1871. *The Descent of Man and Selection in Relation to Sex*. Murray, London.
Emlen, S. T. and L. W. Oring. 1977. Ecology, sexual selection and the evolution of mating systems. *Science* 197:215–223.

Goldberg, S. R. 1971. Reproductive cycle of the ovoviviparous iguanid lizard *Sceloporus jarrovi* Cope. *Herpetologica* 27:123–131.

Hausfater, G. 1975. Dominance and reproduction in baboons: a quantitative analysis. *Contrib. Primat.* Vol. 7. S. Karger, Basel. 150 p.

Lack, D. 1954. *The Natural Regulation of Animal Numbers.* Oxford Univ. Press, Oxford. 343 p.

———. 1968. *Ecological Adaptations for Breeding in Birds.* Methuen, London. 409 p.

LeBoeuf, B. J. 1972. Sexual behavior in the northern elephant seal *Mirounga angustirostris. Behaviour* 41:1–26.

Orians, G. H. 1969. On the evolution of mating systems in birds and mammals. *Am. Nat.* 103:589–603.

Parker, G. A. 1970. The reproductive behavior and the nature of sexual selection in *Scatophaga stercoraria* L. (Diptera: Scatophagidae). IV. Epigamic recognition and competition between males for the possession of females. *Behaviour* 37:113–139.

Parker, W. S. and E. R. Pianka. 1976. Ecological observations on the leopard lizard (*Crotaphytus wislizeni*) in different parts of its range. *Herpetologica* 32:95–114.

Pianka, E. R. 1970. Comparative autecology of the lizard *Cnemidophorus tigris* in different parts of its geographic range. *Ecology* 51:703–720.

Rand, A. S. 1967. Ecology and social organization in the iguanid lizard *Anolis lineotopus. Proc. U. S. Mus.* 122:1–79.

Ruby, D. E. 1976. The behavioral ecology of the viviparous lizard, *Sceloporus jarrovi.* Unpublished Ph.D. thesis, University of Michigan, Ann Arbor. 214 p.

———. 1977. Winter activity in Yarrow's spiny lizard, *Sceloporus jarrovi. Herpetologica* 33:322–333.

———. 1978. Seasonal changes in the territorial behavior of the iguanid lizard *Sceloporus jarrovi. Copeia* 1978:430–438.

Simon, C. A. 1975. The influence of food abundance on territory size in the iguanid lizard *Sceloporus jarrovi. Ecology* 56:993–98.

Stamps, J. A. 1977. Social behavior and spacing patterns in lizards. In C. Gans and D. Tinkle (eds.) *Biology of the Reptilia* 7. p. 265–334.

Stebbins, R. C. 1966. *Field Guide to Western Reptiles and Amphibians.* Houghton Mifflin, Boston. 279 p.

Tinkle, D. W. 1967. The life and demography of the side-blotched lizard, *Uta stansburiana. Misc. Publ. Mus. Zool. Univ. Mich.* No. 132. 182 p.

———. 1969. Evolutionary implications of comparative population studies in the lizard, *Uta stansburiana.* In *Systematic Biology.* National Academy of Sciences, Washington, D.C. p. 133–153.

——— and R. E. Ballinger. 1972. *Sceloporus undulatus:* a study of the intraspecific comparative demography of a lizard. *Ecology* 53:570–84.

Trivers, R. 1972. Parental investment and sexual selection. In B. Campbell (ed.), *Sexual Selection and the Descent of Man.* Aldine, Chicago. p. 136–179.

———. 1976. Sexual selection and resource-accruing abilities in *Anolis garmani. Evolution* 30:253–269.

Turner, F. B., R. I. Jennrich, and J. D. Weintraub. 1969. Home ranges and body sizes of lizards. *Ecology* 50:1076–1080.

Vinegar, M. B. 1975. Comparative aggression in *Sceloporus virgatus, S. undulatus consobrinus* and *S.u. tristichus* (Sauria: Iguanidae). *Anim. Behav.* 23:279–286.

Wiley, R. H. 1973. Territoriality and nonrandom mating in sage grouse *Centrocercus urophasianus. Anim. Behav. Monog.* 6:85–169.

Williams, G. C. 1975. *Sex and Evolution.* Princeton Univ. Press, Princeton, N.J. 193 p.

Wilson, E. O. 1975. *Sociobiology: the New Synthesis.* Harvard Univ. Press, Cambridge.

7.

Population Structure and Social Behavior: Models for Testing the Ecological Significance of Song Dialects in Birds

Robert B. Payne

Locally distinct versions of song or song "dialects" have been described for several species of birds. Neighboring birds may have songs similar to or identical to each other, whereas a few km distant the songs may be distinctively different (Thielcke, 1969). Young songbirds of many species learn their species' songs from older birds, and, in several dialectal species, the young acquire their local songs by learning and copying the songs of local adults (Marler and Tamura, 1964; Marler, 1975; Lemon, 1975).

Although the behavioral mechanisms involved in the development of local traditions have been explored, the ecological significance of the behavior differences among local populations is not well understood. A systematic approach may be useful in testing whether there is any explanation that will apply in general or whether different explanations apply to different species. Here I develop alternative models based on the concept of natural selection and on the random history of local events. Each model leads to certain predictions about the population structure and social behavior of the birds. We can then compare the observed population structure and social behavior of dialectal bird species with these predictions. Developing logical models with alternative properties, subsequently observing behavior in natural populations, and comparing the observed behavior with that predicted from the models is perhaps our most respectable use of the concept of natural selection in explaining social behavior (Platt, 1964). Without direct observations on changing gene frequencies in natural populations and on verified results of the nonrandom mechanics of microevolutionary change, we cannot directly observe the process of natural selection. However, we can develop alternative explanations, each consistent with the concept of natural selection, and then see whether field observations or experiments lead us to reject some explanations as unlikely. The models developed here are compared with field observations in a single species studied intensively and in other species for which some relevant field data are available.

MODELS TO EXPLAIN THE ORIGIN AND MAINTENANCE OF SONG DIALECTS

1. Historical model. Local differences in the songs of birds may be caused by unique historical events. As birds disperse, invade, and colonize new areas, the original founders may have a song variation that is unlike that at the earlier site. Differences in the songs of local populations may then be caused by unrelated, independent founding events. In addition, song copying of young birds may be imperfect, and copy errors may accumulate over generations within a local population. Changes in local song traditions may occur mainly in isolated populations. As a local population expands, opportunities arise for local spread of the song pattern by peripheral dispersal, and a local dialect may occupy an area much more extensive than that of the founding population. This historical model is biologically realistic in its recognition of the importance of dispersal, colonization, and geographic isolation as ecological determinants of local differentiation of populations. The historical explanation has been applied to various bird dialectal populations (Thielcke, 1969, 1973; King, 1972; Baker, 1975; Baptista, 1975, 1977). Versions of the historical model also have traditionally been used in describing the origin and spread of human speech dialects, particularly by dialectologists in the humanities and traditional social sciences (academic departments of linguistics, anthropology, and English). The model has been used in mapping the local distributions of word use in areas of older and more recent settlement to establish routes of migration of people from older centers of language differentiation (e.g., Kurath, 1939; McDavid and McDavid, 1956; Reed, 1967). In some instances a local change in behavior may mark a genetic unit (Burton and Bick, 1972). A local behavior need not imply a genetically distinct population, however, because individuals may change their behavior and social class when they move between local populations (Spielman, et al. 1974; Birdsell, 1973).

2. Racial specialization model. Behavior differences among populations may be related to genetic specialization of the local populations. The song differences themselves may be caused by local traditions of learning, but the populations are specialized for particular habitats, and genetic differences among local populations are assumed to be the result of past natural selection. Choice of a mate by the female may be based on the song of the male, with the resident female choosing a male with a song resembling the song type of her father. In this way the female might assure that she would mate with a local male.

The model includes the following features: (a) Local populations are genetically distinct; (b) genetic differences are nonrandom and are the result of natural selection, with individuals that are genetically specialized in some way having greater survival and reproductive success than others in the local habitat, and these others being eliminated in time; (c) dispersal between dialect areas is ineffective or absent; (d) young birds learn the songs of their home population at an early age; (e) birds remain on their home area by attraction to local songs; (f) females mate selectively with males that sing as do the birds they heard as young females at their birthplace; (g) the preferential response of females to local songs is adaptive because it ensures that her own offspring will be genetically specialized in the same way for the same local environment.

This model is based on reasoning from natural selection theory and therefore attracts the attention of ecologists and evolutionary biologists. Moreover, the model is logical; it allows empirical tests of its validity at several points, and it also leads to corollary hypotheses about the nature of genetic differentiation, habitat specialization, and the importance of local differentiation in speciation (Miller, 1956; Thielcke, 1970; Nottebohm, 1972). Although local behavioral differentiation may be involved in speciation, the process of speciation provides no adaptive explanation for the local differences in terms of natural selection. Ideas useful in developing the model have been discussed by many biologists (Marler and Tamura, 1962; Nottebohm, 1969; Thielcke, 1970; King, 1972; Baker, 1974, 1975), and the reasoning has been developed particularly by Nottebohm (1972).

3. Social adaptation model. Local differences in song behavior may result from social adaptation. Song is a social signal and may be examined in the context of social behavior. Song copying may be explained as intraspecific behavior mimicry, with the song mimic gaining an advantage over non-mimics in his ability to gain and hold a territory and to attract a mate. Birds that copy the song of an established male may have an advantage over other birds, and local song sharing or dialectal populations may result.

The social adaptation model would be an appropriate explanation of song dialects if the following were observed: (a) dialect areas correspond to social units, with song sharers interacting with each other; (b) population differences in song behavior result from individual behavior modification in response to social interaction; (c) differences between populations result from the lack of social interactions between them; (d) birds disperse between dialect areas; (e) songs may be learned well into juvenile or adult life. The social adaptation model implies that males can adjust their song behavior to that of their neighbors, and that this ability to modify behavior may be a result of natural selection though it may be unfeasible to demonstrate a differential success of genotypes related to any individual differences in this behavioral plasticity.

The explanation of song sharing as a social behavior rather than a result of genetic determinism or environmental determinism outside the social context reflects not only a growing interest in the function and developmental flexibility of bird song (e.g., Smith, 1977; Marler, 1975) but also an interest in the social use of human language. It seems reasonable to consider local variations in language in terms of their social use and social consequences and a growing body of observations supports this view (Weinrich, Labov, and Herzog, 1967). Local patterns of language are used and persist in distinct social groups within a single city (Gumperz, 1962; Labov, 1972a). People may switch their speech pattern according to the social context, sometimes shifting towards the speech pattern of the person in a more powerful social position within a group (Labov, 1972a,b), and sometimes preferring the speech pattern of a lower social or economic group when this has its socially rewarding results (Trudgill, 1972, 1974; Tway, 1975; Fishman, 1977). Whether shifts in use of language are directed upward or downward on socioeconomic scales may depend upon the speaker's assessment of the risk of group alienation in switching upwards and the advantages of membership in a coalition as well as the benefits to an upwards switch. Several observations of the social scientists interested in the use of language in its social context may help biologists derive testable hypotheses about the process of the differentiation of behavior.

TESTING THE MODELS: PREDICTIONS

Predictions from the above models may be made to allow an empirical test of these explanations in various species. Several predictions can be made, and in some instances the expected results are mutually exclusive. These are summarized in Table 7–1.

Table 7–1.   Predictions of three models to explain song differences among populations.

Variable	Model		
	Historical	Racial	Social adaptation
Genetic differentiation	sometimes	yes	usually no
Habitat	no relation	patchy, matches dialect	no relation
Population structure			
Dispersal	little	no	yes
Variation in N	high	high	low
Variation in area	high	high	low
Stability	yes	yes	no
Social behavior	(no prediction)	(no prediction)	song sharers interact
Behavior function of song	(no prediction)	intersexual	intrasexual >intersexual
Behavior development	(no prediction)	closed	open and socially conditional

1.   Genetic structure of populations. The racial specialization model assumes that dialectal populations are genetically distinct, not necessarily in regard to the development of song differences but in local genetic adaptations to environmental differences. The historical and social models make no assumptions about genetic distinctiveness. If we find dialectal populations that are not genetically distinct, we may favor these models over the rejected model.

2.   Ecological structure of habitats. The racial model assumes that each population is specialized for a certain habitat. The historical and social models make no predictions of a relationship. If dialect areas are not restricted to different habitats or if dialect boundaries do not correspond with habitat boundaries, then one would tend to reject the racial specialist explanation.

3.   Population structure: dispersal. The racial model assumes that there is no effective dispersal from one dialect population to another. The historical model is based on occasional dispersal from a home population. The social model predicts that individuals may often disperse among populations.

4.   Population structure: population size and area. The racial model predicts that population size and the geographic area of a dialect are highly variable, because the habitat patches of each population are likely to vary in size. The historical model also predicts that population size and area are variable because of local differences in time between founding and population expansion. The social adaptation model, in contrast, predicts that the variation in population size and area of a dialect should be limited and restricted by the number of males that can interact socially on a cost-effective basis within a limited area.

5.   Population structure: stability. If local populations are specialized for local environments, the population should be stable across years, with dialect boundaries being fixed in the absence of environmental shifts and songs themselves remaining unchanged across generations. The racial model predicts stability of boundaries and songs from year to year. The historical model predicts some boundary changes from local expansions and immigrations but no rapid changes in tradition. The social model predicts changes in boundaries and in local song traditions whenever the local social system is perturbed and the birds adjust to a new social order.

6.   Social interaction. The historical and racial models lead to no clear predictions about the nature of social interactions. The social model described is based on the assumptions that song-sharing birds interact socially, that non-sharing birds in the same general area do not, or at least that there is a difference in the interaction between sharers and non-sharers.

7.   Behavioral function of song. Earlier discussions have stressed the likely importance of song in mate choice by the female (Nottebohm, 1972). Hence, an assumption of the racial model is that epigamic function of song is expressed through the local song differences, with females choosing males with songs like those of their parents or neighbors heard when they were young. The social model assumes that intrasexual social interactions among males are important as well. The historical model is of no predictive value regarding song functions.

8.   Behavior development. As far as is known, dialectal differences result from differences in the songs heard and copied by the birds. However, some prediction of differences in development follows from the three models. The racial model assumes that song is a permanent marker of the home area of a bird and that a bird never changes its song and cannot lie about its past. The historical model suggests that song is stable, but no strong prediction is apparent. The social model predicts that song learning is socially conditional. It predicts an asymmetry in song learning, as learners may tend to copy songs in relation to the social behavior of the singing bird. For example, a bird with high mating success may be copied more frequently than birds with no or with low mating success, or immigrants may learn the songs of residents rather than the reverse. The asymmetries would depend upon the nature of the social dynamics of the population, but once this were known, the direction of song change could be specified.

TESTING THE MODELS: OBSERVATIONS OF INDIGOBIRDS

The ecological and behavioral predictions listed here were tested on song populations of village indigobirds, *Vidua chalybeata*. Indigobirds are small brood-parasitic finches living in brushy open woodland in Africa. Each bird has several song types, and often all of the song types are shared locally among neighbors (Payne, 1973). Color-marked individual birds were observed at Lochinvar National Park, Zambia, from 1972 to 1977; songs were tape recorded and audiospectrographed; song types were identified from the audiospectrographs; and the microgeographic distribution of each song type and each set of songs was plotted on aerial photographs. Three major and several minor song dialect populations occur within 40 km². In two years a local song population was closely observed. A song population consisted of birds that repeatedly visited each other and competed for the same set of females. I also sampled songs and populations of unmarked birds in other localities in southern and eastern Africa. The social organization, mating systems, and song behavior have been described (Payne and Payne, 1977; Payne, 1979). Here I shall describe briefly the ecology, population structure, and behavior. The explanatory models above were developed after some field work was complete, but many observations were made after the models were developed and thus constitute a test of the models.

Habitat. Song populations at Lochinvar did not correspond with any obvious habitat patches based on examination of aerial photographs, LANDSAT satellite photographs, local vegetation maps, and local sampling of the vegetation near each singing bird. Nor did dialect areas obviously match any locally different habitats in other areas.

Population structure. From 1972 to 1973, 73 adult or subadult males were color-marked and released. About half (38) were seen in a later year, and, of those, 36 were seen in the same dialect area. Two adult males were found in a dialect other than the one where they were caught. Another adult male shifted from the central area of one dialect to the boundary of that dialect area and an adjacent one within a breeding season, and he acquired some songs from the second dialect area. One female was seen just outside the area where she was originally marked but returned to her home dialect area. Movements of marked birds show limited but apparently effective dispersal of adults between dialect areas. Dispersal is also suggested by the disappearance of all 40 juvenile indigobirds that were ringed at Lochinvar in 1972 to 1974.

The seasonal stability of songs of individual birds allows us to use songs as short-term markers of dispersal. Most commonly each male sang the same 20 distinct song types from year to year. Each song type was generally recognizable from year to year. Song types nevertheless changed slightly in 1–2 notes from year to year, and these changes accumulated over the years in individual marked birds as in the population as a whole. All local birds made the same changes in song from year to year regardless of age. If we assume that birds with songs unlike those of their neighbors are immigrants, we can estimate the proportion of immigrants in the population from these mismatched birds. At Lochinvar, 29 of 191 birds (15 per cent of all birds whose songs were tape recorded) were immigrants by this criterion.

This includes a few bilingual birds. One bilingual bird gave songs of his earlier dialect as well as songs of the bordering dialect a few weeks after he moved 3 km to the border between the populations. Bilingualism appears to be transient as a bird switches song repertoires. In other populations sampled in Transvaal, Botswana, Tanzania, and Kenya, 11 of 84 birds had songs unlike their neighbors—or 13 per cent of the total. I suspect that these figures are minimal estimates of dispersal, because some birds may already have changed their songs to match the local dialect when they were tape recorded. The microgeographic distribution of sets of song types along the Letaba River in Transvaal provides some supporting evidence for local dispersal. Several birds had song types matching those of birds who were not their neighbors, but instead matched songs of males several km distant along the river. Local dispersal followed by the acquisition of some of the local songs by some birds may explain the observed microgeographic pattern of songs.

Population size, area, and stability. The number of birds sharing songs with each other is less than 20 in all dialects at Lochinvar and in other recorded populations. The areas involved are no larger than 10 km². Individual marked birds travel nearly throughout this area within a breeding season, with forays during breaks from singing (Payne and Payne, 1977). However the dialect areas are not all of equal size. The variation may reflect local historical events. During four years of observation at Lochinvar, one dialect population changed in number from 16 singing birds in 1973 to one bird in 1976. The population was replaced by other birds, previously unmarked, who sang the song types characteristic of the neighboring dialect population. Individual birds were encountered with songs unlike those of any others, and these probably immigrated from remote dialect areas. Local immigrations, expansions, and extinctions of song dialect populations occurred at Lochinvar from year to year, thus the consistency of results shows no more than a probable upper limit of about 20 birds and 10 km² for an indigobird dialect song population.

Social interactions. The birds are highly polygynous and one male accounts for more than half of all the matings of the population scattered across several km² within any one year. Singing males chase away intruding males from the areas of their call-sites, where the residents mate with visiting females. Neighboring males usually sing from call-sites more than 100m apart, but a few call sites were closer. These males often countersang, with one bird matching the song type of its neighbor during a part of the countersinging. Social interaction of males typically involved a male flying to a tree near the call-site of another male, listening for several minutes, then visiting another neighbor or returning to his own site and resuming his song. Each male visited call-sites of most other males in his song population but not those in neighboring song populations. When a male disappeared from a call-site where mating had occurred, he was quickly replaced by one of the visiting males. These observations and the fights for occupation of the traditional good call-sites suggest that males that share song types with each other compete for the same call-site, where the females mate (Payne and Payne, 1977).

Behavioral function of song. Males sing throughout the day, advertising their presence on a call-site. Certain songs are associated with particular behaviors, such as chasing other males or courting females, and song in general seems to be directed towards both males and females. However, more interactions were observed of aggressive behavior involving a singing male than of behavior directed towards a female, and it seems likely that intrasexual communication of aggressiveness is a major message of song of the species (Payne and Payne, 1977; Payne, 1979).

Development of song. Experimental results (Payne, unpublished) suggest that males do not imprint upon the fine details of songs of their father or neighbors at an early age. They can improvise a series of songs, but they usually copy other males at a later age after they disperse. In the wild birds, a marked adult male observed to move 5 km from one dialect to another completely changed his song repertoire to match the songs of his new population. Another adult male changed to a new song repetoire when his old neighbors and their songs were replaced by an invading dialect neighborhood from one year to the next. The year-to-year changes in each song type in the marked Lochinvar birds also indicate a life-long ability to modify song. In one instance, the most successful breeding bird developed individual variations of his songs, which other birds appeared to copy. In contrast, the song variations of peripheral birds with no mating success were not copied. The results point to an adaptable song development in which a male may match the songs of the most successful individual in his local adopted population. I suggest that a male may increase his chances of successfully taking over and maintaining a call-site himself, particularly a vacated call-site of the local stud, through mimicking that bird's songs and thereby deceiving the other competing local males.

DISCUSSION

Observations of the indigobird song dialects are more consistent with the social adaptation model than with the genetic differentiation model. The areas in which birds share songs do not correspond with any obvious patches of habitat. The changes in dialect populations over the years at Lochinvar also argue against the concept of stable, genetically specialized, local populations. Variation in the size of populations and the size of the dialect area seems to be limited. Dispersal among populations involves at least 10 per cent to 20 per cent of the singing males per year, and dispersal may be higher in the young. This dispersal would be sufficient to overwhelm any local genetic drift effects or mild selective pressures that one might expect in a small population. The amount of dispersal is sufficiently great that calculation of a genetically effective population size, N_e (Wright, 1969), would approach the number of individuals in the species (Moran, 1962; Lewontin, 1974). Historical considerations may explain immigrations, founding and extinction of new song populations, and the yearly changes in population size and area. Although no direct genetic tests were made for the indigobirds, we can reject the model based on genetic differentiation, because the observations either refuted or did not positively support the other predictions of that model.

Direct genetic tests have been made for two species of dialectal birds, the rufous-collared sparrow, *Zonotrichia capensis*, and the white-crowned sparrow, *Z. leucophrys*. *Z. capensis* has extensive dialects in South America. Dialects are reported to extend in belts along altitudinal and habitat zones for hundreds of kilometers yet change abruptly across steep altitudinal gradients (Nottebohm, 1969, 1975; King, 1972; Handford and Nottebohm, 1976). Biochemical tests for allozymic differences among local populations in the gradients of song change showed some genetic differences among birds, but none related to the song dialect differences (Handford and Nottebohm, 1976). Differences in gene frequencies may occur among geographically remote populations but are not known among neighboring local populations (Nottebohm and Selander, 1972). In coastal California, resident populations of *Z. leucophrys* have well-demarcated song dialects. Dialect borders do not appear to involve shifts from one habitat patch to another. Baker (1975) found significant mean differences in allele frequencies in two of six polymorphic loci in two neighboring dialect areas, but all alleles occurred in both populations, and the same allele was the more frequent one in both populations. Baker (1975) also found differences in allele frequencies along a transect of sparrows in the Rocky Mountains in the absence of any dialect transition. The results do not support the concept of marked genetic differentiation among dialectal populations.

Habitat differences that correspond to local dialects are known in *Z. capensis* (King, 1972; Nottebohm, 1975). Nottebohm suggests that the different acoustical features of these songs may be designed to facilitate the transmission of sound in the corresponding habitats. King however found ''no consistent associations between specific dialects and habitats.'' Local song difference in Z. *capensis* are by no means restricted to local habitat differences in the populations described by Nottebohm (1969). The pampas populations do not have a single song theme that is undifferentiated over hundreds of km, as local song differences or subdialects make groups of neighbors within less than 1 km of each other (Nottebohm, 1969:303). Young sparrows disperse across distances greater than the area of these local subdialects (Miller and Miller, 1968). Hence, even in this species a social explanation of song dialects may be the most appropriate. In some other dialectal species where local habitats have been noted, dialects and habitats do not correspond (Baker, 1975; Baptista, 1977; Payne, 1978a,b).

Song dialects in Z. *leucophrys* occur across several km and may involve hundreds of birds (Marler and Tamura, 1962; Baker, 1975), but local ''subdialects'' are distinguishable within these populations. Baptista (1975), working around the San Francisco Bay area, found local ''subdialects'' involving fewer than six birds. Even within sedentary populations of Z. *leucophrys* in coastal central California, birds sometimes disperse from the population where they were born and settle in a population with a different major dialect (Baker and Mewaldt, 1978). Baker and Mewaldt determined birth-to-breeding distances for 371 birds living in two adjacent dialect areas. In this sample, 15 birds dispersed across the dialect boundary. Baker and Mewaldt chose to exclude from this sample 10 birds that were marked or recaptured very close to the boundary and included them instead as nondispersing individuals, but it seems more straightforward to recognize them as dispersers. Recalculating their figures with the 15 cross-boundary dispersers shows a clear tendency ($x^2 = 4.24$, $.05 > p > .01$) for birds to cross the boundary less often than expected, though not to the degree stated by the authors. Their map suggests local song populations of a few hundred birds. The data suggest a between-population dispersal level of 15/371 birds or 0.040 of the population per generation. This observed dispersal, together with the population size, appears great enough to prevent any marked local genetic differentiation by random processes (Moran, 1962; Lewontin, 1974), and the data on habitats and genetic sampling for these populations (Baker, 1975; Baker and Mewaldt, 1978) do not suggest a strong genetic difference resulting from natural selection; the habitats were remarkably similar as I also have observed. Thus, for Z. *leucophrys* populations breeding in central coastal California, the data available do not strongly support the racial specialization model as developed here. The data are, however, consistent with Baker and Mewaldt's suggestion ''that song dialects reduce migration'' between local populations.

Song dialects might function as signals for assortative mating, thereby maintaining the supposed genetic differences between song populations (Marler and Tamura, 1962; Nottebohm, 1969, 1972). This version of the genetic model is not supported by field observations. In *Zonotrichia leucophrys*, occasional males have a song unlike that of the local dialect, and these males mate and breed successfully (Baptista 1975). Testosterone-induced song of some females mated with males singing alien songs did not match the dialects of their mates but did match the local dialects, indicating that they were local females (Baptista, 1974).

Social adaptation as an explanation of song sharing in dialectal birds seems likely in several other species. In studies of color-marked individual birds, the young of Bewick's wren, *Thryomanes bewickii*, long-billed marsh wrens, *Cistothorus palustris*, rufous-sided towhees, *Pipilo erythrophthalmus*, indigo buntings, *Passerina cyanea*, and New Zealand saddlebacks, *Philesturnus carunculatus* disperse from their birth sites, then settle and sing like their new neighbors, not like their fathers (Kroodsma, 1971, 1974; Verner, 1976; Thompson, 1970; Payne, unpublished observations; Jenkins, 1978). Local song dialects in bobolinks, *Dolichonyx oryzivorus*, a highly migratory and dispersive polygynous species, may change locally from year to year, apparently by local turnover of old males and song copying by young males (Avery and Oring, 1977). Marsh warblers, *Acrocephalus palus-*

tris, share songs locally, but individuals disperse among these populations, so local dialects do not indicate local genetic demes (Lemaire, 1975). Ortolan buntings, *Emberiza hortulana,* sometimes disperse across dialect areas, learning some new songs and introducing novel songs that may be copied by the local residents (Conrads, 1976). In the lek-forming hummingbirds, *Phaethornis longuemarius* and *P. guy,* males in different parts of a group singing assembly all within a single bush may have distinct songs shared only among immediate neighbors. Young males appear to learn these local songs after they arrive at the display area from their birth sites (D. W. Snow, 1968; B. K. Snow, 1974). In another song-dialectal bird of tropical forests, the three-wattled bellbird, *Procnias tricarunculata,* young disperse from their natal area and then learn the local song, as evident from the incomplete vocalizations of immigrant young males (B. K. Snow, 1977; D. W. Snow, 1976). Social effects in song learning are likely in the colonial cacique, *Cacicus cela,* where birds within a colony share their songs. Different colonies have distinct songs, which may change gradually within a season, and new songs may appear in a colony with the arrival of new birds (Feekes, 1977). Young male village weaverbirds, *Ploceus cucullatus,* preferentially model their songs after the songs of the dominant male in the group rather than their father or the most vocal male (Jacobs, 1979). The dialectal tree creepers, *Certhia brachydactyla* and *C. familiaris,* will not learn songs from a tape recorder but only from live birds (Thielcke, 1970). Even the classical dialectal species are not explained simply by a model of nondispersal and primacy in song learning. British chaffinches, *Fringilla coelebs,* have local dialects. Chaffinches defer learning their song until the spring of their first year (Nottebohm, 1968), by which time they may have dispersed. A tenth of the recoveries of ringed birds are from 5–50 km from their birth place (Newton, 1973). Young *Zonotrichia leucophrys* residents in central California sometimes learn the song of seasonal migrants from more northern races (Baptista, 1974; Baptista and Wells, 1975). Occasional birds are bilingual (singing two distinct songs), trilingual, or even quadrilingual, with songs from more than one local dialect (Baptista, 1975). The social aspects of song acquisition in dialectal birds clearly are not restricted to the brood-parasitic indigobirds. Song learning in many birds may depend in part on social interaction not simply on hearing a song at the place of birth.

In birds with several song types, neighboring birds often match their song types while they countersing (Hinde, 1958; Lemon, 1968; Payne, 1973; Baptista, 1975; Verner, 1976). When a male has more than one song type, he often matches the song type heard from a tape recorder in his next song (Hinde, 1958; Payne, 1970; Todt, 1970; Baptista, 1975; Verner, 1976). A male may even anticipate the next song of a determinate song sequence by singing it before the neighbor or the playback tape recorder gives the song (Verner, 1976). Verner suggests that song matching by countersinging males may reflect the "dominance/subordinance relationships between neighbors," with subordinates matching the preceding songs of the dominant bird. Matched countersinging is consistent with the concept of song copying of one neighbor by another as a mechanism of social adaptation.

Why should males model their songs after those of their established neighbors? In experiments on several species, males respond more aggressively to recorded songs of strangers than to the songs of their neighbors with whom they have established territorial boundaries (Falls, 1969; Emlen, 1971; Goldman, 1973; Kroodsma, 1976), and they may habituate to individual songs (Petrinovich and Peeke, 1973). Males habituate to the songs of familiar neighbors and perhaps also to their own songs. If this is true, then a male of a dialectal species may respond less aggressively to his own song or to other birds with songs like his own than to songs from a foreign dialect. In experimental work to date the reverse is true: Birds respond more strongly to songs from their own dialect than to an alien dialect (Thielcke and Linsenmair, 1963; Lemon, 1967; Bertram, 1970; Milligan and Verner, 1971; Harris and Lemon, 1974; Kreuzer, 1974; Becker, 1977). The difference is consistent with a view that song matching is a tactic of intraspecific mimicry if the greater response of the territorial birds is seen to be a countertactic to this behavior, but, if so, this counterselection complicates an analysis of the effect of matching a neighbor's song.

Song dialects in many bird species may result from birds copying their established neighbor's songs after they disperse. The ecological consequences of copying a local song may be a more rapid establishment of a territory, either as a new male is tolerated by the established males or as other males mistake his identity. The number of birds that share songs (size of the "dialect") may vary from 2–5 (e.g., indigo buntings, *Passerina cyanea*, Thompson, 1970; Payne, unpublished) to 10–20 (e.g., village indigobirds, *Vidua chalybeata*, Payne and Payne, 1977; Payne, 1979) or more, depending on species differences in social structure. In contrast to the complex social order of man, where "group identity" or "group solidarity" involves alliances and coalitions of individuals cooperating in their behavior, there is no obvious cooperative social group in these birds, only numbers of competing males. Even the birds with leks, sometimes considered cooperative displays, appear rather to be aggregates of males that compete for the visiting females. Without cooperating groups of "low prestige" males, the social conditions that in humans favor adoption of low-status dialects are nonexistent in the less social birds. Instead, song copying in birds appears to result from some song primacy and, in the dialectal species described here, "upward" shifts of social conditionality by copying established males. We may now focus attention on the costs and benefits of time and breeding success of the song mimic and his model compared with other local birds that do not share these songs, and we can view song dialects as instances of intraspecific mimicry. At the least we can develop this explanatory model, test its predictions on a number of species, and compare the observations with the predictions of alternative models. Perhaps we will find parallels with the social use of language and song among humans and birds.

SUMMARY

Song dialects in birds may be explained by three models: random historical events, environmental determinism, and social adaptation. Mutually exclusive predictions were developed and tested with observations in song populations of the African finch, *Vidua chalybeata*. The observations support the explanation based on social adaptation and suggest that song dialects may be described as social mimicry. Observations on several other dialectal species of birds are consistent with the model of social adaptation. I suggest that biologists interested in the ecological significance of song sharing consider both population structure and the use of song in social behavior.

ACKNOWLEDGEMENTS

I thank Dale Lewis and Karen Payne for assistance with field work. Penelope Eckert suggested references on human sociolinguistics. Luis Baptista, Janet Hinshaw, and Jared Verner commented on the manuscript. My work has been supported by the National Science Foundation (GB29017X, BMS75-03913, BNS78-03178).

REFERENCES

Avery, M. and L. W. Oring. 1977. Song dialects in the bobolink *(Dolichonyx oryzivorus). Condor* 79:113–118.

Baker, M. C. 1974. Genetic structure of two populations of white-crowned sparrows with different song dialects. *Condor* 76:351–356.

———. 1975. Song dialects and genetic differences in white-crowned sparrows *(Zonotrichia leucophrys). Evolution* 29:226–241.

——, and L. R. Mewaldt. 1978. Song dialects as barriers to dispersal in white-crowned sparrows, *Zonotrichia leucophrys nuttalli*. *Evolution* 32: 712–722.

Baptista, L. F., 1974. The effects of songs of wintering white-crowned sparrows on song development in sedentary populations of the species. *Z. Tierpsychol.* 34:147–171.

——. 1975. Song dialects and demes in sedentary populations of the white-crowned sparrow *(Zonotrichia leucophrys nuttalli)*. *Univ. Calif. Publ. Zool.* 105:1–52.

——.1977. Geographic variation in song and dialects of the Puget Sound white-crowned sparrow. *Condor* 79:356–370.

——, and H. Wells. 1975. Additional evidence of song-misimprinting in the white-crowned sparrow. *Bird-Banding* 46:269–272.

Becker, P. H. 1977. Geographische Variation des Gesanges von Winter- und Sommergoldhähnchen *(Regulus regulus, R. ignicapillus)*. *Die Vogelwarte* 29:1–37.

Bertram, B. 1970. The vocal behaviour of the Indian hill mynah, *Gracula religiosa. Anim. Behav. Monogr.* 3:81–192.

Birdsell, J. B. 1973. A basic demographic unit. *Curr. Anthropol.* 14:337-356.

Burton, F. D. and M. J. A. Bick. 1972. A drift in time can define a deme: the implications of tradition drift in primate societies for hominid evolution, *J. Human Evol.* 1:53–59.

Conrads, K. 1976. Studien an Fremddialekt-Sängern und Dialekt-Mischsängern des Ortolans *(Emberiza hortulana). J. Orn.* 117:438–450.

Emlen, S. T. 1971. The role of song in individual recognition in the indigo bunting. *Z. Tierpsychol.* 28:241–246.

Falls, J. B. 1969. Functions of territorial song in the white-throated sparrow, pp. 207–232. In R. A. Hinde, (ed.), *Bird Vocalizations*. Cambridge Univ. Press, Cambridge.

Feekes, R. 1977. Colony-specific song in *Cacicus cela* (Icteridae, Aves): the pass-word hypothesis. *Ardea* 65:197–202.

Fishman, J. A. 1977. The spread of English as a new perspective for the study of 'language maintenance and language drift,' pp. 108–133. In J. A. Fishman, R. L. Cooper, and A. W. Conrad, (eds.), *The Spread of English*. Newbury House, Rowley, Mass.

Goldman, P. 1973. Song recognition by field sparrows. *Auk* 90:106–113.

Gumperz, J. J. 1962. Types of linguistic communities. *Anthropol. Ling.* 4:28–40.

Handford, P., and F. Nottebohm. 1976. Allozymic and morphological variation in population samples of rufous-crowned sparrow, *Zonotrichia capensis,* in relation to vocal dialects. *Evolution* 30:802–817.

Harris, M. A. and R. E. Lemon. 1974. Songs of song sparrows: reactions of males to songs of different localitiès. *Condor* 76:33–44.

Hinde, R. A. 1958. Alternative motor patterns in chaffinch song. *Anim. Behav.* 6:211–218.

Jacobs, C. 1979. Factors involved in mate selection and vocal development in the village weaverbird *(Ploceus cucullatus)*. Ph.D. Dissertation, University of California, Los Angeles.

Jenkins, P. F. 1978. Cultural transmission of song patterns and dialect development in a free-living bird population. *Anim. Behav.* 26:50–78.

King, J. A. 1972. Variation in the song of the rufous-collared sparrow, *Zonotrichia capensis,* in northwestern Argentina. *Z. Tierpsychol.* 30:344–373.

Kreuzer, M. 1974. Réponses comportementales de mâles Troglodytes (Passeriformes) à des chants spécifiques de dialectes différents. *Rev. Comp. Anim.* 8:287–295.

Kroodsma, D. E. 1971. Song variations and singing behavior in the rufous-sided towhee, *Pipilo erythrophthalmus oregonus. Condor* 73: 303–308.

——1974. Song learning, dialects, and dispersal in the Bewick's wren. *Z. Tierpsychol.* 35:352–380.

——1976. The effect of large song repertoires on neighbor "recognition" in male song sparrows. *Condor* 78:97–99.

Kurath, H. 1939. *Handbook of the Linguistic Geography of New England*. Brown Univ. Press, Providence.

Labov, W. 1972a. *Sociolinguistic Patterns*. Univ. Pennsylvania Press, Philadelphia.

——1972b. *Language in the Inner City*. Univ. Pennsylvania Press, Philadelphia.

Lemaire, F. 1975. Dialectal variations in the imitative song of the marsh warbler *(Acrocephalus palustris)* in western and eastern Belgium. *Le Gerfaut* 65:95–106.

Lemon, R. E. 1967. The response of cardinals to songs of different dialects. *Anim. Behav.* 15:538–545.

——1968. The relation between organization and function of song in cardinals. *Behaviour* 32:158–178.

──────1975. How birds develop song dialects. *Condor* 77:385–406.

Lewontin, R. C. 1974. *The Genetic Basis of Evolutionary Change*. Columbia Univ. Press, New York.

Marler, P. 1975. On strategies of behavioral development, pp. 254–275. In G. Barends, C. Beer, and A. Manning (eds.), *Function and Evolution in Behaviour*. Clarendon Press, Oxford.

──────, and M. Tamura. 1962. Song dialects in three populations of white-crowned sparrows. *Condor* 64:368–377.

──────, and M. Tamura. 1964. Culturally transmitted patterns of vocal behavior in sparrows. *Science* 146:1483–1486.

McDavid, R. I. and V. G. McDavid. Regional linguistic atlases in the United States. *Orbis* 5:349–386.

Miller, A. H. 1956. Ecologic factors that accelerate formation of races and species of terrestrial vertebrates. *Evolution* 10:262–277.

──────, and V. D. Miller. 1968. The behavioral ecology and breeding biology of the Andean sparrow, *Zonotrichia capensis*. *Caldasia* 10:83–154.

Milligan, M. M. and J. Verner. 1971. Inter-populational song dialect discrimination in the white-crowned sparrow. *Condor* 73:208–213.

Moran, P. A. 1962. *The Statistical Processes of Evolutionary Theory*. Clarendon Press, Oxford.

Newton, I. 1973. *Finches*. Taplinger, New York.

Nottebohm, F. 1968. Auditory experience and song development in the chaffinch (*Fringilla coelebs*); ontogeny of a complex motor pattern. *Ibis* 110:549–568.

──────1969. The song of the chingolo, *Zonotrichia capensis*, in Argentina: description and evaluation of a system of dialects. *Condor* 71:299–315.

──────1972. The origins of vocal learning. *Amer. Natur.* 106:116–140.

──────1975. Continental patterns of song variability in *Zonotrichia capensis:* some possible ecological correlates. *Amer. Natur.* 109:605–624.

──────, and R. K. Selander. 1972. Vocal dialects and gene frequencies in the chingolo sparrow (*Zonotrichia capensis*). *Condor* 74:137–143.

Payne, R. B. 1970. Temporal pattern of duetting in the Barbary shrike, *Lanarius barbarus*. *Ibis* 112:105–107.

──────1973. Behavior, mimetic songs and song dialects, and relationships of the parasitic indigobirds (*Vidua*) of Africa. *Ornithol. Monogr.* 11.

──────. 1978a. Local dialects in the wingflaps of flappet larks *Mirafra rufocinnamomea*. *Ibis* 120:204–207.

──────. 1978b. Microgeographic variation in songs of splendid sunbirds *Nectarinia coccinigaster:* population phenetics, habitats, and song dialects. *Behaviour* 65:282–308.

──────. 1979. Song structure, behaviour, and sequence of song types in a population of village indigobirds, *Vidua chalybeata*. *Anim. Behav.* 27: 997–1013.

──────and K. Payne. 1977. Social organization and mating success in local song populations of village indigobirds, *Vidua chalybeata*. *Z. Tierpsychol.* 45:113–173.

Petrinovich, L. and H. V. S. Peeke. 1973. Habituation to territorial song in the white-crowned sparrow (*Zonotrichia leucophrys*). *Behav. Biol.* 8:743–747.

Platt, J. R. 1964. Strong inference. *Science* 146:347–353.

Reed, C. E. 1967. *Dialects of American English*. Univ. Massachusetts Press, Amherst.

Smith, W. J. 1977. *The Behavior of Communicating*. Harvard Univ. Press, Cambridge Mass.

Snow, B. K. 1974. Lek behaviour and breeding of Guy's hermit hummingbird, *Phaethornis guy*. *Ibis* 116:278–297.

──────. 1977. Territorial behavior and courtship of the male three-wattled bellbird. *Auk* 94:623–645.

Snow, D. W. 1968. The singing assemblies of little hermits. *Living Bird* 7:47–55.

──────. 1976. The Web of Adaptation. Quadrangle, New York.

Spielman, R. S., E. C. Migliazza, and J. V. Neel. 1974. Regional linguistic and genetic differences among Yanomama Indians. *Science* 184:637–644.

Thielcke, G. 1969. Geographic variation in bird vocalizations, pp.311–339. In R.A. Hinde, (ed.), *Bird Vocalizations*. Cambridge Univ. Press, Cambridge.

──────. 1970. Lernen von Gesang als möglicher Schrittmacher der Evolution. *Z. Zool. Syst. Evolutionsf.* 8:309–320.

──────. 1973. On the origin of divergence of learned signals (songs) in isolated populations. *Ibis* 115:511–516.

──────and K. E. Linsenmair. 1963. Zur geographischen Variation des Gesanges des Zilpzalps, *Phylloscopus collybita*, in Mittel- und Südwesteuropa mit einem Vergleich des Gesanges der Fitis, *Phylloscopus trochilus*. *J. Ornithol.* 104:372–402.

Thompson, W. L. 1970. Song variation in a population of indigo buntings. *Auk* 87:58–71.

Todt, D. 1970. Gesangliche Reaktionen der Amsel (*Turdus merula L.*) auf ihren experimentell reproduzierten Eigengesang. *Z. vergl. Physiol.* 66:294–317.

Trudgill, P. J. 1972. Sex, covert prestige and linguistic change in the urban British English. *Lang. Soc.* 1:179–196.

————. 1974. Linguistic change and diffusion: description and explanation in sociological dialect geography. *Lang. Soc.* 3:215–246.

Tway, P. 1975. Workplace isoglosses: lexical variation and change in a factory setting. *Lang. Soc.* 4:171–183.

Verner, J. 1976. Complex song repertoire of male long-billed marsh wrens in eastern Washington. *Living Bird* 14:263–300.

Weinrich, U., W. Labov, and M. Herzog. 1968. Empirical foundations for a theory of language change, pp. 95-188. In W. P. Lehmann and Y. Malkiel, (eds.), *Directions for Historical Linguistics.* Univ. Texas Press, Austin.

Wright, S. 1969. *Evolution and the Genetics of Populations. Vol. 2, The Theory of Gene Frequencies.* Univ. Chicago Press, Chicago.

8

The Evolution of Sexual Indistinguishability

Nancy Burley

Among pigeons the sexes are not able to distinguish their opposites by sight. The male for example, does not know what the female sex is; he will just as quickly mate with a male as with a female, provided the opportunity is given (Whitman, 1919: 27).

There is an implicit assumption in the biological literature and in the minds of humans that individuals of sexually reproducing species experience little difficulty in discerning the sex of adult conspecifics. Sexual dimorphism is, after all, the natural condition of humankind and many other species. Nevertheless, several observers of one avian subfamily, the Columbidae (pigeons and doves), have concluded that, for some species, individuals are not easily able to tell the sex of conspecifics. C.O. Whitman, quoted at the beginning of this reading, worked extensively with pigeons and doves of known sex, and he observed that sex could not be determined by doves on sight. Wallace Craig (1909) concurred with him. Levi (1967) and numerous pigeon fanciers (pers. commun.) are well acquainted with the fact that pigeons readily engage in courtship with unknown individuals regardless of sex.

My experience with pigeons strongly reinforces Whitman's, Craig's, and Levi's observations. Having difficulty in determining the sex of feral pigeons, I nevertheless initially assumed that pigeons themselves had no such problem. Careful observation of a captive flock of pigeons over a period of two-and-a-half years led me to the opposite conclusion: the sexes are—to pigeons (regardless of their appearance to humans)—morphologically indistinguishable.

My research with pigeons raised the question: why might a species lack morphological markers of sex? In this paper I explore this question. Specifically, my purposes are to (1) provide a definition of sexual indistinguishability, (2) develop the hypothesis that lack of morphological sexual dimorphism may be an evolved trait, (3) suggest one context in which indistinguishability can be expected to occur, and (4) provide limited empirical evidence for the phenomenon.

A DEFINITION OF SEXUAL INDISTINGUISHABILITY

Sexual indistinguishability is defined as the absence of sex-specific, continuously displayed characteristics perceivable by conspecifics during some stage of the life cycle of a species. By contrast, when *morphological* sex-distinctive characteristics permit individuals to determine the sex of nearby conspecifics without ambiguity, the sexes may be termed "distinguishable." Most sex-specific *behavioral* cues, such as auditory and postural signals are displayed discontinuously and, therefore, do not violate the condition of sexual indistinguishability. Indistinguishability entails a lack of obligate sex-identifying cues. An organism that only reveals its sex by behaving in a particular manner (that is, by revealing a morphological cue, singing a song, or posturing a certain way) is otherwise not perceived by conspecifics in sex-appropriate ways. Thus, a sex-indistinguishable organism is essentially concealing its sex except when its behavior indicates otherwise.

The frequency of occurrence of sexual indistinguishability among animals is unknown and, at present, difficult to estimate. With several exceptions (e.g., Mottram, 1915; Huxley, 1934; Tinbergen, 1939; Lack, 1940; 1946; Wolf, 1969; Choat and Robertson, 1975), few investigators have made either a conceptual or an empirical distinction between monomorphism and indistinguishability. "Sexual monomorphism" suggests an overall similarity in appearance, usually among the adults of the two sexes, but does not specify indistinguishability. This lack of distinction has made it difficult to recognize indistinguishability and has inhibited efforts to identify possibly indistinguishable species in the written record. Too, what appears indistinguishable to a human may be distinguishable to organisms with different sensory capacities and vice versa. There are two ways to deal with this problem: (1) select organisms for study that have sensory capabilities similar to humans and catalog a large number of these species according to their distinguishability, assuming cataloging errors are small or cancelling; and (2) experiment with behavior to determine if individuals can actually distinguish sexes. The second method minimizes error but is more difficult and time-consuming.

One possible objection to the proposed definition of indistinguishability is that it creates an artificial distinction between appearance and behavior. For example, Skutch (1976) classifies bird song as a dimorphic characteristic (thus making otherwise monomorphic species dimorphic) rather than as a sex-specific or sex-related trait. While morphology and behavior are highly interrelated, I do not think the distinction is artificial nor does it underplay the importance of behavior. In fact, as will be argued, morphological sexual indistinguishability may correlate with increases in the functional behavioral repertoire.

Another likely criticism is that organisms are able to distinguish conspecifics' sex even though humans are not (e.g., Richdale, 1951). This argument actually has two forms: organisms are sensitive to morphological detail that escapes human attention (e.g., Ingolfsson, 1969); and morphology is unimportant because behavior is a good indicator of sex (e.g., Skutch, 1976). Both positions deny the possibility that individuals in the species involved experience difficulty in determining sex. At the moment it is impossible to resolve these arguments because few studies investigating sex recognition have focused primarily on morphology (but see Noble and Vogt, 1935; Noble, 1936; Marler, 1955; Lewis, 1972; Smith, 1972).

THEORETICAL IMPORTANCE OF SEXUAL INDISTINGUISHABILITY

Two alternative hypotheses may account for indistinguishability: (1) It arises through the presence of identical selection pressures on the two sexes, or (2) it occurs when there is an advantage to individuals of one or both sexes in concealing their sex.

I divide selection pressures into two categories: intra-specific and extra-specific. For extra-specific selection pressures to be identical on the sexes, male and female foraging tactics, abilities, and metabolic needs must be identical. Likewise, their ability to avoid predators and their likelihood of attracting predators must be equal, and all environmental changes must affect the sexes identically. To generate identical foraging tactics and predator attraction, the sex-related roles of species with parental care must be the same. However, considerable evidence has accumulated for the occurrence of sex-related foraging tactics (Selander, 1966; Schoener, 1967; 1968), sex-specific parental roles (see Skutch, 1976 and references therein), and differential mortality patterns (Lack, 1968) even among monogamous species. Numerous ecological factors contribute to sexual dimorphism (see also Rand, 1952; Sibley, 1957; Goodwin, 1960; Hamilton, 1961; Jehl, 1970; Selander, 1972 and references therein). Nevertheless, although identical selection pressures on the sexes seem unlikely, extra-specific selection pressures may be similar enough to result in no obvious morphological differences between the sexes.

Intraspecific selection pressures include within- and between-sex competition; both are related to patterns of parental investment. According to current theory (Trivers, 1972), the sex that invests more per offspring becomes more of a limiting resource for the sex that invests less. Usually the sex investing more is female; the following discussion makes this assumption. Unequal investment patterns mean that the potential reproductive success of a male is greater than that of a female and that reproductive success is more variable among males (Bateman, 1948). Between-sex disparity in parental investment generates strong intrasexual competition among males for access to mates. It also reinforces epigamic selection by females (Fisher, 1930). Sexual selection favors sex advertisement by high-quality individuals of both sexes. As females incur a greater share of the total parental investment, both intrasexual and epigamic selection may enhance sexual dimorphism. Where parental investment patterns are reversed, males should be more selective and females should experience greater intrasexual competition (Trivers, 1972; Burley, 1977b).

It seems likely, therefore, that intraspecific selection pressures are rarely, if ever, identical for the sexes. Even if males and females invest equally in offspring, pressures might not be identical because of differences in the pattern of investment. If, for example, the initial investment by males in their offspring is very low, it may be to a male's advantage to copulate (but not necessarily to pair) with any female (Trivers, 1972). In summary, then, the hypothesis that sexual indistinguishability results from identical selection pressures on the sexes runs counter to theoretical expectation.

Because strong extra- and intra-specific selection pressures favor dimorphism, for indistinguishability to evolve there must be strong contravening pressures. In the following section I argue for the adaptive significance of indistinguishability in social monogamous populations. The evolution of indistinguishability in other groups is dealt with elsewhere (Burley, manuscript).

INDISTINGUISHABILITY IN SOCIAL POPULATIONS

Animals that live or travel with conspecifics during the breeding season may benefit from sexual indistinguishability because sexual competition that results from group living is at some times, at least, disadvantageous to all individuals in the group. In general, organisms that spend time together during the breeding season should experience intensive sexual competition at this time, and organisms that are highly territorial or solitary will largely avoid such competition once territories are firmly established and the breeding season is underway. Although competition between nonbreeding and breeding members of a population will persist throughout the breeding season, interference competition among breeding territory holders may be negligible (e.g., Bertram 1970; Krebs 1971). By contrast, organisms that spend their time during the breeding season in groups, such as colonial breeders and group foragers, are continually subjected to situations that promote sexual competition.

Many variables may contribute to the occurrence of sexual competition in groups. Among polygynous and promiscuous species, fertilization of eggs often takes place in high-density situations. Behaviors that directly result in fertilization are probably more rarely displayed in large groups by monogamous species, because matings may be easily interrupted and intercepted, with resulting confidence of paternity low. Less direct forms of reproductive competition may be commonplace, however; the types and intensity of competition will vary with ecological circumstances and among species. Possible instigators of conflict include widowed or otherwise unmated males, who attempt to impress potential mates with their competitive superiority. Mated males may mimic the behavior of unmated males in order to deceive females. (Many male pigeons, for example, spend a considerable fraction of their time courting unfamiliar conspecifics during periods in which they are also helping to incubate their mate's eggs [personal observation]; this period is relatively undemanding of their parental energies [Burley, 1980]. As hatching date approaches a male's tendency to engage in such courtship declines.) Unmated females may provoke confrontations between males to ascertain superiority. Individuals of both sexes having inferior mates may engage in behaviors that aid in locating and attracting better ones; and the results of repeated interactions may affect an individual's assessment of its current mate's quality.

The consequences of sexual interference competition in groups can be illustrated by considering a feeding flock of birds. Competition within a flock creates disturbances that have at least two effects. First, it lowers the efficiency of food gathering for each individual. This may not be serious in some situations because search and pursuit times within foraging flocks may be quite low (Lack, 1968). However, when young are being fed, it should be more efficient to allocate effort to food-getting rather than to intrasexual competition. Second, competition in flocks reduces attentiveness to predators. Feeding flocks probably often form for protection against predation (Lack, 1954; Buskirk, 1976) as do breeding groups (Lack, 1968; Krebs, 1974) and other associations (Williams, 1964). Birds in flocks must be alert, ready to spot predators and flee; avoiding sexual competition is desirable. However, when increased sexual competition is an effect of aggregating, competition may continue even though it is counterproductive to the function of the aggregation. *This occurs because superior competitors lose less on average than inferior competitors* (Maynard Smith and Price, 1973), although there is a net loss of energy to all individuals in the group from competing. Thus, through natural selection, sexual competition continues and may even escalate.

Individuals may avoid competition without signalling submission in competitive encounters by being sexually unidentifiable. An organism that cannot be sexually identified should be largely ignored by both sexes. For example, imagine a large feeding flock of birds with three phenotypes: F (female), M (male), and O (sex not identifiable; perhaps an organism in juvenile plumage). Within-sex competition is confined to females acting aggressively toward F's and males acting aggressively toward M's. O's will almost certainly be left alone on average more than F's and M's. Being less distracted, O's should be consistently among the first to flee when a predator arrives; they should have a survivorship advantage. Because O's are likely to gather more food per unit time, they should also be better providers of food for their young. For these two reasons, the O phenotype should make superior mates and should spread through the population.

From this reasoning, low-quality individuals appear to benefit most from being indistinguishable. The assertion that superior individuals will lose less from flock competition must be qualified, however. Among social species, there are probably circumstances in which it is to a superior individual's benefit to avoid interference competition as much as possible. For example, a mated male with offspring in the nest may require much time and energy to collect food for offspring. For this male, flock rivalry serves relatively little purpose, and any time spent in competition lessens the amount of resources he can provide to his dependents. An unmated male of lower quality may stand to gain from confrontation; he certainly has less to lose than the mated male. The relative costs and benefits of competition are not merely a function of competitive ability.

In non-social species, individuals may avoid competition to a certain extent by avoiding interactions with others in the population. When confrontations do occur, submission may be signalled without the information being conveyed to a large number of conspecifics. In social species, organisms lack these options. Morphological advertisement of sex conveys information that makes the bearer subject to sexual competition whether or not it is to that individual's best interest.

The liability of advertising one's sex in a population in which other individuals are not doing so may also fix indistinguishability in a population. Imagine a population in which a fraction advertises its sex (F's and M's) and the rest does not (O's). O's are protected by their plumage from disruptive competition. In non-flock competitive encounters O's have an advantage, for they can assess the sex of dimorphic conspecifics although F's and M's are unable to assess the sex of O's. O's can therefore initiate or avoid encounters as advantage dictates. Under the conditions outlined this added advantage to the O phenotype should drive the F and M phenotypes to extinction, leaving a population of indistinguishable individuals.

As the proportion of M's and F's declines in a population, an additional pressure may facilitate their demise. Predators may experience increased ability to fix their attention on these individuals. The smaller the proportion of M's and F's, the greater would be the predator pressure, perhaps insuring the extinction of dimorphic characteristics.

Convergence of phenotypes onto a neutral appearance is only one possible route to indistinguishability. In many populations, males probably experience much more intrasexual competition than do females. The benefits of indistinguishability in these instances would be greater for males (and their mates), and so males should converge onto female appearance. Females should evolve preferences for such males when the quality and quantity of parental care provided by them is sufficient to enhance inclusive fitness more than does the production of dimorphic sons. Other pressures discussed above (the liability of advertising one's sex when others are not doing so, the inverse relationship between predation pressure and frequency of dimorphic traits) would also act to effect the convergence of one sex's phenotype onto that of the other.

CONSTRAINTS ON INDISTINGUISHABILITY

Group size and type of mating system influence the utility of indistinguishability. In small groups recognition of most individuals is possible and advantages to indistinguishability may be small; the benefits conferred by indistinguishability should increase with group size. (For conditions favoring indistinguishability in territorial species, see Wolf, 1969.) Ecological pressures favoring rapid pair formation (Hamilton, 1961; Jehl, 1970) oppose indistinguishability; it is more likely in long-lived species that remain paired to the same individuals for long periods of time.

Monogamous species are more likely to be indistinguishable than polygamous ones. For an individual to benefit by concealing its sex, it must overcome the proximate limitation of lowered physical attractiveness to potential mates. When both sexes select mates partly by the expected quality of parental care, the heightened parental ability of a potential mate should compensate for its lowered physical attractiveness. Indistinguishable individuals may be superior parents and, hence, better mates. Where parental ability is not a criterion of mate choice (as among females of polygynous species), indistinguishability is less likely to be favored.

I have advanced four hypotheses, suitable for within taxon comparisons, regarding the occurrence of sexual indistinguishability in group-living organisms.

1. Populations that breed or feed in groups during the breeding season are more likely to be characterized by sexual indistinguishability than populations that are composed of solitary breeding units.

2. Species that congregate in feeding groups during the breeding season are more likely to

be sexually indistinguishable than organisms that form feeding groups only outside the breeding season, especially when there are no seasonal changes in appearance.

3. Monogamous group-livers are more likely to be indistinguishable than polygamous grouping species.

4. Sexual indistinguishability is more likely to occur in large groups as opposed to small groups.

INDISTINGUISHABILITY AND STATISTICAL DIMORPHISM

Sexual dimorphism can be classified into two types: discontinuous and continuous. Discontinuous dimorphism occurs when morphological traits are confined to one sex as in, for example, the exclusive possession of horns or antlers by males. In continuous dimorphism, the sexes are similar in the traits they possess, but one sex has certain features exaggerated. In some species, for example, both sexes have horns or antlers, but males' antlers tend to be larger (Geist, 1966a and b; Whitehead, 1972). Plumage dimorphisms of many birds fall into this category, with the males tending to be brighter but otherwise similar in appearance.

When sexual dimorphism is discontinuous, all adult conspecifics can be categorized by sex. By contrast, when dimorphism is continuous, several possibilities exist that are best illustrated by example. If, in a species typified by size dimorphism, the range of male size overlaps little with that of females, classification of adults approaches discontinuity. When overlap is somewhat greater, the sexes may still be distinguished, but there is an area of "ambiguity" in which certain individuals could easily belong to either sex. When the size distributions overlap even more, the sex of most individuals is ambiguous. In this last case, phenotypic variability occurs over a trait that has a sex-related component, but an individual's sex cannot be identified by that trait. This condition can be termed "statistical dimorphism." Its significance may be ecological or physiological, but it does not function in sex identification. The phenomenon may be found for various characteristics besides size (e.g., Huxley, 1922).

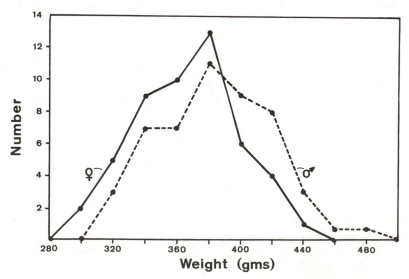

Figure 8–1.   Distribution of weights of 50 male and 50 female pigeons. All birds were non-breeding adults.

Statistical dimorphism is worth noting here because all species can probably be shown to be "dimorphic" in some respect if measured carefully enough. For example, Ingolfsson (1969) examined several species of gulls to determine if sexual dimorphism in size occurs. Measurements taken included culmen length, bill depth, tarsus length, wing length, tail length, and body weight. On most variables, males were somewhat larger, averaging about 102 per cent (tarsus length) to 107 per cent (body weight) the size of females. On wing and tail measurements, males were slightly smaller (about 98 per cent female size). Ingolfsson did note that "the sexes of gulls are indistinguishable in the field;" nevertheless, he concluded that "in gulls sexual dimorphism in size is marked." Furthermore, lacking evidence suggesting sexual specialization on food sources, Ingolfsson ascribed the function of this dimorphism to sex recognition or territorial defense. The problem of how birds detect such small differences was not considered. *Although gulls may be capable of detecting these size variations, we should not assume a priori either that they lack or possess the ability to do so. An equally important question is why species should resort to such distinctions (if they do so) for the purpose of identifying the sexes.* That is, why rely on continuously varying, probabilistic properties for sexual identification, when there is a large set of simple, discontinuous traits (such as eye or leg color) that could have evolved for the same purpose?

SEXUAL INDISTINGUISHABILITY IN PIGEONS

I have undertaken a preliminary study of dimorphism and sex recognition in feral pigeons, *Columba livia*. In many species of pigeons and doves, the sexes are similar in appearance. In *Columba livia,* as among many congeners, males tend to be slightly larger and have more iridescence in their feathers (Levi, 1967; Goodwin, 1970). Although some pigeon fanciers use size as an index of sex, it is not clear that either size or plumage iridescence is a valid indication of the sex of pigeons.

Weight is one index of body size. Although male pigeons are, on average, heavier than females, weight is a quite poor discriminator of sex (Figure 8–1). Among one hundred captive, non-breeding pigeons weighed during one week in November 1976, in Austin, Texas, mean male weight was 379 g, and mean female weight was 361 g. The distribution of weights indicates that throughout most of the size range (320–420 g), an individual might well belong to either sex. Ambiguity is increased because feathers conceal actual body contours. My discrimination threshold for assessing relative weight among Texas pigeons was 35–40 g (Burley, unpublished data).

Obtaining an objective measure of the amount of iridescence is more difficult. When study skins are separated by sex, males generally appear to have somewhat more iridescence. My finding thus concurs with Goodwin (1970). Attempts to classify skins according to sex based on iridescence failed, however, when the exact sex composition of the group of skins was not known *prior* to sorting.

In summary, size and iridescence appear to be inadequate for sex identification, at least by humans. Possibly pigeons could ascertain sex by combining information regarding both traits. However, both are quite affected by behavior. By erecting feathers, individuals increase apparent size and, often, apparent iridescence. By changes in behavior, then, individuals probably affect perception by other birds of their sexual identity.

Of course, if pigeons always acted in sex-specific ways, then their lack of unambiguous morphological identifiers would be trivial. But this is not the case: Many behaviors appear sexually neutral, and even among those that are sex related, there appear to be few restrictions on sexual expression. Females often behave in ways considered typical of males and vice versa (Whitman, 1919; Bennet, 1939; Levi, 1967). Females even initiate courtship in the "male" manner (Burley, 1977a). Such reversals in sexual behavior have been reported elsewhere (Morris, 1952; 1954).

The important question, of course, is whether pigeons can sex conspecifics on sight. Because pigeons, like other birds, appear to know individuals with which they associate closely (Burley, 1977a; Skutch, 1976), one must examine the behavior of birds that are reacting to unknown conspecifics. To determine whether pigeons recognize conspecifics based on appearance alone, I introduced pigeons whose sexes I had previously ascertained through extensive observation, one at a time, into large pens (2.2 x 3.5 x 2.2 m³ or larger) containing from five to nine individuals of one sex and monitored the response of the birds to the stimulus bird for a period of four minutes. Those in the unisexual pens were adults that had been isolated from mates for periods of six weeks to three months. Stimulus birds were either novel (''unknown'') to all or had had extensive prior experience with the majority of individuals in the pen. Prior experience consisted of (1) having been housed together in small groups (12–16 individuals) for an interval of four weeks or longer *or* (2) having been housed together in large groups (60 or more) and having had contiguous nest boxes for six weeks or longer. Breeding pigeons interact frequently with nesting neighbors. Birds with prior experience together are termed ''known'' here. Prior to experimentation ''known'' stimulus birds were separated from test subjects for at least four weeks. Most of the stimulus birds were feral pigeons, but several large French mondains were also used. Prior to the experiments, mondains and ferals were acclimated to each other by housing them together for a month or more. The mondains used in the experiments were housed with birds other than those in the unisexual pens.

Results were classified into four categories. When stimulus birds were placed in the pen, the residents sometimes continued their current activities (e.g., feeding, sunning), paying little or no overt attention to the stimulus bird. This behavior was scored as ''no response.'' The other possibilities were to court the new individual, to behave aggressively, or to retreat from the stimulus bird, often shaking or trembling. During an experiment all birds in a pen were observed at least part of the time. Behaviors were recorded with a tape recorder. Although some behaviors were undoubtedly overlooked, the scoring procedure minimizes the impact of missed behaviors.

Behaviors were scored somewhat differently for males and females. For males, the predominant group activity was scored as the response. For females the predominant activity was always to ''ignore'' the stimulus bird or, at most, to become alert to its presence. In any given case, only a few females might court or act aggressively. For the females, therefore, ''no response'' was scored only if no females reacted to the stimulus bird. Because courtship would seem to be the most sex-specific form of behavior, I have compared each sex's tendency to court stimulus individuals with their tendencies to react in other ways.

Males tended to court females known to them and individuals of either sex not known to them, but they reacted in other ways to males known to them. Except for large pigeons, unknown birds were treated alike regardless of sex (Fisher Exact Test, one-tailed *p, ns;* Table 8–1). Unknowns were not treated differently than known females, but behavior toward known males was significantly different from that toward unknown birds (F.E.T. one-tailed $p < .001$). It appears then, that males cannot assess the sex of unknown individuals, because they treat them all like females. Finally, males generally withdrew from French mondains (Table 8–1).

Females did not behave significantly differently toward any stimulus set (Table 8–1). Occasionally they initiated courtship with known males. One complication is that stimulus males sometimes initiated courtship after only several minutes in the female pen. Because females did not appear to react differentially to known individuals of either sex, it is impossible to interpret whether they can distinguish sexes. Finally, females reacted toward French mondains the same way they treated others. This difference in response of males and females to large birds suggests that males may expect large conspecifics to be males and withdraw because of their own probable inferior competitive ability in encounters.

The behavior of pigeons suggests questions concerning appropriate behavior in interactions with other birds. Under what circumstances should a bird reveal its sex when joining a flock? When should a bird in a familiar area reveal its sex to unknown conspecifics? Would appropriate behaviors be different depending upon whether an individual was alone or in a group?

Why do males routinely treat unknown conspecifics as if they were females? There are several possibilities. Unmated males might gain by advertising their sex and interesting all possible conspecifics. But mated males also court unknown conspecifics, so this cannot be a complete answer. Perhaps all males court to copulate outside their pair bonds. Though this occurs among pigeons, copulation between two birds unknown to each other appears rare (Burley, unpub. data). Male behavior may function to determine the sex of unknown conspecifics by gauging their response to courtship. If this is the case, why not treat some individuals as males, others as females?

A fruitful approach to these questions might consider an individual's options in response to a variety of situations and examine the consequences of its actions. Morphological ambiguity provides the potential for individuals to engage in intra-specific deceit of two forms: withholding sexual identity and misleading others as to one's identity (Otte, 1974). The propensity of sexually indistinguishable organisms to engage in such behaviors may be expected to vary with individual circumstances and environmental conditions.

INDISTINGUISHABILITY IN MONOGAMOUS BIRDS

I have undertaken a preliminary test of the hypothesis that monogamous, social organisms are more likely to be sexually indistinguishable than monogamous, solitary species (Hypothesis 1). Birds were used for two reasons: they have been well described, and their sensory modalities are similar to humans', thus minimizing classification errors. Two types of data were collected on a range of avian species: first, species were categorized as being indistinguishable, barely distinguishable, or easily distinguishable by sex; second, information about the social organization of each species was collected.

Selection of species was based primarily on accessibility of published descriptions. Species were considered "barely distinguishable" when subtle differences between the

Table 8–1.   Reaction of pigeons to introduced conspecifics.

A. Male behavior towards conspecifics.

Type of conspecific	"Ignore"	Court	Aggression	Withdrawal, trembling
"known male"	10	3	3	0
"known female"	0	15	1	0
unknown individual	1	15	2	0
(male)	(0)	(7)	(1)	(0)
(female)	(1)	(8)	(1)	(0)
large individual (unknown)	4	1	0	11

B. Female behavior towards conspecifics.

Type of conspecific	"Ignore"	Court	Aggression	Withdrawal, trembling
"known male"	11	4	1	0
"known female"	9	0	2	0
unknown individual	12	1	1	0
(male)	(7)	(1)	(1)	(0)
(female)	(5)	(0)	(0)	(0)
large individual (unknown)	13	1	0	0

sexes such as iris color occurred regularly. Where doubt remained regarding the status of a species, museum specimens were examined or the species was deleted from consideration. A large number of species, particularly those indistinguishable and barely distinguishable, was eliminated from consideration because of inability to categorize them.

Museum classification involved compilation of a list of "ambiguous" species and the checking of this list against specimens. Ambiguous species were dropped from further consideration when fewer than 12 specimens were available. Where subspecific variability was apparent, each locality was considered separately. Skins were segregated into two piles based on appearance, and then labels were checked to ascertain sex. No consistent morphological characteristic was evaluated; skins were sorted for any trait that appeared variable. A species was classified distinguishable when 90 per cent or more of the skins could be sexed by any trait; barely distinguishable when accuracy was 80–89 per cent; and indistinguishable when accuracy fell below 80 per cent. In a few species almost all skins were male, and the species was eliminated from consideration. Less than 15 per cent of the species reported here were categorized by museum specimens.

After data were collected on appearance, social organization was categorized. This order of data gathering was maintained to avoid influencing the subjective measure of species appearance. Barely distinguishable species were omitted from data analysis for two reasons: There was no hypothesis concerning the functional significance of being "barely distinguishable", and judgments made in assigning species to this group seemed error prone. Therefore, I restricted comparison to the tendency of indistinguishable and distinguishable species to be colonial breeders and/or associate in feeding flocks larger than family groups versus their tendency to be territorial or solitary during the breeding season.

Of more than 400 species examined, 151 species from 12 families were scored on appearance and social structure. Fifty-two species were classified as sexually indistinguishable, 32 as barely distinguishable, and 67 as distinguishable (Table 8–2). Of the 52 indistinguishable species, 47 were colonial breeders and/or flock feeders during the breeding season. Of the 67 clearly dimorphic species, 64 were territorial or solitary. This difference is highly significant ($x^2 = 88.69$; $p < .001$) and supports the hypothesis that grouping species tend more toward indistinguishability.

INDISTINGUISHABILITY AND PREDATION

A topic that I have largely ignored is the possible role of predation in the evolution of indistinguishability. The tendency to flock is often a response to predation pressure (Lack, 1954; Buskirk, 1976). Does the same pressure result in lack of morphological distinctions between the sexes?

I believe that this is an unlikely possibility. Predator pressure on groups operates by selecting for conformity to species-typical appearance. Predators can spot unusual individuals, follow them through crowds, and track them down. However, when two phenotypes are present in a flock in approximately equal proportions, neither phenotype is unusual, and predators are unlikely to be able to follow individuals. Sexual dimorphism per se should not help predators spot potential victims in flocks.

A second attribute often resulting from selection imposed by predation is that of crypsis. Females of many non-monogamous species, and numerous non-social monogamous species appear to be more cryptically attired than males. If males face intense predator pressure, could that not force them into the female appearance?

Again I think that the answer is largely negative. Flocks, after all, are probably not particularly cryptic. Of course, even social animals do not always associate in groups; a lone male (or one in a small group) might well be more vulnerable than a lone female. But it is short-sighted to assume that if males look different from females, they are necessarily less cryptic. There must be many morphological adaptations open to males that would make them unambiguously identifiable as to sex without exposing them to greater risk of preda-

Table 8–2.   Appearances of monogamous birds of known social organization.
I = indistinguishable; BD = barely distinguishable; D = dimorphic.

Avian Family	Appearance			Social Organization	References
	I	BD	D	(All monogamous)	
Antshrikes (Formicariidae)			4	Solitary	Skutch, 1967
Cotingas (Cotingidae)		1	3	solitary, tree-hole nesters	Skutch, 1967 Wetmore, 1964
Finches (Fringillidae)			15	All territorial during breeding; many flock during winter	Wetmore, 1964
		1		solitary (territorial) during breeding season; large flocks in winter	Bent, 1968
	2			colonial breeder; other associates in feeding flocks during breeding season	
Finches (Estrildidae)			4	3 spp. territorial during breeding season (one flocks out of breeding season) 1 sp. forms large flocks during breeding season and is colonial breeder.	Immelmann, 1967
		6		5 spp. solitary in breeding season (3 form large flocks out of breeding season). 1 sp. colonial breeder.	
	7			6 spp. colonial breeders, always associate in flocks; 1 usually seen in small groups.	
Gulls (Laridae)	9			All colonial breeders; some flock on water	Dwight, 1925; Wetmore, 1964; Vaughan, 1972
Parrots (Cacatuidae)			3	Solitary breeders, 2 species feed in small flocks	
		5		1 sp. solitary breeder; 4 spp. found in small groups. Sometimes form large flocks out of breeding season.	Forshaw, 1969; 1978
	2			1 sp. forms large feeding and roosting flocks during breeding season; other is solitary.	
Parrots (Loridae)		3		1 sp. solitary breeder; 1 sp. forms small feeding flocks; 1 sp. feeds in flocks.	Forshaw, 1969, 1978
	4			1 sp. colonial breeder and flock feeder; 2 spp. feed and roost in flocks; 1 sp. forms small groups.	
Parrots (Psittacidae)			26	Solitary breeders; 8 spp. form small flocks out of breeding season.	Dilger, 1960; Forshaw, 1969; 1978
		8		7 spp. solitary breeders; 4 spp. form large flocks out of breeding season; 1 sp. colonial breeder and flock feeder	
	7			4 spp. colonial breeders; 3 feed in flocks.	

Table 8–2.   Continued.

Avian Family	Appearance			Social Organization	References
	I	BD	D	(All monogamous)	
Penguins (Spheniscidae)	9	1		all colonial breeders	Richdale, 1951; Wing, 1956; Welty, 1962
Pigeons (Columbidae)			3	2 spp. colonial breeders and flock feeders; 1 sp. solitary	
		6		4 spp. solitary; 1 sp. forms feeding flocks; 1 sp. forms roosting flocks.	Goodwin, 1970
	15			5 spp. colonial breeders; 8 spp. form feeding flocks; 1 sp. forms roosting flocks; 1 sp. solitary.	
Swallows (Hirundinidae)	6	1		colonial breeder	Wetmore, 1964; Bent, 1942
				5 spp. colonial breeders and flock feeders; 1 sp. solitary.	
Woodpeckers (Picidae)	1		10	Solitary hole nesters	Wetmore, 1964; Lawrence, 1967
				colonial breeder	

tion. For example, clear but subtle ventral markings, such as throat color, breast spotting, and leg color differences in birds would be lost on aerial predators but could be obvious to nearby conspecifics. Thus predator pressure could simultaneously favor the evolution of a flocking tendency and less conspicuous but unambiguous dimorphisms if such were advantageous to their bearers. That such unambiguous markings appear to be lacking in so many social bird species strongly suggests that selection pressures are acting against sex recognition per se and not primarily favoring crypsis.

Earlier I mentioned that predation might accelerate the rate of evolution of sexual indistinguishability in populations in which some individuals were indistinguishable. This occurs because predation merely amplifies the benefits of being indistinguishable. Once sexually distinguishable individuals become rare, predators may be able to cue in on them (if their dimorphisms are not subtle) and, if so, will eliminate them at an ever-increasing rate as their frequency declines.

OPPORTUNISTIC BREEDERS

In this study group-living monogamous birds that are nomadic and breed opportunistically tended to be dimorphic in spite of their social tendency. Species included here (Table 8–2) that fall into this category are the zebra finch (*Poephila guttata*), the flock pigeon (*Phaps histrionica*), and the passenger pigeon (*Ectopistes migratorius*—extinct). These three species account for the entire class of dimorphic flockers. A likely explanation for this phenomenon is that it allows for rapid pair formation and breeding in unpredictable environments (Goodwin, 1960). The rapidity with which zebra finches, for example, breed under favorable conditions is well known (Serventy, 1971). Out of the breeding season, males of these species do not lose their dimorphic plumage; this may also be related to the unpredictability of subsequent favorable periods.

At least one nomadic, opportunistic breeder has evolved seasonal dimorphism. The budgerigar (*Melopsittacus undulatus*—included as barely distinguishable in Table 8–2), nomadic over much of arid Australia, appears indistinguishable out of the breeding season, but females' ceres change from blue to dull red prior to reproduction. This type of seasonal dimorphism is similar to that employed by many fish; it is undoubtedly more rapid and less expensive than molting feathers. One wonders why more birds have not evolved similar adaptations.

INDISTINGUISHABILITY AND TERRITORIALITY

Wolf (1969), noting the occurrence of monomorphism in one species of the typically dimorphic hummingbirds, suggested that monomorphism evolved because male plumage improved female ability to defend territorities. Such benefit would presumably occur in species in which females are normally smaller and weaker, because male plumage may allow females to "bluff" about their defense capabilities. Similar tendencies have been noticed elsewhere (e.g., Lack, cited in Huxley, 1934; Eibl-Eibesfeldt, 1966; Wolf, 1975; Rohwer and Niles, 1977).

This topic is mentioned here because of the paucity of possible examples uncovered in this analysis (Table 8–2). The few territorial indistinguishable species (5 out of 69) may fit such a designation, but the frequency may underrepresent the occurrence of the phenomenon among birds, because only monogamous birds are considered, and the dimorphic species listed tend to be holenesters. Nest defense may be less of a problem among holenesting birds (Lack, 1968), so females may not benefit from appearing to be males (but see Rohwer and Niles, 1977).

SEASONAL MONOMORPHISM AND SEXUAL INDISTINGUISHABILITY

Many temperate bird species that are territorial during the breeding season form large, sometimes multi-species, flocks in the non-breeding season. Populations tend to be dimorphic during the breeding season but monomorphic, possibly indistinguishable, outside the reproductive period. Typically this involves males losing their brighter coloration and taking on "female" appearance (Moynihan, 1958; Hamilton and Barth, 1962; in some species both sexes have breeding and non-breeding plumages, e.g., Salomonsen, 1939).

Two hypotheses have been advanced to explain seasonal monomorphism. One is that conspicuous plumage, of no reproductive advantage when not breeding, attracts predators. If the energetic cost of two molts per year is more than compensated for by lessened risks of predation, two molts would be favored. The second hypothesis states that males lose dimorphic plumage out of the breeding season because it lessens their competition within the flock (Hamilton and Barth, 1962).

In species that are responding to predation pressure, indistinguishability in the non-breeding season may arise through evolutionary conservatism rather than through specific adaptation. Although there may be no reason for males to assume an explicitly female garb, neither is there any reason for them to evolve a particular male winter plumage. As a result, they may simply switch back to an evolutionarily conservative appearance, that characterized by females (and likely similar to juveniles) of their species. In this case monomorphism and indistinguishability are functionally equivalent.

When overwinter survivorship is low, the possible benefits to males in flocks from competing out of the breeding interval appear minimal. Competition probably increases the risk of mortality more than it increases reproductive value, because individuals are not competing for reproductive resources. In these circumstances a likely superior tactic for all individuals is to concentrate on maintenance activities that improve survival chances; it may also be more advantageous to retreat from aggressive advances rather than retaliate. As a result, lack of male competition could evolve without the necessity, associated with seasonal indistinguishability, of incurring two plumage molts per breeding season.

Rohwer (1975) also advanced an hypothesis for plumage types of overwintering birds based on competition within flocks, but his idea related to competition for immediate resources such as food rather than for mates. He hypothesized that individual variability in overwintering plumage evolved to signal the competitive abilities of individuals. He found, for a sample of 29 species, that winter-flocking birds (which compete directly for food) were more likely to show plumage variability than winter-territorial birds (which compete indirectly for resources by defending territories). He predicted that advertisement of status in a flock would lower interference competition, because direct conflict would be limited to individuals of similar competitive ability (also see Geist, 1966b). Sexual identification would be the necessary outcome of this hypothesis only if individuals of one sex were routinely superior competitors for food.

Rohwer examined conflict patterns in overwintering Harris sparrows, (*Zonotrichia guerula*), which display continuous variation in ventral plumage patterns. He found that birds with more black were competitively superior (''studlier''), and although there was some sexual trend in studliness, there was considerable overlap in the appearances of the sexes. Contrary to expectation, Rohwer found that dominance interactions were despotic: High-ranking individuals aim aggression against inferiors rather than against those of equal rank. This is indirect evidence against Hamilton and Barth's hypothesis that plumages converge to lower male–male aggression. If males were to engage in intrasexual rivalry, strong competition should have been evidenced among the blackest individuals, which tended to be males. Rohwer concluded that the function of the despotic activity was the lowering of competition for food through the death of conspecifics. This form of competition has no sex restriction; however, it is reasonable to question what prevents all individuals from assuming a very black winter plumage. Subsequent experiments by Rohwer (1977) indicated that artifically dyed ''studly'' birds are persecuted by true dominants, suggesting that the possibility for deceit is limited.

SUMMARY

Sexual indistinguishability is the absence of sex-specific, external, continuously displayed characteristics in some stage of the life cycle of a species. Monomorphic species may be either distinguishable or indistinguishable.

Indistinguishability evidently does not result passively from the absence of factors favoring dimorphism; instead it seems to occur in spite of such variables and to evolve within dimorphic populations. Factors that promote dimorphism occur in all sexual species; they include fundamental differences between the sexes and different extraspecific selection pressures. Indistinguishability is advantageous to individuals in certain circumstances that favor concealing one's sex.

Continuous sexual dimorphism exists when the two sexes bear the same morphological traits but vary in the degree of expression of traits. Discontinuous dimorphism exists when one sex bears a trait not displayed by the other. Statistical dimorphism occurs in cases of continuous dimorphism in which individuals are nevertheless unable to determine the sex of conspecifics.

One circumstance in which indistinguishability may evolve is found in monogamous, social organisms, where strong sexual competition may persist throughout the breeding season because of the close proximity of neighbors. This competition is an effect of aggregating rather than a function of it and, hence, disadvantageous to at least some individuals in the group. Individuals (of one or both sexes) whose sex is ambiguous may avoid sexual competition (when it is to their benefit to do so) more than those who continuously advertise their sex. This allows them to avoid predators more effectively and to harness energy needed for reproduction more efficiently. As a result, indistinguishable individuals may be superior mates; individuals of one or both sexes may evolve preferences for indistinguishable mates in response to their greater parental ability. Once the indistinguishable trait has become established in a population, its frequency may increase at least in part through the joint effects of predation on unusual phenotypes and the disadvantages of advertising one's sex when others in the population are concealing theirs. Because the benefits of sexual ambiguity are probably greater for males than for females in most circumstances, indistinguishability may often evolve by convergence of the male phenotype onto that of the female rather than by the convergence of the two onto a neutral intermediate.

An hypothesis deduced from this reasoning is that monogamous social organisms are more likely to be indistinguishable than those that are monogamous and solitary. Results of a test of this hypothesis are presented for species from 12 avian families. Using a criterion of distinguishability based on human ability to detect sex differences, data support the prediction that social species are more often indistinguishable. Exceptions are found among opportunistic breeders.

Tests of indistinguishability should ascertain whether species can determine sexes based on appearance alone. Experiments on *Columba livia*, the common pigeon, suggest that individuals rely on behavioral cues elicited over a period of time to establish sex and cannot assess the sex of an unknown conspecific. Two forms of dimorphism that humans sometimes use to ''determine'' sex in pigeons appear statistical in nature: size differences (males are larger) and plumage iridescence patterns (males are brighter).

Morphological indistinguisability increases an individual's functional behavioral repertoire: Under appropriate circumstances, it can reveal, conceal, or mislead others about its sex. Because of previous inattention to the distinction between monomorphism and indistinguishability, it is not presently possible to estimate how widespread a phenomenon it is. However, there may be a large number of circumstances in which it is advantageous for an individual to conceal or disguise its sexual identity, in which indistinguishability may evolve.

ACKNOWLEDGMENTS

My interest in this topic was stimulated through discussions with Daniel Otte, who provided ideas and encouragement throughout the development of this paper. Richard Alexander brought to my attention the possibility that predator pressure could cause the extinction of dimorphic characteristics in populations already partially composed of indistinguishable individuals. Richard Symanski's thoughtful criticism improved the manuscript in innumerable ways.

Behavior experiments were performed at the Brackenridge Field Laboratory of the University of Texas at Austin. The Academy of Natural Sciences, Philadelphia, Pennsylvania, provided access to the museum specimens examined in this study. This research was supported by a grant from the National Science Foundation.

REFERENCES

Bastock, M. 1967. The physiology of courtship and mating behavior. *Advances in Reproductive Physiology* 2: 9–52.
Bateman, A. J. 1948. Intrasexual selection in *Drosophila*. *Heredity* 2: 349–368.
Bennet, M. A. 1939. The social hierarchy in ring doves. *Ecology* 20: 337–357.
Bent, A. C. 1942. *Life Histories of North American Flycatchers, Larks, Swallows and their Allies*. Government Printing Office, Washington. D.C.

_____. 1968. *Life Histories of North American Cardinals, Grosbeaks, Buntings, Towhees, Finches, Sparrows and Allies*. Dover Publications, Inc., New York.

Bertram, B. C. R. 1970. The vocal behaviour of the Indian hill mynah, *Gracula religiosa*. *Animal Behaviour Monographs* 3: 79–192.

Burley, N. 1977a. Mate Choice and Sexual Selection in the Pigeon, *Columba livia*. Unpublished PhD thesis, University of Texas at Austin.

_____. 1977b. Parental investment, mate choice, and mate quality. *Proc. Natl. Acad. Sci.* 74: 3476–3479.

_____. 1980. Clutch overlap and clutch size: alternative and complementary reproductive tactics. *American Naturalist,* 115:223–246.

Buskirk, W. H. 1976. Social systems in a tropical forest avifauna. *American Naturalist* 110: 293–310.

Choat, J. H. and D. R. Robertson. 1975. Protogynous hermaphroditism in fishes of the family Scaridae. Pp. 263–283 in *Intersexuality in the Animal Kingdom,* R. Reinboth, ed. Springer-Verlag, N.Y.

Craig, W. 1909. The expression of emotion in the pigeons. *Jour. Comp. Neur. Psychol.* 19: 29–80.

Dilger, W. C. 1960. The comparative ethology of African parrot genus *Agapornis*. *Z. Tierpsychol.* 17: 649–685.

Dwight, J. 1925. The gulls (*Laridae*) of the world: their plumages, moults, variations, relationships, and distribution. *Amer. Mus. Nat. Hist. Bull.* 52: 63–402.

Eibl-Eibesfeldt, I. 1966. Das Verteidigen der Erablageplatze bei der Hood-Meerechse. *Zeitschrift für Tierpsychol.* 23: 627–631.

Fisher, R. A. 1930. *The Genetical Theory of Natural Selection*. Clarendon Press, Oxford.

Forshaw, J. M. 1969. *Australian Parrots*. Livingston Publishing Co., Wynnewood, Pa.

_____. 1978. *Parrots of the World*. TFH Publications, Neptune, N.J.

Geist, V. 1966a. Evolution of horn-like organs. *Behaviour* 27: 175–214.

_____. 1966b. The evolutionary significance of mountain sheep horns. *Evolution* 20: 558–566.

Goodwin, D. 1960. Sexual dimorphism in pigeons. *Bull. Brit. Ornith Club* 80:45–52.

_____. 1970. *Pigeons and Doves of the World*. 2nd edition. Trustees of the British Museum of Natural History, London.

Hamilton, T. H. 1961. On the functions and causes of sexual dimorphism in breeding plumage characters of North American species of warblers and orioles. *Amer. Natur.* 95: 121–123.

_____, and R. H. Barth. 1962. The biological significance of seasonal change in male plumage appearance in some New World migratory bird species. *Amer. Natur.* 96: 129–143.

Huxley, J. S. 1922. Preferential mating in birds with similar coloration in both sexes. *British Birds* 16: 99–101.

_____. 1934. Threat and warning coloration in birds. *Proceedings of the Eighth International Ornithological Congress:* 430–455.

Immelmann, K. 1967. *Australian Finches in Bush and Aviary*. Angus and Robertson, Sydney.

Ingolfsson, A. 1969. Sexual dimorphism of large gulls. *Auk* 86: 732–737.

Jehl, J. R. 1970. Sexual selection for size differences in two species of sandpipers. *Evolution* 24: 311–319.

Krebs, J. R. 1971. Territory and breeding density in the great tit, *Parus major*. L. *Ecology* 52: 2–22.

_____. 1974. Colonial nesting and social feeding as strategies for exploiting food resources in the great blue heron (*Ardea herodias*). *Behaviour* 51: 99–131.

Lack, D. 1940. Pair-formation in birds. *Condor* 42: 269–286.

_____. 1946. *The Life of the Robin*. H.F. and G. Witherby, Ltd. London.

_____. 1954. *The Natural Regulation of Animal Numbers*. Clarendon Press, Oxford.

_____. 1968. *Ecological Adaptations for Breeding in Birds*. Methuen, London.

Lawrence, L. de K. 1967. A comparative study of four species of woodpeckers. *Ornithological Monographs* 5: 1–156.

Levi, W. M. 1967. *The Pigeon*. Printed by R. L. Bryan Co., Columbia, S.C.

Lewis, D. M. 1972. Importance of face mask in sexual recognition and territorial behavior in the yellowthroat. *Jack Pine Warbler* 50: 98–109.

Marler, P. 1955. Studies of fighting in chaffinches (2). The effect on dominance relations of disguising females and males. *Brit. J. Anim. Behav.* 3: 137–146.

Maynard Smith, J., and G. R. Price. 1973. The logic of animal conflict. *Nature* 246: 15–18.

Morris, D. 1952. Homosexuality in the ten-spined stickleback (*Pygosteus pungitius* L). *Behaviour* 4: 233–261.

――――. 1954. The reproductive behavior of the zebra finch *(Poephila guttata)*, with special reference to pseudofemale behaviour and displacement activities. *Behaviour* 6: 271–322.

Mottram, J. C. 1915. The distribution of secondary sexual characteristics amongst birds, with relation to their liability to the attack of enemies. *Proc. Soc. London* 1915: 663–679.

Moynihan, M. 1958. Some adaptations which help to promote gregariousness. *Proc. 13th Internat. Ornith. Cong.*: 523–541.

Noble, G. K. 1936. Courtship and sexual selection in the flicker *(Colaptes auratus luteus)*. *Auk* 53: 269–282.

――――, and W. Vogt. 1935. An experimental study of sex recognition in birds. *Auk* 52: 278–286.

Otte, D. 1974. Effects and functions in the evolution of signalling systems. *Ann. Rev. Ecol. Syst.* 5: 385–417.

Rand, A. L. 1952. Secondary sexual characters and ecological competition. *Fieldiana (Zoology)* 34: 65–70.

Richdale, L. E. 1951. *Sexual Behavior in Penguins*. Kansas University Press, Lawrence.

Rohwer, S. 1975. The social significance of avian winter plumage variability. *Evolution* 29:' 593–610.

――――. 1977. Status signaling in Harris sparrows: some experiments in deception. *Behaviour* 61:107–129.

――――, and D. M. Niles. 1977. An historical analysis of spring arrival times in purple martins: a test of two hypotheses. *Bird Banding* 48: 162–167.

Salomonsen, F. 1939. *Moult Sequence of Plumages in the Rock Ptarmigan*. P. Haase and Son, Copenhagen.

Schoener, T. W. 1967. The ecological significance of sexual dimorphism in size in the lizard *Anolis conspersus*. *Science* 155: 474–477.

――――. 1968. The *Anolis* lizards of Bimini: resource partitioning in a complex fauna. *Ecology* 49: 704–726.

Selander, R. K. 1966. Sexual dimorphism and differential niche utilization in birds. *Condor* 68: 113–151.

――――. 1972. Sexual selection and dimorphism in birds. Pp. 180–230 in *Sexual Selection and the Descent of Man, 1871–1971*, B. Campbell, ed. Aldine Publishing Co., Chicago.

Serventy, D. L. 1971. Biology of desert birds. In *Avian Biology,* D. S. Farner and J. R. King, eds. Academic Press, London.

Skutch, A. F. 1967. *Life Histories of Central American Highland Birds*. Nuttall Ornithological Club, Cambridge, Mass.

――――. 1976. *Parent Birds and Their Young*. University of Texas Press, Austin.

Sibley, C. G. 1957. The evolutionary and taxonomic significance of sexual dimorphism and hybridization in birds. *Condor* 59: 166–191.

Smith, D. G. 1972. The role of the epaulets in the red-winged blackbird *(Agelaius phoeniceus)* social system. *Behaviour* 41: 251–268.

Tinbergen, N. 1939. The behavior of the snow bunting in the spring. *Trans. Linnean Soc. New York* 5: 1–94.

Trivers, R. L. 1972. Parental investment and sexual selection. Pp. 136–179 in *Sexual Selection and the Descent of Man 1871–1971*, B. Campbell, ed. Aldine Publishing Co., Chicago.

Vaughan, R. 1972. *Gulls in Britain*. U. F. and G. Witherby Ltd., London.

Welty, J. C. 1962. *The Life of Birds*. W. B. Saunders Co., Philadelphia.

Wetmore, A. 1964. *Song and Garden Birds of North America*. National Geographic Society, Washington, D.C.

Whitehead, G. K. 1972. *Deer of the World*. Constable and Co., London.

Whitman, C. O. 1919. *The Behavior of Pigeons*. Vol. 3 in *The Posthumous Works of C. O. Whitman*, H. A. Carr, ed. Carnegie Institution, Washington, D.C.

Williams, G. C. 1964. Measurement of consociation among fishes and comments on the evolution of schooling. *Mich. State Univ. Misc. Publ. Biol. Serv.* 2: 349–384.

Wing, L. W. 1956. *Natural History of Birds*. Ronald Press. Co., New York.

Wolf, L. L. 1969. Female territoriality in a tropical hummingbird. *Auk* 86: 490–504.

――――. 1975. Female territoriality in the purple-throated carib. *Auk* 92: 511–522.

9.

The Evolution of Leks

Jack W. Bradbury

Lek mating systems are associated with some of the most spectacular patterns of male adornment and display known in animals. The inclusion of at least one lek species in nearly all textbooks on animal behavior and good coverage in popular journals belie the fact that lek mating is a rare alternative to more common male strategies such as resource defense or female defense. On the other hand, a few lek species are present in nearly all higher animal taxa. This persistent and perhaps convergent appearance of leks in most higher groups suggests that there may be basic rules governing lek evolution. I should like to outline here the basic questions which I feel must be answered about lek evolution and suggest some testable answers that were suggested by our recent research on lek behavior in bats.

What is a lek? Throughout this chapter, I shall invoke the following criteria to distinguish ''classical'' lek species from those with alternative mating systems (Bradbury, 1977a):

1. There is no male parental care: Males contribute nothing to the next generation except gametes.

2. There is an arena or lek to which females come and on which most of the mating occurs: An arena is a site on which several males aggregate and that does not fill the habitat normally used by the species for other activities such as feeding, roosting, etc.

3. The display sites of males contain no significant resources required by females except the males themselves. This stipulation includes food, water, roosts, nest sites, egg deposition sites, etc.

4. The female has an opportunity to select a mate once she visits the arena.

These criteria are not arbitrary. They are the minimal set required to separate the forms classically called ''lek species'' from what we now recognize as alternative mating systems. For example, the first criterion excludes certain gulls and storks that exhibit mate choice in arenas (called ''clubs''), show no inclusion of resources in the male display sites, and allow for female choice but in which males later assume significant amounts of parental care. We might expect female mate choice to utilize different criteria depending upon whether a male does or does not participate in parental care (Trivers, 1972). The second criterion excludes species in which males have display territories but in which these territories are not clustered to form an arena. In other words, it excludes species in which male territories *fill* the available habitat. The reasons for this criterion will become apparent below. The third criterion is designed to distinguish between species in which female choice of a mate depends only on characteristics of the male (classical lek species), and those in

which female choice includes some assessment of the real estate that each male is controlling (resource defense). It seems probable that there is a continuum between absolute emphasis on the male and absolute emphasis on his real estate. In frogs and fish, where mating
and egg deposition are often contemporaneous, extreme caution is required before assigning a species to one category or the other. Water is a *required* substrate for mating in many
amphibians and hence all male territories must include access to water. The critical issue,
however, is whether there is variation in the quality of the "water" of each male's territory
and whether females do or do not take this into account in their selection of a mate (cf.
Emlen, 1976; Howard, this volume). The final criterion seeks to exclude those species in
which males aggregate but females are not permitted a choice of mate. Mating swarms in
which females seem to have little choice are common in flying insects (Downes, 1969) and
may occur in some mammals (Bradbury, 1977b; R. Payne, personal communication). As
with the prior criteria, there is potentially a continuous gradient in the degree to which a
female can make a choice among a set of males. I have taken the extreme condition in my
definition for classical leks.

The use of these criteria is clearly difficult in a number of cases. I personally do not
think this detracts from the usefulness of making an explicit definition. On the contrary, a
model of lek evolution that incorporates these criteria should be sufficiently broad to identify the intermediate forms and predict when they should evolve. It is often the case that the
mating systems intermediate between two extremes are the best tests for such models. As a
case in point, I would like to turn to "exploded leks." It has become increasingly apparent
that the degree of male clustering in various lek species is highly variable. In groups such as
grouse or the birds-of-paradise, there is a continuum from uniform fields of males on contiguous territories through an intermediate dispersion in which males have somewhat
smaller territories and show a slight clustering to the highly aggregated territories and large
inter-arena distances of classical lek forms (Gilliard, 1969; Hjorth, 1970; Wiley, 1974).
(See Figure 9–1.) The intermediate forms have been called "exploded leks" or "quasi-
leks" because males are often just barely within sight or hearing of each other and the clustering is only apparent as a result of careful mapping. Instead of an oddity, the exploded lek
dispersion is actually quite common in most taxonomic groups that also contain classical
lek species. In the birds-of-paradise, it is more common than the classical lek dispersion (cf.
Gilliard, 1969). These prevalent patterns suggest that models of lek evolution should ex-

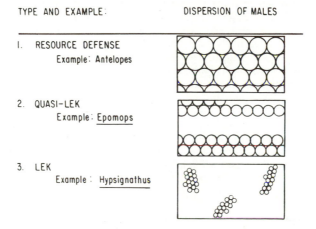

Figure 9–1.   The "continuum" of male dispersion patterns, ranging from a uniform field of males
defending resources (top), through a partially clustered exploded or quasi-lek pattern (center), to the
highly clustered dispersions of classical leks (bottom).

plain *both* (a) why males are clustered on arenas instead of forming uniform fields of territories over resources (a common alternative found in species related to classical lek species), and (b) what determines the degree of clustering as measured by male territory size, number of males per arena, and the distance between arenas. That this gradient of male dispersion exists is probably accepted knowledge on the part of all biologists who have worked with lek species; that it needs to be explained quantitatively seems generally to have gone unnoticed.

In the following pages, I shall examine several current models for lek evolution. In a number of these, conditions for the evolution of leks have been identified, but the question of necessity vs. sufficiency for these conditions has not been assessed. In others, recent comparative studies have suggested that proposed conditions have too little generality to explain lek evolution in different taxa. Finally, I shall add some new conditions and attempt to show how they can be invoked to explain the actual dispersion of males in a quantitative manner.

I.   PRIOR MODELS OF LEK EVOLUTION.

Among the more widely invoked factors leading to leks is the emancipation of males from parental duties (Snow, 1963). Clearly, this is a necessary condition since the time, energy, and morphological structures committed by lek males to attracting females are incompatible with shared parental duties at vulnerable nests. The preoccupation with this factor in previous lek studies is presumably a reflection of the heavy emphasis on lek behavior in birds. In birds, male parental care is the rule and the conditions that favor male emancipation are clearly critical to the evolution of avian leks (Lack, 1968). Paternal care is much less common in other taxa such as mammals and insects, and at least in my reading of the literature, this has not led to a greater occurrence of leks than is found among the birds. In short, it seems clear that while male emancipation is a necessary condition for lek evolution, it is not a sufficient condition.

A second condition that is often suggested for lek evolution is that clusters of males are more ''stimulating'' to females than solitary males and, hence, males gain by clustering. If by more ''stimulating,'' the reference is to greater neural and hormonal excitation of the female, no real solution has been advanced as these proximate mechanisms have themselves been shaped by evolution to insure that females favor clusters over solitary males (Alexander, 1975; Otte, 1974). Alternatively, greater stimulation may be interpreted to mean that more females are likely to be contacted and visit a cluster than would visit a solitary male. For there to be an adaptive advantage for the males, it must be the case that more females *per male* visit clusters than would visit a solitary male (Snow, 1963). There are two ways this could be achieved. In the ''duty-cycle model,'' each male added would increase the fraction of time that signals are being emitted and this would increase the probability that any given female would detect the signals from the aggregation. In the ''active-space model,'' each male added would increase the maximum range that the signals would be detectable and, thus, would increase the number of females that could be potentially drawn to the aggregation. I would like to argue that neither model is likely to attract more females per male than would solitary males *unless,* for other reasons, females have a preference for clusters over dispersed males. That is, there are no direct geometrical or temporal benefits to males of clustering.

Turning first to the duty-cycle model, imagine the best of all possible worlds in which each male added to an aggregation was able to select the phasing of its signal relative to the others currently present. If each male avoided any overlap with others currently displaying, the duty cycle would increase linearly with each male added. Since the probability that a female would encounter a signal is most likely a linear function of the duty cycle, each male added will increase the probability of attracting a given female by an equal increment. Thus with complete facultative manipulation of phasing, the number of females attracted would increase linearly with each male added and there would be no benefit, on a per male basis, over the solitary case. Any other pattern of synchronization (or asynchronization), would result in a slower rise in the probability of attracting females with cluster size and would, thus, be *worse* than the solitary case. By whatever means the increase in the duty cycle is brought about, it will eventually reach 100 per cent, at which point adding further males *decreases* mean male fitness. These considerations, the observations that lek sizes are often much larger than necessary to maximize duty cycles (e.g., Bradbury, 1977a), and the fact that males in some species may adopt synchronization behaviors that *reduce* duty cycles, (Buck and Buck, 1978), all suggest that males gain little individual profit by clustering to increase the fraction of the time that signals are being emitted.

The active-space model is more complicated. We need to consider both (a) whether there are some initial advantages to males that cluster and (b) whether these advantages are maintained when all males are in clusters. I shall consider the former situation first. Here, we presume that the area from which males draw females can increase indefinitely without overlapping that of other clusters. Regardless of sensory modality used, all signals radiate out into the three-dimensional volume around the emitter and, hence, decrease in intensity with increasing distance from the source. For any signal, there will be a maximum distance from the source at which the signal is still above the threshold of detectability. I shall call the circle, coplanar with the earth and having this maximum distance as radius, the ''active space'' of the signaller. In most species with leks, females are not drawn from the entire volume into which the signal radiates but from a smaller volume consisting of the product of the active space and the range of heights that females frequent. Since this latter component is presumably the same whether males are clustered or solitary, it is the relative size of the active space for different numbers of males that determines the number of females drawn to clusters or dispersed males respectively. In Figure 9–2, I have drawn three possible relationships between the number of males per cluster and the active space around a cluster. The curves are all approximated by power functions and differ in whether the exponent i is less than 1, equal to 1 (the linear case), or greater than 1. It should be obvious that males will not gain by clustering when this exponent is 1 or less, because the active space and, hence, the number of females potentially attractable to the cluster, will increase at most in proportion to the number of males. Hence, the number of females per male will not increase with clustering. It is my contention that for nearly all signal systems, it is impossible to get a relationship with i larger than 1, and for many sensory modalities, the rule will be values less than 1.

Consider the case of visual signals. Clustering could increase the range of detectability by (a) increasing the intensity of the visual signal relative to background patterns or by (b) increasing the angle subtended in the visual field of a female and hence the maximum distance of detection. The intensity of the signal at the source cannot increase faster than the contributed intensities of the cluster participants. Thus, this factor will increase linearly with the number of males per cluster. Since light intensity attenuates at least as fast as the

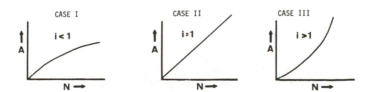

Figure 9–2.   Active space (A) of a lek as a function of the number of males per lek (N). All curves drawn as power functions of the form A = MN^i.

inverse square of the distance, the square of the maximum radius of detection will be directly proportional to the number of males displaying. Because the active space is computed using the square of this radius, it follows that the active space will be a linear function of the number of males displaying and there will be no increase in active space per male. The effect on the subtended angle of the visual field of a female by increasing cluster size depends on the shape of the cluster. If males form a line, the apparent size to a female ranges from that of a single male when the line is seen ''end on'' to that of the entire line. The corresponding active space is an ellipse with a major axis depending on the number of males per cluster and a minor axis independent of that number. The resulting area of this ellipse is proportional to the number of males per cluster, and, thus, there is no net advantage on a per-male basis. Similarly, if males form a filled circle, the cross-sectional diameter will increase with the square root of the number of males (Treisman, 1975). The maximum radius of detection will be proportional to this cross-sectional diameter, and, thus, the area of the active space will be directly proportional to the number of males. Again, there will be no net benefit on a per-male basis of forming clusters. If, as Treisman (1975) argues, increasing cluster size results in an asymptotic probability of detection that is less than one, a cluster size will be reached at which further increase *decreases* male fitness.

For acoustical signals, increasing cluster size will generally increase the intensity of the signal at the source. In the best of all possible worlds, cluster males will emit sounds of identical frequency composition and zero phase differences. In this case, intensity at the source will increase linearly for each male added. As with light, sound intensity decreases with the square of the distance from the source or faster (the result of additional heat and viscous losses). Thus, the active space around a cluster of males emitting sounds will increase in direct proportion to the number of males present. No mean net benefit will accrue to individual males. Because it is highly unlikely that males *can* emit identical sounds in phase, the intensity at the cluster will not be an integral multiple of the number of males present but a lower value. This could well lead to a decrease in mean male fitness for all cluster sizes greater than one male. Thus, clustering provides no advantages for males and most probably is generally disadvantageous.

Olfactory leks have been suggested but remain to be demonstrated definitively. Suppose they do exist. Males might emit odorants in instantaneous puffs or in long bouts of continuous emission. The equations of Bossert and Wilson (1963) for olfactory signal diffusion can be modified to include a dependence on the number of males coordinating odorant emission from a common point. In the single-puff case, it is easy to show that the active space (as defined in the *present* paper) increases with the number of emitting males to the $2/3$ power. Clearly, aggregation is disadvantageous on a per-male basis. If males emit odorant for long periods, the situation is more similar to the continuous emission case of Bossert and Wilson (1963). In this case, it can be shown that the active space increases with the square of the number of males emitting and, hence, *can* lead to a net individual benefit. However, it is also the case that to achieve the maximum radius possible with this system, the amount of time each male must itself emit increases with the square of the number of males in the cluster. Thus, either males must emit for longer periods to achieve the larger radius, or, if they emit for the same periods, they do not achieve the maximum potential radius and there is no net advantage. In addition, the importance of wind and convective movements of the medium make stable distributions increasingly unlikely as the distance from the source increases. Thus, even if males can energetically emit for extended periods, the effective active space will generally be less than that expected by the steady-state model.

The force of the above is that it is very difficult to initiate clusters of males by invoking geometrical advantages to the males themselves. Suppose, however, that such advantages did accrue in a few exceptional cases. Could they be maintained? I should like to argue that they would not. Consider first the alternative male dispersion: A steady-state uniform field of territorial males with contiguous but nonoverlapping territories. Each male produces signals that generate an active space around the male that may or may not be larger than the actual defended territory. One may define a further perimeter around each male, external to that of the active space, that contains the home-range centers of all females that are close enough to touch the active space during normal activities. I shall call this the "drawing area" of the male (see Figure 9–3). The drawing area thus depends on both the size of each male's active space and the average size of a female's home range. The number of females visiting each male can be computed as the product of a male's drawing area and the mean density of females in the region. Because each female may contact the active spaces of several males, male fitness depends not only on how many females contact his active space but also how many competitors he has for mating each of these females. It can be shown that the number of males encountered by each female is equal to the product of mean male density and the average drawing area of each male. The mean mating success of males is thus the ratio of these two values that reduces, not surprisingly, to the overall ratio of female density to territorial male density. This sets the baseline against which the reproductive success of clustered males must be compared: Clustered males must obtain more matings per male than the overall sex ratio would predict to have an advantage over a uniform field of territorial males with the same signal properties.

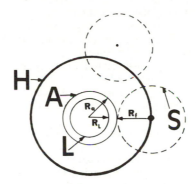

DEFINITIONS:

R_L = Radius of Lek (or of One Male's Territory in Uniform Field)
R_a = Radius of Detection of Lek (or of Single Male)
R_f = Radius of average Female Home Range
L   = Area of Lek (or of Single Male's Territory)
A   = Area of Active Space of Lek (or of Single Male)
S   = Area of One Female Home Range
H   = Drawing Area of Lek (or of Single Male's Territory)
D_m = Density of Territorial or Lek Males Overall
D_f = Density of Females Overall

FITNESS OF AVERAGE MALE IN UNIFORM FIELD:

1. Each male in uniform field encounters
$$D_f \cdot \pi (R_a + R_f)^2 \quad \text{females}$$

2. Each female visits on average
$$D_m \cdot \pi (R_f + R_a)^2 \quad \text{territorial males}$$

3. The average mating success for a male is the number of females visiting divided by the total number of males visited by each female:
$$\frac{D_f \cdot \pi (R_a + R_f)^2}{D_m \cdot \pi (R_a + R_f)^2} = \frac{D_f}{D_m}$$

Figure 9–3.   Steady-state dispersion parameters for solitary or clustered displaying males and computation of mean fitness for solitary males in a uniform field.

In any steady-state model of clustering, the number of males per cluster and the number of clusters combined are limited by the total number of males present. If the number of males per cluster is P, the overall male density D_m, and the average drawing area of each cluster is H, it is easy to show that when drawing areas are not overlapping,

$$\frac{D_m \cdot H}{P} \leq 1.$$

This can be multiplied on both sides by mean female density, D_f, and rewritten to show that

$$\frac{D_f \cdot H}{P} \leq \frac{D_f}{D_m}$$

The left side of this inequality is the mean number of females per male on the cluster, and the right side is the equivalent value for males in the uniform field. It is clear that if drawing areas do not overlap, males do only as well, and may do worse by clustering than by displaying in a uniform field. The case where drawing areas do overlap leads to a similar conclusion. Overlap increases the number of females visiting each cluster but also increases the number of competitors for those females. The result is again the overall sex ratio. In fact, unless some males drop out of the contest for other reasons, there is no way to beat the overall sex ratio with any dispersion of males. Because the uniform field leads to this mating expectation, no other dispersion will be superior in the absence of other factors.

The upshot of the previous section is that it is extremely unlikely that leks first evolved to increase mean male access to females or that, once evolved, they could be maintained for this reason. Instead, it must be the case that it is to the advantage of females to favor clusters over uniform fields of males in certain contexts (see Alexander, 1975). I shall return to why this might be so in a later section.

A final condition that has recently been invoked to explain leks is the nondefensibility of both resources and females (Emlen, 1976; Bradbury, 1977a; Emlen and Oring, 1977). Defense of resources required by females and defense of existing female groups are two common alternative male strategies to lek behavior. The overall rarity of leks and the fact that even in lek-prone groups such as hermit hummingbirds, the occurrence of a defensible resource such as nest sites leads to an abandonment of lek behaviors (B. Snow, 1973b; L. Wolf, personal communication) suggest that leks are a ''default'' strategy adopted by males only when it is impossible to defend resources or females. The previous arguments showing that males generally lose by clustering unless females prefer clusters support this notion. It thus seems likely that nondefensibility is a necessary condition for lek evolution, but again, it is not a sufficient one. Specifically, why is a lek *the* appropriate default strategy instead of some other pattern?

My evaluation of prior lek evolution models is that they have identified a set of necessary conditions for lek evolution, e.g., emancipation of the male from parental duties and the nondefensibility of resources or females, but these do not yet constitute a sufficient set. One is still faced with showing why females should favor clusters over uniform fields of males, *when* they should do so, and what factors determine where on the continuum between uniform fields of males and classical leks the actual dispersion will lie.

II.   SOCIAL DISPERSION AND LEK EVOLUTION.

An increasingly popular view in sociobiological theory and one initiated at the start by John Crook (1964, 1965) is the notion that spatial dispersion of animals is a fundamental locus of selection and that higher social levels, such as mating systems and group composition, evolve contingent upon the existing patterns of group size and spacing (cf. Alexander,

1974; Jarman, 1974). This suggests another whole suite of models of lek evolution in which the primary causes of leks are tied to underlying changes in the overall pattern of dispersion. Contrasts in social dispersion must include at least three parameters, and the most commonly used ones are group size, density, and home-range size (or territory size if home ranges are defended). I shall examine in this section the likelihood that each of these social dispersion parameters can be correlated with lek evolution in a causal way.

A. Group Size and Leks. The most notable attempt to link patterns of group size with the evolution of leks concerns the variable dispersion of males in grouse. It has been noted by numerous authors that grouse using open habitats tend to have classical leks, whereas grouse in forest and woodland tend to have exploded leks or more uniform dispersion of males (Hjorth, 1970; Kruijt et al., 1972; Wiley, 1974). Several explanations have been advanced to explain this correlation between lek size and habitat. The simplest is that displaying males gain advantages through cooperative predator surveillance in open country that do not accrue in forests (Berger, et al., 1963; Koivisto, 1965; Boag and Sumanik, 1969; Hjorth, 1970; Wiley, 1974; Wittenberger, 1978, but see Hartzler, 1974). A second is that grouse forage as groups in open country because of food dispersion patterns, and social bonds formed on the foraging grounds are carried over onto the display sites (Kruijt et al., 1972). Finally, it might be argued that if females form flocks in open sites to avoid predation or maximize foraging efficiency, this might facilitate greater unanimity in mate choice by females and lead to greater centripetal clustering of less successful males around successful ones.

Without dissecting the specific mechanisms proposed above, a major problem with the group-size hypothesis is that it does not fit many other taxa with an equivalent range of male dispersion patterns. Large groups do occur in classical lek species such as the topi (Monfort-Braham, 1975) and the Uganda kob (Buechner and Roth, 1974). However, the full range of male dispersions can also be found in such typically forest species as hummingbirds (B. Snow, 1973b, 1974), manakins (Sick, 1967; D. Snow, 1963), birds-of-paradise (Gilliard, 1969), and epomophorine bats (Bradbury, 1977a). In few of these taxa does either sex move in groups, and where they do, there is no correlation between the presence of such groups and lek size or spacing. This lack of generality immediately raises the question of whether the correlations observed in grouse are causal or, alternatively, the result of joint correlations with some other factors.

B. Density and Leks. Lek species are often common species (e.g., B. Snow, 1973b). This suggests both a reason and mechanism for lek evolution. Imagine an initial dispersion with a uniform field of territorial males defending resources that females require. If male settlement densities can vary independently of the current amount of defensible resource (as in red grouse, Miller et al., 1970), we can imagine that as densities increase, male territory size will gradually decrease. As long as territorial settlement is non-despotic (in the sense of Fretwell, 1972), continued increases in density will lead to smaller and smaller amounts of controlled resource per male. At some critical point, the costs of defense outweigh the benefits of enhanced access to females, and males should adopt alternative strategies. If female defense is not a viable option, males may then shift to ``self-advertisement'' either on leks or in more dispersed patterns. A similar scenario is implied in some models of Emlen and Oring (1977), Monfort-Braham (1975), and Pitelka et al. (1974). The thrust of the argument is that increasing density makes territorial defense of resources a decreasingly viable option for males. Lek species *should* thus be common species. We might also expect to find a gradient from 100 per cent emphasis on resources in low-density species, mixed emphasis on resources and self-advertisement in medium-density species, and 100 per cent self-advertisement in high-density species. The shift to 100 per cent self-advertisement should occur when territories are too small to contain significant amounts of resource. Finally, self-advertising species should not show despotic defense of large territories by males. If they were able to do so, they should not shift to self-advertisement under the density model.

Although the density model is attractive in explaining a variety of issues at once, I do not think it fits the available data any better than does the group-size model. For example, there is no correlation that I can discern between the degree of male clustering in grouse and ambient densities. Grouse with unclustered or loosely clustered males show breeding densities ranging from 7–10 adults/km.[2] in ptarmigan and spruce grouse (Choate, 1963; Ellison, 1973) to 20–40 adults/km.[2] for ruffed grouse (Edminster, 1947). Species with classical leks show breeding densities ranging from 5–6 adults/km.[2] for greater prairie chickens (Robel and Ballard, 1974) to 19 adults/km.[2] for sage grouse (Patterson, 1952). If one focuses just on the adult males, there is still no correlation between ambient densities and male dispersion pattern (Gullion, 1967, 1976; Kirsch et at., 1973; Rippin and Boag, 1974; Patterson, 1952; Hoffman, 1963). Even if I normalize densities according to some allometric function of body weight (e.g., weight to the $2/3$ power), I cannot find a significant relation between density and male dispersion.

The prediction that there is a gradual shift in emphasis on resources vs. self-advertisement along the male dispersion continuum also appears to fail. For example, the exploded lek bat, *Epomops franqueti,* typically shows male territories of about 200 m. or more in diameter. These territories can be shown to be large enough to contain significant amounts of resources required by females. However, the males always place their territories over sites in which female roosting and food resources are rare or absent (Bradbury, unpublished observations). This suggests that male *Epomops* have shifted to 100 per cent self-advertisement although territories are not too small to contain significant resources. A similar separation of habitats used by males in exploded lek species for display and habitats used by females for nesting and foraging has been noted in the bower bird, *Parotia lawesii* (Schodde and McKean, 1973), in ruffed grouse (Gullion, 1976), and in spruce grouse (Ellison, 1971, 1973).

The last prediction, that despotic defense of large territories is unlikely in 100 per cent self-advertisement species, is also not upheld by available evidence. In tetraonids with large territories such as ruffed grouse or spruce grouse, it is clear that there is a large pool of males without territories and that removal of territorial males results in their rapid replacement (Boag and Sumanik, 1969; Ellison, 1971; Archibald, 1976). If the density model were correct, we might expect that the ability to defend a large territory despotically would best be used to defend resources. As we have seen in the previous paragraph, there is considerable evidence that even exploded lek males do not set up territories over resources. Instead, site selection for territories seems directed towards optimizing signal transmission and predator avoidance requirements (Boag and Sumanik, 1969; Gullion, 1976).

C.   Home-Range Size and Leks. I should now like to consider the possibility that female home-range sizes are critical determinants of male dispersion patterns. To my knowledge, this factor has not been previously considered and the behavior of females away from the lek has in general received short shrift by field workers. I begin by considering an initial dispersion of a uniform field of territorial males over some resource required by females. Suppose that selection then favors an increase in average female home-range sizes *without* altering either female densities or territorial male densities. I shall discuss in a later section ecological reasons *why* females might be selected to increase home-range size without any change in density, but I shall assume for now that it leads to some increase in foraging efficiency or predator avoidance. Note that if female densities remain constant as female home ranges increase, the overlap of female home ranges will also tend to increase. There are several possible scenarios for the consequences of this shift to the mating strategies of males. They differ depending on whether the resource defended by males is also one they need to utilize or not. Suppose it is: That is, suppose males defend food sites and females increase home ranges to increase their foraging efficiences. It follows that one of the following will occur:

1. Males will increase their territories so as to maintain the same ratio of female home-range size to male territory size. This will result in some males losing territories but will maintain the same basic mating system.

2. Males cannot increase territory sizes because these are set by male densities. Males will then either (a) continue to defend the original territories but forage in part away from their own territories, (b) continue to defend the original territories and shift to other foods than females, or (c) abandon territorial defense of resources altogether in favor of some alternative strategy. Suppose the initial presumption is not so: That is, males defend one resource needed by females such as nest sites, but females increase their home ranges to gain access to another, such as food. Males could thus afford to continue to defend the initial territory sizes, and feeding ranges would not be related to the size of male territories for either sex.

In short, there are three general outcomes of an increase in female home ranges: (a) Males increase territory size proportionately to the increases in female home-range size and there is no qualitative change in mating strategies; (b) males retain their initial territory sizes and the ratio of female home-range size to male territory size increases; or (c) males abandon resource defense altogether. I am most interested in the second and third outcomes because the first will simply preserve the initial system and we would see no alternative behavior such as leks at all. Because leks do occur, I presume the first case cannot always apply. Both the second and third outcomes make the continued use of resource defense by males a poor strategy. This is clear in the third case but more subtle in the second. Suppose female home-range sizes continue to increase indefinitely relative to the territory sizes of males. Each male encounters more females in his territory than he did when female home-range sizes were smaller. However, each female is visiting more males than previously and thus he has more competitors for each of these females. The net effect on *average* male fitness is zero. (See Figure 9–4.) For the female, on the other hand, the change is significant. Whereas small home ranges allow a single male to withhold access to significant re-

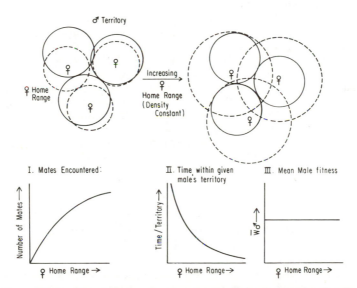

Figure 9–4.   Effects of female home-range size on male and female strategies. Top: Example of increase in female home range size with constant male and female densities and constant male territory sizes. Bottom: Effects of female home range size on number of mates encountered by each sex (I), amount of time a female spends in any one male's territory (II), and mean mating success of males (III).

sources in exchange for sexual access, a female with a large home range has a greater number of territories to choose from and hence can opt for the least dominating males. The combination of a greater number of alternative males and the lower amount of resource per territory combine to "emancipate" the female from the constraints of a resource defense system. This emancipation and the large pool of males to choose from are precisely the conditions that favor a high degree of female choice and the consequent "runaway processes" of sexual selection (Fisher, 1958). A male in such circumstances would do better to invest in self-advertisement than to invest in real estate.

This model thus predicts a shift from resource defense to 100 per cent self-advertisement as a function of the *relative* sizes of female home ranges and male territories, whereas the density model rests on the *absolute* size of male territories. Although absolute and relative sizes of male territories may change together, they need not and examples of self-advertising males on territories large enough to contain substantial resources but placed elsewhere are expected only with the female home-range model. In addition, where male densities are roughly similar, we expect to find increasing probabilities of self-advertisement as female home range size increases.

The prediction of large territories but 100 per cent self-advertisement by the home-range model is definitely met and has been discussed above. For the second prediction, I turn to the grouse. In the monogamous (or occasionally bigamous) red grouse, males form a uniform field of contiguous territories and females pair with males up until hatching of the young. Since females forage almost entirely on the territory of their mate, their home ranges and the size of male territories are commensurate. In Scotland, a very large sample of male territories gave an overall mean of 2.53 ha. per male (and female) with a range of 0.2 to 13 ha. (Watson and Miller, 1971). A similar system and identical values are reported for hazel grouse (Hjorth, 1970), and even smaller male territories and home ranges are recorded for white-tailed ptarmigan (Choate, 1963). The self-advertising but dispersed ruffed grouse, blue grouse, and spruce grouse show monthly female home ranges up to the laying of the clutch of 10–50 ha., a tenfold increase over that of monogamous species (Brander, 1967; Hjorth, 1970; Ellison, 1973; Boag, 1965; Archibald, 1975). Finally, the classical lek species of grouse such as sharp-tailed grouse, sage grouse, and prairie chickens have female home ranges prior to incubation of 200 ha. or more, again a ten-fold increase over the prior category (Hamerstrom and Hamerstrom, 1951; Robel et al., 1970; Wallestad and Pyrah, 1974). Not only do all self-advertising grouse have large female home ranges, but the male dispersions shift towards greater clustering as female home ranges increase. Another test of the model is the topi. In this antelope, different populations show either resource defense of foraging grounds or classical leks (Monfort-Braham, 1975). As the model would suggest, the populations with the largest home ranges are those with the classical leks. The fit is not conclusive however, because both group size and density are higher in the classical lek populations. It is tantalizing that other taxa such as hummingbirds, birds-of-paradise, or manakins in which both lek and non-lek species are present would be ideal as tests of this model. I hope to make a strong enough case in this chapter to encourage the future collection of the relevant data.

III. A QUALITATIVE MODEL AND TRANSITIONAL STAGES OF LEK EVOLUTION

I have argued that an increasing ratio of female home-range size to male territory size should lead to a shift in male strategies from resource defense to self-advertisement. This shift by itself does not necessarily require (a) that males cluster or (b) that they should cluster with some specific pattern of dispersion. If it is not generally advantageous for males to cluster, the fact that they *do* must arise from a preference for clusters on the part of females.

Why should females prefer clusters once a male strategy of self-advertisement has evolved? There are three basic reasons why females should favor clusters over more uniformly dispersed males. The first, and most obvious, is that clustering allows a female to examine a large number of males in the least possible time. This facilitates direct comparison of male phenotypes and may also reduce energy costs of moving between males. This advantage accrues to all females whether they visit the cluster singly or in groups. A second advantage is that males may be coaxed by females into aggregating at locations of maximal accessibility, e.g., at major traffic crossroads or minimally at traditional sites. The exact locations would be the result of the combined preferences and activity ranges of a number of females and hence might not be ideal for any one female. A net advantage would still pertain on a per-female basis. Finally, clustering of males allows females to monitor mate choice by other females. Whether females choose mates on the basis of cues that are correlated with general adaptedness, e.g., age, general vigor, status, size of "handicap" (Zahavi, 1975), etc., or on the basis of some convention uncorrelated with adaptedness (as might evolve when sexual selection leads to high male phenotypic homogeneity), it will be of value for females to know how other females mate. If evaluation of male "adaptedness" rests on experience, younger females will always benefit from the knowledge of how older females have selected males. If uncorrelated cues are used in mate choice, the costs of mating with the "wrong" male may be *greater* than the benefits of mating with the current favorites (cf. Gillespie, 1977, for analogous arguments). Again, clustering will encourage the monitoring of female choice by other females. It has even been suggested that females may attempt to determine and *modify* the choices of other females and that clustering would facilitate this effort (Paul Sherman, personal communication). This final advantage will have its greatest effect in species that favor female groups or in which female visits to clusters are synchronized within narrow time windows. It seems that these three advantages apply in general to most lek species and I can think of no disadvantage to females of preferring clusters (see also Alexander, 1975).

In earlier sections, I argued that clustering led to no net advantage for males in the absence of female preference and in many cases led to geometrical disadvantages. Even where the mean male mating success is not decreased, clustering will in general increase female unanimity of mate choice and the lower ranking males will lose as a result. Thus for some of the males in all systems and all of the males in some systems, clustering is disadvantageous. The shift to self-advertisement thus generates two opposing forces: female preferences for clustered males and a contrary bias on the part of males for more uniform dispersions. The result should be a stable equilibrium dispersion that falls somewhere between the two extremes of classical leks and uniform fields of males (see Figure 9–5). I would now like to examine the evolution of this equilibrium in more detail.

FACTORS DETERMINING MALE DISPERSION PATTERN:

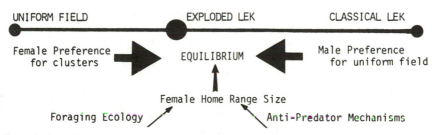

Figure 9–5.   Equilibrium model dispersion patterns assuming that females benefit when males cluster, males lose when they cluster, and the equilibrium point is determined in part by the absolute size of female home ranges.

I begin again with a uniform field of territorial males, but this time the primary male strategy is one of self-advertisement. I presume that within this uniform field, some males cluster and that the disposition of these males to deviate from uniform fields is to some degree heritable. This genetic predisposition to cluster could arise directly through a bias to display near other males, or indirectly through shared biases in preferred display habitats or through secondary male strategies of interference with successful males. Without any female preference for clusters, these aberrant males would be selected against for the reasons noted here. I now suppose that some of the females in the population have a heritable predisposition to favor clusters over uniformly distributed males. For leks to evolve, it must be the case that this bias in favor of clusters leads to some advantage for the females expressing it over females with no bias and over females with the contrary bias favoring uniform males. We have discussed some of the potential advantages above. It is possible that there is an energetic advantage to females when males are clustered. It is also possible that if it is difficult to distinguish between males using phenotypic cues, that an uncorrelated convention, such as the center of a cluster, might have as great an effect in modulating the uniformity of female choice as would the alternative attempt by individual females to discriminate among males using correlated cues. It seems unlikely at this early stage to presume that those males with a disposition to cluster are always the one that females would have chosen for mates using correlated cues. Given that some females favor and benefit from favoring clusters and that some males have a heritable bias to form clusters, there are two basic scenarios for the evolution of leks (see Figure 9–6). In the first case, a subset of the uniform field of males reduces mean territory size to form a cluster. Adjacent males expand their territory sizes to

TRANSITIONAL HISTORIES OF LEK EVOLUTION

CASE I: VACATED SPACE DIVIDED EQUALLY BY UNIFORM MALES:

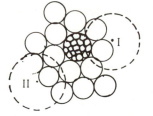

1. Assume that if lek is small enough, once a female contacts the edge of the lek, it is worth her while to examine most or all of it.

2. Type I females gain as they now encounter more males than before clustering. They also can exert a choice.

3. Type II females do not gain and lose but little. They cannot make a choice.

CASE II: VACATED SPACE REMAINS VACANT:

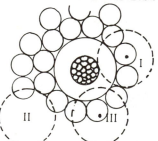

1. Type I females encounter the lek, some empty space, and some males in the uniform field. They also have a choice.

2. Type II females encounter only uniform males and have no choice.

3. Type III females encounter vacant space and uniform males. They do not have a choice.

4. In general, there are more Type III females than Type I if lek is small in size.

5. Once the vacated space is large enough, Type I females encounter only lek males and empty space, no longer have a choice, and are much less numerous than Type III females. This sets limit to size of empty space and numbers of males on lek.

Figure 9–6.   Transitional histories of lek evolution depending on whether the space by clustered males is acquired by noncluster males (Case I) or left vacant (Case II).

take up the vacated space. There are two type of females: Type I females have home ranges so centered that they contact both cluster males and uniformly distributed males; Type II females are farther from the cluster and contact only uniformly distributed males. Type I females gain by the clustering through the advantages outlined above, and moreover, they are in a position to make a choice between clustered and nonclustered males. The consequence of their choice will be an increase in the number of clustered males in the next generation. Type II females lose by the clustering in that they have fewer males to choose from, but because they contact only uniformly distributed males, they cannot make a choice and thus cannot affect the frequencies of clustered vs. nonclustered males in the next generation. The net result is an increase in the frequencies of males that cluster over those that do not. Unchecked, this would lead to one enormous cluster of males. The pattern might be checked internally if increased clustering resulted in some increasing probability of mating by nonclustered males. To see this, consider the fact that clustering is likely to increase the degree of unanimity of mate choice by females and thus increase the skew in mating success among cluster males. As clusters grow in number of males, the mating expectations of low-ranking males should fall. If at the same time, the increase in territory size (or reduction in density) of nonclustered males *enhanced* their chances of getting an occasional mating, a balanced polymorphism would be established when the probability of getting a mating as a low-ranking male on a cluster equalled that for a nonclustered male on a large territory. Such a balance may explain the dispersion patterns of blackcock (Kruijt and Hogan, 1967; Kruijt et al., 1972) and Uganda kob (Leuthold, 1966). On the other hand, if nonclustered males experience lower probabilities of mating as clustering continues (as could arise if females always prefer the higher density sites), the clustering would go on unchecked by internal factors.

In the second case, space vacated by clustering males remains vacant, and uniformly distributed males do not increase their territory sizes. There are three types of females in this case (see Figure 9–6). Type I females contact the cluster, some vacated space, and may contact uniformly distributed males as well. It is easy to show that they always benefit by contacting more males (if they visit an entire cluster once contacting it) than they did before males clustered. In addition, many of these females have a choice between clustered and nonclustered males. Type II females are situated too far from the cluster to be affected either by the cluster or by the vacated space. They neither gain nor lose and contact only one type of male. Type III females encounter nonclustered males and enter vacated space. They lose because they now encounter fewer males but by contacting only a single type of male are not in a position to exert a choice. The result is a net preference for clustered males and a subsequent increase in their relative abundance over time. This model also leads to a continuous increase in the number of males per cluster unless checked by other factors. One internal check could arise if the rate of increase in vacated space were faster than the rate of increase in the cluster active space. Under these conditions, there will be a point at which the area between the perimeter of the cluster's active space and the perimeter of the vacated space can just accommodate an entire female home range. When this point is reached, Type I females no longer contact both types of males and no further preference can be exerted. Clustering should stop at this point. If the area of the cluster's active space increases fast enough, this limit is never reached and the cluster continues to grow indefinitely.

Both of the above models concern a single incipient cluster in a uniform field of territorial males. More realistically, there may be several small clusters from the start, or alternatively, as skew increases on the larger clusters, low-ranking males leave to initiate new clusters elsewhere. As long as there are females whose home ranges do not touch or include a male cluster, the initiation of new clusters will be a viable male strategy. The number of males per cluster and the number of clusters per unit area should thus both increase as the population shifts from nonclustered to entirely clustered males. The option to form new clusters disappears as soon as all females contact at least one cluster. If females have more than one cluster within their home ranges, the advantages favoring clustering in the first place should lead to their selecting one over the others and the gradual dissolution of the others. In the steady state, most females should thus have only a single cluster within their home ranges. Turning this around, this means that at steady state, the outside perimeters of cluster active spaces should be just one female home-range diameter apart (see Figure 9–7). Using the terminology of pp. 143–4 and Figure 9–3, the drawing areas of the clusters should be continguous but nonoverlapping. Thus, a powerful determinant of the final dispersion of males is the absolute size of female home ranges. Note that even if the distance between clusters is determined, there is still an infinite set of male dispersions depending upon the number of males per cluster and the total area occupied by each cluster. In the next section, I wish to develop a quantitative model of lek dispersion that relies on female home-range size as a determinant of inter-lek spacing, on the amount of skew and alternative options as a determinant of the number of males per lek, and on the tendency for males to hold as large a territory as possible as a determinant of the area occupied by a lek.

IV. A QUANTITATIVE MODEL OF LEK EVOLUTION AND STEADY-STATE DISPERSIONS

The dispersion of males in any lek species is totally defined if we know (a) the mean distance between leks, (b) the mean number of males per lek, and (c) the mean area occupied by each lek. The latter parameter can be computed from knowledge of the mean number of males per lek and the mean territory size of each lek male. In the following section, I

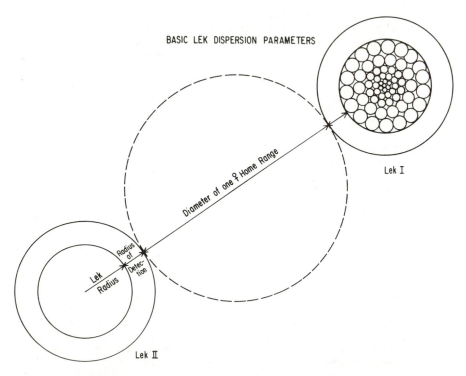

Figure 9–7.   Steady state spacing of leks such that the active spaces of adjacent leks are just one female home range apart.

shall develop models of determination for inter-lek spacing, number of males per lek, and the male territory size following the general arguments of the previous section. For each spatial parameter, I shall examine the available data to see if there is a good fit with the predictions of the models.

A. *Inter-lek Spacing.* The basic relationship has already been defined in the previous section: Active spaces of adjacent leks should be separated by a distance equal to the diameter of the average female's home range. At greater spacings there are females who do not encounter male signals and it is to the advantage of low-ranking males on existing leks to initiate new leks in the interstices. At lesser spacings, the drawing areas of adjacent leks will overlap, and while more females may be encountered, there are more competitors for these females. No gain to males will accrue from drawing area overlap and there may be energetic costs as well. Thus, in the steady state, the drawing areas (defined as the active space plus an annulus of thickness equal to one female home-range radius) of adjacent leks should be contiguous but non overlapping. When this is the case, I shall say that the "contiguity condition" has been met, and the dispersion of leks can be summarized by the relation:

$$\frac{H \cdot D_m}{P} = 1$$

where H is the mean lek drawing area, D_m is the overall density of displaying males, and P is the mean number of males per lek.

There are two types of tests to see whether the contiguity condition is met in real systems. The first is a direct comparison between the typical inter-lek spacings in a population and average female home range diameters. Such comparisons are not easy to make at present. The foremost reason is a dearth of suitable data on female home-range sizes in lek species. A second problem is more subtle. In the prior models, I have assumed a homogeneous habitat in which males are either uniformly distributed or clustered and females are uniformly distributed. If the habitat were not homogeneous but a mosaic of suitable and unsuitable regions, lek spacings might be greater than expected given mean home-range sizes of females. Thus a lack of commensurate values favoring larger lek spacings would not disprove the contiguity condition; the reverse *would* do so. A related complication arises from the fact that the model predicts the distance between the perimeters of the active spaces of adjacent leks not the actual distance between leks. While the latter is often given in the literature, the former is rarely even mentioned, much less estimated. Because the distance between leks should be the sum of one female home-range diameter and twice the distance the lek can be detected, female home ranges will again be an underestimate of the mean distance between leks. Should the reverse be true, the contiguity condition would be called into doubt.

Given these considerations, the available data do tend to support the model. In our own studies on the classical lek bat, *Hypsignathus monstrosus,* the mean distance between 10 adjacent leks was 14 km. (range 5–18 km.) (Bradbury, 1977a). The primary modality used by displaying males is sound, and this attenuates rapidly in the moist lowland atmosphere of our study area. Human ears can detect a *Hypsignathus* lek to about 500 m. distance in forest, and about 700 m. over water. It is possible that female bats can do better although most of the sound energy in the male call occurs at the optimal frequencies for human hearing. We estimated female home-range sizes by radio-tracking 15 adult females during the breeding season. Mean monthly home ranges (the major period a female is likely to visit a lek) averaged about 12 km. in diameter (J. Bradbury, D. Morrison, S. Vehrencamp, A. Miller, unpublished observations). This value plus 1 km. for the limits of the active spaces predict an inter-lek spacing of 13 km. This is very close to the observed value of 14 km. This good fit is to be expected given the relative homogeneity of the habitat in this study area. A related bat species, *Epomops franqueti,* shows exploded lek behavior. Male calls are more whistle-like and can be heard easily by the human ear to 700–900 m. Monthly home ranges for five *Epomops* females ranged from 1.2 to 1.6 km. in diameter. Gaps between clusters of male *Epomops* ranged from 2 to 4 km. in the same study areas. *Epomops* favors various types of second growth over primary forest in Gabon and hence its habitat is a patchy mosaic. Given these facts the fit to the model is fairly good.

Among the tetraonids, sharp-tailed grouse leks are spaced at from 1–2 km.; female home range estimates, though not necessarily from the same areas, range from 1.6 to 3 km. in diameter (Hjorth, 1970; Kirsch et al., 1973; Rippin and Boag, 1974). Greater prairie chicken hens show monthly home ranges prior to laying of about 1.6 km. in diameter; the spacing of three leks in the same area averaged 2.7 km. (Robel et al., 1970; Robel and Ballard, 1974). Where these two grouse species occur sympatrically, there is qualitative agreement with the model in that female home-range sizes are smaller and leks closer together in the sharp-tailed grouse than is the case for the greater prairie chickens (Hamerstrom and Hamerstrom, 1951; Kirsch et al., 1973).

A second test of the contiguity condition is whether females visit more than one lek or not. Basically, the model predicts that *most* females should visit only a single lek in a given season. The notion that each lek has its own female "population" was first suggested by Schwartz (1945) for prairie chickens and later elaborated by Buechner and Roth (1974) for Uganda kob. These studies have been criticized for the group selectionist bias in their interpretations, and Robel and his associates have attempted to disprove the idea by showing that some radio-tracked prairie chicken hens visit more than one lek (Robel et al., 1970). It seems to me that the latter is not a sufficient disproof of the prediction and that an adequate test must be a quantitative one. The contiguity condition predicts that *most* females will encounter signals from a single lek and visit only that lek. A few, however, will have their home ranges centered on the locus of drawing area contiguity, and thus will be equidistant from two adjacent leks. Such females might well visit both leks. An even smaller number of females will be on the points of contiguity of three adjacent leks and might be expected to visit all three. Thus, the demonstration that some females visit more than one lek is not surprising. The exact ratios of females that visit one, two, or three leks will depend on (a) how well males can track female home ranges as these fluctuate from year to year; (b) how much variation exists *within* a year in female home-range size; (c) whether there are patches of unsuitable habitat in some females' home ranges; (d) whether leks are packed hexagonally, rectilinearly, or by some other rule; and (e) how sensitive spring dispersions of males are to winter variations in survival. We need much better longitudinal data than are now available to evaluate these factors.

In spite of this, the overall fit with the data appears good for most lek species. The data on prairie chickens and Uganda kob cited in this section are cases in point. A radio-tracking study of sage grouse by Wallestad and Pyrah (1974) showed that most hens remain near to one lek, some visit two leks, and only 1 out of 31 tracked visited three leks. Lill's studies on manakins (1974a; 1975) showed that, while females may visit different leks in successive years, they are highly faithful to a given lek for a single season. The two major exceptions to the prediction that I could find in the literature were black grouse and ruffs. Kruijt and his colleagues report that 25 per cent of 38 marked black grouse hens visited one lek; 50 per cent visited two leks, and 25 per cent visited three or more leks (Kruijt et al., 1972). Although there is still considerable selectivity by females for a few leks, the ratios are higher than one would expect in a steady-state homogeneous habitat. The latter may in part explain this exception since much of the study area was agricultural land subject to periodic plowing and modifications. Kruijt and his coworkers describe a number of relocations by both sexes as the lands are worked, and this temporal variation would lead to difficulty on the part of the males in tracking female home-range sizes. The second exception occurs in the ruff. Here frequent movements of females between adjacent "leks" have been noted by several workers (Hogan-Warburg, 1966; van Rhijn, 1973 and personal communication). I believe the ruffs may not be a strong exception for the following reason. Ruffs, in addition to having other peculiar characteristics, are unique in showing a clustering of leks. In most studies, ruff leks are not evenly distributed but occur in small clusters with large distances between clusters. It seems to me likely that the cluster itself should be considered the lek and that the individual aggregations are equivalent to the multiple-mating centers described in sage grouse (Wiley, 1973) and hammer-headed bats (Bradbury, 1977a). The critical test would then be to see if inter-cluster distances were as large (or larger given the heterogeneous habitat of the ruff) as expected given female home-range sizes. Such data are not, to my knowledge, currently available.

   B.   Number of Males per Lek. In the qualitative models discussed earlier, I argued that the upper limits to the number of males per lek would be set by the thresholds at which it no longer paid the lowest-ranking males to join or to remain on a lek. The existence of skew in mating success means that once drawing areas are contiguous, further increase in the numbers of males per lek will only result in lowered expectations of matings for the lowest-ranking males. It seems clear that males *do* have the option of not joining a lek as evidenced by the difference between final lek compositions and those during the early season period of lek establishment (personal observations on hammer-headed bats) and by the large pool of nonlek males that exists in most lek species (cf. Wiley, 1973 for review on grouse). In the following section, I wish to develop a quantitive model relating these thresholds for joining a lek with the steady-state numbers of males per lek.

   In most classical lek species, a plot of the percentage of matings obtained by each male versus his rank in getting copulations takes the form of a concave monotonic curve (cf. Bradbury, 1977a; Wiley, 1973; Lill, 1974b). For nine such sets of data, I found that a simple power curve of the form

$$C = BR^{-i}$$

where C is the fraction of copulations obtained on a lek by male of rank R and B and i are constants gave regressions that were highly significant and that explained 70 per cent or more of the variance in C (Bradbury, 1977a; Lill, 1974b, 1975; Wiley, 1973; Floody and Arnold, 1975; Robel, 1966). The constant B in these regressions ranged from 40–90 per cent and the constant i ranged from 1.2 to 1.9. The value of this analysis lies not so much in the observed values of the constants but in the apparently good fit of such a power function to the mating distributions of lek species. Because the summed values of C for all males on a lek of P individuals must equal one, it is easy to show that the constant B depends on i and P as follows:

$$B = \left(\sum_{J=1}^{P} J^{-i}\right)^{-1}$$

This allows me to rewrite the expression for C as a function of the rank of a given male, R, the total number of males on the lek, P, and the constant i:

$$C(R,P) = \frac{R^{-i}}{\sum_{J=1}^{P} J^{-i}}$$

I am most interested in the relative mating success of the lowest ranking male, that is, the one with rank P, and shall denote this by $C'(P)$:

$$C'(P) = \frac{P^{i}}{\sum_{J=1}^{P} J^{-i}}$$

As the value of P is increased, holding i fixed, the value of C' (P) decreases. Similarly, for a fixed value of P, C' (P) is also an inverse function of the value of i. The exponent i is a measure of the degree of unanimity of mate choice by females visiting a lek. The greater the value of i, the greater the degree of unanimity, and the fewer matings the lowest-ranking male will obtain. We might expect i to vary according to whether females visit leks in groups or singly, whether each female devotes many visits or much time per visit to inspecting males, and whether males are highly uniform phenotypically or not. If females rely on a convention for mate choice, such as mating with the most central male (the only unique point in a mass of males), i will vary depending on how difficult it is to identify this locus.

If males distribute themselves to maximize their own fitnesses, we expect that the lowest-ranking male on a lek at steady state has marginally better expectations of lifetime fitness than he would by not displaying on the lek. Using standard procedures (Williams, 1966; Pianka & Parker, 1975), we can divide the lifetime fitness of a male into M, the current year's expectations of mating, and V, the residual lifetime fitness, which depends both on mating success and the chance of survival to older ages. A male that decides to display on a lek this year can expect a lifetime fitness of $M_L + V_L$; a male that decides not to display on a lek can expect a lifetime fitness of $M_0 + V_0$. We expect that for the lowest-ranking male on a lek at steady state

$$M_L + V_L > M_0 + V_0$$

The actual value of M_L can be computed given the drawing area of the lek, H (P), the overall density of females, D_f, and the degree of skew on the lek, C' (P). Substituting this in for M_L and rewriting the conditions, I get

$$D_f \cdot H(P) \cdot C'(P) \geq M_0 + (V_0 - V_L) > D_f \cdot H(P+1) \cdot C'(P+1)$$

In the ensuing discussion, I shall call this the "skew condition."

It is possible to take this derivation one step further by simultaneously invoking the skew condition and the contiguity condition. Specifically, if the drawing areas of adjacent leks are contiguous but nonoverlapping, then the term H in the above expression can be replaced with a combination of P and D_m. The final expression becomes:

$$P \cdot C'(P) \geq \frac{D_m}{D_f} [M_0 + (V_0 - V_L)] > (P+1) \cdot C'(P+1)$$

There are several implications of this result. As long as none of D_m, D_f, M_0, V_0, and V_L are dependent on female home range size (or if they are, as long as these effects cancel each other out when combined), then the number of males per lek will be independent of female home-range size. Secondly, because $P \cdot C'$ (P) is a decreasing function of P, it follows that increasing any of D_m/D_f, M_0, or $(V_0 - V_L)$, without compensating decreases in one of the other terms will lead to reduced numbers of males per lek. Finally, given a fixed sex ratio and set of life history parameters, the model predicts larger numbers of males per lek as female unanimity in mate choice, i, decreases. These relations are summarized in Figure 9–8.

Translating these predictions into direct tests is difficult because the critical variables often covary. The simplest component to examine is the opportunity to mate away from the lek as measured by M_0. In some lek species, this is presumably zero because there are no other energetically feasible alternatives to mating on the lek or simply waiting and doing so later. In other species, it is clear that non-lek males do attempt alternative strategies. For example, male hammer-headed bats have been observed to establish single singing territories near to current food sites used by females or near to major traffic routes. Although females do visit such males and observe their displays, I have never recorded a single copulation in such circumstances (Bradbury, 1977a and unpublished observations). In black-cock, solitarily displaying males at food sites *do* occasionally obtain copulations (Kruijt et al., 1972). Although it is unlikely that all of the other critical parameters are equal in these species, it is of interest that lek size is much larger in the hammer-headed bats than it is in blackcock. This is what would be predicted by the model if the larger value of M_o in black-cock were the only difference between the two species.

Predictions concerning D_m/D_f, and $V_o–V_L$ are complicated by the fact that within limits, these components are probably inversely related (Wiley, 1974; Wittenberger, 1978). Note first that D_m is the density of males displaying on leks, not the overall male density. If some adult males do not join leks (as is often the case), or if males have higher mortality than females, or if males become sexually mature later than females, then D_m/D_f will generally be less than one. When it pays all males to join leks early, D_m/D_f will have its maximal values; where males have alternative strategies that are viable, D_m/D_f will be smaller than this upper limit. Were this ratio the only determinant of the number of males per lek, we would expect to find an inverse relation between the numbers of males per lek and the oper-ational sex ratio, D_m/D_f. Thus, if overall mortality rates were higher for males than females, the number of males per lek would be higher, all other factors being equal. The difficulty is that other things may not be equal because $V_o–V_L$ is also related to the existence of alterna-tive strategies and expectations of survival to various ages. In general, we might expect $V_o–V_L$ to approach zero as (a) the rates of turnover in male status on leks were increased and/or (b) when overall male life expectancy is low regardless of whether males display on leks or not. Either of these conditions will favor a compensating *increase* in D_m/D_f, but this will be limited by the maximal value that this ratio can attain. If D_m/D_f does not increase as fast as $V_o–V_L$ decreases, then the thresholds for joining leks will be reduced and the number of males per lek will be higher. The reverse situation is less predictable: That is, long-lived animals or low turnover rates in status will favor a joint increase in $V_o–V_L$ and decrease in D_m/D_f. Because the latter can continue to decrease until there is only one displaying male in the population, it is much easier for the compensation to be complete and hence there may be no change in number of males per lek. In short, low life expectancies for males and high turnover rates in status may be expected to lead to larger numbers of males per lek, but longer lifetimes and lower turnover rates in status may not alter the number of males per lek at all.

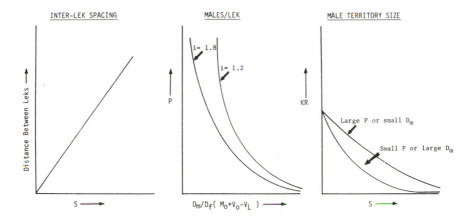

Figure 9–8.   Summary of model relating male dispersion to extrinsic parameters. See text for inter-pretations and definitions of terms.

Most vertebrate lek species have 10–20 males per lek. Exceptions below this value are difficult to assess since they are frequently associated with species on exploded leks where the degree of clustering and number of males per cluster is not known with any certainty. Exceptions above this typical value include the Uganda kob (20–40 males per lek), hammer-headed bats (20–135), sage grouse (9–400), black-and-white manakins (5–70), Wallace's standard-wing bird-of-paradise (30), and several hermit hummingbirds (10–100) (Buechner and Roth, 1974; Bradbury 1977a; Patterson, 1952; D. Snow, 1962; Lill, 1974b; Gilliard, 1969; B. Snow, 1973b). The Uganda kob fits the model in that it exhibits some of the highest rates of turnover in male territorial ownership noted in lek species (Buechner and Roth, 1974; Buechner and Schloeth, 1965). The hammer-headed bat and hermit hummingbirds both show very low annual survival rates for males and thus may be examples of the short longevity effect (J. Bradbury, unpublished observations; L. Wolf, personal communication). Black-and-white manakins have unusually long life expectancies and thus are more difficult to explain. The critical questions, however, are whether they have lower life expectancies than other manakins that have smaller numbers of males per lek, have lower degrees of unanimity in female mate choice than other manakin species, or fewer off-lek options than other species. The sage grouse are also puzzling although the existence of multiple mating centers on large leks reduces the effective skew below that expected if a single mating center were present.

I also wish to note that the model only predicts the *mean* number of males per lek. As stated, it makes no predictions about the variance in the number of males per lek among a set of adjacent leks. It is possible that local stochastic variations in male abundances make the available options different at different lek sites. Where, by chance, a lek has more males than expected given the mean value, its drawing area will be larger than expected. For the contiguity condition to hold, it follows that another adjacent lek must have a smaller than average drawing area and thus fewer males than expected. Although local histories may affect the exact numbers of males on any given lek, the population average should conform to the model at steady state. Critical tests of the model thus do not entail finding a lek with more males than expected (e.g., some of the examples given), but instead finding mean population values that are seriously deviant. Such tests remain to be performed.

C. Male Territory Size on Leks. I have now outlined determinants of the mean spacing between leks and the mean number of males on each lek. It remains to specify the determinants of male territory size. I shall argue below that if the contiguity condition holds and if lek spacing and number of males per lek have been fixed, male territory size is a dependent outcome. To see this, rewrite the contiguity condition in the form

$$H/P = 1/D_m$$

The drawing area of the lek, H, can be shown to be a simple function of the lek active space, A, and female home range area, S:

$$H = A + S + (4AS)^{1/2}$$

For any given lek, I shall define the individual active space A' to be the contribution that each of the P males makes to the overall active space A. Thus $A' = A/P$. This does not necessarily imply that the active space is a linear function of the number of males per lek; that would be true only if A' were the same for a set of lek sizes. Further, I shall define the constant K to be the ratio between each male's contribution to the active space, A', and the area of his territory on the lek, R. Thus $K = A'/R$. If the lek active space is as large or larger than the lek itself (which it must be to be detected), then we expect K to be one or larger. This seems a reasonable assumption because a male must produce a set of signals with enough of an effective range to attract females and keep other males out of his territory. Even where territory sizes are very large relative to the range of a single signal emission, e.g., in exploded lek forms, males typically move about between a variety of signal emission sites and the "effective" active space is at least as large as the territory (B. Snow, 1973a). The value of K depends upon a variety of factors. Suppose a male emits a signal with a certain expenditure of energy on a territory of a certain size. Were the territory to be much smaller but the net energy outlay the same, the active space would be identical and K would automatically be larger in the smaller territory context. If territory size is constant, K will also tend to increase as the energy expended per emission is increased. Finally, a signal emitted with the same energy and from the same sized territory but in different habitats may lead to different values of K depending upon the signal transmission properties of each habitat. All other variables being constant, K should be lower for a visual signal in dense vegetation than in open country.

Given these definitions, the equation for determining territory size becomes

$$KR + S/P + \left(\frac{4kRS}{P}\right)^{1/2} = 1/D_m$$

As P, S, and D_m are determined by extrinsic factors, it follows that the appropriate size of the individual active space, KR, will be completely fixed. This equation allows for a few predictions. First of all, suppose P and D_m are held constant and S is allowed to vary. As S increases, the product KR must decrease to maintain the equality. I have argued that K can only decrease to a value of one in most contexts. It follows that as S gets larger, the value of R must take the brunt of compensation. In other words, when all other factors are equal, male territory size will be an inverse function of female home-range size (see Figure 9–8). At very large values of female home-range size, the active space of the lek is a tiny fraction of the overall lek drawing area, and the absolute size of either male territories or their active spaces may become irrelevant. Secondly, the model predicts that, all other factors being equal, male territory size should be an increasing function of the number of males per lek. This is a rather nonintuitive result of the model. Finally, the size of male territories is quite sensitive to changes in K and will be inversely related to that variable. As noted before, changes in K can cause as well as be caused by changes in male territory size, and this makes more detailed predictions difficult.

The overall prediction that there is an inverse relationship between male territory sizes and female home-range sizes does appear to have generality. The classical lek bat, *Hypsignathus monstrosus*, exhibits male display territories on the lek of 0.008 ha. and female home ranges for a 30–day period of about 10^4 ha. The sympatric and exploded lek bat, *Epomops franqueti*, has male territories of 0.6–0.9 ha. and monthly female home ranges of about 10^2 ha. (Bradbury, 1977a and unpublished observations). Our estimates of density and number of males per lek are similar enough for these two species to expect this good fit. In grouse, too, the model holds up well. Thus ruffed grouse, spruce grouse, and blue grouse all show male territory sizes of 3–10 ha. and female home range sizes (prior to incubation) of 10–20 ha. (Edminster, 1947; Boag, 1965; Gullion, 1967; Brander, 1967; Hjorth, 1970; Ellison, 1971, 1973; Aubin, 1972; Archibald, 1975, 1976). By contrast, sharp-tailed grouse, sage grouse, and greater prairie chickens have male territories of 0.02 ha. or less and female home range sizes of 200–400 ha. (Hamerstrom and Hamerstrom, 1951; Patterson, 1952; Robel et al., 1970; Hjorth, 1970; Kirsch et al., 1973; Wiley, 1973; Rippin and Boag, 1974; Ballard and Robel, 1974; Wallestad and Pyrah, 1974). The densities of males in these species all range from about 0.03 to 0.04 males/ha., and variations in numbers of males per lek seem to be taken up by compensating variations in female home-range sizes (Gullion, 1967; Ellison, 1973; Patterson, 1952; Kirsch et al., 1973). An apparent exception is the capercaillie, which has male territories of about 6–7 ha. and female home ranges of 400 ha. or larger (although the latter have not been measured by radio-tracking) (Hjorth,

1970). This is a case where all things are *not* equal. The densities of displaying males are much lower in capercaillie than in the other grouse; my computations from the data of Hjorth (1970) give a value of D_m of only 0.007 males/ha. These lower densities are not unexpected given the much larger body size of this species. The effect of this lower density, other factors *being* equal, is to increase male territory size above that expected from female home range size alone.

There are currently too few data to test the second prediction for any taxon. As noted, the relations between K and R will be inverse whether K or R is the variable being extrinsically determined. A test of this prediction is suggested by the good correlation between the size of male territories in grouse and the densities of vegetation where they display: That is, open country grouse tend to have small male territories, and forest species tend to have larger territories (Hjorth, 1970; Wiley, 1974). The dissection of causes is difficult in this case because larger female home-range size is also associated with open country habitats. It is interesting to make several specific calculations in this regard. I noted above that the capercaillie, a forest species of grouse, has large male territories of 6–7 ha. each. I have found no references on the exact size of female capercaillie home ranges so I have used two estimates. At the low end, female home ranges ought to be at least as large as those for sage grouse or prairie chickens or about 400 ha. At the upper end, an estimate based on an extrapolation from the larger body size of these birds is 600 ha. Using the above equation, the former estimate leads to a value of K of 3.73, and the latter estimate gives a K value of 1.45. I would like to compare this value to that for other forest grouse. Although there seems to be some uncertainty whether the smaller forest grouse cluster on leks or are simply distributed according to available display habitats, I shall assume for comparison that the clustering that is observed follows the equations outlined above (Gullion, 1967, 1976; Aubin, 1972; Ellison, 1971). For ruffed grouse, this means assuming a mean of 5 males per cluster, a male territory size of 7 ha., a D_m value of 0.04 males /ha., and a female home range size of 20 ha. prior to incubation (Gullion, 1967; Archibald, 1976). The resulting value of K is 1.41. Since territory size is similar for capercaillie and ruffed grouse, this implies that the energetic content and environmental effects on K are similar for the two species (if the lower estimate of 1.45 for capercaillie is accepted) or slightly larger for the larger species (if the larger estimate of 3.73 is used). By contrast, the equivalent calculations for greater prairie chickens using data from Robel and his associates (Robel, 1966; Robel et al., 1970) give a K value of 125 and a total individual active space of about 2.5 ha. Although K is larger for this open country species, the individual active space is actually lower for the prairie chickens than for either of the forest grouse. If the prairie chickens were displaying with the same energy, one would expect the same active space or a larger one given the more open contexts. In fact, the increase in K is not as great as the decrease in R and the product is lower. It is most likely that prairie chickens invest less energy in long-distance signalling than do the forest species. This is reasonable given the fact that lek drawing areas in such high S species depend so little on the actual size of the leks.

D.   Summary of the Model. The model presented above is a dynamic one. By itself, it does not specify *where* leks should be but it does limit the mean number of males per lek, the average spacing between leks, and the size of male territories. If habitats were uniform, stochastic variations in population size might be expected to lead to local extinctions and creations of leks and consequent reshufflings of location to maintain the spacing. One test of the models would be to monitor lek species in uniform habitats to see if spacing parameters are preserved independently of locations. Since habitats are not uniform in many lek species, some modulation of spacing is expected as a function of accessibility to females, signal transmission characteristics, or predator avoidance strategies. In spite of this, the overall correlations between such factors as the degree of clustering and female home-range size should hold.

It is possible to turn these arguments around and suggest that lek spacing is determined strictly by the dispersion of suitable sites, that female home ranges will have to be adjusted by the females to cope with this dispersion of males, and that there will still be some correlation between male dispersions and female movements. A similar conclusion could be reached if lek locations were determined as a result of chance matings by single males and subsequent traditional use of the same sites by both sexes. Although both directions of causality give correlations between male dispersions and female movements, I find it difficult to explain the consistent *direction* of these correlations unless I presume that female home ranges determine male spacings and not vice-versa. In the grouse, female home ranges of 2 ha. are associated with uniform fields of males, ranges of 20 ha. with exploded leks, and ranges of 200 ha. with classical leks. The same patterns appear to hold for bats in spite of radically different types of habitat and radically different diets. In addition, these alternative models ought to lead to many systems in which female home ranges included several leks: Females might increase a foraging range to encompass a distant lek, but they are unlikely to reduce foraging ranges simply because these encompass more than one lek. The available data suggest that more than one lek per female home range is not a common circumstance although much more field work is needed to have an overall picture. In short, the causal sequences outlined by the new models here appear to fit a greater fraction of the data and have greater generality than the alternatives.

V. DETERMINANTS OF FEMALE HOME-RANGE SIZE.

I have concluded above that at least two components of male dispersion, the distance between leks and the sizes of male territories, are functions of the size of female home ranges. Since animals of quite different diets and phylogenies have converged on the lek as a mating strategy, it seems important to ask if there is some common ecological determinant of female home-range size that has favored this convergence. I should like to suggest that, at least for vertebrate lek species, there *is* a common thread in the form of similar foraging strategies.

There are four simple ways in which a change in diet might lead to increased foraging range without concomitant changes in density:

1. A shift to a food that occurs during one season in fewer but richer patches than during other seasons and before the shift.

2. A shift to a food that contains allelochemicals.

3. A shift to a food that is hard to find.

4. A shift to a food with a high within-site variance in particle quality.

The first effect is simply a change in geometry: Where before, food was located in nonoverlapping sets of equally rich and successively available patches, there is now a period in which two adjacent sets share a single larger patch. If animals are distributed passively over such a food dispersion, an initial pattern of small contiguous home ranges will shift to one of larger and overlapping ranges (cf. Bradbury and Vehrencamp, 1976). The second change in diet will cause a foraging animal to leave a located food source before it has satisfied its energy or nutritional needs, and equally importantly, before it has eaten all the available food at that site. The degree of toxicity of the source and the rate of detoxification will determine how much more foraging the animal must attempt and how much food is left at the first site. This will lead to larger and, as other animals may locate the uneaten food, overlapping home ranges. Where diets are altered to include foods that appear in small amounts at unpredictable locations and times, we might expect a forager to miss the next nearest available patch and to travel further than necessary before locating food. Since other animals may find the missed patch, this also leads to larger and more overlapping home ranges than if these food sources were deleted from the diet. Finally, imagine a food source that harbors many food particles or sources per site. Suppose that there is a high variance in the quality of these particles within a site, that an equal pattern obtains at other adjacent sites, and that the locations of all the sites are *known* to foraging animals. These conditions might be expected to lead to "trap-lining" in that foragers would move from site to site selecting the highest quality particles currently present. As long as a forager leaves a current site without exhausting all edible particles, the result will be larger and more over-lapping home ranges than if it remained and ate a wider range of particle qualities at the same site.

As an example of these effects, I wish to summarize unpublished observations on the diets of the classical lek bat, *Hypsignathus monstrosus,* and the exploded lek bat, *Epomops franqueti.* The diets of these two sympatric species are remarkably analogous. Females of each species rely heavily on trap-lined fruit that fits the fourth case cited. In both cases (*Solanum torvum* for *Epomops* and *Anthocleista spp.* for *Hypsignathus*), the plants produce fruit in panicles throughout the year. During the mating seasons of the bats, each plant may

FOODS AND FORAGING OF EPOMOPHORINE BATS

I. CHARACTERISTICS OF FOOD SUPPLY:

FEATURE	TRAP-LINED COMPONENT	OPPORTUNISTIC COMPONENT
1. DENSITY OF PLANTS WITH RIPE FRUIT	10-200/HA.	.05-.10/HA.
2. PERIOD OF AVAILABILITY PER PLANT	ALL YEAR	10 DAYS/1-2 YEARS
3. BATS FEEDABLE/NIGHT/ PLANT	.02-.10	1 OR LESS: 75% 2-30: 25%
4. PREDICTABILITY	HIGH	LOW
5. PROBABILITY OF FINDING NEAREST AVAILABLE PLANT	HIGH	LOW
6. TEMPORAL VARIATION IN NO. RIPE FRUIT/PLANT		
7. RESULTING HOME RANGE	MODERATE	LARGE

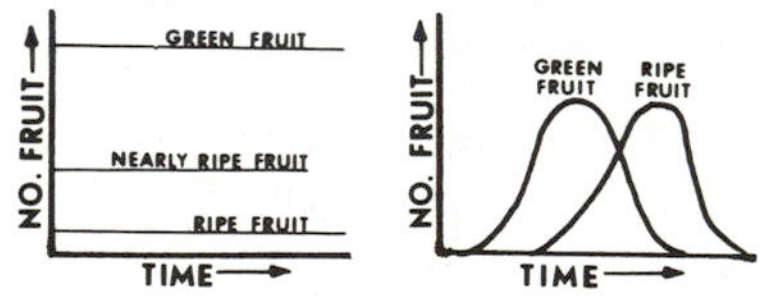

II. TYPICAL FORAGING TRACKS:

A. TRAP-LINED COMPONENT:

B. OPPORTUNISTIC COMPONENT:

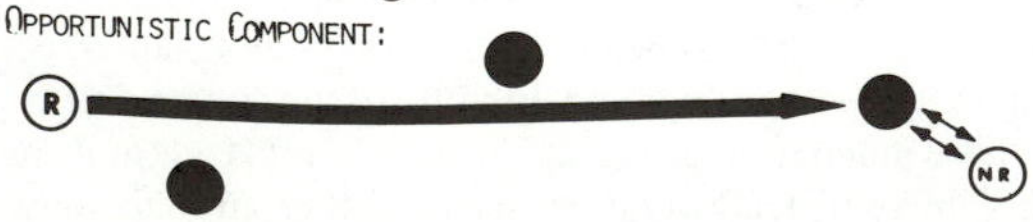

Figure 9–9.   Summary of dispersion characteristics of foods *Hypsignathus monstrosus* and *Epomops franqueti* (I) and resulting patterns of foraging (II).

have hundreds to thousands of fruit, but only 1 per cent–2 per cent are ripe on any one night, a somewhat greater percentage are nearly ripe, and the vast majority are green and sour (Figure 9–9). Radio-tracked females of both bat species fly directly to the same locations on successive nights, remove a few fruit from each plant, and move on to other plants. They frequently return to the first plants later in the night, implying that fruit originally rejected on the first pass becomes more acceptable as the average local quality of fruit declines. Trap-lined fruit constitute the single largest component of the diets of females in both bat species.

The second most important component in the diets are hard-to-find fruit of strangler figs (genus *Ficus*). Our phenological studies of strangler figs in Gabon, continued and elaborated by M. Georges Michaloud, indicate that most forest *Ficus* have small fruit crops that can only feed one or fewer bats for the 5–10 days they have fruit. In addition, the many species of *Ficus* are randomly dispersed in the forest, show intervals between fruiting of from 1–3 years, and are totally asynchronous in fruiting schedules. That this pattern of dispersion makes fruiting *Ficus* hard to find is demonstrated by the missing of nearby fruiting trees by foraging female bats. Once a radio-tracked female bat finds a fig in fruit, she will return nightly to it without fail until it is exhausted. Since the trees are not defended, the failure of a female to stop at a nearby fig in fruit must imply that she did not find it. Thus, in the two most important components of the diets of female *Hypsignathus* and *Epomops*, large overlapping home ranges are favored by the types of foods utilized.

It is possible as well to explain the *differences* in female home-range sizes of these two bats by examining their diets quantitatively. As summarized in Table 9–I, the two species differ in the relative weights given to trap-lined and opportunistic (hard-to-find) plants, the relative abundances of the foods taken, and in body size. There are four reasons why the home ranges of *Epomops* females are found to be a hundred times smaller than those of sympatric *Hypsignathus* females:

1. Female *Epomops* are only about half as large as *Hypsignathus* females and, all other things being equal, should have smaller home ranges.

2. In suitable habitats, the trap-lined component utilized by *Epomops* females occurs at higher local plant densities and matures at an earlier age than that utilized by *Hypsignathus* females.

Table 9–1.   Summary of differences in dietary compositions and home ranges of female *Hypsignathus monstrosus* and *Epomops franqueti*. Diets were determined using seeds and fibers in collected feces and home ranges by radio-tracking adult animals.

I. DIET:	EPOMOPS	HYPSIGNATHUS
1. Trapline Component:	*Solanum torvum*	*Anthocleista spp.*
per cent of Diet:	36%	52%
2. Opportunistic Component:	*Ficus spp.*	*Ficus spp.*
per cent of Diet:	21%	36%
3. Other Components:	*Musanga*, Guava, Banana	*Musanga*
per cent of Diet:	43%	12%
4. Seed Loads (N)	110	135
II. HOME RANGE:	EPOMOPS	HYPSIGNATHUS
1. Area	10^2 Ha.	10^2 Ha.
2. Diameter	1.2–1.6 km.	10–12 km.
3. Females Tracked	7	15
4. Periods Tracked	2–60 Days	10–90 Days

3. Female *Epomops* rely less heavily on strangler figs for food (only 21 per cent of all feces samples) than do *Hypsignathus* females (36 per cent of all feces samples). Since ripe figs occur at densities of only 0.05–0.10/ha. at any time, and ripe trap-lined components occur in both species at densities of 10–200/ha., this should lead to larger home ranges in the species preferring the more dispersed component.

4. Female *Epomops* have a more catholic diet than *Hypsignathus* females, and take a larger number of alternative food sources such as *Musanga, Cecropia,* banana, guava, etc. (43 per cent vs. 12 per cent of all feces samples respectively).

I would like to argue that the dietary preferences of these two species predispose them to have large and overlapping female home ranges and that this leads to self-advertisement and leks as the only viable male mating strategies. The differences in diets and body size change the size of female home-range sizes by two orders of magnitude, and this difference is reflected in the classical lek dispersion of the larger species and the exploded lek pattern of the smaller form.

How well might similar contrasts explain the patterns of male dispersion in other vertebrate groups with leks? As usual, the data are spotty, but I think the overall fit is good. Among the tetraonids, Wittenberger (1978) recently took issue with Wiley's (1973) statements that there were no clear correlations between diet and mating systems in grouse. In particular, Wittenberger cited a general trend towards more varied diets in the monogamous grouse and a bias towards monoculture herbivory in the more promiscuous species. He interpreted the correlations by arguing that abundance of food was lowest for the monogamous forms and "super-abundant" for the promiscuous ones. Although I think the correlation is intriguing, I do not find the interpretations compelling. On the one hand, we might expect to find monogamous grouse at much lower densities if their food was less abundant than that of promiscuous species. This does not seem to be the case. On the other hand, it has been shown by workers on primates (Glander, 1975) and antelopes (Jarman, 1974) that monoculture herbivory rarely leads to a "super-abundance" of food. On the contrary, such herbivores tend to be highly selective about plant part and phenological stage taken, and this may even lead to *lower* effective food abundances than with a more varied diet. In fact, the evidence is strong that grouse are very selective feeders when utilizing plant material (Edminster, 1947; Wiley, 1974; Ellison, 1976).

I believe Wittenberger's correlations can be interpreted and elaborated as follows. With exceptions, there is a general trend towards larger body sizes as grouse move from monogamy through exploded leks to classical leks. This body size component can be explained by arguing that, other factors being equal, we might expect larger female home-range sizes in larger-bodied animals. The exceptions and modulations arise, I suspect, because of different dispersions, not necessarily overall abundances, of foods taken by different grouse species. By analogy with *Epomops* or antelopes (Jarman, 1974), one might expect the smaller grouse to favor a wide variety of foods but to take only the highest-quality items. The combination will lead to small home ranges. The shift to monoculture herbivory leads to greater selectivity for plant part and phenological stage, and, depending upon the degree of local phenological synchrony, larger home ranges as a result. This general trend is paralleled in the antelopes (also in conjunction with increasing body size), and culminates at one extreme with the topi and the Uganda kob. These two species feed on monocultures of plants, show high selectivity for phenological stage, and exhibit classical lek behaviors. In fact, the potential parallels between grouse and African antelopes seem particularly striking to me and I am surprised they did not receive more attention in Geist's (1977) recent review. Exceptions to the overall trend in grouse include the red grouse, which is a monocultural herbivore on small home ranges. This could easily be explained by showing that (a) heather has greater spatial homogeneity in plant phenological stage than sage or (b) that the fraction of edible material is higher per plant in heather than in sage. I do not know if either case is true, but it points up the need to undertake a detailed and quantitative comparison of grouse diets. Were we to have in hand the reasons why a female red grouse can forage in 1 per cent of the area needed by a female prairie chicken, the complete sequence of causation from diet through female home-range size to male dispersion would be available.

In manakins, there is some evidence for trap-line foraging of fruits in several species. The best data are for the long-tailed manakin, which exhibits a dispersed pattern of males with cooperative displays (Foster, 1977a, b). A preferred food for this species is the fruit of *Ardisia revoluta*. These occur on panicles and a single tree may have many thousands of fruit at any one time. The fruit ripen asynchronously resulting in a large variance in fruit quality both within a tree and within a panicle. Foster suggests that the birds know the locations of these trees and J. Radich (unpublished observations) has observed the birds being highly selective about which fruit are taken. Breitwisch and Pliske (1974) report that white-bearded manakins forage on *Anthurium* fruit that are available over long periods and show gradual ripening. Whether the partitioned timing of fruiting in the Melastomes favored by other manakins (D. Snow, 1962) will lead to larger or smaller home ranges is hard to predict without knowing the within-tree variance in ripening and the overall dispersion of the preferred trees.

In a few of the other lek taxa, there is suggestive evidence that foraging modulates female home ranges, but much further study is needed. Hermit hummingbirds are frequently but not always lek species. As noted by Stiles (1975), hermit hummingbirds are also most often trap-lining species, and sympatric nonhermit hummingbirds are territorial. Most of the birds-of-paradise eat both fruit and insects, and the ratios clearly differ among the species (Gilliard, 1969). This would be a particularly interesting group to study because they are large enough to be radio-tracked for home ranges and show a considerable diversity of male dispersions.

I think it is important to note that available data on diets and foraging ranges are often inapplicable for contrasts because they do not separate male and female foraging patterns. This is partly true of the manakin data cited above. It is now clear that dietary preferences and resulting foraging patterns are often different for the two sexes in lek species. In both *Hypsignathus* and *Epomops,* figs constitute a much larger fraction of the male diet (58 per cent of feces samples in *Hypsignathus*) than of the female diet (36 per cent of feces samples in *Hypsignathus*). Female *Hypsignathus* may fly 1–4 km. from their day roosts to feed each night, whereas a foraging male may make nightly flights of 10 km. or more. Male capercaillie feed on different parts of preferred plants and in different areas from females (Hjorth, 1970; Wiley, 1974). These differences are not entirely unexpected. As pointed out in an earlier section, a change in diet that increases female home-range size may not increase male home ranges if the latter do not alter their diets. This will result in both different diets and a shift to self-advertisement strategies by males. It is also possible that differential diets arise as a result of the lek mating system itself. For example, K. Fristrup (personal communication) has suggested that the differences in diet in *Hypsignathus* reflect differences in overall life history strategies for the two sexes. The preferred fruit of males is harder to find but when found provides a local rich patch of food; the food preferred by females is always predictable in location but has a lower average quality because unripe fruit may be taken. Female reproductive strategies are conservative in that a steady output of one young per season will maximize lifetime fitness. Males are more opportunistic and, for the short period following the location of a rich fig crop, a male may be able to garner more matings at once than he will ever achieve having regular access to a more conservative food source. Regardless of the cause, the risk that the two sexes may have highly divergent foraging strategies requires that field observations be kept separate until differences are known to be minimal.

VI. CONCLUSIONS.

I concur that lek evolution requires the meeting of certain necessary conditions such as emancipation of the male from parental duties and the nondefensibility of either resources or female groups. These conditions are favored by certain pre-adaptations and by certain ecological conditions. By themselves, they are apparently not sufficient to favor the evolution of leks. I believe the critical factor that must be added is an increase in female home range size relative to the size of existing male territories. This latter shift can be triggered by a change in diet to either hard-to-find or trap-lined foods. Once it occurs, males are obliged to shift to self-advertisement as a primary mating strategy. Since clustered males actually lose out from a geometrical point of view, whereas females gain if males cluster, a dynamic equilibrium results in which the degree of male clustering depends to a large degree on the size of remale home ranges. Thus, the geometrical costs to males of clustering are just equalled by the preference of females for clusters *and* their abilities to exert a choice. In the steady state, the distance between clusters increases with female home range size while the size of male territories decreases with it. The number of males per cluster depends on the nature of alternative mating opportunities, the degree of unanimity in female mate choice, and the overall life history expectations of males. The degree to which the male dispersion fits these predictions will vary depending on the heterogeneity of the habitat utilized, the seasonal fluctuations in male densities and female home ranges, and the stability of life history expectations for males. All of these predictions are for *mean* values in a large population: They thus allow for considerable local variation through history as long as the average dispersion parameters are constant.

ACKNOWLEDGEMENTS.

The author wants to thank Douglas Morrison, Amasa Miller, and Georges Michaloud for access to unpublished results. Sandra Vehrencamp and Kurt Fristrup played major roles in the development of the models. Helpful comments and criticisms were provided by many of my colleagues at UCSD. This work was supported by NSF Grant BNS-7604400.

REFERENCES

Alexander, R. D. 1974. The evolution of social behavior. *Ann. Rev. Ecol. System* 5:325–383.
———. 1975. Natural selection and specialized chorusing behavior in acoustical insects. pp. 35–77, in *Insects, Science and Society,* D. Pimentel, ed. New York: Academic Press.
Archibald, H. L. 1975. Temporal patterns of spring space use by ruffed grouse. *J. Wildl. Mgmt.* 39:472–481.
———. 1976. Spatial relationships of neighboring male ruffed grouse in spring. *J. Wildl. Mgmt.* 40:750–760.
Aubin, A. E. 1972. Aural communication in ruffed grouse. *Can. J. Zool.* 50:1225–1229.
Ballard, W. B., and R. J. Robel. 1974. Reproductive importance of dominant male greater prairie chickens. *Auk* 91:75–86.
Berger, D. D., F. Hamerstrom, and F. N. Hamerstrom. 1963. The effect of raptors on prairie chickens on the booming grounds. *J. Wildl. Mgmt.* 27:778–791.
Boag, D. A. 1965. Population attributes of blue grouse in southwestern Alberta. *Can. J. Zool.* 44:799–814.
Boag, D. A. and K. M. Sumanik. 1969. Characteristics of drumming sites selected by ruffed grouse in Alberta. *J. Wildl. Mgmt.* 33:621–628.
Bossert, W. H., and E. O. Wilson. 1963. The analysis of olfactory communication among animals. *J. Theor. Biol.* 5:443–469.

Bradbury, J. 1977a. Lek mating behavior in the hammerheaded bat. *Zeit. Tierpsych.* 45:225–255.

———. 1977b. Social organization and communication. Pages 1–72 in W. Wimsatt, ed. *The Biology of Bats*, Vol. 3. Academic Press, New York.

Bradbury, J., and S. Vehrencamp. 1976. Social organization and foraging in emballonurid bats. II. A model for the determination of group size. *Behav. Ecol. Sociobiol.* 1:383–404.

Brander, R. B. 1967. Movements of female ruffed grouse during the mating season. *Wilson Bull.* 79:28–36.

Breitwisch, R., and M. Pliske. 1974. *Anthurium* fruits as a food of white-bearded Manakins. *Ibis* 116:365.

Buck, J., and E. Buck. 1978. Toward a functional interpretation of synchronous flashing by fireflies. *Amer. Nat.* 112:471–492.

Buechner, H. K., and H. D. Roth. 1974. The lek system in Uganda kob antelope. *Amer. Zool.* 14:145–162.

Buechner, H. K., and R. Schloeth. 1965. Ceremonial mating behavior in Uganda kob (*Adenota kob thomasii*). *Zeit. Tierpsych.* 22:209–225.

Choate, T. S. 1963. Habitat and population dynamics of white-tailed ptarmigan in Montana. *J. Wildl. Mgmt.* 27:684–699.

Crook, J. H. 1964. The evolution of social organization and visual communication in the weaver birds (Ploceinae). *Behaviour,* Suppl. 10:1–178.

———. 1965. The adaptive significance of avian social organizations. *Symp. Zool. Soc. Lond.* 14:181–218.

Downes, J. A. 1969. The swarming and mating flight of Diptera. *Ann. Rev. Entomol.* 14:271–298.

Edminster, F. C. 1947. *The Ruffed Grouse*. The Macmillan Co., New York. 385 pp.

Ellison, L. N. 1971. Territoriality in Alaskan spruce grouse. *Auk* 88:652–664.

———. 1973. Seasonal social organization and movements of spruce grouse. *Condor* 75:375–385.

———. 1976. Winter food selection by Alaskan spruce grouse. *J. Wildl. Mgmt.* 40:205–213.

Emlen, Stephen T. 1976. Lek organization and mating strategies in the bullfrog. *Behav. Ecol. Sociobiol.* 1:283–313.

Emlen, S. T. and L. W. Oring. 1977. Ecology, sexual selection, and the evolution of mating systems. *Science* 197:215–223.

Fisher, R. A. 1958. *The Genetical Theory of Natural Selection*. 2nd Edition. Dover Publications, New York. 291 pp.

Floody, O. R. and A. P. Arnold. 1975. Uganda kob (*Adenota kob thomasii*): territoriality and the spatial distributions of sexual and agonistic behaviors at a territoritial ground. *Zeit. Tierpsych.* 37:192–212.

Foster, M. S. 1977a. Odd couples in manakins: a study of social organization and cooperative breeding in *Chiroxiphia linearis*. *Amer. Nat.* 111:845–853.

———. 1977b. Ecological and nutritional effects of food scarcity on a tropical frugivorous bird and its fruit source. *Ecol.* 58:73–85.

Fretwell, S. D. 1972. Populations in a seasonal environment. Monograph #5: *Monographs in Population Biology. Princeton University Press,* Princeton, 217 pp.

Geist, V. 1977. A comparison of social adapations in relation to ecology in gallinaceous bird and ungulate societies. *Ann. Rev. Ecol. Syst.* 8:193–207.

Gillespie, J. H. 1977. Natural selection for variances in offspring numbers: a new evolutionary principle. *Amer. Nat. 111:1010–1014.*

Gilliard, E. T. 1969. *Birds of Paradise and Bower Birds*. Weidenfeld and Nicolson, London. 485 pp.

Glander, K. E. 1975. Habitat description and resource utilization: a preliminary report on mantled howling monkey ecology. Pages 37–57 in R. H. Tuttle, ed. *Socioecology and Psychology of Primates*. Mouton, The Hague/Paris.

Gullion, G. W. 1967. Selection and use of drumming sites by male ruffed grouse. *Auk* 84:87–112.

———. 1976. Reevaluation of "activity clustering" by male grouse. *Auk* 93:192–193.

Hamerstrom, F. N. and F. Hamerstrom. 1951. Mobility of the sharp-tailed grouse in relation to its ecology and distribution. *Amer. Midl. Nat.* 46:174–226.

Hartzler, J. E. 1974. Predation and the daily timing of sage grouse leks. *Auk* 91:532–536.

Hjorth, I. 1970. Reproductive behavior in Tetraonidae. *Viltrevy* 7(4):184–596.

Hoffman, D. M. 1963. The lesser prairie chicken in Colorado. *J. Wildl. Mgmt.* 27:726–732.

Hogan-Warburg, A. J. 1966. Social behavior of the ruff *Philomachus pugnax. Ardea* 54:1–45.

Jarman, P. J. 1974. The social organization of antelope in relation to their ecology. *Behaviour* 48:215–267.

Kirsch, L. M., A. T. Klett, and H. W. Miller. 1973. Land use and prairie grouse population relationships in North Dakota. *J. Wildl. Mgmt.* 37:449–453.

Koivisto, I. 1965. Behavior of the black grouse, *Lyrurus tetrix* during the spring display. *Finnish Game Res.* 26:1–60.

Kruijt, J. P. and J. A. Hogan. 1967. Social behavior on the lek in black grouse. *Ardea* 55:203–240.

Kruijt, J. P., G. J. deVos, and I. Bossema. 1972. The arena system of black grouse. Pages 399–423. *Proc. XVᵗʰ Intl. Ornith. Cong.* E. J. Brill, Leiden.

Lack, D. 1968. *Ecological Adaptations for Breeding in Birds.* Chapman and Hall, London.

Leuthold, W. 1966. Territorial behavior of Uganda kob. *Behav.* 27:255–256.

Lill, A. 1974a. Social organization and space utilization in the lek-forming white-bearded manakin (*M. manacus trinitatis*). *Z. Tierpsych.* 36:513–530.

———. 1974b. Sexual behavior of the lek-forming white-bearded manakin (*M. manacus trinitatis*). *Z. Tierpsych.* 36:1–36.

———. 1975. Lek behavior in the golden-headed manakin (*Pipra erythrocephala*) in Trinidad (West Indies). *Forts. Verhaltensforsch.*, Heft 18. Verlag Paul Parey, Berlin/Hamburg.

Miller, G. R., A. Watson, and D. Jenings. 1970. Responses of red grouse populations to experimental improvement of their food. Pages 323–334 in A. Watson, ed. *Animal Populations in Relation to Their Food Resources,* Blackwell Scientific Publications, Oxford/Edinburgh.

Monfort-Braham, N. 1975. Variations dans la structure sociale du topi *Damaliscus korrigum* Ogilby, au Parc National de l'Akagera, Rwanda. *Z. Tierpsych.* 39:332–364.

Otte, D. 1974. Effects and functions in the evolution of signalling systems. *Ann. Rev. Ecol. System.* 5:385–416.

Patterson, R. L. 1952. *The Sage Grouse in Wyoming.* Sage Books, Denver.

Pianka, E. R., and W. S. Parker. 1975. Age specific reproductive strategies. *Amer. Nat.* 109:453–464.

Pitelka, F. A., R. T. Holmes, S. F. MacLean. 1974. Ecology and evolution of social organization in Arctic Sandpipers. *Amer. Zool.* 14:185–204.

Rhijn, J. G. van. 1973. Behavioral dimorphism in male ruffs, *Philomachus pugnax. Behav.* 47:153–229.

Rippin, A. B. and D. A. Boag. 1974. Recruitment to populations of male sharp-tailed grouse. *J. Wildl. Mgmt.* 38:616–621.

Robel, R. J. 1966. Booming territory size and mating success of the greater prairie chicken *(Tympanuchus cupido pinnatus).* Anim. Behav. 14: 328–331.

Robel, R. J. and W. B. Ballard. 1974. Lek social organization and reproductive success in the Greater Prairie Chicken. *Amer. Zool.* 14:121–128.

Robel, R. J., J. N. Briggs, J. J. Cebula, N. J. Silvy, C. E. Viers, and P. G. Watt. 1970. Greater prairie chicken ranges, movements, and habitat usage in Kansas. *J. Wildl. Mgmt.* 34:286–306.

Schodde, R., and J. L. McKean. 1973. The species of the genus *Parotia* (Paradiseidae) and their relationships. *Emu* 73:145–156.

Schwartz, C. W. 1945. The ecology of the prairie chicken in Missouri. *Univ. Missouri Stud.* 20:1–99.

Sick, H. 1967. Courtship behavior in the manakins (Pipridae): a review. *Living Bird* 6:5–22.

Snow, B. K. 1973a. Notes on the behavior of the White Bellbird. *Auk* 90:743–751.

———. 1973b. The behavior and ecology of hermit hummingbirds in the Kanuku Mountains, Guyana. *Wilson Bull.* 85:163–177.

———. 1974. Lek behavior and breeding of Guy's hermit hummingbird *Phaethornis guy. Ibis* 116:278–297.

Snow, D. W. 1962. A field study of the black and white manakin, *Manacus manacus*, in Trinidad. *Zoologica* 47:65–104.

———. 1963. The evolution of manakin displays. *Proc. 13ᵗʰ Intl. Ornith. Cong.*, Vol. I, pp. 553–561.

Stiles, F. G. 1975. Ecology, flowering phenology, and hummingbird pollination of some Costa Rican *Heliconia* species. *Ecol.* 56:285–301.

Treisman, N. 1975. Predation and the evolution of gregariousness. I. Models for concealment and evasion. *Anim. Behav.* 23:779–800.

Trivers, R. L. 1972. Parental investment and sexual selection. Chap. 7 in B. Campbell, ed. *Sexual Selection and the Descent of Man.* Aldine Press, Chicago.

Wallestad, R., and D. Pyrah. 1974. Movement and nesting of sage grouse hens in Central Montana. *J. Wildl. Mgmt. 38:630–633.*

Watson, A., and G. R. Miller. 1971. Territory size and aggression in a fluctuating red grouse population. *J. Anim. Ecol.* 40:367–383.

Wiley, R. H. 1973. Territoriality and non-random mating in sage grouse, *Centrocercus urophasianus*. *Anim. Behav. Monographs* 6:85–169.

———. 1974. Evolution of social organization and life history patterns among grouse (Aves:Tetraonidae). *Quart. Rev. Biol.* 49:201–227.

Williams, G. C. 1966. Natural selection, the costs of reproduction, and a refinement of Lack's principle. *Amer. Nat.* 100:687–690.

Wittenberger, J. F. 1978. The evolution of mating systems in grouse. *Condor* 80:126–137.

Zahavi, A. 1975. Mate selection—a selection for a handicap. *J. Theor. Biol.* 53:205–214.

III

Parental Strategies in Vertebrates

10

Natural Selection and the Evolution of Interspecific Brood Care in Fishes

Kenneth R. McKaye

It is theory which decides what we can observe.

Einstein to Heisenberg 1926 (Heisenberg, 1971)

INTRODUCTION

Most recent theories concerning the evolution of social systems have drawn support from or have addressed questions pertinent to the social insects, mammals, and birds (Wilson, 1975). Until recently (Barlow, 1974; Blumer, 1979; Perrone and Zaret, 1979; Rohwer, 1978) little attention has been paid to fish social systems. The aqualung, however, has greatly facilitated direct field observations of fish behavior, which can begin to make important contributions to sociobiological theory.

Fish exhibit modes of sociality usually attributed only to higher vertebrates. These behaviors include territoriality (Clarke, 1970), biparental care of young (Fryer and Iles, 1972), and "lekking" or breeding arena behavior (Loiselle and Barlow, *in press*), along with seemingly "altruistic behavior" (McKaye, 1977; 1979). The wide range of breeding strategies employed by fishes (Breder and Rosen, 1966; Perrone and Zaret, 1979) bears witness to this diversity of behavior. The hamlets, Family Serranidae, are simultaneously hermaphroditic (E. Fischer, pers. comm.), with individuals changing male and female roles while courting. Still others are parthenogenetic but require insemination by males of another species to activate the eggs (White, 1970).

Cichlids and catfishes are unique among fishes in that both parents often participate in the guarding of the fry (Breder and Rosen, 1966). The cichlids, in particular, are interesting because of their diversity of parental care. This care can vary from biparental care with close cooperation between parents in defending the young to uniparental care with either the female or the male tending the brood (Fryer and Iles, 1972). Other fishes of different families exhibit no parental care, simply releasing their eggs into the pelagic environment (Breder and Rosen, 1966).

Fishes, for practical reasons alone, are an ideal vertebrate group in which to test many sociobiological and ecological theories as well as to expand general knowledge of vertebrate social systems. In their natural habitats, many species are easy to observe at close range. Specimens can be collected in large numbers without having a major detrimental effect upon the population. Furthermore, fishes, as contrasted to birds and mammals, can be studied relatively realistically and inexpensively under laboratory or semi-natural pond conditions.

Interspecific brood care and nest utilization among fishes are behavioral phenomena of direct interest to studies of vertebrate social systems and the evolution of cooperative behavior. Although these behaviors are widespread among fishes they are not well known to sociobiologists (Wilson, 1975) or even to individuals commenting upon interspecific brood care by fishes (anonymous, 1977; Ribbink, 1977; Coyne and Sohn, 1978). Often when interspecific brood care is noted, analogies to bird brood parasitism are made by claiming that the adopted young are parasitic upon their foster parents. This adopting behavior is presumed not to have been a product of natural selection, but rather it is supposed that the host simply makes a mistake (anonymous, 1977; M. H. Carr, 1942; A. Carr, 1946; Coyne and Sohn, 1978; Ribbink, 1977).

This view arises from studies of birds. Interspecific brood care and brood parasitism in birds have been the subject of considerable research (see Payne, 1977, for a review of the subject). Brood parasites lay their eggs in the nests of host species who then incubate and rear young to whom they are not genetically related. Such parasitic action usually depresses the reproductive success of the host parent, and, hence, ought to be disadvantageous for the host birds. Most species engaging in brood parasitism are cuckoos—Family Cuculidae—thus this form of parasitism is often termed "cuckoo behavior." For example, there are Hymenoptera known as cuckoo bees of the genus *Psithyrus* that parasitize the nest of social bumble bees (Askew, 1971). Ants and wasps also engage in alien brood substitution; this behavior has been called both "cleptoparasitism" and "cuckooism" (Wilson, 1971). The term "cuckoo behavior," with the inference of social parasitism reducing the host's reproductive potential, has also been recently used to describe interspecific brood adoptions by three cichlid species in Lake Malaŵi, Africa (anonymous, 1977; Coyne and Sohn, 1978; Ribbink, 1977).

The cuckoo hypothesis, however, is inadequate to explain the existence of interspecific brood care by certain fishes. I will review the relevant literature (Table 1) in light of three general hypotheses: (1) the cuckoo hypothesis (e.g., Ribbink, 1977); (2) the mistaken-identity hypothesis (Coyne and Sohn, 1978); and (3) the adaptive or mutualistic hypotheses (McKaye and Hallacher, 1973; McKaye and McKaye, 1977). I will argue that

Table 10–1.   Interspecific brood care by fishes observed in the field.

Alien Young	Foster Parents	Author and Date
Haplochromis sp.	*Tilapia saka* or *squamipinnis*	Lowe, 1952
Tilapia melanopleura	*Tilapia mariae*	Burchard, 1967
T. mariae	*T. melanopleura*	Burchard, 1967
Etroplus suratensis	*Etroplus maculatus*	Ward & Wyman, 1975, 1977
E. maculatus	*E. suratensis*	Ward & Wyman, 1975, 1977
Haplochromis chrysonotus	*Haplochromis polystigma*	Ribbink, 1977
	H. macrostoma	Ribbink, 1977
	Serranochromis robustus	Ribbink, 1977
Cichlasoma citrinellum	*Neetroplus nematopus*	McKaye & McKaye, 1977
	Cichlasoma longimanus	McKaye & McKaye, 1977
C. longimanus	*C. nicaraguense*	McKaye & McKaye, 1977
N. nematopus	*C. citrinellum*	McKaye & McKaye, 1977
Cichlasoma dovii	*C. nicaraguense**	McKaye & McKaye, 1977
Haplochromis taeniolatus (?)	*Haplochromis kiwinge*	This paper
H. kiwinge	*H. heterodon* (?)	This paper
Lethrinops sp.	*H. heterodon* (?)	This paper
Unidentified 3-spot cichlid	*H. heterotaenia* (?)	This paper
Lepomis gibbosus	*Esox niger**	Shoemaker, 1947
Notemigonus crysoleucas	*Lepomis punctatus*	M. H. Carr, 1946
Erimyzon sucetta	*Micropterus salmoides*	M. H. Carr, 1942

22 examples of the use by cyprinids of the nests of other species Hunter & Hasler, 1965.

(?) Species identification uncertain.

*   Foster parent observed defending pure brood of another species with none of their own young present.

the third hypothesis, in which natural selection is presumed to be the driving force behind the evolution of interspecific brood care by fishes, is most likely to be correct. This hypothesis states that fish who adopt nonrelated young are often more successful in rearing young of their own than are fish who do not adopt. However, this relative increase in success will be dependent upon an interplay between parents or young for limited resources. I will further argue that behavioral plasticity ought to be evident in acceptance or rejection of nonrelated young in a variable biological environment.

EXAMPLES OF INTERSPECIFIC BROOD CARE BY FISHES

Largemouth bass

M. H. Carr (1942) was one of the first to describe interspecific brood care in fishes and the first to explain the interactions in terms of brood parasitism. In her study she observed largemouth bass, *Micropterus salmoides,* defending the eggs and young of the lake chubsucker, *Erimyzon sucetta.* She followed this work with observations on interspecific brood care of the young and eggs of the golden shiner, *Notemigonus crysoleucas,* by the spotted sunfish, *Lepomis punctatus* (M. H. Carr, 1946). In both cases she attributed this phenomenon to social parasitism comparable to that between "the cowbird (*Molothrus ater ater*) and various host birds" (M. H. Carr, 1942). Fortunately, M. H. Carr (1942, Table 10–1) presents data that permit a reexamination of her conclusion that chubsuckers are parasites upon the bass.

Male largemouth bass remain on the nest for up to 30 days. If they succeed in rearing eggs and fry, they defend the fry for 8–9 days after hatching. M. H. Carr (1942) reports that the adopted fish and the parents' own young "were indistinguishable (to her) on the basis of swimming activity, schooling habits, and color pattern." If brood parasitism is occurring, the care of heterospecific fry should directly depress the reproductive success of largemouth bass. This depression might result from competition between alien and host young for food or for parental attention.

Of 22 largemouth bass nests in which eggs were spawned, 5 had chubsucker eggs and 17 did not. Of 14 continuously observed nests without chubsucker young, the fry of only one nest survived. Four of the five broods of young with chubsucker fry present survived to leave the nest! Rather than demonstrating parasitism (disadvantage to the host parent), Carr's data clearly show that largemouth bass that cared for chubsucker eggs had a higher brood survival rate (80 per cent vs 7 per cent) than those that did not.

I am not familiar with the system that Carr studied; therefore, I can only speculate as to why bass with chubsucker eggs were more successful in rearing their eggs and young than those without chubsucker eggs. M. H. Carr (1942) could not recognize the factors that led to bass success, but it is possible that chubsuckers can sense which bass might be successful and deposit their eggs in such nests. This explanation would be consistent with the cuckoo-parasitism hypothesis if the chubsuckers chose potentially successful bass and actually reduced the host's reproductive potential in a manner that is not readily discerned. Another hypothesis is that the addition of chubsucker eggs is advantageous to the largemouth bass in reducing predation by bluegills, *Lepomis macrochirus,* upon the parents' own eggs. Given an attack upon a nest by bluegills, the presence of chubsucker eggs in the nest might reduce the probability that eggs or fry of the largemouth bass would be eaten. M. H. Carr (1942) states that because the male bass left their nests so frequently, an "abnormally great mortality of eggs and fry resulted." This second hypothesis is consistent with McKaye and McKaye's (1977) view that "between species and within species adoptions of unrelated individuals should occur when predation pressure is intense and predation upon the parent's young can be reduced."

Kramer and Smith (1960) also observed interspecific brood care by largemouth bass. They found that over a three-year period in two environments—a lake and an adjoining slough—from 4 per cent to 75 per cent of the active bass nests in the lake and from 40 per cent to 94 per cent of those in the slough had eggs of a cyprinid fish, the golden shiner, in them. The proportion of golden shiner eggs ranged from 0.006 to 0.784 of all eggs present in the nests. They also reported that in two different years the behavior of male bass toward golden shiners varied. In one year the males did not interfere with the shiners attempting to spawn in their nests but in the second year the males tried to drive shiners away. These different responses explain the varying proportions of golden shiner eggs in bass nests and indicate that bass may regulate the number of foreign eggs deposited and that the defense of shiner eggs is unlikely to be the result of mistaken recognition. The authors further report that golden shiner reproduction was highest in successful bass nests and that the number of golden shiner young "was directly proportional to the percentage of bass nests utilized for spawning in the spring." Consequently, largemouth bass can apparently regulate the population size of golden shiners by allowing or not allowing adult shiners to drop eggs into their nests.

The tending of shiner eggs by largemouth bass as described by Kramer and Smith (1960) seems to be in the best interest of the golden shiner. The question remains, are golden shiners "parasitic" upon largemouth bass or is there some actual advantage to bass who defend foreign eggs or fry? Unfortunately, data on the success of bass in relation to deposition of shiner eggs are not given. The authors do, however, cite Richardson's (1913) report that bass fingerlings seek protection from predators in schools of golden shiners.

Cyprinids

Cyprinids have been the most extensively reported family of fishes who engage in interspecific utilization of nests or brood adoptions. This is probably because cyprinids often spawn above nests (Hunter and Hasler, 1965) and their eggs drop into the nests of other species. Because cyprinids do not always directly lay eggs upon a substrate, spawning over a nest is a useful adaptation to any fish who has another tend its young. This form of spawning enhances the interspecific relationship regardless of whether it is ultimately parasitic or mutualistic to the host. If the relationship between a cyprinid and a nonrelated nesting adult is mutualistic, dropping eggs from above then prevents predation by the alien, cyprinid parent on the host's eggs.

Hunter and Hasler (1965) list 22 examples of interspecific nest utilization by cyprinids, and I will refer the reader to their excellent review rather than repeat the details here. Occasionally the host species attempts to drive the cyprinid away and eat the cyprinid eggs (M. H. Carr, 1946), but often the host species shows no aggression toward the alien cyprinid parent (Hunter and Hasler, 1965). Hankinson (1920) even observed mutualistic interactions and a division of labor between the hornyhead chub, *Hybopsis biguttata,* and the common shiner, *Notropis cornutus.* In this case, the male hornyhead transported pebbles to the nest while the common shiner only guarded the nest.

Pickerel–Pumpkinseed

Shoemaker (1947) is probably the first person to have considered interspecific brood care in fishes as an adaptive "mutualistic coaction." He observed chain pickerel, *Esox niger,* defend the eggs and young of the pumpkinseed, *Lepomis gibbosus,* from predation by golden shiners, *N. crysoleucas.* The presumed advantage to the pickerel is the increased availability of edible golden shiners as they approach the nest, and the advantage to the sunfish is the greater survivorship of its own young. Shoemaker speculates that "more sunfish survive when there are pickerel present to keep the golden shiners in check.'' Such a mutualistic relationship would be similar to the increased survivorship documented for *Cichlasoma dovii* young defended by *Cichlasoma nicaraguense* (McKaye, 1977, and *in press*).

Cichlids

Many of the known examples of interspecific brood care in fishes involve cichlids (Burchard, 1967; Lowe, 1952; McKaye, 1977; McKaye and Hallacher, 1973; McKaye and McKaye, 1977; Ribbink, 1977; Ward and Wyman, 1975, 1977). Cichlids are now becoming well known for defending young that are not their own, and complementary studies have demonstrated that cichlids can also distinguish their own young from conspecific and heterospecific young on the basis of chemical cues (Kuhme, 1963; Kuenzer, 1964; McKaye and Barlow, 1976; Myrberg, 1966). Noble and Curtis (1939) first demonstrated the ability of cichlids to recognize their own young on the basis of color patterns. It therefore seems unlikely that the observed defense of foreign young involves the inability of the parents to distinguish their own young from those of others. Rejection or acceptance of foreign young by cichlids varies (Burchard, 1965; Collins and Braddock, 1962; Greenberg, 1963a, b; Myberg, 1964, 1966; Noakes and Barlow, 1973; Noble and Curtis, 1939.) Like the largemouth bass (Kramer and Smith, 1960), cichlids appear behaviorally flexible in their acceptance or rejection of foreign young into their broods: Acceptance is dependent upon biological parameters such as intensity of predation, competition, and number of individuals already in the brood (McKaye and McKaye, 1977).

Coyne and Sohn (1978), without referring to any other interspecific brood adoptions by fishes, attempt to use Ribbink's (1977) cuckoo hypothesis to support their contention that interspecific brood care is a mistake. The hypothesis that a given behavior is motivationally a mistake is untestable because the animal can never answer why it is performing that behavior. One can ask, however, whether cooperative behavior can be explained by chance or whether such behavior depresses the animal's reproductive success. When these questions are asked of Ribbink's (1977) observations, alternative interpretations are suggested. Although Ribbink (1977) concludes that it is a ''mistake'' for adopting parents to care for these foreign young, he states: ''As mixed broods were found on several occasions with each of the three parental species, it is unlikely that foreign fry were included by chance.'' Although he concludes that this is a case of social parasitism by *Haplochromis chrysonotus* upon three predatory cichlids, he neither explains the mechanism by which the young of *H. chrysonotus* are deposited into the brood of these predatory mouthbrooding cichlids nor demonstrates that this presumed parasitic behavior reduces the reproductive success of the host parents.

In addition to Ribbink's Lake Malaŵi observations, my coworkers and I have observed, while scuba diving at West Thumbe Island in the southern portion of Lake Malaŵi, three more instances of interspecific brood care by cichlids. S. Twombly and I observed a large predatory cichlid, tentatively identified as *Haplochromis heterotaenia,* defending a mixed brood of its own young and the young of an unidentified three-spot cichlid species. The female, disturbed by our presence, fled the area and all of her brood were consumed by predators. D. Lewis and I saw *H. kiwinge* defend, along with its own brood, the young of a species tentatively identified as *H. taeniolatus.* As did Ribbink (1977), we observed the guarding parent retrieve the mixed brood but not until predators attacking the brood had eaten some of the *H. taeniolatus* and *H. kiwinge* fry. S. Twombly and I made further observations of a fish, tentatively identified as *H. heterodon,* defending the young of *H. kiwinge* and *Lethrinops* spp. We observed the female retrieve her own young first, consistent with Ribbink's (1977) observation that ''on occasion'' the parents claimed ''their own young with greater facility than the foreign individuals.''

DISCUSSION

The understanding of fish social systems is rudimentary at best (Barlow, 1974). Theories derived from other better-studied vertebrate groups have been used to explain seemingly analogous patterns of morphology, color, or behavior in fishes (Lorenz, 1962). Cuckoo behavior in birds, for example, has been employed to describe interspecific brood care by fish. Upon closer examination of interspecific brood care in both fishes and birds, it is obvious that parental birds and parental fish are doing many things differently and for different reasons (Table 10–2).

1.   Size of brood. The most significant difference between bird and fish broods is in the number of young tended. Birds usually care for less than half a dozen chicks, whereas parental fish may guard hundreds or thousands of eggs or fry.

2.   Predation. When a bird nest is found by a predator, all the nestlings are usually taken (Lack, 1968). However when a predator attacks a school of fry the entire brood is not consumed; the result of a predatory attack is only a fractional loss of the brood. This difference is one of the primary factors resulting in mutualistic interspecific interactions in fish.

3.   Foraging by young. Because nestlings are confined to their nest, they are unable to forage themselves and must be fed by their parents. In contrast, food for young fish is often carried to them by currents laden with plankton. As the fry can forage themselves, the parents are relieved of the responsibility of feeding their young.

Table 10–2.   Some comparisons between interspecific brood care in birds (parasitic) and fishes (mutualistic). See text for discussion.

	Birds	Fishes
1. size of brood	small	large
2. predation	attack by predator usually leads to total loss of brood	attack by predator leads to fractional loss of brood
3. foraging by young	food brought by parents	food not provided by parents often brought by currents (plankton)
4. energetic input by foster parents into feeding alien young	high	none or very low
5. foraging by parents	leave young at nest	can move and forage with young
6. intra- and interspecific competition	yes—for both parental attention, food and space in the nest	probably low
7. behavior of alien young or its natural parent	may remove host's nest eggs or kill host's young	no removal or replacement ever observed
8. active incorporation of alien young into brood (kidnapping or egg stealing)	no	yes
ultimate "adaptive" response	rejection of alien eggs or young	active acceptance and search for nonrelated young

4.   Energetic input by foster parent into feeding alien young. Because young nestlings are incapable of feeding themselves, adult birds must provide all the food necessary for the survival of young. The addition of alien young to the nest requires increased energy expenditure if the parent spends additional time obtaining food for unrelated young. Parental fish do not usually actively feed fry (see Noakes and Barlow, 1973 for an exception).

5.   Foraging by parents. Parental birds leave the young in the nest when they forage for food and must consequently return to the nest to feed the young. With greater food requirements of the young, more time is spent away from the nest and more energy is expanded in gathering food. Furthermore, the young might be more susceptible to predators when the parents are away. In contrast, many parental fish are able to move fry to more productive areas and thus can forage with their young and provide a defense from predators at all times.

6.   Intra-and interspecific competition for resources by young. Competition for food, parental attention, and space in the nest is high among nestling birds (Payne, 1977). Competition for food among fish fry is often low because the parents can move the brood to more productive spots and because currents continually supply new food sources (plankton) to young. However, when competition among fish for food does become high, we might expect the relationship between host and alien fish to become ''parasitic'' or to see parents reject alien fry.

7.   Behavior of alien young or behavior of alien young's parents. It is frequently reported in studies of bird brood parasites that the parasitic mother may remove the host's own eggs from the nest (Payne, 1977). In the case of cuckoos, the young cuckoo often pushes the host parent's eggs over the edge of the nest. This active removal of host eggs from the nest by an alien fish and replacement with alien eggs has never been observed.

8.   Active incorporation of alien young into brood (kidnapping or egg stealing). Active stealing of foreign eggs and young and incorporation of these ''stolen'' young into a host species nest to be cared for have never been reported in birds. McKaye and McKaye (1977) reported kidnapping of fry and incorporation of orphaned fry into cichlid broods. Egg stealing by male sticklebacks and the subsequent incorporation of these eggs into their nests have been observed several times (see Rohwer, 1978).

Among birds parental care of young is energetically costly to the parents. Predation upon a brood usually results in the destruction of the entire brood. Alien young and their parents often kill the host's own young. The evidence suggests that under most circumstances care of alien young by parental birds lowers the reproductive success of the parents and, hence, the interaction is truly parasitic (Payne, 1977). Such may not always be the case among fish when: (1) the energetic cost of rearing alien young is minimal; (2) brood sizes are large, and when a predator attacks the brood, it does not take the entire brood, and (3) in the cases where adoptions do occur, the alien young or their parents pose no threat to the host's young. Adoptions, therefore, might be adaptive if the addition of foreign fry to a brood of fish reduces the probability of the parent's own young being taken by a predator (McKaye and McKaye, 1977).

Although data concerning interspecific brood care by fishes have not yet been collected systematically or in vast quantities, we do have evidence that the mutualistic hypothesis is correct. Carr's (1942) data on largemouth bass caring for eggs and young of the chubsucker lend support to the idea that the reproductive success of largemouth bass foster parents was enhanced by the addition of foreign fry. Kramer and Smith's (1960) study indicates that largemouth bass will, at times, accept eggs deposited by golden shiners and that bass can regulate the number of eggs introduced into the next by golden shiners. Anecdotal reports of mutualistic interactions and division of labor among heterospecific cyprinids indicate cooperation rather than antagonism between fishes. This is in marked contrast to the hostile interactions observed between parasitic and host parental birds. Cichlids lend the best support to the adaptive nonparasitic hypothesis because they are known to incorporate young into their broods.

I suggest that selection for caring for nonrelated young is dependent upon an interplay between (1) competition, (2) the behavior of alien young and their parents to the host's young, and (3) a reduction in predation upon the host's young. Therefore, circumstances should exist where fish that accept foreign young will be selected against, and birds that accept foreign young will be favored. For example, fish should not accept foreign young (1) when competition for food or space is high, (2) when the behavior of alien young or their parents is a threat to the host's young, or (3) when predation upon young is low. Birds, conversely, might accept foreign young if the behavior of the young was in some way advantageous to their own young (Smith, 1968). The behavioral flexibility of parents in adopting interspecific young can be tested by comparative field studies along with controlled laboratory experiments where the food resources and predation pressures are varied.

Field evidence currently available indicates that parental fish are selective in the adoption of foreign fry. Those fry that are large enough to eat the host parent's own young or eggs are consistently rejected from broods by parental cichlids (McKaye and McKaye, 1977; Noakes and Barlow, 1973). Also, alien parents who could be construed by parental cichlids as a threat to eggs or fry are chased away. Because most fish are potential predators, they are generally prevented from coming near eggs or young. It is unlikely that any parental fish would allow another to come close to its own eggs, as the potential for egg predation by the alien parent would be great. Not surprisingly, all examples of interspecific egg care by fishes involve the care of cyprinid eggs. Cyprinids are able to release eggs up in the water column and have them drop into the host's nest. No examples of interspecific cichlid egg care have been observed in either mouthbrooders or substratum spawners. Foreign young are generally incorporated into a cichlid brood of freeswimming young two to three weeks after hatching.

All of our examples of interspecific brood care in fishes come from freshwater species. There are no reported examples among marine fishes. This difference seems not to be an artifact of data collection but a result of the fact that marine fishes engaging in parental care lay demersal eggs that are affixed to the substrate. Consequently, there are no opportunities for eggs to be dropped into nests from the water column—as in cyprinids—and any other fish that tried to court and to lay eggs in another species nest would constitute a real predatory threat to the host's eggs. Furthermore, few marine fishes actually defend freeswimming fry for any extended period of time, thus further limiting possibilities for interspecific care.

The classical example of "parasitism" being advantageous to host birds is that reported between cowbirds and oropendolas in Panama (Smith, 1968). In this case the alien young of the giant cowbird, *Scaphidura oryzivora,* remove botfly larvae from the young of *Zarhynchus wagleri* and *Cacicus cela.* This behavior increases the survivorship of the hosts' young. In host colonies where it is advantageous to take care of cowbird young, the parent oropendolas do not discriminate against cowbird eggs in the nest nor do they chase adult cowbirds away from the colony. This is in marked contrast to the behavior of oropendola parents in colonies located near wasps or bees that also provide protection from botfly larvae. In these latter colonies, cowbirds reduce the reproductive potential of their hosts, and the oropendolas respond by tossing cowbird eggs from the nest and actively chasing female cowbirds from the colony. When oropendola colonies are not located near wasp or bee nests, it is clearly advantageous for them to accept cowbird young; interspecific brood care is advantageous to both species, hence mutualistic.

Concerning hosts of the supposed "cuckoo fish" of Lake Malaŵi—*Haplochromis chrysonotus*—it has been asked "why have the foster parents not developed some sort of defense against this form of parasitisation (sic)?" (anonymous, 1977). The answer to this question may be that the premise is incorrect. The interaction is not parasitic; consequently, defense is not relevant.

CONCLUSION

Evolution by natural selection has been described as a tautological, nonfalsifiable theory that is of little value because it explains everything and hence explains nothing (Peters, 1977)—a view that has been challenged by many (Caplan, 1977; Castrodeza, 1977; Ferguson, 1976; Maynard Smith, 1969; Stebbins, 1977). Darwin himself (1859), however, provided us with the ultimate and simple test of the validity of his theory of natural selection: "If it could be proved that any part of the structure of any one species had been formed for the exclusive good of another species, it would annihilate my theory, for such could not have been produced through natural selection."

Interspecific interactions involving brood care provide ideal systems for empirically testing Darwin's theory of evolution by natural selection, and for this reason deserve special attention. It should be possible to measure the relative reproductive success of individuals of different species and to examine directly their behavior and ecology. From such data one could determine whether a given behavioral pattern is adaptive, the result of parasitism, or evolved for the good of another species. If a given interspecific interaction is adaptive, then the reproductive success of individuals engaging in cooperative behavior should be greater, and these individuals should actively "encourage" the interspecific relationship. If the interaction is parasitic, the reproductive success of the host species should be lower than those not parasitized, and the host should actively discourage the relationship. If the interaction exists solely for the good of another species (the alien species rather than the host species), the reproductive success of the host should be lowered and at the same time, the host should actively encourage the relationship. If this last relationship were to persist through time we could say that the theory of natural selection had been falsified. Unlike most studies that attempt to test the adaptiveness of a given behavior in a single species, the result of interspecific studies will never be clouded by kin or group selection arguments that claim that a seemingly maladaptive behavior has really evolved to help one's relatives or species. I suspect, however, that Darwin's theory will withstand this test because it is correct rather than because it is tautological.

I hope that this review will encourage others who come upon seemingly rare and unusual behavior in nature not to be convinced by those such as Coyne and Sohn (1978) who question "whether *every* behavior, however infrequent, demands an evolutionary explanation" (italics theirs). If we do not recognize *all* the evidence available to deduce an evolutionary explanation for observed behavior, then there are no scientifically constructive alternatives to studying nature. Because most behavioral acts are self-centered, examples of reciprocal altruism, altruism as a result of kinship, or cooperative behavior for whatever reason will be relatively rare in nature but perhaps very important in the structuring of communities (McKaye, 1977).

In the future, studies of interspecific interactions will make an important contribution to our understanding of selfishness, altruism, cooperation, and spitefulness. Unlike studies involving intraspecific interactions, investigators will not have to speculate about or hedge their explanations in terms of group or kin selection. Williams (1966) maintains "that adaptation need almost never be recognized at any level about that of a pair of parents and associated offspring." This is certainly true for our understanding of interspecific brood care in fishes. I suspect that it will be shown to hold true for most examples of intra- and interspecific cooperation among vertebrates.

ACKNOWLEDGEMENTS

I wish to thank George Barlow, Richard Harrison, G. Evelyn Hutchinson, and Charles Sibley for helping me develop ideas concerning the parasitic-mutualistic dichotomy between interspecific brood care by birds and fishes. Assistance from Tony Bledsoe, Joe Germano, Tim Goldsmith, Richard Grossberg, Digby Lewis, and Michael Oliver in reviewing the manuscript is gratefully acknowledged. David Eccles, Digby Lewis and Michael Oliver's aid in tentatively identifying Malaŵi cichlids was invaluable. My greatest debt of gratitude goes to Saran Twombly who worked with me in Malaŵi and spent innumerable hours discussing and reviewing the ideas presented in this paper. Her remarkable patience is greatly appreciated. Nevertheless, not everyone of them agrees with all the opinions or ideas expressed, and I am the sole one responsible for the errors that may remain. The research in Malaŵi is supported by NSF Grant DEB 76-04920.

REFERENCES

Anonymous. 1977. Cuckoo fish. *New Scientist* 74: 1054.

Askew, R. R. 1971. *Parasitic Insects*. New York. Elsevier.

Barlow, G. W. 1974. Contrasts in social behavior between Central American cichlid fishes and coral-reef surgeon fishes. *Amer. Zool.* 14: 9–34.

Blumer, L. 1979. Paternal care in the bony fishes. *Quart. Rev. Biol.* 54: 149–161.

Breder, C. M., and D. E. M. Rosen. 1966. *Modes of Reproduction in Fishes*. Natural History Press, Garden City, New York.

Burchard, J. E. 1965. Family structure in the dwarf cichlid *Apistogramma trifasciatum* Eigenmann and Kennedy. *Z. Tierpsychol.* 22: 150–162.

Burchard, J. E. 1967. The family Cichlidae. In *Fish and Fisheries of Northern Nigeria* (ed. W. Reed), p. 128–144. Min. Agric. Northern Nigeria.

Caplan, A. L. 1977. Tautology, cicularity, and biological theory. *Amer. Nat. 111: 390–393.*

Carr, A. 1964. *Ulendo, Travels of a Naturalist in and out of Africa*. New York: Alfred A. Knopf.

Carr, M. H. 1942. The breeding habits, embryology, and larval development of the large-mouth black bass in Florida. *Proc. New England Zool. Club* 20: 43–77.

Carr, M. H. 1946. Notes on the breeding habits of the eastern stumpknocker, *Lepomis punctatus punctatus* (Cuvier). *J. Florida Acad. Sci.* 101–106.

Castrodeza, C. 1977. Tautologies, beliefs and empirical knowledge in biology. *Amer. Nat.* 111: 393–394.

Clarke, T. A. 1970. Territorial behavior and population dynamics of a pomacentrid fish, the Garibaldi, *Hypsopops rubicunda. Ecol. Mon.* 40: 189–212.

Collins, H. L., and J. C. Braddock. 1962. Notes of fostering experiments with the cichlid fishes *Tilapia sparmanni* and *Aequidens portalegrensis* (abstract). *Amer. Zool.* 2: 400.

Coyne, J. A., and J. J. Sohn. 1978. Interspecific brood care in fishes: Reciprocal altruism or mistaken identity? *Amer. Nat.* 112: 447–450.

Darwin, C. R. 1859. *On the Origin of Species by Means of Natural Selection or the Preservation of Favoured Races in the Struggle for Life*. John Murray, London.

Ferguson, A. J. 1976. Can evolutionary theory predict? *Amer. Nat.* 110: 1101–1104.

Fryer, G., and T. D. Iles. 1972. *The Cichlid Fishes of the Great Lakes of Africa: Their Biology and Evolution*. Oliver & Boyd, Edinburgh.

Greenberg, B. 1963a. Parental behavior and imprinting in cichlid fishes. *Behaviour* 21: 127–144.

Greenberg, B. 1963b. Parental behavior and recognition of young in *Cichlasoma biocellatum. Anim. Behav.* 11:572–582

Hankinson, T. L. 1920. Report on the investigations of fish of the Galien River, Berrien County, Michigan. *Occ. Pap. Mus. Zool. Univ. Mich.* 89: 1014.

Heisenberg. 1971. *Physics and Beyond*. Harper & Row. New York.

Hunter, J. R., and A. D. Hasler. 1965. Spawning association of the redfin shiner, *Notropis umbratilis*, and the green sunfish, *Lepomis cyanellus*. *Copeia* 1965 (3) 265–281.

Kramer, R. J. and L. L. Smith, Jr. 1960. Utilization of nests of largemouth bass, *Micropterus salmoides*, by golden shiners, *Notemigonus crysoleucas*. *Copeia* 1960 (1): 73–74.

Kuenzer, P. 1964. Weitere Versuch zer Auslosung der Nachfolgereaktion bei Jungfischen von *Nannacara anomala* (Cichlidae). Naturwissenschaften 5: 419–420.

Kuhme, W. 1963. Chemisch ausgeloste Brutpflege und Schwarmreaktionen bei *Hemichromis bimaculatus*. *Z. Tierpsychol.* 20: 688–704.

Lack, D. 1968. *Ecological Adaptations for Breeding in Birds*. Metheun, London.

Loiselle, P. V., and G. W. Barlow. Do fishes lek like birds? *Contrasts in Behavior*. eds. E. S. Reese & F. Lichter. *in press*.

Lorenz, K. 1962. The function of colour in coral reef fishes. *Proc. Roy. Inst. Great Britain* 39: 282–296.

Lowe, R. H. 1952. Report on the *Tilapia* and other fish and fisheries of Lake Nyasa 1945–47. *Colon. Off. Fish. Publ.*, IX (2).

Maynard Smith, J. 1969. The status of neo-Darwinism. Pages 82–89 in C. H. Waddington, ed., *Towards a Theoretical Biology*. Vol. 2 Aldine, New York.

McKaye, K. R. 1977. Defense of a predator's young by a herbivorous fish: An unusual strategy. *Amer Nat.* 111: 301–315.

McKaye, K. R. 1979. Defense of a predator's young revisited. *Amer. Nat.* 114: 595–601.

McKaye, K. R., and G. W. Barlow. 1976. Chemical recognition of young by the Midas cichlid *Cichlasoma citrinellum*. *Copeia* 1976 (2): 276–282.

McKaye, K. R., and L. E. Hallacher. 1973. The Midas cichlid of Nicaragua. *Pacific Discovery* 25: 1–8.

McKaye, K. R., and N. M. McKaye. 1977. Communal care and kidnapping of young by parental cichlids. *Evolution* 31: 674–681.

Myrberg, A. A. 1964. An analysis of the preferential care of eggs and young by adult cichlid fishes. *Z. Tierpsychol.* 21: 53–98.

Myrberg, A. A. 1966. Parental recognition of young in cichlid fishes. *Anim. Behav.* 14: 565–571.

Noakes, D., and G. W. Barlow. 1973. Cross-fostering and parent-offspring response in *Cichlasoma citrinellum* (Pisces, Cichlidae). *Z. Tierpsychol.* 33: 147–512.

Noble, G. K. and B. Curtis. 1939. The social behavior of the jewel fish *Hemichromis bimaculatus* Gill. *Bull. Amer. Mus. Nat. Hist.* 76: 1–46.

Payne, R. B. 1977. The ecology of brood parasitism in birds. *Ann. Rev. Ecol. Syst.* 8: 1–28.

Perrone, M., and T. Zaret. 1979. Parental care patterns of fishes. *Amer. Nat.* 113: 351–361.

Peters, R. H. 1976. Tautology in evolution and ecology *Amer. Nat.* 110: 1–12.

Ribbink, A. J. 1977. Cuckoo among Lake Malawi cichlid fish. *Nature* 267: 243–244.

Richardson. 1913. Observations on the breeding habits of fishes at Havana, Illinois, 1910 and 1911. *Bull. Ill. Nat. Hist. Surv.* 9: 405–416.

Rohwer, S. 1978. Parent cannibalism of offspring and egg raiding as a courtship strategy. *Amer. Nat.* 112: 429-440.

Shoemaker, H. H. 1947. Pickerel and pumpkinseed coaction over the sunfish nest. *Copeia* 3: 195–196.

Smith, N. G. 1968. The advantage of being parasitized. *Nature* 219: 690–694.

Stebbins, G. L. 1977. In defense of evolution: Tautology or theory? *Amer. Nat.* 111: 386–390.

Ward, J. A., and R. A. Wyman. 1975. The cichlids of the resplendent isle. *Oceans* 8: 42–47.

Ward, J. A., and R. L. Wyman. 1977. Ethology and ecology of cichlid fishes of the genus *Etroplus* in Sri Lanka: preliminary findings. *Env. Biol. Fish.* 2:137–145.

White, M. J. D. 1970. Heterozygosity and genetic polymorphism in parthenogenetic animals. In *Essays in Evolution and Genetics in Honor of Theodosius Dobzhansky*, pp. 262–273, M. K. Hecht and W. C. Steere, eds., New York, Appleton-Century-Crofts.

Williams, G. C. 1966. *Adaptation and Natural Selection*. Princeton, Princeton Univ. Press.

Wilson, E. O. 1971. *The Insect Societies*. Belknap Press. Harvard.

Wilson, E. O. 1975. *Sociobiology: The New Synthesis*. Belknap Press. Harvard.

11.

Parental Behavior of Male and Female Frogs

Kentwood D. Wells

Vertebrate parental behavior has been investigated extensively by comparative psychologists, ethologists, and field naturalists for decades and is receiving increasing attention in the sociobiological literature (Williams, 1966, 1975; Trivers, 1972; Wilson, 1975; Dawkins, 1976; Dawkins and Carlisle, 1976; Maynard Smith, 1977, 1978; Grafen and Sibly, 1978; Ridley, 1978; Perrone and Zaret, 1979; Blumer, in press). Although parental behavior was long viewed as a prime example of cooperation between males and females, the emphasis has now shifted to potential evolutionary conflicts in the reproductive interests of males and females (Trivers, 1972; Maynard Smith, 1977) or parents and offspring (Trivers, 1974). It is increasingly clear that the evolution of parental care must be viewed in the broader context of overall male and female reproductive strategies.

In this paper I review the parental behavior of anuran amphibians (frogs and toads) in light of recent theoretical discussions of parental investment and the evolution of parental care. I attempt to define conditions that favor the evolution of paternal or maternal care by relating parental behavior to the social organization and mating systems of particular species. I also examine possible relationships between parental care and the reversal of sex roles in courtship and agonistic behavior.

PATTERNS OF ANURAN PARENTAL CARE

A comprehensive review of anuran parental care is difficult because most of the available literature consists of anecdotal natural history notes of uncertain reliability. In most cases we can only guess the possible functions of parental care, because experimental studies designed to determine the contribution of the adult to egg or larval survivorship are lacking (exceptions are studies of *Hyla rosenbergi* by Kluge (1978) and *Centrolenella* by McDiarmid (1978). Most of the available information on anuran parental care has been summarized in recent reviews (Salthe and Mecham, 1974; Lamotte and Lescure, 1977; Wells, 1977a; McDiarmid, 1978; Ridley, 1978) and will not be repeated in detail here. Nevertheless, a brief review of general patterns will be useful as background information for subsequent evolutionary arguments.

Parental care is uncommon in anurans occurring in only 10% of all species, but some form of parental care has been reported in fourteen families (McDiarmid 1978). Although there are scattered reports of parental care in aquatic breeders, it occurs most frequently in terrestrial breeders from the humid tropics. In fact, most examples of parental care are part of a broader pattern of non-aquatic oviposition in tropical frogs, a possible evolutionary response to predation in aquatic environments (Salthe and Mecham, 1974; Crump, 1974; Lamotte and Lescure, 1977; McDiarmid, 1978).

McDiarmid (1978) recognized twelve categories of anuran parental care, based on oviposition habitat (aquatic or terrestrial), site of parental investment (nest, burrow, or on the parent), nature of the larval stage (free-swimming or direct development), and sex of the care-giving parent. I combine these into four major categories: (1) egg attendance, (2) tadpole attendance, (3) egg transport, and (4) tadpole transport. The few ovoviviparous or viviparous frogs are not considered (see Lamotte and Lescure, 1977, for a review).

Egg Attendance

Egg attendance is the most common form of parental behavior in frogs. It occurs in at least twelve families (Salthe and Mecham, 1974; Lamotte and Lescure, 1977; McDiarmid, 1978). Several possible functions of egg attendance have been proposed. Male *Nectophryne afra* (Bufonidae) swim in place and direct a stream of water toward eggs to aerate them (Scheel, 1970). Male *Hyla rosenbergi* (Hylidae) guard mud nests against conspecifics to prevent disturbance of the egg surface film. If eggs are disturbed, they sink to the bottom and die (Kluge, 1978). Female *Leptodactylus ocellatus* (Leptodactylidae) guard eggs in a foam nest at the water's surface against predators (Vaz-Ferreira and Gehrau, 1975). McDiarmid (1978) suggested that male *Centrolenella valerioi* (Centrolenidae) protect their eggs from predatory wasps, but he did not observe frogs attacking predators. For other terrestrial breeders, such as *Eleutherodactylus* (Leptodactylidae), *Dendrobates* (Dendrobatidae), and some microhylids, there is circumstantial evidence that egg attendance prevents desiccation or inhibits mold growth (Wager, 1965; Myers, 1969; Blommers-Schlösser, 1975; Tyler 1976; Wells, 1978), but there have been no controlled experimental studies.

In some species, the presence of an adult may be incidental to other aspects of reproduction and may provide little protection to the eggs. Woodruff (1977) suggests that male *Pseudophryne* (Myobatrachidae) remain in their burrows after oviposition to attract additional females but provide no care for the eggs. Some dendrobatids remain with eggs until they hatch and then carry the tadpoles to water, but they may or may not care for the eggs themselves (Lüddecke, 1974; Van Meeuwen, 1977).

Tadpole Attendance

Tadpole attendance is rare in frogs, probably because most adults are terrestrial whereas tadpoles are aquatic. The best documented example is *Leptodactylus ocellatus*. The tadpoles form a school after hatching. The female follows the school and guards it from predators (Vaz-Ferreira and Gehrau, 1975). Male *Nectophryne afra* also remain with tadpoles for some time after hatching (Scheel, 1970). Balinsky and Balinsky (1954), Rose (1956), and Poynton (1957) reported that the African ranid *Pyxicephalus adspersus* guards tadpoles from predators, but other authors questioned this interpretation (Wager, 1956, 1965; Lambiris, 1971).

Egg Transport

Egg transport on a parent's body is uncommon but has evolved independently in at least four families. In the midwife toad, *Alytes obstetricans* (Discoglossidae), the male carries eggs entwined around his legs and releases tadpoles into a pond (Boulenger, 1912). All other cases of egg transport involve females. In *Pipa* (Pipidae), a totally aquatic genus, females carry eggs in spongy tissue on the back. Eggs hatch as tadpoles *(P. carvalhoi)* or small frogs *(P. pipa)* (Rabb and Rabb, 1961; Lamotte and Lescure, 1977). In various hylids, including *Gastrotheca, Nototheca, Hemiphractus, Cryptobatrachus,* and *Stefania,* eggs are carried exposed on the female's back or in dorsal brood pouches; there they hatch into aquatic larvae or undergo direct development (Salthe and Mecham, 1974; Lamotte and

Lescure, 1977). One of the most bizarre adaptations is found in the Australian myobatrachid *Rheobatrachus silus*. The female carries eggs and larvae in her stomach (Corben et al., 1974).

Tadpole Transport

Tadpoles may be transported from a terrestrial oviposition site to water, or they may metamorphose on the adult. Tadpole transport on the back of an adult has been reported in three families. It is well documented only in dendrobatids *(Dendrobates, Colostethus, Phyllobates),* where it has been reported for both males and females (Wells, 1977a, 1977b, 1978, and references therein). Male sooglossids from the Seychelles Islands are reported to carry tadpoles on their backs (Salthe and Mecham, 1974), but recent attempts to confirm this in the field have been unsuccessful (Ronald Nussbaum, personal communication). There is one report of *Rana microdisca,* from Borneo, carrying tadpoles, but details are unknown (Lamotte and Lescure, 1977). Other examples include transport of tadpoles in the male's vocal sac in *Rhinoderma* (Rhinodermatidae) (Cei, 1962; Busse, 1970; Lamotte and Lescure, 1977) and male transport of tadpoles in inguinal brood pouches in the Australian myobatrachid *Assa darlingtoni* (Ingram et al., 1975).

THE EVOLUTION OF ANURAN PARENTAL CARE

Mate Desertion and Parental Care

Most recent theoretical discussions of parental care are based on models of mate desertion, which attempt to determine which parent will desert offspring first, leaving the other to desert or care for offspring alone (Trivers, 1972; Dawkins, 1976; Dawkins and Carlisle, 1976; Maynard Smith, 1977, 1978; Grafen and Sibly, 1978; Ridley, 1978). Such models assume that the strategy adopted by individuals of one sex is determined by the activities of members of the opposite sex as well as those of other members of the same sex (Maynard Smith, 1977; Grafen and Sibly, 1978).

One difficulty with these models is that they show how a set of evolutionary strategies could be maintained in a population but do not explain how such strategies originated. Several alternative strategies might be evolutionarily stable, and the behavior that actually evolves may depend on initial conditions (Maynard Smith, 1977). For more frogs and teleost fishes, the most probable initial condition is no parental care, so desertion by one parent probably does not require the other to care for eggs. The scarcity of any form of parental care in frogs suggests that desertion by both parents has been a frequent evolutionarily stable strategy. Maynard Smith (1977) conceded that his models could not explain many specific examples of parental care in anurans or teleost fishes.

I assume that in frogs the tendency for one parent to desert has little or no effect on the tendency of the other to care for eggs. I then attempt to identify conditions that favor parental care by one sex or the other by considering separately the potential costs and benefits to individual males and females. There are difficulties with this approach as well. Quantitative estimates of costs and benefits are not available in the literature and are difficult to obtain in the field. Consequently, the following discussion depends largely on subjective evaluations of potential costs and benefits.

Mode of Fertilization and Parental Care

Parental care by males alone is more common in animals with external fertilization than in those with internal fertilization (Trivers, 1972; Ridley, 1978). Among vertebrates, parental care by the male alone is uncommon in mammals, birds, reptiles, and salamanders with internal fertilization but is relatively widespread in teleost fishes with external fertilization and in frogs (Williams, 1975; Maynard Smith, 1977; Wells, 1977a; McDiarmid, 1978; Ridley, 1978).

Two non-exclusive explanations of this relationship have been proposed. First, with external fertilization, males must be present when eggs are laid and therefore would be available to assume parental duties (Williams, 1966, 1975; Trivers, 1972; Wells, 1977a; Maynard Smith, 1978). Second, a male is unlikely to care for another male's offspring by mistake because of the high probability that all eggs in a clutch are his own (Williams, 1966, 1975; Trivers, 1972; Maynard Smith, 1978; Ridley, 1978; Perrone and Zaret, 1979; Blumer, in press; R. Shine and M. Gross, personal communication). This would reduce selective pressure opposing male parental care but is not a sufficient condition for its evolution.

The reliability of paternity hypothesis may have been overemphasized in some discussions of parental care. Maynard Smith (1978) pointed out that if paternity is uncertain, the value of obtaining additional mates, an alternative to parental care, is reduced as well. Furthermore, external fertilization may explain why male parental care is more likely to evolve in anurans and fishes than in mammals, birds, and reptiles, but it provides no explanation for the diversity of parental strategies in frogs and fishes. If external fertilization favors the evolution of male parental care, then we still must explain why some species have male parental care, whereas others in the same family or genus have female parental care.

Territoriality and Parental Care

Many forms of male parental care in teleost fishes probably evolved as a consequence of male territoriality (Williams, 1975; Ridley, 1978; Perrone and Zaret, 1979; Blumer, in press) and the same may be true for frogs (Wells, 1977a; McDiarmid, 1978; Ridley, 1978). The argument is as follows: when a male defends a territory around an oviposition site, he controls a resource that enhances his attractiveness to females and thereby increases his reproductive success. After one clutch is deposited in the territory, a male might continue to attract females while giving the eggs some protecton. Thus, the cost of parental care to the male in reduced opportunities for future matings would be relatively low (Trivers, 1972; Williams, 1975; Wells, 1977a; Woodruff, 1977; McDiarmid, 1978).

There is little doubt that this general scheme explains many instances of male parental care in frogs, but several factors must be considered before a direct link between territoriality and male parental care is established. First, one cannot assume that a male remaining at an oviposition site protects the eggs. In green frogs *(Rana clamitans)* and bullfrogs *(Rana catesbeiana)*, males remain in their territories and continue to call after fertilizing eggs (Wells, 1977c; Howard, 1978), but there is no evidence that this is advantageous to the eggs. Egg attendance in burrows by male *Pseudophryne* is frequently cited as a case of parental care, but it has not been established that the male actually enhances egg survivorship (Woodruff, 1977).

Second, a correlation between male parental care and territoriality is expected only if males defend oviposition sites. Ridley (1978) stated that if males are territorial and fertilization is external, then females will lay eggs in a male territory. This is not necessarily true for frogs. In many species, males defend shelters, feeding sites, or calling perches but not oviposition sites. Often a female will approach a male at a calling site, enter amplexus, and then carry the male to another site for oviposition (Wells, 1977a). If a male were to give up a choice calling site to remain with an egg clutch laid somewhere else, then his opportunities for future matings might be greatly reduced. Hence selection would oppose the evolution of male parental care.

Finally, the type of parental care provided must be considered. The argument deriving male parental care from territoriality assumes that parental care does not interfere with territory defense. Some forms of parental care may make territory defense impossible, and the advantages of parental care would be balanced against the disadvantages of losing the territory. I will discuss this point in more detail when I consider specific types of parental care.

Other Factors Affecting the Evolution of Parental Care

The potential costs of parental care for females probably are not the same as those for males. The chief cost for males would be decreased opportunities for attracting females, whereas the major cost for females would be decreased opportunities for renewing energy reserves needed to produce additional eggs (Trivers, 1972; Williams, 1975). If females assume parental duties only when costs are minimal, then female parental care is most likely to occur when females feed while caring for eggs or when the time required for parental care is short compared to the time needed to produce another clutch.

Unfortunately, quantitative studies of species with female parental care are almost non-existent. Presumably such forms of care as egg transport in *Pipa* and *Gastrotheca* or tadpole transport in *Dendrobates* and *Colostethus* do not greatly reduce a female's ability to feed, but nothing is known about relative feeding rates of parental and non-parental females. Almost nothing is known about the number or frequency of egg clutches laid by individual females, so it is impossible to compare the time required for parental care with that needed to produce a second clutch. Furthermore, data needed to compare the benefits of caring for eggs with the costs of abandoning them are not available, so it is almost impossible to predict whether female parental care will or will not occur in specific cases.

In the following discussion, I focus on the question of which sex cares for offspring when some form of parental care occurs, but I do not attempt to explain why parental care occurs in some species but not in others in the same family or genus. Because so few reports of tadpole attendance are available, I consider only egg attendance, egg transport, and tadpole transport.

Egg Attendance

Examples of egg attendance are summarized in Tables 11–1 and 11–2. The genus *Eleutherodactylus* would be a good one for detailed comparisons of parental strategies, because the genus contains species with male, female, and no parental care. Information presently available suggests an association of male parental care with territorial defense of tree holes, crevices, rolled palm leaves, or other ovipositon sites. In contrast, species with female egg attendance typically lay eggs in leaf litter, coconut husk piles, or similar sites. Males usually call from bushes, trees, fence posts, walls, or other elevated sites separated from oviposition sites (Table 11–1). Although additional data are needed, these observations support the hypothesis that males care for eggs only if they can continue to attract additional females. In at least two species, *E. coqui* and *E. hedricki,* males are known to attend more than one clutch at a time (Drewry, 1970, 1974).

Species in other families show a similar trend (Table 11–2). In almost all species exhibiting male egg attendance, males call from tree holes, burrows, rock cavities, specially constructed nests, or other oviposition sites likely to be in short supply. Active territorial defense of these sites has been reported in seven species and probably occurs in others. In nine species, males have been observed attending more than one clutch or are known to continue calling while attending eggs. Female egg attendance occurs primarily in species that lay eggs in burrows constructed by the female, in foam nests formed by pairs in amplexus, or other sites not likely to be defensible by males (Table 11–2).

One exception to the pattern of males continuing to attract females while attending eggs is *Hyla rosenbergi*. Previous papers predicted that males should fertilize clutches of more than one female in the same nest (Wells, 1977a; McDiarmid, 1978), but this is not correct. The necessity of protecting the surface film from disturbance apparently makes this impossible (Kluge, 1978). Futhermore, the male cannot re-use a nest until all previous tadpoles have left because of the danger of cannibalism (A. Kluge, personal communication). In this species, the costs of not guarding eggs apparently are so great that they override the cost of not obtaining additional mates immediately.

Egg Transport

Egg transport is almost exclusively a female activity in frogs, and there are several possible reasons for this. McDiarmid (1978) suggested that as females usually are larger than males, they might be better able to transport eggs on their bodies because they could accommodate complete clutches. However, a similar argument should apply to tadpole transport. Tadpole transport in dendrobatids occurs at least as often in males as in females, and in most *Phyllobates* and *Colostethus* the entire clutch is carried at once (Lüddecke, 1974, 1976; Silverstone, 1976; Wells, 1977a, 1977b, unpublished observations). Therefore, the ability to carry an entire clutch of eggs probably does not limit egg transport to males.

At least two other factors may be important. First, if males defend territories needed for courtship and mating, then they are unlikely to carry eggs because this would interfere with territory defense. Male *Pipa pipa* and *P. carvalhoi* defend mating territories in captivity (Rabb and Rabb, 1963; Weygoldt, 1976), but whether they do so in nature is unknown. Male *Nototheca fitzgeraldi* do not appear to be territorial (personal observations), but nothing is known about male behavior in other egg-transporting species.

Perhaps even more important is the fact that males of most species probably could not carry more than one clutch at a time, so opportunities for future matings would be reduced. McDiarmid (1978) pointed out that in the midwife toad, the only species with male egg transport, a male can carry more than one clutch at a time, thus providing an exception that proves the rule. Boulenger (1912) reported field observations of males carrying one or two clutches successfully courting additional females.

There is another unusual feature of this species' reproductive biology that may reduce the costs of parental care for males. As in other discoglossids, the breeding season of *Alytes* is divided into several separate breeding periods. The pattern seems to be determined by an endogenous hormonal cycle (Obert, 1974). In one population, mating occurred in four one- to two-week periods, separated by intervals of two to four weeks (Heinzmann, 1970). Usually eggs are carried for two to three weeks (Hellmich, 1962). Therefore, a male can complete care of several clutches in one breeding period before additional mating opportunities arise.

Table 11–1.   Examples of egg attendance in *Eleutherodactylus*. Sources are given in parentheses with species names.

Species	Oviposition Site	Calling Site	Parent
E. coqui (3, 4, 9)	Tree hole or rolled palm leaf*	Oviposition site or nearby perch	Male
E. hedricki (3, 4)	Tree hole*	Oviposition site or nearby perch	Male
E. cooki (3, 4)	Under rock	Tops of rocks	Male
E. cundalli (8, 9)	Litter	Shrubs, tree trunks, banks	Female
E. johnstonei (4, 9)	Litter	Shrubs, fences, tree trunks	Female
E. nubicola (6)	Under rock	Tops of rocks, embankments	Female
E. martinicensis (1, 5)	Under rock	Shrubs, walls, tree trunks	Female
E. decoratus (2)	Under rock	Not reported	Female
E. caryophyllaceus (7)	Exposed leaf	Shrubs	Female

* Males defend sites and attend more than one clutch at a time.
Sources: 1) Adamson, et al. 1960; 2) Bogert 1969; 3) Drewry 1970; 4) Drewry 1970; 5) Lemon 1971; 6) Lynn and Grant 1940; 7) Myers 1969; 8) Stewart, in press; 9) M. Stewart, personal communication.

Tadpole Transport

Previous authors usually considered egg attendance and tadpole transport together. For example, McDiarmid (1978) stated that male territoriality in many dendrobatids probably accounts for the prevalence of male parental care in these species. In fact, female parental care is known in a number of species with territorial males, and male parental care occurs in the absence of male territoriality (Wells, 1977b, 1978). Predictions about parental care in egg-attending species cannot be applied to tadpole-transporting species because the costs of the two forms of care are quite different.

A frog carrying tadpoles is unlikely to defend a territory because of potential injury to the young. If a male's territory is essential for courtship and mating, then giving up the

Table 11–2.   Examples of egg attendance in frogs other than *Eleutherodactylus*. Species that also transport tadpoles are not included. Sources are given in parentheses with species names.

Species	Oviposition Site	Calling Site	Parent
Myobatrachidae			
Pseudophryne dendyi	Burrow[a,b]	Burrow	Male
P. semimarmorata			
P. bibroni (9, 13)			
Adelotus brevis (8)	Hole, crevice[c]	Hole, crevice	Male
Lymnodynastes dorsalis (8)	Burrow[c]	Burrow	Male
Leptodactylidae			
Hylactophryne augusti (3)	Under rock[c]	Under rock	Male
Leptodactylus ocellatus (11)	Foam nest in shallow water	Shallow water	Female
L. fuscus (6)	Foam nest in burrow near water	Not reported	Female
Bufonidae			
Nectophryne afra (6)	Shallow water	Shallow water	Male
Hylidae			
Hyla rosenbergi (2, 4, 5)	Mud nest built by male	Mud nest	Male
Centrolenidae			
Centrolenella valerioi	Leaves over stream[a,b]	Leaves over stream	Male
C. colymbiphyllum (7)			
Microhylidae			
Platyhyla grandis (1)	Tree hole[a]	Tree hole	Male
Plethodontohyla notosticta (1)	Tree hole[a]	Tree hole	Male
Plethodontohyla tuberata (1)	Burrow	Not reported	Female
Anodontohyla boulengeri (1)	Tree hole[b]	Tree hole	Male
Probreviceps rhodesianus (10)	Burrow	Usually open ground	Female
Breviceps adspersus (12)	Burrow	Usually open ground	Female
B. sylvestris (12)	Burrow	Usually open ground	Female

Notes: (a) males defend oviposition sites, (b) males attend more than one clutch at a time, (c) males continue to call while attending eggs.

SOURCES: (1) Blommers-Schlösser, 1975; (2) Breder, 1946; (3) Jameson, 1950; (4) Kluge, 1978; (5) A. Kluge, personal communication; (6) Lamotte and Lescure, 1977; (7) McDiarmid, 1978; (8) Moore, 1961; (9) Pengilley, 1971; (10) Poynton and Pritchard, 1976; (11) Vaz-Ferreira and Gehrau, 1975; (12) Wager, 1965; (13) Woodruff, 1977.

territory to carry tadpoles might severely limit future mating opportunities. Of course, the cost of such behavior would vary depending on the time required for larval transport and the intensity of territorial competition.

I predict that tadpole transport by males will be rare or absent when male–male competition for mating territories is intense, unless the time required for tadpole transport is very short. If tadpole transport occurs at all, it should be performed by females. When competition for mating territories is less intense or when males are not territorial, then either sex might carry tadpoles. The costs and benefits to males and females would be similar to those governing the evolution of egg attendance.

Some information on both territoriality and tadpole transport is available for nine species of dendrobatids (Table 11–3). These fit predicted patterns reasonably well. Males compete vigorously for all-purpose territories in *Colostethus inguinalis,* with some males remaining at the same sites for at least six months. Females carry tadpoles for up to eight or nine days. Although females sometimes defend temporary feeding territories, such behavior is largely confined to the dry season when little reproduction takes place (Wells, unpublished). In *C. pratti,* males defend territories, and I have observed marked individuals at the same sites for several months. Females carry tadpoles and show no signs of territorial behavior (Wells, unpublished). Similarly, frequent male–male territorial encounters have been reported in *D. pumilio* (Duellman, 1966; Bunnell, 1973). Females are the principal tadpole carriers although males occasionally carry tadpoles (Silverstone, 1975; R. G. Zahary, personal communication; A. S. Rand, personal communication).

In *Dendrobates auratus,* there is no evidence of male territoriality in the field or in captivity, but males sometimes fight while attempting to attract the same female (Wells, 1978). Males carry tadpoles, one or two at a time, to bromeliads and other temporary accumulations of water and can care for more than one clutch at a time (Senfft, 1936; Dunn, 1941; Eaton, 1941; Wells, 1978). The behavior of *D. azureus* seems to be similar, but this species has been studied only in captivity (Polder, 1974).

The situation is more complex in *Colostethus trinitatis, C. collaris, C. palmatus,* and *C. nubicola.* Males are aggressive toward one another in all four species but also carry tadpoles (Test, 1954; Sexton, 1960; Duellman,1966; Lüddecke, 1974, 1976; Durant and Dole, 1975; Van Meeuwen, 1977; Wells, 1977b). However, the occurrence of aggressive encounters between males does not necessarily mean that males defend long-term territories. I marked male *Colostethus trinitatis* along a stream in Trinidad and found that although particular calling perches were used over and over again, they frequently were occupied by different individuals on successive days. I found no evidence that males defended particular sites because of resources they contained. Males turn black while courting females and sometimes attack other black males, but in contrast to *C. inguinalis* males, they do not attack females or non-calling males (Wells, 1977b, unpublished).

Interpretation of parental behavior in *C. trinitatis, C. collaris,* and *C. palmatus* is further complicated by the fact that females appear to be more aggressive than males. In *C. trinitatis* and perhaps in other species, females defend long-term territories (Test, 1954; Sexton, 1960; Wells, unpublished). This agrees with the expected pattern; female territoriality should be more common when males carry tadpoles. However, it is not clear whether females can defend long-term territories because they do not carry tadpoles, or cannot carry tadpoles because of the disadvantages of leaving their territories. Additional studies on the permanence of female territories and the types of resources being defended are needed before this system will be fully understood.

Parental Care and Sex Role Reversal

Williams (1966), Trivers (1972), and others suggested that high male parental investment may lead to reversal of the usual sex roles in reproductive behavior, with females competing among themselves for access to males. Dendrobatids have been cited repeatedly

Table 11–3.   Parental care and territoriality in dendrobatid frogs.

Species	Habitat	Principal Tadpole Carrier	Tadpole Habitat	Territoriality Male	Territoriality Female	Source
Colostethus						
inguinalis	Rocky streams	Female	Streams	+	+[1]	Wells, unpublished
pratti	Forest floor	Female	Streams	+	–	Wells, unpublished
nubicola	Forest floor	Male	Streams	+	–	Wells, unpublished
collaris	Rocky Streams	Male	Streams	–[2]	+[2]	Durant & Dole, 1975
trinitatis	Rocky streams	Male	Streams	–	+	Test 1954; Sexton, 1960; Wells, unpublished
palmatus	Rocky streams	Male	Streams	+[3]	+	Lüddecke, 1974, 1976
Dendrobates						
pumilio	Forest floor	Female	Bromeliads	+	–	Bunnell, 1974; Silverstone, 1975
auratus	Forest floor	Male	Tree holes; Bromeliads	–	–	Senfft, 1936; Eaton, 1941; Wells, 1978
azureus	Rocky streams	Male	Streams	–[4]	–[4]	Polder, 1974

[1]Female *C. inguinalis* defend only temporary territories. [2]male–male encounters infrequent, female–female encounters frequent in *C. collaris*; data on marked individuals not available. [3]Data on marked *C. palmatus* in field not available. [4]Data for *D. azureus* from captive studies.

as possible examples of sex role reversal because males often provide parental care and females of some species are more aggressive than males (Trivers, 1972; Wilson, 1975; Barash, 1977; Ridley, 1978). However, no conclusive evidence of sex role reversal exists for any dendrobatid although the behavior of at least one species is consistent with the hypothesis (Wells, 1978).

Some authors tend to equate male parental care with high male parental investment (e.g., Ridley, 1978), but this is not necessarily valid. Parental investment is defined in terms of decreased investment in future offspring (Trivers, 1972), something that is virtually impossible to quantify. Many forms of parental care in anurans may provide considerable advantages to offspring while costing the parent little in future reproductive success. The fact that males carry tadpoles does not necessarily imply that male parental investment exceeds that of females.

In order for sex role reversal to occur, male parental care must be so expensive that it significantly inhibits males from obtaining additional mates and thereby decreases the availability of males in the population. Female reproductive success then might be limited by their ability to find mates, and females would actively court males or compete among themselves for access to males (Trivers, 1972). The following types of data are the minimum required to demonstrate a relationship between male parental investment and sex role reversal in dendrobatids: (1) at any given time, receptive females should outnumber receptive males, (2) the shortage of males must be related to male parental investment and not simply to an unequal population sex ratio, (3) there should be instances of more than one gravid female approaching the same calling male, (4) female–female aggressive encounters should be related to competition for males and not solely to competition for ecological resources such as feeding sites or shelter, (5) females should take the more active role in courtship, and (6) males should discriminate between females when given a choice of mates.

Conditions leading to these types of behavior are most likely to occur when females lay many small clutches of eggs in rapid succession and the time required to care for each clutch is longer than the interval between clutches. Even if males accept more than one clutch at a time, female egg production could outstrip the ability of the males to care for them, and a shortage of males would result. In *Dendrobates auratus*, females do produce small clutches at frequent intervals. Several females have been observed following single calling males and fighting among themselves for access to males, but females are not territorial. Males call to attract females, but females appear to court males. Male mate discrimination has not been demonstrated (Wells, 1978). The behavior of *D. auratus* is consistent with the sex role reversal hypothesis, but many additional observations are needed before alternative explanations can be eliminated.

Several species of *Colostethus* have been cited as possible examples of sex role reversal (Barash, 1977; Ridley, 1978), but I find no evidence to support this interpretation for any species. In *C. trinitatis*, females are territorial and more brightly colored than males (Test, 1954; Sexton, 1960). However, I never observed females competing among themselves for access to individual males, nor did I see more than one female following the same calling male (Wells, unpublished). On any given day, there were between one and two dozen males calling along a 20 to 30 m stretch of stream, but few females approached these males for courtship, suggesting that there was no shortage of available males in the population. Females did not engage in the sort of active courtship of males observed in *D. auratus*. Territoriality in this species appears to be related to competition for feeding sites and shelter (Test, 1954; Sexton, 1960; Wells, unpublished), but not to reproductive competition. Females leave their territories to mate and follow males to oviposition sites up to several meters away (Wells, unpublished). Although these observations are not conclusive, they suggest that caution is required in postulating widespread sex role reversal in dendrobatids.

CONCLUSIONS

I hope this review has demonstrated that parental care, although an unusual reproductive strategy in anurans, is nevertheless of interest to behaviorists and sociobiologists. If anuran parental care is to be integrated into broader evolutionary discussions of vertebrate parental strategies, it is essential that the fundamental differences between anuran parental care and that of birds and mammals be understood. Some theoretical discussions of parental behavior have ignored these differences, as well as differences in costs associated with various forms of parental care in frogs.

In mammals and most passerine birds, parental care is a physiological necessity, without which no young are likely to survive. The dominant feature of mammalian reproduction is the nutritional contribution to the young by the female in the form of internal gestation and lactation. Since males have no way of making an equivalent contribution, desertion by the male and polygynous mating systems are the rule in mammals. In birds, on the other hand, the energetic demands of producing a large endothermic juvenile from a small ectothermic hatchling have led to widespread bi-parental care. In both groups, the costs of abandoning offspring and the costs of caring for them are high.

This is not necessarily true for frogs or teleost fishes. With the exception of viviparous species, frogs do not feed their young, nor do most teleost fishes. Most frogs do not guard their eggs or young against predators as large as themselves although this form of parental care is relatively common in fishes (Perrone and Zaret, 1979). In short, parental care in frogs and fishes often is relatively inexpensive and is best viewed as an adaptation to specific ecological conditions, not as a necessary condition for offspring survival. Parental care may increase the proportion of young surviving, but in most species it seems unlikely that all deserted young perish.

This suggests that parental care should vary as ecological conditions vary, just as social organizations and mating systems vary with changing ecological conditions. I would expect many species to exhibit facultative parental care, particularly when simple egg attendance is involved. An adult might remain with eggs during dry periods or when predators are abundant but abandon them when moisture is adequate or predators scarce.

A beautiful example of facultative parental care has been discovered in *Hyla rosenbergi* by Arnold Kluge (personal communication). When population densities are high, most males guard their nests against conspecifics. When densities are low and the probability of intrusion by conspecifics is reduced, males rarely guard their nests. These results demonstrate the need for additional long-term studies under a variety of ecological conditions and for comparative studies of different populations of the same species. Such investigations would move the study of anuran parental care from the realm of anecdotal natural history into quantative evolutionary biology.

ACKNOWLEDGEMENTS

I am grateful to the following individuals for supplying me with unpublished information or manuscripts: Larry Blumer, Mart Gross, Arnold Kluge, Ronald Nussbaum, A. Stanley Rand, Richard Shine, Margaret Stewart, and Robert Zahary. For comments on the manuscript, I thank Larry Blumer, Arnold Kluge, and Roy McDiarmid. Field work on dendrobatid frogs was supported by a Smithsonian Postdoctoral Fellowship and a grant from the University of Connecticut Research Foundation.

REFERENCES

Adamson, L., R. G. Harrison, and I. Bayley. 1960. The development of the whistling frog, *Eleutherodactylus martinicensis*, of Barbados. *Proc. Zool. Soc. London* 133:453–469.

Balinsky, B. I., and J. B. Balinsky. 1954. On the breeding habits of the South African bullfrog, *Pyxicephalus adspersus*. *S. Afr. J. Sci.* 51:55–58.

Barash, D. P. 1977. *Sociobiology and Behavior*. Elsevier, New York.

Blommers-Schlösser, R. M. A. 1975. Observations on the larval development of some Malagasy frogs, with notes on their ecology and biology (Anura: Dyscophinae, Scaphiophryninae, and Cophylinae). *Beaufortia* 24:7–26.

Blumer, L. S. Male parental care in the bony fishes. *Q. Rev. Biol.*, in press.

Bogert, C. M. 1969. The eggs and hatchlings of the Mexican leptodactylid frog, *Eleutherodactylus decoratus* Taylor. *Amer. Mus. Novit* (2376):1–9.

Boulenger, G. A. 1912. Observations sur l'accouplement et la ponte de l'Alyte accoucheur, *Alytes obstetricans*. *Bull. Class. Sci. Acad. Roy. Belgique* 1912:570–579.

Bunnell, P. 1973. Vocalizations in the territorial behavior of the frog *Dendrobates pumilio*. *Copeia* 1973:277–284.

Busse, K. 1970. Care of the young by male *Rhinoderma darwini*. *Copeia* 1970: 395.

Cei, J. M. 1962. *Batracios de Chile*. Universidad de Chile, Santiago.

Corben, C. J., G. J. Ingram, and M. J. Tyler. 1974. Gastric brooding: unique form of parental care in an Australian frog. *Science* 186:946–947.

Crump, M. L. 1974. Reproductive strategies in a tropical anuran community. *Univ. Kansas Misc. Publ. Mus. Nat. Hist.* 61:1–68.

Dawkins, R. 1976. *The Selfish Gene*. Oxford University Press, New York.

———, and T. R. Carlisle. 1976. Parental investment, mate desertion and a fallacy. *Nature* 262:131–133.

Drewry, G. 1970. The role of amphibians in the ecology of Puerto Rican rain forest, pp. 16–85. In *Puerto Rico Nuclear Center Rain Forest Project Annual Report*. Puerto Rico Nuclear Center, San Juan.

———. 1974. Ecology of *Eleutherodactylus coqui* Thomas in montaine rain forest of eastern Puerto Rico (abstract). *54th Annual Meeting, Amer. Soc. Ichthyol. Herpetol.*, p. 5.

Duellman, W. E. 1966. Aggressive behavior in dendrobatid frogs. *Herpetologica* 22:217–222.

Dunn, E. R. 1941. Notes on *Dendrobates auratus*. *Copeia* 1941:88–93.

Durant, P., and J. W. Dole. 1975. Aggressive behavior in *Colostethus (= Prostherapis) collaris* (Anura: Dendrobatidae). *Herpetologica* 31:23–26.

Eaton, T. H. 1941. Notes on the life history of *Dendrobates auratus*. *Copeia* 1941:93–95.

Grafen, A., and R. Sibly. 1978. A model of mate desertion. *Anim. Behav.* 26:645–652.

Heinzmann, U. 1970. Untersuchungen zur Bio-Akustik und Okologie der Geburtshelferkröte, *Alytes o. obstetricans* (Laur.). *Oecologia* 5:19–55.

Hellmich, W. 1962. *Reptiles and amphibians of Europe*. Blanford Press, London.

Howard, R. D. 1978. The evolution of mating strategies in bullfrogs (*Rana catesbeiana*). *Evolution* 32:850–871.

Ingram, G. J., M. Anstis, and C. J. Corben. 1975. Observations on the Australian leptodactylid frog, *Assa darlingtoni*. *Herpetologica* 31:425–429.

Jameson, D. L. 1950. Development of *Eleutherodactylus latrans*. *Copeia* 1950:44–46.

Kluge, A. G. 1978. Sexual selection, territoriality, and the evolution of parental care in *Hyla rosenbergi* (abstract). *Joint Annual Meeting*, ASIH-SSAR-Herp. League, Tempe, Arizona.

Lambiris, A. J. L. 1971. A note on "parental care" in the bullfrog, *Pyxicephalus a. adspersus*. *J. Herp. Assoc. Africa* (8):6.

Lamotte, M., and J. Lescure. 1977. Tendances adaptives a l'affranchissement du milieu aquatique chez les amphibiens anoures. *Terre et Vie* 31:225–312.

Lemon, R. E. 1971. Vocal communication by the frog, *Eleutherodactylus martinicensis*. *Can. J. Zool.* 49:211–217.

Lüddecke, H. 1974. Ethologische Untersuchungen zur Fortpfanzung von *Phyllobates palmatus* (Amphibia, Ranidae). Ph.D. dissertation, Johannes Gutenberg-Universitat, Mainz.

———. 1976. Einige Ergebnisse aus Feldbeobachtungen an *Phyllobates palmatus* (Amphibia, Ranidae) in Kolumbien. *Mitt. Inst. Colombo-Aleman Invest. Cient.* 8:156–163.

Lynn, W. G., and C. Grant. 1940. *The Herpetology of Jamaica*. The Institute of Jamaica, Kingston.

Maynard Smith, J. 1977. Parental investment: a prospective analysis. *Anim. Behav.* 25:1–9.
────. 1978. *The Evolution of Sex.* Cambridge University Press, New York.
McDiarmid, R. W. 1978. Evolution of parental care in frogs, pp. 127–147. In G. M. Burghardt and M. Beckoff, eds. *The Development of Behavior. Comparative and Evolutionary Aspects.* Garland Publishing, Inc., New York.
Moore, J. A. 1961. The frogs of eastern New South Wales. *Bull. Amer. Mus. Nat. Hist.* 121:149–386.
Myers, C. W. 1969. The ecological geography of cloud forest in Panama. *Amer. Mus. Novit.* (2396):1–52.
Obert, H. 1974. Untersuchungen zur hormonalen Steurrung der Rufaktivität von Fröschen und Kröten der Familien Ranidae, Discoglossidae, Hylidae, und Bufonidae. *Zool. Jb. Physiol.* 78:219–241.
Pengilley, R. K. 1971. Calling and associated behavior of some species of Pseudophryne (Anura: Leptodactylidae). *J. Zool. London* 163:73–92.
Perrone, M., and T. M. Zaret. 1979. Parental care patterns of fishes. *Amer. Natur.* 113:351–361.
Polder, W. N. 1974. Pflege und Fortpflanzung von *Dendrobates azureus* und anderer Dendrobatiden. II. *Aquarien Terrarien Z.* 27:28–32.
Poynton, J. C. 1957. Bullfrog guardians. *Afr. Wildlife* 11:80.
────, and S. Pritchard. 1976. Notes on the biology of *Breviceps* (Anura: Microhylidae). *Zool. Afr.* 11:313–318.
Rabb, G. and M. S. Rabb. 1961. On the mating and egg laying behavior of the Surinam toad, *Pipa pipa. Copeia* 1961:271–276.
────. 1963. Additional observations on breeding behavior of the Surinam toad, *Pipa pipa. Copeia* 1963:636–642.
Ridley, M. 1978. Paternal care. *Anim. Behav.* 26:904–932.
Rose, W. 1956. Parental care in batrachians. *Afr. Wildlife* 10:257.
Salthe, S. N. and J. S. Mecham. 1974. Reproductive and courtship patterns pp. 209–521. In B. Lofts, ed., *Physiology of the Amphibia,* II. Academic Press, New York.
Scheel, J. J. 1970. Notes on the biology of the African tree-toad, *Nectophryne afra* Buchholz and Peters, 1875 (Bufonidae, Anura) from Fernando Po. *Rev. Zool. Bot. Afr.* 81:225–236.
Senfft, W. 1936. Das Brutgeschäft des Baumsteigerfrosches (*Dendrobates auratus* Girard) in Gefangenschaft. *Zool. Gart.* 8:122–136.
Sexton, O. J. 1960. Some aspects of the behavior and of the territory of a dendrobatid frog, *Prostherapis trinitatis. Ecology* 41:107–115.
Silverstone, P. A. 1975. A revision of the poison-arrow frogs of the genus *Dendrobates* Wagler. *Nat. Hist. Mus. Los Angeles County Sci. Bull.* 21:1–55.
────. 1976. A revision of the poison-arrow frogs of the genus *Phyllobates* Bibron in Sagra (Family Dendrobatidae). *Nat. Hist. Mus. Los Angeles County Sci. Bull.* 27:1–53.
Stewart, M. M. The role of introduced species in a Jamacian frog community. *Proceedings, IV Symposium Internacional de Ecologica Tropica,* Panama, in press.
Test, F. H. 1954. Social aggressiveness in an amphibian. *Science* 120:140–141.
Trivers, R. L. 1972. Parental investment and sexual selection, pp.136–179. In B. G. Campbell, ed. *Sexual Selection and the Descent of Man.* Aldine Press, Chicago.
────1974. Parent-offspring conflict. *Amer. Zool.* 14:249–264.
Tyler, M. J. 1976. *Frogs.* Collins, London.
Van Meeuwen, H. M. 1977. De Trinidadse beekkikker *Colostethus trinitatis. Lacerta* 36:3–11.
Vaz-Ferreira, R. and A. Gehrau. 1975. Comportamiento epimeletico de la rana comun, *Leptodactylus ocellatus* (L.) (Amphibia, Leptodactylidae). I. Attencion de la cria y actividades alimentarias y agresivas relacionades. *Physis* 34:1–14.
Wager, V. A. 1956. Parental care in batrachians. *Afr. Wildlife* 10:341–343.
────1965. *The Frogs of South Africa.* Purnell and Sons, Capetown.
Wells, K. D. 1977a. The social behaviour of anuran amphibians. *Anim. Behav.* 25:666–693.
────1977b. The courtship of frogs, pp. 233–262. In D. H. Taylor and S. I. Guttman, eds., *The Reproductive Biology of Amphibians.* Plenum Press, New York.
────1977c. Territoriality and male mating success in the green frog (*Rana clamitans*). *Ecology* 58:750-762.
────1978. Courtship and parental behavior in a Panamanian poison-arrow frog (*Dendrobates auratus*). *Herpetologica* 34:148–155.
Weygoldt, P. 1976. Beobachtungen zur Biologie und Ethologie von *Pipa* (*Hemipipa*) *carvolhoi* Mir. RiB. 1937. (Anura, Pipidae). *Z. Tierpsychol.* 40:80–99.

Williams, G. C. 1966. *Adaptation and Natural Selection*. Princeton University Press, Princeton.
———1975. *Sex and Evolution*. Princeton University Press, Princeton.
Wilson, E. O. 1975. *Sociobiology: The New Synthesis*. Harvard University Press, Cambridge, Massa-
    chusetts.
Woodruff, D. S. 1977. Male postmating brooding behavior in three Australian *Pseudophryne* (Anura:
    Leptodactylidae). *Herpetologica* 33:296–303.

12.

Reproductive Cost and the Sex Ratio in Red-Winged Blackbirds

Kent L. Fiala

The study of the sex ratio occupies a unique place in evolutionary biology. Darwin himself (1871) recognized the sex ratio as an attribute that should be explicable by natural selection, yet after reviewing a wide variety of data, he remained unable to find a selective advantage for one sex ratio over another and explicitly left the problem to future generations to solve. It remained unsolved until 1930, when Fisher (1958) hypothesized that natural selection would adjust the sex ratio so as to equalize parental expenditure in the two sexes. Williams (1966a, p. 21) singled out this hypothesis as a major generalization connecting evolutionary theory and observation and apparently considered the sex ratio to be the major solved problem of evolutionary biology (ibid., p. 272).

Yet, although Fisher's principle has been repeatedly modelled mathematically (Shaw and Mohler, 1953; Bodmer and Edwards, 1960; Kolman, 1960; Mac Arthur, 1965; Verner, 1965; Leigh, 1970; Emlen, 1973; Charnov, 1975) and extended to special cases, including local mate competition (Hamilton, 1967), facultative control (Trivers and Willard, 1973; Werren and Charnov, 1978), and parent-offspring conflict (Trivers, 1974; Trivers and Hare, 1976), it has not received rigorous empirical study. In accounting for the generality of the 1:1 sex ratio and for the independence of the sex ratio from the breeding system, it is consistent with a mass of data, but it is not the only hypothesis that might be so. One might argue that the sex ratio is simply an unmodifiable effect of meiosis (Maynard Smith, 1978). That reasoning, similar to Fisher's accounts for skewed sex ratios in haplodiploid organisms (Hamilton, 1967), gives the genetic aspect of Fisher's principle additional credence, but the aspect of equality of expediture has remained little studied. This inattention is probably largely because few organisms have offspring that clearly receive parental care differentially according to sex and because parental care is difficult to quantify.

In the first part of this paper, I develop a general model of natural selection of the sex ratio, incorporating an operational concept of "parental expenditure" (here called reproductive cost). In the second part I report an experimental test of the model in a sexually dimorphic species.

THEORY

A fundamental assumption of life history theory is that natural selection tends to maximize the malthusian parameter or genotypic rate of increase, m (Fisher, 1958). It has been shown (Schaffer, 1974a; Taylor et al., 1974) that a life history that maximizes m also maximizes reproductive value v_x/v_0 at any age x, in the sense that any feasible departure from the optimal life history will decrease both m and v_x/v_0. This result simplifies the modelling of life histories, for it proves to be easier to model the maximization of reproductive value than of m.

Fisher (1958, p. 158) originally pointed out that "the problem of the influence of Natural Selection on the sex-ratio may be most exactly examined by the aid of the concept of reproductive value," and following this lead, the several subsequent approaches to expressing Fisher's principle symbolically (cited above) have all made use of some equivalent of reproductive value. Also like Fisher, nearly all have used some concept of expenditure; still this latter concept remains nebulous. Fisher himself did not carefully define parental expenditure but referred to expenditures of nutriment, time, and activity. But the maximization of reproductive value implies that the effects of such expenditures are subsumed as effects on reproductive value, making it necessary to express expenditure in the same terms as reproductive value.

A useful approach to the problem has been to partition reproductive value at the onset of the breeding season into two components, that accruing to the parent through the expected reproduction of its offspring produced at that time (current reproductive value) and that retained by the parent (residual reproductive value, the present value of all future reproduction (Williams, 1966b; Schaffer, 1974a)). Any event or behavior may be said to be costly to an organism if it decreases either or both of the components of the organism's reproductive value. In particular, any behavior that decreases residual reproductive value while tending to increase current reproductive value may be said to impose a reproductive cost, even if the net effect is to increase total reproductive value. The magnitude of a reproductive cost is the present value of the future reproduction "foregone" (in the sense that the expectation of future reproduction has been reduced) in order to accomplish the increase in current reproductive value. Thus the overall cost of a particular reproductive episode is the present value of all future reproduction foregone in order to reproduce at that time (Hirshfield and Tinkle, 1975). This cost concept is in keeping with the economic concept of opportunity cost, which is that the true cost of any action can be measured by the value of the best alternative that must be foregone when the action is taken (Nicholson, 1972).

I will regard a parent's current reproductive value, C, and its residual reproductive value, R, both measured at the time of conception of offspring, as continuous functions of the numbers of sons, M, and daughters, F, conceived:

$$C = f_1(M,F); R = f_2(M,F).$$

Total reproductive value of the parent is then $V = C + R$. The benefit and cost of producing an offspring will be expressed as the resultant changes in C and R, respectively. I will also use the term "reproductive investment" to mean the incurring of a reproductive cost or the cost incurred.

The model specifically refers to the time of conception because it is only then that a gene influencing the sex ratio can be expressed. Whether or not investment is in any sense "equalized" by the end of parental care is essentially an incidental effect of selection at conception. Note that this restriction reduces such disparate cost factors as differential mortality and "differential demands" to a common basis. Greater demands by one sex on the parent tend to increase that sex's expected cost, while greater mortality of one sex tends to lower its expected cost, owing to the greater probability that the full cost will not be incurred.

A population's primary sex ratio will be in selectively stable equilibrium when the total differential of reproductive value with respect to the mean numbers of sons and daughters,

$$dV = \left(\frac{\partial C}{\partial M} + \frac{\partial R}{\partial M} \right) dM + \left(\frac{\partial C}{\partial F} + \frac{\partial R}{\partial F} \right) dF$$

equals zero. If this were not so, then there would be some sex ratio other than the average that would give a selective advantage to those genotypes producing it. Assuming $dV = 0$ and rearranging,

$$\frac{-dM}{dF} = \frac{\dfrac{\partial C}{\partial F} + \dfrac{\partial R}{\partial F}}{\dfrac{\partial C}{\partial M} + \dfrac{\partial R}{\partial M}} \tag{1}$$

This result implies a functional relationship between M and F, the nature of which depends on additional constraining assumptions. In all related previous models, the assumed constraint has been that the total investment is fixed, and that clutch size then varies with the sex ratio (assuming that there is cost dimorphism). In the present context, this is equivalent to fixing R. Assuming this, then by the implicit function theorem,

$$\frac{\partial R / \partial F}{\partial R / \partial M} = \frac{-dM}{dF} ,$$

and by substituting into (1) and rearranging, the sex ratio is found to be stable when

$$\frac{-dM}{dF} = \frac{\partial R / \partial F}{\partial R / \partial M} = \frac{\partial C / \partial F}{\partial C / \partial M} . \tag{2}$$

From this it may be seen that a more general way of stating Fisher's principle is that the population sex ratio will be stable when the ratio of marginal costs of the two sexes equals the ratio of their marginal values.

A complementary model that has not been previously examined but which may be more appropriate for many organisms (e.g., birds) is that in which the clutch size is fixed, and cost varies according to the sex ratio. In this case, $dM = -dF$ and therefore, at equilibrium

$$\frac{\partial C}{\partial F} + \frac{\partial R}{\partial F} = \frac{\partial C}{\partial M} + \frac{\partial R}{\partial M} .$$

Both models give the same sex ratio for the globally optimal clutch size because at that point $\partial C / \partial F = -\partial R / \partial F$ and $\partial C / \partial M = -\partial R / \partial M$. However, the two cases predict different paths toward equilibrium from non-equilibrial states. In general, the stable sex ratio is nearer 50 per cent under clutch size constraint than under investment constraint for smaller-than-optimal clutch size and further from 50 per cent for greater-than-optimal clutch size.

It remains to determine the functional relationships between value and cost, respectively, and clutch composition. Although the contrary assumption is commonly made (it is implicit in Fisher's principle), both functions cannot be linear. If they were, the optimal clutch size would in all instances be either zero or infinite. (But the stable sex ratio would be independent of investment. This allows the success of linear models such as those of Fisher and of Bodmer and Edwards (1960) and others.) For the purposes of modelling sex ratio optimization, it has proven instructive to consider the implications of assuming current reproductive value to be a linear function of clutch composition, i.e., that each offspring in a population makes the same contribution to its parents' current reproductive value as any offspring of the same sex regardless of the number or sexes of its siblings.

This assumption has been analyzed by Shaw and Mohler (1953), whose argument may be briefly summarized as follows. Consider a population in which the mean individual sex proportion (probability that a given offspring will be male) is p. Since the collective amount of reproduction by males must exactly equal that by females, each sex has half the cohort's collective reproductive value. Then, if the population produces n clutches, each averaging M males and F females, collective reproductive value equals $n(M + F)$, and

$$\text{mean reproductive value per son} = \frac{n(M + F)}{2nM} = \frac{1}{2p}$$

$$\text{mean reproductive value per daughter} = \frac{n(M + F)}{2nF} = \frac{1}{2(1 - p)}.$$

If the population contains a small subpopulation in which the mean individual sex proportion is p', then the expected reproductive value of one of its offspring is $V = \frac{1}{2}(p'/p + (1-p')/(1-p))$.

By finding dV/dp' and equating it to zero, the stable sex proportion (ignoring cost) is found to be one half. That the second derivative is zero shows that the equilibrium is not at a maximum of V (in fact the function has neither maximum nor minimum) but at a line toward which the population is drawn as individuals are selected for higher values of V and along which there is no variance of fitness between sex proportions. Thus, a population has an equilibrial but not an optimal sex ratio; an individual may have an optimal sex ratio but only if the population sex ratio is not at equilibrium. The equilibrial nature of the stable sex ratio is best appreciated graphically (Figure 12–1).

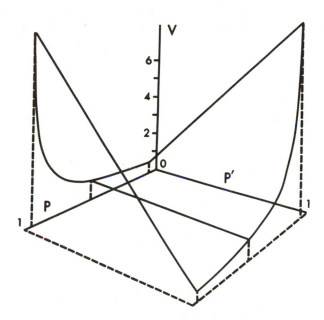

Figure 12–1.   The function $V = \frac{1}{2}(p'/p + (1-p')/(1-p))$. Note that when $p < \frac{1}{2}$, the optimal p' is 1, when $p > \frac{1}{2}$, the optimal p' is 0, and when $p = \frac{1}{2}$, all values of p' are equally fit.

The male and female reproductive values derived above may be substituted for $\partial C / \partial M$ and $\partial C / \partial F$ in equation (1), giving

$$-\frac{dM}{dF} = \frac{\dfrac{M + F}{2F} + \dfrac{\partial R}{\partial F}}{\dfrac{M + F}{2M} + \dfrac{\partial R}{\partial M}}$$

Making the same substitution into (2) shows the equilibrial sex ratio under investment constraint to be given by

$$-\frac{dM}{dF} = \frac{\partial R / \partial F}{\partial R / \partial M} = \frac{\partial C / \partial F}{\partial C / \partial M} = \frac{M}{F} \cdot$$

Specification of the form of the cost function is a more difficult task. But note that with the assumptions of fixed R and linear C, an expression ($-dM/dF = M/F$) for the equilibrial sex ratio exists that contains only M and F and neither R nor C. This has the important consequence that in an empirical study of investment with respect to sex ratio it is, in principle, sufficient to measure investment on an ordinal scale, i.e., all that is needed is to know what different family compositions have the same cost, so that dM/dF may be calculated (Figure 12–2). Unfortunately, the empirical difficulties of distinguishing small differences between adjacent isocosts may lead to considerable imprecision in the estimate of the slope of the isocosts.

The above conclusion that $M/F = -dM/dF$ is formally identical to that reached by Mac Arthur (1965), but the underlying model is different in an important way. Mac Arthur's

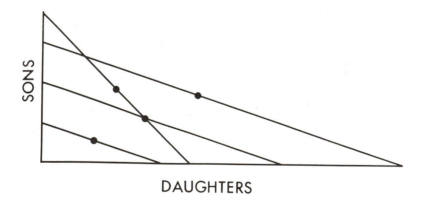

Figure 12–2.   Hypothetical cost and value functions. The cost of any particular combination of sons and daughters could be shown in a third dimension, depicted here by three representative contour lines or isocosts. Since the isocosts have a slope $dM/dF = -1/3$, the stable sex ratio is 1 male to 3 females. The reproductive values of the family compositions can be depicted by isovalues, of which one representative is shown here, crossing the isocosts. The slope of the isovalues is the negative of the ratio of males to females; the mean sex ratio occurs at the midpoints of the isovalues. Selection will adjust the sex ratio so that the isovalues are coincident with the isocosts.

model is restricted to discrete generations and thus does not actually incorporate anything corresponding to reproductive cost as I have defined it; rather it simply divides all family compositions into those that are "permitted" by a given genotype and those that are not. The identity of our conclusions rests on the similarity of the boundary of the set of permitted family compositions to an isocost. This similarity breaks down in the case of clutch size constraint, to which Mac Arthur's model does not extend because of its lack of recognition of a tradeoff between present and future reproduction. The clutch size constraint model seems more realistic, as fixing investment, given sexual dimorphism, requires exacting control over the sex of offspring, which is apparently unknown among diploids with genetic sex determination. But this model lacks the analytic tractability of the investment constraint model, and because both give the same optimal mean family composition, the latter serves as a first approximation. A possible inadequacy of it will be discussed below.

FIELD STUDY

A test of the theory requires a study organism with young that are decidedly sexually dimorphic during the period of parental care. Relatively few species meet this requirement; some of the most promising are certain raptorial birds and icterids. I studied one of the latter, the red-winged blackbird, *Agelaius phoeniceus*, because it can be found in abundance, and a great deal is already known about its breeding biology, including the sexual dimorphism of nestlings, which has been documented in four previous studies (Williams, 1940; Haigh, 1968; Holcomb and Twiest, 1970; Laux, 1970).

The size dimorphism is prima facie evidence for cost dimorphism but, in view of the importance of cost dimorphism to the model, a major objective of this study was to document it more thoroughly. Doing so was especially necessary because cost is properly measured in terms of parental reproductive value rather than physiological requirements of offspring. The two quantities are not necessarily proportional; however, the former can be measured much less precisely than the latter, and effects on parental reproductive value, especially those that depend on the sex of offspring, will certainly be related at least qualitatively to offspring requirements. Therefore, I attempted to estimate isocost slope, dM/dF, using both more precise, but perhaps less accurate, physiological comparisons, and more accurate, but perhaps less precise, comparisons of assumed correlates of residual reproductive value. This approach at least permits testing of the null hypothesis that the sexes are equally costly and provides rough estimates of the expected sex ratio for comparison with the actual sex ratio, the second main objective of the study.

Methods. The study was conducted from 1974 to 1978, principally in four marshes in or near the E. S. George Reserve, Livingston Co., Michigan, and ranging in size from 2.3–6.8 ha. During the breeding season, these marshes were searched thoroughly to find as many nests as possible, which were then followed until they became inactive. Most nests were found before egg-laying was complete and nearly all before hatching. Once young hatched, they were individually marked by clipping one toenail or, at later ages, plucking one primary feather. Nestlings were regularly weighed to the nearest 0.1 gm with a 50 gm Pesola spring balance and a tared mesh bag. I attempted to concentrate on weighings on days 0, 2, 5, and 8 after hatching, but strict adherence to this schedule was not feasible.

During the first three years of the study, the sex of nestlings was determined by weight on or after day 8. Near the end of the third year, I developed a laparotomy technique (Fiala, 1979) for sexing very young nestlings, and in 1977 and 1978, 545 nestlings were sexed in this manner at an average age of 2.27 days.

In 1975 and 1976, I hand-raised a total of 28 nestlings from late-season nests for varying lengths of time. The birds were fed a homogeneous diet, and the food for each was kept separately and replenished in weighed units so that total food consumption of each individual could be measured. The diet was the nestling softbill mix of Lanyon (1979), except that in the first year only half the amount of turkey starter mash was used. In 1976 the daily fecal production of some of the nestlings was collected. Both food and feces were analyzed by bomb calorimetry.

In 1977 the total metabolism of five male and six female nestlings was measured under field conditions using doubly-labelled water (Mullen, 1973). Usually one bird of each sex in a brood of four was labelled on day 5 or 7. Samples of cloacal fluid were then collected in capillary tubes at 12-hour intervals for up to 36 hours (Fiala and Congdon, in prep.).

Early sexing by laparotomy permitted brood manipulations involving the sex composition as well as size of broods. Such manipulations were usually done the day or the day after the birds involved were laparotomized. To observe the success of enlarged unisexual broods, in 1977 I assembled five broods of five males each and five broods of five females; and in 1978, 11 broods of five males, seven broods of five females, and two broods of six females, all in nests with an original clutch of four eggs. To compare feeding frequencies between family compositions, in 1977 I assembled 16 unisexual broods of two to five young in nests with original clutches of three to four eggs and including some of the broods mentioned above. These broods were watched for one-hour intervals, and the number of feeding trips by the parents recorded. One brood in which a male died during the period of observation was counted as both a brood of five and of four. Also, one opposite-sex pair of broods of three and one opposite-sex pair of broods of four were each nearly synchronous, and about halfway through the respective observation periods I interchanged the two broods so that the feeding frequencies of the same broods could be compared between two "mothers." These five broods counted twice gave a total of 21 mother-brood combinations.

Most statistical calculations were made using the Michigan Interactive Data Analysis System or other programs supported by the University of Michigan Statistical Research Laboratory.

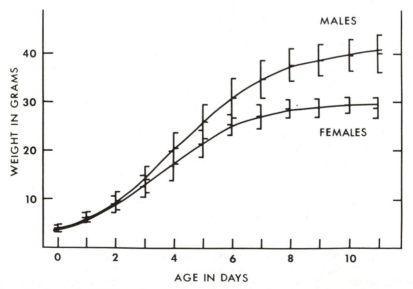

Figure 12–3.   Growth of nestling red-wings. Vertical bars show one standard deviation on either side of the mean. Sample sizes range from 79 to 353. The logistic curves were fitted by least squares regression.

Table 12–1.   Logistic regressions of weight on age.*

Sex	a	b	c	n'	ems''
Males	41.4±.218	9.85±.265	.564±.00805	2042	9.25
Females	30.5±.137	7.34±.156	.577±.00748	2033	4.17

*Weight at age x, $W(x) = a/(1 + be^{-cx})$. Coefficients shown ±1 asymptotic standard deviation.
'Number of weighings.
"Error mean square.

Estimation of cost dimorphism. The sexes are not significantly different in weight on days 0 and 1 after hatching, but males are significantly heavier at all later ages (Figure 12–3); by day 8 there is virtually no overlap. The growth data were well fit by logistic functions obtained by least squares regression (Tables 12–1,12–2). There are apparently no statistical tests for comparisons of non-linear regressions, but support-plane confidence intervals can be calculated for individual parameters (Conway et al., 1970). Of the three logistic parameters, there is a clear sexual difference in a, the upper asymptote, and in b, which is equal to the weight to be gained after hatching divided by hatching weight; but there is no clear difference in c, a measure of the rapidity with which the asymptote is attained though there is some suggestion that females tend to have a higher c. Thus the growth curve for each sex has the same shape, but that for females is lower for any given position on the curve and, in addition, is shifted to the left relative to the male curve.

This leftward displacement reflects the fact that in hatching at essentially the same weight as males, females hatch at a higher percentage of their asymptotic weight. This head start is maintained through the nestling period; females give the impression of gaining coordination and alertness more rapidly than do males and tend to fledge slightly sooner (Holcomb and Twiest, 1970). I cannot report fledging ages because my handling of older nestlings tended to precipitate fledging, but one observation conveys the sexual difference: Of birds still in the nest or near enough to be captured and weighed on days 10 or 11, the proportion of males was significantly higher than at younger ages ($X^2 = 25.1$, 1 d.f., p <.00001).

The hand-raising experiments were done to investigate the possibility that the sexual differences in growth arise from differences in efficiency rather than food intake. Substantial retardation of growth relative to that of wild nestlings as well as considerable individual variation, rendered the analysis of the growth patterns of the hand-raised birds rather fruitless. However, the wet weight of daily food consumption was found to be a quadratic function of morning body weight in each sex (Figure 12–4). The regression for males is food $= -2.43 + .823$ wt $- .00848$ wt^2 ($r^2 = .56$, p <.0001, n $= 149$); for females, food $= -1.75 + .776$ wt $- .0101$ wt^2 ($r^2 = .37$, p <.0001, n $= 206$). Neither intercept is significantly different from zero. Analysis of covariance of food consumption with weight and its square showed the regression coefficients to be significantly different between the sexes (p <.0005), i.e., for a given weight males consume more food than do females.

The food used in the first year contained 37.12±.55 per cent dry matter, with 5.297±.112 kcal/gm dry weight. The second year's mix was 46.21 ± .64 per cent dry, with 5.107 ± .103 kcal/gm dry weight. Curiously, a two-way analysis of covariance of the feeding data with food consumption converted to calories showed the same sex effect each year but also a significant difference between years; i.e., more calories were consumed on the richer diet. The biological significance of this is not clear. Possibly the birds' hunger was regulated by mass consumed rather than by energy, but it is also possible that an unconscious preconception of the birds' requirements biased my perception of their hunger (I did not know which diet had the higher energy content at the time).

Table 12–2. Logistic regressions of weight on age in broods of four.*

Sex Ratio ♂♂♀♀	Male Regressions					Female Regressions				
	a	b	c	n	ems	a	b	c	n	ems
0 4						30.9 ± .650	8.20 ± .942	.614 ± .0403	109	6.35
1 3	42.3 ± 1.55	9.28 ± 1.29	.532 ± .0447	80	12.6	30.1 ± .484	6.81 ± .392	.542 ± .0221	219	3.94
2 2	42.3 ± .700	10.1 ± .806	.562 ± .0255	170	7.71	30.9 ± .523	7.12 ± .569	.567 ± .0292	158	5.02
3 1	40.1 ± .680	10.5 ± .985	.611 ± .0285	202	10.4	30.0 ± .776	8.21 ± 1.25	.623 ± .0512	65	5.48
4 0	42.1 ± .652	9.85 ± 1.11	.609 ± .0332	54	4.37					

* see footnotes to Table 1.

The linear regression of caloric value of daily fecal production on daily food consumption has an intercept not significantly different from zero, so it was recalculated to pass through the origin. The resulting regression equation is fecal calories = .261 food calories (r^2 = .407, p <.0001, n = 14). There is no significant difference in the regressions (and hence in digestive efficiency) between sexes (analysis of covariance, p <.4).

Because the growth of the hand-raised birds was different from that of wild nestlings and because of the possibility of bias in the way they were fed, I used doubly-labelled water to measure metabolic rate directly in the next year. The measured rates of CO_2 production were not significantly different between sexes; assuming the same respiratory quotient in both sexes, the rates of O_2 consumption are likewise not significantly different.

Experimental tests of the hypothesis that cost dimorphism exists took the form of asking whether different family compositions within a brood size could be considered to lie on the same isocost. The relevance to the model of such tests depends on the validity of the model's assumption that the reproductive value of an offspring is independent of the sex of its siblings, at least in normal clutch sizes, i.e., that any sexual differences in offspring requirements are reflected only in the mothers' residual reproductive value and not in the offsprings' own fitness. To test this assumption, nestlings' weights were grouped by brood composition and logistic growth curves were calculated for each group by least squares regression. The results for broods of four are shown in Table 12–2 and indicate that there is apparently no effect of sex ratio on growth. Thus, for example, an individual of either sex is no worse off if its three nestmates are brothers than if they are sisters. Similarly, stratifying the data by brood size, regardless of family composition, shows no apparent effect of brood size on the sex-specific regressions. Interpretation of this absence of a sibling effect on growth as an absence of an effect on offspring fitness requires the assumption that offspring fitness is dependent on body weight. There is support for this assumption in that, of 20 males individually marked as nestlings and recaptured in a subsequent year, 16 were above

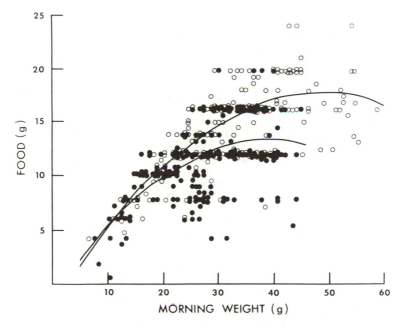

Figure 12–4.   Hand-raised nestlings' daily food consumption (grams wet weight) as a function of body weight at the beginning of the day. Open circles: males. Solid circles: females.

the mean weight for their age when last weighed and only three were below ($X^2 = 8.89$, 1 d.f., p <0.005). (The hatching date of the remaining male was not accurately known. Too few females were recaptured for a similar comparison.)

Because the growth pattern did not vary with sex ratio in normal-sized broods, parents apparently respond to normal variation in offspring demands by providing the appropriate amount of food. There is evidence that this parental adaptability does not fully extend to enlarged broods, which presumably place the parents under greater stress than it is optimal for them to incur. In much of their range, redwings have only two common clutch sizes, three and four (196 and 391, respectively, of 640 clutches in this study; cf. Crawford, 1977; Francis, 1975; Robertson, 1973), and reproductive success of both naturally large and ex-perimentally enlarged broods appears to be reduced (Francis, 1975; Robertson, 1973). In the present study, natural clutches of five in which all eggs hatched accounted for a dispro-portionate number of presumed starvation deaths (Table 12–3). I attempted to exploit the possibility that response to enlarged broods would not be entirely adequate for the nest-lings' needs by assembling enlarged unisexual broods. Under the null hypothesis that males and females are equally costly, the success of enlarged all-female broods should be equally reduced as that of enlarged all-male broods, but under the hypothesis that cost is related to physiological requirements, male broods of five could be expected to have more severely lowered success than female broods of five which have about the same biomass as a normal-sized brood of four males.

In 1977, one of the enlarged all-female broods was predated before any results could be observed. In the other four broods of five females, all young grew well and fledged, except for one individual late in the season. On the other hand, only one of the five broods of five males had all young survive, the single exception being a brood that the "father" helped feed. In three other broods, one male died, and in the last brood, also a late-season nest, two males died. These data suggested greater difficulty in raising males, especially because starvation deaths are rare (Tables 12–3,12–4), but they are too few to be signifi-cant.

In the following year's repeat of the experiment, 10 of the 20 nests were predated, but 14 survived until at least day 8. Unlike the previous year, there were no starvation deaths in any of these nests (Table 12–3). Furthermore, in neither sex were growth curves signifi-cantly different from those of control birds that had also been laparotomized but not placed in enlarged broods.

A second experiment was designed to compare the relative effects of sex and number of offspring on feeding frequency. Although feeding frequency is an imprecise measure of offspring requirements because of variation in the amount of food delivered each trip (Roy-ama, 1966), it may be a more satisfactory measure of parental stress and, hence, investment than is the rate of food delivery. In any case, feeding frequency has usually been found to

Table 12–3.   Presumed starvation mortality.

	Starved[1]	Not Starved[2]
Natural broods of 5	5	40
Experimental broods		
of 5: 1977	6	39
of 5 or 6: 1978	0	102
All other broods	48	1,287
Total	59	1,468

[1] Found dead in nest or vanished from nest.
[2] Fledged or hatched but predated.

Table 12–4.   Fate of eggs in completed clutches.

Unhatched:	Predated	520
	Hatching failure	138
	Other	133
Hatched:	Predated	522
	Collected	119
	Died or vanished	59
	Other	44
	Fledged	818
		2,353

Table 12–5.   Hourly feeding frequencies at experimental nests.

Sex		Brood size			
		2	3	4	5
Male:	Mean		12.5	14.2	11.3
	SD		.69	.74	.92
	Hours		41	31	12
	Nests		5	5	2
Female:	Mean	12.9	12.6	13.8	10.5
	SD	1.25	1.51	1.37	.94
	Hours	9	7	11	20
	Nests	2	2	2	3

increase with brood size (see Klomp, 1970 for a review) and thus a comparable increase with sex ratio should be expected.

Most feedings were by females, but males fed during most observations at three nests containing five males, five females, and three males, respectively; and rarely at three other nests. Most observations were made after nestlings were at least five days old, and age did not contribute significantly to the variation.

Within brood size-sex combinations, there were significant differences in feeding rate between nests (two-level nested ANOVA). These differences and unequal sample sizes from different nests preclude a complete analysis of variance. A two-way ANOVA of mean feeding frequencies at each mother–brood combination (excluding the broods of two females because there were no broods of two males) showed neither brood size nor sex to be a significant factor (Table 12–5).

The estimates of $-dM/dF$ that follow from these results fall into two groups, those based on metabolic requirements of the young and those based on observable effects of the young on their parents. The simplest estimate, the ratio of the asymptotic weight of females to that of males, is .737. Even if metabolic requirements vary with the .724 power of weight, as found by Lasiewski and Dawson (1967) in between-species comparisons of standard metabolic rate, the estimate increases only to .802. Alternatively, an index of food consumption by each sex at each age can be obtained from the regressions of food consumption on weight in hand-raised birds and the regressions of weight on age in wild birds, and an index of total requirements for each sex can be obtained by summing the daily indices. The ratio of these sums is .776. The sex ratios expected from these relative cost estimates are 42.4, 44.5, and 43.7 per cent males, respectively. The apparent lack of effect of sex of offspring on parental behavior, on the other hand, provides no basis for rejecting the null hypothesis that the sexes are equally costly, i.e., that $-dM/dF = 1$. From this hypothesis, the stable sex ratio is expected to be 1:1.

Table 12–6.   Sex ratios of nestling redwings.

	Males	Females	% Males	X^2
Williams (1940)	57	62	47.9	
Haigh (1968)	206	225	47.8	
Holcomb & Twiest (1970)	50	68	42.4	
Laux (1970)	162	166	49.4	
Knos & Stickley (1974)	35	38	48.0	
Subtotal	510	559	47.7	2.25
This study: 1974	77	93	45.3	
1975	69	61	53.1	
1976	145	151	49.0	
1977	113	132	46.1	
1978	164	198	45.3	
Subtotal	568	635	47.2	3.73 p < .054
Grand total	1078	1194	47.4	5.92 p < .02

Mean sex ratio. Previous to the present study, five investigators had published sex ratios of nestling redwings (Table 12–6), all based on nestlings sexed by weight or tarsal length late in the nestling period. All the reported sex ratios are very similar, and all show fewer males than females. However, the proportions are not significantly different from 50 per cent.

In four of the five years of my study, the sex ratio was likewise biased in favor of females (Table 12–6); there is some reason to discount the single exception because there is a small seasonal decrease in the sex ratio (Fiala, in prep.), and I did not sample through to the end of the season in 1975. The overall sex ratio is as near significance at the 5 per cent level as is possible without being significant; if a single male had been a female instead, the male proportion would be significantly different from 50 per cent. The combined sex ratio of all the studies is significantly less than 50 per cent (Table 12–6).

These are not direct measurements of either the primary or secondary sex ratio. The first three years' data are based almost entirely on birds that survived to day 8 or later. The last two years' data are largely based on birds sexed by laparotomy at an average age of just over 2 days. (This incidentally makes them a more nearly complete sample of the population, and it is noteworthy that these two samples together do contain significantly less than 50 per cent males (X^2 = 4.63, 1 d.f., p <0.05).) Whether or not these sex ratios represent the primary or secondary sex ratios depends on whether or not differential mortality occurred before sexing. Note (Table 12–4) that very nearly all the post-hatching mortality is the result of predation. There is no reason to suppose that this might affect the sexes differentially because the whole brood is virtually always taken at once. Furthermore, of those few birds that were assumed to have starved, there is no apparent sex bias (Table 12–7). Therefore, I conclude that my data are representative of the sex ratio at hatching. It is impossible to estimate the primary sex ratio (Fiala, 1980) because the rate of hatching failure is high (Table 12–4) and no method of sexing an egg is known. In order for the primary sex ratio to have been exactly 50 per cent, it would have been necessary for male egg hatching failure to exceed that of female eggs by about three or four to one, but a much less dramatic bias could have been sufficient to account for the statistical significance of the observed sex ratio.

Discussion. Although the growth and physiological data provide compelling evidence for sexual dimorphism in offspring requirements, the data on the effect on the parents of this dimorphism are at best ambivalent. From the theoretical model it is known that the marginal

Table 12–7.   Sex of presumed starvation mortalities.

	Males	Females	Unknown
Vanished nestlings	6	9	24
Dead nestlings	10	8	2
	16	17	26

rate of transformation of the sexes, $-dM/dF$, rather than absolute costs, determines the stable sex ratio, at least under investment constraint, so that inability to distinguish slight differences does not rule out the possibility that they exist and have an important effect on the sex ratio. Nevertheless, the difference in the amount of dimorphism implied by the two kinds of data is puzzling.

It is possible that the experiments on the parents gave the less accurate assessment of cost dimorphism. Much of the lack of significant differences in effects on the experimental mothers may be because actual effects on future reproduction could not be directly observed. The females who successfully raised broods of five males might, contrary to my expectation, have done so exclusively at the cost of reduced survival probability, rather than a combination of the latter and reduced offspring survivorship. Likewise, the small variation in feeding frequency between sexes or number of offspring might have been accomplished in part by a decrease in the mother's own food consumption.

Conversely, it is likely that physiological dimorphism exceeds reproductive cost dimorphism. The slightly greater precocity of females can have a bearing on this in two ways. First, it may slightly reduce the difference in food requirements. Still greater precocity of the smaller sex has been observed in the sparrowhawk, *Accipiter nisus,* with the net results being an apparent absence of a difference in food intake (Newton, 1978) and no effect on the sex ratio (Newton and Marquiss, 1979). Second, because of high mortality (Young, 1963; Table 12-4), at conception, the expected length of parental care probably extends only to several days beyond hatching, when, because of the advancement of female growth, the full degree of sexual dimorphism is not yet established. This would tend to reduce the disparity in expected costs at conception, but the importance of the reduction is difficult to evaluate, because even though the probability of requiring the full amount of parental care is small, the amount required in the later stages probably sufficiently outweighs that received earlier to make a substantial contribution to the expectation at conception. Growth resumes after fledging; the exact pattern of this later growth is unknown, but fledging weight in both sexes is roughly only two thirds of adult weight, and observation of hand-raised birds suggests that most of the additional weight is gained during the post-fledging period of parental care.

Depending on how it is given, male parental care could be expected to influence differentially maternal reproductive costs. From the mother's point of view, if her mate's assistance is given unpredictably or at least independently of the sex of her nestlings, then his expected contribution is simply another resource, with no differential effect on cost or sex ratio. However, if the mother is more likely to obtain assistance by producing sons, then the disparity in the costs of the two sexes is reduced for the mother, and the optimal proportion of sons is raised. Although the father would be, in effect, manipulated into investing excessively in sons, if their fitness would be unduly low under the mother's care alone, then the marginal value of helping them may be sufficiently great to justify it.

Time constraints did not permit study of the male role, but males were observed feeding at both male and female broods in the 1977 feeding frequency experiment. In the 1978 brood enlargement experiment, males were observed making at least some contribution at several (probably a greater than expected proportion) enlarged broods of either sex. Thus, males may preferentially feed large broods, but there is no clear evidence of a sex preference. A non-significant trend toward higher male proportion in male-assisted broods has been observed in another population (C. B. Patterson, pers. comm.), and a significantly higher male proportion in primary nests, which are consistently male-assisted, has been observed in the yellow-headed blackbird, *Xanthocephalus xanthocephalus* (C. B. Patterson, pers. comm.).

There can be little doubt that there is some degree of cost dimorphism of the sexes, and that the marginal rate of transformation of the sexes lies between the physiologically-based estimates of about .75 and the null hypothesis of 1. The observed male proportion of 47.2 per cent does lie about halfway between the proportions predicted from these two dimorphism estimates. But although the deviation from 50 per cent is in the predicted direction, it is suspiciously small, given the uncertainty of the true degree of dimorphism, and the conclusion that it is adaptive, not merely fortuitous, can be accepted only with reservations.

It is possible that cost dimorphism is as extreme as implied by the physiological data but that the model used to predict the sex ratio is not applicable. The intermediacy of the sex ratio suggests parent–offspring conflict in the determination of sex (Trivers, 1974) as an intriguing, if not very parsimonious, alternative hypothesis, but such conflict seems unlikely with female heterogamety, as the mother never produces a genotype different from her own that does not already have its sex determined.

Finally, environmental uncertainty of breeding success has been shown in theory to reduce optimal brood size relative to the optimum for mean conditions (Schaffer, 1974b), and the clutch size constraint model suggests that such a reduction might increase the stable sex ratio. For example, the discrepancy between the incidence of brood reduction in natural and artificial broods of five suggests that the reason for the rarity of broods of five may not lie in the inability of parents to raise them but in the uncertainty of the last-hatched young's becoming established in competition with its older siblings. If so, it could be advantageous for the mother who is capable of raising five young to invest in a more certain brood of four, but with an increased sex ratio.

SUMMARY

A theoretical model predicts that a population's sex ratio will equilibrate so that the ratio of the marginal costs of the two sexes equals the ratio of their marginal values. From this it follows that the equilibrial sex ratio can be predicted from the marginal rate of transformation of the sexes, $-dM/dF$. In principle, this can be measured, but empirical problems make imprecision likely.

Male and female nestling red-winged blackbirds were shown to have markedly different metabolic requirements, but experiments designed to test whether or not $dM/dF = -1$ gave ambivalent results. The sex ratio was found to be significantly biased at hatching. The results are interpreted as a qualitative but not quantitative verification of theory.

ACKNOWLEDGEMENTS

I thank the members of my dissertation committee, R. B. Payne, R. D. Alexander, G. F. Estabrook, and D. W. Tinkle for advice during the study and for comments on various drafts of the manuscript. D. De Steven and C. J. Martin also offered constructive criticism of the manuscript. S. Sferra did much of the recording of feeding frequencies. J. Congdon collaborated in the work involving labelled water, and instructed me in calorimetry. During parts of the study, I received support from an NSF graduate fellowship, a Rackham dissertation grant, and a Hinsdale scholarship.

REFERENCES

Bodmer, W. F., and A. W. F. Edwards. 1960. Natural selection and the sex ratio. *Ann. Hum, Genet.* 24:239–244.

Charnov, E. L. 1975. Sex ratio selection in an age-structured population. *Evolution* 29:366–368.

Conway, G. R., N. R. Glass, and J. C. Wilcox. 1970. Fitting nonlinear models to biological data by Marquardt's algorithm. *Ecology* 51:503–507.

Crawford, R. D. 1977. Breeding biology of year-old and older female red-winged and yellow-headed blackbirds. *Wilson Bull.* 89:73–80.

Darwin, C. R. 1871. *The Descent of Man and Selection in Relation to Sex.* John Murray, London.

Emlen, J. M. 1973. *Ecology: An Evolutionary Approach.* Addison-Wesley, Reading, Mass.

Fiala, K. L. 1980. On estimating the primary sex ratio from incomplete data. *Amer. Natur.,* 115:442–444.

⸺. A laparotomy technique for nestling birds. *Bird–Banding* 50:366–367.

Fisher, R. A. 1958. *The Genetical Theory of Natural Selection.* Dover, New York.

Francis, W. J. 1975. Clutch size and nesting success in red-winged blackbirds. *Auk* 92:815–817.

Haigh, C. R. 1968. Sexual dimorphism, sex ratios and polygyny in the red-winged blackbird. Ph.D. thesis, University of Washington.

Hamilton, W. D. 1967. Extraordinary sex ratios. *Science* 156:477–488.

Hirshfield, M. F., and D. W. Tinkle. 1975. Natural selection and the evolution of reproductive effort. *Proc. Nat. Acad. Sci.* 72:2227–2231.

Holcomb, L. C., and G. Twiest. 1970. Growth rates and sex ratios of red-winged blackbird nestlings. *Wilson Bull.* 82:294–303.

Klomp, H. 1970. The determination of clutch-size in birds. A review. *Ardea* 58:1–124.

Knos, C. J., and A. R. Stickley, Jr. 1974. Breeding red-winged blackbirds in captivity. *Auk* 91:808–816.

Kolman, W. A. 1960. The mechanism of natural selection for the sex ratio. *Amer. Natur.* 94:373–377.

Lanyon, W. E. 1979. Development of song in the wood thrush *(Hylocichla mustelina),* with notes on a technique for hand-rearing passerines from the egg. *Amer. Mus. Nov.* 2666:1–27.

Lasiewski, R. C. and W. R. Dawson. 1967. A re-examination of the relation between standard metabolic rate and body weight in birds. *Condor* 69:13–23.

Laux, L. J., Jr. 1970. Non-breeding surplus and population structure of the red-winged blackbird *(Agelaius phoeniceus).* Ph.D. thesis, University of Michigan.

Leigh, E. G., Jr. 1970. Sex ratio and differential mortality between the sexes. *Amer. Natur.* 104:205–210.

Mac Arthur, R. H. 1965. Ecological consequences of natural selection. In T. Waterman and H. Morowitz (eds.), *Theoretical and Mathematical Biology.* Blaisdell, N.Y.

Maynard Smith, J. 1978. *The Evolution of Sex.* Cambridge University Press, Cambridge.

Mullen, R. K. 1973. The $D_2{}^{18}O$ method of measuring the energy metabolism of free-living animals. In J. A. Gessaman (ed.), *Ecological Energetics of Homeotherms.* Monogr. Series 20, Utah State Univ. Press, Logan.

Newton, I. 1978. Feeding and development of sparrowhawk *Accipiter nisus* nestlings. *J. Zool.* 184:465–487.

⸺, and M. Marquiss. 1979. Sex ratio among nestlings of the European sparrowhawk. *Amer. Natur.* 113:309–315.

Nicholson, W. 1972. *Microeconomic Theory.* Dryden Press, Hinsdale, Ill.

Robertson, R. J. 1973. Optimal niche space of the red-winged blackbird. III. Growth rate and food of nestlings in marsh and upland habitat. *Wilson Bull.* 85:209–222.

Royama, T. 1966. Factors governing feeding rate, food requirement and brood size of nestling great tits *Parus major. Ibis* 108:313–347.

Schaffer, W. M. 1974a. Selection for optimal life histories: The effects of age structure. *Ecology* 55:291–303.

⸺1974b. Optimal reproductive effort in fluctuating environments. *Amer. Natur.* 108:783–790.

Shaw, R. F. and J. D. Mohler. 1953. The selective significance of the sex ratio. *Amer. Natur.* 87:337–342.

Taylor, H. M., R. S. Gourley, C. E. Lawrence, and R. S. Kaplan. 1974. Natural selection of life history attributes: An analytical approach. *Theor. Pop. Biol.* 5:104–122.

Trivers, R. L. 1974. Parent-offspring conflict. *Amer. Zool.* 14:249–264.

————, and H. Hare, 1976. Haplodiploidy and the evolution of the social insects. *Science* 191:249–263.

————, and D. E. Willard. 1973. Natural selection of parental ability to vary the sex ratio of offspring. *Science* 179:90–92.

Verner, J. 1965. Selection for sex ratio. *Amer. Natur.* 99:419–421.

Werren, J. H., and E. L. Charnov. 1978. Facultative sex ratios and population dynamics. *Nature* 272:349–350.

Williams, G. C. 1966a. *Adaptation and Natural Selection*. Princeton Univ. Press, Princeton.

————. 1966b. Natural selection, the costs of reproduction, and a refinement of Lack's principle. *Amer. Natur.* 100:687–690.

Williams, J. F. 1940. The sex ratio in nestling eastern red-wings. *Wilson Bull.* 52:267–277.

Young, H. 1963. Age-specific mortality in the eggs and nestlings of blackbirds. *Auk* 80:145–155.

IV

Cooperative Breeding in Birds

13.

Altruism, Kinship, and Reciprocity in the White-Fronted Bee-Eater

Stephen T. Emlen

INTRODUCTION

The evolution of apparent ''altruism'' presents one of the most interesting and important questions in the new field of sociobiology. Altruism is here defined as any behavior performed by an individual that benefits a recipient while incurring a cost to the donor (Hamilton, 1964; Wilson, 1975). Such behavior is not only of general biological and anthropological interest; it also poses an evolutionary dilemma as it appears to contradict the fundamental theorems of individual natural selection.

Altruism, outside of a parent–infant context, is presumed to be rare in the animal kingdom. It is commonplace only among the social insects and reappears spottily among the vertebrates. Here it reaches its highest development among primates, social carnivores, and certain tropical, cooperatively breeding birds.

Evolutionary biologists define fitness in terms of genetic contribution to succeeding generations. Consequently, the ultimate in seemingly altruistic behavior (outside of sacrificial death) would be to forego breeding and, instead, to aid other individuals in their reproductive efforts. Cases of such behavior have been reported in over 150 species of birds (see compilations by Skutch, 1961; Rowley, 1968, 1976; Harrison, 1969; Fry, 1972; Grimes, 1976; Woolfenden, 1976; and Emlen, 1978) and, until recently, have been lumped under the designation of ''helpers at the nest.''

Most current theory on the evolution of cooperative breeding stresses two points. The first point is ecological saturation. Many species of cooperative breeders are sedentary and inhabit stable and restricted environments. As population numbers increase, all suitable habitat becomes filled or ''saturated,'' until a portion of the population is forced to remain as non-breeders. Unoccupied territories are nonexistent, and vacancies or turnovers are rare. Thus the options for independent breeding are severely limited, and one strategy is to remain at home on the natal territory until such a breeding vacancy presents itself. The second point is kin selection. Most known cases of helping involve yearling birds that remain at home and aid their parents in the rearing of later broods. This raises the possibility that the gain in inclusive fitness realized by helping raise siblings might more than offset the cost in individual fitness incurred by such helping behavior.

These ideas have emerged from detailed studies of group-territorial species; indeed the overwhelming majority of known cases of helping behavior occur in group-territorial species. But a few kinds of birds nest colonially as well as cooperatively. Nest sites and general spaces for breeding are not limited for such colonial breeders. Thus, ecological saturation and the scarcity of vacant breeding territories may be relatively unimportant to an understanding of their helping behavior. The more gregarious the species, the greater the frequency with which individuals will come in contact with others who are neither close kin nor members of the same cooperative sub-groups. Such interactions could lead to opportunities for the development of more complex forms of social bonding and societal organization (Emlen, 1978).

Normally, we think in terms of social advantages that stem from colonial living. But what appear to be cooperative and harmonious societies on the surface often are expected to be extremely competitive underneath. The presence of large numbers of interacting individuals and the close proximity of large numbers of active nests open opportunities for various subtle forms of behavioral manipulation and cheating (Alexander, 1974; Zahavi, 1976; Emlen, 1978). A very complicated network of subtle and competitive as well as friendly and cooperative, interactions thus should be expected in any society that is both colonial and cooperative.

For these reasons I believe that studies of highly gregarious cooperative breeders offer unique opportunities to gain a new perspective on questions of the evolution of "altruism."

THE WHITE-FRONTED BEE-EATER

Only a handful of avian species currently are known to be both colonial and cooperative. Such social organization is found among a few kingfishers, a few swifts, and many members of the Old World family, Meropidae, the bee-eaters.

Several years ago, Natalie J. Demong and I initiated an intensive study of the white-fronted bee-eater (*Merops bullockoides*) in the Rift Valley of Kenya. We first studied the breeding biology and the role of helpers in this species in the spring and fall of 1973. We returned to investigate the dynamics of social interactions during the spring of 1975. And, together with the assistance of Robert E. Hegner and Carolyn E. Miller, we initiated a comprehensive, longitudinal study of a population of individually marked birds that has been in continuous operation since January of 1977.

Our study area comprises roughly 30 square kilometers in the southern end of Lake Nakuru National Park, Kenya. Over 500 birds have been captured, sexed (by laparotomy), and marked for individual identification (both by leg rings and by unique saflag patagial tags). Intense behavioral observations are concentrated on approximately 150 "focal" birds, whose locations, social interactions, group membership and status, and breeding contributions are regularly recorded. These data are complemented by demographic information on survival (calculated from monthly census records), dispersal, and fecundity (obtained by monitoring the success of all breeding attempts).

White-fronted bee-eaters are common inhabitants of the savannahs of eastern and southern Africa. They are medium-sized (30 to 40 grams), colorful, sexually monomorphic birds that are social throughout the year. They breed in dense colonies comprised of from 50 to 500 birds and from 20 to 150 nests. Nests consist of burrows extending 0.5 to 2.0 meters into vertical cliffs along river banks or other ravines. Each nest is dug, tended, and roosted in by a small group of from two to seven birds. Each bee-eater is a member of one of these small, relatively cohesive groups that travel and forage in the same area during the day, and roost together in the same nest chamber at night. All individual bee-eaters that forage over a large geographic area (10 to 20 square kilometers) converge in the late afternoon to socialize and roost at the colony sites.

Thus the primary social unit in white-fronted bee-eater society is the small cooperative breeding group of from two to seven individuals. In four years of study, group size has averaged 3.0 individuals; 58 per cent of nests have had helpers present, and 72 per cent of all bee-eaters have lived in groups comprised of more than two members (Figure 13–1). Stated another way, from 20 to 50 per cent of the adult population are foregoing breeding themselves and aiding others to rear young in any given reproductive season. Such non-breeders share in virtually all aspects of nesting, from digging and constructing the nest chamber, to incubating the eggs, feeding the nestlings, and tending and defending young during the eight-week transition to independence that follows initial fledging from the nest.

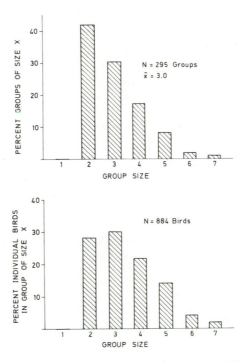

Figure 13–1.   Frequency histograms of group size. Data from twelve different colonies breeding between February 1973 and June 1978 are included.

ALTRUISM?

Hamilton (1964) defined four basic types of interactions that might occur between organisms: altruistic, cooperative, selfish, and spiteful (Figure 13–2). Both altruistic and spiteful behaviors pose theoretical paradoxes as they result in a lessening of the fitness of the individual donor. Note that to be altruistic, a behavior must both confer a benefit to the recipient *and* incur a cost to the donor. Does helping behavior in the white-fronted bee-eater meet these two criteria?

The Contribution of Helpers to Breeding Success

Non-breeding bee-eaters are observed to assist in all phases of reproduction but most noticeably in the incubation of eggs and feeding of young. The magnitude of any benefit accrued by a breeder through the actions of a helper can be measured by comparing the number of fledglings produced by pairs, with similar productivity values from groups with one or more helpers.

In four years of study, we have collected such data from 12 different breeding colonies. These include breeding attempts initiated just prior to or during the anticipated long rains of 1973, 1975, 1977, and 1978 as well as during the short rains of 1977. Environmental conditions and reproductive success in the different seasons were variable enough as to invalidate a simple pooling of all the data. We examined the contribution of non-breeding helpers by comparing the reproductive success and the production of fledglings in nests tended by pairs alone with those from nests tended by groups. Nests that were lost as a result

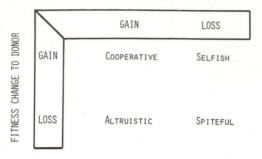

Figure 13–2.   Schematic representation of types of behavioral interactions (defined in terms of individual, not inclusive, fitness).

of chance catastrophic effects (to safari ants or flooding, where group size could play no role in influencing success) were omitted from analysis.

The mean number of fledglings produced per nest is histogrammed as a function of group size for the January through May breedings of 1977 and 1978 in Figure 13–3. (These were the only two seasons that were similar enough to justify pooling.) It is apparent that helpers do play a significant role in increasing the successful production of young, with groups of four rearing over twice the number of young as pairs alone. Similar trends were apparent in the data from 1973 and 1975, but the magnitude of the differences as well as the overall mean reproductive success differed in the different seasons.

Observations of feeding rates at nests containing comparable numbers and ages of young indicate that nestlings being tended by pairs with helpers receive approximately 30 per cent more food per hour than nestlings fed by pairs alone (Hegner et al., in press). It thus appears that non-breeding helpers play an important role in increasing the reproductive output of breeders, and one major way in which this is accomplished is by increasing the amount of food brought to the young.

The Options Available for Independent Breeding

Does helping involve an actual sacrifice or loss of fitness to the helper? There are two aspects to this question. First, what are the alternate options available to a non-breeding helper? Is it forfeiting opportunities to breed on its own by remaining a helper? And second, what are the actual costs or risks involved in helping behavior?

Many tropical insectivorous birds time their breeding to coincide with the rainy seasons. Bee-eaters, however, frequently initiate breeding during the tail end of the harsh dry season, apparently anticipating the rains. In this way the period of hatching and nestling growth may be timed to the early rains, which bring with them a flush in insect food availability. Such a strategy can lead to high productivity in areas with predictable rainfall such as West Africa (Fry, 1972; Dyer and Fry, in press) and southern Africa (Emlen and Demong, unpublished data).

But the white-fronted bee-eater in Kenya is faced with a more unpredictable and, often, a more harsh environment than its southern or western counterparts. Although textbooks describe Kenya as having two rainy seasons, the long rains of March, April, and May and the short rains of October and November, the visitor is most impressed by the tremendous variability in both the timing and the amount of rain that falls during any given year. Equally astonishing is the spatial heterogeneity of rainfall—monthly values frequently differ significantly at locations only kilometers apart.

If *Merops bullockoides* is adopting the strategy of anticipating the rains, many such "anticipations" are unsuccessful as the rains come late or fail to materialize altogether. Many reproductive attempts are unsuccessful and losses due to nestling starvation can be impressively high. Conversely, when rains are unusually heavy, rivers rise rapidly and can reach the point of covering the nesting holes and drowning the eggs or nestlings inside. The contents of two entire breeding colonies have been lost in this manner.

It is difficult to use the general terminology found in the literature on cooperative breeding and speak in terms of "nesting vacancies" or "breeding openings," because nest chambers are not a limiting resource and can be dug at any time. But the highly variable and often harsh environment of the Rift Valley suggests that very different levels of parental (or group) investment might be needed to successfully rear young during different seasons. Assessing the harshness of these ecological conditions shquld be extremely important to individual bee-eaters that presumably are weighing the costs and benefits of the strategies of independent breeding versus joining or remaining in a breeding group as a helper.

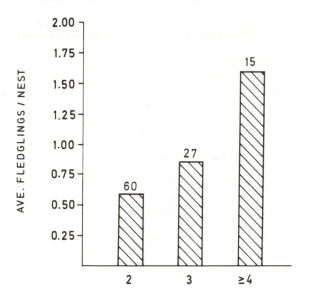

Figure 13–3.   The relationship between nesting productivity and group size. The numbers at the top of each histogram represent the sample size (number of nests). In the lower contingency table, "successful" denotes the number of nests that reared at least one young to fledging age. (All data from colonies MBAA, MB, ESII, and AB from 1977 and MM1 and MM2 from 1978 are included.)

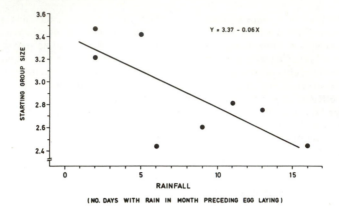

Figure 13–4.   The relationship between average starting group size and rainfall in the month preceding egg laying. Each point represents the mean starting group size for a single breeding colony.

It is not possible to test this idea experimentally, but one can examine the relation between group size and environmental harshness. To do this I calculated the average starting group size for all breeding units in each colony. These values were plotted as a function of the number of days of rainfall occurring in the month prior to egg laying in Figure 13–4. (A more realistic indicator of environmental harshness would be insect availability during the time prior to egg laying; insects have been sampled regularly, and these data are being compiled but are not yet available for presentation.) The significant negative regression ($r = .714$; $p < 0.05$) between group size and environmental harshness shown in Figure 13–4 is consistent with the hypothesis that individual bee-eaters are assessing the ecological potential for successful breeding and choosing to remain as helpers when conditions are harsh and the chances for successful independent reproduction are low but are opting to leave established units and initiate breeding independently when ecological conditions (here being estimated by rainfall alone) appear favorable.

The Costs and Benefits of Helping

When observing bee-eaters in the field, the researcher is struck by the large amount of time and energy that helpers spend tending the nests and rearing the young of the breeders. It is not surprising that attention has been focused on the costs and risks involved in such helping behavior rather than considering the more subtle and often more indirect, benefits that could potentially accrue to individuals engaged in such behavior. In actuality, potential benefits to a helper may be many; four that appear to be of importance to white-fronted bee-eaters are listed briefly below. (For a fuller discussion of the various costs and benefits of helping, the reader is referred to Emlen, 1978 and Brown, 1978.)

First, a bird may gain valuable experience in the caring and rearing of young while being a helper. In long-lived species that frequently are subjected to harsh breeding conditions, such experience could be extremely beneficial, especially among younger birds. Preliminary results suggest that reproductive success is lower among inexperienced pairs than those with prior breeding experience and also is lower among experienced members of pairs of recent formation (where a prior mate has died and been replaced by a new individual).

Second, several advantages accrue merely from living in groups rather than solitarily. Such benefits stem from the increased security afforded by group predator vigilance and defense, from guaranteed access to the resources or specialized foraging area of the group, and from improved competitive and social status achieved via group rather than individual defense and agonistic interactions at the colony. Presumably such group benefits lead to an enhanced survival probability over the long run and to lower energetic costs of daily life in the short run. Our study has not been of sufficient duration to quantitatively test most of these points. Stallcup and Woolfenden (1978), however, have been able to document an increased annual survival among breeders with helpers compared to breeders nesting alone in the Florida scrub jay (*Aphelocoma coerulescens*).

Third, through helping and general group membership, an individual forms social bonds and close friendships with other conspecifics. In the white-fronted bee-eater, these bonds appear to enhance the probability of acceptance in other groups, of recruitment of other birds who may serve as helpers later in life, and of reciprocal receipt of helping from others (see following section on reciprocity).

Fourth, an individual bee-eater might maximize its *inclusive* fitness by helping, by increasing the indirect component of its fitness by raising young that are close genetic relatives (see following).

These major points—(1) that helping does benefit breeders, (2) that helping occurs primarily when alternate options for independent breeding are few, and (3) that several potential benefits exist that might accrue to the helper—lead me to conclude that helping behavior in the white-fronted bee-eater should be considered as "cooperative" rather than "altruistic."

KINSHIP

In the past decade, kin selection has become the topic of much discussion and debate (Hamilton, 1964, 1972; Lin and Michener, 1972; Alexander, 1974; Brown, 1974; West-Eberhard, 1975, this volume; Evans, 1977; Ligon, this volume; Woolfenden, this volume). The fundamental question is not whether selection operates at the level of kin but whether the kin-component of natural selection ever assumes major importance and leads to predictions fundamentally different from those arrived at by models of selection operating at the level of the individual alone. Has kinship been a *necessary* feature in the evolution of helping behavior?

As mentioned previously, altruism and spite, behaviors that decrease the fitness of the individual performing the acts, pose an evolutionary dilemma because they are not expected to evolve through the process of natural selection. The expansion of the theory of natural selection to include kin partially alleviates this paradox. Many cases of apparent altruistic behavior "become" cooperative if a donor and recipient are close kin. Similarly, many apparently spiteful acts "become" selfish.

It is a general finding in studies of group-territorial species that helpers generally are young from previous breeding attempts that remain with, and assist, the family unit. The social unit, thus, is relatively "closed" and helpers and breeders are close kin. Is the same true in the white-fronted bee-eater?

Since bee-eaters are long-lived, and our intensive study of known kinship interactions began only in January of 1977, it is impossible to trace the genetic relationships between breeders and helpers except in those instances involving young birds. Unfortunately, the sample is not large, because reproductive success has been low, and mortality during the period prior to independence (the first four months after fledging) is high. Thus only 21 young produced in 1977 survived as yearlings at the time of breeding in 1978. Of these, 13 remained with or rejoined their parents and aided in their breeding attempts. Two helped at the nests of one surviving parent and a stepparent, while two others helped birds other than their parents. Two took mates and bred on their own (one being aided by its father, its mother having died in the intervening year). The remaining two are still roosting with their parents, but the parents have not renested as of this writing.

I have already demonstrated that helpers make a significant contribution to increasing the reproductive success of breeders. The few data presented here suggest that helpers and breeders usually are close kin. These results are certainly consistent with the hypothesis that kinship is important in understanding the cooperative social system seen in the white-fronted bee-eater. But, in the absence of many additional types of information, the data are insufficient to answer the question of the relative importance or possible essentiality of the kinship component to the explanation of the evolution and functioning of this social system.

RECIPROCITY

Reciprocity is a concept that has received little attention in the literature of cooperative breeding. It refers to cases of apparently altruistic behavior that are, in fact, based upon a selfish probabilistic expectation of a reciprocal return of helping in the future. The concept has been known for years in the social sciences but first received a detailed formulation in the biological literature by Trivers (1971). The idea has not received wide support among sociobiologists because (1) reported cases of such reciprocity are rare (but see Packer, 1977; Ligon and Ligon, this volume), and (2) the intellectual capabilities required to prevent ''cheating'' have been considered by many to preclude the widespread existence of reciprocity in anything other than the higher primates (West-Eberhard, 1975).

White-fronted bee-eaters, by roosting and nesting gregariously, interact frequently with many individuals from both within and outside their direct social units. The social bonds that may be formed in this manner add a level of complexity to the societal organization. As discussed earlier, such multi-faceted social relationships present opportunities for various subtle forms of behavioral competition, manipulation, and cooperation—including the development of reciprocal helping interactions.

By following individually marked birds over long periods of time, we are building up individual dossiers of the social friendships and social interactions of birds of known sex, age, kinship, and group membership. What is emerging is a picture of a fascinatingly complex animal society. The bee-eater social system represents a mixture of openness and fluidity of group membership on the one hand, with stability and fidelity of certain social bonds on the other. Thus, bee-eater groups have a fluid and dynamic membership, in which individuals regularly leave the group, visit, mix with, or join other units but then frequently return in later months or years to roost or nest again with individuals with whom they have shared a prior common membership in the past.

Often, if their nesting attempt fails, the breeding group will no longer remain together but will split up. When this occurs, one or more individuals of the original unit may join a different group at another hole where breeding is in progress. In such cases, the late joiners not only roost socially with their new group but actively contribute to rearing the young at this new nest.

Figure 13–5 summarizes our current information on the frequency of such redirected helping behavior. The phenomenon was first discovered in 1975, when our own human disturbance caused desertion of several nesting attempts. We were surprised when the group membership shifted and certain individuals joined and began feeding young at other nesting holes in the colony. During 1977 and 1978 we have systematically collected data on the subsequent behavior of all individuals belonging to groups in which nesting has failed. These have been subdivided in the table into cases where breeding failure was the result of natural causes and cases where failure was caused by catastrophic flooding.

An examination of the social interactions of individuals whose groups failed from natural causes (primarily starvation) shows that in 21 of the 33 groups (64 per cent), individuals joined other nests and showed surrogate or redirected helping behavior.

In one colony each in 1977 and 1978 massive rains caused river waters to rise to the

RECIPROCITY ?

FOLLOWING   NESTING FAILURE,   BREEDERS
MAY JOIN ANOTHER ACTIVELY
BREEDING   GROUP AND CONTRIBUTE
TO THE REARING OF THEIR YOUNG

CAUSE OF FAILURE	FREQUENCY OF REDIRECTED HELPING
CATASTROPHIC FLOODING	2 OF 72 GROUPS 3 %
NATURAL CAUSES	21 OF 33 GROUPS 64 %

point where virtually all nests were inundated and the contents drowned. The result was that of 79 nests actively breeding at the times of the floods, only 7 survived the flooding and continued attempting to rear young. Of the 72 cases of failure, in two instances individuals joined and redirected helping behavior at other nests. I feel that this low rate of occurrence is the result, in part, of the fact that only seven recipient nests were available. By contrast, natural failures occur asynchronously in colonies, and a large number of potential recipient nesting groups are reproductively active following such failures.

These shifts, where a breeder becomes a helper at another nest, demonstrate a very important point: that an individual adult bee-eater is not locked into a specific strategy of either breeding or helping for the entirety of its lifetime. In most cooperative species studied to date, helping is a transitory phase in the behavioral maturation of the individual. It is primarily younger animals or individuals that have not yet attained the social status or dominance necessary to attract a mate or take over a territory that engage in helping behavior. Once a breeding opportunity arises and the individual has attained sufficient experience or dominance to compete successfully for that vacancy, the individual becomes a breeder. For example, in his eleven-year study of Florida scrub jays, Glen Woolfenden has documented the general pattern that young birds remain as helpers with their parents for from one to three years. But once a bird has become a breeder, it remains such for the remainder of its life. Out of hundreds of breeding records that Woolfenden and his collaborators have collected, in only two instances has a breeder reversed its social status and later become a helper (G. Woolfenden, pers. comm.).

In contrast, such role reversals are commonplace among white-fronted bee-eaters. Numerous individuals have already been followed as they have shifted from helper to breeder to helper, and vice versa (for some detailed examples, see the next section). If future years' observations corroborate our present findings, it may be the rare, exceptional bee-eater that retains the same social status of either breeder or helper for the majority of its adult life.

When a breeding attempt fails and a bee-eater shifts over and becomes an accepted member of a different, reproductively active group, who are the recipients of the redirected helping behavior? As a result of the individual life history information that we are accumulating, it is possible to trace the past social interactions and memberships of many of the individuals that showed such changes of membership following breeding failures in 1978. Of 13 birds involved in group membership changes and redirected helping activity in 1978 (for which prior information is available), 11 (85 per cent) joined groups that contained individuals with whom they had shared prior social memberships or close friendship ties during the past ten to fourteen months. Thus the rejoinings were by no means randomly distributed throughout the colony. Rather they appeared to represent a reestablishment of social (and perhaps kinship) ties that had been cemented in the past life histories of these individuals.

These three facts—the fluidity of group membership and mobility between groups, the frequent alteration of social status from helper to breeder and vice versa, and the non-random reestablishment of bonds with individuals with whom one has shared prior past memberships—form the essential basics necessary for the operation of a system of reciprocation.

SOCIAL DYNAMICS OF THE WHITE-FRONTED BEE-EATER SOCIETY

The interactions of numerous cooperatively breeding units all living within a highly gregarious and social colony give rise to an extremely complex form of social organization in the white-fronted bee-eater. The surprising degree of fluidity and openness of group memberships has already been mentioned. Social interactions in a bee-eater colony are intricate and involve at least three levels of social bonding between individuals. The primary and most cohesive social unit is the cooperatively roosting and breeding group. But most individuals also have close friendships with (and direct access to) one or two other birds residing in other holes and belonging to other breeding units. These secondary social ties grant immunity from attack and allow frequent visitations to be made to specific other nesting chambers. And superimposed on all these close social alliances is a looser bond with most, if not all, other bee-eaters in the colony.

In our study we continuously monitor the social membership, status, and interactions of a large number of individuals. For each such individual, a monthly summary is made of its membership in any given social group and its visitations and temporary roostings with individuals from other groups. Records also are kept of all breeding attempts by the group, together with the status and relative contribution of each individual. From these monthly summaries, we generate ''flow diagrams'' that trace the friendships and social interactions as well as the breeding contributions of each individual across time. In order to provide a better understanding of the complexity of bee-eater social interactions as well as to provide concrete examples of some of the points discussed above, a ''flow diagram'' of the locations and group memberships of a small subsample of individuals is shown in Figure 13–6. This diagram interweaves the histories of three small groups as they shifted over a 14-month period between several successive breeding attempts. Seven specific individuals will be traced to illustrate some of the types of dynamic interactions that have been mentioned in the text.

Let us focus our attention first on female 46 and male 116, a breeding pair that nested at hole number 7 at MBAA colony in April 1977. Shortly after their eggs hatched, the colony was flooded by high river waters. Both birds left the colony site, wandered 300 meters downstream, and joined with two other bee-eaters roosting in a new hole at this new sub-colony, MB. The male, 116, occasionally also roosted in a second chamber coinhabited by an additional male and female. In November of 1977, several months after the completion of breeding at the MB colony, most of the bee-eaters in the area moved two and one half kilometers upstream, and a new colony, called MM, was formed. Female 46 and male 116 remained together and took up residence in hole number 65 at MM. In late January of 1978, this pair initiated breeding, but their small nestlings were again destroyed by floods in March. During the non-breeding interim from May to December of 1977, each bird mixed and roosted with other individuals of both sexes; yet they showed mate fidelity when renesting in the following year. (After the nesting failure at MM, female 46 moved to hole 300, a shift that will be discussed more fully below.)

Female 84 was first seen as an accepted visitor to female 46 and male 116 at their active nest at MBAA. However, it did not join this group but traveled the few hundred meters to the MB sub-colony, where, together with male 360, it bred in hole 94. They were joined later by a female helper and, together, successfully reared two offspring (363 and 364).

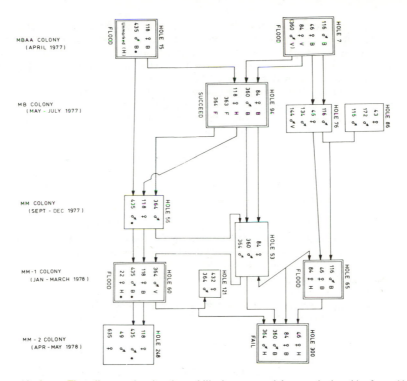

Figure 13–6.   Flow diagram showing the mobility between social groups in the white-fronted bee-eater. Each box represents a breeding (double outline) or roosting (single outline) chamber. The birds residing at that location are identified by band number, sex, and status. B denotes breeder; H denotes helper; V denotes visitor; and F denotes young fledged from that nest. Parentheses indicate presumed rather than confirmed status. An asterisk identifies ''yellow morph'' individuals. For a detailed explanation of the fates of selected individuals, see text.

In November, 84 and 360 joined with the rest of the population in moving to the new colony site, MM. They remained together, roosting in hole 53, but failed to breed when the majority of the colony nested in January and February of 1978. However, both birds occasionally visited female 46 and male 116 and, when this latter pair hatched young and began feeding small nestlings, female 84 shifted much of her attention away from her mate in hole 53. She became a major feeding contributor at hole 65. When heavy rains caused the drowning of these young, female 84 returned to her mate. The kinship hypothesis would predict that she was returning for a second year to help her genetic parents. But, in the interim, she had mated, bred, and successfully reared two offspring. She thus illustrates two important principles of bee-eater society: the combination of fluidity and stability that characterize group membership and the shift between breeding and helping status.

Shortly thereafter, female 84 and her mate, 360, renovated a new hole (300) in the MM colony and in April of 1978 began nesting. Two young were hatched in late April, and at this point female 46 moved in, joining 84 and 360 as a helper. She brought significant amounts of food to the young, greeted and socialized with the breeders, and regularly roosted as part of the group. Here we have a clear case of reciprocal helping. Female 84 had been a helper to female 46 during her breeding attempt in January and February; now 46 was reciprocally helping female 84 in her attempt in April.

An additional scenario is provided by female 118, first shown breeding at colony MBAA in April 1977. Her nest, with its contents of three small young, also was destroyed by the flood waters. Her group split up following the nesting failure, and she not only left her original group but moved to the adjacent MB colony where she redirected help to hole 94 where breeding already was in progress. Thus, her path and those of female 84 and male 360 converged at this point. Following the successful rearing of the two fledglings from this nest, female 118 divided her time, sometimes roosting with her new social group and sometimes returning to roost with her original mate (435) in a nearby hole. When the population moved upstream to the new colony, MM, female 118 and male 435 took up residence first in hole 56 and later in hole 60, while female 84 and male 360 resided in hole 53. At this point the fledglings divided their time, being greeted and socializing with both adult groups, and roosting first with one group and then the other. By November of 1977, one of the fledglings had died, and the remaining youngster (364), spent most of its time with the foster group (118 and 435). This group was joined by another adult female and initiated breeding in late January.

Two points should be stressed here. First, female 118 and male 435 provide yet another example where a mated pair split following a nesting failure, wandered and socialized with a wider set of individuals in the intervening months, yet showed fidelity and formed the core of a new social unit that bred in the following year.

Equally interesting is the social bonding of the surviving yearling, 364. It maintained a close social tie to female 118 and established a social bond with her mate, a bird that had not been a participating member of the group that had helped to rear it. This raises the fascinating question of whether helpers might ''recruit'' young by establishing close social bonds during the nestling and early fledgling period that lead to a joining or reciprocation with the former helper at a time later in life when the helper has now itself become a breeder. Unfortunately, this must remain purely speculative for the moment. The yearling was forming still another social bond during the month of January, this one with a yearling female (a presumptive mate). The two yearlings split off from their respective groups, examined several unoccupied holes together, and took up residence at hole 121 just at the time when breeding was getting under way in hole 60. Thus we cannot say whether or how much 364 would have contributed to the breeding attempt of its former helper if it had not become engaged in the process of pair formation.

To make the story more complex, 364 left hole 121 and its presumptive mate later in March and shifted back to hole 300 where its parents were tending recently hatched nestlings. The grown offspring joined and made a significant feeding contribution to this group. Thus the same individual fledgling that might have exemplified a case of recruitment as a future helper by a former helper, also stands as an example of a yearling helping its genetic parents in the rearing of a later brood.

Finally, I would like to mention female 22. She is a rare ''yellow throat'' morph that comprises 0.5 per cent of the population. She enters the diagram as a late helper, who joins female 118 and male 435 in their breeding attempt at hole 60 in January of 1978. The interesting point is that the breeding male in this hole (435) also is a ''yellow throat'' morph. Our records show no interaction of female 22 and male 435 in the months prior to this point. No information is yet available on the genetic basis of the rare yellow morph, or on the possible kin relationships of these two individuals. But their interaction again prompts the speculation that perhaps kin split for long intervening periods, only to regroup and reciprocally redirect help in later breeding attempts.

CONCLUSION

Many other flow diagrams could have been presented. But the basic trends that are beginning to emerge would remain the same. Bee-eater social organization combines a large measure of openness and fluidity of group membership and frequent changes between breeding and helping status with a stability imposed by the reestablishment and fidelity of certain social bonds. This stability may be based in large part upon kinship ties. Or, perhaps, it is based on the reestablishment of past friendship ties alone. The two may be interwoven, as most friendships could be formed, at least initially, via membership in social groupings that have kinship ties at their basis. But whatever the nature of the formation of such bonds, it is the faithfulness of their reestablishment that gives the stability and the pattern to the fabric of bee-eater society.

Biologists often seek to study "systems" that are sufficiently simple as to be amenable to detailed analysis yet complex enough to warrant being useful as models for more complex "systems" in higher organisms.

The simplicity of bee-eater society stems from its being an avian society. Most avian displays are stereotyped and thus easy to interpret. Information on paternity and the success of breeding attempts can be monitored accurately. And the relatively short avian life span makes the collection of demographic and lifetime fitness data obtainable in less than the full life span of the researcher.

The complexity of bee-eater society stems from the fluidity of group memberships and the existence of several different levels of social bonding between individuals. These traits, in turn, result from the bee-eaters' combination of gregarious, colonial living with cooperative, helping behavior at the nest.

It is my belief that the dynamics of bee-eater society will prove to be interpretable in terms of a general set of predictive rules and selective pressures. My hope is that these rules will be generalizable and will prove valuable in generating models that will increase our knowledge of the inner workings of other complex animal societies as well as lead us toward a better understanding of the evolution and functioning of cooperative behavior.

ACKNOWLEDGMENTS

I thank the government of Kenya, the Ministry of Tourism and Wildlife, and the officials at Lake Nakuru National Park for permission to conduct our studies. I also thank the John Simon Guggenheim Foundation, the National Geographic Society, the Chapman Fund of the American Museum of Natural History, and the National Science Foundation (BMS-76-81921) for financial support. The information presented was collected and analyzed with the assistance of Natalie J. Demong, Robert E. Hegner, Carolyn E. Miller, and Nancy E. Schrempf.

REFERENCES

Alexander, R. D. 1974. The evolution of social behavior. *Ann. Rev. Ecol. Syst.* 5:325–383.

Brown, J. L. 1974. Alternate routes to sociality in jays—With a theory for the evolution of altruism and communal breeding. *Amer. Zool.* 14:63–80.

———. 1978. Arian communal breeding systems. *Ann. Rev. Ecol. Syst.* 9:123–155.

Dyer, M., and C. H. Fry. In press. The origin and role of helpers in bee-eaters. *Proc. XVII Int. Orn. Congr.* (Berlin).

Emlen, S. T. 1978. The evolution of cooperative breeding in birds. In: *Behavioural Ecology: An Evolutionary Approach.* J. Krebs and N. Davies, Eds., Blackwell Scientific Publications Ltd., Oxford, England, pp. 245–281.

Evans, H. E. 1977. Extrinsic versus intrinsic factors in the evolution of insect sociality. *BioScience* 27:613–617.

Fry, C. H. 1972. The social organization of bee-eaters (Meropidae) and cooperative breeding in hot-climate birds. *Ibis* 114:1–14.

Grimes. L. G. 1976. The occurrence of cooperative breeding behaviour in African birds. *Ostrich* 47:1–15.

Hamilton, W. D. 1964. The genetical evolution of social behaviour, I and II. *J. Theoret. Biol.* 7:1–52.

————. 1972. Altruism and related phenomena, mainly in social insects. *Ann. Rev. Ecol. Syst.* 3:193–232.

Harrison, C. J. O. 1969. Helpers at the nest in Australian passerine birds. *Emu* 69:30-40.

Hegner, R. E., S. T. Emlen, N. J. Demong, and C. E. Miller. 1979. Helping at the nest in the White-fronted Bee-eater. *Scopus.*

Ligon, J. D. Demographic patterns and communal breeding in the Green Woodhoopoe, *Pheoniculus purpureus.* This volume.

————, and S. H. Ligon. 1978. Communal breeding in Green Woodhoopoes as a case for reciprocity. *Nature.* 276:496–498.

Lin, N., and C. D. Michener. 1972. Evolution of sociality in insects. *Quart. Rev. Biol.* 47:131–159.

Packer, C. 1977. Reciprocal altruism in *Papio anubis. Nature* 265:441–443.

Rowley, I. 1968. Communal species of Australian birds. *Bonn. Zool. Beitr.* 19:362–370.

————. 1976. Cooperative breeding in Australian birds. *Proc. XVI Int. Orn. Congr.* (Canberra, Australia), pp. 657–666.

Skutch, A. F. 1961. Helpers among birds. *Condor* 63:198–226.

Stallcup, J. A., and G. E. Woolfenden. 1978. Family status and contributions to breeding by Florida Scrub Jays. *An. Behav.* 26:1144–1156.

Trivers, R. L. 1971. The evolution of reciprocal altruism. *Quart. Rev. Biol.* 46:35–57.

Wilson, E. O. 1975. *Sociobiology: The New Synthesis.* Cambridge, Massachusetts: Harvard University Press.

West-Eberhard, M. J. 1975. The evolution of social behavior by kin selection. *Quart. Rev. Biol.* 50:1–33.

————. 1980. Intragroup selection and the evolution of insect societies. This volume.

Woolfenden, G. E. 1976. Cooperative breeding in American birds. *Proc. XVI Int. Orn. Congr.* (Canberra, Australia), pp. 674–684.

————. This volume. Selfish behavior by Florida scrub jay helpers.

Zahavi, A. 1976. Cooperative nesting in Eurasian birds. *Proc. XVI Int. Orn. Congr.* (Canberra, Australia), pp. 685–693.

14.

Demographic Patterns and Communal Breeding in the Green Woodhoopoe, *Phoeniculus purpureus*

J. David Ligon

INTRODUCTION

Communal or cooperative breeding in birds is characterized most conspicuously and typically by the presence in discrete flocks of both non-breeding and breeding individuals. The non-breeders, generally referred to as helpers (following Skutch, 1961), contribute food and protection to the offspring of the breeding pair or pairs. Helpers frequently are related to the nestlings they aid, often being older sibs (Brown, 1974). As a consequence, nest helpers have been considered as manifestations of kin selection (Maynard Smith, 1964; Hamilton, 1963, 1964) with the assumption, explicit or implicit, that such aid was phenotypically altruistic (Alexander, 1974), in that it reduces the aid-giver's lifetime production of offspring. In such cases the beneficent bird was thought to be compensated in an evolutionary sense by the success of genes it shared with the recipient of its beneficence (Brown, 1970, 1974; Ricklefs, 1975; West-Eberhard, 1975). An alternate view first proposed by Zahavi (1974) is that helpers actually are following a strategy for personal gain within the confines of the social setting in which they find themselves and that helpers may not enhance the reproductive success of the breeding pair. Brown (1975a) challenged Zahavi's interpretation of the data he presented but elsewhere suggested that helping behavior might indeed be a strategy for direct reproductive gain (Brown, 1975b). Woolfenden (1975) has shown that helpers do enhance reproductive success of the breeders in Florida scrub jays *(Aphelocoma c. coerulescens),* and Woolfenden and Fitzpatrick (1978) have demonstrated that male helpers, in particular, gain breeding status (their own territorial space) by helping to increase group size and thus territory size via production of young jays.

Currently, the interpretation of several writers is that both personal reproductive gain ("classical component" of inclusive fitness, West-Eberhard, 1975) and increased success of genes shared with other relatives (''kinship component,'' West-Eberhard, 1975) are involved in the evolution of helping behavior (e.g., Brown, 1978; Emlen, 1978; Woolfenden and Fitzpatrick, 1978). Although this may be correct, it is important to attempt to evaluate the relative significance of each: Is one the ''driving selective force'' and the other a more or less inevitable correlate, or are both of major importance? Because, with a few exceptions (e.g., Rowley, 1965,1978; Woolfenden, 1973, 1975; Woolfenden and Fitzpatrick, 1978), long-term data have not been available for any communal bird, it has not been possible to recognize and assess the kinds of overall selective pressures on individuals of different age, sex, and social status, and the life-time adaptive strategies they follow. As a result kin selection has perhaps been too readily invoked to ''explain'' avian helper systems.

In interpreting the data to be presented here I have attempted to adhere to the caution of Williams (1966), who admonished against invoking the concept of adaptation at any higher level than the evidence demands. It seems to me that application of this doctrine is as important when considering kin selection interpretations as when considering group selection interpretations of biological phenomena. For example, if one can account for the aid provided by an individual bird to another as a strategy critical to its own personal reproductive gain, is it parsimonious to assume that a more complex system, with less certainity of evolutionary repayment, such as kin selection, is the driving force behind the phenomenon of helping?

Here I describe patterns of mortality, natality, emigration, and immigration for a communal bird, the green woodhoopoe *(Phoeniculus purpureus),* that my wife Sandra and I have studied in Kenya over the past three years and consider how these demographic features might be related to the overall reproductive strategies of individual woodhoopoes. I also address in a preliminary manner the question: Who gains by the presence of helpers and how?

The Birds

Green woodhoopoes belong to the Family Phoeniculidae (Order Coraciiformes), a small group restricted to sub-Saharan Africa. The geographic range of this species is large—from East to West Africa, and south to southernmost South Africa (see Davidson, 1976, Figure 3). Throughout their range green woodhoopoes apparently are communal (Rowan, 1970; Grimes, 1975).

Social units or flocks number from two to sixteen and contain a single breeding pair. Other flock members, usually relatives of one or both breeders, serve as nest helpers, bringing food to the incubating female and later to nestlings. Helpers also defend nestlings and fledglings from predators, engage in territorial encounters against neighboring groups, and exhibit complex behavioral interactions with the young birds. In short, helpers are full participants in all flock activities except breeding.

All suitable habitat is "owned" by one group or another; thus unoccupied space suitable for new territory establishment rarely is available. Probably related to this is the extremely sedentary nature of most woodhoopoes. Breeders and juveniles (birds up to about fifteen months by our criteria) of both sexes almost never move from their original territory and adult male helpers, when they emigrate, rarely move farther than to an adjacent territory. Adult female helpers are more prone to disperse, but they, like their male counterparts, often attain breeding status in their original territory or in an adjacent one. Ligon and Ligon (1978b) provide a detailed account of the general life history of this species.

STUDY SITES AND METHODS

We have studied green woodhoopoes at three sites near Lake Naivasha in central Kenya at about 0°41′ S, 36°23′ E, at an elevation of approximately 1,950 meters. Here the birds occupy open, flat, park-like woodland, consisting almost entirely of one tree species, the yellow-barked acacia *(Acacia zanthophloea).* The understory is composed of grasses, with forbs occurring only in heavily-shaded spots. The simple vegetational characteristics of this habitat are advantageous in that various parameters of the birds' environment can be readily quantified.

This study began in July 1975. Our first priority at that time was to mark all the birds in many adjacent flocks individually with colored plastic bands and uniquely numbered alumimum rings. During the course of eleven months of fieldwork, July 1975 to May 1976, 148 woodhoopoes were so marked. Subsequent fieldwork in January and June to August 1977 and 1978 has resulted in a total of 257 individually marked birds. Capture techniques and other procedural details are described elsewhere (Ligon and Ligon 1978b).

For several reasons we believe that most disappearances of individuals meant that the bird had died. This is an especially important point when considering demographic patterns, thus we elaborate here on the rationale for equating most disappearances with death.

1. Since the begining of the study in 1975, no breeding bird is known to have left its original territory, with two exceptions (one male, one female). After their mates disappeared, each moved to an adjacent territory where a breeding vacancy was available.

2. All non-breeding males that have left the group in which they were originally banded have moved into a portion of the parental territory (also see Woolfenden and Fitzpatrick, 1978) or into an immediately adjacent territory, almost always in groups of two or three.

3. Despite careful search with the aid of taped vocalizations, we have rarely (twice) recorded a banded bird in areas adjacent to the study sites. Female woodhoopoes, as in some other communal species (e.g., Woolfenden, 1973, 1975; Zahavi, 1974), are more prone to move about than are males, and we have documented one instance of long-distance (ca. 10 mi) movement by a female. However, like male emigrants, females often emigrate as small groups into an adjacent territory. Our evidence thus indicates that movement by breeders, adult male helpers, and juveniles is extremely conservative. Therefore, we conclude that birds in these categories that cannot be accounted for probably have died.

4. The remains of several banded birds noted as having ''disappeared'' subsequently were found (see Ligon and Ligon [1978b] for details of predation and mortality).

Another major point critical to development of an understanding of kinship and behavioral relationships within and between flocks is knowledge of parentage of young birds. All of our observations indicate that certainty of paternity is as high in green woodhoopoes as in other monogamous birds. The male breeder assiduously guards his mate before the eggs are laid, and copulation is of long duration (up to 2.5 min). This is important in that quick, ''stolen'' copulations probably cannot be accomplished by secondary males because of the proximity of the alpha male. Certainty of maternity is probably even higher than certainty of paternity. The behavioral (and probably physiological) changes preceding egg laying are exhibited only by the breeding or alpha female; other females do not interact with a mate and thus ovarian development probably does not occur (Lofts and Murton, 1973). The female breeder remains in or near the nest cavity before and during egg laying and thus would almost surely intercept and thwart any female flock member that attempted to enter the nest at this time. In addition, there is no evidence that clutches are larger when more females are present in the flock. Because some eggs regularly fail to hatch, both in flocks containing only one female and in flocks containing several, it is unlikely that the unhatched eggs are laid by a second female.

In short, all of our evidence suggests that breeders of both sexes behave in ways designed to insure that all offspring produced are theirs. See Ligon and Ligon (1978b) for additional details concerning certainty of parentage.

Although our study has lasted for only three years (July 1975 to August 1978), turnover of individuals has been high (for adults about twice as great per year as for the Florida scrub jay, Woolfenden, 1973) and has thus produced fair knowledge of genetic relationships. As of August 1978, 63 per cent of the marked woodhoopoes in 22 flocks were hatched in 1975, 1976, or 1977 and are of known age, social background, and parentage.

RESULTS

Group Composition

Flock size in the woodhoopoes we have studied ranges from two to sixteen throughout the year, averaging between five and seven birds per flock. Only one breeding pair is

Table 14–1.   Size and sex composition of the same 19 flocks of marked Green Wood-hoopoes, at about 6-month intervals.

	July '75[1]	Jan. '76[2]	May '76	Jan. '77	Jun. '77	Jan. '78	Jun. '78
Total No. Individuals	102	126	114	118	97	125	119
Mean Flock Size	5.37	6.63	6.00	6.21	5.10	6.58	6.26
(Range)	(3-9)	(4-16)	(3-15)	(2-10)	(2-8)	(3-11)	(3-11)
♂/♀ Ratio	1	.94	1	.84	.67	.79	.75
Percent ♂♂	50	48	50	46	40	44	43

[1] Minimum No. Estimate for Four Flocks.
[2] Minimum No. Estimate for Two Flocks.

present in each flock; other flock members are usually, but not always, offspring or sibs of the breeders. A typical newly-formed flock may consist of a breeding pair and a sib or two of one or both breeders. Occasionally, unrelated birds of the same sex unite to form a new unit (Ligon and Ligon, 1978a).

Mean flock sizes vary in time as does the sexual composition of flocks (Table 14–1). There is a tendency for female helpers to outnumber males (cf. Hamilton, 1972: 201), unlike the situation in some other communal systems (Brown, 1974; Woolfenden, 1976). This probably is related to (1) somewhat higher male mortality (see next section) and (2) a tendency for more female than male young to be produced in small and/or newly-formed flocks (Ligon and Ligon, unpublished data).

Mortality

Individually marked woodhoopoes disappear at a high rate, unlike the general picture described by Ricklefs (1973:379) for tropical land birds. Likewise, the disappearance rate is about twice as high in adults as that described for another communal breeder, the Florida scrub jay (Woolfenden, 1973). Perhaps most unusual is the fact that mortality is similar in juveniles and adults and in various social and sexual categories (Table 14–2). However, males in all categories fare somewhat worse than females. This probably is related to the larger size of males and the consequent usage by them of roost cavities that are less predator proof than those most often used by females.

Table 14–2.   Summary of minimal annual survival over two years, 1 Jan. 1976–1 Jan. 1978, in 22 flocks of Green Woodhoopoes.

	No. 1 Jan. '76 ♂♂	♀♀	No. 1 Jan. '77 ♂♂	♀♀	No. 1 Jan. '77 ♂♂	♀♀	No. 1 Jan. '78 ♂♂	♀♀
Social Category:								
Breeders	22	22	13	15	22	22	11	14
Helpers	33	28	21	17	24	29	15	21
Juveniles[1]	16	18	11	14	14	25	8	16

Mean Annual Survivorship				
♂♂	Breeders:	55%	♀♀ Breeders:	66%
♂♂	Helpers:	63%	♀♀ Helpers:	67%
♂♂	Juveniles:	63%	♀♀ Juveniles:	70%

[1] Immature birds 2–5 months old on their first January.

The woodhoopoes seem to support Ricklefs' (1975) suggestion that rapid turnover of individuals can occur in populations limited by resources (i.e., ''K-selected'', MacArthur and Wilson, 1967). Since juveniles survive as well as adults, general inexperience probably is not a major factor in mortality. This supports other available evidence that suggests that most mortality results from nocturnal predation at roost cavities. In contrast, in the communal Florida scrub jay, juveniles (birds up to one year of age) die over twice as fast as adults on an annual basis (Woolfenden, 1973), and in a pattern similar to those of other small land birds (Ricklefs, 1973:381).

Some evidence also suggests that woodhoopoes are more likely to die of disease (in the broad sense) than many other birds. In nature dead birds are rarely found (von Haartman, 1971); however, we have recorded dead or sick birds on five occasions. We have picked up the dried bodies of two individuals, one banded 2.5 years earlier and one unbanded, in our study area. Neither had been damaged; instead, they apparently fell to the ground and died or vice versa.

On two occasions, in July 1977 and August 1978, we observed single breeding females that appeared to be very sick. Each flew only with great effort, perched with the wings hanging loosely, and spent a lot of time apparently sleeping. The sick female recorded in 1977 has not been seen again. The 1978 bird had a swollen and closed eye but had not succumbed by the time we left Kenya in mid-August. This bird had a nine-day-old nestling that apparently died of exposure (its stomach was full) when its mother became sick and ceased brooding.

Whatever the exact combination of factors leading to the frequent disappearance of woodhoopoes, the resulting high turnover of individuals has several ramifications relevant to the communal social organization of this species. These are considered in the following section.

Fates of Breeders

One obvious and important aspect of high mortality is the resulting short-term nature of the mateships of most pairs of woodhoopoes. By following the fates of 23 individually marked breeding pairs we found that, from January 1976 to August 1977, 28 breeders had disappeared (1.47/mo) and 91 per cent of the original pair bonds were broken within that 19-month period (Table 14–3).

This has important implications concerning the kinship ties of helpers and nestlings; it means that many helpers are not full sibs of the nestlings they feed. Thus, this species, at least, does not strongly support the argument that high survival rates and the concomitant long-term nature of the pair bond are critical factors favoring communal breeding (Ricklefs, 1975). Rather, these data suggest that helping behavior is not invariably closely linked to a high degree of genetic relatedness.

Table 14–3.   Mortality of breeders alive and well, January 1976.

No. breeders, Jan. 1976	No. Dead by 1 August, 1977
46	28
(23 Flocks)	

From 1 January, 1976 to 1 August, 1977, the 46 original breeders died at a rate of 1.47/month.

By 1 August, 1977, only 2 original pairs intact[1]
    1 dead in 12 flocks
    both dead in 8 flocks
    1 pair left original territory and split up (both living, August 1978)

[1]2 pairs still intact as of August 1978.

Fates of Non-Breeders

Since January 1976 we have followed the histories of 94 marked non-breeding woodhoopoes (helpers and juveniles hatched in 1975). To date 39 have attained breeding status; 27 are known or thought to be alive as non-breeders; and 28 probably died before attaining breeding status. Brown (1974) has suggested that a major aspect of communal breeding is the prospect that a helper eventually will inherit breeding status in the (parental) territory. Woolfenden and Fitzpatrick (1978) have found that male Florida scrub jay helpers do indeed acquire breeding space by the "budding off" of a portion of the parent's territory. Our data, too, indicate that this is one pay-off for remaining in the parental flock; half of the birds becoming breeders have done so in the flock in which they were banded and/or hatched, either by inheriting the original territory intact or by acquiring a portion, or "bud," of the original territory. However, unlike Florida scrub jays, female woodhoopoes as well as males may attain breeding status in the parental flock, and both sexes also seem to become breeders in other flocks with about equal success. Stallcup and Woolfenden (1978) have shown that in Florida scrub jays adult male helpers provide far more aid than either younger males or any female helpers. They attribute this to the fact that older male helpers will gain breeding space as a direct result of increased flock size and concomitant increase in territory size, whereas females do not have this option. In the woodhoopoes, both sexes can potentially gain breeding space in the parental territory and sexual differences in helping behavior are not apparent (Ligon and Ligon 1978b).

Lifetime Reproductive Success

Even when a woodhoopoe survives long enough to become a breeder, its reproductive success is far from assured. During the course of this study 20 marked birds have attained breeding status in an established territory and subsequently disappeared. More than half of these left no offspring (Table 14–4). Among the nine birds that did produce young, variation in lifetime reproductive success was great (0–7).

Similar variation is seen when the reproductive success of the 46 breeders alive in January 1976 is analyzed. Of the 87 independent young produced by these birds, 1975–77, 61 (70 per cent) are the offspring of only 13 (28 per cent) of the marked breeders. Ten of these 13 breeders were still alive in August 1978. Fourteen breeders (30 per cent) in this class died, leaving no known young; however, some flock members present in 1975 possibly were the offspring of these birds. Of the remaining 19 breeders (41 per cent) alive in January 1976, 11 are dead (leaving 1 to 4 young) and eight are living (with 0 to 3 young). Because 18 of the original 46 breeders are still alive and possess breeding status, these figures will change; however, the general pattern of great individual variation in lifetime reproductive success will not be altered by the future efforts of these birds.

Table 14–4.   Lifespan after attaining breeding status in an established flock and number of offspring produced.

No. birds attaining breeding status and dying, Aug. 1976–Aug. 1978	20
Approximate lifespan as a breeder	10.95 mo.
$\bar{x}$ No. breeding seasons[1]	.95 (0-2.5)
$\bar{x}$ Lifetime no. of independent young	1.55 (0-7)[2]
$\bar{x}$ No. young surviving to date	1.20 (0-5)

[1] Breeding season June–December. Potentially two broods per season.
[2] 11/20 (55%) left no young.

The overall conclusion to be drawn from the data accumulated to date is that a few woodhoopoes provide a disproportionate share of the succeeding generation, that many more or less replace themselves, and that a very large percentage of those birds attaining breeding rank leave no independent offspring.

Emigration and Immigration

For any demographic equation to balance, the effects of emigration and immigration must be considered. We have recorded immigrants and emigrants onto and off of our main study area, Morendat Farm (Table 14–5). Birds that simply moved to an adjacent territory on the farm are not considered in this analysis. Over the three-year period 16 females came onto Morendat and entered established flocks or joined a lone male (2 cases). During this same interval eight mature non-breeding females are known to have left their original flocks (they were seen after having departed) and 12 others disappeared; some of these probably emigrated. Three marked males, known brothers, came from a territory adjacent to Morendat and one male left Morendat but remained on a territory adjacent to his father's. This actually was a case of territorial budding at the arbitrarily designated margin of our study area. Thus, it appears reasonable to assume that immigration and emigration are equal in green woodhoopoes. Woolfenden (1973) concluded the same for Florida scrub jays.

Overall, we have noted only two cases where two unrelated males joined to form the nucleus of a new flock; in both, the first male present was older than the other and conspicuously dominant to it. Unrelated females have merged on seven occasions. Zahavi (1974) and Gaston (1976) describe similar group formation by unrelated females. Thus woodhoopoes in general follow the pattern of greater female dispersal and greater male sedentariness described for other communal birds (Rowley, 1965; Woolfenden, 1973; Zahavi, 1974; Gaston, 1976). In addition, female woodhoopoes, like males, can inherit the parental territory or gain breeding status in an adjacent flock; thus females of this species appear to employ more options regarding the procurement of breeding status than either male woodhoopoes or members of either sex in other communal species.

Recruitment of Young

In our study area woodhoopoes typically have two potential breeding periods per year, June to August and October to December. However, there is much annual flock-to-flock

Table 14–5.   Emigration and immigration of Green Woodhoopoes on Morendat Farm.

	Aug. 1975	Jan. 1976	May 1976	Jan. 1977	Jun. 1977	Jan. 1978	Aug. 1978
No. stable flocks	12	13	12	13	14	14	14
No. resident birds	72	85	77	80	69	94	89
Mean flock size	6.0	6.5	6.4	6.2	4.9	6.7	6.4
(Range)	(2–12)	(2–16)	(3–15)	(3–10)	(4–8)	(4–11)	(5–11)
							Totals
No. emigrants[1]	3	2 (+1)	0 (+4)	2 (+4)	2 (+2)	0 (+1)	9 (+12)[1]
No. immigrants[2]	2	0	4	13	2	1	22[2]

[1] Numbers in parentheses indicate females that disappeared and possibly emigrated. Only one emigrant was a male, and this is actually a case of "budding" to an area just off Morendat.

[2] 16 females and 6 males have immigrated onto Morendat. Three males were marked sibs from an adjacent territory, and two unmarked males that came together may have come from just outside the boundary.

Table 14–6.   Production and survival of independent young, 1975–1977.

	Class of:		
	1975	1976	1977
No. flocks	22	22	22
Mean flock size at onset of nesting season	5.8[1]	5.6	4.8
Mean no. young produced/flock	1.5	1.9	2.4
(Range)	(0-7)	(0-6)	(0-6)
Percent survival through the following year	73	61	94[2]

[1] Approximate. Most flocks not censused until August or later.
[2] Through August 1978.

variation in reproductive effort and success, especially during the first period. Because some flocks produce two (in one case three) broods of young in this seven-month interval, whereas others produce one or none, flock-to-flock variance in productivity is great on an annual basis. Moreover, year-to-year variation in overall reproductive success is high, averaging from 1.5 to 2.4 per flock over a three-year period. Thus far, there is an inverse relationship between mean flock size and mean number of young produced per flock. In 1975 mean flock size was one bird higher and mean production of young was about one per flock less than in 1977 (Table 14–6). The relevant factors are complex and varied, but precipitation patterns and subsequent food abundance differed in those two years.

DISCUSSION

Helpers as a Parental Strategy

One of the questions most frequently asked by student of communal birds relates to the effect of helpers on the reproductive success of the breeders (e.g., Zahavi, 1974; Brown, 1975a; Woolfenden, 1975). Because helpers or more helpers do not always enhance reproductive success (Emlen, 1978, Brown, 1978) the selective basis for their presence is sometimes obscure. We hold the view that natural selection favors retention of helpers in the territory of the breeding (and dominant) pair only if it leads to a net increment in the breeders' overall or lifetime reproductive success (cf. Zahavi, 1974). We suggest that in woodhoopoes allowing the grown young to remain in an established territory is primarily a form of extended parental care. This view contrasts with most published analyses of the effects of helpers, where positive correlations between number of helpers and production of fledglings are sought (see Emlen 1978 and Brown 1978 for summaries of these data).

The critical data for communal systems pertain not to number of young fledged per nest or per year or even yearly survival but to the lifetime success of breeders in establishing their own young in breeding positions. In many temperate zone species, this apparently is best achieved by producing large numbers of young that disperse widely. However, in tropical situations where territory availability does not change seasonally and where the habitat for a given species tends to be more or less filled on a permanent basis, other parental strategies must develop. One such strategy exhibited by breeding green woodhoopoes is retention of the young, followed by an emigration of several sibs to a known or potential territorial vacancy. This group movement has several ramifications. From the parent's viewpoint it ensures that one of their offspring will acquire breeding status; several birds, males for example, can more readily gain and defend a newly acquired territory than can a singleton. Thus, sequestering young can be a sound parental strategy, whether or not the grown offspring (helpers) significantly enhance the parent's subsequent reproductive output, i.e., whether or not helpers help to rear more babies than would be produced without them. One prediction following from this suggestion is that most birds becoming established as breeders will come from larger rather than smaller social units. Larger flocks generally are composed primarily of grown offspring of the breeders. Table 14–7 shows that most (90 per cent) known emigrants come from larger than average flocks and that such units do not permit outsiders to join their groups. In contrast, all immigrants enter smaller than average units and very few emigrating birds originate from the smaller groups (also see Rowley, 1978).

Do Helpers Increase Subsequent Reproductive Success?

The line of argument that I am following suggests that retention of young, and thus increasing flock size, is a parental strategy primarily related to the survival and eventual procurement of breeding space by their offspring and that larger flocks may or may not be correlated with greater subsequent production of young birds. Our data for 1975, 1976, and 1977 indicate a significant positive correlation between flock size and number of young produced per year only in 1975 and then only if certain failed nests are eliminated from analysis and by the thus-far unique occurrence of three broods by one flock. Thus we conclude, on current evidence, that in green woodhoopoes the adaptive significance of helpers is not principally related to production of increased numbers of young. To the extent that this relationship does hold, however, it should further increase the selective advantage to parents of retaining young birds in the flock.

Why Do Helpers Help?

The discussion thus far presents the retention of grown young in woodhoopoe flocks as a parental strategy related to acquisition of breeding space by their offspring. However, this does not address the question posed by Brown (1978) of why helpers provide attention to nestlings and fledglings, such as feeding, grooming, and vocalizing to them, as well as protecting them from predators. Since helpers and nestlings often are related, shared genes or kin selection is a readily invoked explanation. However, other factors may be of equal or greater importance. Our evidence suggests that *reciprocity* also may be involved (Ligon and Ligon, 1978a; also see Brown, 1975b:208).

Table 14–7.   Flock sizes and emigrations and immigrations at six-month intervals.

Flock Size	Total Known Emigrants	Total Known Immigrants	Mean No. Flocks/Six-month Interval
Six or more	36	0	11.5
Two to five	4	40	9.8

Summary:
   1. Larger flocks have produced 90 per cent of the emigrants to new flocks. Most of these move in unisexual groups of 2–4.
   2. Larger flocks receive *no* outsiders.
   3. Only smaller groups (e.g., decimated flocks, newly forming flocks) have received immigrants.

First, a helper may gain directly by the production of younger flockmates, especially those of its own sex. Helpers of both sexes use younger birds of the same sex, often sibs, to gain entry to and establishment in a new territory (Ligon and Ligon, 1978b). These younger birds subsequently become provisioners for the oldest former helper's own young. Thus young woodhoopoes in the nest can be viewed as an essential resource that can be utilized by the current helpers for their own personal gain (Ligon, in press; Ligon and Ligon, 1978a,b).

Second, younger birds (beta) may gain by emigrating with an older, dominant bird (alpha) of the same sex. Kin selection may be involved to some extent, as offspring of the alpha bird are related to the beta individual by an average of 0.25 (if alpha and beta are full sibs). However, we feel that the high and unpredictable mortality described earlier provides a more important answer. The beta individual has as good or better chance of attaining successful breeding status as the alpha bird. In seven of nine cases where unisexual groups have emigrated to a new territory, or where two males were found in small or new flocks, the alpha bird died first and without surviving offspring, whereupon the beta bird inherited

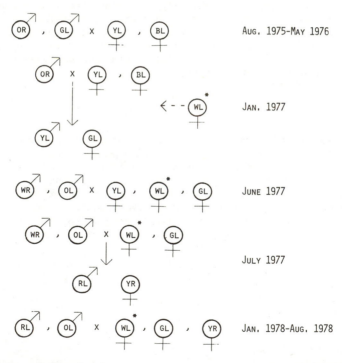

HISTORY OF THE H5 FLOCK, ILLUSTRATING HOW A NEWCOMER MAY INHERIT

TERRITORY OWNERSHIP, BREEDING STATUS, AND HELPERS

Figure 14–1.   Outline of territory procurement, attainment of breeding status and helpers by a newly arrived female (WL*) unrelated to the previous breeders. The young female, GL, became an active helper for WL's nestlings after her mother, YL, disappeared. Males OL and WR, known sibs, joined this group following the disappearances of the previous males, OR and YL. Mated pairs are indicated by the X between individuals; all others are non-breeders. The vertical arrows indicate offspring of the mated birds.

Table 14–8.   Food contributions in one flock by related and unrelated helpers.

	1977 Food Units/Hr. Obs.[1] Incub. (13)[2] Nestling (16)			1978 Food Units/Hr. Obs. Incub. (12) Nestling (3)		
H5 Flock						
[3]p-♂OL	7.85	9.93	p-♂OL	7.58	6.66
*-♀GL	2.46	7.13	*-♀GL	7.25	4.66
u-♂WR	0	2.06	fs-♀YR	2.92	5.66
			fs-♂RL	3.58	3.00

[1] Food units are based on size categories of food brought to the nest: large (3), medium (2), small (1) x feeding visits.

[2] Numbers in parentheses indicate hours of observation.

[3] p indicates parent, *-unrelated helper, u-uncle, fs-full sib.

breeding status and other flock members as helpers and bred successfully.

Finally, in a third situation, reciprocity in the absence of kinship ties may be primarily responsible for helping behavior. Helpers unrelated to either member of the breeding pair occur in a small number of flocks (at least two of 22 flocks in 1977 and at least four of 22 flocks in 1978) and may provide a great deal of aid to the incubating female and especially to the nestlings. In addition to the difficult-to-measure advantages of participating in the flock's activities per se, this behavior can benefit such a helper in that if the breeder of its sex dies, it may inherit a mate, territory, and helpers (Ligon and Ligon, 1978a,b). In one flock, a newly arrived female (WL), unrelated to either breeder, soon acquired territory ownership, breeding status, and a younger female (GL) as a helper for her young (Figure 14–1). In this flock, the unrelated helper GL later made greater food contributions than did related birds (Table 14–8). Thus, in situations such as these, effort expended in helping behavior is not related to genetic ties; rather, it appears to be a long-term, indirect strategy for procurement of breeding status and helpers. Recently, Rood (1978) has described a parallel behavior pattern in the communal dwarf mongoose (*Helogale parvula*), where an unrelated female ''babysitter'' provided a great deal of care of young. Rood, too, suggests that this is a long-term strategy for procurement of breeding status and helpers.

CONCLUSIONS AND SUMMARY

Green woodhoopoe populations are stable over time although annual mortality is high and is similar in breeders, helpers, and juveniles. Males as a group survive somewhat less well than do females, probably because the roost holes available to them are often less secure from predators than those of females.

The high mortality rate does not accord well with some theoretical predictions concerning the role of K-selection in communal breeding nor is it similar to the mortality pattern of either small land birds in general or of tropical birds (Ricklefs, 1973). The frequent turnover of breeders has several important implications as regards communal breeding. (1) Nest helpers are frequently less than full sibs of the nestlings they feed, perhaps raising questions about kin selection arguments for this phenomenon. (2) Many individuals that survive to adulthood die before obtaining a breeding opportunity. (3) Of those acquiring breeding status, a small number produce a disproportionately large share of the next generation, and many leave no surviving offspring.

Overall, it appears that emigration and immigration are about equal on our study sites. Females disperse for greater distances than do males, as is true of other communal species.

Most emigrants are from larger flocks (six or more) and all immigrants join smaller social units (two to four). In many cases emigrants leave as unisexual groups; often these are sibs. In small, decimated, or newly forming flocks unrelated individuals of the same sex sometimes merge to form a new social unit. If subsequent emigration or mortality does not occur, non-breeders become helpers to unrelated nestlings.

Because most members of larger flocks are offspring of the breeding pair and because these are the flocks that produce most new breeders, it appears that retention of young is a sound parental strategy. This is viewed as more fundamental to the helper system of green woodhoopoes than subsequent production of additional young by the breeders. Our data over three years do not convincingly demonstrate that more helpers per flock yield more surviving young woodhoopoes. Rather, many factors affect reproductive success of breeders, and it is thought that differential mortality between flocks is a more powerful force than differential reproduction in determining overall success of breeders over time.

Our evidence suggests that helping behavior in green woodhoopoes is a means of promoting personal gain. First, older helpers clearly gain by helping to produce younger flock mates in that the younger birds can be "used" to obtain breeding status for the older (former) helper and to feed and otherwise care for the older bird's own nestlings. As a result of the high mortality, the "used" individual also may gain; more often than not the younger, subordinate bird acquires breeding status and helpers as a result of having accompanied the older, dominant individual to a new territory, aiding in territorial acquisition and defense, and helping to rear the older bird's offspring. Second, the presence in a few flocks of helpers unrelated to the nestlings they aid also casts doubt on interpretations of helping behavior based on kin-selected altruism. Rather, such individuals, like those related to nestlings, can procure breeding status, a territory, and helpers by first being a helper.

Thus, as a result of (1) the payback received by older helpers in procuring breeding status, (2) the personal gain to some younger helpers, and (3) the presence of hard-working helpers unrelated to nestlings, we view helping behavior in green woodhoopoes as a special kind of strategy for personal gain and as not necessarily nepotistic.

ACKNOWLEDGEMENTS

Several persons and agencies have made this research possible. I wish to thank W. and R. Hillyar, R. and B. Terry, and G. Backhurst for invaluable logistical support in Kenya, F. Bisleti for allowing us to work on his farm, R. E. Leakey, National Museums of Kenya, and E. K. Ruchiami and the Government of Kenya for providing research permits, and R. Thornhill for helpful criticisms of the manuscript. Field work has been supported by grants from The National Geographic Society, the National Science Foundation, the U.S. National Fish and Wildlife Laboratory, The American Museum of Natural History, and the University of New Mexico.

Most of all, I acknowledge with thanks the efforts of Sandra H. Ligon, who has participated fully in all aspects of the field work (except the tree climbing).

REFERENCES

Alexander, R. D. 1974. The evolution of social behavior. *Ann. Rev. Ecol. Syst.* 5:325–383.

Brown, J. L. 1970. Cooperative breeding and altruistic behavior in the Mexican jay, *Aphelocoma ultramarina. Anim. Behav.* 18:366–378.

―――. 1974. Alternate routes to sociality in jays—with a theory for the evolution of altruism and communal breeding. *Amer. Zool.* 14:63–80.

―――. 1975a. Helpers among Arabian Babblers *Turdoides squamiceps. Ibis* 117:243–244.

―――. 1975b. *The Evolution of Behavior.* Norton and Co., Inc. New York.

_____. 1978. Avian communal breeding systems. *Ann. Rev. Ecol. Syst.* 9:123–155.

Davidson, N. C. 1976. The evolution and systematics of the Phoeniculidae. *Bull. Nigerian Orn. Soc.* 12:2–17.

Emlen, S. T. 1978. The evolution of cooperative breeding in birds. In: *Behavioral Ecology: an Evolutionary Approach.* J. Krebs and N. Davies, eds. Sinauer Assoc., Inc., Sunderland, Mass.

Gaston, A. J. 1976. Factors affecting the evolution of group territories in Babblers (*Turdoides*) and Long-tailed Tits. D. Phil. Thesis, Oxford University.

Grimes, L. G. 1975. Notes on the breeding of the Kakelaar at Legon, Ghana. *Bull. Nigerian Orn. Soc.* 11:65–67.

Hamilton, W. D. 1963. The evolution of altruistic behavior. *Amer. Nat.* 97:354–356.

_____. 1964. The genetical evolution of social behaviour. I, II. *J. Theor. Biol.* 7:1–52.

_____. 1972. Altruism and related phenomena, mainly in social insects. *Ann. Rev. Ecol. Syst.* 3:193–232.

Ligon, J.D. In press. Communal breeding in birds: an assessment of kinship theory. *Proc. XVII Intern. Ornith. Congress* (West Berlin, West Germany).

_____, and S. H. Ligon. 1978a. Communal breeding in green woodhoopoes as a case for reciprocity. *Nature* 276:496–498.

_____, and S. H. Ligon. 1978b. The communal social system of the green woodhoopoe in Kenya. *Living Bird* 16:159–197.

Lofts, B., and R. K. Murton. 1973. Reproduction in birds. pp. 1-107. In: *Avian Biology.* Vol. III., D. S. Farner and J. R. King, eds. Academic Press, New York.

MacArthur, R. H., and E. O. Wilson. 1967. *The Theory of Island Biogeography.* Princeton University Press, Princeton, N. J.

Maynard Smith, J. 1964. Group selection and kin selection. *Nature* 20:1145–1147.

Ricklefs, R. E. 1973. Fecundity, mortality, and avian demography. pp. 366–435. In *Breeding Biology of Birds.* D. Farner, ed. National Academy of Sciences, Washington, D.C.

_____. 1975. The evolution of co-operative breeding in birds. *Ibis* 117:531–534.

Rood, J. P. 1978. Dwarf mongoose helpers at the den. *Z. Tierpsychol.* 48:277–287.

Rowen, M. K. 1970. Communal nesting in Redbilled Woodhoopoes. *Ostrich* 38:257–258.

Rowley, I. 1965. The life history of the Superb Blue Wren, *Malurus cyaneus. Emu* 64:251–297.

_____. 1978. Communal activities among White-Winged Choughs (*Corcorax melanorhamphus*). *Ibis* 120:178–197.

Skutch, A. F. 1961. Helpers among birds. *Condor* 63:198–226.

Stallcup, J. A., and G. E. Woolfenden. 1978. Family status and contributions to breeding by Florida scrub jays. *Anim. Behav.* 26:1144–1156.

von Haartman, L. 1971. Population dynamics. pp. 392–461. In *Avian Biology.* Vol. 1, D. S. Farner and J. R. King, eds., Academic Press, New York.

West-Eberhard, M.J. 1975. The evolution of social behavior by kin selection. *Quart. Rev. Biol.* 50:1-33.

Williams, G. C. 1966. *Adaptation and Natural Selection.* Princeton University Press, Princeton, N.J.

Woolfenden, G. E. 1973. Nesting and survival in a population of Florida scrub jays. *Living Bird* 12:25–49.

_____. 1975. Florida scrub jay helpers at the nest. *Auk* 92:1–15.

_____. 1976. Cooperative breeding in American birds. *Proc. XVI Intern. Ornith. Congress* (Canberra, Australia), pp. 574–584.

_____, and J. W. Fitzpatrick. 1978. The inheritance of territory in group-breeding birds. *BioScience* 28:104–108.

Zahavi, A. 1974. Communal nesting by the Arabian Babbler. A case of individual selection. *Ibis* 116:84–87.

15.

Kin Selection and Individual Selection in Babblers

Jerram L. Brown and Esther R. Brown

The popularity of the concept of inclusive fitness (Hamilton, 1964, 1975) lies in the faith that many social phenomena can be explained more completely and parsimoniously with it than with the classical concept of individual fitness alone. Inclusive fitness differs from classical individual fitness by the addition of a quantity that we name indirect fitness. Therefore in evaluating the usefulness of inclusive fitness as an explanatory principle for social behavior we must examine indirect fitness critically. In this paper we attempt to evaluate some of the components of indirect fitness in a natural population.

Because we have found the existing terminology of inclusive fitness theory to be awkward and used inconsistently, we have found it valuable to introduce the new terms "direct" and "indirect" as adjectives to qualify concepts of fitness, selection, reproductive value, and other ideas in population biology. We divide inclusive fitness into two components as shown in Figure 15–1. The first, *direct fitness,* is mediated through the genes in an individual's own offspring. For the individual, direct fitness equals classical individual fitness. The second component, *indirect fitness,* is mediated through copies of the same genes in the offspring of other individuals. An individual can increase its indirect fitness by increasing the direct fitness of others who carry the same genes but who are not its offspring. An individual can be conceived as bestowing direct and indirect influences on offspring and others respectively and as receiving direct and indirect influences from its parents and others respectively.

The term "kin selection" is in use by some authors (e.g., West-Eberhard, 1975) as a synonym for indirect selection, but it is unsatisfactory for the following reasons:

1. Kin selection was defined by Maynard Smith (1964) as including parental care, and it is still used by some authors in that way (e.g., Dawkins, 1976; Brown, 1978).

2. Kin selection implies relatedness, whereas it is not necessary for two individuals to be related for them to carry the same genes.

3. Indirect selection does not require altruism or sacrifice (in terms of net effect on direct fitness) by the donor. Use of "kin selection" may (e.g., Ligon and Ligon, 1978) or may not (e.g., Brown, 1974) imply altruism, depending on the author.

4. Indirect selection does not require precise discrimination of degrees of relatedness, a feature that some authors (e.g., Ligon and Ligon) regard as implicit in kin selection, but others do not (e.g., Maynard Smith, 1976; Brown, 1974).

An appropriate social behavior with which to examine indirect fitness is helping behavior in birds (defined and reviewed in Skutch, 1961; Brown, 1978). By definition a

FITNESS PATHWAYS

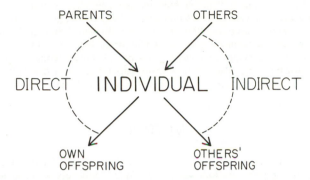

Figure 15–1.   The inclusive fitness of an individual may be divided into two components, *direct fitness*, which is mediated through the genes in an individual's own offspring, and *indirect fitness*, which is mediated through copies of the same genes in the offspring of other individuals. Similarly, an individual's inclusive fitness is affected by influences from its parents (direct path) and from others (indirect path). These paths converge on the individual, where they are blended and expressed as the individual's direct and indirect fitness.

helper aids in some empirically measurable way another individual who is neither its own offspring nor its mate. Thus the helper's efforts, if they raise the recipient's direct fitness and if the recipients carry genes carried by the helper, would raise the helper's indirect fitness. The questions for the field biologist are as follows: Does helping raise the direct fitness of recipients? If so, then how much and by what mechanisms?

An opportunity to study the contribution of helpers to their indirect fitness came with a year of academic leave in 1976–77. Our team of field workers was composed of a mated pair and one non-breeding helper from a previous brood — namely, ourselves and our daughter Sheryl. With generous aid from an unrelated helper, D. D. Dow, we located a study area in Meandarra, Queensland, Australia on which we lived during the breeding season and on monthly visits thereafter. We were joined in the field for several days each month by Dow. Travel and supplies were paid for by a research grant from the U.S.P.H.S. (MH 16345). Detailed accounts of that year's work are in various stages of preparation or publication (e.g., Brown et al., 1978; Brown, 1979). We present here an overview and progress report.

BACKGROUND

We chose grey-crowned babblers *(Pomatostomus temporalis)* for this study because they live in communal social units that seem nearly ideal for testing hypotheses involving indirect fitness. They are easy to watch and inhabit open, level woodland that allows a large number of social units to be monitored. They live all year in groups of from 2 to 13 or more that defend all-purpose territories. Between the territories are zones where the home ranges of neighboring units may overlap; and occasionally a large unit may penetrate far into the territory of a smaller one. But for the most part the territories are, as required by definition, exclusive of rival units. Within each unit there is typically only one breeding pair, often distinguishable by its yellow eyes. The non-breeding birds are in most cases offspring of the breeding pair from preceding years (our observations), and they usually have brown eyes.

In this population individuals normally breed first at the age of 3 or 4 years (King, 1974), spending the first few years as helpers for their parents or their replacements. In our study we found no unit with more than one breeding pair, but units with more than one laying female in one nest are well known (Counsilman, 1977; Dow, pers. com.). The most frequent unit sizes at the start of the 1976 breeding season were 4 through 7. Most and probably all non-breeders performed some kind of help for the breeders. This often took the form of feeding young or carrying nest material to the nest, but in some individuals it might conceivably be little more than alarm calling. In this paper we average the contributions of non-breeders to breeder fitness and refer to them collectively as helpers.

METHODS

Because this is a summary paper, methods will be only briefly stated. Details may be found in the main reports. We followed the reproductive success, survival and movements of each individual in 46 social units for 12 months. Of the 279 birds present in these units at the start in August 1976, 238 were subsequently color-banded. In addition, 136 nestlings were banded. Birds could be aged approximately by eye color (King, 1974; Counsilman and King, 1977). Adults were easily sexed by behavior and incubation patch, but one- and two-year olds could not usually be reliably sexed.

FACTORS CORRELATED WITH REPRODUCTIVE SUCCESS

In this paper fitness will be estimated from reproductive success. Effects of survival on fitness in units of different size will be considered later. For indirect fitness to exceed zero it is necessary (but not sufficient) that breeders helped by non-breeders reproduce more than unaided breeders. For *P. temporalis* a positive correlation between reproductive success and size of social unit would satisfy this criterion. As a convenient measure of reproductive success, the number of young raised to the age of fledging (21–24 days, Brown, 1979) in the breeding season of 1976 will be used (henceforth referred to as FTOT, for fledgling total). As an index of the number of non-breeders (potential helpers) the size of the social unit early in the breeding season (late August: AUGSIZ) will be used. Other indices of reproductive success, such as young alive at the end of the breeding season, and other indices of unit size, such as unit size in September 1976, yield similar results.

In a sample of 36 units not used in removal experiments a positive correlation was found between FTOT and AUGSIZ ($r = 0.50, P = 0.002, \hat{y} = 1.02 + 0.50\,\mathrm{AUGSIZ}$). This result is in line with the finding of Rowley (1965) and later authors that reproductive success is greater in the presence of non-breeding helpers than in their absence. An extension of this finding provided by our study is that success is correlated with the number of non-breeders over a relatively wide range, not just with their presence or absence.

In order to prove that helping raises indirect fitness it is necessary to show that helping behavior causes increased direct fitness in the breeders. Simple correlations such as this one do not prove cause-effect relationship. At least two other sets of variables must be examined before the importance of helpers in this context can be estimated (Lack, 1968). The first set, territory suitability, including area, quality, and their correlates, was demonstrated to be important by Brown and Balda (1977) in communal babblers. The second set, age of parent and correlates of age, was shown by Woolfenden (1975) to be important in communal jays. Territory suitability has two components, size and quality. An optimally suitable territory need not be unusually large if it is of good quality; and a large territory might not be suitable if it contained only low-quality vegetation.

Territory Area. Territory size is correlated with unit size in some species having helpers (e.g., Parry, 1973), and the role of unit size in territory defense is likely to be important in communal birds (Brown, 1969). In *P. temporalis* there is inconsistent evidence of a correlation between area and unit size (King, unpub. ms.). We plotted home ranges of each unit on a map of the study area, but we observed no dramatic or consistent correlations with unit size. We agree with King that territory size is not a good indicator of suitability in *P. temporalis* because large areas of the territory are unsuitable for foraging. These are mainly, large, open, grassy areas.

Territory Quality. Grey-crowned babblers are the size and shape of curve-billed thrashers *(Toxostoma curvirostre)*. Similarly, they forage a great deal on the ground for small to large insects but also on tree trunks and branches. When alarmed they fly to trees and shrubs. These babblers build domed, dormitory nests in which the entire social unit may sleep in all seasons. A suitable territory for *temporalis* must provide a moderate number of tall, leafy trees in which to build several large, bulky nests. When foraging, *temporalis* rarely uses areas that are densely wooded or that lack trees altogether. Densely wooded areas have little herbaceous vegetation, and grassy areas have few of the shrubs and trees needed for protection from predators and miners *(Manorina)*, which frequently attack babblers. A suitable territory, therefore, does not have extremes of tree cover or grass but provides both in moderation and appropriately mixed.

The foods of *temporalis* are difficult to census efficiently and accurately. Therefore, we concentrated on measures of cover likely to reflect the kinds of areas where *temporalis* frequently foraged. After screening a large number of potential variables as possible indices of territory quality we found two that were correlated with unit size and reproductive success. LE30 is the number of grid squares on an aerial photograph of the territory in which no less than 20 per cent and no more than 30 per cent of the square was covered with woody vegetation. BRIGALOW is the number of times that this species of tree *(Acacia harpophylla)* was counted in standardized, on-the-ground transects in each territory. No perfect index of territory quality for *temporalis* is known. We used these two because they agreed with our field observations of what good foraging and nesting areas were and because they were correlated with measures of unit size and success.

In our study of *temporalis* FTOT was correlated not just with the size of the social unit but also with an index of mother's age (EYEF) and two indices of vegetation (LE30 and BRIGALOW), as shown in Table 15–1. When four variables are positively correlated with reproductive success, it is hypothetically possible that any of them alone or in any combination might be responsible for the variation in FTOT. Parental age and habitat variables are well known to influence reproductive success in various species, and unit size might merely

Table 15–1.   Simple Pearson correlation coefficients for variables discussed in text. FTOT = total number of young fledged per unit in the 1976 breeding season. AUGSIZ = size of unit in August 1976 at the start of the season. BRIGALOW = number of brigalow trees per territory. LE30 = number of grid squares with 20–30 per cent tree-and-shrub cover per territory. EYEF = index of age of breeding female by eye color. N = 36 social units.

	FTOT	AUGSIZ	BRIGALOW	LE30	EYEF
FTOT	—	0.50**	0.34*	0.33*	0.35*
AUGSIZ		—	-0.10	0.28	0.44**
BRIGALOW			—	0.29	-0.22
LE30				—	0.12

$**P < 0.01$

$*P < 0.05$

reflect these influences as a result, not as a cause of the variation in FTOT.

To estimate the relative importance of these three sets of variables we employed two, methods, stepwise multiple regression and experimental removal of non-breeders.

ESTIMATION OF IMPORTANCE OF HELPERS BY PARTIAL CORRELATION AND REGRESSION

The results of the stepwise regression analysis are shown in Table 15–2. The partial regression coefficient for AUGSIZ indicates that on the average for each additional helper a unit fledged an additional 0.46 young when the effects of the other relevant variables were held constant statistically. The index of maternal age, EYEF, was not significantly correlated with FTOT when the effects of the vegetation variables were removed ($P = 0.08$), but its inclusion in the regression equation would lower the regression coefficient for AUGSIZ to 0.36.

To examine the influence of AUGSIZ in the absence of complications due to EYEF, units with younger mothers (less than four years old; eyes not fully yellow) were excluded from the data, and the remaining 24 units were subjected to stepwise regression. AUGSIZ was again the most highly correlated variable ($r = 0.65; P < 0.01$), with a slope of 0.53 fledglings per helper. When younger breeders of both sexes were excluded, the sample was reduced to 17 units, but the partial correlation and regression coefficient for AUGSIZ remained similar. These results suggest that the correlation of reproductive success with number of helpers is not attributable to age of parent or to the habitat variables considered, but they do not exclude the possibility that other variables not measured might be importantly involved.

ESTIMATION OF IMPORTANCE OF HELPERS BY THEIR EXPERIMENTAL REMOVAL

If helpers make a positive contribution to reproduction, their removal should diminish success relative to unaltered units. If helpers make a negative contribution, their removal should enhance reproduction. To enable comparisons 20 units of equivalent size (6, 7 and 8 members) were divided into two groups, matched as nearly as possible with respect to size. The main advantage of the experiment over the regression approach is that any variable correlated with unit size whether known or unknown, measured or not, would be expected not to differ significantly between the two groups. A difference in success between the two groups could then be attributed only to the difference in number of helpers or to an interaction of helpers with another variable (e.g., time spent foraging or in territorial defense). In each of the experimental units all non-breeding individuals except one yearling were removed. The control units were netted and handled just as the remaining experimentals. Later analysis showed that control and experimental units did not differ significantly in age-related or vegetation variables.

Since the removals were done after the first known nesting of the 1976 season but before the second no difference between experimentals and controls in number fledged from first known nests was expected or found. For the sum of young fledged in each unit after the removal (second and subsequent nests in the breeding season of 1976) the control units averaged roughly twice as many fledgings as the experimentally reduced units of the same original size (2.4 vs. 0.8 young; $P < 0.05$, separate t). With only 9 experimental units and 10 controls, a high level of statistical significance was not achieved. The number of fledglings attributable to an average helper can also be estimated from the experiment. The

Table 15–2.   Results of stepwise regression analysis with FTOT (number of fledglings) as dependent variable. *Y* intercept = −0.95.

	Entry Order	Partial Regression Coefficient	Partial Correlation Coefficient	Increase in r^2
AUGSIZ	1	0.46	0.57**	0.25
BRIGALOW	2	0.09	0.46**	0.16

**$P < 0.01$

result, 0.44 fledglings per helper, agrees with the estimate of 0.46 arrived at independently by stepwise multiple regression on 36 units (which included the 10 controls but not the 9 experimentals). The results of both regression analysis and experiment suggest that reproductive success is causally related to the number of helpers. The mechanisms by which these effects might be mediated will be discussed below.

WHAT IS THE MECHANISM BY WHICH HELPERS BENEFIT BREEDERS?

The data presented so far strongly indicate a causal relationship between unit size and fledging success. But unless the mechanism of these effects can be found, the effects themselves will remain questionable. To search for mechanisms we examined feeding rates of nestlings as a function of the number of helpers. Perhaps more nestlings could be reared with more helpers because more food could be brought to them. Previous studies were inconclusive on this point because they did not control important variables. In our study we screened over 30 variables for possible significance. We controlled selected variables statistically by partial correlation and experimentally by standardizing observations and pairing nests (Brown et al., 1978).

The rate at which food was brought to the nest by all breeders and non-breeders combined was independent of the number of feeders. It was dependent on the size and number of nestlings and on environmental variables, such as temperature and recent rain. The clearest benefit to breeders of an increased number of helpers was the reduction of feeding rates by the breeders (Figure 15–2). Over a range of unit sizes from 2 to 8, as the unit size increased, the percentage of total feeding visits by mothers, fathers, and individual helpers taken separately decreased. Similiarly, absolute feeding rates of parents and helpers decreased as unit size increased.

Several lines of evidence suggest that one reason for the positive correlation between number of fledglings and helpers is in the frequency of new clutches rather than in the rate of success per clutch. Table 15–3 shows that clutch size, fledglings per egg, and fledglings per nest varied little and inconsistently as a function of unit size, while the number of clutches, interval between clutches, and date of first known clutch were related to unit size. Larger units typically started earlier, renested sooner, and initiated a larger number of clutches in the same period of time than smaller units.

PARTITIONING REPRODUCTIVE SUCCESS: HELPERS VS. BREEDERS

On a population basis the total production of fledglings in the 1976 breeding season (FTOT) can be partitioned into fledglings attributable to the breeders as if they had no helpers and fledglings in excess of this number, i.e., attributable to helpers. The basis for

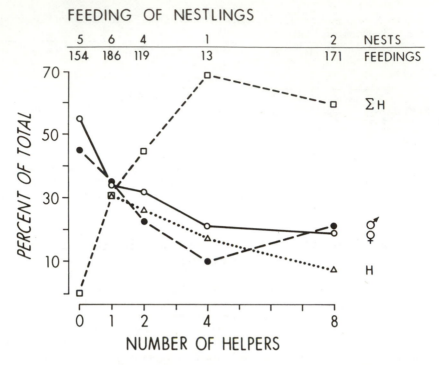

Figure 15–2.   The feeding of nestlings expressed as percentage of the total number of feedings. ΣH, total feedings by helpers. ♂, feedings by father. ♀, feedings by mother. H, feedings per helper. The number of nests watched and total number of feedings at those nests are shown for each number of helpers. From Brown et al. 1978.

this is the regression equation for the estimated number of fledglings $y = +0.82 + 0.46$ AUGSIZ, which is derived from the equation in Table 15–2 by substituting the mean value of BRIGALOW. Substituting the unit size of two for AUGSIZ (i.e., a breeding pair without helpers), the estimated average number of fledglings per unit attributable to the breeders is 1.74. (Four actual units of 2 averaged 2.25 fledglings and four actual units of 3 also averaged 2.25). The total of fledglings in the 36 units attributable to parents alone can be estimated as the product, 36 x 1.74 = 63 fledglings. Subtracting 63 from 122, the total production of fledglings by the 36 units, we obtain 59 fledglings as the estimate of fledglings attributable to helpers. This estimate is 49 per cent of the total and 95 per cent of the estimated average production of unaided pairs. More conservatively, using 2.25 fledglings attributable to unaided pairs, the number attributable to helpers is 41 or 34 per cent of the total and 51 per cent of the production of unaided pairs. In either case the contribution of the helpers both to the population and to the breeders as individuals seems to be biologically important.

OPTIONS FOR THE NON-BREEDER

If we compare the number of fledglings a babbler can rear as a full adult with helpers (3.62) with the number he can rear as a helper (0.46), it is clear that helping is a poor alternative to breeding with helpers. Yet most babblers do not breed at all until 3 or 4 years old

Table 15–3.   Reproductive starts, scheduling of clutches, and success as functions of unit size. Start = start of incubation of a new clutch. Clutch dates are expressed as days of the year. Intervals between clutches are in days. Columns are means. Sample sizes are in parentheses. A more comprehensive analysis of these data is in progress. Variation among groups of units was tested with one-way ANOVA.

Unit Size	N Units	Starts per Unit**	Fledglings per Start	Fledglings per Egg	Size of Clutch	Date 1st Clutch*	Interval to Next Clutch**
2,3	8	0.9	1.9	1.0(8)	2.4	241(6)	334(6)
4,5	13	1.4	1.1	0.6(29)	2.3	248(10)	192(9)
6-8	11	2.3	1.3	0.6(29)	2.4	217(11)	105(11)
10+	4	2.3	2.0	0.6(19)	2.8	205(4)	73(4)

**$P < 0.01$

*$P < 0.05$

(Table 15–4, Figure 15–3). Instead, they behave as helpers for 1–3 years. Failure to breed is presumably related to dominance because only the oldest bird of each sex breeds in most units and age is correlated with dominance in captive units (King, 1974).

Success in breeding at the younger ages is summarized in Table 15–4. One-year-olds had tiny gonads and were never seen to breed. Two-year-olds had moderate-sized gonads, and very few achieved breeding status. Three-year-olds had fully adult gonads and frequently bred. Birds four or more years old almost invariably bred. The average breeding success of those younger birds that did breed was nearly that of full adults and clearly exceeded the average contribution by helpers. This pattern suggests that inability to rear young successfully is not the cause of the delay. A more likely hypothesis would be inability to achieve dominance and control of suitable space.

Table 15–4.   Age-specific survival and reproduction of banded *P. temporalis*.

Age (x)	Eye*	Survival s_x	1_x	Number Individuals	Per cent Breeding	Fledglings per Breeder	Fledglings per Individual
0	F	0.623	1000	122	0	—	—
1	DB	0.689	623	88	0	—	—
2	MB	0.762	429	21	19	2.0	0.38
3	LB,Y–	0.667	327	34	62	2.3	1.44
4+	Y	0.904	218+	50	100	3.6	3.62

*F = fledgling; DB = dark brown; MB = medium brown; LB = light brown; Y– = flecked yellow; Y = pure yellow

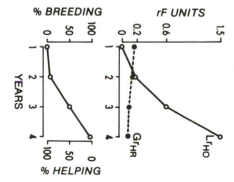

% BREEDING   rF UNITS

Figure 15–3.   Genetic gains by helping vs. losses by not helping as a function of age, assuming all non-breeders are helpers. After 4 years of age all birds are breeders. *Above:* Gr_{HR} = average genetic gain by helping in rF units (see text). Lr_{HO} = average genetic success for all individuals (including breeders and non-breeders) in rF units. *Below:* Percentages of babblers breeding and helping by age.

RELATEDNESS OF HELPER TO RECIPIENT FLEDGLINGS

We determined relatedness of yearling non-breeders to the breeders in their unit in 1977 by color-banding nestlings of the year-class of 1976 and their parents and then observing their associations in 1977. Although during the year a few young became separated from their parents, and a few parents disappeared, by the 1977 breeding season all banded 1976 offspring that were in the population ($N = 45$) were still in their natal territory and with both their parents. The 1975 year class showed similar faithfulness to social unit though not as impressively. Our information on dispersal of 1974 and older birds is spotty, but there was no electrophoretic evidence of inbreeding (M. Johnson, pers. comm); so dispersal for breeding must be effective by the age of attainment of breeding status. The principal factor reducing the relatedness of a helper to the breeders in its unit is the disappearance of a parent and its replacement by an unrelated bird.

The decline in average relatedness of a helper to the young it feeds ($\bar{r}_{HR}$) can be calculated from the number of families with 0, 1, or 2 parents missing ($\bar{r}_{HR} = 1/2, 1/4, 0$ respectively). If s is the rate of survival of its parents in the same territory as the helper, then the average relatedness of a helper to recipient fledglings after n successive years can be estimated as $\bar{r}_{HR} = s^n/2$. For birds of breeding age, s is likely to be essentially independent of age, as is typical of birds. For these calculations I have assumed $s = 0.80$. Actually from August 1976 to August 1977 the observed values for full adults were higher (see Y in Table 15–4). These rates probably represent better than average survival, for conditions were relatively good in 1976 (Dow, pers. comm.).

THE CHOICE IN rF UNITS

To compare the options open to a non-breeder in terms of inclusive fitness, we must take into account its relatedness to the fledglings it might feed. In Figure 15–3 we have converted numbers of fledglings to rF units by multiplying the number of fledglings, F, by the appropriate value of r. By this means we may compare the potential genetic contributions to its inclusive fitness for the breeding and helping options in terms of comparable units.

Except in the first two years the average contribution to inclusive fitness made by breeding far outweighs that made by helping. It must be emphasized that this graph shows only the averages; it does not suggest that an individual should remain a helper at any time if it can become a breeder, and there is no good reason to think that individuals refrain from breeding in order to remain helpers. In fact, the gap in rF units between the helping and breeding strategies is so great that any behavioral ploy that aids achievement of breeding status should be strongly favored. Only if the bird cannot breed successfully does the helping tactic become a desirable option.

DISCUSSION

Removals. Since removal experiments have not been previously used in studies of communally breeding birds, a few more words of interpretation may be desirable. The primary goal of the experiment was to establish whether the correlation between number of helpers and reproductive success was due to a cause-effect relationship involving the manipulated variable or not. The results strengthened the view that a cause-effect relationship existed, but they did not indicate how helpers cause increased reproductive success, nor did they eliminate other possible causal factors.

Among the relevant changes possibly effected by the removals are the following:

1. The amount of effort that the breeders had to devote to caring for their offspring from an earlier brood might have been increased because the helpers, who could have cared for them, were not present.

2. The amount of effort that the parents had to devote to territorial encounters might have been increased.

3. The rate at which a female might prepare herself physiologically for a following brood (e.g., fat build-up) might have been slowed because of 1 and/or 2. These considerations suggest that similar experiments combined with observations on the time-energy budgets of breeding females (especially with attention to care of earlier broods and to territorial defense) might provide critical clues to the mechanisms by which non-breeders benefit breeders.

rF *Currency.* We compared helping and breeding options in *rF* units. This currency has some defects. First, it does not include effects of the helpers on survival of the fledglings and other unit members. The importance of such effects is unknown. Consequently, helping might have a greater effect on indirect fitness than revealed in this paper. Second, if different ages in the life of an individual are being compared, *rF* units are unsatisfactory because they ignore the probability of death of the helper before attaining reproductive status. Using the rates given in Table 15–4, the probability that a one-year-old helper would reach the age of 3 is only 0.5. Thus, at the risk of oversimplifying, for an average yearling helper a fledgling produced by helping in the present is worth 2 or more produced by breeding in the future. Furthermore, the reproductive value of a young reared by a helper is greater than that of a young reared by the same individual as a breeder one or more years in the future because the helper-reared young reaches maturity sooner. In view of these considerations the fledglings produced by a yearling helper are much more valuable to the average helper than their small number might at first suggest.

RRV. In thinking about the options open to a non-breeder for the allocation of its resources it may be helpful to employ the dichotomy suggested by Williams (1966). He divided fitness into a part manifested in present reproduction and a part manifested in the future, the residual reproductive value (*RRV*). An interesting outcome of our analysis is a new way to look at the "costs of reproduction." In non-communal birds reproductive efforts are frequently assumed to decrease the *RRV* of the breeders. But in *P. temporalis* the net effect of production of offspring by a breeder may be to *increase RRV* because the young produced may cause the unit to be larger the next year. Such positive effects on *RRV* require that definitions of "parental investment," such as that of Trivers (1972), be revised to allow for increase in *RRV* resulting from parental effort.

Not Altruism. We employ Hamilton's (1964:15) original concept of altruism, which we illustrate in Figure 15–4A. Note that the mere giving of aid is not necessarily altruism unless it lowers the direct fitness of the altruist and raises the direct fitness of the recipient. Thus, altruism must on average lower the total number of the altruist's offspring that reach maturity. The term altruism has often been used for avian helping behavior, but this practice was never more than speculative and now seems unwise, simply because there is still no persuasive evidence that helpers reduce their own direct fitness (see discussion in Brown, 1978). More generally, it remains to be shown in any vertebrate that an individual helper is ever typically altruistic. The behaviors that are sometimes referred to as altruistic by others involve sacrifice that is demonstrable when measured in terms of commodities or services (operational altruism, Brown, 1975). But in virtually none of these can the loss be translated to a loss in direct fitness because the latter is likely to be so small as to be unmeasurable in practice. Extending the discussion for a moment to include all vertebrates and perhaps invertebrates, in view of the difficulty of proving (or disproving) the existence of altruism perhaps too much attention has been paid to altruism by theorists and too little to the role of indirect selection where it is likely to be important in nature, namely in the quadrant designated as cooperation in Figure 15–4A or in the gray area between altruism and cooperation.

Fitness Space. In order to illustrate graphically some limitations in our knowledge of helping behavior in relation to inclusive fitness theory, D. S. Wilson's (1975) fitness-space diagrams may be useful. As shown in Figure 15–4A, Hamilton's (1964) four types of fitness relationships between participants in a dyadic encounter can be represented in the four quadrants. In Figure 15–4B the dashed line separates relationships that can be achieved in a single population by direct selection (on the right) from those that require indirect selection (left). Interestingly, this line bisects the cooperation quadrant, meaning that cooperation is divided into two types: (1) that in which the recipient benefits more than the donor (requiring indirect selection) and (2) that in which the recipient benefits less than the donor (not requiring indirect selection). The former has been named R-cooperation and the latter D-cooperation (Brown, 1978). The line dividing them designates strict reciprocity.

Where does helping behaviour in *P. temporalis* fall in this scheme? Figure 15–4C shows the possibilities. We have shown that parents raise 0.5 more fledglings for each helper than they would alone. Therefore, using fledglings as the unit of direct fitness and designating either parent as recipient, the y-coordinate is 0.5. It is the value of the x-coordinate about which we are in doubt. For a helper the x-coordinate corresponds to its change in *RRV*. No quantitative estimates of the change in a non-breeder's *RRV* as a consequence of helping have been made for any species, so we can only list the possibilities and make educated guesses.

If x were negative, helping would be altruism (AL in Figure 15–4C). For reasons given (and in Brown, 1978), we regard this as unlikely. The only remaining possibility is cooperation (including reciprocity and mutualism). Whether helping should be regarded as D-cooperation or R-cooperation or reciprocity cannot even be intelligently guessed at present.

Because cooperation may involve individuals expending effort to raise their own direct fitness, some authors have suggested on this basis alone that "complicated mechanisms such as kin selection are unnecessary" (Zahavi, 1977). In this view the indirect benefit to the genotype achieved by helping is an ineffective byproduct. Unfortunately, for this argument half of the fitness space for cooperation in Figure 15–4 requires indirect selection (the alarm-call model of Wilson, 1975, 1977). In other words, even unquestionable proof that helpers raise their own *RRV* by helping would not prove that indirect selection was unnecessary. Furthermore, even in D-cooperation, indirect selection may be involved.

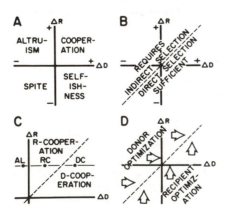

Figure 15–4.   Fitness space diagrams. ΔR = change in direct fitness of recipient. ΔD = change in direct fitness of donor. A. Hamilton's (1964) categories of behavior based on direct fitness. B. Cost-benefit conditions for direct selection. C. Hypothetical locations of helping behavior: AL = altruism; RC = R-cooperation; DC = D-cooperation. For further explanation of fitness space diagrams see D. S. Wilson (1975). D. Directions of donor optimization and recipient optimization.

For example, given two genotypes showing the same increase in helper *RRV* by helping, the one with the larger recipient-benefit would win, provided it helped close relatives selectively. In other words, even a small difference in indirect fitness could be crucial.

Optimizing Cooperation. This example suggests some principles: when donor benefit or cost is fixed, selection will maximize benefit to recipient as long as recipients are closely related (recipient optimization in Figure 15–4D). Similarly, when recipient benefit is fixed, selection will maximize donor net benefit, minimizing donor cost (donor optimization, Figure 4D). Whether participant benefit or cost is fixed or not, these forces should (1) *eliminate altruism wherever possible* and (2) adjust benefits to donor and recipient (helper and parent) optimally with respect to relatedness, reproductive value, and representation of competing genotypes in the population. This view is based on Hamilton's (1964: 8) that "average inclusive fitness . . . will always increase."

This view of cooperation in nature emphasizes the flexibility of phenotypic response of genotypes. The winning genotype is the one that responds appropriately to each situation when the individual is a donor *and* when it is a recipient. There are no simple rules, such as "the amount of helping is determined only by the parent" or "only by the helper" or "there are only winners and losers." Recent modeling suggests the inadequacy of such simple rules (Stamps, et al., 1978; Parker and MacNair, 1978; O'Connor, 1978).

The Individual. Hamilton's (1964) theory of inclusive fitness and later, more comprehensive theories involving indirect pathways (e.g., D. S. Wilson, 1975) were theories of the genotype primarily and the individual only secondarily. Our data indicate that indirect fitness is important and, therefore, justify the theoretical emphasis on the genotype rather than exclusively on the individual's direct fitness. Emphasis on individual fitness (direct fitness) at the expense of indirect fitness by some authors in this symposium seems to us to result in part from confusion over the components of individual fitness. Figure 15–1 illustrates the potential for confusion. *The individual's direct fitness actually results in part from indirect influences acting on that individual.* For example, a bird that acquires a territory with the help of sibs increases its direct fitness through indirect influence from relatives. In attempting to maximize its direct fitness the individual can be expected to make use of whatever indirect benefits are available. Consequently, in assessing the importance of indirect pathways *both* the indirect influences on the individual and the individual's indirect effects on others must be considered.

SUMMARY

The fitness pathways leading to and from an individual may be divided into two categories, direct (from parent to offspring) and indirect (from an individual to others who are not its offspring). We attempted to estimate the importance and the mechanism of the indirect pathway in a study of helping behavior in the grey-crowned babbler (*Pomatostomus temporalis*). This paper is a progress report of the results from a one-year study.

By stepwise multiple regression it was shown that number of helpers and structure of vegetation were the two variables most strongly correlated with production of fledglings. By experimental removal of helpers it was shown that they were an important cause of variation in production of fledglings. The mechanism by which helping benefits breeders probably does not involve increased rates of feeding of nestlings. It may involve savings in effort by the breeding female in caring for her young.

Reproduction was partitioned at the population level into a fraction attributable to the parents as if unhelped and a fraction attributable to the helpers. The former fraction was predominant but the latter was large. Helpers were closely related to the young they cared for. Comparisons of inclusive fitness expressed in rF units (see text) suggested that for the first year helping represents a better strategy than attempting to breed, but in later years helping is inferior to breeding if a chance to breed exists. We recommend caution in the use of "altruism" to refer to helping behavior.

REFERENCES

Brown, J. L. 1969. Territorial behavior and population regulation in birds. *Wilson Bull.* 81: 293–329.
––––––. 1974. Alternate routes to sociality in jays—with a theory for the evolution of altruism and communal breeding. *Amer. Zool.* 14:63–80.
––––––. 1975. *The Evolution of Behavior.* W.W. Norton and Co., New York, N.Y.
––––––. 1978. Avian communal breeding systems. *Ann. Rev. Ecol. Syst.* 9: 123–155.
––––––. 1979. Growth of nestling grey-crowned babblers, with notes on determination of age in juveniles. *Emu* 79: 1–6.
––––––, and R. P. Balda. 1977. The relationship of habitat quality to group size in Hall's babbler (*Pomatostomus halli*). *Condor* 79: 312–320.
––––––, D. D. Dow, E. R. Brown, and S. D. Brown. 1978. Effects of helpers on feeding of nestlings in the grey-crowned babbler (*Pomatostomus temporalis*). *Behav. Ecol. Sociobiol.* 4: 43–59.
Counsilman, J. J. 1977. Groups of the grey-crowned babbler in central southern Queensland. *Babbler* 1: 14–22.
––––––, and B. King. 1977. Aging and sexing the grey-crowned babbler (*Pomatostomus temporalis*). *Babbler* 1: 23–41.
Dawkins, R. 1976. *The Selfish Gene.* Oxford Univ. Press. Oxford and New York.
Hamilton, W. D. 1964. The genetical evolution of social behavior. I, II. *J. Theor. Biol.* 7: 1–52.
––––––. 1975. Innate social aptitudes of man: an approach from evolutionary genetics. In Fox, R. (ed.) *Biosocial Anthropology.* Wiley, New York.
King, B. 1974. Communal breeding and related behaviour in the grey-crowned babbler *Pomatostomus temporalis*, in south-east Queensland. M. Sc. Thesis, University of Queensland, Queensland, Australia.
Lack, D. 1968. *Ecological Adaptations for Breeding in Birds.* Methuen, London.
Ligon, J. D., and S. H. Ligon. 1978. Communal breeding in green woodhoopoes as a case for reciprocity. *Nature* 276: 496–498.
Maynard Smith, J. 1964. Group selection and kin selection. *Nature* 201: 1145–1147.
––––––. 1976. Group selection. *Quart. Rev. Biol.* 51: 277–283.
O'Connor, R. J. 1978. Brood reduction in birds: selection for fratricide, infanticide and suicide. *Anim. Behav.* 26: 79–96.
Parker, G. A., and M. R. MacNair. 1978. Models of parent-offspring conflict. I. Monogamy. *Anim. Behav.* 26: 97–110.
Parry, V. 1973. The auxiliary social system and its effect on territory and breeding in kookaburras. *Emu* 73: 81–100.
Rowley, I. 1965. The life history of the superb blue wren *Malurus cyaneus*. *Emu* 64: 251–297.
Skutch, A. F. 1961. Helpers among birds. *Condor* 63: 198–226.
Stamps, J. A., R. A. Metcalf, and V. V. Krishnan. 1978. A genetic analysis of parent-offspring conflict. *Behav. Ecol. Sociobiol.* 3: 369–392.
Trivers, R. L. 1972. Parental investment and sexual selection, p. 136–179. In B.G. Campbell (ed.), *Sexual Selection and the Descent of Man* (1871–1971). Aldine-Atherton, Chicago.
West-Eberhard, M. J. 1975. The evolution of social behavior by kin selection. *Quart. Rev. Biol.* 50: 1–33.
Williams, G. C. 1966. Natural selection, the costs of reproduction, and a refinement of Lack's principle. *Amer. Natur.* 100: 687–690.
Wilson, D. S. 1975. A theory of group selection. *Proc. Nat. Acad. Sci.* USA 72: 143–146.
––––––. 1977. Structured demes and the evolution of group advantageous traits. *Amer. Natur.* III: 157–185.
Woolfenden, G. E. 1975. Florida scrub jay helpers at the nest. *Auk* 92: 1–15.
Zahavi, A. 1977. Reliability in communication systems and the evolution of altruism, p. 253–259. In B. Stonehouse and C. Perrins (eds.), *Evolutionary Ecology*. University Park Press, Baltimore.

16

Selfish Behavior by Florida Scrub Jay Helpers

Glen E. Woolfenden

Group-breeding birds are characterized by the existence of helpers, helpers being individuals who assist birds other than their own offspring or mate. It is difficult to demonstrate that helpers really do help, but for the few species studied in detail it appears to be true (Rowley, 1965; Woolfenden, 1975), and no proof to the contrary exists.

If the assistance that helpers provide decreases their own production of offspring then the helpers are behaving as fraternal altruists. However, if the assistance provided increases their production of offspring, then the helpers are behaving selfishly. Hamilton (1963, 1964) and Maynard Smith (1964) describe an evolutionary force termed kin selection, a component of which is fraternal altruism. Theoretically, helpers can evolve as fraternal altruists if their aid increases their inclusive fitnesses in the same way that parents increase their inclusive fitnesses through parental altruism. Under the assumption that avian helpers and the recipients of their aid have close genetic relatedness, kin-selected fraternal altruism was offered as an explanation for helping behavior in birds (Brown 1970, 1974).

Information obtained from a long-term and continuing study of the Florida scrub jay (*Aphelocoma c. coerulescens*) has been useful for studying the evolutionary forces that control group breeding. Several papers, mostly recent and one in press, detail the information obtained thus far (see Woolfenden and Fitzpatrick, 1978 and references therein). This report analyses some new data but is based primarily on these published works.

The Florida scrub jay is stenoecic, sedentary, long-lived, and both nearly permanently monogamous and permanently territorial (Woolfenden, 1974). Through the years about half of the breeders have had helpers. For pairs with helpers their number has ranged from one to six, with 1.8 the mean. Close inbreeding is rare because breeding pairs are not formed of birds who were previously contemporary occupants of the same territory.

Florida scrub jay helpers participate in certain nesting activities but not others. They feed young, mob nest predators, and defend territorial boundaries. They do not build nests, incubate eggs, or brood young. They do appear to help. Based on reproductive data from ten consecutive years (Table 16–1), 79 per cent of all pairs with helpers succeed in fledging at least one young per season. Only 61 per cent of the pairs without helpers succeed. Pairs with helpers fledge 2.3 young; those without only 1.5. The differences are highly significant.

Numerous weaknesses exist when all breeders are included in the analyses. For some bird species it is known that novice breeders tend to produce fewer young than experienced pairs, and novice jay pairs tend to have no helpers. Perhaps more critical, by including all pairs in the analyses, variation in territory quality and genetic constitution are ignored. Table 16–1 includes separate calculations designed to eliminate or at least weaken these factors. Several pairs, all experienced at fledging young, have in later years attempted

Table 16–1.   Reproductive success, 1969–1978.

	With Helpers		Without Helpers	
	All 141 Pairs	24 Prev. Succ. Prs.	All 125 Pairs	17 Prev. Succ. Prs.
Seasonal breeding success	79%**	79%^{ns}	61%**	59%^{ns}
Fledglings per pair per season	2.3**	2.5*	1.5**	1.5*

*Significant at 5 per cent.
**Significant at 1 per cent.

Table 16–2.   Whom helpers help—based on 152 known-age helpers during 229 seasonal breedings.

Breeders		Helper Seasons		
Male	Female	Male	Female	Sex?
Father	Mother	60	65	17
Father	Non-related	14	8	5
Brother	Non-related	5	1	0
Prob. brother	Non-related	3	0	1
Half brother	Non-related	3	1	0
Grandfather	Mother	1	0	0
First cousin	Mother	1	1	0
Prob. uncle	Grandmother	1	0	0
Non-related	Mother	5	12	4
Non-related	Non-related	1	4	0
Unknown	Non-related	7	0	0
Unknown	Unknown	5	3	1
		106	95	28

breeding essentially on the same territory both with and without helpers. Seasonal breeding success for these pairs, both with and without helpers, is similar to the all-inclusive sample, but the difference is not statistically significant. Fledgling production also is similar, and here the difference is significant.

The presence of helpers in Florida scrub jays also appears to lower the mortality of breeders. During the years 1969–1976 breeders with helpers sustained only a 13 per cent annual mortality; breeders without helpers died at the rate of 20 per cent per annum (Stallcup and Woolfenden, 1978). The difference is significant.

Based on our analyses of the reproductive success and survival of breeders, it is concluded that Florida scrub jay helpers do help.

Table 16–2, reproduced from Woolfenden and Fitzpatrick (in press), shows the familial relationships of 152 helpers to the breeders they assisted. Clearly helpers tend to help both of their parents. But because of the mortality of breeders and the duration of some jays as helpers, many individuals assist breeders other than their parents. Furthermore, because of the vicissitudes of family and territory stability, jays sometimes help certain breeders when genetically closer relatives exist nearby. Regardless of the causes, many times Florida scrub jays give aid to individuals with whom they do not share a high degree of relatedness, and these results suggest an evolutionary explanation other than kin-selected fraternal altruism.

In Table 16–3, row 3 shows the reproductive output of helpers beyond one helper. Clearly the effort expended by any helpers beyond one is wasted if their only gain is through inclusive fitness. Thus when more than one non-breeder lives with a breeding pair the opportunity is available to cheat on the system by not investing effort in raising young. However, we find no evidence of this. Indeed, feeding rates by individuals, and other contributions to breeding seem unaffected by many variables including number of helpers and number of young (Stallcup and Woolfenden, 1978).

Florida scrub jays increase the representation of their genes in the population by fledging their own young or by helping fledge the young of close relatives. Using the jay data from 1969 to 1977, Stephen T. Emlen and I attempted to discover whether breeding or helping produced the greatest increase in a jay's genes. To do this we compared (1) success at fledging young by breeders for which (a) one and (b) both members of the pair were novices with (2) success at fledging young attributable to the helper of a breeding pair. The results indicate that, regardless of the age or experience of the individual or its mate, becoming a breeder is the best way for a jay to increase the representation of its genes in the population (Emlen, 1978). These results, together with the frequency with which jays help individuals who are not close relatives, lead to the question: Do helpers profit as individuals from helping?

Non-breeding helpers probably live longer by remaining on familiar ground with familiar jays than by dispersing. The familiar ground most available to them usually is occupied by the family that raised them. Although survival probably is thus enhanced, the opportunities for the non-breeding helpers to become breeders in their home territories are very low. Florida scrub jays circumvent this problem, in part, by executing dispersal forays. When searching for a breeding space, helper jays visit the numerous other families in their neighborhood. When not searching, they live in the presumed safety of their home territory.

Increased survival may explain why Florida scrub jays remain on familiar ground with familiar jays, but it does not explain why they help. Recently Woolfenden and Fitzpatrick (1978) outlined a series of events that seems to explain why male helpers help. Briefly the sequence is as follows: (1) helpers increase the family size of the breeders they assist. (2) as the family grows, its territory increases in size. (3) following territorial expansion, the dominant male helper often becomes sole occupant of a segment of the territory he helped establish. Here, with a mate from outside the family, the former helper becomes a breeder. These events imply the existence of a dominance hierarchy, which indeed does exist (Woolfenden and Fitzpatrick, 1977). Thus, for males at least, we suggest that helpers help raise young because increasing family size increases their own chances of becoming breeders.

Female helpers rarely gain directly in this manner. However, females also invest less in helping in that they remain as helpers for fewer years (Woolfenden and Fitzpatrick, 1978) and when present they deliver less food (Stallcup and Woolfenden, 1978). Increased survival may be sufficent to explain why females remain at home. In addition it also may be that an intrafamilial dominance system exists among helper females. If so, then helping to

Table 16–3.   Fledgling production and number of helpers, 1969–1978.

	Number of Helpers				
	0	1	2	3	4-6
Sample size	125	63	50	18	10
Fledglings per pair per season	1.5	2.3	2.1	2.6	2.4
Reproductive gain per helper above one helper	—	—	− 0.2	0.2	0.0
Fledglings per feeder per season	0.8	0.8	0.5	0.5	0.4

produce more female young would not tend to decrease breeding opportunities for the older helper females.

Florida scrub jays rarely breed before age two years. Many do not breed for the first time until several years later. Inability to attain sexual maturity seems an unlikely reason for delayed breeding. Birds their size, including jays of the same species found in western North America, apparently regularly breed during their first breeding season post hatching (Brown, 1963). Furthermore, one Florida scrub jay of each sex has bred successfully in our study tract at age one year. Lack of ecological opportunity to breed seems the more likely reason for the delay. Florida scrub jays are extremely habitat specific (see map in Westcott, 1970). It may be that acceptable habitat for breeding often is saturated. Under such conditions remaining at home and helping may be the best way for a jay to become a breeder, as well as the only way for it to reproduce before breeding.

Based on the information available at present I offer the following conclusions. As non-breeders, Florida scrub jays increase their inclusive fitness by helping. If by helping, the jays also maximize their opportunities to become breeders, then helping certainly is not entirely altruistic and may not be altruistic at all. Helping may be a form of selfish behavior, namely selfishness through cooperation. If this reasoning is valid, then such aspects of helping behavior in these jays is similar to mutualism as described by West-Eberhard (1978) and reciprocal altruism as proposed by Trivers (1971).

REFERENCES

Brown, J. L. 1963. Social organization and behavior of the Mexican jay. *Condor* 65: 126–153.

———. 1970. Cooperative breeding and altruistic behaviour in the Mexican jay, *Aphelocoma ultramarina. Anim. Behav.* 18: 366–378.

———. 1974. Alternate routes to sociality in jays—with a theory for the evolution of altruism and communal breeding. *Am. Zool.* 14: 63–80.

Emlen, S. T. 1978. The evolution of cooperative breeding in birds. Chap. 9, pp. 245–281 in *Behavioural Ecology: An Evolutionary Approach* (Krebs, J. R., and N. B. Davies, eds.). Sunderland, Mass., Sinauer Assoc.

Hamilton, W. D. 1963. The evolution of altruistic behaviour. *Am. Nat.* 97: 354–356.

———. 1964. The genetical evolution of social behaviour. I and II. *J. Theor. Biol.* 7: 1–52.

Maynard Smith, J. 1964. Group selection and kin selection. *Nature* 201: 1145–1147.

Rowley, I. 1965. The life history of the superb blue wren, *Malurus cyaneus. Emu* 64: 251–297.

Stallcup, J. A., and G. E. Woolfenden. 1978. Family status and contributions to breeding by Florida scrub jays. *Anim. Behav.* 26:1144–1156.

Trivers, R. L. 1971. The evolution of reciprocal altruism. *Q. Rev. Biol.* 46: 35–57.

West-Eberhard, M. J. 1978. Temporary queens in *Metapolybia* wasps: non-reproductive helpers without altruism? *Science* 200: 441–443.

Westcott, P. W. 1970. Ecology and behavior of the Florida scrub jay. unpubl. Ph. D. thesis, Univ. of Florida.

Woolfenden, G. E. 1974. Nesting and survival in a population of Florida scrub jays. *Living Bird* 12: 25–49.

———. 1975. Florida scrub jay helpers at the nest. *Auk* 92: 1–15.

Woolfenden, G. E., and J. W. Fitzpatrick. 1977. Dominance in the Florida scrub jay. *Condor* 79: 1–12.

———. 1978. The inheritance of territory in group-breeding birds. *BioScience* 28: 104–108.

———. In press. The selfish behavior of avian altruists. *Proc. 17th Int. Ornithol. Congr.*

17.

Ecological Factors and Kin Selection in the Evolution of Cooperative Breeding in Birds

Walter D. Koenig and Frank A. Pitelka

A question central to current thought regarding the evolution of cooperative breeding in birds concerns the relative importance of ecological versus genetical factors (Hamilton, 1964; Brown, 1974; West-Eberhard, 1975; E. O. Wilson, 1975). Specifically, does kinship or the degree of genetic relatedness among cooperators *per se* act as a crucial factor in the selection process of cooperative breeding? The ensuing review dealing with this question was triggered by ongoing research on the social system of the acorn woodpecker (*Melanerpes formicivorus*) in central coastal California. Earlier work by MacRoberts and MacRoberts (1976) has been continued, and more recent results to which reference is made here are presented in detail elsewhere (Koenig, 1978). Our review is in two parts: After a brief section on definitions, we first consider ecological factors, discussing in detail one hypothesis that we view as particularly important to the evolution of cooperative breeding. We then deal more directly with kinship, offering arguments in support of the focus on ecological factors.

DEFINITION OF COOPERATIVE BREEDING

A species in which individuals additional to a male-female pair assist in production of young at a single nest can be considered a cooperative breeder. Three variations on this theme are now recognized in birds: In the most common class, one or more non-breeding "helpers at the nest" assist a breeding pair to raise its young. Many examples will be cited in the text which follows. In the second, less frequent class, more than a single pair participate in gamete production; species in which this occurs may be said to be true "communal breeders." Two distinct types of communal systems are those in which reproduction involves (1) two or more males and a female who lays a single clutch, presumably fathered in part by both males (*Tribonyx*, Maynard Smith and Ridpath, 1972; *Parabuteo*, Mader, 1975; *Buteo*, de Vries, 1975); and (2) two or more females who lay eggs simultaneously in a nest and are mated in pairs to an equal number of males (*Crotophaga*, Vehrencamp, 1977), or apparently promiscuously to a variable number of males (*Melanerpes*, Koenig, 1978; *Corcorax*, Rowley, 1965b, 1978). A third class of cooperative breeding also often considered to be "communal" occurs in courtship display rather than nesting: Two or more males display together to attract mates (*Chiroxiphia*, Foster, 1977; *Meleagris*, Watts and Stokes, 1971), and the females of these species go on to raise their offspring by themselves, independently of either their mate(s) or other females.

Each of these systems meets three criteria: (1) three or more birds must take part in gamete production and/or the care of young; (2) the offspring originate from a single nest; and (3) a significant degree of assistance or cooperation must be rendered among the birds in the group, especially among those of the same sex. For example, the polyandrous Tasmanian native hen (*Tribonyx mortierii*) is a cooperative breeder because two males frequently mate with a single female who produces only a single nest cared for by all three birds. The polyandrous northern jacana (*Jacana spinosa*), however, cannot be considered cooperative because in this species, two or more males again mate with a female, but a separate clutch is laid for each male, none of whom assist each other in any known way (Jenni and Collier, 1972). Thus neither criterion 2 nor 3 is met. Another type of situation not quite qualifying as cooperative breeding is presented by starlings (*Sturnus vulgaris*) in Scotland (Yom-Tov *et al.*, 1974). In these birds, intraspecific nest parasitism is common, with the result that some clutches are the product of two or more females. Since no known assistance is rendered by the parasitic females, however, this species does not meet criterion 3.

Thus, the distinction of a "cooperative breeder" often rests on the criterion of whether or not individuals are *assisting* in the production or raising of young. The application of this criterion will not always be easy; some subtle forms of cooperation may elude detection except with extensive study.

ECOLOGICAL FACTORS

Crook (1965), Lack (1968), and Brown and Orians (1970) all suggested that the spacing pattern or social system of a population can often be inferred from knowledge about the food resources it uses and about the kinds of predation pressure to which it is exposed. More recently, Alexander (1974) and Hoogland and Sherman (1976) have pointed out that no automatic advantages are conferred by group living and that only three general classes of effects may provide the selection pressure necessary to counteract the inherent disadvantages to group behavior: (1) defense against predators, (2) characteristics of the food supply, and (3) localization of some resource other than food. Each of these classes can be subdivided as shown in Table 17–1. We concur with the authors cited that they provide our only options for explaining the evolutionary contexts favoring group living.

To date, finding similarities among cooperative breeders, much less pinpointing any single one of the factors listed in Table 17–1 as providing the selective background for the evolution of cooperative breeding, has proved discouraging (Fry, 1972a, 1977; Brown, 1974; Ricklefs, 1975). This situation has led Zahavi (1976) to suggest, perhaps facetiously, that the only common denominator among cooperative breeders may be that " ... there is always more than a pair at the nest." Rather than attempt to discuss all the hypotheses listed in Table 17–1, however, we point out a dichotomy among them which may be an important

Table 17–1.   Ecological factors that might select for group living.

1. Predator defense.
   a. Deterrence of nest predators.
   b. Overall increased vigilance reducing day-to-day predation rate.
   c. "Selfish herd" effect.
2. Exploitation pattern.
   a. Food supply short and unpredictable in time; more than two birds needed to start and complete nesting cycle within narrow "window" of good times.
   b. Food supply scattered and clumped; more than two birds defend food supply better and/or exploit patches more efficiently.
   c. Food items very large or ferocious; more than two birds needed to catch and/or subdue them.
3. Localization of a limited resource.
   a. Habitat (see text).
   b. Other suggested localized resources: nest holes, mates.

clue relevant to selection for cooperative breeding. As noted by Alexander (1974), individuals in groups gain by the presence of others in the first two general cases (predator defense and food exploitation pattern) but in the third they do not. Thus, in a species that has evolved cooperative breeding for any reason listed under 1 or 2 of Table 17–1, the genetic contributions of individuals in groups to the overall gene pool of the population should be greater, on a *per capita* basis, than that of just pairs, and individuals in larger groups, at least to some optimal size, should be more successful than those in smaller groups. If this is not the case, individuals will gain by splitting off and reproducing on their own and cooperative breeding or some other form of group living should not evolve unless resource localization (item 3, Table 17–1) forces individuals to remain in groups.

As long as all group members have a good chance of breeding while in the group, the above generalization is straightforward in its application to groups composed of related individuals. (It does not apply if groups are composed entirely of unrelated individuals, and breeding success of some members is strongly and consistently higher than others. No cooperative system is known conclusively to follow this pattern, however.) When group members are related (as is the case in most cooperative species), the proof of the above statement is rather more complex. Analysis of such situations can be carried out using benefit/cost analysis (West-Eberhard, 1975, modified after Hamilton, 1964). This method makes use of the ratio (K_i) of the relatedness of the concerned individual (= "ego") to the donor's (altruist's) potential offspring

$$(r_{EA_y})$$

and the relatedness of ego to the recipient's (beneficiary's) potential offspring

$$(r_{EB_y}),$$

as a measure of how advantageous a specific altruistic act is from the point of view of ego. For our purposes here, ego is either the altruist or the beneficiary, but West-Ebehard's model has more general applicability.

The first case of interest is that of "helpers" aiding their parents to raise full siblings. Such a situation for a hypothetical species in which the reproductive rate for pairs alone is .5 offspring/bird/year and the opportunity to enter the breeding population is unlimited is presented in Figure 17–1. From the parents' (beneficiary) point of view,

$$r_{EA_y} = .25, r_{EB_y} = .5,$$

and thus $K_t = .5$. Thus, given the *per capita* reproductive rate of .5 offspring/bird (1.0 offspring per pair), each parent will break even in terms of his or her inclusive fitness (Hamilton, 1964) whether the helper "helps" or breeds independently, and they should encourage helping only if each helper allows the production of at least .5 *extra* young per breeding season, thereby maintaining the *per capita* fecundity of .5 offspring/bird for trios. If helpers do not contribute at least this much to their parents' reproductive success, they would improve both their own and their parents' inclusive fitnesses by dispersing and breeding on their own.

Note, however, that from the helper's (altruist) point of view,

$$r_{EA_y} = .5, r_{EB_y} = .5,$$

and $K_t = 1.0$. Thus, given the reproductive regime above, and assuming a helper's survival is the same whether it disperses or not (see beyond), a helper should *voluntarily* disperse unless he can cause his parents to produce >1.0 extra offspring as a consequence of his aid, thereby increasing the *per capita* reproductive rate of trios to >2.0/group, or $>.67$/bird, even higher than the .5/bird rate for pairs alone in the population. If the reproductive increment is only 1, the helper is merely breaking even, providing no compelling reason to stay and help.

A. No helping

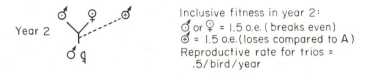

Inclusive fitness in year 2:
♂ or ♀ (parent) = 1.0 + .5 = 1.5
    offspring equivalents (o.e.)
⊕ (offspring) = 1.0 + 1.0 = 2.0 o.e.
Reproductive rate for pairs alone =
    .5/bird/year

B. Helping occurs, parent breaks even

Inclusive fitness in year 2:
♂ or ♀ = 1.5 o.e. (breaks even)
⊕ = 1.5 o.e. (loses compared to A)
Reproductive rate for trios =
    .5/bird/year

C. Helping occurs, offspring breaks even

Inclusive fitness in year 2:
♂ or ♀ = 2.0 o.e. (comes out ahead,
    compared to A)
⊕ = 2.0 o.e. (breaks even compared
    to A)
Reproductive rate for trios =
    .67/bird/year

Figure 17–1.   Reproductive rate necessary for helping to be advantageous from a parent's (beneficiary) or offspring's (helper or altruist) point of view; reproductive rate is .5 bird/year for pairs alone
and must exceed the rate calculated for trios for helping to be advantageous for the concerned individual, either and separately a parent or the helper.

    Two points of interest emerge from this analysis. (1) from either the altruist's or benefi-
ciary's point of view, the reproductive rate of groups (pairs plus helpers) must be higher on a
per capita basis than that of pairs without helpers, for helping to increase inclusive fitness.
(2) There is a basic asymmetry in the genetic interests of parents and helpers in cooperative
groups: The threshold for cooperative breeding to occur is less for breeders than for helpers
(see also Emlen, 1978). The option of "helping" is not advantageous to all parties concerned unless the *per capita* reproductive rate of groups greatly exceeds the rate for pairs
alone (in the case of Figure 17–1, trios must do 33 per cent better than pairs for helpers to
break even). In other words, from both the altruist's and beneficiary's points of view, helping should occur only if the reproductive rate of groups (pairs plus helpers) is higher, on a
per capita basis, than that of pairs without helpers, *given that the opportunity for dispersal
and breeding elsewhere is present.*
    A comparable analysis is presented in Figure 17–2 for the second type of reproductive
cooperation, that of two or more siblings forming a cooperating unit, and provides the same
qualitative conclusions as the prior situation: (1) the reproductive rate per bird in groups
must be greater than that for members of pairs for group living to be advantageous; and (2) a

A. No helping or cooperation

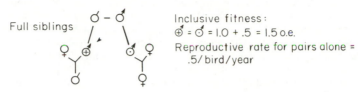

Inclusive fitness:
♂ = ♂ = 1.0 + .5 = 1.5 o.e.
Reproductive rate for pairs alone =
.5/bird/year

B. Helping by one sib, breeder breaks even

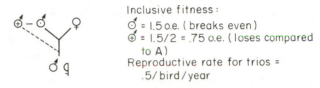

Inclusive fitness:
♂ = 1.5 o.e. (breaks even)
♂ = 1.5/2 = .75 o.e. (loses compared
to A)
Reproductive rate for trios =
.5/bird/year

C. Helping by one sib, helper breaks even

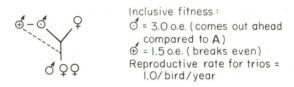

Inclusive fitness:
♂ = 3.0 o.e. (comes out ahead
compared to A)
♂ = 1.5 o.e. (breaks even)
Reproductive rate for trios =
1.0/bird/year

D. "Wife-sharing," sibs break even

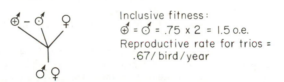

Inclusive fitness:
♂ = ♂ = .75 x 2 = 1.5 o.e.
Reproductive rate for trios =
.67/bird/year

Figure 17–2.   Reproductive rate necessary for helping or ''wife-sharing'' to be advantageous for siblings; reproductive rate is .5 bird/year for pairs alone and must exceed the rate calculated for trios for either type of cooperation to be advantageous to either sib. For D, either sib is certain of fostering ½ of the group offspring, and thus their inclusive fitnesses are $[(1 \times 1.0) + (1 \times .5)]/2 = .75$ offspring equivalents for each group offspring.

similar asymmetry exists between the genetic interests of breeders and helpers. Similar conclusions via a somewhat different model were obtained for the case of sibling cooperation by Maynard Smith and Ridpath (1972).

Several circumstances may affect these conclusions. Here we discuss four that we feel are potentially the most important: First are delayed maturity and a biased sex ratio. If birds of a given species are physiologically unable to reproduce for one or more years after birth, their reproductive output in that interval if they dispersed would necessarily be zero, and *any* increase in per group reproductive success by help to their parents could provide an advantage to cooperative breeding. Similarly, if the sex ratio is biased, individuals of the ''surplus'' sex unable to obtain mates are excluded from breeding, and again, any help they render to breeding relatives could yield a selective advantage. Both factors have frequently been invoked as important to the evolution of cooperative breeding (*e.g.,* Brown, 1974, 1978; Fry, 1972a; Maynard Smith and Ridpath, 1972; Orians *et al.,* 1977; Emlen, 1978).

We believe these conclusions are flawed for at least two reasons. First, study of several cooperative species that had previously been thought to exhibit delayed maturity has now shown that first-year individuals can and do breed under appropriate circumstances (*Aphelocoma,* Stallcup and Woolfenden, 1978; *Melanerpes,* Koenig, 1978). Similarly, several cooperative species have apparently even or near even sex ratios (*Gymnorhinus,* Carrick, 1972; *Porphyrio,* Craig, 1976; *Pomatostomus,* Councilman, 1977b; also possibly *Corcorax,* Rowley, 1978). Thus, neither of these factors is necessary for the evolution of cooperative breeding. In other words, biased sex ratio and/or delayed maturity in cooperative species may be a result rather than a cause of cooperative breeding. Delayed maturity may be favored if few first-year birds ever have the opportunity to breed because of habitat limitation. Delayed maturity among most or all first-year birds would then be a side effect of the primary ecological factor selecting for cooperative breeding, namely, habitat saturation. Similarly, differential female dispersal is likely to be the result of differing options for gaining reproductive status available to males vs. females within cooperative groups (see, for example, Woolfenden and Fitzpatrick, 1978). To the extent that this is the case, biased sex ratio is then also a side effect.

Third, the situations outlined in Figures 17–1 and 17–2 change in an inbred population, when an altruistic individual remaining in his natal group may then be more closely related to the young of other group members (coefficient of relationship $r > .5$) than he would be to his own young if he were to mate at random outside of the group ($r = .5$). This is part of the hypothesis used by Brown (1974) as the basis for a model of the evolution of cooperative breeding systems. This hypothesis has recently been retracted (Brown, 1978), and despite considerable recent work a significant amount of inbreeding has yet to be reported in any cooperative species. Furthermore, work on the Florida scrub jay *Aphelocoma c. coerulescens* (Woolfenden, 1976; Woolfenden and Fitzpatrick, 1978) and the acorn woodpecker (Koenig, 1978) suggests that these species have well-developed behavioral mechanisms to avoid close consanguineous matings, despite the extended family nature of their groups. Thus, there is no *a priori* reason to assume an unusual amount of inbreeding to occur in cooperative species, and the following discussion considers exogamy to be the norm.

Finally, a fourth factor potentially altering conclusions of Figures 17–1 and 17–2 is the limiting effect of territories or some other resource in short supply, making it impossible for offspring to go off freely and breed on their own. The ecological circumstances in such a situation will be discussed in detail.

The dichotomy discussed therefore provides a theoretically straightforward test of whether a particular cooperative breeding system has been selected as a result of either predator defense and/or some aspect of the food resources it exploits. This test is the lifetime reproductive success of grouped *versus* ungrouped individuals. Unfortunately, it is almost impossible to obtain an unambiguous measure of lifetime reproductive success of individuals in any unbounded natural population. Instead, inconclusive measures of success, such as number of young fledged, or at best, number of young raised to independence, are usually substituted. With only one exception, these data present a consistent pattern: Reproductive success is inversely related to group size (*Tribonyx,* Maynard Smith and Ridpath, 1972; *Merops,* Fry, 1972a; *Dacelo,* Parry, 1973; *Turdoides,* Zahavi, 1974; *Aphelocoma* [calculated from data in Woolfenden, 1975]; *Passer,* Sappington, 1975; *Crotophaga,* Vehrencamp, 1978; *Turdoides,* Gaston, 1978a; *Melanerpes,* Koenig, 1978; an exception is *Malurus,* Rowley, 1965a). A negative correlation betwen group size and *per capita* reproductive success is not unique: A similar decrease in reproductive efficiency with increasing size of colonies has been observed in the social Hymenoptera (Michener, 1964). Of course, unless interyear variations are statistically controlled (e.g., Koenig, 1978), they may obscure a significant pattern in all but the longest studies. More importantly differential survivorship, through either direct predation or starvation, between the time at which reproductive "success" is measured and the time at which dispersal and breeding occur, may completely reverse the apparently consistent results found in the data cited above. That is, increased survivorship among broods or adults in larger groups as a result of either better predator defense or greater efficiency in resource exploitation (or both) might ultimately result in higher reproductive success per bird within groups despite their initial disadvantage as measured by simple fecundity.

There are at least two complicating factors in discerning the effect of larger groups on reproductive success. The first is differential territory quality: If large groups tend to live on superior territories, then any enhancement of reproductive success in large groups might reflect the quality of the territory rather than the effect of more individuals *per se* (Zahavi, 1974, 1976). The distinction between these two factors can be quite difficult to make in practice; thus, if large groups are merely those that, living on good territories, have produced many young in the past, and groups that have produced many young are defined as reproductively more successful, then the observation that large groups are more successful than small groups is circular. The positive correlation between group size and habitat quality in Hall's babblers (*Pomatostomus halli*), for example, might be the result of either increased productivity by larger groups or increased productivity of groups living on better territories with no direct positive effect of group size (Brown and Balda, 1977). Attempts to control for the importance of territory quality have now been made in several studies. Woolfenden (1975) compared four experienced pairs of Florida scrub jays and found that their reproductive success in years when they had helpers was greater than when they bred alone, suggesting that differential territory quality was not an important consideration. In the jungle babbler (*Turdoides striatus*), the grey-crowned babbler (*Pomatostomus temporalis*), and the acorn woodpecker, however, differential territory quality appears to be an important contributing factor to the variance in reproductive success of groups (Gaston, 1978a; Brown and Brown, this volume; Koenig, 1978; see also Ligon, this volume). In some cooperative species, therefore, differential territory quality decreases the probability that larger groups are inherently more successful on a *per capita* basis than smaller groups.

The second complicating factor is the differing amount of reproductive experience that different-sized groups are likely to have had. Similar to the effect of differential territory quality, this factor, unless controlled, will result in an overestimate of the true contribution of helpers to the reproductive success of breeding groups. This is because small groups, especially pairs, often consist of young, inexperienced birds. On the other hand, the presence of helpers in large groups are themselves good evidence that the group's breeding birds have bred successfully in prior years and are experienced. Woolfenden (1975) separated Florida scrub jay pairs breeding for the first time from pairs that had bred previously but had lost their offspring and found that prior experience enhanced reproductive success. Similarly in the acorn woodpecker (Koenig, 1978), groups with no turnover in breeding group membership during the prior year reproduced significantly better than those with turnover.

The data regarding reproductive success are thus ambiguous. Little information is as yet available with which to evaluate and compensate for the problems of differential territory quality, prior breeding experience, or differential survivorship in cooperative species; and analysis of the ecological conditions favoring cooperative breeding will remain speculative until these problems can be dealt with quantitatively. The observations, however, that in most cooperative breeders, groups are not more fecund per bird than are pairs and that at least in three instances the effects of group size on number of offspring surviving through their first year on a *per capita* basis is negative (*Aphelocoma* [data from Woolfenden, 1975]; *Corcorax*, Rowley, 1978; *Melanerpes*, Koenig, 1978) suggest that for many cooperative breeders, resource localization in some form (item 3, Table 17–1) may provide some or all of the selective basis for group living. By "some," we allow for the possibility that all three classes of factors (Table 17–1) may contribute to that selective basis. Here we stress the hypothesis of resource localization, and we risk the impression that one hypothesis of causality can apply with equal force to all three types of cooperative breeding, but this is unlikely, and our main goal here is to explore the possible selective role of resource localization in general terms. This is a useful and even necessary first step toward any ensuing insights as to its strengths and limitations. The idea that cooperative breeding is selected for by habitat limitation or saturation has recurred a number of times (Selander, 1964; Brown, 1974, 1978; Ricklefs, 1975; E. O. Wilson, 1975; Emlen, 1978; Gaston, 1978b), but it has never been examined in detail.

THE HYPOTHESIS OF HABITAT-FORCED COOPERATIVE BREEDING

We propose that among cooperative species there is a lack of areas that are ''marginal'' with regard to access to or amount of some limiting resource. This hypothesis is presented graphically in Figure 17–3 for the easily visualized case of a species with an all-purpose territory (for species that do not maintain such territories, substitute ''resource'' for ''area''). The abscissa ranks all inhabitable areas from worst to best; the ordinate represents the relative quality of the areas or, alternatively, the fitnesses of the individuals inhabiting each particular area. Given that the distribution of resources (the habitat gradient slope) follows curve A, the population surplus that is produced by individuals occupying the ''good'' areas is essentially sacrificed if these young disperse to ''bad'' areas, where their fitness would be very low. In contrast, given the habitat gradient slope B or C, a population surplus excluded from ''good'' areas can still move to more or less marginal areas good

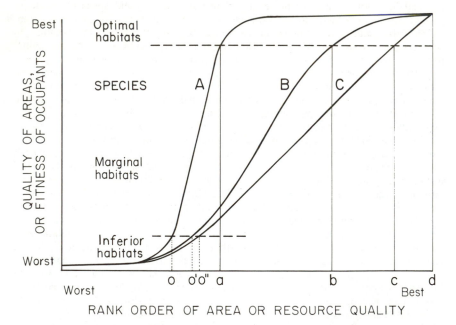

Figure 17–3.   A graphical representation of the hypothesis of habitat localization for the evolution of cooperative breeding in permanently territorial species (see text). Those (such as A) whose habitat gradient slopes are steep will show communal tendencies; those (B, C) whose habitat gradient slopes are flatter will not. The threshold for communal breeding will thus be some ratio of optimal to suboptimal habitats between gradient slopes of species A ($^{ad}/_{oa}$) and species B ($^{bd}/_{o'b}$).

enough to allow successful reproduction, at least in some areas at the higher ranks, and in any event serving as way stations before shifts to better areas are made as these become available. Because for curve A the "good" areas are all relatively very good, all territories within such habitat will usually be filled, and surplus young will be produced on a regular basis. The critical feature here is the ratio of "marginal" to "optimal" habitat. As this ratio decreases, opportunity to disperse decreases until young are almost entirely excluded from productive dispersal to unoccupied habitat. At this point they will be better off on the average to remain in their natal group, moving to another "good" area if and when a vacancy occurs. The current situation with post doctorals and the job market provides a useful analogy: The job market contracts; the optimal habitats fill; students "post-doc" with their academic parent or with academic relatives and do so longer while waiting to disperse to a suitable site to independently enhance their professional fitness.

This scenario thus provides what seems to us to be all the essential features of a potential cooperative system: A surplus of individuals effectively unable to disperse to unoccupied habitat and therefore ecologically "forced" to remain on their natal territories for an indeterminate length of time, during which period they may defer reproduction and assist in the raising of subsequent group offspring. We stress that the absolute size of the surplus is not important to this model: Even a small average number of surplus young might opt to remain as helpers if no marginal habitats exist to which they can disperse. Examples of resources that might be localized in a way to select for cooperative behavior are nest sites in hole-nesting species that do not excavate their own nest holes or the habitat itself in a territorial species. In acorn woodpeckers in California, for example, each group caches acorns in the fall in specially modified trees or granaries: the presence of these acorns affects both the breeding success of the group the following spring and the subsequent survivorship of the young during the summer (Koenig, 1978). Groups that do not have granaries in their territories rarely breed because such groups have few places to store acorns and, thus, are unlikely to have a supply of stored acorns lasting through the winter (MacRoberts and MacRoberts, 1976). As a result, the number of territories in an area suitable for breeding is to some extent directly limited by the number of granaries contained in that area, and the cooperation in this species possibly results from this interdependence of woodpeckers, granaries, and acorns (Koenig, 1978). Other forms of habitat or resource localization of this sort are suggested for numerous species in the literature by such observations as that a species has " ... extremely narrow habitat tolerances" (Woolfenden, 1973); or that in cooperative species in general, the " ... possibility of young birds entering the breeding population on their own is restricted" (Ricklefs, 1975); or that cooperative breeding seems to evolve in populations "... with few suitable vacant territories" (Brown, 1974).

On the other hand, we hypothesize that in non-cooperative species, surplus individuals produced by those inhabiting "optimal" habitat have a good probability of acquiring a territory that is marginal with either productively exploitable levels of resource supply or levels adequate simply for maintenance. Though their reproductive success may be below that of their parents as long as they occupy a marginal area, it would still often be higher than that of an individual opting to remain with his/her parents to "help" raise other siblings. Because both reproduction and survivorship among inhabitants of marginal areas should be less than those in optimal sites, areas of such habitat could act as a "sink" readily accommodating a variable surplus from year to year. Birds dispersing initially to these marginal areas would not be excluded from shifting to better areas in subsequent seasons as openings arose through attrition. The net effect for the individual would be an alternative superior to "helping."

An important feature of this hypothesis is that it is concerned with proximate rather than ultimate factors selecting for cooperative breeding. Most forms of the resource localization that we propose as a basis for cooperative breeding can ultimately be linked with other factors such as predator escape, food exploitation, or competition, all of which might affect the habitat/resource gradient curve in a way such that "marginal" habitat would be rare relative to "optimal" habitat. Thus, as discussed, a species that is extremely habitat specific and never found in habitat other than the preferred type might be forced to live in groups because of the absence of marginal habitat; but the ultimate cause of such a pattern could be the species' specialization on a food resource found only in the preferred habitat. In other words, the habitat gradient slope of a territorial species (or the comparable resource gradient slope of a species for any limited and localized resource, territorial or not) is ultimately determined by other factors, very often the exploitation pattern and/or the predation it experiences. In addition, for permanently resident species (which most known cooperative breeders are), subhabitats in the overall habitat area that are seasonally strongly varying and unpredictable will contribute to the steepness of the habitat gradient slope. Thus, while here emphasizing resource localization, we recognize that all three classes of factors (Table 17–1) can figure in the evolution of a particular cooperative breeding system.

PREDICTIONS

The hypothesis presented here, that cooperative behavior may be selected for on the basis of a limited and localized resource resulting in a low ratio of marginal to optimal habitat, permits the formulation of several predictions. These predictions are in several cases different from those which follow from the two alternative hypotheses (predation and characteristics of the food supply). Each of the predictions is considered in detail below and summarized in Table 17–2.

Choice of alternative strategies. The strategy of "helping" should, in all cases where resource localization is the primary selective force behind it, be adopted by an independent offspring only as a last resort strategy. Prospective helpers should always disperse and set up territories of their own whenever they can acquire enough of the critical resource to make their success likely. Data from two carefully studied species support this prediction. In Flor-

Table 17–2.   Predictions of three alternative hypotheses for the ecological factors selecting for cooperative breeding.

Variables	Hypotheses		
	Habitat or Resource Localization	Predation	Characteristics of the Food Supply
Per capita success of large groups compared to smaller groups	Less	Greater (increased survivorship)	Greater (greater fecundity and/or increased survivorship)
Strategic preference of independent individuals	Always leave and reproduce on own	Sometimes stay and help	Sometimes stay and help
Floaters	Not present	Not present	Not present
Cooperative breeding common in migratory species?	No	Yes	Yes
Variation in territory quality among groups	Less than in non-cooperative species	No prediction	No prediction

ida scrub jays, the most dominant helpers (and therefore those most likely to remain in the group if that option were preferred) are the first to disperse or annex part of their parents' territory to breed on their own (Woolfenden and Fitzpatrick, 1977). In acorn woodpeckers, groups are composed of two or more breeders along with their offspring from up to three or more years in the past. Our data suggest that group offspring are literally just "helpers," breeding in their natal groups only in special circumstances. Should the breeding bird(s) of one sex die or disappear in a group, they create a vacancy that is filled by former helpers from *another* group after a period of display lasting up to several days and involving 20 or more birds from numerous surrounding groups (Koenig, 1978). The opportunity to fill such a vacancy, and in doing so giving up one's status as a helper elsewhere, is clearly a desirable one. Both these examples show that helping *per se* is not the preferred option of non-breeders in the population. Neither pattern would necessarily be expected if these species were cooperative because of predator defense or some aspect of the food supply. In either of these alternative cases individuals might be expected to gain by remaining a member of their natal group rather than risking immigration to new territories of often unknown quality, even when open territories happened to be available.

A corollary to this prediction that "helping" is a last-resort strategy is that areas containing any significant amount of the critical resource should be occupied virtually at all times. Any areas vacant as a result of attrition or changing conditions should be filled rapidly or at least by the following breeding season by former helpers dispersing from their natal territories. This situation is well documented in the Australian magpie *Gymnorhina tibicen* (Carrick, 1972), Florida scrub jay (Woolfenden and Fitzpatrick, 1977), and acorn woodpecker (MacRoberts and MacRoberts, 1976; Koenig, 1978), and has been previously suggested by Brown (1974) and Ricklefs (1975).

Absence of floaters. In territorial cooperative species, "floaters" should be scarce or lacking altogether. This follows from the pattern of territory quality as proposed above: Birds would in general be better off to remain in established territories. Young, potential "floaters" are in effect absorbed within their natal groups rather than pushed out to find their territories all at once, as is normal for most non-cooperative species. The lack or near-lack of a floating population has been noted for several cooperative species (e.g., *Melanerpes*, MacRoberts and MacRoberts, 1976; *Aphelocoma*, Brown, 1974, Woolfenden and Fitzpatrick, 1977), where virtually all individuals are members of a territorial flock at all times. A similar lack of floaters is predicted by hypotheses 1 and 2 (Table 17–1) for cooperative breeding, however, because under either, lone individuals are presumably at a disadvantage compared to birds belonging to a group.

In contrast, a floating population in a non-cooperative species might evolve when extensive marginal habitat exists that is suitable at least for survival or both survival and breeding as in Californian populations of the scrub jay (Pitelka, ms). Under such a regime, young birds disperse and live non-territorially in marginal habitat where increased mobility and less time spent in territorial defense probably permit them to find vacancies in good habitat faster and over a wider area.

A unique combination of cooperative breeding habits concurrent with a large floating population occurs in only one species of which we are aware, the Australian magpie (Carrick, 1972). In this species, no breeding occurs in the non-territorial flocks, which apparently serve as temporary "clubs" pending openings in suitable breeding habitat. It is significant that successful breeding is accomplished only by birds living in territories spanning a narrow range of habitat quality, and that competition for such territories is intense. Possibly flocking of floaters superimposed on cooperative breeding may have been selected for if (1) competition for openings is heavy so that non-breeders must spend considerable time searching over a wide area, (2) selection (by factors of predation or food) for group living on non-breeders acts independently of cooperative breeding. If the latter, selection for flocking will be facilitated by non-breeding *per se*.

Territoriality. Cooperative breeding on the basis of habitat or resource localization is more likely in permanently territorial species than in migratory, seasonally territorial species. In migratory species, every individual has a new chance of acquiring a suitable territory each year, regardless of the actual fraction of individuals that successfully acquire such territories in any one year. In contrast, a dispersant in a permanently territorial species never gets equal opportunity to compete for sites with established territorial occupants; instead, it must wait and try to fill a vacancy whenever one occurs. This prediction does not hold for non-territorial but cooperative species (e.g., *Merops, Chaetura*) where the hypothesized localized resource is something other than space for an all-purpose territory. If, on the other hand, cooperative breeding were selected for on the basis of either predation or characteristics of the food supply, there would be no reason to expect there to be an absence of cooperative breeders among migratory, seasonally territorial species. The advantages of cooperative breeding are, after all, equally available to migratory and resident species. A correlation between cooperative breeding and permanent territoriality was pointed out by Brown (1974), but he hypothesized that it was the result of kinship (to be discussed) rather than localization of habitat suitable for breeding.

Quality of territories. Breeding territories should vary less in quality in cooperative species compared to closely related non-cooperative species. This follows once again from the difference in shape of the resource gradient slope (Figure 17–3). Specifically, we expect that the variance in reproductive success of breeding groups in cooperative species may be less than that of breeding pairs of a comparable but non-cooperative species, because in the latter a significant fraction of the population, at least in some years, would be breeding in marginal habitat. Such marginal habitat is, under our hypothesis, rarely available for breeding in cooperative species, and only in a very few species available for even temporary non-breeding occupancy (e.g., the Australian magpie). Considerable comparative demographic data will have to be acquired on both cooperative and comparable non-cooperative species before this hypothesis can be adequately tested.

KINSHIP AND KIN SELECTION

Kinship has been hypothesized to be important to the evolution of cooperative systems by several authors (e.g., Brown, 1974; Ricklefs, 1975). There are at least two ways in which kinship might act to promote group living. The first results from differences in breeding structure (Ricklefs, 1975). In any monogamous, outbred diploid population, parents are related to their offspring (and the siblings, on the average, to one another) by an identical amount ($r = .5$). Thus, selection based on relatedness *per se* is of little value in predicting which of two similarly monogamous species might be cooperative: In both cases, a potential helper is related by an equal amount to both his own offspring and to his younger siblings. This situation changes when the breeding system of a group becomes more complex, such as would occur if the breeding unit consisted of more than one male and/or female. In a group with a breeding unit of two females and a male, for example, two offspring have a 50 per cent chance of sharing the same mother (and thus being full sibs), and a 50 per cent chance of having different mothers (thus being half sibs if the two female breeders are unrelated, or $3/4$ sibs if the two females are full sisters). On the average, any two such siblings are less closely related to each other than are two siblings of a monogamous pair in which both offspring normally share the same two parents. Thus one might predict that given the choice of "helping" to raise younger siblings and dispersing to breed on his or her own, an offspring of this cooperative polygamous trio would be more likely to disperse, because he or she would not, on the average, be aiding individuals sharing as many of his genes as if his or her parents had been monogamous.

Nevertheless, "helping" by offspring occurs in species polygamous in exactly the way we have discussed. In Californian acorn woodpeckers, for example, two females frequently nest communally in a group. Yet offspring in this species usually stay and help raise subsequent broods of siblings for one or more years after fledging (Koenig, 1978). Other species with helpers whose breeding units are believed to be composed commonly of two or more females include the white-winged chough, *Corcorax melanorhamphus* (Rowley, 1978), the grey-crowned babbler (Councilman, 1977a), and pukeko *Porphyrio porphyrio* (Craig, 1975). Additionally, helping by offspring occurs in several cooperative species in which more than one male breeds in a group as well (*Melanerpes*, Koenig, 1978; *Tribonyx*, Ridpath, 1972a; and *Manorina*, Dow, 1978). Such complex mating systems can be very difficult to detect, and we further suspect that they may be more common and widespread among cooperative breeders than is presently believed. Thus, these species and others similar to them in breeding structure maintain helpers that aid in raising siblings who are *less* closely related to themselves than they would be in a typically monogamous species. The point is strengthened by the fact that of typically monogamous species, only a small percentage have helpers at the nest.

A second way in which relatedness might affect the probability of cooperative breeding in a species is by survivorship affecting the probability that parents might die and leave offspring from prior years to aid half-sibs (or less) rather than full sibs (Ricklefs, 1975). By this criterion alone, species with the highest survival rates might be expected to be cooperative, because their offspring are always most likely to be aiding full sibs in subsequent breeding seasons. Cooperative breeding, however is not found predominantly among the very largest, presumably longest-lived birds, but rather is found within a diversity of families representing a wide range of demographic patterns (Brown, 1978). In our view, increased longevity (like biased sex ratios and delayed maturity), to whatever extent it characterizes cooperative breeders, is more a result than a cause of selection for cooperative breeding.

We therefore find no good evidence that selection based on relatedness is useful in predicting conditions leading to cooperative breeding behavior in birds. Instead, the ultimate explanation for why a species lives in groups or has helpers at the nest must be sought among various ecological factors (e.g., Table 17–1).

Kin selection does become potentially important when considering why a specific behavior occurs in a cooperative species. Consider, for example, the two behaviors for which kin selection is most frequently invoked: (1) the cooperation of unisexual sibling units in certain cooperative species and (2) the phenomenon of ''helping'' by presumed nonreproductive individuals within a group,

1.   *Adult (sibling) cooperation.* This phenomenon has thus far been discussed in detail only in the Tasmanian native hen (Maynard Smith and Ridpath, 1972), the plain turkey *Meleagris gallopavo* (Watts and Stokes, 1971), and the acorn woodpecker (Koenig, 1978), but no doubt occurs at least occasionally in other cooperative species as well. Fraternal groups of two or more males both live and mate with a single female in the Tasmanian native hen; reportedly fraternal groups display communally in turkeys. In the acorn woodpecker, however, both males and females emigrate in unisexual sibling units. Maynard Smith and Ridpath (1972) discuss the hypothesis that such sibling cooperation is an example of kin selection. Their analysis is based on the finding that the reproductive success of trios compared to pairs was not enough to justify the persistence of such trios on that basis alone and proceeded to develop a model, later generalized by West-Eberhard (1975), relating the increase in reproductive success necessary for the behavior to be advantageous given that the cooperating males are or are not full siblings. If, however, this cooperative behavior has been selected for by resource or habitat localization, it is to be expected that the reproductive success per individual is less in trios than in pairs. In addition, it seems likely to us that under a regime of habitat localization, competition among ''surplus'' individuals to fill vacancies occurring through the deaths of birds in ''good'' areas might be intense. If such competition occurs, entrance into a good area or access to the limited resource might be

greatly enhanced when more than one individual cooperates to acquire it. Thus, cooperating groups might be selected for not on the basis of any increased reproductive success *per se*, but rather on the basis of their increased likelihood of being able to acquire or maintain access to the limiting resource, and therefore of reproducing at all. Data for both the Tasmanian native hen and the plain turkey lend some support to this interpretation: In the former, 22 first-year groups censused over three years by Ridpath (1972b) consisted of 15 pairs and 7 (32 per cent) multi-male groups (mostly trios); whereas of 46 mature groups, 22 were pairs and 24 (52 per cent) multi-male groups. There are at least two possibilities which could account for this increasing proportion of trios. First, many groups starting out as pairs might later be joined by a third bird whose mate had died. Though no specific mention is made of the fate of paired birds whose mates die, the stability of group composition reported by Ridpath (1972b) argues against this hypothesis. A second explanation is that multi-male trios are more persistent or successful than pairs, possibly because they are able to defend their territories better or because the territories acquired by such groups are superior to those settled by pairs in the first place. This is an ''advantage'' distinct from those listed under items 1 and 2, Table 17–1. Such a situation would provide considerable selective pressure for cooperation between two or more birds when attempting to acquire a territory regardless of the genetic relatedness among the cooperating individuals. And the possibility remains that a Tasmanian native hen would still be better off if he could obtain and maintain a territory on his own without sharing it with a second male.

A similar argument may be made for the plain turkey: In this species, numerous possibly fraternal groups display together at each lekking ground. There is a distinct inter-group and intra-group dominance hierarchy, and usually only the dominant individual(s) in the most dominant group mates. This elaborate dominance system is apparently largely determined within the juvenile flocks, where the fraternal group with the largest number of members usually wins dominant status. There is thus a considerable advantage to being a group member, operating above and beyond that accruing as a result of the individuals within groups apparently being brothers.

As discussed by Ridpath (1972b), cooperation between males requires a level of mutual tolerance and familiarity that is far more likely to be achieved between individuals who have grown up together in the same family group than between individuals from separate family groups. This being the case, the fact that cooperating multi-male units are often composed of siblings may be largely a result of the intimacy of birds having grown up together rather than of any genetic advantage gained by cooperation among relatives. In a sense, then, the brotherhood may be a coincidence that gives two comfortably associated individuals an advantage over singletons; two affiliated foster brothers would enjoy the same advantage. We venture this point notwithstanding the generally accepted view that kin knowledge is nearly always incidental or circumstantial.

Further support for this line of argument comes from cases of mate sharing. The hypothesis that certain ecological situations favor a bird sharing a mate with an unrelated individual has been put forth convincingly for the evolution of polygyny (Verner and Willson, 1966; Orians, 1969; Wittenberger, 1976; Pleszczynska, 1978), a situation not meeting the criteria for cooperative breeding but nonetheless sharing many features with the type of male–male cooperation found in Tasmanian native hens and the female–female cooperation found in acorn woodpeckers (Koenig, 1978). Furthermore, evidence in some species suggests that adult cooperating groups may consist primarily of unrelated individuals. In the long-tailed manakin (*Chiroxiphia linearis*) males form long-term bonds and cooperate in performing elaborate displays to attract females. Though proof is lacking, the small clutch size, low reproductive success, and dispersal pattern of this species suggest that the males in cooperating groups are not likely to be closely related (Foster, 1977). Additional evidence, though also not conclusive, suggests that adult females in groups of several cooperative breeders may not be related (*Turdoides*, Zahavi, 1974; *Crotophaga*, Vehrencamp, 1978; *Phoeniculus*, Ligon and Ligon, 1978).

We suggest that a more profitable approach to the question of the importance of kinship would be to look for evidence of individuals, in the Tasmanian native hen, for example, who *avoid* forming a multi-male group if unrelated. If the competitive environment makes union of unrelated birds advantageous, the absence of such unions would provide evidence that in fact kinship is critical to the evolution of cooperation.

2. Helpers at the nest. Many of the "helpers at the nest" that have thus far been investigated are usually the former offspring of the breeding pair and therefore are generally "helping" to raise their full siblings. This, as we have seen, has led several authors to conclude that such helping evolved through kin selection. But again, in review, the non-dispersal of young may result from ecological considerations. Group living may be either individually desirable (items 1 and 2, Table 17–1) or individually necessary through the inferior alternative of dispersal resulting from resource localization (item 3). Non-dispersal is thus viewed as independent of genetic relatedness among the birds involved.

Even for a non-dispersing youngster, however, there are numerous potential costs to helping, and there are similar potential costs to birds who accept help (Orians et al., 1977). Despite these possible disadvantages on both sides, young remaining for a year or more in their natal territories in group-living species are remarkably consistent in their tendency to help at the nest (Brown, 1975). Woolfenden and Fitzpatrick (1978) hypothesize that the helping done by surplus birds in the Florida scrub jay is a selfish act that increases their own fitness by making the group territory (whose size is correlated with the size of the group) larger, thereby increasing their own probability of eventually being able to annex a part of it for their own use. In some situations, it is possible that by helping, a bird is permitted access to communal resources that would otherwise be denied to him by more dominant individuals (for a possible example, see Craig, 1976). Such a situation might constitute a form of reciprocal altruism (Trivers, 1971), a phenomenon again not dependent upon relatedness between participants though beset by more complexities than kin selection. Reciprocity as an important factor selecting for helping at the nest irrespective of genetic relatedness has recently been advocated by Gaston (1978b) and supported by data from the green woodhoopoe (Ligon and Ligon, 1978) and the white-fronted bee-eater (Emlen, this volume). Certainly, at the very least, helpers are likely to gain valuable experience that aids them later during their own reproductive careers (Skutch, 1961; Rowley, 1965b; Lack, 1968; Fry, 1972a; Ricklefs, 1975; West-Eberhard, 1975), though this effect has yet to be demonstrated in any natural population.

An additional possibility is that "helper" males may occasionally cuckold the alpha male and "helper" females may sometimes parasitize the alpha female. Both would be most likely when the individuals involved are not related, inasmuch as within a family group there would be a considerable risk of inbreeding. Thus, this factor is not likely to be important in the extended families of many permanently territorial cooperative species but could provide a partial rationale for "helping" among nomadic or migratory species in which groups may not always be composed of family units. In *Merops bulocki,* a cooperatively breeding, colonial bee-eater, two females may lay in the same nest, and Fry (1975) suggests that the clutches of these second females, who otherwise behave as typical "helpers," are, in fact, parasitic. Fry (1972b) further observed occasional copulations between male "helpers" and female breeders. If cuckoldry by "helper" males is sometimes successful, their confidence of paternity in the young they are helping to raise, however small, might be enough to select for typical (though probably reduced) parental behavior in what otherwise seems like a non-breeding auxiliary. In this regard, note that in species with male–male cooperating pairs, both males usually copulate with the female, resulting most likely in the situation where the confidence of paternity is fairly evenly split between them (*Tribonyx,* Ridpath, 1972b; *Buteo,* de Vries, 1975; *Parabuteo,* Mader, 1975). Thus, neither male is a "helper"; both are merely tending offspring who are presumably partially their own.

In contrast to the foregoing is the hypothesis that "helping" is a kin-selected trait by virtue of the relatedness generally found between helpers and the birds they are helping (Lack, 1968; Brown, 1974, 1975; Ricklefs, 1975; West-Eberhard, 1975). We agree that this is a viable hypothesis but feel that merely showing that "helpers" are usually related to the individuals they assist does not prove that kin selection is necessary and sufficient. It may, however, have a significant additive evolutionary role if helping tends to be restricted to kin even if other factors trigger the evolution of helping. Evidence for or against our hypothesis seems to us to be most objectively sought in those cooperative breeders that are non-territorial, nomadic, or otherwise very different in social organization during the non-breeding season. If kin selection is not a critical factor in the evolution of helping, then we can expect in such species that helpers will usually be unrelated.

At this time, we are aware of only two studies fitting the foregoing specifications and allowing an evaluation of the relative frequency of related *versus* unrelated helpers. In the white-fronted bee-eater (*Merops bullockoides*), Emlen (this volume) suggests that helpers are frequently relatives of those they help. But results from a study of house sparrows (*Passer domesticus*) in Mississippi (Sappington, 1975, 1977) differ. They live in loose colonies in which helpers are commonly observed. Of 59 helpers of known origin, only 16 (27 per cent) aided one or both their parents. Meanwhile, 36 (61 per cent) aided birds in their natal colony other than their parents, and 7 (12 per cent) were individuals from outside the colony itself. The transient pair bonding and sequential polygyny frequently observed in the population further decrease the average genetic relatedness that might be expected between helpers and beneficiaries. Thus, preliminary evidence indicates that the high genetic relatedness commonly observed within flocks of permanently territorial cooperative breeders may be of considerably less importance to the evolution of helping at the nest than has been commonly assumed.

The crux of the kin selection issue is whether or not helping at the nest or sibling cooperation reduces the Darwinian fitnesses of the "helpers" (the altruists). At present, data do not permit a clear answer. Even if they did, several alternative hypotheses exist and cannot, as yet, be rejected. One such alternative, that of reciprocal altruism, was mentioned above. By helping, an individual may gain access to communal resources that would otherwise be denied to him by the dominant group members. Such a reciprocal arrangement assumes no necessary relatedness between individuals.

Another alternative is that of parental manipulation when cooperating individuals are related. Alexander (1974) points out that "If the individuals ... are not receiving genetic benefits overcompensating their altruism to siblings, then the genetic relatedness of the siblings may be incidental to their altruism, since they are all similarly related to the individual being helped, i.e., the mother." This is potentially applicable to both behaviors discussed, that is, siblings cooperating and offspring helping their parents. We can think of no easy way to test the hypothesis of parental manipulation, however, except by examining the asymmetries or conflicts that may exist in such altruistic behaviors that might be attributable to the differing genetic interests of those involved (Trivers, 1974). One such conflict, for example, might arise from the probability of aiding only half sibs rather than full sibs, in which case the related parent might be expected to "manipulate" his or her offspring to act more altruistically toward their half sibs than their actual genetic relatedness would justify (Hamilton, 1964). Difficulties in separating the potential effects of kin selection and parential manipulation are discussed fully by West-Eberhard (1975).

Presently a theoretical base is being built for the idea of altruistic traits evolving via Darwinian selection among individuals not necessarily related (Matessi and Jayakar, 1976; D. S. Wilson, 1975, 1977). These models are based on a formulation of group selection that might result in the evolution of individually disadvantageous but group-advantageous traits. One crucial condition to be met for these models to be effective is small deme size (Matessi and Jayakar, 1976), which most cooperative breeders at least superficially possess. Despite this and other limitations of these models (Alexander and Borgia, 1978), their potential importance to this discussion is that they provide a mechanism by which altruistic traits might evolve among unrelated individuals. Nonetheless, the conditions for the evolution of altruism are certainly less stringent when cooperating individuals are close relatives than when they are distantly related (Matessi and Jayakar, 1976; West-Eberhard, 1975). This means that one must be very cautious before drawing a link between the empirical observation that cooperating individuals are related and an evolutionary mechanism based on kinship. Given a choice, an individual should always cooperate with a close relative rather than a less closely related individual (Hamilton, 1964; Alexander, 1974; West-Eberhard, 1975). But when the possibility for close relatives to associate occurs frequently, as it does in many cooperative species, the fact that beneficial interactions occur between related individuals is not proof that their evolution is dependent on such kinship. All hypotheses must be carefully evaluated and examined before conclusions can be objectively drawn on the role or importance of any one of them to the behavior and the species in question. And yet more realistically, considerable effort and time will be needed to sort out critically the ecological effects in natural populations we emphasize here as foundational to an understanding of the diversity and evolution of cooperative breeding systems in birds.

SUMMARY

Cooperative breeders are species in which three or more individuals assist in the production of young at a single nest. Among birds, three common forms of cooperative breeding have been described: "Helping at the nest," adult (sibling) cooperation, and cooperative courtship. The ecological bases for these behaviors are unclear. Here we discuss the hypothesis that resource localization and, in the particular case of many permanently territorial cooperative species, habitat localization may provide the selective background for these types of group living. We propose a model for cooperative breeding postulating a relative scarcity of "marginal" habitats compared to "optimal" habitats. This low ratio of marginally occupiable habitats to optimal habitats selects against the dispersal and independent breeding effort of young birds after the short period it takes them to attain self-sufficiency. Accordingly, they associate with territorially established birds, usually their parents. An important prediction from this hypothesis is that reproductive success of groups compared to pairs (or larger groups compared to smaller groups) need not be greater on a *per capita* basis. Preliminary evidence in numerous species now supports this prediction. Other predictions are discussed as they relate to competing hypotheses for the ecological bases of cooperative breeding.

The evolutionary mechanisms responsible for some of the apparently altruistic traits observed in most cooperative species are also obscure. In particular, the hypothesis that kin selection is an integral factor in the evolution of either sibling cooperation or helping at the nest requires careful re-evaluation. In any case, kin selection itself is unlikely to be an important cause of group living but may be an additive or bonus factor contributing to the evolution of particular altruistic behaviors within groups. The relative importance of selfish individual selection in cooperative systems is easily overlooked, but it is likely to be at least as important as kin selection in the evolution of many cooperative behaviors. Other mechanisms potentially important and in need of critical evaluation as they pertain to avian breeding systems are the hypotheses of reciprocal altruism, parental manipulation, and group selection.

ACKNOWLEDGMENTS

We would like to thank J. P. Myers, D. B. Wake, R. L. Mumme, F. S. Dobson, and especially P. W. Sherman for critically reading this manuscript. R. D. Alexander suggested the "post-doc" analogy. J. N. Sappington allowed access to his unpublished data. R. W. Dexter also provided information. We are indebted to Dr. John Davis for use of facilities and other assistance at the Hastings Natural History Reservation. Our work on acorn wood-peckers has been aided by an NSF doctoral dissertation improvement grant. Later phases of the preparation of this paper were supported by NSF grant DEB-78-08764.

REFERENCES

Alexander, R. D. 1974. The evolution of social behavior. *Ann. Rev. Ecol. Syst.* 5: 325–383.

————, and G. Borgia. 1978. Group selection, altruism, and the levels of organization of life. *Ann. Rev. Ecol. Syst.* 9: 449–474.

Brown, J. L. 1974. Alternate routes to sociality in jays—with a theory for the evolution of altruism and communal breeding. *Amer. Zool.* 14: 63–80.

————. 1975. Helpers among Arabian Babblers, *Turdoides squamiceps. Ibis* 117: 243–244.

————. 1978. Avian communal breeding systems. *Ann. Rev. Ecol. Syst.* 9: 123–155.

————, and R. P. Balda. 1977. The relationship of habitat quality to group size in Hall's Babbler (*Pomatostomus halli*). *Condor* 79: 312–320.

————, and G. H. Orians. 1970. Spacing patterns in mobile organisms. *Ann. Rev. Ecol. Syst.* 1: 239–262.

Carrick, R. 1972. Population ecology of the Australian Black-backed Magpie, Royal Penguin, and Silver Gull. *U.S. Dept. Int. Wildl. Res. Rep.* 2: 41–99.

Councilman, J. J. 1977a. Groups of the Grey-crowned Babbler in central southern Queensland. *Bird Behaviour (Babbler)* 1: 14–22.

————. 1977b. A comparison of two populations of the Grey-crowned Babbler (Part 1). *Bird Behaviour* 1: 43–82.

Craig, J. L. 1975. Co-operative breeding of Pukeko. *Emu* 74 (suppl.): 308.

————. 1976. An inter-territorial hierarchy: an advantage for a subordinate in a communal territory. *Z. Tierpsychol.* 42: 200–205.

Crook, J. H. 1965. The adaptive significance of avian social organizations. *Symp. Zool. Soc. London* 14: 181–218.

Dow, D. D. 1978. Reproductive behavior of the Noisy Miner, a communally breeding honeyeater. *Living Bird* 16 : 163–185.

Emlen, S. T. 1978. The evolution of cooperative breeding in birds. Pp. 245–281 in J. R. Krebs and N. D. Davies (eds.), *Behavioural Ecology: An Evolutionary Approach.* Blackwell Scientific Publications, Oxford.

Foster, M. S. 1977. Odd couples in manakins: a study of social organization and cooperative breeding in *Chiroxiphia linearis. Amer. Nat.* 111: 845–853.

Fry, C. H. 1972a. The social organization of Bee-eaters (Meropidae) and co-operative breeding in hot climate birds. *Ibis* 114: 1–14.

————. 1972b. The biology of African Bee-eaters. *Living Bird* 11: 75–112.

————. 1975. Cooperative breeding in Bee-eaters and longevity as an attribute of group-breeding birds. *Emu* 74 (suppl.): 308–309.

————. 1977. The evolutionary significance of cooperative breeding in birds. Pp. 127–135 *in* B. Stonehouse and C. M. Perrins (eds.), *Evolutionary Ecology.* University Park Press, Baltimore.

Gaston, A. J. 1978a. Demography of the Jungle Babbler, *Turdoides striatus. J. Anim. Ecol.* 47: 845–870.

————. 1978b. The evolution of group territorial behavior and cooperative breeding. *Amer. Nat.* 112: 1091–1100.

Hamilton, W. D. 1964. The genetical evolution of social behavior. I, II. *J. Theor. Biol.* 7: 1–52.

Hoogland, J. L., and P. W. Sherman. 1976. Advantages and disadvantages of Bank Swallow (*Riparia riparia*) coloniality. *Ecol. Mono.* 46: 33–58.

Jenni, D. A., and G. Collier. 1972. Polyandry in the American Jacana (*Jacana spinosa*). *Auk* 89: 743–765.

Koenig, W. D. 1978. Ecological and evolutionary aspects of cooperative breeding in Acorn Woodpeckers of central coastal California. Ph. D. diss., Univ. California, Berkeley.

Lack, D. 1968. *Ecological Adaptations for Breeding in Birds.* Methuen, London.

Ligon, J. D., and S. H. Ligon. 1978. Communal breeding in Green Woodhoopocs as a case for reciprocity. *Nature* (London) 276: 496–498.

MacRoberts, M. H., and B. R. MacRoberts. 1976. Social organization and behavior of the Acorn Woodpecker in central coastal California. *Ornith. Mono.* 21: 1–115.

Mader, W. J. 1975. Extra adults at Harris' Hawk nests. *Condor* 77: 482–485.

Matessi, C., and S. D. Jayakar. 1976. Conditions for the evolution of altruism under Darwinian selection. *Theor. Pop. Biol.* 9: 360–387.

Maynard Smith, J., and M. G. Ridpath. 1972. Wife-sharing in the Tasmanian Native Hen, *Tribonyx mortierii:* a case of kin selection? *Amer. Nat.* 106: 447–452.

Michener, C. D. 1964. Reproductive efficiency in relation to colony size in hymenopteran societies. *Insectes Sociaux* 11: 317–341.

Orians, G. H. 1969. On the evolution of mating systems in birds and mammals. *Amer. Nat.* 103: 589–603.

———, C. E. Orians, and K. J. Orians. 1977. Helpers at the nest in some Argentine blackbirds. Pp. 137–151 in B. Stonehouse and C. M. Perrins (eds.), *Evolutionary Ecology.* University Park Press, Baltimore.

Parry, V. 1973. The auxiliary social system and its effect on territory and breeding in Kookaburras. *Emu* 73: 81–100.

Pleszczynska, W. K. 1978. Microgeographic prediction of polygyny in the Lark Bunting. *Science* 201: 935–937.

Ricklefs, R.E. 1975. The evolution of co-operative breeding in birds. *Ibis* 117: 531–534.

Ridpath, M. G. 1972a. The Tasmanian Native Hen, *Tribonyx mortierii*. I. Patterns of behavior. *CSIRO Wildl. Res.* 17: 1–51.

———. 1972b. The Tasmanian Native Hen, *Tribonyx mortierii*. II. The individual, the group, and the population. *CSIRO Wildl. Res.* 17: 53–90.

Rowley, I. 1965a. The life history of the Superb Blue Wren, *Malurus cyaneus*. *Emu* 64: 251–297.

———. 1965b. White-winged Choughs. *Aust. Nat. Hist.* 15: 81–85.

———. 1978. Communal activities among White-winged Choughs, *Corcorax melanorhamphus*. *Ibis* 120: 178–197.

Sappington, J. N. 1975. Cooperative breeding in the House Sparrow (*Passer domesticus*). Ph. D. diss., Mississippi State University.

———. 1977. Breeding biology of House Sparrows in North Mississippi. *Wilson Bull.* 89: 300–309.

Selander, R. K. 1964. Speciation in wrens of the genus *Campylorhynchus*. *Univ. Calif. Publ. Zool.* 74: 1–305.

Skutch, A. F. 1961. Helpers among birds. *Condor* 63: 198–226.

Stallcup, J. A., and G. E. Woolfenden. 1978. Family status and contributions to breeding by Florida scrub jays. *Anim. Behav.* 26: 1144–1156.

Trivers, R. L. 1971. The evolution of reciprocal altruism. *Quart. Rev. Biol.* 46: 35–57.

———. 1974. Parent-offspring conflict. *Amer. Zool.* 14: 249–264.

Vehrencamp, S. L. 1977. Relative fecundity and parental effort in communal nesting Anis, *Crotophaga sulcirostris*. *Science* 197: 403–405.

———. 1978. The adaptive significance of communal nesting in Groove-billed Anis (*Crotophaga sulcirostris*). *Behav. Ecol. Sociobiol.* 4: 1–33.

Verner, J., and M. F. Willson, 1966. The influence of habitats on mating systems of North American passerine birds. *Ecol.* 47: 143–147.

de Vries, Tj. 1975. The breeding biology of the Galapagos Hawk, *Buteo galapagoensis. Le Gerfaut* 65: 29–57.

Watts, C. R., and A. W. Stokes. 1971. The social order of Turkeys. *Sci. Amer.* 224: 112–118.

West-Eberhard, M. J. 1975. The evolution of social behavior by kin selection. *Quart. Rev. Biol.* 50: 1–33.

Wilson, D. S. 1975. A theory of group selection. *Proc. Nat. Acad. Sci.* 72: 143–146.

———. 1977. Structured demes and the evolution of group-advantageous traits. *Amer. Nat.* 111: 157–185.

Wilson, E. O. 1975. *Sociobiology: The New Synthesis.* Harvard Univ. Press, Cambridge.

Wittenberger, J. F. 1976. The ecological factors selecting for polygyny in altricial birds. *Amer. Nat.* 110: 779–799.

Woolfenden, G. E. 1973. Nesting and survival in a population of Florida scrub jays. *Living Bird* 12: 25–49.

———. 1975. Florida scrub jay helpers at the nest. *Auk* 92: 1–15.

––––––. 1976. Co-operative breeding in American birds. *Proc. 16th Int. Ornith. Congr.* [1974]: 674–684.

––––––, and J. W. Fitzpatrick. 1977. Dominance in the Florida scrub jay. *Condor* 79: 1-12.

––––––, and J. W. Fitzpatrick. 1978. The inheritance of territory in group-breeding birds. *BioScience* 28: 104–108.

Yom-Tov, Y., G. M. Dunnet, and A. Anderson. 1974. Intraspecific nest parasitism in the Starling *Sturnus vulgaris. Ibis* 116: 87–90.

Zahavi, A. 1974. Communal nesting in the Arabian Babbler. A case of individual selection. *Ibis* 116: 84–87.

––––––. 1976. Co-operative nesting in Eurasian birds. *Proc. 16th Int. Ornith. Congr.* [1974]: 685–693.

V

Social Behavior
and
Life Histories in Mammals

18.

Nepotism and Cooperative Breeding in the Black-tailed Prairie Dog (Sciuridae: *Cynomys ludovicianus*)

John L. Hoogland

INTRODUCTION

Cooperative breeding occurs whenever certain individuals relinquish their own breeding and assist the breeding of others (Brown, 1974, 1978). As emphasized by Emlen (1978), explaining cases of apparent altruism (Alexander, 1974; Wilson, 1975) such as cooperative breeding is one of the most important issues faced by evolutionary biologists. Cooperative breeding is especially common among the social insects (Wilson, 1971) but also occurs in numerous vertebrates. Studies of cooperatively breeding species have usually shown that nonbreeding, cooperating individuals ("helpers at the nest" or "alloparents") are genetically related to the breeding adults. Theories to explain cooperative breeding have nonetheless been numerous and diversified (e.g., Fry, 1972; Gaston, 1976, 1978; Zahavi, 1976; Brown, 1978; Emlen, 1978; Woolfenden and Fitzpatrick, 1978). In this report, I investigate cooperative breeding in the black-tailed prairie dog (*Cynomys ludovicianus*). My purpose is fourfold: (a) to examine the genetic relationships among the members of a cooperatively breeding unit known as a *coterie,* (b) to quantify alarm calling and both intra- and inter- coterie interactions (fights, chases, allogrooming, etc.), and to determine if these behaviors involve preferential treatment of genetic relatives, (c) to examine the effect of coterie size on annual reproductive success of adult males and females, and (d) to examine several relevant hypotheses that might explain the observed relationship between coterie size and the annual reproductive success of adult females.

MATERIALS AND METHODS

The Study Animal

Black-tailed prairie dogs are large (700–1500 g), diurnal, colonial rodents of the squirrel family (Sciuridae) and are among the most social of the vertebrates. Black-tails live in short grass prairies at altitudes of 900–1600 m, and are found in a narrow western belt of North America that extends from southern Canada to central Texas. Males and females of northern latitudes do not first breed until at least two years old; in any particular year, numerous adults (≥ 2 years old) of both sexes do not breed (see below). Sexual dimorphism is slight, with males being approximately 5 per cent–10 per cent larger than females. Unlike prairie dogs of the subgenus *Leucocrossuromys,* black-tails (subgenus *Cynomys*) do not hibernate. Breeding in northern latitudes occurs in February and March. The usual litter size at these same latitudes is 1–5 ($\overline{X} \pm SD = 2.90 \pm 1.07; N = 83$), and the first emergences of weaned juveniles from their natal burrows occur in May and June. An accurate life table has yet to be computed for black-tails. Survivorship during the first year is approximately 50 per cent for both sexes; females that survive the first year commonly live for 5–6 years, and males that survive the first year commonly live for 3–4 years (Hoogland, unpubl.).

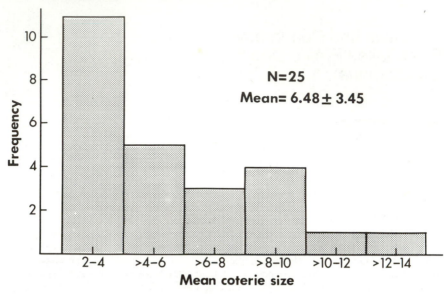

Figure 18–1.   Histogram of mean coterie sizes at the study ward.

Unlike ground-dwelling mammals such as pocket gophers (Geomyidae) and moles (Talpidae), black-tails spend much of their time aboveground; during sunny weather at temperatures above 0°C, for example, individuals spend as much as 80 per cent–95 per cent of their time aboveground. Thus, numerous behavioral interactions (probably most of them) can be observed easily.

The typical black-tail colony is usually subdivided into two or more *wards* (King, 1955), or subcolonies, by a hill, a row of trees, a small stream, etc. Residents of one ward can sometimes see or hear residents of an adjacent ward, but movements and communications between wards are uncommon. Ward densities from studies of marked individuals range from 7.52 to 32.7 adults and yearlings per hectare (ha), with a mean $\pm$ *SD* of 14.8 $\pm$ 9.67 (Hoogland, 1977, 1981a).

The most conspicuous feature of the black-tail social system is the organization of individuals within wards into units called coteries (King, 1955). Coterie size ranges from 2 to 15 ($\overline{X} \pm SD$ = 6.48 $\pm$ 3.45; see Figure 18–1), and the "average" coterie contains 1.33 $\pm$ 0.73 adult males, 3.23 $\pm$ 2.04 adult females, and 1.84 $\pm$ 2.05 yearlings of both sexes (this study; c.f. King, 1955). The number of (a) adult males (see below and Figure 18–2b), (b) adult females (r = .800, P <.001), and (c) yearlings (r = .211; P = .038) all increase directly with coterie size. As will be discussed, black-tails are generally friendly to coterie members and hostile to noncoterie members (King, 1955, 1959; Tileston and Lechleitner, 1966; Smith et al., 1973). Coterie members restrict essentially all of their activities to a well-defined *coterie territory*. The mean size of a coterie territory is 0.26 $\pm$ 0.12 ha (N = 25; c.f. King, 1955). Each territory contains 30–100 burrow entrances; some of these entrances within the same territory are connected by underground tunnels, but entrances of different coterie territories are never connected. As noted by Wilson (1975), a striking feature of the black-tail coterie territory is that it remains constant in size from year to year and from generation to generation.

Within a coterie, yearlings of both sexes and many of the $\geq$2-year-old females do not breed in any particular year. Nonbreeding adults and yearlings usually assist the breeders with territorial defense (King, 1955), and such "helpers" interact amicably (as will be described) with juveniles that have recently emerged from their natal burrows. Brown (1978) argued that "The diagnostic feature [of cooperative breeding] is the presence of individuals in a social unit who behave as parents but are not the genetic parents of the offspring whom they aid." [and] " ... diagnostic behaviors include nestbuilding, incubation, feeding off-spring, and defense of the territory." I have chosen to label black-tails as cooperative breeders even though black-tail helpers do not assist breeders to the same degree as do helpers in most avian cooperative breeders. For example, unlike most avian helpers (e.g., Rowley, 1965; Woolfenden, 1975), black-tail helpers do not assist with the feeding of small juveniles: a black-tail mother does not allow other individuals to enter the burrow system containing her unweaned young (King, 1955; Hoogland, unpubl.), and communal nursing (e.g., as observed by Bertram, 1976, in Lions, *Panthera leo*) does not occur. Of Brown's (1978) list of diagnostic behaviors, black-tail helpers show only defense of the territory.

Black-tail coloniality involves both costs and benefits. Probable costs include in-creased aggression and increased transmission of diseases and ectoparasites (Hoogland, 1979a). The most important benefit of black-tail coloniality is probably increased protec-tion from predators such as coyotes (*Canis latrans*), bobcats (*Lynx rufus*), badgers (*Taxidea taxus*), long-tailed weasels (*Mustela frenata*), black-footed ferrets (*Mustela nigripes*), and various birds of prey (*Aquila* spp., *Buteo* spp., and *Falco* spp.). Individuals of large wards detect predators more quickly than do individuals of smaller wards (Hoogland, 1977, 1981a), and also are able to devote proportionately less time to individual alertness (i.e., watching for predators) and proportionately more time to feeding (Hoogland, 1979b, 1981a).

In 1978, five field assistants and I attempted to figure out the black-tail mating system. Specifically, we attempted to determine if a female copulates only with the male(s) within her coterie. Unfortunately, almost all copulations occured underground, so it was difficult to specify exactly when a particular female copulated. However, three behaviors often made it possible to identify copulating pairs: (a) Just before and during estrus, a female was unusually hostile to any conspecific, even one of her own coterie, that approached too closely (c.f. King, 1955, and Figures 4a and 4b). (b) While sexually receptive (for 2–3 hours in late afternoon), an estrous female went into a burrow with a single adult male for 10–30 min before emerging and eventually submerging into a burrow for the night. Before submerging for the night, a nonestrous female never went into a burrow with an adult male for more than a few seconds. (c) Just before and/or just after submerging with an estrous female for 10–30 min, an adult male usually gave a special "mating call" that was heard only rarely at other times (and was never heard after all the females had bred). The single copulation that was observed aboveground lasted 16.5 min and was characterized by behav-iors (a) and (c). Observations from 22 estrous females from 15 coteries indicate that 17 of the females copulated only with a single male within the home coterie, 2 copulated both with a single male within the home coterie and with a single male from an adjacent coterie, and 3 copulated only with a single male from an adjacent coterie. That is, 19 of the 22 estrous females (86.4 per cent) probably copulated at least once with a male within the home coterie. Put another way: the resident adult male(s) copulated at least once with at least one of his females in 14 of the 15 coteries containing estrous females (93.3 per cent). These data suggest (a) that an estrous female usually copulates with an adult male within her home coterie, and (b) that an adult male, therefore, usually sires most or all of the offspring within his coterie during any particular year. Paternities inferred from behavioral observa-tions are being checked by an electrophoretic analysis of blood samples taken from all the adults and juveniles at the study ward in 1978; this analysis has not yet been completed.

The Study Ward

The study ward is located in Wind Cave National Park, Hot Springs, South Dakota, at a distance of approximately 10 km from King's (1955) study ward. The study ward is approximately rectangular in shape, with a length of 500 m, a width of 150 m, and an area of 6.60 ha (see Hoogland, 1977). For 1976–1978, the mean number of adults and yearlings was 134 ± 11.5, the mean number of weaned juveniles was 83.7 ± 15.6, and the mean number of coteries was 24.0 ± 1.00. In May of 1976, there were 1,591 burrow entrances at the study ward, and this number varied by less than 1 per cent–2 per cent over the next two years (see also King, 1955, and Tileston and Lechleitner, 1966). Each year, all but five of the coterie territories were bound on at least one edge by peripheral, unused habitat: thus I made no attempt to examine possible effects of intraward position (e.g., center vs. edge) on individual reproductive success. The closest ward to the study ward is 0.5 km away, and the next closest ward is approximately 1.5 km away. Other details of the study ward will be discussed.

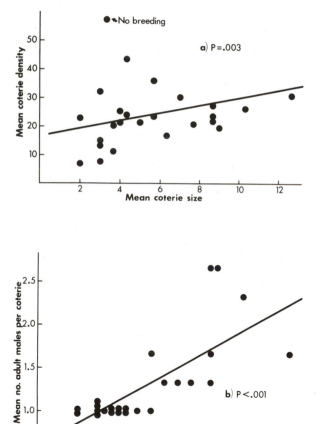

Figure 18–2.   Relationship between mean coterie size and (a) mean coterie density (the mean number of adults and yearlings per ha) and (b) the mean number of adult males per coterie. The coterie with the highest mean coterie density was the only coterie in which there was no breeding in either 1976, 1977, or 1978.

Methods and Procedures

My methods for live-trapping, handling, and marking prairie dogs are outlined elsewhere (Hoogland, 1977, 1979a).

As indicated above, black-tails usually do not breed until at least two years old. Actually, first breeding for both sexes can occur as early as February or March of the second year, 20–22 months after weaning. In this report, I use the term "adult" to indicate individuals that have been weaned for ≥20 months, and I use the term "yearling" to indicate individuals that have been weaned for 8–14 months.

Data in this report were collected in April–June of 1976, April–June of 1977, and November–December, and February–July of 1978. The 1978 interactions depicted in the various figures were classified as either prebreeding (15 February–10 March), early breeding (11 March–17 March), late breeding (18 March–3 April), lactation (1 May until date for each coterie when the first juvenile emerged from its natal burrow), or postweaning (date for each coterie when the first juvenile emerged until 3 July). No data were collected between 3 April and 1 May.

Intra- and inter- coterie interactions were categorized as either hostile or friendly. Hostile interactions included fights, chases, and territorial disputes (see Hoogland, 1979a). Friendly interactions included allogrooming, play, and the identification kiss (King, 1955; Hoogland, 1977). When a series of hostile or friendly interactions occurred in rapid succession between the same two individuals (fight + chase + fight, for example, or kiss + allogrooming + kiss), that series was scored as a single interaction. When a hostile interaction occurred in the same series with a friendly interaction (kiss followed by a fight, for example), that series was scored as a single hostile interaction.

Coterie density (i.e., the number of adults and yearlings per ha) varies directly with coterie size ($r = .325$, $P = .003$) (Figure 18–2a). I made no attempt to distinguish between effects resulting mainly from coterie size and effects resulting mainly from coterie density. In this report I only discuss possible effects of coterie size.

In this report, I use the term *nepotism* to indicate preferential treatment of close genetic relatives.

To investigate black-tail alarm calling, I performed experiments with a stuffed badger mounted on a plastic sled. Under undisturbed conditions, the badger was introduced from a brown cloth bag to which the prairie dogs had become habituated over several days and was pulled at a constant rate (18 cm per sec) across the study ward by means of fishing wire. For a particular coterie, individual alarm calling was recorded only when the badger was in the territory of the home coterie. I assumed that black-tails responded to the stuffed badger as though it was alive, and limited observations during attacks by live badgers indicate that this assumption was justified.

Statistical Procedures

For most of the analyses reported herein, I used conventional parametric statistics. I assumed that the usual assumptions for parametric procedures were met in each case, but I did not rigorously investigate possible violations. Differences that proved to be significant by parametric statistics were also usually significant by nonparametric statistics.

In several figures (e.g., Figures 18–9a, 18–9b, 18–9c, and 18–10a, 18–10b, 18–10c) the horizontal axis is labeled mean coterie size and the vertical axis is labelled the mean of a particular variable. In these figures, each data point indicates for each coterie the relevant mean values for three years' data; that is, each data point indicates the mean for both coterie size and the variable in question for three years' data. The significance levels in these figures resulted from analyses involving approximately 75 data points (three years' data for each of 25 coteries). To correct for differences in sample sizes among the various coteries, weighted mean proportions (Remington and Schork, 1970) were used in the preparation of figures.

All significance levels in this report resulted from one-tailed statistical analyses. Numbers in the text and tables indicate means $\pm$ SD (one standard deviation); numbers and lines in figures indicate means $\pm$ SE (one standard error). Numbers above SE lines indicate sample sizes; ''r'' indicates Pearson's correlation coefficient.

GENETIC RELATIONSHIPS AMONG COTERIE MEMBERS

Data from several species of squirrels indicate sexual differences with respect to dispersal, with males tending to disperse farther (see references in Sherman, 1977). For blacktails, similarly, data from King (1955) suggest that males tend to disperse from the natal coterie territory while females tend to remain there. To investigate this possibility, I marked all the young at the study ward in 1976 and 1977 (N = 145 from 50 litters, 22 coteries) and followed their movements. I was only able to record movements within the study ward.

Of 53 1976–1977 female young that were still in the study ward until April of their first year, all 53 (100 per cent) were still in the natal coterie territory (Figure 18–3a). Of 18 female young of 1976 that were still in the study ward until April of their second year (1978), 16 (88.9 per cent) were still in the natal coterie territory (Figure 18–3a). The two 2-year-old females that moved were full sisters: they emigrated together from the natal coterie territory with another coterie member, an unrelated 2-year-old male who had immigrated into the coterie approximately 6 months earlier, and founded a new colony 200 m north of the study ward. This colonization followed the forceful eviction of the male and the two sisters (as well as the sisters' mother, father, and brother, all of whom disappeared) by three invading prairie dogs from an adjacent coterie territory. In other words, I have not yet detected a single case in which a black-tail female has emigrated from her natal coterie territory of her own apparent initiative. The data of Figure 18–3a indicate a remarkably low probability of dispersal by black-tail females during their first two years.

In April of 1976, there were 85 $\geq$ 2-year-old females at the study ward. In an attempt to determine the probability of dispersal by older black-tail females, I followed the intraward movements of these females over the next two years (Figure 18–3b). Of the original 85, 69 were still in the study ward in April of 1977, and 68 of these (98.6 per cent) were still in the coterie territory where first trapped in 1976. The single observed movement (by RB3) is questionable, because it is not clear to what coterie RB3 belonged in 1976. In April of 1978, 51 of the original 85 females were still in the study ward, and 48 of these (94.1 per cent) had not moved during the second year from the coterie territory where they were first trapped in 1976. One of the three movements involved a mother (Cross), who, along with the five other coterie members described above, was forcefully evicted from her coterie territory; Cross established her own peripheral territory on the northwest edge of the study ward, approximately 300 m from her original coterie territory, and died there shortly afterward (reason unknown). The other two movements of $\geq$ 4-year-old females involved two females who, with a $\geq$ 4-year-old male, were responsible for the eviction of Cross and her coterie members in March of 1978; the two females were probably close genetic relatives because they had lived together in the same coterie for at least 2.5 years prior to their takeover. The data of Figure 18–3b indicate that, like younger black-tail females, > 2-year-old females are also unlikely to disperse.

Like females, black-tail males also are likely to remain in the natal coterie territory during their first year (Figure 18–3a). But the likelihood is not so striking for males: of 35 1976–1977 black-tail male young still in the study ward until April of their first year, 30 (85.7 per cent) were still in the natal coterie territory. The probability of male intraward movement during the first year, though slight, is significantly higher than that for females (P <.025, chi-square). By contrast, black-tail males are almost certain to be gone from

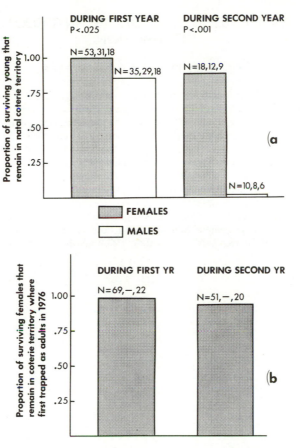

Figure 18–3.   Dispersal patterns of (a) males and females during their first two years and (b) older females. Numbers above bars indicate numbers of surviving individuals, numbers of litters from which these survivors originated, and numbers of coteries from which the survivors originated, respectively.

their natal coterie territory by the end of their second year: of 10 1976 young males that were still in the study ward until March of their second year (1978), all 10 (100 per cent) had emigrated from the natal coterie territory ($P < .001$ for male-female difference during second year, chi-square). Intraward movements of > 2-year-old males are also common ($N = 17$ for 1977–1978).

As has been indicated, I am only able to record individual movements within the study ward. I do not yet have a way to follow movements of individuals that leave the study ward. In 1975–1978, 3 adult or yearling females and 6 adult or yearling males immigrated into the study ward and successfully established residence there; 2 other females and 1 other male (all adults or yearlings) immigrated into the study ward and remained temporarily. Thus, it is clear that males and females disperse long distances, at least occasionally. Significantly, none of the three immigrant females that established residence was accepted into any coterie: two established their own territories at the periphery of the study ward, and the third evicted a single female from her coterie territory and then took over that territory. Because intraward dispersal of females is so rare, it seems unlikely that females would commonly attempt long-distance dispersal to other wards, but I cannot yet rule out this possibility.

QUANTIFICATION OF INTRA- AND INTERCOTERIE INTERACTIONS

Nepotism Involving Adult Females

Adult female–adult female interactions. Data from Figures 18–3a and 18–3b indicate that adult females within a coterie are close genetic relatives. If nepotism is important, it follows that adult females should be more altruistic towards other adult females within the home coterie than towards adult females of other coteries. To test this prediction, I recorded friendly and hostile interactions at the study ward during five stages of the 1978 annual cycle (Figure 18–4a). Within coteries, the weighted mean proportion of friendly interactions ranged from 0.139 to 0.977; between coteries, the range was from 0.000 to 0.111. At each stage intracoterie interactions were significantly more friendly than intercoterie interactions ($P < .001$ for all, chi-square), and this trend suggests the importance of nepotism to black-tail adult females when interacting with other adult females. Similar nepotism in adult female–adult female interactions has been observed among Richardson's ground squirrels (*Spermophilus richardsonii*) (Yeaton, 1972) and Belding's ground squirrels (*S. beldingi*) (Sherman, 1976).

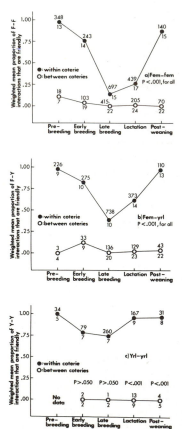

Figure 18–4.   Intra- and inter- coterie interactions involving (a) adult females only, (b) adult females and yearlings, and (c) yearlings only. Numbers above dots indicate numbers of observations; numbers below dots indicate numbers of coteries from which data were available.

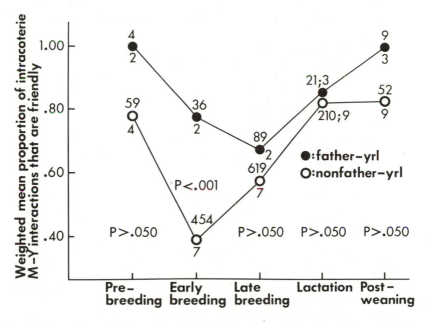

Figure 18–5.   Intracoterie interactions between fathers and yearlings and nonfathers and yearlings. Numbers above dots indicate numbers of observations; numbers below dots indicate numbers of coteries from which data were available.

Adult female–yearling interactions. Because young of both sexes usually remain in the natal coterie territory during the first year (Figure 18–3a), intracoterie interactions between adult females and yearlings will usually involve genetic relatives, whereas intercoterie interactions will not involve such relatives. To investigate the possible importance of nepotism in adult female–yearling interactions, I examined the weighted mean proportion of interactions that were friendly both within and between coteries (Figure 18–4b); all data were collected in 1978. Intracoterie proportions ranged from 0.386 to 0.978, whereas intercoterie proportions ranged from 0.000 to 0.121. At each stage of the annual cycle, intracoterie interactions were significantly more friendly than intercoterie interactions ($P < .001$ for all, chi-square), and again there is a suggestion of the importance of nepotism to adult black-tail females.

Nepotism Involving Adult Males

Adult male–yearling interactions. After moving into a new coterie, an adult male usually remains there for 1–2 years (King, 1955; Hoogland, as follows and unpubl.). During his first year in a new coterie, an adult male is usually unrelated (or only distantly related) to any yearlings therein. During his second year in a new coterie, on the other hand, an adult male is usually the father of most of the yearlings therein. If nepotism is important, then adult black-tail males should be more friendly to related yearlings within the home coterie than to unrelated yearlings there; that is, a male should be more friendly to yearlings during his second, rather than his first, year in a new coterie. To test this prediction, I compared intracoterie father–yearling interactions with intracoterie nonfather–yearling interactions for five stages of the 1978 annual cycle (Figure 18–5). I assumed that any adult male that was in the same coterie during the breeding, pregnancy, and lactation stages of both

Table 18–1.   Composition of all-male groups that entered new coteries.

1. 1 Yearling male and 1 unrelated yearling or adult male.
2. 2 Full-brothers and 1 half-brother (all 2-year olds).
3. 2 Half-brothers (both 2-year olds).
4. Father and 1 2-year old son.
5. Father and 1 yearling son.
6. Father and 1 yearling son.

1977 and 1978 sired at least some of the 1978 yearlings in that coterie (except immigrant male yearlings). During all five stages, father–yearling interactions were more friendly than nonfather–yearling interactions (a trend which in itself is significant: $P = .031$, sign test), but the difference was significant only during early breeding ($P < .001$, chi-square). Sample sizes for intracoterie father–yearling interactions were small because only 3 of the 24 coteries in 1978 contained fathers and their yearlings (by contrast, there were seven coteries containing fathers and their yearlings in 1977, when I did not monitor behaviors).

Coterie take-overs by groups of males. When a yearling or adult black-tail male enters a new coterie, he usually does so alone ($N = 40$ for 1977–1978). Such entry may occur while the resident adult male is still there or after his disappearance. Occasionally, however, males enter a new coterie in groups ($N = 6$, all in 1978). In 5 of the 6 cases, members of the group were close genetic relatives (Table 18–1). It seems likely that groups of related males are more likely than single males to successfully defend and retain a new coterie after take-over, but I do not yet have any direct evidence on this point. Similar cooperative take-overs of females by groups of presumably related males have been observed in lions (Bertram, 1976) and Hanuman langurs (*Presbytis entellus*) (Hrdy, 1977).

Nepotism Involving Yearlings

Yearling–adult female and yearling–adult male interactions. Though adults may be friendly to yearlings, the converse does not necessarily follow. Data from Figures 18–4b and 18–5 indicate not only that black-tail adult females and adult males are nepotistic toward yearlings, but also that yearlings are nepotistic towards adult females and adult males.

Yearling–yearling interactions. Because male and female black-tails usually remain in the natal coterie territory during their first year (Figure 18–3a), intracoterie interactions between yearlings should be more friendly than intercoterie interactions between yearlings if nepotism is important. Relevant data, from both male and female yearlings, are shown in Figure 18–4c. For all four stages of the 1978 annual cycle for which data were available, intracoterie weighted mean proportions of friendly interactions were higher than intercoterie proportions, and two of these differences were significant ($P < .001$ for both, chi-square). Frequencies of yearling–yearling interactions, especially intercoterie frequencies, were low (e.g., compare Figures 18–4a and 18–4c) for three reasons. First, yearlings are not aboveground and active as much as adults, especially during cold weather. Second, yearlings do not defend coterie territory boundaries as often as do adults. Third, intra- and/or inter-coterie interactions between yearlings were impossible in some coteries because 10 of 1978's 24 coteries contained no yearlings, and 4 others contained only 1 yearling.

It is possible that male and female yearlings respond differently to adults and to other yearlings. There were no obvious sexual differences, at least, but I did not investigate this possibility.

Because of occasional movements into new coteries by yearling males (Figure 18–3a), coteries sometimes contain yearling males that are not closely related to the adult females and other yearlings therein. There is an indication that both adult females and yearlings are more friendly to related yearlings than to unrelated yearlings that have immigrated into the home coterie territory, but sample sizes are still too small for analysis (in 1978, for example, only two unrelated yearling males immigrated into a new coterie prior to the breeding season, and both immigrated into the same coterie).

Nepotism and Alarm Calling

When a predator approaches a black-tail ward, there is usually a chorus of alarm calls (King, 1955; Hoogland, 1981a). That alarm calling is nepotistic has been suggested by several recent studies of squirrels (Barash, 1975; Dunford, 1977; Sherman, 1977; Leger and Owings, 1978; Smith, 1978; see Sherman, 1977, for more references). In 1978, I attempted to investigate the possible importance of nepotism for black-tail alarm calling. I conducted experiments with a stuffed specimen of a natural predator, the badger, and recorded which individuals gave alarm calls. I categorized all individuals as either (a) with genetic relatives in the home coterie or (b) without such genetic relatives; I only recorded data while the badger was in the home coterie territory. Conclusions were based on 1004 observations of 108 different individuals from 22 coteries (Figure 18–6). Adult and yearling females with relatives in the home coterie called more often than did females without such relatives (41.8 per cent vs. 32.1 per cent), but the difference was not significant ($P > .050$, chi-square). Similarly, adult and yearling males with relatives in the home coterie called more often than did males without such relatives (43.4 per cent vs. 22.5 per cent), but the difference here was significant ($P < .001$, chi-square). Among those individuals with relatives in the home coterie, neither sex was more likely to give an alarm call ($P > .400$, chi-square).

Although nepotism has evidently been important in the evolution of black-tail alarm calling (Figure 18–6), other factors must also have been important (see Sherman, 1977, for

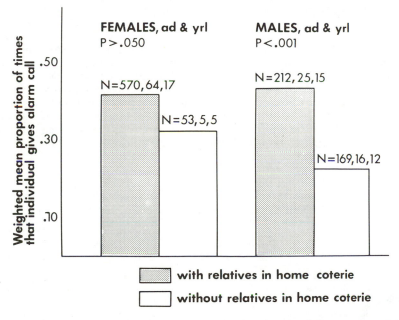

Figure 18–6.   Alarm calling by males and females. Numbers above bars indicate numbers of observations, numbers of individuals observed, and numbers of coteries containing observed individuals, respectively.

a list of other factors) as evidenced by the fact that adult and yearling females without nearby relatives called 32.1 per cent of the time in response to the badger. I am currently investigating the relevance of factors other than nepotism for black-tail alarm calling.

Other Nepotistic Behaviors

Communal sleeping. Groups of black-tails commonly sleep together in the same burrow system at night. In fact, only females ready to give birth and lactating females regularly sleep alone (King, 1955; Hoogland, unpubl.). The advantages of communal sleeping are not readily obvious, but two possibilities come quickly to mind. First, communal sleeping probably helps conserve individual body heat, especially during cold weather (Muul, 1968). Consistent with this is the observation that black-tail communal sleeping groups are larger in autumn and winter than in spring and summer (Hoogland, unpubl.). Second, through either increased ''selfish herd'' effects (Hamilton, 1971), an increased ability to detect predators (Pulliam, 1973; Hoogland, 1979b), or an increased ability of large groups to somehow deter predators (Hoogland and Sherman, 1976; Hoogland, 1981a), communal sleeping might increase an individual's defense against predators such as badgers that sometimes attack at night. Accompanying these possible benefits of communal sleeping are probably several costs, such as increased competition for sleeping sites and increased transmission of diseases and ectoparasites (see Hoogland, 1979a, for relevant arguments).

To investigate the possible importance of nepotism in communal sleeping, I recorded those burrow entrances into which individuals submerged for the last time at night or from which they emerged for the first time in the morning (Table 18–2; see also King, 1955). I assumed that two individuals that submerged into or emerged from the same burrow entrance slept together in the same nest chamber, and this assumption seems reasonable since most underground tunnel systems probably contain only a single nest chamber (King, 1955; Sheets et al., 1971). Data from Table 18–2 indicate that communal sleeping among black-tails is nepotistic because it is restricted almost entirely to members of the same coterie.

Construction of mounds. Black-tail burrow entrances are characterized by conspicuous mounds. Mounds are of at least two types (King, 1955), and each type requires periodic construction and maintenance to retain its form. One type of mound (the ''rim crater'') ''is made of the top soil scraped into a pile from the surface of the ground about the entrance and molded by the feet and noses of the prairiedogs to form a compact structure. Sometimes the dirt for this mound is scraped from an area with a radius of as much as five or six feet.'' (King, 1955, p.18–19). Especially after rain, individual black-tails work on mounds singly or in groups of 2–4 for as long as 30 min. Mounds are used as vantage points (Hoogland, 1977, and references therein) and might also facilitate the movement of fresh air through burrow systems (Vogel et al., 1973).

Table 18–2.   Communal sleeping patterns for adult females, adult males, and yearlings. For all three classes, the small number of cases that involved sleeping with noncoterie members were all doubtful, and most were probably errors in individual identification.

	Adult Females (N = 120 from 20 Coteries)	Adult Males (N = 30 from 20 Coteries)	Yearlings (N = 50 from 20 Coteries)
No. times individual sleeps in same burrow with *coterie* member	1200	300	300
No. times individual sleeps in same burrow with *noncoterie* member	< 5	< 5	< 5

Table 18–3.   Excavation patterns for adult females, adult males, and yearlings.

	Adult Females (N = 43 from 21 Coteries)	Adult Males (N = 19 from 18 Coteries)	Yearlings (N = 20 from 11 Coteries)
No. times individual digs burrow or constructs rim crater *within* coterie territory	115	56	50
No. times individual digs burrow or constructs rim crater *outside* coterie territory	0	0	0

In 1978, I recorded the mounds worked on by various black-tails (Table 18–3). Individuals worked alone or in groups only on those mounds within the home coterie territory. That is, individuals worked only on those mounds used by themselves or their genetic relatives, and this indicates that the construction of mounds is nepotistic.

Construction of nests. Individual black-tails, especially pregnant and lactating females, commonly take dry grass into burrow systems (King, 1955; Sheets et al., 1971). This grass is presumably used to increase the warmth and/or comfort of underground nests, although I cannot rule out the possibility that it is sometimes used for food. To determine if the building of nests is nepotistic, I recorded all burrow entrances into which each individual was observed to carry nest material (Table 18–4). Individuals only carried nest material into burrow entrances within the home coterie territory, and each burrow with a presumed nest (except those of pregnant or lactating females, who build their nests alone and sleep there alone with their young [King, 1955; Hoogland, unpubl.]) was slept in by at least two different coterie members sometime shortly after nest building was observed there. Table 18–4 does not include data from pregnant or lactating females. Evidently, the construction of black-tail nests is also nepotistic.

Nepotistic Variations in Social Organization

"Split" coteries. As I have indicated, the typical black-tail coterie contains a single adult male and an indefinite number of adult females and yearlings. Occasionally, a second adult male will enter a coterie, usually a large coterie, and divide the coterie territory with the adult male already there: each adult male now defends a well-defined section of the original coterie territory from the other adult male. When this happens, the adult females and yearlings continue to interact for the most part as if nothing has happened: they remain friendly among themselves and move freely over the entire original coterie territory but are still hostile to unrelated adult females and yearlings of other coteries (Figure 18–7a; see also King, 1955). Observations from such "split" coteries indicate that intracoterie cooperation

Table 18–4.   Nest building patterns for adult females, adult males, and yearlings.

	Adult Females (N = 58 from 20 Coteries)	Adult Males (N = 15 from 13 Coteries)	Yearlings (N = 16 from 10 Coteries)
No. times individual builds nest in burrow slept in by other *coterie* members	91	25	23
No. times individual builds nest in burrow slept in by other *noncoterie* members	0	0	0

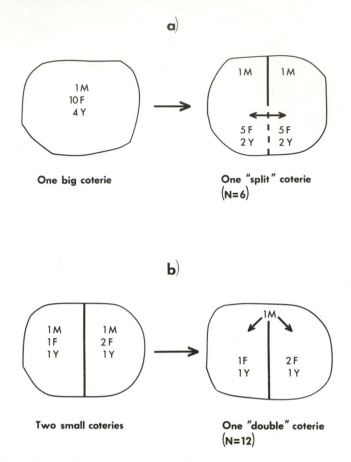

Figure 18–7.   Nepotistic variations in social organization.

among adult females and yearlings (Figures 18–4a, 18–4b, and 18–4c) is based on nepotism rather than on some sort of friendliness within the confines of a particular territory belonging to a particular male. Of the 25 coteries at the study ward, 6 (24.0 per cent) were ''split'' at least once in either 1976, 1977, or 1978.

"Double" coteries. When the adult male of a coterie disappears, the adult male of an adjacent coterie sometimes takes over the vacated coterie and its territory, while still maintaining control over his first coterie and its territory. When this happens, the adult females and yearlings of the two original coteries continue to interact for the most part as if nothing has happened: within each coterie they remain friendly but they are still hostile to the adult females and yearlings of the other coterie with whom they now share their adult male. Further, the adult females and yearlings within each coterie continue to use only their original coterie territory (Figure 18–7b). Data from such ''double'' coteries, both coteries of which are usually small, again suggest that cooperation among adult female and yearling blacktails is best explained by nepotism rather than by some sort of friendliness imposed by an adult male on individuals within his territory. Of the 25 coteries at the study ward, 12 (48.0 per cent) were parts of ''double'' coteries at least once in either 1976, 1977, or 1978. In

1977 there was one "triple" coterie, in which a single adult male controlled what had previously been three distinct coteries in three distinct territories. Hrdy (1977, pp. 146–152) apparently observed groupings similar to "double" coteries among hanuman langurs, whose social organization resembles that of black-tails in several respects.

THE EFFECT OF COTERIE SIZE ON ANNUAL REPRODUCTIVE SUCCESS OF ADULT MALES AND FEMALES

Annual Reproductive Success of Adult Males

Figures 18–8a, 18–8b, and 18–8c, which summarize data from 1976, 1977, and 1978, indicate that the number of litters per coterie ($r = .453$, $P < .001$), the number of young per coterie ($r = .311$, $P = .004$), and the number of surviving yearlings per coterie ($r = .211$, $P = .038$) all increased directly with coterie size. These figures might suggest that the annual reproductive success of adult males also increased directly with coterie size since the typical coterie contains a single adult male who probably sires most of the off-

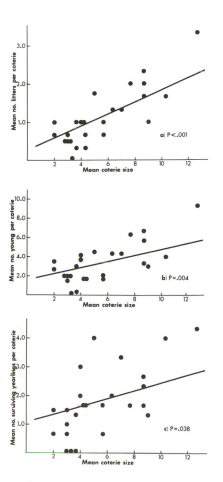

Figure 18–8.   Relationship between mean coterie size and (a) mean number of litters per coterie, (b) mean number of young per coterie, and (c) mean number of surviving yearlings per coterie.

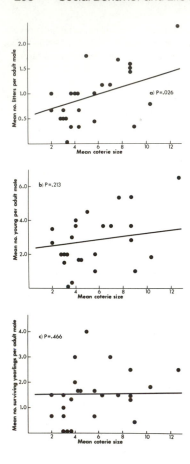

Figure 18–9.   Relationship between mean coterie size and (a) the mean number of litters per adult male, (b) the mean number of young per adult male, and (c) the mean number of surviving yearlings per adult male.

spring therein. But the probability of a second adult male within a coterie (i.e., the probability of having to share copulations with another male) also increased directly with coterie size ($r = .564$, $P < .001$) (Figure 18–2b). To compare annual reproductive success of adult males with coterie size, I assumed that paternity was shared equally among the adult males within a coterie; behavioral observations in 1978 indicate that paternity probably is shared, although probably not equally, among the adult males of a multi-male coterie, and I am awaiting the results of the electrophoretic analysis of blood samples for further confirmation or refutation. As shown in Figures 18–9a, 18–9b, and 18–9c, the number of litters per adult male increased directly with coterie size ($r = .230$, $P = .026$), but there was no significant relationship between coterie size and either the number of young per adult male ($r = .095$, $P = .213$) or the number of surviving yearlings per adult male ($r = .010$, $P = .466$). These data indicate that the annual reproductive success of black-tail adult males does not increase directly with coterie size. Data from 1976–1978 coteries containing only a single adult male suggested a similar conclusion: although both the number of litters per adult male ($r = .461$, $P = .001$) and the number of young per adult male ($r = .282$, $P = .018$) increased directly with coterie size, the best estimate of fitness, the number of surviving yearlings per adult male, did not significantly increase directly with coterie size ($r = .094$, $P = .245$).

Practically every relevant study has suggested a positive correlation between harem size and the annual reproductive success of adult males (e.g., Holm, 1973; Martin, 1974; Emlen and Oring, 1977; and references therein). For Yellow-bellied Marmots (*Marmota flaviventris*), Downhower and Armitage (1971) suggested that the annual reproductive success of adult males correlates positively with harem size only up to a certain harem size, after which it declines. Thus, it might seem surprising that the annual reproductive success of black-tail adult males does not obviously increase directly with harem size (which varies directly with coterie size). This result is better understood after an examination of the annual reproductive success of black-tail adult females.

Annual Reproductive Success of Adult Females

The relationships between coterie size and the various estimates of annual reproductive success for black-tail adult females for 1976–1978 are shown in Figures 18–10a, 18–10b, and 18–10c. The number of litters per adult female, a measure that is equivalent to both the proportion of adult females per coterie that reared litters and the probability of rearing a litter for any particular adult female, varied inversely with coterie size ($r = -.206$, $P = .042$). The number of young per adult female ($r = -.329$, $P = .003$) and the number of surviving yearlings per adult female ($r = .269$, $P = .012$) also varied inversely with coterie size.

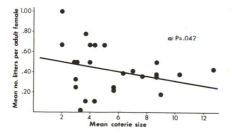

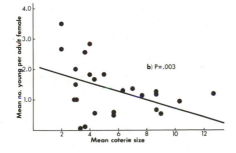

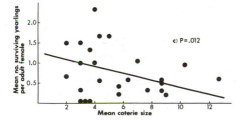

Figure 18–10.   Relationship between mean coterie size and (a) the mean number of litters per adult female, (b) the mean number of young per adult female, and (c) the mean number of surviving yearlings per adult female.

If adult females in large coteries experience such poor annual reproductive success, who do they remain there? Why don't they force their daughters or other females to disperse, or why don't they disperse themselves? Coupled with the dispersal strategy of black-tail females (Figures 18–3a and 18–3b), the inverse relationship between coterie size and the annual reproductive success of adult females does not readily follow from traditional treatments of the theory of natural selection. Relevant hypotheses that might explain these results are discussed as follows.

RELEVANT HYPOTHESES

The adult females and yearlings within a black-tail coterie are close genetic relatives (Figures 18–3a and 18–3b) that cooperate with each other in numerous ways (Figures 18–4a, 18–4b, and 18–4c; Tables 18–2, 18–3, and 18–4). Because of this nepotistic cooperation, I predicted at the outset of my study that annual reproductive success of adult females would increase directly with coterie size. But my three estimates of annual reproductive success of adult females all varied inversely with coterie size (Figures 18–10a, 18–10b, and 18–10c). I will discuss possible complicating factors and possible explanations for these results.

Possible Complicating Factors

As discussed here, the results of Figures 18–10a, 18–10b, and 18–10c might have been biased by either (a) unnatural or disturbed conditions at the study ward or (b) female age.

Unnatural or disturbed conditions at the study ward. The study ward has contained black-tails since at least 1951 (Lovaas, 1973), and probably much longer. By being in a National Park, it is protected from many forms of human disturbance. Periodic poisoning campaigns have been carried out at Wind Cave, but the study ward has probably only rarely, if ever, been victimized by such campaigns (A. L. Lovaas, pers. comm.). Though large for research purposes, (e.g., c.f. King, 1955), the study ward is relatively small and isolated when compared with other wards (e.g., see Linder and Hillman, 1973), and this condition might have inhibited female dispersal. As indicated above, the nearest other ward is approximately 0.5 km to the north. The east and west edges of the study ward are bordered by trees, but areas just north and south of the ward appear suitable for expansion; in fact, three black-tails in 1978 did temporarily (March–June) live 200 m north of the study ward from which they originated.

Wind Cave is a small National Park (114 km²). Though predators such as coyotes, badgers, bobcats, and golden eagles are protected in the park, they are intensively hunted when they wander outside park boundaries. The study ward is near one of the park boundaries, and the density of predators there is probably unnaturally low; also, park records suggest that black-footed ferrets have always been rare (and probably absent in most years) at Wind Cave. Further, my presence might sometimes deter predators when I am conducting research at the study ward. This condition of low density of predators could lead to unnaturally large coteries at the study ward. Alternatively, if the observed coteries are not unnaturally large, it is possible that individuals in large coteries would be proportionately better protected than individuals in smaller coteries if predators and predation were more common (thereby, perhaps, reversing the trends in Figures 18–10a, 18–10b, and18–10c).

Live-trapping probably causes considerable disturbance within a coterie. But such disturbance could not have accounted for the trends in Figures 18–10a, 18–10b, and18–10c unless large coteries were systematically disturbed by trapping more than were smaller co-

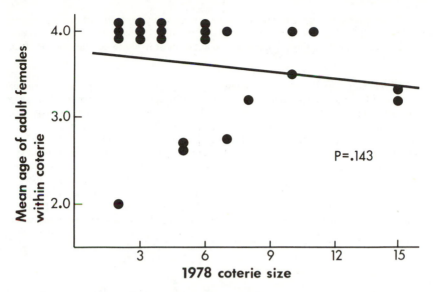

Figure 18–11.   The relationship between 1978 coterie size and mean age of adult females.

teries. Unfortunately, this possibility remains open since the time necessary to trap all coterie members, and probably the total disturbance that results, increases directly with coterie size.

In summary, there are several possible unnatural or disturbed conditions at the study ward that might have biased my examination of the annual reproductive success of adult females, and none of these possibilities can be rigorously discounted.

Female age. On theoretical grounds (e.g., Hamilton, 1966; Emlen, 1970), annual reproductive success is expected to vary with age. Such age-related variation has been observed in numerous species (e.g., Davis, 1975; Coulson and Horobin, 1976; and references therein). For squirrels, such variation occurs in Belding's ground squirrels (Sherman, 1976) and possibly also in Uinta ground squirrels (*S. armatus*) (Slade and Balph, 1974). To this point, I have detected no effects of female age on annual reproductive success of females, but accurate ages are known for relatively few individuals (at the study ward in April of 1978, for example, there were 23 1-year-old females, 15 2-year-olds, and 53 ⩾ 4-year-olds). Data in Figure 18–11 indicate that the female age does not vary systematically with coterie size ($r = -.130, P = .143$), but small sample sizes for certain ages and the combining of so many individuals into one '' ⩾ 4-year'' category might have masked a possible correlation. However, the strong tendency for females to remain in the natal coterie territory, probably for their entire lives (Figures 18–3a and 18–3b), means that old or young females do not commonly seek out females of similar ages and form new coteries. In summary, there is no evidence to this point that the trends in Figures 18–10a, 18–10b, and 18–10c result because female age varies systematically with coterie size. Similarly, male age does not seem to vary systematically with coterie size (Hoogland, unpubl.).

Possible Explanations

If data from the study ward are representative despite possible complications such as those discussed above, how can the results of Figures 18–10a, 18–10b, and 18–10c be explained? Nine possible explanations that are not necessarily exclusive of one another are considered below. This list of possibilities is by no means exhaustive (e.g., see Emlen, 1978) but rather includes those possibilities that are most likely to be relevant for black-tails.

The learning hypothesis. The possible importance of breeding experience to annual reproductive success has been indicated for several bird species (e.g., Woolfenden, 1975; Wooler and Coulson, 1977; see also Le Boeuf, 1979, for mammals). Since helpers of cooperatively breeding bird species usually help with feeding of the young, defense of the nest, and a variety of other parental duties, numerous investigators have emphasized the possible importance of learning and experience for the helpers. For individuals of a long-lived species, it is easy to see how experience gained early in life could potentially compensate for a lost year of breeding. For long-lived black-tails, the learning hypothesis might apply to nulliparous yearling helpers and to older nulliparous helpers but probably would not apply to multiparous helpers, which are common (in 1978, for example, there were at least 13 primiparous or multiparous females that did not breed, and 7 of these were in coteries where

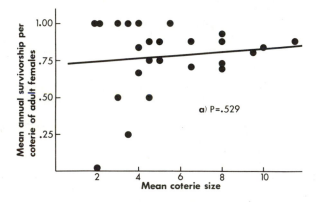

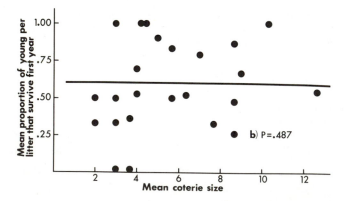

Figure 18–12.   The relationship between mean coterie size and (a) the mean annual survivorship for adult females and (b) the mean proportion of young per litter that survived the first year.

at least one female successfully weaned a litter). To this point, I have been unable to compare the reproductive successes of experienced and nonexperienced breeders, mainly because almost all females help at least once before breeding. If differences do exist, they will be difficult to separate from age-related differences.

Increased survivorship. Though *annual* reproductive success of females varies inversely with coterie size (Figures 18–10a, 18–10b, and 18–10c), *lifetime* reproductive success of females may not vary similarly. More specifically, the survivorship of adult females may correlate positively with coterie size (because of "selfish herd" effects, increased ability to detect predators, decreased individual alertness, etc.), such that females in large coteries are able to rear more offspring over their lifetimes than are females of smaller coteries. Elliott (1975) argued similarly for yellow-bellied marmots. For data from April of 1976 to April of 1978, there was no significant relationship between coterie size and the annual survivorship of adult females (i.e., the proportion of adult females that survived from one April to the next) (Figure 18–12a). Evidently, black-tail young during their first year also do not experience increased survivorship in larger coteries (Figure 18–12b, which includes data for both males and females). Finally, females during their second year do not seem to survive better in large coteries ($P > .100$ for t-test that compared coterie sizes of survivors and non survivors; data from 29 females from April of 1977 to April of 1978). Thus, data to this point indicate that neither adult females of large coteries nor their offspring experience increased survivorship as possible compensation for the former's reduced annual reproductive success. However, the possibility remains that there are particular years or particular circumstances when survivorship of adult females or their offspring increases directly with coterie size: if so, then defining the relevant conditions may require several more years of study.

Parental manipulation. By a process of parental manipulation, Alexander (1974) proposed that parents might sometimes reduce the reproduction of some of their offspring in order to increase their own reproduction via other offspring. He suggested that helpers at the nest might sometimes result from such parental manipulation. Because helpers in a coterie are commonly offspring of (and are always closely related to some extent to) the breeding members, parental manipulation might apply to black-tails.

If parental manipulation is important, then it follows that breeders with helpers should rear more offspring than should breeders without helpers: otherwise, parents should not bother to manipulate their offspring into serving as helpers. Increased reproduction in the presence of helpers has been shown for numerous bird species: of twelve cooperatively breeding species cited by Emlen (1978), for example, helpers led to increased parental success in every case, although not all of the differences were significant (see also Brown, 1978). To investigate the possibility of parental manipulation in black-tails, I examined the relationship between coterie size and (a) the litter size of breeding females (Figure 18–13a) and (b) the number of surviving yearlings per breeding female (Figure 18–13b). For both (a) ($r = -.326$, $P < .001$) and (b) ($r = -.210, P = .029$), there was an inverse relationship with coterie size: that is, the annual reproductive success of breeding females in large coteries (with numerous helpers) was *lower* than that of breeding females in smaller coteries (with fewer helpers). To my knowledge, this is the first case involving numerous data for which the annual reproductive success of breeding females seems to vary inversely with the size of the cooperatively breeding unit (see Brown, 1978; Emlen, 1978). These data suggest that black-tail cooperative breeding does not result from parental manipulation of offspring.

Kin selection. Groups of cooperating relatives immediately suggest kin selection. When helping leads to increased reproductive success of those individuals that breed, it is possible that the fitness of nonbreeding helpers (more specifically, their inclusive fitness)

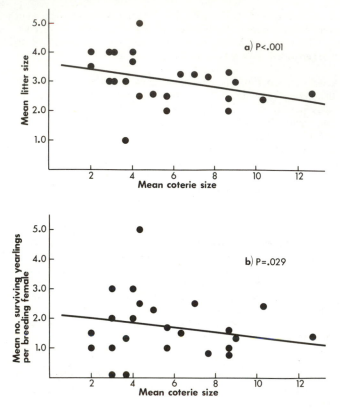

Figure 18–13.   The relationship between mean coterie size and (a) mean litter size and (b) the mean number of surviving yearlings per breeding female.

will exceed that of nonhelping individuals that attempt to breed alone (Hamilton, 1964). That is, the best reproductive strategy under some circumstances might be to assist with the rearing of nieces and nephews, for example, rather than to attempt to breed alone. Data presented above for parental manipulation (Figures 18–13a and 18–13b) indicate that breeding females in large coteries reared fewer offspring than did breeding females in smaller coteries. This suggests that black-tail cooperative breeding probably cannot be ex- plained by kin selection. Only when helping leads to increased reproductive success of the breeders can kin selection (acting alone, at least) be considered a viable explanation.

Reciprocal altruism. Because of an increased protection from predators, colonial black-tails probably fare better (i.e., are more likely to survive and reproduce) than are solitary individuals. As evidenced by the fact that individuals within wards are invariably organized into coteries, there also must be one or more (still undetermined) benefits associ- ated with membership in a coterie. Individual black-tail females might therefore sometimes be selected via reciprocal altruism (Trivers, 1971) to assist breeding females and forego their own breeding in exchange for acceptance into the coterie. Gaston (1978) argued simi- larly for birds. If reciprocal altruism is important, then two predictions follow: (a) breeding females should evict incompetent helpers from the coterie, and (b) breeding females should sometimes accept genetically unrelated helpers into the coterie. Regarding (a), only once have I seen a female evicted from her coterie by other coterie members; this single eviction was a gradual process that took place over several days, so it is likely that I would have seen other evictions if they were common. It is possible that more evictions of this type do not occur simply because helpers are regularly competent, but this seems unlikely. Regarding (b), data from Figures 18–3a and 18–3b indicate that unrelated female helpers are almost never allowed admission into a coterie. Thus, reciprocal altruism (including Brown's (1978) "unconscious" reciprocity) probably cannot account for cooperative breeding among black-tails.

The usurpation hypothesis. When the breeding individuals within a group of breeders and nonbreeders rear more offspring than do solitary breeders, a female might sometimes be selected to enter a group because of the probability that she will be one of the breeders through either chance or usurpation. This hypothesis probably does not apply to black-tails simply because breeders in groups do not rear more offspring than do solitary breeders (Figures 18–13a and 18–13b). Further, the usurpation hypothesis predicts that groups should sometimes contain females that are unrelated or only distantly related to other females within the group: such groups of unrelated females do not occur among black-tails (Figures 18–3a and 18–3b).

Increased reproductive success of sons. Adult females in large coteries might be compensated for their lowered annual reproductive success by an unusually high reproductive success experienced by their sons (which disperse before breeding; see Figure 18–3a). Such high reproductive success might result if the presumably more social environment of large coteries leads to a production of males that are more aggressive (and perhaps therefore better able to secure a coterie territory) or more parental, for example, than males of smaller coteries; or it might result if large coteries attract the best males and the heritability of male fitness is high. If so, then females of large coteries should be selected to bias their litters in favor of males (Trivers and Willard, 1973; Alexander, 1974; Dickemann, 1979). Figure 18–14 indicates that there is no significant correlation between intralitter sex ratio and cote-

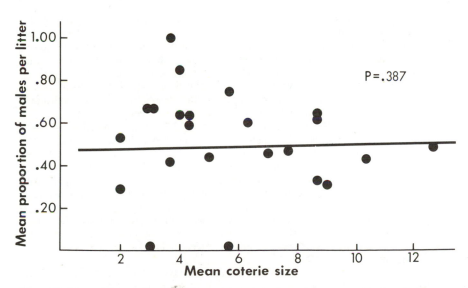

Figure 18–14.   The relationship between mean coterie size and the mean proportion of males per litter.

rie size. Further, to this point there is no indication that males originating in large coteries are unusually successful as adults, but sample sizes are still small (in 1978, for example, there were only 9 adult males, all 2-year-olds, at the study ward for which I knew natal coterie sizes; the most successful of these, #28, originated in a coterie consisting of only a single adult male and a single adult female).

Group size vs. territory size and territory quality. For the Florida scrub jay *(Aphelocoma c. coerulescens)*, Woolfenden and Fitzpatrick (1978) reported that the territory of a cooperatively breeding unit grows as the unit grows. Among other factors, this is important because ''with a large territory, a male's chance to bud off part of it for his own breeding efforts increases'' (Woolfenden and Fitzpatrick, 1978, p. 107). While it is true that coterie territory size increases directly with coterie size ($r = .624, P <.001$), coterie density also increases directly with coterie size (see above and Figure 2a). More importantly though, Woolfenden and Fitzpatrick's (1978) argument (see also Brown, 1978) probably does not apply to black-tails simply because coterie territories do not commonly expand and contract as they do for Florida scrub jays and most other territorial animals: of the 25 coteries at the study ward, there were only five changes in coterie territory size during 1976-1978; of these five changes, three were expansions, and only two of these correlated with increases in coterie size.

For several cooperatively breeding bird species, both group size and the annual reproductive success of adult females increase directly with territory quality (see references in Brown, 1978). For black-tails, the inverse relationship between coterie size and the annual reproductive success of adult females might result if territory quality also varies inversely with coterie size (assuming that territory quality has some effect on female reproductive success). Since coterie density varies directly with coterie size (Figure 18–2a), such an inverse relationship between territory quality and coterie size might result from increased competition for food. I do not yet have any information on the quality of coterie territories. If territory quality for black-tails varies inversely with the size of the cooperatively breeding unit, then, to my knowledge, this would be the first species for which this is known to be true.

Shortage of suitable habitat. Almost every study of cooperative breeding has emphasized the possible importance of habitat shortages (e.g., see Emlen, 1978, and Koenig and Pitelka, 1981). If suitable habitat openings are rare, then offspring might be selected to stay at home, and parents selected to keep them there, until such openings appear or until the offspring or the parents themselves are in a better position to disperse and compete for whatever is available. Note that this hypothesis might easily involve selected aspects of some of the alternative hypotheses discussed above, such as kin selection (e.g., Why is it that only *relatives* are retained in the home coterie?), learning, parental manipulation, etc.

In a study of prairie dog coloniality (Hoogland, 1977, 1981a), I concluded that black-tails are probably not physically forced into colonies because of a shortage of suitable habitat. Though suitable habitat away from colony sites seems to be available, however, colonization of such habitat (excavation of burrows, clipping of tall vegetation, etc.; e.g., see King, 1955) might involve considerable danger. That is, it might be almost suicidal for a mother or her daughter to leave the home coterie territory and try to colonize a new area, however suitable it may be. If so, then the best strategy for mothers and their daughters might be to remain in the home coterie territory and wait until other coterie territories within the home ward become vacant. This might be the best strategy for both breeders and related nonbreeders even if the breeders consistently experience reduced annual reproductive success as a result.

Coterie territories within the home ward do rarely become vacant. For example, in 1978 (the only year when such vacancies occurred), all the females of three different coteries disappeared: two of the vacated coterie territories were quickly appropriated by some or all of the females from an adjacent coterie, and the third territory was appropriated by an invading female from another ward. Disappearance of females from at least two of the original three coteries followed eviction by prairie dogs from other coteries. Appropriation of a coterie territory by strange females probably never occurs until all the resident females of that coterie have either died or been evicted (Figures 18–3a and 18–3b).

One hypothesis that follows from these arguments is that members of large coteries should be more likely than members of smaller coteries to acquire vacated coterie territories within the home ward. This might be true for two reasons: (a) because of simple probability (i.e., large coteries contain more potential dispersers), and (b) if taking over and successfully defending a vacated coterie territory following either disappearance or eviction of the residents usually requires (or is usually most successful with) a squad of several members, then large coteries are probably in a better position to send out such squads. If this hypothesis is relevant to black-tails, then the *lifetime* reproductive success of adult females in large coteries might exceed the lifetime reproductive success of adult females in smaller coteries, despite the opposite trend in *annual* reproductive success (Figures 18–10a, 18–10b, and 18–10c). At the study ward, more data are needed to test this hypothesis.

DISCUSSION

Do individual black-tails cooperate with close genetic relatives per se or merely with coterie members? I cannot yet distinguish between these two possibilities, simply because the two relevant variables covary so closely. That is, for females and yearling males, coterie members are almost always close genetic relatives, and close genetic relatives are almost always coterie members. However, numerous other social systems and dispersal patterns could have evolved. I suggest that the black-tail coterie system is a *mechanism* (in the sense of Williams, 1966) to insure that benefits are dispensed mainly to close genetic relatives.

Is nepotism of the sort that I have observed (Figures 18–4—18–7 and Tables 18–1—18–4) important to individual black-tails? For females, data to this point (Figures 18–10a, 18–10b, 18–10c, 18–13a, and 18–13b) indicate that adult females with numerous helpers rear fewer offspring than do adult females with fewer helpers. But this does not necessarily mean that the observed nepotism is of no importance. The crucial question is this: What would be the reproductive success of adult females in large coteries if other coterie members were *not* nepotistic? In other words, how would adult females in large coteries fare if their coterie members were hostile, rather than friendly, to them? (Do helpers really help?) I do not yet have an answer to this question for females, nor can I yet evaluate the importance of nepotism to black-tail males. The extent of nepotistic cooperation varies from one coterie to another: perhaps a comparison of the reproductive success of individuals from equal-sized coteries that differ in the extent of nepotistic cooperation will provide possible answers.

It is possible that there is an ''optimal'' coterie size at which annual and lifetime reproductive success of adult females is maximized. Figures 18–10a, 18–10b, 18–10c, 18–13a, and 18–13b suggest that the smallest coterie sizes (2–4) might be the ''optimal'' coterie sizes for adult females. Perhaps it is also significant that the smallest coterie sizes are also the most frequent coterie sizes (Figure 18–1). However, even though the smallest coterie sizes are the most frequent, most black-tails are found in the larger coteries: for 1976–1978, only 22 per cent of the black-tails were in coteries with 2–4 members, whereas 78 per cent were in coteries with 5–15 members (53 per cent were in coteries with 2–7 members whereas 47 per cent were in coteries with 8-15 members). Whether or not there is an ''optimal'' coterie size for black-tailed adult females, the paradox remains: if annual reproductive success for adult females is maximal in small coteries, why are so many adult females in large coteries?

It is possible that several questions raised in this report could be quickly answered by manipulating coterie sizes. For example, one way to determine if individuals of large coteries are more likely than individuals of smaller coteries to acquire vacated coterie territories would be to remove all the members of several coteries. But manipulating coterie sizes would interfere with other objectives of this study. No manipulations are planned at the present time.

Several times in this report I have alluded to the possible importance of lifetime reproductive success for an understanding of cooperative breeding among black-tails. I am currently trying to determine such lifetime reproductive success for individuals at the study ward.

SUMMARY

In 1976–1978, I investigated the social behavior of a cooperatively breeding squirrel, the black-tailed prairie dog (Sciuridae: *Cynomys ludovicianus*). A female black-tail usually remains in her natal coterie territory from birth until death: by contrast, a male usually remains in his natal coterie territory only during his first year and disperses sometime during his second year. Thus, adult females (≥ 2 years old) and yearlings of both sexes within a coterie are usually close genetic relatives. Behavioral interactions (fights, chases, allo-grooming, etc.) indicate that adult females, adult males, and yearlings are all nepotistic. For both sexes, individuals with close genetic relatives in the home coterie are more likely to give an alarm call during a predatory attack than are individuals without such nearby relatives. Two variations in social organization ("split" and "double" coteries) further emphasize the importance of nepotism. Annual reproductive success of adult males probably does not increase directly with coterie size. Contrary to expectation, annual reproductive success of females varies inversely with coterie size. Several possible explanations for the latter inverse relationship are discussed.

ACKNOWLEDGEMENTS

I received financial support for my research from The National Science Foundation, The National Geographic Society, The American Society of Mammalogists, Sigma Xi, The Center For Field Research, The Theodore Roosevelt Memorial Fund, The University of Michigan, The University of Minnesota, my brother, my parents, and my parents-in-law.

Since I started studying prairie dogs in 1974, twenty-seven persons have assisted me in the field, and my research would have been impossible without their help. Those field assistants who were especially involved with the research reported herein include Charles Bertsch, Diane Boyd, Kim Campbell, Craig Flory, Judy Hoogland, Mike Killebrew, Dirk Miller, Lori Reich, and Vera Wong.

The Superintendent of Wind Cave National Park, Lester F. McClanahan, provided housing, and he and his staff also provided constant encouragement and cooperation.

More than anyone else, Richard D. Alexander is responsible for generating my interest in questions such as those examined in this report.

The following persons read an earlier version of this manuscript and made helpful suggestions: Richard Alexander, Donna Baird, George Barrowclough, Nate Flessness, Warren Holmes, David Ligon, John King, Ann Pace, Harry Power, Mark Stromberg, and Donald Tinkle.

REFERENCES

Alexander, R. D. 1974. The evolution of social behavior. *Annu. Rev. Ecol. Syst.* 5:325–383.

Barash, D. P. 1975. Marmot alarm-calling and the question of altruistic behavior. *Am. Midl. Nat.* 94: 468–470.

Bertram, B. C. R. 1976. Kin selection in Lions and in evolution. In Bateson, P. P. G., and R. A. Hinde (eds.). *Growing Points in Ethology.* Cambridge Univ. Press, Cambridge. viii + 548 pp.

Brown, J. L. 1974. Alternate routes to sociality in jays—with a theory for the evolution of altruism and communal breeding. *Amer. Zool.* 14: 63–80.

———. 1978. Avian communal breeding systems. *Ann. Rev. Ecol. Syst.* 9: 123–155.

Coulson, J. C., and J. Horobin. 1976. The influence of age on the breeding biology and survival of the Arctic Tern *Sterna paradisaea. J. Zool.,* London 178: 247–260.

Davis, J. W. F. 1975. Age, egg-size and breeding success in the Herring Gull *Larus argentatus. Ibis* 117: 460–473.

Dickemann, M. 1979. Female infanticide and the reproductive strategies of stratified human societies: a preliminary model. In Chagnon, N. A., and W. Irons (eds.). *Evolutionary Biology and Human Social Behavior: an Anthropological Perspective.* Duxbury Press, Massachusetts.

Downhower, J. F., and K. B. Armitage. 1971. The Yellow-bellied Marmot and the evolution of polygamy. *Am. Nat.* 105: 355–369.

Dunford, C. C. 1977. Kin selection for ground squirrel alarm calls. *Am. Nat.* 111: 782–785.

Elliott, P. F. 1975. Longevity and the evolution of polygamy. *Am. Nat.* 109: 281–287.

Emlen, J. M. 1970. Age specificity and ecological theory. *Ecology* 51: 588–601.

Emlen, S. T. 1978. The evolution of cooperative breeding in birds. In Krebs, J. R., and N. Davies (eds.). *Behavioural Ecology: an Evolutionary Approach.* Sinauer Associates, Sunderland, Massachusetts. xi + 494 pp.

———, and L. W. Oring. 1977. Ecology, sexual selection, and the evolution of mating systems. *Science:* 197:215–223.

Fry, C. H. 1972. The social organization of Bee-eaters (Meropidae) and cooperative breeding in hot-climate birds. *Ibis* 114: 1–14.

Gaston, A. J. 1976. Group-territorial behaviour in Long-tailed Tits and Jungle Babblers. *Ibis* 118: 304.

———. 1978. The evolution of group territorial behavior and cooperative breeding. *Am. Nat.* 112: 1091–1100.

Hamilton, W. D. 1964. The genetical evolution of social behaviour. I, II. *J. Theor. Biol.* 7: 1–52.

———. 1966. The moulding of senescence by natural selection. *J. Theor. Biol.* 12: 12–45.

———. 1971. Geometry for the selfish herd. *J. Theor. Biol.* 31:295–311.

Holm, C. H. 1973. Breeding sex ratios, territoriality, and reproductive success in the Red-winged Blackbird *(Agelaius phoeniceus). Ecology* 54: 356–365.

Hoogland, J. L. 1977. The evolution of coloniality in White-tailed and Black-tailed Prairie Dogs (Sciuridae: *Cynomys leucurus* and *C. ludovicianus).* Ph.D. dissertation, University of Michigan. xiii + 292 pp.

———. 1979a. Aggression, ectoparasitism, and other possible costs of prairie dog (Sciuridae: *Cynomys* spp.) coloniality. *Behaviour* 69: 1–35.

———. 1979b. The effect of colony size on individual alertness of prairie dogs (Sciuridae: *Cynomys* spp.). *Anim. Behav.* 27:394–407.

———. 1981a. The evolution of coloniality in prairie dogs (Sciuridae: *Cynomys* spp.). *Ecology* (in press).

———. 1981b. Why do animals live in groups? In Barash, D., J. MacCluer, and K. Schlesinger (eds.). *Encounters in Sociobiology.* (in prep).

———, and P. W. Sherman. 1976. Advantages and disadvantages of Bank Swallow *(Riparia riparia)* coloniality. *Ecol. Monogr.* 46: 33–58.

Hrdy, S. B. 1977. *The Langurs of Abu.* Harvard Univ. Press, Cambridge. xviii + 361 pp.

King, J. A. 1955. Social behavior, social organization, and population dynamics in a Black-tailed Prariedog town in the Black Hills of South Dakota. *Contr. Lab. Vert. Biol.,* Univ. Mich., No. 67: 1–123.

———. 1959. The social behavior of prairie dogs. *Sci. Am.* 201:128–140.

Koenig, W. D., and F. A. Pitelka. 1981. Ecological factors and kin selection in the evolution of cooperative breeding in birds. (this volume).

LeBoeuf, B. J. 1979. Female competition and maternal success in Elephant Seals. (in preparation).

Leger, D. W., and D. H. Owings. 1978. Responses to alarm calls by California Ground Squirrels: effects of call structure and maternal status. *Behav. Ecol. Sociobiol* 3: 177–186.

Linder, R. L., and C. N. Hillman (eds.). 1973. *Proceedings of the Black-footed Ferret and Prairie Dog Workshop*. South Dakota State University, Brookings. v + 208 pp.

Lovaas, A. L. 1973. Prairie dogs and Black-footed Ferrets in the national parks. In Linder, R. L., and C. N. Hillman (eds.). *Proceedings of the Black-footed Ferret and Prairie Dog Workshop*. South Dakota State University, Brookings. v + 208 pp.

Martin, S. G. 1974. Adaptations for polygynous breeding in the Bobolink, *Dolichonyx oryaivorous*. *Am. Zool.* 14: 109–119.

Muul, I. 1968. Behavioral and physiological influences on the distribution of the Flying Squirrel, *Glaucomys volans*. *Misc. Publ. Mus. Zool.*, Univ. Mich. 134: 1–66.

Pulliam, H. R. 1973. On the advantages of flocking. *J. Theor. Biol.* 38: 419–422.

Remington, R. D., and M. A. Schork. 1970. *Statistics with Applications to the Biological and Health Sciences*. Prentice-Hall, Englewood Cliffs. xi + 418 pp.

Rowley, I. 1965. The life history of the Superb Blue Wren *Malurus cyaneus*. *Emu* 64: 251–297.

Sheets, R. G., R. L. Linder, and R. B. Dahlgren. 1971. Burrow systems of prairie dogs in South Dakota. *J. Mammal.* 52: 451–453.

Sherman. P. W. 1976. Natural selection among some group-living organisms. Ph.D. dissertation, University of Michigan. xvi + 256 pp.

_____. 1977. Nepotism and the evolution of alarm calls. *Science* 197: 1246–1253.

Slade, N. A., and D. F. Balph. 1974. Population ecology of Uinta Ground Squirrels. *Ecology* 55: 989–1003.

Smith, S. F. 1978. Alarm calls, their origin and use in *Eutamias sonomae*. *J. Mammal.* 59: 888–893.

Smith, W. J., S. L. Smith, E. C. Oppenheimer, J. G. Devilla, and F. A. Ulmer. 1973. Behavior of a captive population of Black-tailed Prairie Dogs. Annual cycle of social behavior. *Behaviour* 46: 189–220.

Tileston, J. V., and R. R. Lechleitner. 1966. Some comparisons of the Black-tailed and White-tailed Prairie Dogs in north-central Colorado. *Am. Midl. Nat.* 75: 292–316.

Trivers, R. L. 1971. The evolution of reciprocal altruism. *Q. Rev. Biol.* 46: 35–57.

_____, and D. E. Willard. 1973. Natural selection of parental ability to vary the sex ratio of offspring. *Science* 179: 90–92.

Vogel, S., C. P. Ellington, and D. L. Kilgore. 1973. Wind-induced ventilation of the burrow of the prairie-dog, *Cynomys ludovicianus*. *J. Comp. Physiol.* 85: 1–14.

Williams, G. C. 1966. *Adaptation and Natural Selection*. Princeton Univ. Press, Princeton. x + 307 pp.

Wilson, E. O. 1971. *The Insect Societies*. Harvard Univ. Press, Cambridge. x + 548 pp.

_____. 1975. *Sociobiology*. Harvard Univ. Press, Cambridge. ix + 697 pp.

Woolfenden, G. E. 1975. Florida scrub jay helpers at the nest. *Auk* 92: 1–15.

_____, and J. W. Fitzpatrick. 1978. The inheritance of territory in group-breeding birds. *Bioscience* 28: 104–108.

Wooller, R. D., and J. C. Coulson. 1977. Factors affecting the age of first breeding of the Kittiwake *Rissa tridactyla. Ibis* 119: 339–349

Yeaton, R. I. 1972. Social behavior and social organization in Richardson's Ground Squirrel *(Spermophilus richardsonii)* in Saskatchewan. *J. Mamml.* 53: 139–147.

Zahavi, A. 1976. Cooperative nesting in Eurasian birds. *Proc. XVI Int. Ornithol. Congr.* (pp. 685–693).

19

Reproductive Competition and Infanticide in Belding's Ground Squirrels and Other Animals

Paul W. Sherman

On July 6, 1974 I witnessed the following incident at Tioga Pass, California, where I was studying Belding's ground squirrels *(Spermophilus beldingi):*

8:50 A.M.   1-year-old male #22 goes down a hole 5 m. south of female #X's burrow (20 m. from my observation tree).

8:53 A.M.   Male #22 emerges from the main entrance of female #X's burrow at a run, carrying something in his mouth. He carries the object about 10 m. to beside rock #25.

8:56 A.M.   Male #22 picks up and drops the object several times. The thing is *alive,* and it squeaks occasionally. It looks like a vole or perhaps a juvenile ground squirrel??

8:58 A.M.   Male #22 bites its victim's head, then drops it. Repeat. The squeals stop. Then #22 eats the animal's head.

9:13 A.M.   I chase male #22 away from the carcass. The dead animal is a newborn ground squirrel (a female)! Incredible! It must be only a few days old: its eyes are not open, its toes are still webbed, and it is about 6 cm. long. The brain, neck, and upper thoracic areas have been eaten away. *Why* did this killing occur? So much to think about. . . .

(transcribed from field notes)

These startling and intriguing events alerted me to infanticide, the killing of conspecific young, at the beginning of my four-year study (1974–1977). In the 3,817 hours of observation since then, I have seen ground squirrels attack juveniles of their own species 55 times and witnessed 26 infanticides. During the 25 to 28 days between birth and weaning, 89 of (an estimated) 308 (29 per cent) juveniles died. Of these, 26 (29 per cent) were preyed on by conspecifics, so at least 8 per cent of all young born were infanticide victims. During this study more young were killed by conspecifics than by any other known predator species.

In this paper I investigate which animals perpetrate infanticide, the circumstances under which it occurs, and how young are protected from it. In addition I enumerate and give examples of nine evolutionary contexts in which infanticide might occur. After reviewing observations of infanticide, particularly among ground squirrels (genus *Spermophilus*), I conclude that it may be a more important mortality source and a more widespread form of reproductive competition than is currently recognized.

Infanticide is a well-known but little-studied phenomenon. There are at least four reasons why it has been largely ignored. First, it is usually regarded as a rare or unusual behavior, deserving neither extensive investigation nor evolutionary interpretation (e.g., Beach, 1978, p. 119; see also Sherman, 1978). This point has recently been countered by E. O. Wilson (1978, p. 40), who notes that:

311

> For the moment the existence of even a few cases [of infanticide] suggests the need
> for a reexamination of the phenomenon with close attention to biological theory.

Second, even if infanticide were common, it might seldom be seen because to avoid detection killers probably behave surreptitiously, thus incidentally making their behavior difficult for humans to observe or interpret. Third, infanticide is usually viewed as a pathological response to an evolutionarily recent habitat disturbance (such as crowding), therefore without adaptive significance (Curtin and Dolhinow, 1978). This view is sustained largely because of the ease with which infanticide is induced by artificially overcrowding insects (Park et al., 1965; Young, 1970), rodents (Southwick, 1955; Calhoun, 1956, 1962), rabbits (Myers et al., 1971), and primates (Zuckerman, 1932). Finally, because killing of infants is frequently a socially repugnant topic, infanticide is often ignored or concealed. As M. Dickemann has noted (1975, p. 111 and p. 107):

> Until recently, such matters as cannibalism, warfare, human sacrifice, wife capture, torture, slavery, sexual mutilation, and infanticide were either largely neglected or became the subjects of embarrassed dispute. . . . The practice of infanticide has been widespread in human cultures, yet, perhaps more than any other means of population regulation, it has been neglected by anthropologist, historian, and demographer.

Individuals investigating human population regulation were the first to suggest that infanticide might have adaptive significance. They argued that killing of children is one of a suite of mechanisms from sexual abstinence to head-hunting that promote group survival by reducing population size to the environment's carrying capacity (e.g., Carr-Saunders, 1922; Dorjahn, 1958; Wynne-Edwards, 1962; Douglass, 1966; Schrire and Steiger, 1974; Wind, 1978). For example, anthropologists W. T. Divale and M. Harris recently argued (1976, p. 527) that:

> . . . the most parsimonious explanation for the prevalence of warfare in band and village societies is that war was formerly part of a distinctively human system of population control. The principal component in this system was the limitation of the number of females reared to reproductive age through female infanticide, the benign and malign neglect of female infants, and the preferential treatment of male children.

Such explanations stimulated interest in and focused attention on infanticide. However the realization that selection acts most powerfully on individuals not groups (Williams, 1966; Wiens, 1966; Lewontin, 1970; Alexander and Borgia, 1978) led to explanations other than population regulation. R. A. Fisher was one of the first to link infanticide to individual fitness (also Krzywicki, 1934). In 1930, Fisher suggested (p. 218) that:

> ... the practice of infanticide is somewhat widespread among uncivilized peoples. If we consider the perils of savage life, and the extreme hardships to which uncivilized peoples are from time to time exposed, it would, I believe, be a mistake to regard this practice as altogether a maladaptation. Wherever the mortality in infancy and childhood is extremely high, the reproductive value ... of a new-born infant, must be small compared to that of a young and fertile woman. In times of famine, or of urgently enforced migration, an attempt to spare the life of the child would not only be often unsuccessful, but would certainly endanger the more valuable life of its mother.

Since then infanticide has been analyzed in terms of enhancing ''inclusive fitness'' (Hamilton, 1964) in humans (Birdsell, 1968; Chagnon, 1968; Alexander, 1974; Dickemann, 1979; Chagnon, Flinn, and Melancon, 1979) and other animals (birds: O'Conner, 1978; lemmings: Mallory and Brooks, 1978; primates: Hrdy, 1974, 1977; Goodall, 1977). Data and arguments presented by these authors and others (e.g., Williams, 1966; Alexander, 1971, 1975; Wilson, 1975) suggest that infanticide is most appropriately studied in the context of reproductive competition among individuals rather than groups.

There are two major categories of infanticide in nature. In the first, parents *gain* from the demise of certain offspring. Indeed they either kill the young themselves or acquiesce in such killing by close relatives. Most human infanticide falls in this category (Dickemann, 1975, 1979; Odenheimer, ms.). Reasons underlying such killings include deformed young, young born during ecological crises or too close together (often twins; Sumner, 1906), and young of an inappropriate sex (Alexander, 1974; Dickemann, 1979; Chagnon, Flinn, and Melancon, 1979). In the second category, parents *lose*, again in terms of their inclusive fitness, from having offspring killed. They and their relatives vigorously defend dependent young. Intraspecific competition for food, mates, nesting sites, or other resources are important factors underlying such infanticide (Fox, 1975). The Belding's ground squirrel infanticide I observed falls exclusively within the second category; I never saw them prey on their own or related young and they always resisted conspecifics' attempts to kill their offspring.

Infanticide in Belding's ground squirrels is more properly viewed as a manifestation of individual reproductive competition than as a social pathology or a mechanism of population regulation. In particular it seems inappropriate to dismiss the single most important source of juvenile mortality as a social pathology when (1) it occurred every year in a free-living population, (2) circumstances leading to killing are identifiable and not unusual in evolutionary time, (3) behaviors characteristic of killers are recognizable and predictable, (4) not all age and sex categories of animals commit infanticide equally frequently, (5) related young are not killed, and (6) the frequency of infanticide is unrelated to population density. The last point deserves further mention. To test for density-dependent effects I determined per capita infanticide rate and density for each year of the study. I found no correlation ($P = .17$, Kendall's Rank Correlation Test) between intraspecific killings/female and animals/hectare. These considerations lead me to discuss infanticide in terms of effects on the reproduction of its perpetrators and those attempting to thwart it.

STUDY ANIMALS AND TECHNIQUES

Belding's ground squirrels (Rodentia: Sciuridae) are diurnal, group-living rodents that inhabit mountain meadows in the Sierra Nevada and southern Cascades. Fifteen field assistants and I studied them in a species-typical habitat at the 3,040 m. summit of Tioga Pass, Mono County, California. Descriptions of the study area are given by Morton (1975) and Sherman (1976, 1977). Ground squirrels are active there from May through September, hibernating the rest of the year (Morton, Maxwell, and Wade, 1974; Morton, 1975). Females rear only one litter per season, are reproductively mature at age one, and usually live four to six years. Males usually live only two to three years, and are not reproductively mature until they are two (Morton and Gallup, 1975; Sherman, 1976).

Exact age and matrilineal relationships among conspecifics are known for most study animals. Between 1969 and 1973, M. L. Morton and his students individually toeclipped 731 ground squirrels. During 1974–1977, my assistants and I double-eartagged another 1551, including all 651 young from 138 litters. We captured juveniles within three days of their first emergence above ground and took precautions to ensure that all young were captured and unambiguously assigned to sibling groups.

Behavioral data were gathered during 3,817 hours of direct observation over four summers: 16 May–25 August, 1974 (4 observers, 916 hours), 17 May–23 September, 1975 (6 observers, 1639 hours), 1 May–18 July, 1976 (6 observers, 527 hours), and 22 April–1 August, 1977 (7 observers, 735 hours). Ground squirrels were observed from platforms in trees or from 2–3 meter tall tripods, usually with binoculars, and data were recorded in notebooks.

Animals were live-trapped about once a week. All trapping was done during 3000 +

non-observation hours. Ground squirrels were permanently marked by attaching a numbered metal fish fingerling tag to each ear. Those losing eartags were toeclipped. Animals were also marked uniquely with fur dye for individual identification at a distance. For marking they were hand-held and no anesthetic was used (Sherman, 1976). I looked for but discovered no differences in behavior of marked and unmarked animals and in behavior of the same animal with different marks.

Female Belding's ground squirrels are more sedentary than males, and they live significantly closer to female relatives than do males (Sherman 1977, 1980). Males permanently disperse from their birthplaces before their first winter's hibernation and thereafter live about ten times farther from natal burrows and kin than females. About the time young are born the most polygynous males leave their mates' vicinities and establish nest burrows elsewhere. Once settled in the new areas, these males are sedentary until after attempting to mate the following spring. One result of such post-mating dispersal is that males do not interact with mates or mates' offspring and they do not behave parentally. In addition, they never mate consanguineously. Post-weaning dispersal by juvenile males and post-mating dispersal by adults probably functions to reduce inbreeding as does similar dispersal in some birds (Greenwood, Harvey, and Perrins, 1978; Greenwood, 1980).

Coyotes and badgers prey on many juveniles every year. They usually dig out females' nest burrows at night; if they reach the nest, they invariably eat the entire litter. I separated mortality caused by coyotes from that caused by badgers on the morning after the predation. As evidenced by tracks and droppings, coyotes excavate round holes, usually 25 cm. or larger in diameter, and spray the dug-out earth into dome-shaped piles. Badgers dig more eliptical holes, usually less than 15 cm. high and 20–30 cm. wide, and leave a furrow through the mound of dug-out soil (probably from pushing their bodies through it).

Because I did not dig out and count litters prior to their demise, I do not know how many young died when a nocturnal predator excavated their nest. Therefore I estimated mortality based on the relationship between maternal age and litter size of undisturbed females (Sherman, 1976): one-year olds have 3–4 young, two- to five-year olds have 6–8, and six- to eight-year olds have 3–4. In order to avoid underestimating the number of young killed by coyotes and badgers, I assumed that the litter size of each female whose young were destroyed was one standard deviation above the mean litter size for females her age.

The number of juvenile deaths attributable to weasels, raptors, drowning, and miscelaneous other causes was determined by direct observation. Each year between 15 and 22 females' nest burrows were observed daily. Observations were particularly intense from parturition (signalled by a sudden drop in maternal body weight) until weaning, which takes place about the time the young appear above ground (i.e., 25–28 days after parturition). All burrow openings were known from watching females' activities, and all were marked with sticks or rocks. Because reproductive females always nested alone (Sherman, 1976), trespassers were conspicuous.

I did not attribute a death to infanticide unless the killing had been seen and, in most cases, the carcass examined. For example, I did not ascribe five recently-dead juveniles I found to infanticide, even though all bore tooth marks that could have been inflicted by conspecifics. When a ground squirrel other than the owning mother entered a nest burrow, all openings were observed until it reemerged. If it was carrying a juvenile when it reappeared its behavior was watched especially closely. Such potentially infanticidal animals were not disturbed unless they began to drag their victims out of sight (often down burrows). If this happened, I ran to the victim and without handling it determined if it were dead, the nature and extent of its external injuries, its body length, and sex. Then I resumed unobtrusive observations. Usually killers returned a few minutes after my departure and often fed on the carcass.

Unless otherwise indicated, all significance levels are for two-tailed nonparametric statistical tests. Two-sample comparisons were made with the Mann-Whitney U statistic. Correlations were analysed with Kendall's Rank Correlation Test.

PREVALENCE OF INFANTICIDE

Of the estimated 308 young born to 72 study females in 1974–1977, 89 (29 per cent) are known to have died before weaning (Figure 19–1). Most of these were killed by coyotes, badgers, and conspecifics. Several were killed by weasels and hawks, a few drowned in torrential rainstorms, one was killed by hail, one died following convulsions and paralysis, I accidently stepped on one, and five others died of unknown causes. Conspecifics cause more deaths than any other predator species (Figure 19–1). Of the 89 juveniles that died, 26 (29 per cent) were infanticide victims. Thus conspecifics kill 8 per cent of all pups born. In 1974 and 1975, intraspecific killing was the major mortality source; in 1976 and 1977, respectively, it ranked third and second. For the reasons previously outlined these figures probably underestimate the frequency of infanticide at Tioga Pass. Additionally, there were sometimes gaps in my observations ranging in length from several minutes to several hours. Obviously infanticides that might have occurred during these absences went unrecorded. Note also that intraspecific killing was only observable when young were brought above ground, so the extent of subterranean mortality is unknown. Thus my estimate of infanticide frequency (Figure 19–1) is probably conservative with regard to the actual prevalence and therefore the potential significance of the behavior.

Young are in jeopardy from birth to weaning. The youngest victim died on June 11, 1976. It was nearly hairless, its toes were webbed, and its eyes and ears were not open. It measured 5.5 cm. from crown to rump and weighed 8.4 g. I estimate that this infant was one to three days old, based on Morton and Tung's (1971) table of body weights and linear measurements for known age juveniles from Tioga Pass. At the other age extreme, a juvenile that was captured, eartagged, and dye-marked on August 2, 1975, its second day above ground, was killed on the afternoon of August 4, when it was 27 to 29 days old. I never saw older juveniles killed by conspecifics. Thus infanticide ceases when young become capable of fleeing and defending themselves. Post-weaning young also give loud shrill squeals when attacked, and these draw nearby females, usually their mothers, to the defense.

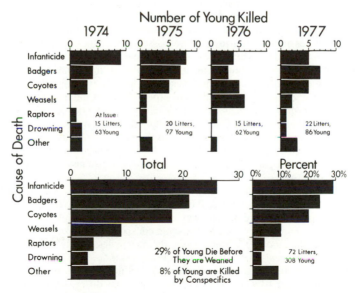

Figure 19–1.   Extent of mortality from birth to weaning and causes of death for juvenile Belding's ground squirrels at Tioga Pass, California, 1974–1977.

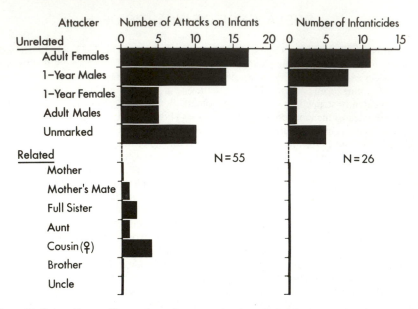

Figure 19–2.   Conspecific attackers of post-weaning juvenile Belding's ground squirrels and perpetrators of infanticide on nursing pups, divided by sex and age class. All conspecific predators were adults (i.e., one-year-old or older). Note that ground squirrels seldom attacked and never killed related juveniles.

Trespassing ground squirrels never entered a nest burrow when the owning female was on her territory. This is because they were chased by the owner or her closest female kin 80 per cent to 90 per cent of the times they trespassed; on the other occasions they left before being chased (Sherman, 1976, 1980). Indeed only when territory holders were either absent from their territories or in their burrows did trespassers remain for more than a few seconds. On such occasions trespassers usually behaved as if searching for the nest burrow, looking down and sniffing successive holes until it was located. If the owner was in her burrow when a trespasser entered, the latter was attacked and quickly evicted. If the owner was not present, the trespasser usually remained below ground for a few minutes. On 26 of 78 occasions (33 per cent) when a nonrelative entered a female's undefended burrow a juvenile was brought above ground and killed. On five more of these occasions the marauder reemerged without a carcass but with a red substance, probably blood, around its mouth. Killing was usually accomplished by quick, repeated bites to the victim's head and chest. Of eight juveniles I autopsied, five apparently died of head wounds, two had punctured hearts, and one had a severed spine.

After the infanticide, killers usually either dragged their victim away and began feeding on it (especially one-year-old males) or returned for another pup (especially females). Often killers departed or were driven away after only one infanticide. However on four occasions two juveniles were killed by the same conspecific; once a single female killed four pups. Other than looking at and sniffing them, females usually paid no attention to their dead offspring; occasionally they fed on the carcasses.

There was a small sex bias among infanticide victims. Of 23 dead young, 13 (57 per cent) were females and 10 were males. These proportions differ slightly ($.01 < P < .05$) from the sex ratio of young weaned at Tioga Pass from 1974 through 1977 (47 per cent females, 53 per cent males; $N = 651$).

Table 19–1.   Frequency of various sex and age classes of Belding's ground squirrels at Tioga Pass and their proportional representation in observations of infanticide.

Category of Animal	Proportion in the Population**	Proportion in Observations of Infanticide***
Nonresident* adult females	7%	42%
Adult males	14%	4%
Nonresident* one-year-old females	4%	4%
One-year-old males	11%	31%
Unmarked animals	5%	19%
Resident adult females	59%	0%

*Defined in the text.

**Mean frequency of observations of these animals during the time between the birth of the first litter and the appearance above ground of the last one, 1974–1977.

***See Figure 19–2.

WHICH ANIMALS PERPETRATE INFANTICIDE?

Members of all sex, age, and kinship classes occasionally attacked post-weaning young, but only nonrelatives brought nursing pups out of their nests and killed them (Figure 19–2). Although it is conceivable that females occasionally kill their own young or those of relatives and do not bring out the carcasses, there is no evidence of such behavior. Of all classes, adult females, one-year-old males, and unmarked animals were the most frequent attackers and killers (Figure 19–2). They committed infanticide more often than expected solely on the basis of their frequency in the population (i.e., greater than random expectation; Table 19–1), while adult males killed less often than expected and one-year-old females did so roughly in proportion to their frequency. None of the adult females that killed resided on the area where the infanticide occurred. That is, they had never lived within 100 m. of their victims' burrows, and observers had either never previously seen them or had seen them only once or twice prior to the killing. Unmarked killers (Figure 19–2) definitely did not reside near victims' burrows, but they were otherwise unidentifiable.

UNDER WHAT CIRCUMSTANCES DOES INFANTICIDE OCCUR?

Because one-year-old males and adult females perpetrate most infanticides and because therefore data are most numerous for them, I investigated their pre-and post-killing behavior in detail. At Tioga Pass one-year-old males are not faithful to particular nest burrows. Rather, they wander widely, sometimes spending successive nights in burrows several hundred meters apart. Their movements are predictable only in that they never return to the area where they were born (Sherman, 1976, 1977, 1980). One-year-old males often prey on young near their (temporary) residences. The distance between a burrow in which a yearling male spent the night previous to commiting infanticide and its victim's burrow was 28.6 ± 11.7 m. (S.D.; $N = 4$). Infanticide does not cause predators to cease wandering. For example, the distance between a deceased youngster's nest and the burrow of its (yearling male) killer during mating the following spring was 186.0 ± 20.3 m. ($N = 5$).

Yearling males usually kill only one juvenile per episode (in 7 of 8 cases). Upon discovering an undefended nest burrow, they enter and quickly return to the surface (1.0 ± 0.3 min., $N = 6$). Whether or not the owner returns, they immediately drag their victim several meters away. Then they kill it and usually eat the carcass (Table 19–2). They

Table 19–2.   Carnivory among one-year-old male and adult female Belding's ground squirrels that committed infanticide.

Class of Perpetrator	Number of Young Killed	Number of Young Eaten by Perpetrator
One-year-old males (N = 7)	8	6 (75%)
Adult females (N = 8)	11	1 (9%)

behave as if the carcass were valuable to them and, if surprised by the dead juvenile's mother or another animal, they try to flee with the body. Five times yearling males fought over a pup killed by one of them; in every case the fight winner fed on the carcass.

Carnivory has been observed in many ground squirrel species (for a review see Morton and Sherman, 1978), but the age and sex of the meat-eaters is usually unknown. At Tioga Pass meat seems to be especially important to one-year-old males. For example, during this study ground squirrels stalked live gophers, voles, moles, and insects 36 times. On 19 of these occasions (53 per cent) the hunter was a yearling male, and they made eight of 13 successful kills (62 per cent). Additionally, 34 of 51 (67 per cent) marked animals seen feeding on roadkills were one-year-old males. These data suggest that yearling males are more carnivorous than other sex and age classes, because their proportional representation in observations of carnivory far exceeds their relative frequency in the population (Table 19–1). Because male copulatory success depends on fighting ability, which in turn is positively correlated with body weight (Sherman, 1976), one-year-old males that grow the largest are most likely to copulate successfully the following spring. Furthermore, there is a positive correlation between overwinter survivorship and body weight among one-year-old males, but not among adults (Sherman, unpubl. data). Perhaps meat is particularly important to yearling males for these reasons.

Adult females that perpetrate infanticide behave differently. As already noted, females are usually sedentary within and between years. They emigrate from their natal area only if all their offspring are destroyed by interspecific predators (usually coyotes or badgers). Whereas 16 of 48 females (33 per cent) whose young were not preyed on changed burrows within a season, 14 of 20 females (70 per cent) whose young were destroyed did so (Table 19–3). Additionally females losing young moved significantly farther ($P < .001$; Table 19–3). The presence of close relatives appears to affect emigration among females losing their litters. Of the 14 females that emigrated, only three (21 per cent) had a living mother, sister, or adult offspring. By contrast all of the six nonmigrating females had at least one living sister or adult offspring, and four of the six had at least three close female kin alive.

Only females that had lost their young to interspecific predators and then emigrated committed infanticide, and they never killed offspring of relatives (i.e., first cousins or

Table 19–3.   Effects of interspecific (coyote and badger) predation on emigration and infanticide among female Belding's ground squirrels.

Category of Reproductive Females	Number	Number Moving Within a Season	Distance Moved (m.)	Number (%) Committing Infanticide
Those losing their entire litters to coyotes or badgers	20	14 (70%)*	114.7 ± 36.9m.	8 (57% of those moving)
Those not losing their litters	48	16 (33%)*	20.4 ± 11.3m.	0

*Difference in proportions significant, $P < .001$.

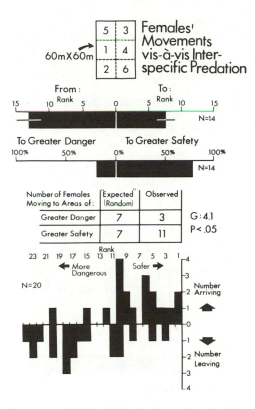

Figure 19–3.   Emigration pattern of 14 female Belding's ground squirrels that lost their litters to interspecific predators, and tests for randomness of movement vis-à-vis safety from such predators (see text). In test 1, females left dangerous areas (average rank = 13.6) and settled in safer ones (rank = 7.2; P <.01). In test 2, 79 per cent of females moved to safer areas while only 21 per cent moved to more dangerous ones or ones of equal danger (P <.05). Test 3 confirms test 2, using the "G" statistic. Finally (bottom), a graphical presentation of the females' movements shows clearly that they left (below the center line) more dangerous areas and settled in safer ones. For this latter graph I included all 20 females whose litters were destroyed by coyotes or badgers.

closer).[1] Of the 14 females that emigrated, eight (57 per cent) preyed on conspecific young. The distance between a female's destroyed nest burrow and that of her victim(s) was 99.3 ± 19.7 m., significantly farther (P< .001) than the distance between previous night residences of one-year-old males and their victims' burrows. In contrast to yearling males, females seldom ate their victims (Table 19–2), and sometimes they killed more than one pup from a single litter. Young were usually killed at the mouth of the victim's burrow. Because females spent 2.4 ± 0.8 min. (N = 9) in victim's burrows, considerably longer (P< .01) than yearling males, it is possible that more young were killed underground. If surprised by the victim's mother, infanticidal females usually fled without a carcass. They did not behave as if meat were valuable to them and only twice fought for possession of a dead juvenile's body.

In further contrast to one-year-old males, females that killed settled near their victims'

[1] In July 1979, near Tioga Pass, Kay Holekamp (pers. comm.) saw a lactating female *S. beldingi* kill and eat a juvenile conspecific.

burrows. I located six of the eight predatory females the summer following their infanticides. They nested 31.4 ± 8.9 m. from their victims' burrows, significantly closer
($P < .001$) than yearling males settled to their victims' nests. Of the six other females that
lost all their young, emigrated, but did not commit infanticide, I located three the following
summer. All nested in areas that had previously been uninhabited (i.e., no conspecific had a
burrow within 30 m. of them).

Did the females that emigrated following the total loss of their litters (Table 19–3)
move randomly? To investigate this question I divided the study meadow into 24, 60
m. × 60 m. quadrats. I chose 60 m. squares because that is the maximum distance away
from their nest burrows females move to forage. For each year of the study I ranked these 24
quadrats on the basis of per capita predation rate (burrows excavated/females present) and
food abundance (per cent coverage with edible vegetation). The latter was determined by
sampling 25 randomly chosen 50 cm. × 50 cm. subplots (see Sherman, 1976). Using
three slightly different measures I tested whether females moved randomly with regard to
either factor. The results (Figures 19–3 and 19–4) were that females immigrated to quadrats

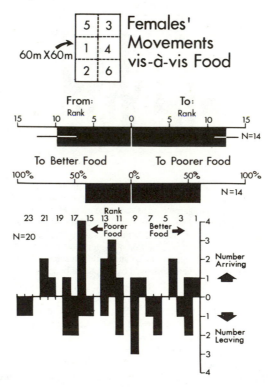

Figure 19–4.   Emigration pattern of 14 female Belding's ground squirrels that lost their litters to
interspecific predators, and tests for randomness of movement vis-à-vis food abundance (see text). The
tests are the same as those shown in Figure 19–3. In test 1, there was no difference ($P > .10$) in food
abundance between areas females left and those on which they settled. In test 2, about the same fraction
moved to areas of more (43 per cent) and less (57 per cent) abundant food. Finally (bottom) a graphical
presentation of the females' movements shows that they did not leave areas of less abundant food in
order to settle on richer areas. For this graph I included all 20 females whose litters were destroyed by
coyotes or badgers. I also tested (not shown) for randomness of movement and found that females did
not move to quadrats with more food than those they left ($P > .20$, "G" statistic).

safer from interspecific predators without regard to food abundance there. These results obviously leave open the possibility that females move nonrandomly with regard to food plant species, food quality, or some other environmental factor or factors. Regardless, they clearly move to areas safer from digging predators (Figure 19–3) following the death of their litters, and they show no similar preference for areas of abundant food (Figure 19–4). In terms of per capita predation rate (and food abundance) there were significant positive correlations ($P < .05$) between years in quadrat rank order during 1974–1977. Thus females moving to safer areas (Figure 19–3) were likely to experience reduced interspecific predation in subsequent years.

I do not know what proximate factors cause immigrating females to preferentially settle on safer quadrats. Perhaps excavated burrows or the lingering scent of predators divert females away from the most dangerous areas. I also do not know what physical features made some quadrats safer. Neither the (1) number of exposed rocks, (2) number of fallen trees, (3) number or size of bushes, nor (4) mean height of the grass (measured at 25 randomly chosen spots) differed significantly ($P > .08$, all tests) between territories females left and those on which they settled, and territories in the center of the meadow (i.e., surrounded by conspecifics) were no safer than those on the edges. Perhaps subterranean obstacles or soil density made some areas more inaccessible to digging predators than others.

Taken together, these data suggest that by killing young, females might eliminate current and future competitors for preferred nest sites. This hypothesis implicates intrasexual competition for nest burrows safe from coyotes and badgers in the expression of infanticide among females. If potential killers can distinguish between male and female juveniles, the hypothesis predicts a female sex bias among young killed by females because only juvenile females (not males) are sedentary and could thus represent competitors for space. Unfortunately, my sex ratio data are too sparse to permit a convincing test of this corollary. However it appears (Table 19–4a) that females do kill more female than male juveniles and that there is no similar sex bias among young preyed on by one-year-old males. The sex bias among females' infanticide victims is opposite the sex ratio bias among juveniles in the population at large (Table 19–4b), but the difference is not significant.

Table 19–4a.   Sex ratio of juvenile ground squirrel infanticide victims during 1974–1977 at Tioga Pass, California.

Age, Sex of Killer	Number of Juvenile Males Killed	Number of Juvenile Females Killed
One-year males*	4	3
Adult females	4	7
Unknown	2	3
	10 (43%)	13 (57%)

Table 19–4b.   Sex ratio bias among juvenile ground squirrels killed by adult females.

Sex of Juvenile Killed by Adult Females	Number "Expected" to be Killed**	Number Observed to be Killed
Male	6	4
Female	5	7
		($.10 > P > .05$; "G" statistic)

*One juvenile killed by a yearling male was not sexed (see Figure 19–2).

**Number "expected" if juveniles were killed randomly, in proportion to their frequency in the population (47% females, 53% males).

HOW ARE JUVENILES PROTECTED AGAINST INFANTICIDE?

Female ground squirrels with dependent young attack and chase all conspecifics except close female relatives away from their nest burrow and an area or territory (sensu Burt, 1943) surrounding it. Such territories range in size from 100m² to 1,640 m² and females delineate their boundaries with scent marks. Territorial defense is particularly vigorous during lactation when neonatal young are present (Sherman, 1976). Close kin cooperate to secure and guard territories. For example, females seldom fight with adult daughters or sisters when establishing nest burrows, and these relatives share and codefend portions of the same territories, allow each other nearly unmolested access to unambiguously owned portions of their territories, and jointly chase away trespassers (Sherman, 1980).

Is there a link between territorial defense and infanticide? In 1968 R. J. Burns witnessed infanticide among Uinta ground squirrels (*Spermophilus armatus*) and that incident plus the observation that females defend territories only during lactation led him to suggest (1968, p. 31) that " ... one function of female territoriality is to protect the young." Seven sorts of information suggest that the adaptive significance of Belding's ground squirrel territoriality also lies in thwarting infanticide. Because my data and arguments are presented in detail elsewhere (Sherman, 1976, 1980, ms.) I will only summarize the evidence here. Territoriality probably represents nepotistic defense of neonatal young because:

1. Territorial defense is most pronounced (in terms of frequency of chases and fights) from parturition to weaning, when young are in jeopardy. Females cease defending when their young come above ground and begin to fend for themselves.
2. Only lactating females defend territories; neither males nor nonreproductive females do so. Females whose litters are totally destroyed cease defense soon after the loss.
3. Nonresident adult females and one-year-old males, animals shown to perpetrate infanticide most frequently (Figure 19–2), are chased significantly farther and longer than other conspecifics (Figure 19–5).
4. Nest burrows are usually located in the geometric center of territories rather than near the edges, suggesting that territories represent a protected radius surrounding each female's young.
5. When females are experimentally restrained so that they cannot defend their territories, the rate of infanticide rises sharply.
6. There is an inverse correlation between territory size and likelihood of losing young to conspecific predators. This effect probably occurs because the largest, most vigorous females are able to keep unrelated animals farthest from their nest burrows (i.e., they defend the largest territories).
7. Because of joint territorial defense, females with adult offspring or sisters living adjacent lose fewer offspring to infanticide than females with no living kin.

It is possible that territoriality also functions to reduce some of the other disadvantages of breeding in proximity to potential competitors (see Alexander, 1974; Hoogland and Sherman, 1976; Davies, 1978). However, no evidence suggests that territoriality diminishes intrasexual competition for mates or matings, possibilities for misdirecting parental care, likelihood of contracting ectoparasites, or interspecific predation. Because females often feed on their territories, the possibility that they are defending food resources cannot be rejected easily. However there is no evidence of food shortages at Tioga Pass. Animals never fight over feeding sites away from nest burrows, and the transient males and sedentary nonreproductive females obtain food without defending it. Furthermore, variations in the timing, intensity, and specificity of territorial defense (points 1–7 and Figure 19–5) are more parsimoniously interpreted under the hypothesis of thwarting infanticide than sequestering food.

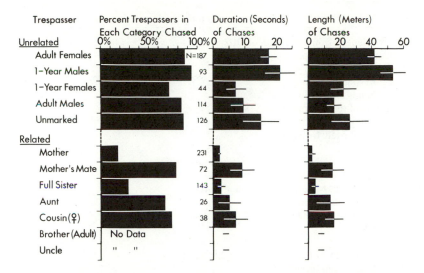

Figure 19–5.   Vigor with which various sex and age classes of conspecific ground squirrels are excluded from territories by lactating females. In the first column, *N* is the number of times individuals in each category trespassed when the resident was above ground. In the second and third columns the duration and length of chases are shown, with means as thick bars and standard deviations as thin lines. In the latter two columns, the means differ significantly ($P < .001$, Analysis of Variance) and the first two classes of animals differ significantly from the others but not from each other ($P < .05$, Student-Newman-Keuls a posteriori tests).

REPRODUCTIVE COMPETITION AND INFANTICIDE

There are nine different circumstances in which infanticide might occur (Table 19–5; also Sherman, 1976). These are divisible into two categories, based on whether parents gain or lose from the deaths of their offspring. Parents might benefit from the demise of young under three circumstances (Table 19–5; Alexander, 1974). First, they may gain from terminating investment in young that are congenitally deformed or handicapped, weak or sickly (e.g., humans; Dickmann, 1975). Second, if vital resources such as food vary greatly in abundance, parents may kill dependent young or allow them to starve during sudden periods of scarcity. Among predatory birds for example, when food becomes scarce the youngest or smallest nestlings are often terminated (O'Conner, 1978); frequently siblings do the killing and eat the carcass (Ingram, 1959; Meyburg, 1974; Parsons, 1975; Proctor, 1975; Gargett, 1978). Similarly, if young are conceived too frequently parents may gain by killing those that impose an intolerable drain on familial resources or that, if permitted to live, would be doomed to retarded development by lack of food. The infrequency with which human twins are reared (Sumner, 1906; Grantzberg, 1973; Odenheimer, ms.) suggests the importance of infanticide as a spacing mechanism. In a slightly different vein, among many fishes males protect eggs and fry (Perrone and Zaret, 1979; Blumer, 1979), and tending males occasionally eat their charges (Rohwer, 1978). By sustaining themselves males are able to remain with their broods continuously, thereby preventing an even greater loss to cannibalistic conspecifics or other predators. Third, parents might gain by rearing only young of the appropriate sex. As Alexander has recently noted (1974, p.369; also Trivers and Willard, 1973), the mating system can affect which sex is "appropriate":

Table 19–5.   Nine circumstances in which infanticide occurs in nature.

I. Parents Benefit from the Death of Offspring
    1. Congenitally Handicapped Young
    2. Young Born During Ecological Crises
       a. Resource Scarcity
       b. Young Born Too Close Together
    3. Young of the Inappropriate Sex
       a. Polygyny and Societal Stratification
       b. Local Mate Competition

II. Parents Do Not Benefit from the Death of Offspring
    4. Male-Male Reproductive Competition
    5. Avoidance of Misdirecting Parental Care
    6. Predation and Cannibalism
    7. Removal of Current or Future Competitors
    8. "Spite"
    9. Accidents
       a. By-Product of Selection in Another Context
       b. Inadvertent Infanticides
       c. Product of Habitat Disturbance

> For example, most human societies allow polygynous units, and even if they do not
> they develop polygynous breeding systems ... It follows that the reproductive vari-
> ance among men is increased over that of women ... Under such circumstances
> advantage is generally gained from emphasizing one's male ancestors .... these
> considerations generate ... the obvious prediction that female-preferential infanti-
> cide is more likely among women married to high-ranking men and less likely
> among women married to low-ranking men or not legitimately married at all.

In support of this hypothesis, Dickemann (1979) has shown that in stratified human societies, female children of high-ranking mothers are preferentially killed. Another factor that
might affect the "appropriateness" of an offspring's sex is local mate competition (Hamilton, 1967; Alexander and Sherman, 1977). If members of either sex compete most intensely with close relatives for mates, the result will be a devaluation of the sex in greater
competition. Under such circumstances of intrafamilial strife, parents might gain by reducing investments in the sex competing locally, in favor of rearing more offspring of the opposite sex. The frequency with which local mate competition creates situations favoring sex-
specific infanticide in nature remains to be explored.

The second major category of infanticide (Table 19–5) includes all circumstances in
which reproductive interests of parents and perpetrators do not coincide (i.e., infanticide
reduces inclusive fitness of parents but not killers). First, among some polygynous species
that live exclusively in single-male groups, usurpers may gain by killing (unrelated) dependent offspring if by doing so they cause lactating females to resume sexual cycling. Thus,
infanticide has recently been linked to male–male competition among lions (*Panthera leo*;
Schaller, 1972; Bertram, 1975, 1978) and some primates (Hrdy, 1974, 1977; Struhsaker,
1977; Angst and Thommen, 1977; but see Curtin and Dolhinow, 1978; Boggess, 1979).
The Bruce effect (Bruce, 1960, 1963) suggests that infanticide might be a more widespread
form of intrasexual reproductive competition than is currently recognized. It is well known
that when unfamiliar males or their urine are introduced, pregnant females in many rodent
species spontaneously abort (Stehn and Richmond, 1975) or kill nursing young (Mallory
and Brooks, 1978). Perhaps such females have been selected to terminate investment in
young that will probably be killed by the new male regardless of attempts at defense.

Second, when misdirected parental care is likely to occur if young mix, parents may kill unrelated juveniles that attempt to insinuate themselves into their broods. For example chicks that wander into nonfamilial nests in colonial sea birds (Armstrong, 1947; Ashmole, 1963; Hunt and McLoon, 1975; Hunt and Hunt, 1976) and northern elephant seal pups (*Mirounga angustirostris*) that attempt to suckle from unrelated females (LeBoeuf, Whiting, and Gantt, 1972; LeBoeuf and Briggs, 1977) are frequently infanticide victims.

Third, among species that are at least occasionally carnivorous, conspecific juveniles may be easily discovered, caught, and subdued. Cannibalism occurs in a wide variety of species (reviewed by Fox, 1975), including insects (Fox, 1975), corvid (Yom-Tov, 1974) and larid birds (Parsons, 1971), bears (Troyer and Hensel, 1962), ground squirrels (this study), marmots (*Marmota flaviventris;* Armitage, Johns, and Andersen, 1979), and chimpanzees (*Pan troglodytes;* Goodall, 1977; Nishida, Uehara, and Nyundo, 1979).

Fourth, infanticide might function to remove current or future (expected) competitors. For example long-billed marsh wrens (*Telmatodytes palustris*) destroy each other's nests and eggs (Picman, 1977a, b), thereby causing abandonment; similar behavior occurs among various species of frigate-birds (*Fregata*) (Nelson, 1975). Likewise, female northern elephant seals leave crowded pupping beaches if their young are killed by conspecifics (Christenson and LeBoeuf, 1978; LeBoeuf and Briggs, 1977). Infanticide may also dispose of juvenile competitors. Thus dominant female wild dogs (*Lycaon pictus*) sometimes kill other pack females' offspring, thereby reducing the number of young the group must feed (van Lawick-Goodall and van Lawick-Goodall, 1968, 1971; van Lawick, 1974).

Fifth, W. D. Hamilton has suggested that under certain circumstances an individual might gain by being "spiteful," ready (1970, p. 1218) " ... to harm itself in order to harm another more." He also noted that unambiguous cases of spiteful behavior have never been observed in nature, and that most behaviors that harm others benefit the harming individual more. Rothstein (1979) has recently pointed out several theoretical barriers to the evolution of spite. Therefore a case of infanticide that may implicate spite is particularly interesting. In the lesser black-backed gulls (*Larus fuscus*) studied by Davis and Dunn (1976), parents that fail to breed or lose their broods before fledging frequently kill conspecific juveniles. They do not eat the carcasses and do not derive any obvious benefit from the dead chicks' parents or their nests. Davis and Dunn conclude (1976, p.72) that:

> The motivation behind this spiral of inter-neighbour aggression is not clear though it is worth noting that, in terms of gene frequency, any individual losing its own progeny still stands to gain some selective advantage by eliminating the progeny of conspecifics.

This intriguing case deserves further investigation, particularly with regard to spite and selfishness.

Finally, infanticide might be a by-product of selection for some other behavior, an accidental occurrence, or a result of evolutionarily recent habitat disturbances (e.g., see Curtin and Dolhinow, 1978; Beach, 1978). The breeding biology of northern elephant seals may offer examples of each. Probably to avoid predators these animals breed on offshore islands. The scarcity of suitable islands, coupled with a recent population explosion (LeBoeuf and Panken, 1977), has forced them into dense aggregations for mating and pupping. On one island studied by LeBoeuf and Briggs (1977), between 13 per cent and 26 per cent of pups died before weaning. Some were crushed when females huddled to avoid high waves accompanying storms. Others were squashed during male–male confrontations over females (Bartholomew, 1952; LeBoeuf, Whiting, and Gantt, 1972; LeBoeuf and Briggs, 1977). No evidence suggests that such behavior by females or males is the result of selection directly favoring infanticide. Instead pup mortality is probably an accidental consequence of intrasexual reproductive competition at population densities that may never have been so high in the species' evolutionary past.

Belding's ground squirrels never kill related young, and infanticide is consistently resisted by mothers and their kin. Therefore, infanticide in this species may occur because of benefits to its perpetrators (i.e., category II, Table 19–5) but not because of benefits to parents (category I). One-year-old males probably kill to obtain nutritious food (context 6, Table 19–5), while nonresident females may benefit from the removal of competitors for nesting sites safe from interspecific predators (context 7). Adult males seldom commit infanticide, and regardless of the loss of their litters females are sexually receptive only once per season. Thus infanticide is not related to elimination of offspring of males' reproductive competitors (context 4). Because most infanticides occur before young mingle and because killers seldom have living juveniles, infanticide does not reduce possibilities of misdirecting parental care (context 5). Killers may derive immediate (food) or possibly future benefits (nest sites) from infanticide, so their behavior appears to be more "selfish" than "spiteful" (context 8; Hamilton, 1970). Finally, no evidence suggests that infanticide in this species is accidental or a result of habitat disturbance (context 9).

How common is infanticide among other ground squirrels (genus *Spermophilus*)? Among free-living populations, infanticide has been reported in eight of eleven species (Table 19–6). Males most frequently injure or kill (unrelated) young in species that live in harem groups such as Columbian ground squirrels (*S. columbianus;* Steiner, 1970a, b, 1972) and Arctic ground squirrels (*S. undulatus;* Steiner, 1972). Females most frequently perpetrate infanticide in nonharem species like Uinta (Burns, 1968), Richardson's (*S. richardsonii;* Quanstrom, 1968), and Belding's ground squirrels. Infanticide also occurs in Townsend's (*S. townsendi;* Alcorn, 1940), Franklin's (*S. franklinii;* Sowls, 1948), and probably California ground squirrels (*S. beecheyi;* Linsdale, 1946), but the killers' sexes are unknown.

Richardson's ground squirrels deserve special consideration. Quanstrom (1968, p. 51) observed infanticide in this species. However Michener (1973a) reported that infanticide does not occur in *S. richardsonii* because during a three-year study she neither observed it

Table 19–6.   Field observations of infanticide among ground squirrels (genus *Spermophilus*). Although infanticide has been studied specifically in only a few species, the behavior has been reported frequently, suggesting that intraspecific killing of young may be even more common in this genus than the table indicates.

Infanticide Observed	
Species	*Reference*
S. armatus	Burns, 1968
S. beecheyi*	Linsdale, 1946
S. beldingi	this study
S. columbianus	Steiner, 1970b, 1972; McLean, 1979
S. franklinii	Sowls, 1948
S. undulatus	Steiner, 1972
S. richardsonii**	Quanstrom, 1968
S. townsendii	Alcorn, 1940

Infanticide Not Observed***

S. lateralis
S. tereticaudus
S. tridecemlineatus

No Field Data

S. brunneus, S. mexicanus, S. mohavensis, S. spilosoma, S. variegatus, and S. washingtoni

*Author observed unexplained disappearances of young and attributed them to intraspecific killing.
**See text for further discussion of this species.
***At least two field studies were published on their behavior, but infanticide was not observed.

nor found injured or dead juveniles. I also seldom discovered mutilated young, probably because they were quickly eaten by carnivorous conspecifics or other predators, and I might therefore have failed to emphasize the behavior had I not observed it. Because Michener (1973a, p. 1002) reports data from only 40 hours of " … intense observations … between 16 June (when juveniles were about six weeks old) and 3 July (after which adult males ceased above-ground activity) … ", it is conceivable that she missed any infanticide that might have occurred. The likelihood that neonatal young may sometimes be killed in *S. richardsonii* is seemingly increased by Michener's report (1973b) that, in the laboratory, six of seven virgin females and one of six nonlactating adults attacked or killed conspecific juveniles presented to them.

These examples indicate that infanticide may commonly occur in at least one taxonomic group, the ground squirrels. Indeed this report suggests that infanticide may occur more frequently and in a greater array of animals than has previously been realized. I suggest therefore that further studies of the circumstances and prevalence of infanticide are warranted.

SUMMARY

During the summers of 1974 through 1977, fifteen field assistants and I spent 3,817 hrs. studying the behavior of free-living Belding's ground squirrels at Tioga Pass, California. We discovered that between birth and weaning, more juveniles are killed by conspecifics than by any other predator species. Of 89 neonatal young that perished (29 per cent of an estimated 308 born), 26 (29 per cent) were infanticide victims. Thus at least 8 per cent of all young born were preyed on by conspecifics.

Although members of all sex and age classes occasionally perpetrated infanticide, the majority was done by females and one-year-old males. Individuals never killed young of relatives (i.e., cousins or closer kin), and infanticide frequency was unrelated to population density. Yearling males usually (1) preyed on young near their residences, (2) killed only one juvenile per episode, (3) fed on the carcass, and (4) did not permanently settle near the victim's burrow. Females in contrast usually (1) killed young far from their residences, (2) killed as many young as possible, (3) did not feed on the carcasses, and (4) settled permanently near their victim's burrows. These differences suggest that yearling males and females may derive different benefits from infanticide. Probably one-year-old males obtain sustenance, and adult females increase the likelihood of obtaining nest sites safe from coyotes and badgers by removing potential competitors. Lactating females defend territories surrounding their nest burrows, probably to thwart infanticide.

A literature survey reveals that infanticide occurs in nine different contexts. These are separable into two categories, depending on whether or not parents benefit from the loss of young (Table 19–5). Infanticide occurs in free-living populations of eight of eleven ground squirrel species (genus *Spermophilus*). The widespread occurrence of the behavior suggests that further studies of reproductive competition and infanticide are warranted.

ACKNOWLEDGEMENTS

I thank my field assistants: L. Blumer, K. Dunny, M. Flinn, S. Flinn, S. Gurkewitz, C. Kagarise, J. Kenrick, D. Knapp, D. Kuchapsky, B. Mulder, J. Odenheimer, M. Roth, B. Schultz, D. Weber, and C. Wood. A preliminary version of this paper forms chapter 4 of my doctoral dissertation (Sherman, 1976). For assistance with it I thank R. Alexander, J. Hoogland, S. Hrdy, C. Kagarise, M. Morton, J. Neel, R. Payne, and D. Tinkle. For help with the present paper I thank M. Dickemann, P. Dolhinow, S. Glickman, W. Holmes, C. Kagarise, K. Holekamp, J. Hoogland, B. Ivins, F. Pitelka, L. Rask, D. Tinkle, and S. West. J. Odenheimer allowed me to cite her unpublished manuscript on human infanticide. My studies were financially supported by the National Science Foundation, the National Institutes of Mental Health, the American Philosophical Society, the Museum of Zoology at the University of Michigan, and the Museum of Vertebrate Zoology and the Miller Institute at the University of California. The U.S. Forest Service allowed me to study ground squirrels on their land. The Southern California Edison Company provided housing, and the Clairol Company donated hair dye. R. Alexander and D. Tinkle made possible my participation in the October 1978 symposium on ''Natural Selection and Social Behavior,'' where this paper was first presented.

ADDENDUM

After this manuscript was submitted, S. Hrdy sent me a paper entitled ''Adaptive and nonadaptive classes of infanticide,'' that was prepared for the VIIth (1979) International Congress of the Primatological Society. In this manuscript Hrdy classifies cases of infanticide in a different but complementary way to that given in Table 19–5; the paper was recently published in *Ethology and Sociobiology* (1979, 1:13–40) under the title ''Infanticide among animals: a review, classification, and examination of the implications for the reproductive strategies of females.''

REFERENCES

Alcorn, J. R. 1940. Life history notes on the Piute ground squirrel. *J. Mammal.* 21: 160–170.
Alexander, R. D. 1971. The search for an evolutionary philosophy of man. *Proc. Royal Soc. Victoria* 84: 99–120.
————. 1974. The evolution of social behavior. *Ann. Rev. Ecol. Syst.* 5: 325–383.
————. 1975. The search for a general theory of behavior. *Behav. Sci.* 20: 77–100.
————, and G. Borgia. 1978. Group selection, altruism and the levels of organization of life. *Ann. Rev. Ecol. Syst.* 9: 449–474.
————, and P. W. Sherman. 1977. Local mate competition and parental investment in social insects. *Science* 196: 494–500.
Angst, W., and D. Thommen. 1977. New data and discussion of infant killing in old world monkeys and apes. *Folia Primatol.* 27: 198–229.
Armitage, K. B., D. Johns, and D. C. Andersen. 1979. Cannibalism among yellow-bellied marmots. *J. Mammal.* 60: 205–207.
Armstrong, E. A. 1947. *Bird Display and Behavior: An Introduction to the Study of Bird Psychology,* 2nd ed. Drummond, London.
Ashmole, N. P. 1963. The biology of the wideawake or sooty tern *Sterna fuscata* on Ascension Island. *Ibis* 103b: 297–364.
Bartholomew, G. A. 1952. Reproductive and social behavior of the northern elephant seal. *Univ. of Calif. Publ. Zool.* 47: 369–472.
Beach, F. A. 1978. Sociobiology and interspecific comparisons of behavior. In M. S. Gregory, A. Silvers, and D. Sutch (eds.), *Sociobiology and Human Nature.* Jossey-Bass, San Francisco, pp. 116–135.
Bertram, B. C. R. 1975. Social factors influencing reproduction in wild lions. *J. Zool.* (London) 177: 463–482.
————. 1978. *Pride of Lions.* Scribner's, New York.
Birdsell, J. B. 1968. Some predictions for the pleistocene based on equilibrium systems among recent hunter-gatherers. In R. B. Lee, and I. DeVore (eds.), *Man the Hunter.* Aldine, Chicago, pp. 229–240.
Blumer, L. S. 1979. Male parental care in the bony fishes. *Quart. Rev. Biol.* 54: 149–161.
Boggess, J. 1979. Troop male membership changes and infant killing in langurs (*Presbytis entellus*). *Folia Primatol.* 32: 65–107.

Bruce, H. M. 1960. A block to pregnancy in the mouse caused by proximity of strange males. *J. Reprod. Fertil.* 1: 96–103.

———. 1963. Olfactory block to pregnancy among grouped mice. *J. Reprod. Fertil.* 6: 451–460.

Burns, R. J. 1968. The role of agonistic behavior in regulation of density in Uinta ground squirrels (*Citellus armatus*). Unpubl. Ms. thesis, Utah State Univ., Logan.

Burt, W. H. 1943. Territoriality and home range concepts as applied to mammals. *J. Mammal.* 24: 346–352.

Calhoun, J. B. 1956. A comparative study of the social behavior of two inbred strains of mice. *Ecol. Monogr.* 26: 81–103.

———. 1962. Population density and social pathology. *Sci. Amer.* 206: 139–149.

Carr-Saunders, A. M. 1922. *The Population Problem: A Study in Human Evolution*. Clarendon, Oxford.

Chagnon, N. A. 1968. *Yanomamö, The Fierce People*. Holt, Rinehart, and Winston, New York.

———, M. V. Flinn, and T. F. Melancon. 1979. Sex ratio variation among the Yanomamö indians. In N. A. Chagnon and W. Irons (eds.), *Evolutionary Biology and Human Social Behavior: An Anthropological Perspective*. Duxbury Press, Mass., pp. 290–320.

Christenson, T. E., and B. J. LeBoeuf. 1978. Aggression in the female northern elephant seal, *Mirounga angustirostris*. *Behaviour* 64: 158–172.

Curtin, R., and P. Dolhinow. 1978. Primate social behavior in a changing world. *Amer. Sci.* 66: 468–475.

Davies, N. B. 1978. Ecological questions about territorial behavior. In J. R. Krebs and N. B. Davies (eds.), *Behavioural Ecology: An Evolutionary Approach*. Sinauer, New York, pp. 317–350.

Davis, J. F. W., and E. K. Dunn. 1976. Intraspecific predation and colonial breeding in lesser black-backed gulls *Larus fuscus. Ibis* 118:65–77.

Dickemann, M. 1975. Demographic consequences of infanticide in man. *Ann. Rev. Ecol. Syst.* 6: 107–137.

———. 1979. Female infanticide, reproductive strategies, and social stratification: A preliminary model. In N. A. Chagnon and W. Irons (eds.), *Evolutionary Biology and Human Social Behavior: An Anthropological Perspective*. Duxbury Press, Mass., pp. 321–367.

Divale, W. T., and M. Harris. 1976. Population, warfare, and the male supremacist complex. *Amer. Anthropol.* 78: 521–538.

Dorjahn, V. R. 1958. Fertility, polygyny, and their interrelationships in Temne society. *Amer. Anthropol.* 60: 838–860.

Douglass, M. 1966. Population control in primitive groups. *Brit. J. Sociol.* 17: 263–273.

Fisher, R. A. 1930. *The Genetical Theory of Natural Selection*. Oxford Univ. Press, Oxford.

Fox, L. R. 1975. Cannibalism in natural populations. *Ann. Rev. Ecol. Syst.* 6: 87–106.

Gargett, V. 1978. Sibling aggression in the black eagle in the Matopos, Rhodesia. *Ostrich* 49: 57–63.

Goodall, J. 1977. Infant killing and cannibalism in free-living chimpanzees. *Folia Primatol.* 28: 259–282.

Grantzberg, G. 1973. Twin infanticide—a cross-cultural test of a materialistic explanation. *Ethos* 1: 405–412.

Greenwood, P. J. 1980. Mating systems, philopatry and dispersal in birds and mammals. *Anim. Behav. in press*.

———, P. H. Harvey, and C. M. Perrins. 1978. Inbreeding and dispersal in the great tit. *Nature* 271: 52–54.

Hamilton, W. D. 1964. The genetical evolution of social behaviour, I and II. *J. Theoret. Biol.* 7: 1–52.

———. 1967. Extraordinary sex ratios. *Science* 156: 477–488.

———. 1970. Selfish and spiteful behavior in an evolutionary model. *Nature* 228: 1218–1220.

Hoogland, J. L., and P. W. Sherman. 1976. Advantages and disadvantages of bank swallow (*Riparia riparia*) coloniality. *Ecol. Monogr.* 46: 33–58.

Hrdy, S. B. 1974. Male–male competition and infanticide among the langurs (*Presbytis entellus*) of Abu, Rajasthan. *Folia Primatol.* 22: 19–58.

———. 1977. *The Langurs of Abu*. Harvard Univ. Press, Mass.

Hunt, G. L., Jr., and M. W. Hunt. 1976. Gull chick survival: The significance of growth rates, timing of breeding, and territory size. *Ecology* 57: 62–75.

———, and S. C. McLoon. 1975. Activity patterns of gull chicks in relation to feeding by parents: their potential significance for density-dependant mortality. *Auk* 92: 523–527.

Ingram, C. 1959. The importance of juvenile cannibalism in the breeding biology of certain birds of prey. *Auk* 76: 218–226.

Krzywicki, L. 1934. *Primitive Society and Its Vital Statistics*. Macmillan, London.

van Lawick, H. 1974. *Solo: The Story of an African Wild Dog*. Houghton-Mifflin, Boston.

van Lawick-Goodall, H., and J. van Lawick-Goodall. 1968. *Miss Goodall and the Wild Dogs of Africa*. 16 mm. color, sound film, National Geographic Society (Swan Productions, Ltd., London).

————, and J. van Lawick-Goodall. 1971. *Innocent Killers*. Houghton-Mifflin, Boston.

LeBoeuf, B. J., and K. T. Briggs. 1977. The cost of living in a seal harem. *Mammalia* 41: 167–195.

————, and K. J. Panken. 1977. Elephant seals breeding on the mainland in California. *Proc. Calif. Acad. Sci.* 41: 267–280.

————, R. J. Whiting, and R. F. Gantt. 1972. Perinatal behaviour of northern elephant seals and their young. *Behaviour* 43: 121–156.

Lewontin, R. C. 1970. The units of selection. *Ann. Rev. Ecol. Syst.* 1: 1–18.

Linsdale, J. M. 1946. *The California Ground Squirrel*. Univ. of Calif. Press, Berkeley.

Mallory, F. F., and R. J. Brooks. 1978. Infanticide and other reproductive strategies in the collared lemming, *Dicrostonyx groenlandicus*. *Nature* 273: 144–146.

McLean, I. G. 1979. Paternal behaviour and intra specific killing by the Arctic ground squirrel. *Amer. Zool.* 19:936.

Meyburg, B-U. 1974. Sibling aggression and mortality among nestling eagles. *Ibis* 116:224–228.

Michener, G. R. 1973a. Intraspecific aggression and social organization in ground squirrels. *J. Mammal.* 54: 1001–1003.

————. 1973b. Maternal behaviour in Richardson's ground squirrel (*Spermophilus richardsonii richardsonii*): Retrieval of young by nonlactating females. *Anim. Behav.* 21: 157–159.

Morton, M. L. 1975. Seasonal cycles of body weights and lipids in Belding ground squirrels. *Bull. South. Calif. Acad. Sci.* 74: 128–143.

————, and J. S. Gallup. 1975. Reproductive cycle of the Belding ground squirrel (*Spermophilus beldingi beldingi*): Seasonal and age differences. *Great Basin Natur.* 35: 427–433.

————, C. S. Maxwell, and C. E. Wade. 1974. Body size, body composition, and behavior of juvenile Belding ground squirrels. *Great Basin Natur.* 34: 121–134.

————, and P. W. Sherman. 1978. Effects of a spring snowstorm on behavior, reproduction, and survival of Belding's ground squirrels. *Can. J. Zool.* 56: 2578–2590.

————, and H. L. Tung. 1971. Growth and development in the Belding ground squirrel (*Spermophilus beldingi beldingi*). *J. Mammal.* 52: 611–616.

Myers, K., C. S. Hale, R. Mykytowycz, and R. L. Hughes. 1971. The effects of varying density and space on sociality and health in animals. In A. H. Esser (ed.), *Behavior and Environment*. Plenum, New York, pp. 148–186.

Nelson, J. B. 1975. The breeding biology of frigate birds—a comparative review. *Living Bird* 14: 113–156.

Nishida, T., S. Uehara, and R. Nyundo. 1979. Predatory behavior among wild chimpanzees of the Mahale Mountains. *Primates* 20: 1–20.

O'Conner, R. J. 1978. Brood reduction in birds: Selection for fratricide, infanticide and suicide? *Anim. Behav.* 26: 79–96.

Odenheimer, J. B. ms. Infanticide in human societies: A cross-cultural study. Unpubl. Honors Thesis (1975), Biology Department, Univ. of Michigan, Ann Arbor.

Park, T., D. B. Mertz, W. Grodzinski, and T. Prus. 1965. Cannibalistic predation in populations of flour beetles. *Physiol. Zool.* 38: 289–321.

Parsons, J. 1971. Cannibalism in herring gulls. *Brit. Birds* 64: 528–537.

————. 1975. Asynchronous hatching and chick mortality in the herring gull *Larus argentatus*. *Ibis* 117: 517–520.

Perrone, M., Jr., and T. M. Zaret. 1979. Parental care patterns of fishes. *Amer. Natur.* 113: 351–361.

Picman, J. 1977a. Destruction of eggs by the long-billed marsh wren (*Telmatodytes palustris palustris*). *Can. J. Zool.* 55: 1914–1920.

————. 1977b. Intraspecific nest destruction in the long-billed marsh wren, *Telmatodytes palustris palustris*. *Can. J. Zool.* 55: 1997–2003.

Proctor, D. L. C. 1975. The problem of chick loss in the south polar skua *Catharacta maccormicki*. *Ibis* 117: 452–459.

Quanstrom, W. R. 1968. Some aspects of the ethoecology of Richardson's ground squirrel in eastern North Dakota. Unpubl. Ph.D. Thesis, Univ. of Oklahoma, Norman.

Rohwer, S. 1978. Parent cannibalism of offspring and egg raiding as a courtship strategy. *Amer. Natur.* 112: 429–440.

Rothstein, S. I. 1979. Gene frequencies and selection for inhibitory traits, with special emphasis on the adaptiveness of territoriality. *Amer. Natur.* 113: 317–331.

Schaller, G. B. 1972. *The Serengeti Lion.* Univ. of Chicago Press, Chicago.

Schrire, C., and W. L. Steiger. 1974. A matter of life and death: An investigation into the practice of female infanticide in the Arctic. *Man* 9: 161–184.

Sherman, P. W. 1976. Natural selection among some group-living organisms. Unpubl. Ph.D. Thesis, Univ. of Michigan, Ann Arbor.

———. 1977. Nepotism and the evolution of alarm calls. *Science* 197: 1246–1253.

———. 1978. Comparative review of S. B. Hrdy's "The langurs of Abu," and J. A. Kurland's "Kin selection in the Japanese monkey." *Quart. Rev. Biol.* 53: 491–493.

———. 1980. The limits of ground squirrel nepotism. In G. W. Barlow, and J. Silverberg (eds.). *Sociobiology: Beyond Nature/Nurture?*. Westview Press, Boulder, pp. 505–544.

———. ms. Territoriality, infanticide, and population regulation in Belding's ground squirrels. Paper presented at XVIth Int. Ethol. Congr. (1979).

Southwick, C. H. 1955. Regulatory mechanisms of house mouse populations: Social behavior affecting litter survival. *Ecology* 36: 627–634.

Sowls, L. K. 1948. The Franklin ground squirrel *Citellus franklinii* (Sabine) and its relationship to nesting ducks. *J. Mammal.* 29: 113–137.

Stehn, R. A., and M. E. Richmond. 1975. Male-induced pregnancy termination in the prairie vole, *Microtus ochrogaster. Science* 187: 1211–1213.

Steiner, A. L. 1970a. Étude descriptive de quelques activités et comportements de base de *Spermophilus columbianus columbianus* (Ord) I. Locomotion, soins de corps, alimentation, fouissage, curiosité et alarme, reproduction. *Rev. Comp. Animal* 4: 3–21.

———. 1970b. Étude descriptive de quelques activités et comportements de base de *Spermophilus columbianus columbianus* (Ord). II. Vie de groupe. *Rev. Comp. Animal* 4: 23–42.

———. 1972. Mortality resulting from intraspecific fighting in some ground squirrel populations. *J. Mammal.* 53: 601–603.

Struhsaker, T. T. 1977. Infanticide and social organization in the redtail monkey (*Cercopithecus ascanius schmidti*) in the Kibale Forest, Uganda. *Zeits. für Tierps.* 45: 75–84.

Sumner, W. G. 1906. *Folkways.* Ginn and Co., New York.

Trivers, R. L., and D. E. Willard. 1973. Natural selection of parental ability to vary the sex ratio of offspring. *Science* 179: 90–92.

Troyer, W. A., and R. J. Hensel. 1962. Cannibalism in brown bear. *Anim. Behav.* 10: 231.

Wiens, J. A. 1966. On group selection and Wynne-Edwards' hypothesis *Amer. Sci.* 54: 273–287.

Williams, G. C. 1966. *Adaptation and Natural Selection.* Princeton Univ. Press, Princeton.

Wilson, E. O. 1975. *Sociobiology.* Harvard Univ. Press, Mass.

———. 1978. *On Human Nature.* Harvard Univ. Press, Mass.

Wind, J. 1978. Abortion, ethics, and biology. *Persp. Biol. Med.* 21: 492–504.

Wynne-Edwards, V. C. 1962. *Animal Dispersion in Relation to Social Behaviour.* Hafner, New York.

Yom-Tov, Y. 1974. The effect of food and predation on breeding density and success, clutch size and laying date of the crow *Corvus corone* L. *J. Anim. Ecol.* 43: 479–498.

Young, A. M. 1970. Predation and abundance in populations of flour beetles. *Ecology* 51: 602–619.

Zuckerman, S. 1932. The Social Life of Monkeys and Apes. Kegan Paul, London.

20.

Correlations Among Life History Characteristics of Mammalian Species Exhibiting Two Extreme Forms of Monogamy

D. G. Kleiman

INTRODUCTION

The form of social organization exhibited by monogamous mammals ranges from a dispersed social system (the pair is rarely seen together or with the young) to a pair bonded condition (the pair is usually seen together, with the nuclear family a temporary phenomenon) to a permanent nuclear or extended family (the pair is always seen together with different-aged offspring and sometimes other kin) (see Figure 20–1). The purpose of this paper is to examine the similarities and differences in the behavior of monogamous mammals, to determine whether there are correlations among different behavioral characteristics, depending upon the form of social organization exhibited. The chief behavioral characteristics to be discussed here include the form, intensity, and direction of interactions between and within the sexes, the condition of young at birth and during ontogeny, parental care systems, dispersal mechanisms, and sex differences in territorial behaviors such as scent marking.

BACKGROUND

A recent merging of evolutionary and ecological theory has produced testable hypotheses concerning the factors promoting the evolution of different mating systems (for recent reviews see Emlen and Oring, 1977; Clutton-Brock and Harvey, 1978). It has been suggested that monogamy may evolve when males cannot defend either groups of females or monopolize those resources sufficiently to attract several females. Such conditions are most likely to occur when essential resources are sparse but evenly distributed, thus leading to a wide dispersion of females. The ecological adaptations of many monogamous mammals generally support this hypothesis. For example, callitrichids are frugivore/omnivores, depending on small packets of high-energy foods such as fruits, insects, and small vertebrates that are relatively evenly dispersed in space and time (Dawson 1977; Izawa 1978). The monogamous elephant shrews (Macroscelididae) and dik-diks (*Madoqua* spp.) depend on invertebrates and high-quality browse, respectively (Rathbun, 1979; Hendrichs and Hendrichs, 1971), high-energy diets that are also dispersed in small packets.

The evolution of a modal group size, social tolerance, and ultimate social organization is, however, influenced by factors independent of the mating system itself. For example, social tolerance may be negatively influenced by the following factors:

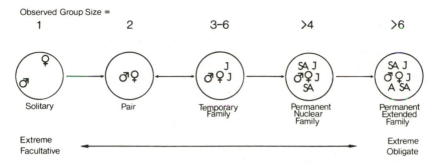

Figure 20–1.   Observed group size and composition in different forms of monogamy ranging from the facultative (dispersed social system) to the obligate (cohesive social system) type. Note that the pair may temporarily become a nuclear family, depending upon reproduction. ♂ and ♀ represent the reproductively active male and female. J refers to juvenile offspring, SA to subadult offspring, and A to adult offspring or other adult relatives of the breeding pair.

1. Intersexual competition: Social tolerance may be selected against if the sexes must themselves compete for limited resources. For example, rufous elephant shrew females (*Elephantulus rufescens*), although monogamous, aggressively defend from males (including the mate) areas of termite surface activity; these concentrations of foraging termites occur erratically (Rathbun, 1979) but are a temporarily rich food resource.
2. Cryptic anti-predator strategy: For species that depend on crypsis to avoid predation, social contact may be disadvantageous to all individuals (Eisenberg and McKay, 1974). The monogamous elephant shrews and agoutis (*Dasyprocta punctata*) are cursorial species, which are heavily preyed upon by a variety of small predators (Rathbun, 1978; Smythe, 1978). Presumably, susceptibility to predation would be increased with a larger group size. Selection against a social group has even influenced the form of maternal care in these species, in that mother-young contact is rare, with neonates spending the majority of time in isolation, hiding.

Although group foraging and feeding is usually more disadvantageous than advantageous, thus promoting social intolerance, food acquisition and defense may in some cases be improved by a larger group size (Eisenberg, 1966; Alexander, 1974). In some of the smaller monogamous canid species, cooperative hunting *may* occasionally improve foraging success, thus benefiting more than one individual (Kleiman and Eisenberg, 1973). This would result in selection for greater social tolerance. Another condition that would select for greater social tolerance is an anti-predator strategy based on group defense.

Given that there are factors that independently select for and against social tolerance, variations in group size and social structure in monogamous mammals should parallel the variation seen in polygynous mammals. Indeed, among monogamous mammals, group size may vary from 1 to 15 individuals while social structure ranges from an essentially solitary condition to extended families in which several adult males and females as well as juveniles and sub-adults co-exist (Figure 20–1).

Examples of relatively asocial monogamous species include the elephant shrews (Macroscelididae) (Rathbun, 1976, 1979) and dik-diks (*Madoqua* spp.) (Hendrichs and Hendrichs, 1971) where individuals are usually seen alone or as pairs, and young usually disperse from the parental home range before a subsequent birth. In the more social monogamous mammals, the group is essentially a nuclear family, although in some species siblings of the reproductive pair (and perhaps other close relatives) are also part of the social group, resulting in an extended family with only one set of reproductive adults. Offspring may not disperse until after puberty, thus young of different ages may be present simultaneously. Examples of species exhibiting this form of monogamy may be found in the primate family Callitrichidae, the marmosets and tamarins (Epple, 1975a; Rothe, 1975); pack-hunting canids like the wolf, *Canis lupus,* and hunting dog, *Lycaon pictus,* also show these characteristics (Mech, 1970; van Lawick, 1971; Frame and Frame, 1976; Kleiman and Brady, 1978).

I have previously termed the two most extreme forms of monogamy in mammals facultative (asocial) and obligate (highly social) (Kleiman, 1977a). The adjective facultative is defined by *Webster's New Collegiate Dictionary* (1977) as ''showing the typical life style under some environmental conditions but not under others.'' The use of this qualifier reflects the probability that polygyny in asocial monogamous mammals is prevented by ecological constraints, i.e., the dispersion of resources in an average environment reduces the probability that a male can defend the territories (or home ranges) of more than one female and thus increase his reproductive success. Obligate is defined as ''restricted to one particular mode of life'' (Webster's, 1977). As used here, it suggests that polygyny is prevented less by ecological constraints than by the reduced probability that a female can rear young successfully without the *direct* aid of a male. Thus, direct male parental care appears to have less effect on female reproductive success in asocial monogamous mammals than on female reproductive success in the highly social species despite the fact that the monogamy is still the modal mating system, i.e., a male and female tend to mate exclusively with each other through several reproductive efforts.

This implies that the quality and quantity of parental investment by males, like the degree of social tolerance, are influenced by factors other than the mating system itself. For example, the degree of close contact between a male and female should affect the frequency and type of parental investment by males. Where social tolerance is high and pair mates interact frequently, direct paternal care by males is more likely as paternity is more certain. In relatively asocial species, paternity may be in question because the pair mates are rarely in contact. Thus, one would expect less active paternal care. Finally, the quality and quantity of parental care will be influenced by the degree to which such behavior is advantageous in the rearing of offspring.

Correlated Life History Characteristics and their Analysis

In Table 20–1, I suggest the probable correlations among eight life history characteristics in extreme facultative and extreme obligate monogamy. These correlations are based on a combination of expectations from theory and known facts. The function of these correlations is to provide a framework whereby comparisons can be made, with the same questions being asked of many different species.

A. Behavior towards adult conspecifics

1. Relationship within the bonded pair:

The term ''pair bond'' is a frequently and loosely used phrase for which there is not yet an operational definition. For example, Wilson (1975), in his glossary, defines ''pair bonding'' as ''a close and long-lasting association formed between a male and female'' (p. 590). This definition, however, does not specify the character of the association or its duration. Nor has there been an attempt to do so by most authors, even though intuitively, both ethologists and others recognize that pair bond ''strength'' varies from species to species and that there should be a method of quantifying such variability (see Eisenberg, 1966).

Among species exhibiting facultative monogamy where there may be selection against social tolerance, one would expect a ''weaker'' pair bond. Among species with obligate monogamy, where there is either no selection against social tolerance or selection favoring social tolerance, pair bonds should be ''stronger.'' To examine differences in pair bond

Table 20–1.   Correlations of behavioral characteristics in extreme facultative and extreme obligate monogamy.

	Facultative Monogamy	Obligate Monogamy
1. Behavior towards adult conspecifics		
a. Relationship between bonded pair	weak pair bond; more aggressive than affiliative behaviors; female aggressive to male?	strong pair bond; more affiliative than aggressive behaviors; female aggressive to male?
b. Behavior towards other adults	male–male aggression greater than female–female aggression; occasional polygamy	female–female aggression equal to or greater than male–male aggresson; polygamy uncommon
2. Relation to space and time		
a. Distribution of territorial behaviors between mates	males more than females	males and females equal
b. Synchrony of pair activities	asynchronous	synchronous
3. Quality and quantity of parental care		
a. Paternal care	less developed, mainly indirect	well-developed, mainly direct
b. Parental care by juveniles	not present	present
4. Ontogeny		
a. Sequence of development	rapid social weaning; early puberty	late social weaning; delayed puberty
b. Mechanisms of dispersal	parental aggression towards young	sibling aggression; parental aggression rarer

"strength," the following characteristics could be investigated.

(a) Paired individuals could exhibit both agonistic and affiliative behaviors towards each other, regardless of the interaction rate. One would expect that the ratio of affiliative to agonistic behaviors would be higher, the stronger the bond between the pair. Weakly bonded individuals would be expected to exhibit relatively higher rates of agonistic or conflict behavior and avoidance. Affiliative behaviors would include (i) those that promote proximity between paired individuals, e.g., courtship displays and vocal signals that maintain auditory contact during independent foraging and (ii) those involving long periods of body contact, such as sleeping together, huddling, allogrooming, and sexual contacts.

(b) The process of pair-bond formation as measured by the length of time it takes for pair interactions to reach an equilibrium as well as the degree to which reproduction (i.e., sexual activity) alters that equilibrium could also be an indicator of pair-bond quality. In weakly bonded species pair interactions might be expected to reach an equilibrium rapidly but be more easily altered or upset than in strongly bonded species. Moreover, species in which only weak bonds are formed might exhibit relatively higher levels of courtship behavior by the male prior to sexual activity because of the generally low levels of interactive behavior at other times. Increased courtship prior to copulation would also aid in ensuring paternity because the female would be monopolized during the receptive period. Fewer changes in interactions before mating might characterize species with a stronger bonding tendency.

(c) The degree of synchrony in routine daily activities could also be used to distinguish between strong and weak pair bonds. Species exhibiting strong pair bonds are likely to be characterized by a high level of synchrony in such activities as foraging, feeding, scent marking, nest-building, etc., with the reverse true for weakly bonded species.

(d) The duration of the pair's association may be a measure of pair-bond strength.

However, this characteristic must be related to longevity and frequency of reproduction and can only be determined from long-term field observations. It is likely that in more strongly bonded species, mate changes will be relatively less frequent.

In species exhibiting facultative monogamy, where social tolerance may be disadvantageous for ecological reasons, pair bonds may be weak and I would predict that pairs would exhibit a higher ratio of agonistic and conflict behavior relative to affiliative behavior, less behavioral synchrony, and would reach an interaction equilibrium faster after pair bond formation than in obligate monogamy. Data already available seem to confirm this expectation. For example, in the rufous elephant shrew, *Elephantulus rufescens,* interactions between pair mates are characterized by agonistic behavior or avoidance, except before the female's estrus. Pairs infrequently sleep at the same location and never forage together (Rathbun, 1979). Similar observations have been reported by Smythe (1978) for the agouti, *Dasyprocta punctata.* Females rarely permit the pair mates to approach and also become extremely aggressive shortly after birth. Smythe observed very rare cases of affiliative behavior, such as mutual grooming of the ear region. Foraging was conducted independently, and pairs did not sleep in contact, although they were occasionally in close proximity.

By contrast, pair interactions are of a more affiliative nature in species exhibiting obligate monogamy. For example, among lion tamarins (*Leontopithecus rosalia*), which live in nuclear or extended family groups, agonistic interactions are rarely seen within the members of a pair. Moreover, pair mates regularly rest and sleep in close body contact and allogroom on a regular basis (Kleiman, 1977b). There is synchrony in feeding and resting behavior, and pairs are rarely out of visual or vocal contact with each other. Courtship behavior by the males during estrus is inconspicuous relative to the driving behavior described for elephant shrews (Rathbun, 1979) and agoutis (Smythe, 1978).

There are species in which pair bonds appear to be intermediate in "strength," suggesting that the gradation in group size reflects a gradation in the degree of social tolerance among monogamous mammals. Such variability undoubtedly depends on the strength of the various ecological pressures, e.g., feeding strategies, either favoring or selecting against social tolerance.

A species intermediate in pair bond strength is the crab-eating fox *(Cerdocyon thous)* where pairs are usually seen together although they may forage separately and exhibit intermediate levels of close body contact and affiliative behaviors. Agonistic interactions occur mainly during the early stages of pair bond formation (Kleiman and Brady, 1978). Courtship is conspicuous, as in elephant shrews and agoutis.

One characteristic of a pair bond that is unrelated to group size and social structure is the dominance relationship within a pair. I have already suggested that in some monogamous mammals, females appear to be more assertive and aggressive than males in heterosexual interactions (Kleiman, 1977a), a characteristic that is rare in polygynous mammals. If monogamous females compete with males for scarce resources, and these resources are critical for the female's reproductive success, one would predict a reversal of the more typical form of male-dominated heterosexual interaction. Such a condition need not be specific to monogamous mammals but may be accentuated with this reproductive strategy as the male's reproductive success is closely aligned with the female's reproductive success. Such critical resources might include a burrow system, cached food, or food resources that are rich but sparsely distributed in the home range. The scattered food hoards of the agouti are such a resource (Smythe, 1978), and female agoutis tend to dominate the mate.

The female also tends to be dominant over the male in rufous elephant shrews (Rathbun, 1979), bush dogs (*Speothos venaticus*) (Drüwa 1976, 1977), beavers *(Castor fiber)* (Wilsson, 1971), and green acouchis *(Myoprocta pratti)* (Kleiman, 1977a) although it is not known whether the causes of the female dominance are the same in all cases. Female dominance may be associated with females being nearly as large or larger than males, although this is not the case in dik-diks, *Madoqua* (Ralls, pers. comm.)

2. Relationship with adults other than the mate:

With a monogamous reproductive strategy, male-male competition should be less intense than in polygyny. However, there may still be considerable variation in the degree of intrasexual competition among both males and females in monogamous mammals, and these may derive from differences in group size and social tolerance. Moreover, the degree of exclusivity of the mating relationship may differ. I would expect that in species exhibiting facultative monogamy where pair members are dispersed, the degree of intrasexual competition will be greater in males than in females and will parallel what is seen in polygynous mammals because of the relatively lower certainty of paternity. By contrast, in species exhibiting obligate monogamy where the certainty of paternity is higher, males and females will be more similar in the degree of aggression shown towards same-sexed conspecifics. This trend will be paralleled by a tendency for facultative species to have potentially less exclusive mating relationships (although still with a high percentage of monogamous matings) while mating outside the pair bond may be rarer in obligate species.

In species exhibiting facultative monogamy, males seem to be more aggressive to male strangers than females are to female strangers, e.g., dik-dik, *Madoqua kirki* (Hendrichs and Hendrichs, 1971), elephant shrews, *Rhynchocyon chrysopygus* (Rathbun, 1979), and agoutis, *Dasyprocta punctata* (Smythe, 1978). Females do, however, defend the territory against female strangers.

Among some mammals exhibiting obligate monogamy, it has been reported that competition or aggression among females is more intense than among males, e.g., saddle-backed tamarin, *Saguinus fuscicollis*, (Epple, 1977); wolf, *Canis lupus*, (Zimen, 1975); hunting dog, *Lycaon pictus*, (van Lawick, 1971, 1973; Frame and Frame, 1976, 1977; Frame et al., 1980). This reversal of the normal mammalian pattern of intense male–male competition is predicted to occur only in species where males are the limiting sex, i.e., in polyandry where males have a greater parental investment than females. With internal gestation and lactation female mammals always provide more parental investment than males and therefore are the limiting sex. The intense female–female competition in some monogamous mammals suggests that females may be competing for groups of males that exhibit good paternal care even though only a single male may contribute gametes to the future offspring. Such a condition is more likely where the males are genetically related, e.g., brothers, and does appear to exist among hunting dogs, *Lycaon pictus*, where females (usually sisters) compete intensely for the loyalty of groups of related males (Frame and Frame, 1976, 1977). Groups of related males are usually monopolized by and rear the offspring of a single dominant female who apparently only mates with the most dominant male. Other females are prevented from achieving reproductive success by (1) the dominant female's aggression during estrus that prevents copulations, (2) the dominant female destroying the offspring of sisters and (3) males refusing to feed a subordinate female and her litter. Competition among females also results in females being the primary dispersers from social groups (Frame and Frame, 1976, 1977; Frame et al., 1979; van Lawick, 1971, 1973).

Since facultative monogamy involves little assurance of paternity because of the low levels of social tolerance, it is likely that males may opportunistically try to mate with other females. However, aggression from the female pair-mate towards other transient or neighboring female adults may limit the success of such attempts. Observations of elephant shrews (Rathbun, 1979) suggest that intersexual relations among neighbors are usually amicable. Rathbun did observe an *R. chrysopygus* male attempting to mate with a neighboring female who had lost her mate.

In obligate monogamy, attempts to mate outside the pair bond may be much rarer, since pairs are in close association and usually jointly attack territorial intruders (e.g., tamarins, Dawson 1977; Neyman, 1977; wolves, Mech, 1970). Among family members, the dominant pair suppresses reproduction in siblings or offspring by both behavioral and physiological means. In marmosets and tamarins, it is already clear that sexual behavior is restricted to the bonded pair in families and artificial groups (Epple, 1972; Rothe, 1975; Kleiman, 1979) without aggression being common between same-sexed adults *if* they have been previously habituated to each other. Hearn (1977) has shown that daughters will not exhibit an ovarian cycle as long as they remain in the presence of their mother. Among wolves and dwarf mongooses (*Helogale undulata*), matings of subdominant animals may be prevented by direct aggression (Rabb et al., 1967; Rasa, 1973a), and in African wild dogs, reproductive dominance occasionally may be achieved through killing the offspring born to a subordinate female (van Lawick, 1973).

Clearly, in assessing how and why mating exclusivity is achieved, one must determine (1) whether mating outside the pair bond occurs and (2) if not, whether it is prevented by the pair-mate or simply not attempted. There are no data available on the frequency of polygyny (or polyandry) for any typically monogamous mammal.

B. Behavior with respect to space and time

1. Distribution of territorial behaviors between mates:

Mammals may use a variety of behavior patterns to indicate their presence to conspecifics without a direct confrontation. These include signals such as scent marking and long-distance vocalizations that probably provide information about an individual or group's identity and location.

The majority of monogamous mammals appear to be territorial in that they defend exclusive use of an area from neighboring conspecifics and advertise their presence by scent marking and vocalizing.

The greater degree of intra-male aggression suggested for species exhibiting facultative monogamy should be paralleled by sex differences in the frequency of ''territorial'' behaviors such as scent marking, with males exhibiting more marking than females. Among elephant shrews (Rathbun, 1979), dik-diks (Hendrichs and Hendrichs, 1971; Kranz, unpublished), and agoutis (Smythe, 1978), this is indeed the case.

In obligate monogamy, sex differences in these behaviors should be reduced. Among several species of marmosets and tamarins, males and females tend to scent mark at similar frequencies (Kleiman and Mack, 1980; Epple, 1977; Box, 1977a), and females occasionally scent-mark more than males. Although Rasa (1973b) reports that in dwarf mongooses the dominant male marks significantly more than the dominant female (p. 300), these results were obtained during experimental tests, and Figure 6 in Rasa (1973b) suggests that there is little sex difference with longitudinal observations. Among bush dogs the female consistently urine-marks at much higher levels than the male (Drüwa, 1976, 1977; Kleiman and Brady, unpublished), indicating a reversal of the typical sex role and paralleling the high levels of intrasexual competition among females in this species.

With respect to long-distance vocalizations, hylobatid males and females jointly vocalize on a daily basis. The calls of males and females differ, with the female's great call dominating the duet in some species (Marshall and Marshall, 1976).

2. Synchrony of pair activities

Because the males and females of species exhibiting facultative monogamy are not often in contact, it is likely that they will carry out most maintenance activities alone and will rarely jointly perform behavior patterns that promote spacing.

Under obligate monogamy, pairs should synchronize their activities, including foraging and feeding, resting, and the execution of ''territorial'' behaviors. Such synchronous activity has been remarked upon by many authors for species such as siamangs (*Symphalangus syndactylus*) (Chivers, 1975) and titi monkeys (*Callicebus* spp.) (Robinson, 1979; Kinzey et al., 1977). Long-distance vocalizations may be performed as duets (e.g., lion tamarins, McLanahan and Green, 1977; some hylobatids, Marshall and Marshall, 1976; titi monkeys, Robinson, 1979; Kinzey et al., 1977), and scent-marking may be performed in alternation (or sequentially) at the same location (canids, Kleiman and Brady, 1978; Golani and Keller, 1975; Frame et al., 1979; marmosets and tamarins, Mack and Kleiman, 1979). Wolf howls, although performed by an entire family, are undoubtedly derived from the joint calling of the dominant breeding male and female of a pack.

Among species exhibiting facultative monogamy, pairs appear to carry out most maintenance activities alone and rarely perform together behavior patterns that promote spacing. This trend has already been noted for scent-marking in elephant shrews (Rathbun, 1976, 1979), agoutis (Smythe, 1978), and dik-diks (Hendrichs and Hendrichs, 1971).

C. Quality and quantity of parental care

1. Paternal investment:

A critical expectation already mentioned is that the males of species exhibiting facultative monogamy will exhibit less parental care than males of species exhibiting obligate monogamy, because the former are less assured of paternity as a result of their asocial tendencies. Unfortunately, it is difficult to compare species directly with respect to parental investment by both sexes because one must consider, for each type of behavior pattern, the time and energy output, the cost or risk to the parent (with respect to future reproduction) of such an activity, and the contribution to the survivorship of offspring by the behavior. Moreover, indirect forms of parental care, such as territorial defense, that contribute to survivorship of young must be considered in addition to direct forms of investment such as feeding young (Ralls, 1977). Finally, physical differences must be considered as some species cannot provide a form of parental care that is common in others. However, the time devoted to specific behavior patterns could be compared among species and the *relative* contribution by males and females to rearing young within each species can be roughly assessed. It is clear that an individual female mammal will assume a greater parental burden than a single male regardless of the species' reproductive strategy because female mammals both gestate young and feed them with milk until the time of weaning.

The total time in contact with young is a minimal measure of potential contribution to an infant's survival. Whether and how often young are fed (by males and females after weaning), played with, or carried are also important measures.

Changes in the degree of intolerance to strange conspecifics in both adult sexes when young are born may also indicate the degree to which a male or female becomes more territorial during reproduction. This may be an important measure of parental investment for facultative species.

I have already suggested that male parental investment is highest in obligate monogamy although the index used was somewhat arbitrary because of the sketchy data (Kleiman, 1977a). In species showing facultative monogamy, although the male's direct contribution appears low, total parental investment by males cannot easily be determined since indirect investment may be considerable. In facultative species, males expend considerable time and energy in patrolling the territory. Protectiveness towards the young has also been reported (e.g., in elephant shrews, Rathbun, 1979, and dik-diks, Simonetta, 1966). It is worth noticing that many of the species exhibiting facultative monogamy produce precocial young that are "hiders" during the early post-natal period. Thus, lack of close contact between the male and his offspring or direct paternal care is paralleled by reduced mother–young contact or maternal care.

The heavy parental investment by males in species exhibiting obligate monogamy has been documented in several species, e.g. marmosets and tamarins (Epple, 1975b; Hoage, 1977; Box, 1977b), dwarf mongooses (Rasa, 1977), and canids (van Lawick, 1971, 1973; Mech, 1970; Moehlman, 1979) and may be correlated with larger and/or heavier litters as well as more altricial young.

2. "Parental" investment by kin:

One of the basic differences between the two extreme forms of monogamy is that older juveniles may remain with the parents after weaning (and even puberty) in the obligate condition and aid in rearing the young of subsequent litters of their parents (Kleiman, 1977a). In facultative monogamy young tend to disperse prior to the next birth or at least avoid the parents after weaning (e.g., elephant shrews, Rathbun, 1979) if they remain on the parental territory. There are differences, however, within obligate monogamy in whether a nuclear or extended family is maintained. For example, among golden and black-backed jackals

(*Canis aureus, C. mesomelas*) (van Lawick, 1971; Moehlman, 1979), the helpers all appear to be offspring of the adult pair while among wolves (Mech, 1970), African wild dogs (van Lawick, 1971, 1973; Frame and Frame, 1976) and possibly marmosets and tamarins (Dawson, 1977), other kin may aid in rearing infants. Group size and composition seem to be positively correlated with the breeding female's reproductive success, both within and between species. Two mammalian families in which such predictions could be examined are the Canidae and Callitrichidae.

For direct parental investment by kin to be possible, several behavioral traits are required. First, parents must exhibit continued tolerance towards weaned young (or brothers and sisters) so that there is an opportunity for them to interact with infants, and second, the older juveniles (or other kin) must have a positive attraction for young. Third, reproductive activity in kin must be suppressed. For these behavioral traits to evolve, there must be clear benefits to both parents and relatives. These benefits have recently been discussed by Blaffer–Hrdy (1976), mainly for polygynous primates. The benefits to parents include increased reproductive success, i.e., survival of more offspring (this has been shown for the black-backed jackal by Moehlman, 1979). The helpers benefit by gaining experience in parental care, gaining protection and access to resources while remaining in the family, and helping in the survivorship of close relatives, which increases their inclusive fitness (Hamilton, 1964).

D. Ontogeny

1. Sequence of development:

The condition of neonates, e.g., altricial or precocial, and ontogenetic parameters were not found to be correlated with a monogamous reproductive strategy in any specific way (Kleiman, 1977a). However, Rathbun (1979) has suggested that facultative species that are cursorial as an anti-predator strategy tend to bear more precocial young. Correlated with this characteristic are rapid development, early weaning, and early puberty.

In species exhibiting obligate monogamy young may remain dependent on the parents long after nutritional weaning, which would be expected if young are to remain with the parents beyond a subsequent birth. Moreover, sociosexual maturity should be delayed in reproductive-age animals as long as they are in the presence of their parents. Delayed puberty or reproductive suppression have been reported for callitrichids (Epple, 1975), dwarf mongooses (Rasa, 1973a), and canids (Mech, 1970; Kleiman and Brady, 1978).

A comparison of the two extreme forms of monogamy with respect to aspects of behavioral development such as delayed puberty requires data on growth rates, earliest and typical age at first reproduction, reproductive cycle, litter size, and age at reproductive senility (i.e., total lifetime productivity). These data are not yet available for many species (but see Eisenberg, in press).

2. Mechanisms of dispersal:

A comparison of this behavioral characteristic in monogamous species is of major importance because a determination of when and why young leave their parents is essential to understanding how a nuclear or extended family can develop and persist.

Among species exhibiting facultative monogamy, it is expected that young will disperse after the development of social intolerance by the parents, when young begin to compete for essential resources. The young may be expected to remain on the parental territory as long as the parents tolerate them, despite a lack of parent-offspring contact. Among elephant shrews, parental aggression towards young and dispersal have been observed in *Elephantulus rufescens* but in *Rhynchocyon chrysopygus*, occasional young were tolerated on the parental territory without aggression for as long as seven months (Rathbun, 1979). In both species, young rarely interact with parents after a subsequent birth. Among agoutis, parental aggression to older offspring tends to be sex specific and exacerbated by food scarcity. Older juveniles appear to be chased out of the parental territory unless fruit is abundant (Smythe, 1978). Among dik-diks, Hendrichs and Hendrichs (1971) have also described

parents chasing offspring from the territory. In all of the above species, the post-weaning period is one of the greatest periods of mortality—until juveniles and subadults gain access to their own territory.

In extreme obligate monogamy, parental aggression towards young should be rare as long as offspring (or other kin) "help" with rearing subsequent litters and do not threaten the reproductive dominance of the pair. However, as young mature and as the carrying capacity of the family group's home range is approached, conflicts should develop. The nature of the conflicts is likely to depend on the age and sex composition of the family group, and the result will depend on the available options for the non-reproductive kin. Offspring may often remain within the family group because helping to raise younger siblings increases their inclusive fitness and decreases their potential mortality. In general, however, I suggest that sibling conflict may be a greater promoter of dispersal than parent-offspring conflict since siblings not only increase their inclusive fitness by remaining but have the potential to achieve breeding status if a parent dies.

Clearly, conflict will be within each sex class, and heterosexual fighting should be rare. Conflict should also be more common within each age class, as at any given point the reproductive value of littermates is similar. Offspring should not challenge parents until parents approach reproductive senescence and their reproductive future is uncertain. The decision to remain with the family or disperse will depend on the degree of competition within the family balanced with other available options. Options will differ depending upon the overall population density and the degree of saturation of the habitat. Females should have more serious conflicts than males because they may be competing for "helpers" as well as mates.

There is already evidence that competition among same-sexed, same-aged siblings is high in obligate forms. In common marmosets, *Callithrix jacchus*, twin same-sexed siblings are reported to fight as juveniles (Sutcliffe, 1979; Rothe, 1979), while in lion tamarins, *Leontopithecus rosalia*, it has been noted that aggression within family groups often can be traced to sibling interactions (Kleiman, 1979), usually at the time of the mother's estrus. Conflict is more commonly expressed among twin or sibling males in *Leontopithecus*, although conflict between twin females is more serious and has resulted in fatal attacks on females with the mother strongly implicated in the deaths (Kleiman, 1979).

Captive studies may distort the nature of family conflict, depending on a researcher's measures of conflict. For example, among lion tamarins, conflict among males has been observed most frequently, both between father and sons and between siblings. Yet, the only deaths resulting from family conflict were of females. This suggests that real conflict is greater among females than males. Neyman's (1977) field study indicates that more females (*Saguinus oedipus*) than males are transient or leave groups, which supports the above suggestion.

Among wild dogs, sibling competition is also most severe among female littermates and results in an initial dispersal of females from the natal pack and a secondary dispersal of non-reproductive sisters when one female sibling in a group begins reproducing (Frame and Frame, 1977; Frame, et al., 1979).

SUMMARY

Evidence from mammals indicates that there are two extreme forms of monogamy in this class, with gradations based on the degree of sociality in a species. In facultative monogamy (dispersed social system), the pair bond is weak and polygyny may occasionally occur when opportunities arise. Mated pairs interact rarely and occasionally are antagonistic. Parental investment by males is mainly indirect, i.e., the male defends the essential resources of the home range from conspecifics. Development of young is rapid, and matur-

ing juveniles leave the parental territory and reach reproductive maturity at a relatively early age. Although there is little sexual dimorphism in size, males and females exhibit sex role differences, with males exhibiting higher levels of intrasexual aggression and territorial behaviors. Parent-offspring conflict is mainly responsible for juvenile dispersal.

Within extreme obligate monogamy, sex role differences are smaller and in some species sex roles are almost reversed, especially with respect to intrasexual competition (females may be more aggressive than males) and territorial maintenance (females may be more active than males). In comparing facultative and obligate monogamy it appears that the lack of sexual dimorphism in size, a general characteristic of both types, is not a good indicator of the degree of sex role differentiation.

In obligate monogamy, males exhibit parental care, as do many juveniles and siblings of the breeding pair. Young remain dependent but also help their parents, often beyond the age of sexual maturity. The pair bond is strong and characterized by synchronous behavior of the pair members and the frequent display of affiliative behaviors such as mutual grooming. Sexual infidelity may be prevented by intrasexual aggression towards strangers but also by the reproductive inhibition of juveniles and siblings of the breeding pair, both behaviorally and physiologically. Dispersal of young may be initiated mainly through intrasexual sibling aggression.

Species exhibiting facultative monogamy were often thought to be solitary and polygynous in nature while obligate forms appeared to be social and polygynous. In both cases, the mating system has only become apparent after detailed field and laboratory studies. Clearly, a species' mating system cannot be deduced only from data on group size and composition.

The major force promoting monogamy in mammals is the inability of a male to defend groups of reproducing females. The group size and therefore type of monogamy in mammals depends on the interaction of several factors selecting for and against sociality. In some cases, obligate monogamy may have evolved from the need for increased paternal investment.

ACKNOWLEDGMENTS

The author's research has been supported by NIMH 25242 and 27241 and the Smithsonian Research Foundation. I am extremely grateful to the following persons for their comments on this manuscript as well as previous drafts: John F. Eisenberg, Katherine Ralls, Christen Wemmer, Eugene Morton, Galen Rathbun, and the editors of this volume. My thanks also to Gail Hill who patiently typed several early drafts of this paper.

REFERENCES

1   Alexander, R. D. 1974. The evolution of social behavior. *Ann. Rev. Ecol. Syst.* 5:325–383.
2.   Blaffer-Hrdy, S. 1976. The care and exploitation of nonhuman primate infants by conspecifics other than the mother. *Adv. Study Behav.* 6:101–158.
3.   Box, H. O. 1977a. Social interactions in family groups of captive marmosets (*Callithrix jacchus*). pp. 239–249. In D. G. Kleiman (ed.), *The Biology and Conservation of the Callitrichidae.* Smithsonian Institution Press, Washington, D.C.
4.   ———. 1977b. Quantitative data on the carrying of young captive monkeys (*Callithrix jacchus*) by other members of their family groups. *Primates* 18:475–484.
5.   Chivers, D. G. 1975. The siamang in Malaya: A field study of a primate in a tropical rain forest. *Contrib. Primat.* 4:1–335.
6.   Clutton-Brock, T. H., and P. H. Harvey. 1978. Mammals, resources, and reproductive strategies. *Nature* 273:191–195.

7. Dawson, G. A. 1977. Composition and stability of social groups of the tamarin, *Saguinus oedipus geoffroyi,* in Panama: ecological and behavioral implications. pp. 23–37. In D. G. Kleiman (ed.), see Reference #3.

8. Drüwa, P. 1976. Beobachtungen zum Verhalten des Waldhundes (*Speothos venaticus,* Lund 1842) in der Gefangenschaft. Ph.D. Dissertation, Universität Bonn.

9. _____. 1977. Beobachtungen zur Geburt und Naturlichen Aufzucht von Waldhunden (*Speothos venaticus*) in der Gefangenschaft. *Zool. Gart. N. F. Jena* 47:109–137.

10. Eisenberg, J. F. 1966. The social organizations of mammals. *Handbuch der Zoologie,* VIII (10/7), Lieferung 39. De Gruyter, Berlin.

11. _____. (In press). *The Mammalian Radiations: A Study in Adaptation, Evolution and Behavior.* University of Chicago Press.

12. Eisenberg, J. F., and G. M. McKay. 1974. Comparison of ungulate adaptations in the New World and Old World tropical forests with special reference to Ceylon and the rain forests of Central America. In V. Geist and F. Walther (eds.), *The Behaviour of Ungulates and its Relation to Management.* pp. 585–602, IUCN Publ. #24, Morges.

13. Emlen, S. T., and L. W. Oring. 1977. Ecology, sexual selection, and the evolution of mating systems. *Science* 197:215–223.

14. Epple, G. 1972. Social behavior of laboratory groups of *Saguinus fuscicollis.* In D. D. Bridgwater (ed.), *Saving the Lion Marmoset,* pp. 50–58. Wild Animal Propagation Trust, Wheeling, West Virginia.

15. _____. 1975a. The behavior of marmoset monkeys (Callithricidae). In L. A. Rosenblum (ed.), *Primate Behavior,* Vol. 4, pp. 195–239. Academic Press, New York.

16. _____. 1975b. Parental behavior in *Saguinus fuscicollis* ssp. (Callithricidae). *Folia Primatol.* 24:221–238.

17. _____. 1977. Notes on the establishment and maintenance of the pair bond in *Saguinus fuscicollis.* pp. 231–237. In D. G. Kleiman (ed.), see Reference #3.

18. Frame, L. H., and G. H. Frame. 1976. Female African wild dogs emigrate. *Nature* 263:227–229.

19. _____. 1977. The Plains Pack. *Anim. Kingdom* 80:13–25.

20. Frame, L. H., J. R. Malcolm, G. W. Frame, and H. van Lawick. (1979). Social organization of African wild dogs (*Lycaon pictus*) on the Serengeti Plains, Tanzania, 1967–1978. *Z. Tierpsychol.* 50:225–249.

21. Golani, I., and A. Keller. 1975. A longitudinal field study of the behavior of a pair of golden jackals. In M. W. Fox (ed.), *The Wild Canids,* pp. 303–335. Van Nostrand Reinhold, New York.

22. Hamilton, W. D. 1964. The genetical theory of social behaviour. I, II. *J. Theoret. Biol.* 7:1–16; 17–52.

23. Hearn, J. P. 1977. The endocrinology of reproduction in the common marmoset, *Callithrix jacchus.* pp. 163–171. In D. G. Kleiman (ed.), see Reference #3.

24. Hendrichs, H., and U. Hendrichs. 1971. *Dikdik und Elefanten: Okologie und Soziologie zweier afrikanischer Huftiere.* R. Piper and Co., Munich.

25. Hoage, R. J. 1977. Parental care in *Leontopithecus rosalia rosalia:* sex and age differences in carrying behavior and the role of prior experience. pp. 293–305. In D. G. Kleiman (ed.), see Reference #3.

26. Izawa, K. 1978. A field study of the ecology and behavior of the black-mantle tamarin (*Saguinus nigricollis*). *Primates* 19:241–274.

27. Kinzey, W. G., A. L. Rosenberger, P. S. Hersler, D. L. Prowse, and J. S. Trilling. 1977. A preliminary field investigation of the yellow handed titi monkey, *Callicebus torquatus torquatus,* in Northern Peru. *Primates* 18:159–181.

28. Kleiman, D. G. 1977a. Monogamy in Mammals. *Quart. Rev. Biol.* 52:39–69.

29. _____. 1977b. Characteristics of reproduction and sociosexual interactions in pairs of lion tamarins (*Leontopithecus rosalia*) during the reproductive cycle. pp. 181–190. In D. G. Kleiman (ed.), see Reference #3.

30. _____. 1979. The development of pair preferences in the lion tamarin (*Leontopithecus rosalia*): male competition or female choice. In H. Rothe, H. J. Wolters, and J. P. Hearn (eds.), *Biology and Behaviour of Marmosets,* University of Göttingen.

31. _____. 1979. Parent-offspring conflict and sibling competition in a monogamous primate. *Am. Naturalist.* 114:753–760.

32. Kleiman, D. G., and C. A. Brady. 1978. Coyote behavior in the context of recent canid research:

problems and perspectives. pp. 163–188. In M. Bekoff (ed.), *Coyotes: Biology, Behavior, and Management*. Academic Press, N.Y.

33. Kleiman, D. G., and J. F. Eisenberg. 1973. Comparisons of canid and felid social systems from an evolutionary perspective. *Anim. Behav.* 21:637–659.

34. Kleiman, D. G., and D. S. Mack. 1980. The effects of age, sex, and reproductive status on scent marking frequencies in the golden lion tamarin (*Leontopithecus rosalia*). *Folia primatol.* 33:1–14.

35. Mack, D. S., and D. G. Kleiman. 1979. Distribution of scent marks in different contexts in captive lion tamarins, *Leontopithecus rosalia* (Primates). In H. Rothe, H. J. Wolters, and J. P. Hearn (eds.), *Biology and Behaviour of Marmosets*, University of Göttingen.

36. Marshall, J. T., Jr. and E. R. Marshall. 1976. Gibbons and their territorial songs. *Science* 193:235–237.

37. McLanahan, E. B., and K. M. Green. 1977. The vocal repertoire and an analysis of the contexts of vocalizations in *Leontopithecus rosalia*. pp. 251–269. In D. G. Kleiman (ed.), see Reference #3.

38. Mech, L. D. 1970. *The Wolf: Ecology and Social Behavior of an Endangered Species*. Natural History Press, N.Y.

39. Moehlman, P. D. 1979. Jackal helpers and pup survival. *Nature* 277:382–383.

40. Neyman, P. F. 1977. Aspects of the ecology and social organization of free-ranging cotton-top tamarins (*Saguinus oedipus*) and the conservation status of the species. pp. 39–71. In D. G. Kleiman (ed.), see Reference #3.

41. Rabb, G. B., J. H. Woolpy, and B. E. Ginsburg. 1967. Social relationships in a group of captive wolves. *Am. Zoologist* 7:305–312.

42. Ralls, K. 1977. Sexual dimorphism in mammals: avian models and unanswered questions. *Am. Naturalist* 111:917–938.

43. Rasa, O. A. E. 1973a. Intra-familial sexual repression in the dwarf mongoose *Helogale parvula*. *Die Naturwiss.* 60:303–304.

44. ———. 1973b. Marking behaviour and its social significance in the African dwarf mongoose, *Helogale undulata rufula*. *Z. Tierpsychol.* 32:293–318.

45. ———. 1977. The ethology and sociology of the dwarf mongoose (*Helogale undulata rufula*). *Z. Tierpsychol.* 43:337–406.

46. Rathbun, G. B. 1976. The ecology and social structure of the elephant-shrews, *Rhynchocyon chrysopygus* Günter and *Elephantulus rufescens* Peters. Ph.D. Thesis, University of Nairobi.

47. ———. 1978. Evolution of the rump region in the golden-rumped elephant shrew. *Bull. Carnegie Mus.*, No. 6:11–19.

48. ———. 1979. The social structure and ecology of elephant-shrews. *Z. Tierpsychol., Advances in Ethology Supplement*. No. 20:1–80.

49. Robinson, J. G. 1979. An analysis of the organization of vocal communication in the titi monkey *Callicebus moloch. Z. Tierpsychol.* 49:381–405.

50. Rothe, H. 1975. Some aspects of sexuality and reproduction in groups of captive marmosets (*Callithrix jacchus*). *Z. Tierpsychol.*, 37:255–273.

51. ———. 1979. Structure and dynamics of captive *Callithrix jacchus* groups. In H. Rothe, H. J. Wolters, and J. P. Hearn (eds.), *Biology and Behaviour of Marmosets*, University of Göttingen.

52. Simonetta, A. M. 1966. Osservazioni etologiche ed ecologiche sui dik-dik (*Madoqua;* Mammalia, Bovidae) in Somalia. *Monit. Zool. Ital.*, 74:1–33.

53. Smythe, N. 1978. The natural history of the Central American agouti (*Dasyprocta punctata*). *Smithson. Contrib. Zool.* No. 257:1–52.

54. Sutcliffe, A. 1979. Scent marking and piloerection behaviours in social groups of the common marmoset *Callithrix jacchus jacchus*. In H. Rothe, H. J. Wolters, and J. P. Hearn (eds.), *Biology and Behaviour of Marmosets*, University of Göttingen.

55. van Lawick, H. 1971. Golden jackals, In H. and J. van Lawick-Goodall (eds.), *Innocent Killers*, pp. 105–149. Houghton-Mifflin Co., Boston.

56. ———. 1973. *Solo*. Houghton-Mifflin Co., Boston.

57. Wilson, E. O. 1975. *Sociobiology: The New Synthesis*. Harvard University Press, Cambridge.

58. Wilsson, L. 1971. Observations and experiments on the ethology of the European beaver (*Castor fiber* L.). *Viltrevy*, 8(3):115–266.

59. Zimen, E. 1975. Social dynamics of the wolf pack. In M. W. Fox (ed.), *The Wild Canids*, pp. 336–362. Van Nostrand Reinhold Co., New York.

21

Some Applications of Computer Models to the Study of Primate Mating and Social Systems

Glenn Hausfater, Carol D. Saunders, and Michael Chapman

INTRODUCTION

This paper describes three applications of computer modeling to the analysis of primate mating and social systems. Many of the most interesting and important questions in the biology of mating systems, especially among primates, concern aspects of individual life-history, for example, total lifetime reproductive success. Likewise, many contemporary theories of social behavior and its evolution, for example, kin selection and reciprocal altruism, are actually hypotheses about the social or genetic relationships between individual life-histories. Thus, the models reviewed in this paper are focused upon understanding the structure of and interactions between life-histories and, as such, have been developed in relation to longitudinal studies of natural primate populations. Most important in this regard has been our own longitudinal study of yellow baboons (*Papio cynocephalus*) in the Amboseli National Park of Kenya (Hausfater, 1975; Altmann et al., 1977). Also influential in shaping this work have been the longitudinal studies of Sade (1972) on the Cayo Santiago population of rhesus monkeys (*Macaca mulatta*) and long-term studies of several other primate species including the research of Imanishi (1957, 1960), Kawai (1965) and numerous other workers on Japanese monkeys *(M. fuscata),* the research of Goodall (1968) and coworkers on chimpanzees *(Pan troglodytes)* in the Gombe Stream National Park, Tanzania, and the research of Hrdy (1977b) on Hanuman langurs (*Presbytis entellus*) at Mt. Abu, Rajasthan, India.

The defining characteristic of these longitudinal studies has been that some set of individuals has been followed through all or a substantial portion of their life-cycle. As a result, these studies have revealed information on the structuring of life-histories that could not have been obtained through even a large number of cross-sectional studies of shorter duration. Nevertheless, given an estimated twenty to forty years longevity for many species of Old World monkeys, it is obvious that these longitudinal studies are almost always long-term undertakings and that numerous important aspects of data analysis and hypothesis testing will be completed only after many years of investigation.

Computer modeling can by no means alleviate the need for such long-term research nor replace longitudinal studies as a research strategy. However, when developed in conjunction with longitudinal studies, computer models allow us to test hypotheses about the operation of a system based on our "state-of-the-art" understanding of the system. Development and analysis of computer models provides information on the probability of various end states or configurations for a system and often also results in the formulation of sensitive measures of system performance. Additionally, by systematically changing the value of variables and parameters of the model, we are able to determine the relative contribution of specific variables to overall system performance and outcome. Generally, variables that have large effects on the outcome or performance of a computer model can be presumed to have large effects on the outcome and performance of real life systems as well. Obviously, both field data acquisition and more formal mathematical models might be profitably focused on these high-strength variables.

Furthermore, computer models also allow us to ask questions about a system concerning the effects of certain rare, hypothetical, but, nevertheless, evolutionarily important events, particularly events that we might otherwise have to wait years to observe in real life or which, if they occurred in real life, might destroy the very system we seek to understand. In sum, computer models make a major contribution to longitudinal research by generating testable predictions concerning the operation and end states of a system, by producing information on the relative importance of specific variables or parameters of a system, and, more generally, by providing novel insights about, say, life-history structuring and interactions that guide all stages of data acquisition and systems analysis.

In each of three cases in this paper, we will attempt to sketch a biological problem to which we have applied simulation techniques or other forms of computer modeling. We will then discuss the relationship between the computer model and the biological problem, stating explicitly the rationale, assumptions, and parameters of the model. Next, we will endeavor to give a non-technical description of the operation of the model or simulation, emphasizing important or unusual aspects of programming technique and program structure. Finally, we will discuss the results of our analyses of the model and attempt to show how the model has provided new insights into the operation of its corresponding real life system as well as generated testable research hypotheses concerning that system.

THE MODELS

Differential Reproduction with Respect To Dominance Rank Among Adult Male Baboons

The Problem. Variance in reproductive success among males of different dominance ranks over a short period of time has been cited as evidence of sexual selection in numerous primate species (DeVore, 1965; Conaway and Koford, 1964). However, in long-lived species, such as baboons, other monkeys, apes and humans, individual males change rank or social status several times during their reproductive career (Hausfater, 1975; Sade, 1972). Thus, the actual sequence of ranks or statuses occupied in a lifetime as well as associated rank or status specific rates of reproduction are the necessary data for demonstration of differential reproduction among males. Unfortunately, no lifetime study of dominance in baboons or other primate species has yet been completed, and thus we decided to apply simulation techniques to the analysis of sexual selection in baboons (Saunders and Hausfater, 1978).

Briefly, both social and demographic factors cause adult male baboons to change dominance rank frequently throughout their lifetime. In our field work and analyses, we label as "demographically-induced" any rank change resulting from such phenomena as maturation to adulthood of juvenile males, deaths, and intergroup migration of males. Similarly, we label as "agonistically-induced" any rank change resulting from the actual defeat in an agonistic bout of one male by another, typically closely-ranked, individual. The interplay of these various social and demographic factors thus determines the sequence of ranks occupied by a particular male in his lifetime. Likewise, insofar as differences in rank occupancy sequences exist among males, there is also likely to be differential reproduction among males. The purpose of this simulation was to determine the relative contribution of various social and demographic factors to the extent of differential reproduction among males, to isolate those factors showing the greatest effects on the extent of differential reproduction, and, more generally, to obtain both a set of rank occupancy sequences and measures of system performance against which field data from ongoing longitudinal studies could be compared.

Rationale, Assumptions, and Parameters of the Simulation. The rationale of this simulation was to generate lifetime sequences of dominance rank occupancy for individual adult males and, then, using rank-specific rates of reproduction, to evaluate the reproductive success associated with each rank occupancy sequence. To accomplish this task, we modeled dominance rank transitions among adult males as a first-order Markov process. In a first-order Markov process, the probability of transiting from any given rank to any other rank depends only on a male's current rank and not on any more extensive aspect of life-history. The rank transition matrix used in this simulation was estimated from actual field data on Amboseli baboons (Hausfater, 1975) as shown in Table 21–1.

Other important parameters of this model were also estimated from field data on Amboseli baboons, including the rate of agonistically-induced rank changes, rank-specific rates of reproduction, and rates of death, emigration, and immigration. Specifically, we programmed one agonistically-induced rank change, on average, every 527.6 adult male dyad-days of simulation, and one death, emigration, or immigration, i.e., demographic change, on average, every 504.8 days of simulation. The maturation rate in all versions of the simulation was set equal to the death rate and thus the simulated population was maintained in a steady-state condition.

The rank transition matrix shown in Table 21–1 deserves several comments. First, a Markov transition matrix must have row values that sum to 1. To obtain such a matrix from the transition matrix calculated from field data, as shown in Table 21–1, we merely divided each cell value by its corresponding row marginal total. Second, in the simulation, males were scheduled for a rank change based upon the overall rate of agonistically- and demographically-induced rank changes and not by consulting the matrix shown in Table 21–1. Rather, once a male was assigned to the rank change queue, the row-normalized matrix obtained from Table 21–1 was used to decide the specific rank to which a male transited. Thus, the absence of values along the main diagonal of Table 21–1 reflects the fact that this matrix was utilized only after a rank transition was scheduled to occur in the simulation population and does not indicate that males were in some way unable to remain stationary within their current rank position.

Furthermore, it will also be noticed that males had a zero probability of transiting more than two ranks at any given change. This arrangement of transition probabilities was not an arbitrary assignment on our part, but reflected the actual state of affairs among Amboseli baboons: Changes of rank typically involved the exchanging of ranks between males who were otherwise very closely ranked in the dominance order. At a more general level, we do

Table 21–1.   Proportion of all rank changes in which an adult male occupying rank shown by row number transited to rank shown by column number as calclulated from published field data on Amboseli baboons (Hausfater, 1975). See text for explanation of zero cell values and absence of entries on main diagonal.

OLD RANK	NEW RANK							
	1	2	3	4	5	6	7	8
1	–	.054	0	0	0	0	0	0
2	.027	–	.162	.081	0	0	0	0
3	.027	.216	–	.027	0	0	0	0
4	0	0	.081	–	.027	0	0	0
5	0	0	0	.027	–	0	0	0
6	0	0	0	0	.027	–	.081	0
7	0	0	0	0	0	.054	–	.054
8	0	0	0	0	0	0	.054	–

not really believe that no aspects of a male's life-history, other than current rank, influence the next rank that he will occupy. Rather, we make the assumption of a first-order process for heuristic purposes only, but it should be noted that in doing so, we are able to generate rank occupancy sequences that match, quite closely, sequences obtained from our ongoing longitudinal study.

Structure of the Simulation: Preliminary Version. In our initial version of the simulation, we generated dominance rank transitions and reproductive success values for forty males within a population of five groups, each group beginning with eight adult males. The target individuals for each demographic change and rank transition were selected at random and without regard to age, current rank, or rank at onset of reproduction (hereafter referred to as "initial rank"). Typically, we generated twenty-year sequences of rank occupancies, but not all males necessarily survived for the full twenty years. In fact, longevity in this preliminary version of the simulation averaged about eight simulation years (i.e., years of adulthood or the equivalent of sixteen to eighteen total years of life, a figure not inconsistent with our field estimates of lifespan. Forty such twenty-year runs of the simulation were carried out in four separate blocks of ten runs each. The reproductive success values for males of initial ranks 1 through 8 were averaged across all groups and then plotted as cumulative proportion of offspring attributable to males of each initial rank as a function of years of adulthood. Although most of our analyses utilized cumulative reproductive success values averaged across many males, the generated rank transition sequences for individual males also provided another useful form of simulation output and will eventually be compared to actual rank occupancy sequences abstracted from the field data.

Results of the Simulation: Preliminary Version. An example of output from a preliminary version of the simulation is shown in Figure 21–1. The convergence of reproductive success values through time was an automatic consequence of the use of a Markov model. Of interest here, however, is the rate of convergence through time of reproductive success values as well as differences in reproductive success between males of high and low initial rank at the end of an average lifespan of eight years. With demographic factors operating randomly with respect to age, current rank, and initial rank, the simulation demonstrated that by the end of an average lifespan, a male who began reproduction at initial rank 1 produced 57 per cent more offspring than a male of initial rank 8 (Figure 21–1). Overall, longevity had the effect of diminishing but never completely eliminating differential reproduction among males. In sum, this preliminary version of the simulation served to pinpoint longevity and initial rank as key determinants of male lifetime reproductive success.

In part, the power of the above conclusion stems from the fact that demographic processes are unlikely to operate randomly with respect to rank or age in natural populations. Essentially, by programming random operation of demographic processes, we created conditions in favor of equal rank occupancy, and thus equal reproductive success, among males. In fact, even under these rather drastic conditions, differential reproduction among males, based on initial rank and attenuated by longevity, was evident.

In a modification of this simulation, demographic parameters were programmed to favor either high- or low-ranking males. Specifically, the favored class of males had a reduced probability of death or emigration and an enhanced probability of obtaining a high rank following a change of groups. As might be expected, when males of high rank were favored demographically, the extent of differential reproduction increased substantially. More interestingly, however, when low ranking males were given a sizeable assist through the skewed operation of demographic parameters, differential reproduction among males could be diminished but never completely eliminated. In other words, even with a fairly liberal demographic cost to reproductive benefit ratio for low-ranking males, our simulation model was unable to completely eliminate differential reproduction among males on the basis of initial rank.

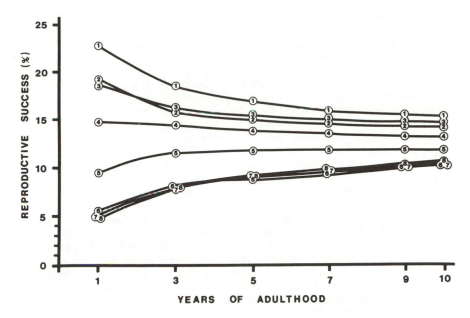

Figure 21–1.   Reproductive success, measured as mean per cent of offspring attributable to males of each initial rank (circled numbers), as a function of years of adulthood. See text for further explanation.

Simulation Structure: Advanced Version. A major problem with the preliminary version of the simulation was that its structure still did not fully reflect the structure of sexual selection in natural populations. Specifically, the raw material of sexual selection is differences between individuals in competitive abilities or mate attraction, but our preliminary simulation model did not include any program features analogous to individual differences. One reason for the absence of such program features was that the inclusion of individual differences in a simulation model often has the effect of reducing the overall utility and robustness of the model. For the purposes of illustrating this point, suppose that we introduced individual differences by programming the computer to utilize completely different transition matrices and different rates of rank change for each of three classes of males corresponding to, say, individuals of high, medium, and low genetic quality. As a result of this modification, males within any simulation run would indeed show meaningful individual differences based upon genetic quality, but, likewise, whole versions and runs of the simulation would also differ in their overall transition matrix and rates of rank change. In particular, each version or run of the simulation would be characterized by a unique set of average demographic and social parameter values, which in turn would be heavily dependent upon the particular starting composition of males in that version or run.

It is interesting to note that field studies of behavior are subject, in analogous fashion, to this same problem of skewed initial conditions, because most studies involve only a single, probably nonrandom, population or group of subjects. A discussion of the general problem of the sensitivity of simulation models and field studies to differences in the starting composition of the study population or other aspects of initial conditions is outside the scope of the paper. However, to minimize such effects in the advanced version of our simulation model, we introduced individual differences into the model through a more complex procedure than that described above, but, importantly, a procedure that assured comparability between versions and runs of the simulation with respect to both generated sequences of rank occupancies and overall population level demographic and social parameter averages. In particular, we introduced individual differences into the advanced version of the simulation through the use of modifier matrices.

Briefly, a modifier matrix was of the same size and shape as the main transition probability matrix shown in Table 21–1. One set of modifier matrices was constructed to correspond to each class of attributes by which males might differ from each other as individuals. For example, it has often been speculated that males in natural populations differ in social skills and experience and that such factors affect in important ways a male's ability to acquire mates or high social status. Thus, based upon age, each male in our simulation was classed as young, prime, or senile and a separate modifier matrix corresponded to each of these conditions. When an individual male was scheduled for a rank change, his age class was first determined and then the appropriate modifier matrix added to the main transition matrix to obtain a new, transformed matrix specific to the male under consideration. Yet another class of individual differences was labeled ''inherent characteristics'' and corresponded to non-age dependent attributes of the male, presumably acquired by genetical or cultural (say, through association with a high-ranking maternal genealogy) means. For example, perhaps some males, regardless of age, are born leaders and others born losers. We thus established eight levels of inherent characteristics ranging from males of the very highest quality, Level 1, to males of the very lowest quality, Level 8. As in the case of age-dependent individual differences, this set of eight inherent characteristic levels corresponded to a set of eight modifier matrices.

From a simulation programming point of view, the most important feature of the modifier matrices was that cell values were both signed and of very small absolute value, averaging about .02 in the advanced simulation version. Additionally, the signed cell value totals above and below the main diagonal of any single modifier matrix exactly canceled each other. Likewise, the sum of all cell values taken across all modifier matrices representing all levels or conditions within any attribute class, e.g., age-dependent characteristics, also summed to zero. Given this ''zero-sum'' constraint, the expected value of all modifier matrices was a null matrix and thus the expected effect of a large number of modifier operations on the main transition probability matrix was merely to add that matrix to the null matrix. Thus, while each male utilized an individually tailored set of transition probabilities, the overall average of transition probabilities within and between simulation runs remained constant. In similar fashions, modifier operations were also carried out to produce individual differences in the rates at which males underwent demographic and social changes. In other words, each male in the simulation underwent a rank occupancy sequence determined by his specific age and inherent characteristics but did so within an otherwise stable social and demographic context.

Results of the Simulation: Advanced Version. Figure 21–2 is an attempt to evaluate in systematic fashion the effects of age-related and inherent differences among males on the extent of sexual selection. Shown in the figure are the cumulative reproductive success curves for males of initial rank 1 (top row) and initial rank 8 (bottom row) in three sets of simulation runs. As noted above, all simulation runs and thus the resultant reproductive success curves are strictly comparable as the result of the use of modifier matrices. For comparative purposes, data from Figure 21–1, in which demographic factors operated randomly with respect to age and rank, are shown in the rightmost panel of the figure. After eight years of adulthood in the random model and, of course, with no individual differences operating, males of the highest initial rank contributed about 15 per cent of all offspring compared to only about 10 per cent for males of the lowest initial rank.

In subsequent runs of the simulation, individual differences were introduced first as inherent characteristics (center panel, Figure 21–2) and then as both inherent and age-related characteristics (leftmost panel, Figure 21–2). The result of introducing individual

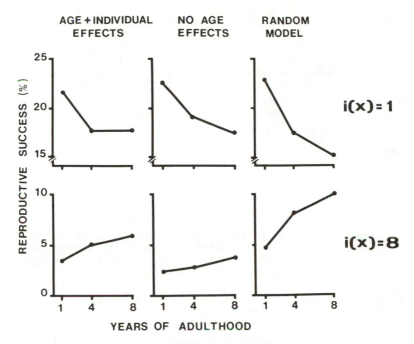

AGE + INDIVIDUAL
EFFECTS

NO AGE
EFFECTS

RANDOM
MODEL

REPRODUCTIVE SUCCESS (%)

YEARS OF ADULTHOOD

Figure 21–2.   Reproductive success for males of initial ranks 1 (upper row) and 8 (lower row) compared in three versions of the advanced simulation model. Right panel shows results obtained from preliminary model of the simulation (Figure 21–1) in which demographic factors operated randomly with respect to age, current rank, and initial rank. Center panel shows results obtained when inherent, but not age-dependent, individual differences were added to the model. Left panel shows results when both inherent and age-related individual differences were incorporated into the model. Note differing scales on upper and lower ordinate; other conventions as in Figure 21–1. See text for further explanation.

differences into the model as inherent characteristics was to substantially increase the extent of differential reproduction and, thus, sexual selection among males. Thus, at the end of an average lifespan, males of the highest initial rank (and also high inherent characteristics level) contributed nearly 20 per cent of all offspring for their cohort, while males of the lowest initial rank (and thus also low inherent characteristics level) contributed less than 5 per cent of all offspring. In general, then, the effect of even very small inherent differences between males was to greatly increase the extent of differential reproduction. In contrast, inclusion of age-related individual differences (left panel, Figure 21–2) resulted in a decrease in the extent of sexual selection among males.

At present, we have used only very small modifier matrix cell values in our simulations. This is so both for heuristic reasons and because we suspect that elements of real-life situations analogous to such values are also very slight. Nevertheless, this advanced version of the simulation allows us to examine systematically the influence of various kinds of patterns of individual differences on the extent of differential reproduction among males. More generally, with this simulation model, we are able to explore the role of inherent and ontogenetic factors in all aspects of individual life-histories while at the same time producing any desired social and demographic context within which the life-histories interact and unfold. As such, we believe that this current version of the simulation provides an extremely useful and powerful tool for exploring the relationship between the structure of individual life-histories, demography, and evolution.

The Reproductive Consequences of Infanticide: A Computer Model

The Problem. Consider now a special case of the rank-ordered social and mating system modeled above. This special case encompasses those species for which the typical reproductive unit contains several adult females but only one adult male. A male's life-history is then somewhat analogous to an indicator variable, composed of periods of group life and high reproductive potential, alternated with periods of solitary or bachelor group life with little or no reproductive potential. Such a system is common in Old World primates (Eisenberg et al., 1972), including many species of Colobines, a subfamily of monkeys characterized by a specialized ruminant-like digestive system (Jolly, 1972). In at least one Asian group of Colobines, the genus *Presbytis* or langur monkeys, not only are so-called one-male groups a typical reproductive unit but changes in the resident male of the unit are marked by a very interesting and as yet poorly understood phenomenon—infanticide (Sugiyama, 1964; Hrdy, 1974). Much speculation has been carried out on the basis of infanticide in primates (Hrdy, 1977a), even its very existence questioned (Curtin and Dolhinow, 1978), but for both langurs and a range of other species, we believe the evidence to be quite good that a high frequency of accidental or intentional infant deaths follows a change in the resident male of a one-male unit. The question that we addressed in our computer model concerned the precise consequences of infant death for the reproductive success of the new resident male (Chapman and Hausfater, 1978). More generally, we are interested in exploring the possibility that a few simple demographic and reproductive parameters characteristic of langur monkeys could account for the peculiar behavior of infanticide, whether it be adaptation or pathology.

Rationale, Assumptions, and Parameters. In most monkey species, with the exception of highly seasonal breeders, the death of an unweaned infant results in the mother of that infant resuming sexual cycles shortly thereafter (Altmann et al., 1978). Obviously, given a period of lactational amenorrhea that may exceed two years in some species, the waiting time to next estrus for a particular female is decreased to a greater or lesser extent, by early infant death, even if through infanticide, compared to conditions of spontaneous termination of amenorrhea following weaning. Thus, the overall effect of infanticide accompanying change of the resident male in a langur group is to decrease the new male's waiting time for insemination of those females whose infants have been lost. For langurs, we estimate that infanticide would typically have a shortening effect on the time to next conception for nearly 60 per cent of all females in a group, and, moreover, that a new resident male, if infanticidal, would be able to inseminate nearly 70 per cent of all females in the group within just a few months of his entry (Chapman and Hausfater, 1978).

More precisely, the reproductive advantage that may accrue to an infanticidal male depends upon several demographic and reproductive parameters. Of primary importance are (1) male tenure, T, defined as the interval between successive replacements of the resident adult male in a bisexual group of langurs or other appropriate species, (2) the interval, I, between successive conceptions for an individual female, referred to as the interconception interval, (3) the month, m, in which replacement occurs relative to the most recent conception of a particular female, and (4) the likelihood that the new resident male will himself eventually be replaced by a male who is infanticidal, referred to in our model as the replacement condition. In essence, the purpose of our computer model and analysis was to determine the effects of these variables on the number of offspring that are sired by an infanticidal or noninfanticidal resident male with respect to a particular female and that survive beyond the male's own replacement. For convenience this number of offspring is referred to as the male's reproductive success, r, with respect to the female and as such is a *per capita* measure.

For the purposes of this model, we have assumed that lactational amenorrhea among females terminates simultaneously with the death or weaning of an infant. Under this simplifying assumption, the interconception interval can be thought of as composed of three nonoverlapping segments: gestation, a period of lactational amenorrhea terminated by death or weaning of the infant, and one or more month-long menstrual cycles prior to the next conception. Furthermore, we have also assumed that rates of miscarriage, spontaneous abortion, and other forms of infant mortality are independent of any infanticidal or noninfanticidal tendencies on the part of the resident male. Thus, these sources of infant mortality would be expected to affect the reproductive success of infanticidal and noninfanticidal males equally and are ignored in the model.

Given these few simplifying assumptions and specific values for the lengths of various segments of any sequence of consecutive interconception intervals, we were able to calculate the reproductive success obtained by infanticidal and noninfanticidal males after any period of tenure and under either replacement condition. These calculations were carried out by reference to four sets of conditional equations. For example, for a noninfanticidal male replaced by another noninfanticidal male after T months tenure in a group, offspring production with respect to a female showing consecutive interconception intervals of known length can be calculated as follows:

$$\text{If } T < I_1 - (m - \tfrac{1}{2}), \; r = 0\,;$$

$$\text{If } I_1 - (m - \tfrac{1}{2}) \leqslant T < I_1 - (m - \tfrac{1}{2}) + I_2, \; r = 1\,;$$

.

.

.

$$\text{If } I_1 - (m - \tfrac{1}{2}) + I_2 + \ldots + I_{n-1} \leqslant T <$$

$$I_1 - (m - \tfrac{1}{2}) + I_2 + \ldots + I_n, \; r = n - 1\,;$$

where $I_{1,2\ldots,n}$ are n consecutive interconception intervals of any length such that I_1 is the interconception interval in progress at the time of initial male replacement and I_n is the interconception interval in progress when the resident male is himself replaced and where the quantity $I_1 - (m-1/2)$ is equal to the portion of I_1 remaining after the initial male replacement. We call m the month of entry of that male into the female's current interconception interval and 1/2 is subtracted from m in the above equations as a correction for continuity in replacement times: Replacement is considered to occur midway through the mth month of interconception interval I_1.

The conditional equations for the cases of an infanticidal resident male, infanticidal successor male, or both, required information on the exact duration of the three component segments of interconception interval length—gestation, lactation, and sexual cycles—as well as all of the same information required by the equations given. Nevertheless, it should be clear that through the use of such equations, offspring production (r) could be readily calculated for both infanticidal and noninfanticidal males under any replacement condition and given specific values for male tenure, the lengths of interconception interval components, and the male's month of entry (m) within the first such interval.

Structure of the Computer Model. Calcuation of offspring production for infanticidal and noninfanticidal males is a straightforward application of the conditional equations given when reproductive cycles for individual females, for the populaton, or species are of constant duration. However, in most natural populations, reproductive parameters vary both within and between females. In our general model, as applied to langurs, we attempted to calculate the average or expected number of offspring (per female) produced by an infanticidal or noninfanticidal male when female interconception intervals varied over a range of values. Specifically, we calculated reproductive success values for infanticidal and noninfanticidal males under both replacement conditions for tenure values of one to eighty months and with interconception interval lengths geometrically distributed from twenty to thirty-one months. To do so, we fixed the duration of amenorrhea and gestation at thirteen and seven months, respectively, and, consequently, all variability in interconception interval length was solely the result of variability in the number of sexual cycles prior to conception. Furthermore, we assumed that male replacements in bisexual groups occurred independently of the reproductive states of females in the group or, in other words, that the probability of a male replacement was equally likely for all months in the first of any series of consecutive interconception intervals.

Once the probability distributions of various interconception interval lengths and times of entry were determined, the computation of expected reproductive success, $E(r_T)$, over a range of T values was completed through the use of the preceding conditional equations and the following iterative procedure:

$$E(r_T) = \sum_{I_{1,2,\ldots,n}=k}^{K} \sum_{m=1}^{I_1} \prod_{j=1}^{n} P(I_j)\, P(m)\, r_{m.T.I_{1,2,\ldots,n}} \, ,$$

where

$$\prod_{j=1}^{n} P(I_j)$$

represents the joint probability of n consecutive interconception intervals of lengths I_1, I_2, . . .,I_n, such that $k \leqslant I_j \leqslant K$. The variables k and K are the lower and upper limits on interconception interval length, which in the present case were twenty and thirty-one months, respectively. $P(m)$ equals the probability that initial male replacement occurs during the mth month following conception in the first of these n interconception intervals and

$$r_{m.T.I_{1,2,\ldots,n}}$$

is merely the reproductive success resulting from any specific set of values for the subscripted parameters as determined from the appropriate set of conditional equations. Obviously, the number of computations necessitated by this formula increased exponentially with every additional consecutive interconception interval and was thus prohibitive for use with any device other than a high-speed computer. The output from such an iterative determination of expected reproductive success for infanticidal and noninfanticidal males under conditions of subsequent replacement by an infanticidal male is graphed in Figure 21–3.

Results of the Model. It is intuitively obvious that under conditions of subsequent replacement by a noninfanticidal male, infanticide by a new resident male will always be advantageous. At the very worst under these conditions, the reproductive success of an infanticidal male will equal that of a noninfanticidal male. More usually, an infanticidal male replaced by a noninfanticidal will have substantially higher reproductive success than a noninfanticidal male replaced under the same conditions. In particular, analyses of our computer model showed that an infanticidal male replaced by a noninfanticidal male obtains maximum reproductive advantage compared to his noninfanticidal counterpart at tenures of 3, 26, 48 and 70 months, respectively. In short, our model clearly demonstrated that an infanticidal male will almost always have a reproductive advantage compared to other males in a predominantly noninfanticidal population.

Of more interest, however, are the results shown in Figure 21–3. This figure compares expected reproductive success for infanticidal and noninfanticidal males under conditions of subsequent replacement by another male who is himself infanticidal. As such, this figure may be thought of as demonstrating the reproductive consequences of infanticide once the behavior has become fully established in a population, i.e., when a resident male of either type will almost always be replaced by an infanticidal successor. Under these conditions, infanticide was not shown to be reproductively advantageous at all male tenures. In fact, at values of T between 8 and 19, between 32 and 40, between 54 and 61, and between 77 and 80, inclusive, infanticidal males actually had a lower expected reproductive success than their noninfanticidal counterparts. Briefly, these intervals demarcated tenures that terminated during periods when the current male's infants were likely to be unweaned and thus subject to infanticide by the successor male. In contrast, at values of T near 26, 47, and 69 months, respectively, infanticidal males were at a substantial reproductive advantage relative to noninfanticidal males.

More general conclusions of this analysis and model are discussed elsewhere (Chapman and Hausfater, 1978), but suffice it to note that infanticide, at least under most naturally occurring demographic conditions, constitutes an evolutionarily stable strategy (Maynard Smith, 1974). Also, the distribution of infanticide among langur populations would not be expected to show density dependence *per se* (cf. Eisenberg et al., 1972), but would be expected to vary regularly in relation to both the mean and variance in male tenure for a population as well as the proportion of males living outside of bisexual groups. Unfortunately, most published data on langur populations are barely adequate for testing either the above or any more extensive predictions of our model. Thus, as is often the case, the value of a computer model or any other rigorous formulation may lie as much in demonstrating precisely what data are necessary to answer a meaningful question about behavior as in actually providing the answer itself.

A Simulation Model of Dominance Relations Among Adult Female Primates

The Problem. Thus far, our computer models have been concerned with dominance relations and reproductive success among adult male primates. However, there is a growing

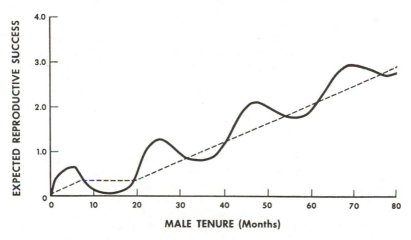

Figure 21–3.   Expected reproductive success, $E(r_T)$ with respect to a given female for infanticidal (solid line) and noninfanticidal (broken line) males as a function of their tenure, T, in months under conditions of subsequent replacement by an infanticidal male.

body of evidence indicating that dominance rank is also an important determinant of reproductive success for adult female primates. Specifically, age at onset of first reproduction, duration of lactational amenorrhea, and probability of infant mortality have all been shown to be related to dominance rank among females (Drickamer, 1974; Altmann et al., 1978) and, in such a way as to confer higher reproductive success on higher-ranking females (Sade et al., 1976). Thus, patterns of rank change, mechanisms of dominance rank acquisition, and the overall stability or consistency of dominance relations among adult females are topics of great interest and importance in the study of primate mating systems.

At first glance, there seem to be two distinct patterns of dominance relations and rank acquisition among adult female primates. Generally, in macaque groups, adult females form a stable linear dominance hierarchy (Sade, 1967), and changes in the rank order of adult females result only from death or maturation. Specifically, at about the time of a macaque female's first estrus, she typically enters the rank order of adult females at a position just beneath that of her mother. As a result, the female members of a matrilineal genealogy will all rank close to each other in the dominance order, and, moreover, younger sisters will rank above their older female siblings (Sade, 1972). Other than this age-reversed rank order of sisters, the dominance ranking of adult female macaques shows little relationship to age.

In contrast, a highly age-graded system of adult female dominance relations has been reported for langur monkeys (Hrdy and Hrdy, 1976). Specifically, as females mature, they apparently defeat older females in the rank order such that, in general, there is a strong inverse correlation between age and dominance rank (Hrdy and Hrdy, 1976). Even though the langur data suffer from some vexing sample size problems, we still considered it instructive to carry out a systematic examination and comparison of the operation of age-graded and nepotistic dominance systems. In particular, we were interested in determining in a method analogous to our simulations of adult male dominance relations the relative importance of various demographic and social factors in the operation of age-graded and nepotistic dominance systems.

Rationale, Parameters, and Assumptions. Our simulation analysis of adult female dominance relations focused on the question of whether two such seemingly disparate systems as the age-graded and nepotistic patterns of adult female organization might actually be derived from or generated by a single set of simple rules governing life-history interactions among females. As in the simulation of adult male dominance relations, our procedure was to vary key social and demographic parameters of the model but to do so without changing the few basic rules of life-history interaction upon which the model was predicated. In conjunction with these analyses, we hoped to formulate measures, applicable to both field and computer studies, for assessing the relative degree of nepotism and age-gradedness in the operation of a dominance system.

The first and most important of the basic rule of life-history interaction in this simulation was that no female ever defeated her mother in an agonistically-induced rank change. Secondly, at maturity, a daughter assumed a dominance position among adult females equal to that of her mother *at the time of the daughter's birth,* hereafter called ''maternal rank.'' However, if, at maturity, that particular rank number were currently held by the mother, then the recently matured daughter assumed the rank position immediately beneath that of her mother. The final interactional rule merely stated that in agonistically-induced rank changes among adult females, younger females always defeated older females, except in the case of mother–daughter pairs as governed by the first rule above.

The key parameters for this simulation were rates of maturation, death, and agonistically-induced rank change. In each of two versions of the simulation discussed below, maturation rate was set equal to death rate at 14 per cent *per annum.* In the first version of the simulation, modeling langur monkeys, the rate of agonistically-induced rank change averaged one such change per year. In contrast, in the second version of the simulation, modeling rhesus macques, the rate of agonistically-induced rank change averaged one such change every seven years.

Structure of the Simulation. Briefly, each run of the simulation began with a group of ten linearly ranked adult females. These founding females formed the core of a group whose size was subsequently augmented through births and maturation and decreased through the death of adult females. Births, deaths, and maturation of daughters were programmed to occur randomly with respect to years of adulthood, current dominance rank, and maternal rank. Daughters of the founding females and all subsequent adult female participants in the simulation entered the group after a maturational period of four years and promptly assumed a dominance rank dependent upon maternal rank and dictated by interactional rule two. Obviously, however, prior to a daughter's maturation to adulthood, her mother or any other female already in the simulated group might be subject to an agonistically-induced rank change or some other demographic event. Thus, by the time of a daughter's maturation, her mother might still be occupying the maternal rank, might have fallen in rank to a younger female, or might have been entirely eliminated from the simulated group through death.

Each simulation run was continued until fifty females had passed through the simulated group from maturation to death. Five such runs were completed for each simulation version and results pooled across runs for the purposes of system description and analysis. As in the case of our work on adult male dominance relations, the present simulation model also provided output in the form of lifetime rank occupancy sequences for individual females, and, eventually, these simulated sequences will be compared to the rank occupancy sequences of real individuals as abstracted from field data on natural primate populations. However, at present, we find it most useful merely to compare the results of several different simulation versions on the basis of two summary measures of system performance. Specifically, for each year of the simulation model, we determined the average number of females in the group for whom current rank number differed from maternal rank number as well as the magnitude of the difference between these two rank assignments. Although adult female dominance relations for several different primate species were characterized in this way, the following discussion focuses only on two versions, referred to in short-hand fashion as "rhesus" and "langurs."

Results of the Simulation. Figure 21–4 compares summary measures of system performance for the rhesus and langur versions of our simulation model of adult female dominance relations. In the rhesus version, just over 20 per cent of all females in any year held a dominance rank higher than that of their mother at the time of birth. In contrast, in the langur version of the model, over twice as many females on average, as compared to the rhesus version, occupied a rank higher than that of their maternal rank ($X^2 = 24.2$, $d.f. = 2$, $p < .001$). Likewise, in the langur version the average difference in any year between a female's current rank and her maternal rank was significantly greater than the comparable difference in the rhesus version ($t = 2.1$, $d.f. = 168$, $p < .05$). Thus, at least with respect to a .05 significance level, these two simulated dominance systems would be accepted as differing substantially from each other—one version obviously age-graded, the other obviously nepotistic—even though both systems are operating under precisely the same set of social rules or principles of life-history interaction.

Work with other versions of this simulation model has demonstrated that we can produce nearly any desired degree of nepotism or age-grading merely by selecting appropriate values for the death rate and the rate of agonistically-induced rank changes. For example, baboons appear to have a dominance system characterized by slightly less strict nepotism than that of rhesus monkeys (Moore, 1978). Such a system can be readily generated by our simulation model merely by increasing the rate of agonistically-induced rank changes, the death rate, or both, compared to the rhesus version. One implication of these simulation analyses is that, contrary to prevailing opinion in primate sociobiology (Jolly, 1972; Wilson, 1975), dominance relations among adult females in many different primate species may actually be based on a unitary set of interactional rules. If so, then, in theory, only one set of explanatory principles should be required to account for the entire array (or gradient) of dominance systems reported for adult female primates. In sum, these models demonstrate that apparent differences between species in dominance, mating, or other social systems may actually reflect habitat- or species-specific differences in demographic parameters rather than intrinsic differences between species in underlying patterns of life-history interaction. As such, it is then these differences in demographic parameters that require explanation, rather than differences in the structure of the social or mating system *per se*. In any event, at the very least, this simulation model of adult female dominance relations points out the importance of obtaining basic demographic data in long-term field studies of dominance relations or other aspects of female life-history.

CONCLUSIONS

Long-term or longitudinal studies are essential means of testing many important theories in sociobiology and, more generally, for increasing our understanding of animal social behavior and individual life-histories. Unfortunately, such long-term endeavors often proceed in relatively unstructured fashion and rely heavily on analytical techniques and research questions derived from short-term or cross-sectional studies. By reviewing several simulation and computer models of primate mating and social systems, we have tried to demonstrate the valuable role that these computer techniques can play in guiding and structuring long-term, particularly longitudinal, field research.

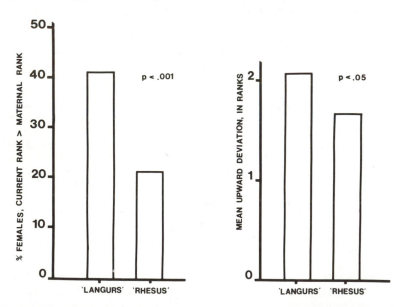

Figure 21–4.   Proportion of all adult females in any year whose current rank exceeded their maternal rank as produced by versions of a computer simulation modeling dominance relations in langur monkeys and rhesus macaques. Rightmost figure shows the mean number of ranks by which daughter's current rank exceeded maternal rank in these same simulation versions. See text for further explanation and statistical test results.

Simulations and other forms of computer modeling are essentially compact research projects that can be carried out in a matter of milliseconds as compared to the years of work often required by a field study. As such, these computer techniques provide us with the opportunity to analyze and test hypotheses about social and mating systems, as well as to gain insights into the structure of male and female life-histories, in a much shorter period of time than required for completion of a field research project. However, it is very unlikely that a systems analyst observing the behavior of a simulation model in a computer center will ever replace the field biologist observing the behavior of real animals in the wild. Nevertheless, insofar as both groups of workers are oftentimes attempting to understand the same phenomena—the evolution and dynamics of social and mating systems—closer collaboration and cooperation might very likely result in more efficient and effective use of research time for all concerned.

ACKNOWLEDGMENTS

A list of scientists too numerous to name has provided helpful criticisms and suggestions for the improvement of the models reviewed in this paper. At various points, comments by Stuart and Jeanne Altmann, Irwin Bernstein, and Wolfgang Schleidt have been particularly influential in the development of our models of adult male dominance relations. Sarah Hrdy generously provided insights into langur infanticide thus influencing the development of that model, and, together with Jim Moore, Donald Sade, Robert Seyfarth and Dorothy Cheney also contributed to the development of our models of adult female dominance relations. Conversations with the participants at a 1978 Wenner–Gren conference on baboon social behavior also helped to clarify various points concerning these models and their presentation. Finally, this paper benefited greatly from critical readings by Jeff Stelzner, Ginny Hayssen, and, of course, Bw. Aardwolf. The participation of all of these individuals in this research endeavor is gratefully acknowledged as is financial support from the National Science Foundation and the National Institutes of Health.

REFERENCES

1. Altmann, J., Altmann, S. A., Hausfater, G., and McCuskey, S. A. 1977. Life-history of yellow baboons: Physical development, reproductive parameters, and infant mortality. *Primates,* 18: 315–330.
2. Altmann, J., Altmann, S. A., and Hausfater, G. 1978. Primate infant's effects on mother's future reproduction. *Science,* 201: 1028–1029.
3. Chapman, M., and Hausfater, G. 1979. The reproductive consequences of infanticide in langurs: A mathematical model. *Behavioral Ecology and Sociobiology,* 5:227–240.
4. Conaway, C. H., and Koford, C. B. 1964. Estrous cycles and mating behavior in a free-ranging band of rhesus monkeys. *J. Mammal.,* 45: 577–588.
5. Curtin, R., and Dolhinow, P. 1978. Primate social behavior in a changing world. *Am. Sci.,* 64:468–475.
6. Eisenberg, J. F., Muckenhirn, N. A., and Rudran, R. 1972. The relation between ecology and social structure in primates. *Science,* 176: 863–874.
7. DeVore, I. 1965. Male dominance and mating behavior in baboons. In *Sex and Behavior,* F.A. Beach (ed.), John Wiley and Sons, New York, pp. 266–289.
8. Drickamer, L. C. 1974. A ten-year summary of reproductive data for free-ranging *Macaca mulatta. Folia Primat.,* 21: 61–80.
9. Goodall, J. Van Lawick. 1968. The behaviour of free-living chimpanzees in the Gombe Stream Reserve. *An. Behav. Mongr.,* 1(3): 165–311.
10. Hausfater, G. 1975. Dominance and reproduction in baboons *(Papio cynocephalus)*: A quantitative analysis. *Contributions to Primatology,* 7: 1–150.
11. Hrdy, S. B. 1974. Male-male competition and infanticide among the langurs *(Presbytis entellus)* of Abu, Rajasthan. *Folia primat.,* 22: 19–58.

12. _____. 1977a. Infanticide as a primate reproductive strategy. *Am. Sci.*, 65: 40–49.
13. _____. 1977b. *The Langurs of Abu: Male and Female Strategies of Reproduction.* Harvard University Press, Cambridge, Mass., 361 pp.
14. _____, and Hrdy, D. B. 1976. Hierarchial relations among female Hanuman langurs (Primates: Colobinae, *Presbytis entellus*). *Science,* 193: 913–915.
15. Imanishi, K. 1957. Social behavior in Japanese monkeys, *Macaca fuscata. Psychologia* 1: 47–54.
16. _____. 1960. Social organization of sub-human primates in their natural habitat. *Current Anthropology,* 1: 393–407.
17. Jolly, A. 1972. *The Evolution of Primate Behavior.* Macmillan Co., New York, 397 pp.
18. Kawai, M. 1965. On the system of social ranks in a natural troop of Japanese monkeys: (I) Basic rank and dependent rank. In *Japanese Monkeys,* S. A. Altmann (ed.), Published by the Editor, Atlanta, Georgia, pp. 66–86.
19. Maynard Smith, J. 1974. The theory of games and the evolution of animal conflicts. *J. Theor. Biol.,* 47:209–221.
20. Moore, J. 1978. Dominance relations among free-ranging female baboons in Gombe National Park, Tanzania. In *Recent Advances in Primatology, Vol. 1: Behaviour,* D. J. Chivers and J. Herbert (eds.), Academic Press, New York, pp. 67–70.
21. Sade, D. S. 1967. Determinants of dominance in a group of free-ranging rhesus monkeys. In *Social Communication Among Primates,* S. A. Altmann (ed.), University of Chicago Press, Chicago, pp. 99–114.
22. _____. 1972. A longitudinal study of social behavior of rhesus monkeys. In *Functional and Evolutionary Biology of Primates,* R. Tuttle (ed.), Aldine, Chicago, pp. 378–398.
23. _____, Cushing, K., Cushing, P., Dunaif, J., Figueroa, A., Kaplan, J. R., Lauer, C., Rhodes, D., and Schneider, J. 1976. Population dynamics in relation to social structure on Cayo Santiago. *Yearbook of Physical Anthropology,* 20: 253–262.
24. Saunders, C. D., and Hausfater, G. 1978. Sexual selection in baboons *(Papio cynocephalus)*: A computer simulation of differential reproduction with respect to dominance rank in males. In *Recent Advances in Primatology, Vol. 1: Behaviour,* D. J. Chivers and J. Herbert (eds.) Academic Press, New York, pp. 567–571.
25. Sugiyama, Y. 1964. Group composition, population density and some sociological observations on Hanuman langurs *(Presbytis entellus).* *Primates,* 5: 7–37.
26. Wilson, E. O. 1975. *Sociobiology: The New Synthesis.* Belknap Press, Cambridge, Mass., 697 pp.

VI

The Problem of Sexuality

22

Fluctuation of Environment and Coevolved Antagonist Polymorphism as Factors in the Maintenance of Sex

William D. Hamilton, Peter A. Henderson, and Nancy A. Moran

INTRODUCTION

At this symposium there seem to be no papers on the social behavior of procaryotes. The large long-lived species that tend to attract study by behaviorists and ethologists—those species, no doubt, which are considered to have social behavior worth discussing—are almost always eucaryotes and *sexual*. This fact, intrinsically curious, poses a dilemma for genetical kinship theory. Our outline of the dilemma can be starting point and justification for the somewhat non-social theme of natural selection that follows.

The theory has it that the strongest positive social interactions will occur between the closest relatives: in the most straightforward view, then, clonal relatives ought to be the most cooperative. This prediction is fulfilled admirably in the very diverse and integrated behavior shown by the cells of the metazoan body; but it is fulfilled rather poorly in a diversity of other cases—for example, in the behavior of aphids, rotifers, armadillos and human monozygotic twins. An excuse has commonly been offered that these clonal situations are too short-lived in evolutionary time or too rare for much progress with social development to be made before they end. But if this is true, why? At once, in so far as it is acceptable, the excuse confronts us with the problem of sex.

Data bearing on the excuse are of mixed import. It is satisfactory, for example, that aphids have now yielded at least a few cases of a sacrificial and sterile soldier caste (Aoki, 1977; Aoki, Yamane, and Kiuchi, 1977); aphids are a group where the lease of survival can be considered renewed each year in the annual generation of sex. Rotifers on the other hand contribute a negative impression: the order Bdelloidea has undergone considerable adaptive radiation without, apparently, any sex at all, and such radiation surely implies quite enough time for formation of social colonies in suitable situations of non-panmixia if relatedness were the main controlling factor.

Even with such dialectical items aside, acceptance of the excuse merely transfers us to another kind of difficulty about relatedness. If sex is so important then our reliance on coefficients of relatedness in genetical kinship theory is placed in doubt: the coefficients of relatedness currently used fail to assess special advantages possessed by sexual progeny through which, so the excuse claims, they eventually outlast the progeny of clones. In purporting to explain why identical twins cooperate as little as they do we are forced the more to wonder why husband and wife cooperate so much, or to put the main issue more precisely, to wonder what ultimate value it is that females get from the act of mating and from the production of unprovenly useful sons. This second horn of the dilemma sharpens a little as further facts come to light concerning how males, beyond mere idleness, sometimes indifferently trample juveniles to death in the course of their fighting and mating (elephant seals) or even deliberately kill them (langurs).

Evidently the question of sex has bearing on many fine details of social behavior. Issues of mate choice, for example, might be understood better if we understood first, from an evolutionary point of view, why mating occurs at all.

PREVIOUS VIEWS

Interest in the evolutionary problem of sex took renewed impetus in the mid-1960's. It came to be realized that as regards any *constant* selection pressure asexuals have less disadvantage in their speed of adaptive response than had previously been supposed (Crow and Kimura, 1965, 1969; Maynard Smith, 1968; Felsenstein, 1974). In fact, in some circumstances they have an advantage (Karlin, 1973; Eshel and Feldman, 1970).

In general the rate of response is much more dependent on the rate of occurrence of new mutuations of the right kind than on how sexual mechanism or lack of it allows the mutations to be assembled. About the same time in the 1960's genetical kinship theory bought into focus the fact that a sexual offspring is only a ''half'' offspring to its parent, so raising the spectre of a widespread and often powerful selection incentive for females to produce ''full'' offspring instead—by parthenogenesis. Obviously the incentive exists only to the extent that parental investment by males is absent (Trivers, 1976), for if the sexes invest equally the half-as-many ''full'' offspring that a female could produce working alone would give no advantage over the full number of ''half'' offspring she could have through cooperation with a mate. While blatantly uninvolved fathers are sufficiently common in the living world for the problem of sex to remain very acute, this point about male investment cautions against magnifying the problem too much. Unobvious forms of investment by the male might be more common than is realized. For example, it is tempting to connect the generally very low rate of incidence of parthenogenesis in moths (compared to other insects) with the long-mooted suspicion that males may contribute importantly to the food reserves of eggs through materials transferred in copulation. Such transfer has recently been demonstrated in a heliconiine butterfly (Gilbert, 1976)[1].

Returning from these asides to the main problem, from the renewed doubts and from the rather limited success of models referring to unequivocally ''good'' and ''bad'' mutations, which, when present at different loci, could be either in ''positive'' or ''negative'' linkage disequilibrium (LD), it is a fairly obvious step to argue that if constant evolution in one direction cannot give advantage to sex then the advantage is likely to come from some sort of *varying* selection pressure that continually favors different combinations among a set of alleles already present in the population. Actually this type of ''reassortment theory'' of sex began long before the 1960s (indeed can be dated back to Weismann in the last century, see Thompson, 1976). Yet in most versions of the reassortment view, environmental patchiness is considered to determine the need for continual reassortment rather than any population-wide and inter-generational changes (Williams, 1975; Maynard Smith, 1976). Where such changes are admitted, they are thought to pose ''qualitatively new challenges'' rather than simply to rehash old ones (Maynard Smith, 1978).

It hardly need be said that our own model will differ in these various respects. It will have no unequivocally ''good mutations,'' its only patches will be temporal and coextensive with the whole population; and they will be endlessly rehashed, giving by themselves no progressive evolution at all—no more, basically, than amounts to a permit to the species to stay alive. The view of sex that the model implies approaches that of Treisman (1976) and, most of all, that of Jaenike (1978). It also approaches the view of Thompson (1976), who emphasized a function of sex in *slowing down* adaptive responses to environment changes. However, whereas Thompson's discussion was openly group selectionist and disclaimed attempt on the problem of short-term advantage against mutant asexual strains, our models can show such advantage on a short time scale—not, admittedly, the scale of a single generation but with definite advantage to sex achieved in a few.

[1]If such transfer is important generally in Lepidoptera, a recently reported case of parthenogenesis in moths (Mitter and Futuyma, 1977) strengthens the point made here. The case was of gynogenesis; thus, even though the females seemed not to have the option of not mating, they could be considered cheating the males in an evolutionary sense if males indeed contribute substantially to the eggs.

When environmental autocorrelation is incorporated (although this development is not reported here), the general model of this paper will bear some resemblance to another of Maynard Smith's models (1971, 1976)—one which requires that correlations between different environmental features change signs between generations, generating a negative heritability of fitness. He considered this requirement unrealistic; however, he emphasized abiotic factors that, admittedly, are expected to show correlation, which at best is zero, and otherwise is positive, over generations. The reactivity that is possible in the biotic environment provides a more plausible basis for the type of environmental change required.

Returning to other recent versions of the reassortment approach, it has to be admitted that models with even shorter-term advantages to sex have already been obtained (Williams and Mitton, 1973; Williams, 1975; Maynard Smith, 1976). What were these models and why do we still seek others? The models in question postulated patchy environments, possibly but not necessarily, also fluctuating over generations and also had an essential element of sibling competition. While they had outstanding success in rendering sex immune to inroads of parthenogenesis in the short term, such success, unfortunately, could be claimed only for a rather special class of life styles: competition had to be very intense and consequently minimum fecundities had to be very high. Since in nature large long-lived species—which are, to repeat, the favorites of symposia on animal behavior—are often of low fecundity and yet monotonously fail to abandon their male sex, whether this is industriously paternal, polygynous, or promiscuous, these existing successful models fail rather awkwardly just where, in a sense, they are most needed. And it is certainly unappealing to have to believe that the pervasive uniformity of meiosis and fertilization is propped up by various different causes in different parts of the eucaryote kingdom.

TEMPORAL FLUCTUATION

The idea that "varying selection pressure" or "environmental heterogeneity" might support sex is really a compound idea; variation, heterogeneity, can be either in place or in time. The preceding successful models emphasize the spatial variation. Because it is known that temporal fluctuation of selection can have quite different results from spatial variation (see review in Felsenstein, 1976), we decided to try to extend some of the models of temporally fluctuating selection beyond the question of polymorphism, which has been their usual focus in the past, to the problem of sex. Two principal considerations encouraged this approach.

One arose out of a model on the problem of sex proposed by Treisman (1976). The underlying idea here is very simple and can be explained without reference to details of the model—indeed, it had been roughly stated in connection with the disadvantageous inflexibility of asexual strains many times before (Thompson, 1976). If for the range of variability manifested in a species, *every* genotype sooner or later encounters a state of environment where its fitness is zero, then every asexual clone that a sexual species is capable of producing must correspondingly die out; on the other hand, with suitable adjustment of the "sooner or later" (so that the sexual species is not itself forced to extinction during the period while clones are flourishing) the sexual species may well survive all of the crises that are deadly for individual genotypes.

If clones continually die out like this and the sexual species survives, there is a slow selection of genes that preclude the option of parthenogenesis more and more thoroughly—a process somewhat analogous to Darwin's evolutionary loss of wings in insects of windy sea-girt islands. In fact even death of clones is unnecessary for this selection (instead a clone might become, for example, almost permanent in some part of the original niche); it is merely necessary that clones have no possibility to recontribute to the sexual gene pool. Thus, except insofar as facultative parthenogenesis occurs, a certain metastability of sex is to be expected. This expectation may help to explain why disappearances of hopeful clones are not as common as the model suggests they should be. Actually we do not know of a single clear case of re-establishment of a sexual strain in an area previously occupied by an apomict strain. And apomictic strains often seem too demographically stable and geographically uniform relative to their nearest sexual congeners to satisfy this view although admittedly the evidence is equivocal (Maynard Smith, 1978), and many of the most uniform are somewhat unnatural outbreaks into new continents arising from human activity, so that it seems possible that more natural situations in which various clones spring up, flourish, and wither in succession as offshoots from a persistent stolon of sexuality may still await recognition. Perhaps some cases of claimed facultative parthenogenesis may prove to be of this kind—actually cases of the sexual parent species in process of reoccupying the subniche taken from it by a derived parthenomorph.

The second consideration that directed us to models with temporal fluctuation of environment derives from recent reviews of the ecological circumstances of known cases of parthenogenesis. Evidence accumulates to suggest factors of the *biotic* environment as being particularly supportive of sex (Glesener and Tilman, 1978; Jaenike, 1978; Levin, 1975; Ghiselin, 1975; Cuellar, 1977): it seems that a species is more likely to go asexual in parts of its range where the variety of its important interactant species is reduced. This suggests that we entertain the possibility of certain kinds of *reactivity* in the environmental fluctuations. Whether the biotic interactions involved present themselves as prey evasions, food qualities, or tactics of predators or parasites, all are subject to frequency- and density-dependent jostling of the kind that theoretical community ecology has sought to analyze. Even the possibility of "chaotic" fluctuations involving two or more species implies at least some degree of autocorrelation of the environment of each species involved, and of course much more regular patterns fairly easily occur in simple models.

Limit cycles in the interaction of polymorphic host and parasite have recently been emphasized by Clarke (1976). Clarke's paper also well reviews the literature on parasite selection, and frequency-dependence more generally, as sources of polymorphism. He concludes that proper appreciation of this kind of selection will largely exorcise the difficulties that lend favor to the "neutralist" view on the abundance of protein polymorphism. Of most interest in the present context, however, is the demonstrated robustness of limit cycles as contrasted to conditions of final stasis—i.e., balanced polymorphism or allele fixation—in this kind of selection situation.

As well as a possibility of regular and quasi-regular types of limit cycle, the so-called "chaotic" interaction (May, 1974) has been found in theoretical models where one host species is exposed to a variety of pathogens (Eshel, 1977) and also where a prey's (or host's) genotype array was matched as regards evasion and susceptibility by a corresponding array of variation in a predator (or parasitoid) (Auslander, Guckenheimer, and Oster, 1978). The last-mentioned study took as a possible real counterpart a recorded case of irregular fluctuation in an insect host and parasitoid (See Hassell and Huffaker, 1969 and Figure 1 in Auslander et al., 1978): it was suggested that the variation might concern the depth to which the parasitoid had to probe for host larvae in the medium. Actually the postulated variation in the parasites as to preferred depth of probing for prey cannot apply to the Hassell–Huffaker experiment because the parasite they used is thelytokous. Nevertheless, in general, a guess about depth of prey as a crucial variable in a host–parasitoid would not be unreasonable because polymorphisms in ovipositor length, very possibly arising out of agonistic coevolution of the kind postulated, are known in other parasitoids (Askew, 1971; Hamilton, 1978a). Auslander and his coworkers did not relate their findings to the problem of sex. However, a similar two-species system (with a true predator, not parasitoid) was discussed independently by Hubbell and Norton (1978) in connection with the very unusual occurrence of parthenogenesis in a cave cricket.

Coincidental to the variation that Auslander et al. hypothesized, with the cave cricket depth of burial in a substrate is known to be a factor in escaping the predator (a carabid beetle) although here the ovipositor in the story belongs to the prey and appears to be the device through which the prey's eggs partially escape predation. The ovipositor has proved to be of significantly greater mean length in caves where the predator is present. Data are not given on whether it is also relatively more variable in such caves. Hubbell and Norton draw attention to the absence of the predator from caves inhabited by the parthenogenetic strain in contrast to its usual presence in the caves occupied by the sexual counterpart, and they tentatively link this absence to the thesis of a connection of sex with biotic diversity (Glesener and Tilman, 1978). Obviously any linkage with the mixed strategies and cyclical and strange chaotic attractors of Auslander et al., must as yet be even more tentative. It will be shown later there is reason to suspect that one predator alone would not easily provide sufficient complexity of selection to ensure the retention of sex.

The biotic environment of the parthenogenetic cricket may well be simple not only as regards its predators but also in one sense as regards its own food. Although it is a very omnivorous scavenger, it hardly takes any food that is alive. A survey of feeding habits in relevant animal groups suggests that a diet of dead organisms or detritus is disproportionately common in the known cases of parthenogenesis. Of course, dead food and detritus (apart from associated fungi and microorganisms—which might sometimes gain from at least contact with a feeder for the sake of dispersal) have no interest in trying to avoid being eaten and hence do not co-evolve in a manner likely to select for genetic diversity in whatever feeds on them. Live foods on the contrary not only are expected to flee from or oppose, in an evolutionary sense, any important feeder (Olson and Pimental, 1974) but also are expected to diversify their evasive behavior, toxins, etc., within the species (Clarke, 1976). To pursue this kind of strategy they have to retain sex themselves and in retaining it may impose a similar retention by the predator. Some hint of the degree to which living foods tend to demand specialist feeders (implying, within the more generalist species, specialist genotypes maintained in polymorphism) is perhaps illustrated by the contrast between the insect faunas of living and dead trees (Elton, 1966; Hamilton, 1978b).

As regards living foods, the idea of the constant and generally hostile co-evolution going on between these species and those which feed on them leading to diversification of species, and within species, to adaptive polymorphisms, has been well reviewed by Levin (1975). Although his main concern was with why recombination is kept so open (i.e., linkage so loose), Levin included parthenogenesis as the extreme beyond inbreeding of a trend that he identified as towards genetic conservatism in biotically simpler habitats. The problem of sex versus non-sex was not clearly focused, however, perhaps because of inclination to a group-oriented view of natural selection. Before Levin, other authors had already documented enough cases of genotype-for-genotype resistance–susceptibility situations in parasites and hosts to suggest that, if searched for with the thoroughness so far devoted only to agricultural and disease situations, such interacting polymorphic systems will be found to be abundant almost everywhere (Day, 1974; Dolinger et al., 1973; see also Edmunds and Alstad, 1978; Dunn and Kempton, 1972; Barr, 1975; Richards, 1975; Rutter et al., 1975; Clarke, 1976). We must emphasize the ''almost everywhere'' here—this paper, of course, endorses cited previous suggestions that such interactions will be found to be less abundant at the margins of a species' range and wherever else adoption of extreme sex-ratios and parthenogenesis is apt to occur. The initial theoretical viewpoint hardly differs from that explained recently by Jaenike (1978); but where some statements of Jaenike were unquantified and could be considered theoretically doubtful, we here attempt to provide confirmatory models. These will now be described. In brief preview it may be stated that their outcomes somewhat complicate the notions outlined here by showing that at least *two* factors of fluctuating selection may be needed to stabilize sex on a reasonable basis. Looking back, for example, the Auslander model as it stands, based on single-factor differences, seems almost certain to be insufficient. Real cave crickets likewise may need a second genetic hassle with a predator—over, it might be, distastefulness of eggs as well as that already indicated concerning depth of burial—if the one predator is to provide a sufficient basis for retaining sex. In general our models suggest improved hopes of a given species for stable sexuality if it faces two important antagonist species rather than one.

THE MODELS

We confine attention to models based on two simplifying assumptions. First, we assume that asexual strains arise easily from the sexual species, so that for every genotype of the sexual species there exists a corresponding asexual clone. Admittedly, this assumption out-does reality in favor of the clones, but it gives impartial symmetry to the analysis and, in the light of various large-scale tests of apparently non-parthenogenetic invertebrates, a viewpoint of this kind seems currently fairly acceptable (White, 1973, pp. 701–703).

Preparing for our second assumption, consider statistical descriptors that permit assessment of clone and species growth, "mean fitness," and natural selection in the fluctuating environment. Consider the multiplication of any one of the asexual clones over a series of generations: let the sequence of fitnesses in the varying successive environments be $A_1, A_2, A_3, \ldots$ At the end of the nth generation the population of this clone will have grown from its initial value by a factor equal to the product

$$A_1 A_2 A_3 \ldots A_n$$

Thus the fitness which, if expressed constantly, would have given the same total product is

$$(A_1 A_2 A_3 \ldots A_n)^{1/n}$$

The ideal "mean fitness" that assesses the growth or decline of a clone would use this expression evaluated for the limit $n \to \infty$. Similar expressions, which will be referred to as LGMFs (long-term geometric mean fitnesses), can be found for the other clones; and if they differ, comparison of magnitudes would show which clone will win.

The second simplifying assumption of our models, then, is that the LGMFs of all our clones are equal; fitness parameters and frequencies for the various states of environment are to be applied such that this occurs. This second assumption is obviously even more artificial than the first. Its aim is to de-emphasize competition between clones and bring to focus the one other LGMF that is crucial to assessing the role of sex, the LGMF of the sexual population as a whole. For this sexual *geometric* mean, obtained over generations in the same way as the last, the A_i in the formula will themselves be means over the various genotypes within the ith generation, these being the more familiar *arithmetic* means of genotype fitnesses (e.g., $w = p^2 a + 2pqb + q^2 c$ under random mating). The separate applications of geometric and arithmetic means for between- and within-generation contexts of selection are well known (Crow and Kimura, 1970; Felsenstein, 1976). Our present account combines such applications and its limited achievement with respect to sexuality depends implicitly on a fundamental inequality, $AM > GM$, which holds whenever the means are composed from positive numbers.

For sex to be "stable" we assume that the LGMF of the sexual species must be higher than the highest LGMF among the clones. Suppose that the highest such LGMF is M, and that this is a number within, or at least not far outside, the range 1 to 2. M is to be related to an LGMF of the corresponding sexual genotype that is set at 1, so that the excess of M above 1 represents the cost of meiosis in the species. In other words, when the asexual female is producing M offspring it is supposed that the corresponding sexual female produces two— of which, on average, only one is female. Obviously M will sink towards 1 insofar as male parental care is important (the unhelped parthenogenetic female producing fewer offspring), and insofar as the apomictic process is imperfect; but M could also conceivably rise above 2, as when, for example, mate-finding is a particularly limiting difficulty for the sexual species. It is arranged that, in all the models that follow, all clones have an LGMF of M.

One-locus Models

We show first a simple model demonstrating a theoretical possibility for a sexual species to outcompete its clones in spite of (a) low maximum fecundity (in contrast to models of Williams and of Maynard Smith) and (b) no fitnesses that are zero (in contrast to Treisman's model). It is supposed that the environment has two states conferring fitnesses on the clones and sexual genotypes as follows:

	Sexual species			Clones		
	gg	gG	GG	gg	gG	GG
Environment "A"	r	r^{-1}	r	Mr	Mr^{-1}	Mr
Environment "B"	r^{-1}	r	r^{-1}	Mr^{-1}	Mr	Mr^{-1}

In accord with our assumption the LGMF of all the clones is M. Thus the analytic task is to determine the demographic behavior of the sexual population under a specified pattern of successive environments: does the LGMF of the sexual population exceed M? Figure 22–1 shows at once how the chosen fitness sets hold out a hope for sexuality in the fact that at any given gene frequency other than 0 or 1 the LGMF of the sexual species is greater than unity. The heavy-line GM mean curve is shown for the assumption that the two environments occur with equal frequency irrespective of gene frequency. Obviously at any non-terminal gene frequency LGMF >2 can be obtained by a sufficient increase of r. However, gene frequency may change—and perhaps by large steps if r is high—because of the selection process, so our focus quickly transfers to the problem of the stochastic behavior of gene frequencies over a long series of generations. Is there a steady state distribution and if so is this sufficiently concentrated centrally to allow stability of sex at values of r that are biologically feasible?

It is easily seen from symmetry that a gene-frequency at $q = .5$ is an equilibrium, and it turns out that this equilibrium, although not "protected" in the sense of Felsenstein (1976), is stable both for a regular alternation of the two environments and for random sequences based on equal frequency. Thus, the final state is concentrated ideally for giving advantage to sex, and the LGMF is simply $\frac{1}{2}(r + r^{-1})$. When $r = 4$, as in Figure 22–1, this is 2.125, so sex is stable even against a full cost of meiosis ($M = 2$) for a fecundity of 8, and this is about as low as any known for a sexual species.

The problem with this model is, of course, that there is neither evidence nor *a priori* plausibility to the postulated pattern of fitnesses: even with $r = 4$ the degree of over- and under-dominance is extreme compared to known natural cases, and nothing like the supposed switching from over- to under-dominance has ever been recorded. Worse than this, such artificialiity seems ineradicable. It appears to be impossible in a one-locus model to modify fitness patterns or sequence of environments so as to retain the desired high LGMF in a more realistic setting. Beyond the problem of retaining a stable and central-peaked distribution, which can be overcome if necessary by bringing in frequency dependence in the occurrence of the environmental states, other more drastic difficulties loom in the fact that the most hopeful patterns of symmetry in fitness coefficients force conditions where stability implies that alleles must have LGMF's of unity.

Consider for example the regular sequence of fitness patterns:

$$(r^{-2}, r, r) \longrightarrow (r^{-2}, r, r) \longrightarrow (r, r^{-2}, r^{-2})$$

This model has a more plausible pattern of dominance and the sequence gives a stable cycle of gene frequencies. The stable cycle has been achieved through reduction of the

LGMF of one homozygote. The main point, however, is that even with such reduction allowed, the model remains hopeless for sex, for it is easily seen that allele G is experienceing always the same sequence of fitness, r, r, r^{-2}, etc., irrespective of tenure in heterozygote and homozygote: hence its branching process cannot grow. Next consider an even simpler and more attractive pair of patterns:

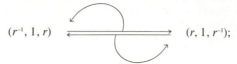

$$(r^{-1}, 1, r) \quad \rightleftharpoons \quad (r, 1, r^{-1});$$

and suppose here that environments occur in some regular or random pattern that ensures a non-terminal stable distribution. Almost the same drawback operates as before: an allele

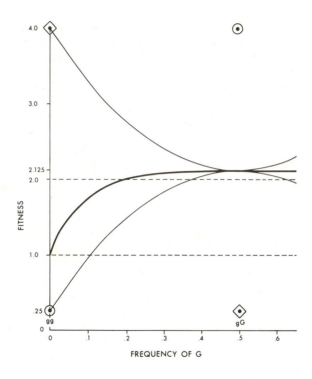

Figure 22–1.   A model giving evolutionary stability of sex at low fecundity.
    The environment has two states occurring with equal frequency. One state, ◇, gives fitnesses 4, $1/4$, 4 to genotypes gg, gG and GG; the other state gives fitnesses $1/4$, 4, $1/4$. Diagram shows various relevant fitnesses over half the gene-frequency range, the other being mirror image of that shown. Symbols show genotype fitnesses, thin curves show population mean fitnesses as function of gene frequency for each environment, the thick curve is the geometric mean between thin curves as appropriate to showing expected contribution to multiplicative growth rate of population at given gene frequencies.
    Dashed lines show the probable range of mean fitnesses of clones derivable from the three sexual genotypes. It can be seen that over a broad range of gene frequencies (~.2 to 8) the growth rate of the sexual population exceeds the likely fitness maximum of two for the clones; and under alternation of environments described gene frequency moves asymptotically towards .5, assuring eventual renewed superiority of the sexual population after disturbance.

must, while in the homozygous state, meet the two types of environment, in the long run, with equal frequency; on occasions when it escapes from this state it gets only the standard unit; so overall its LGMF is one.

In the light of such examples it appears unlikely that a viable one-locus model for maintenance of sex based on fluctuation of environment can be devised. This at least gives some cool comfort with regard to traditional views of sex. If a one-locus model had proved plausibly ''sufficient'' an equally important problem would be left outstanding, that of explaining the near universality of crossing over. Even more important, such a model based on special values of the three diploid genotypes would have failed to explain the persistence of sex in the many eucaryote groups that spend almost their entire lives as haploids. In these organisms (for example, green algae, bryophytes, and fungi), the advantages of sex must depend on effects of recombination between loci; from this point of view a generally applicable model needs to treat at least two loci. In the many primarily haploid organisms that are isogamous, the cost of meiosis is eliminated, reducing the magnitude of the advantage needed to maintain sex (Williams, 1975, p. 113). Still, many forms exist that combine anisogamy and a predominance of haploidy, for example, the genera *Pleodorina* and *Volvox* of the green algae. It is also noteworthy here that, as with aphids, rotifers, and many plants, most largely haploid species possess mechanisms for asexual reproduction; thus, the argument that sex is a maladaptive vestige, maintained only because wholly asexual lines fail to arise, is particularly weak. In addition, the fact that sex probably originated in haploids makes it especially desirable that a theory with pretensions to generality should cover life cycles that are still primarily haploid.

Two-locus Models

Success in the first described one-locus model, such as it was, was caused by the possibility under sex that an allele over a series of generations can slip from homozygosity to heterozygosity and back in ways that take some advantage of the changing favorabilities of the diploid associations. As presented each environment occasioned special production of the genotype or genotypes that will be most successful in the next environment. With two segregating loci the number of avenues open to an allele for ''changing alliance'' is greatly expanded. As already indicated cyclical patterns of environmental change, ranging from regular to chaotic, strongly suggest themselves as providing advantage to continual change of alliance. It is intuitively plausible that the modes of such regrouping would themselves range correspondingly from regular to ''chaotic,'' so that the randomness of segregation and crossing over could partly reflect a prevalence of chaotic cycling in nature. These issues remain vague in the present account as work in progress on two-locus models has not yet covered the promising role foreseen for cyclicity in changes of environment. The results to be presented here aim to clear the ground respecting *necessity* for frequency dependence or cyclicity in gaining stability for sex.

Our main question so far addressed to our model is whether a *purely random* sequence of environments is capable of stabilizing sex on a reasonable basis. The concept of null gene pair at a different locus along with our first one-locus model shows that stability certainly can be obtained: but can it occur more realistically? The answer, obtained first from simulation studies and later backed by analysis (see appendix), has been a limited ''yes.'' The new best model state described as follows is somewhat less incredible; yet on present evidence is hardly to be described as actually realistic. The result once more suggests that while the trick can just be done with the materials allowed, much more impressive and satisfying effects await when autocorrelations in the environmental sequence can be brought in.

The model has two alleles at each of two loci. Because of the usual analytical difficulties we have used mainly monte-carlo simulation of the genetical-demographic process. So far we have investigated only random sequences involving four states of environment supposed to favor the four types of double homozygote, AABB, AAbb, aaBB, and aabb: we shall refer to these as the ''AB,'' ''Ab''. ''aB,'' and ''ab'' environments.

Consider the construction of a symmetrical 3×3 fitness matrix that generalizes the property chosen for the one-locus case, namely, that the LGMF of every genotype taken individually should be unity. Let there be symmetry with respect to the different environments: each environment produces the same fitness pattern but favors different alleles. Such symmetry at once excludes forms analogous to that which gave the only success in the one-locus case.

The symmetries required in the construction of the matrix are most easily seen if the *logarithms* of fitness are shown: set out in such a form the most general matrix, given as for an "AB" environment, can be presented as follows:

	bb:	bB:	BB:
aa:	$(-1 - y + z)\delta$	$(-\frac{1}{2} + y)\delta$	$(0 - z)\delta$
aA:	$(-\frac{1}{2} + y)\delta$	0	$(\frac{1}{2} - y)\delta$
AA:	$(0 - z)\delta$	$(\frac{1}{2} - y)\delta$	$(1 + y + z)\delta$

Adequacy of three parameters is set by the degrees of freedom, but in choosing three to apply as shown here we are guided by the intention of the e^δ can serve like the multiplicative fitness factor r in the simpler no-dominance model, so setting a general "slope" to the present log fitness matrix, or equivalently, a general "degree of concavity" to the matrix of fitness itself. But, as the log fitness expression for AABB shows, e^δ does not any longer necessarily set the highest fitness attained: indeed, when either or both of y and z are negative AABB might not be, even in its best environment, the genotype with the highest fitness. In searching the now extensive parameter space for realistic models relevant to sex, however, it seemed reasonable to constrain y and z against patterns of co-epistasis that seem too bizarre, and we therefore mainly confine attention to cases where a specific rule of "no over- or under-dominance" applies. That is, apart from a few trial excursions, we treat only cases where fitness of the favored double homozygote is *at least as high* as any other. This rule confines (y, z) to a kite-shaped region around the zero point, corners at ($\frac{1}{2}$, 0), (0, $\frac{1}{2}$), ($-\frac{1}{4}$, 0), (0, $-\frac{1}{2}$). The zero point ($y = z = 0$) has fitness interactions multiplicative both within and between loci. It is well known that this pattern of selection makes behavior of the two loci effectively independent: any initial linkage disequilibrium dies away. Thus, the possibility of success of sex under any pattern of environmental change where the selection on one locus is uncorrelated with selection on the other is excluded by the argument already given for the one-locus case. Likewise, by an argument used already for the one-locus examples, possibility of success is excluded at the kite's extreme corner at ($\frac{1}{2}$, 0) where the fitness pattern has r^{-1} and r at opposite corners of the matrix and units everywhere else.

For our trial study of the behavior of the model by computation, we assumed non-overlapping generations and an infinite random-mating population. Fitness was assumed to affect mortality although, given certain assumptions about breeding system, the parameters could be considered to include effects on gamete output as well. A parameter was provided for the recombination fraction between the two loci. With these assumptions and any state of the 3×3 fitness matrix and any four initial frequencies of chromosome types ab, aB, Ab, and AB, the chromosome frequencies in the next generation are easily calculated. Using a pseudo-random number generator to give sequences of the four states of the environment we followed movements of gene frequency and linkage disequilibrium over long series of generations. So far effects of autocorrelation or gene frequency dependence in the sequence of environments have not been studied. During the runs logarithms of population mean fitness were accumulated with a view to forming at the end, as antilog of the total, a geometric mean fitness for the whole run.

Even if gene frequencies terminalize, the expected LGMF falls only to 1. Thus values close to 1 (or, in occasional runs, just below—these caused by, presumably, accidentally hostile sample sequences) were taken to indicate failure to establish polymorphism. Interest focused on parameter states giving high GMFs, especially when these could be shown to be repeatable and steady for longer runs.

It was found that compared to the one-locus successful model fairly high best fitnesses (i.e., $\delta > 5$ or $e^{\delta} > 45$) were necessary to get any GMFs above 2; however, the really novel feature was that certain patterns having highest fitnesses of this order could predictably produce LGMF>2 under pure stochasticity of environment; in other words such LGMFs >2 are possible *at stable equilibria*. The first result can be understood if thought is given to the maximum value that the GMF curve or surface attains as more loci enter: although important, this point will not be expanded here. The second result was more surprising in view of statements in theoretical literature that seemed to give minimal plausibility to any kind of continuing polymorphism when there is no overdominance in geometric mean fitness for any heterozygous genotype (Felsenstein, 1976). Before giving further attention to this, it is convenient to mention that the linkage parameter played no important part in specifying the region where polymorphism is possible. Starting from a mid-range linkage value, we found that tighter linkage lowers any otherwise promising GMF, while less linkage, on the other hand, makes hardly any difference—such change as was shown in the monte-carlo simulations was once more downward although very slight. Such findings are not very surprising in view of the disadvantage that tight linkage of alleles is expected to confer in models with varying combination optima like ours (Charlesworth, 1976). Therefore in most runs we used $c = .25$, and this value is also assumed in the discussion that follows.

Within our "kite" of (y, z)—this being, to repeat, the region that excludes all overdominance, corners at $(\frac{1}{2}, 0)$, $(0, \frac{1}{2})$, $(-\frac{1}{4}, 0)$, and $(0, -\frac{1}{2})$—we found almost no suggestion of possible polymorphism when $0 \leqslant y \leqslant \frac{1}{2}$. Nor was any favorable suggestion obtained in trials of larger values of y (i.e., outside the kite). Increase of z along $y = 0$ gave even less positive indication than increase of y along $z = 0$; increase of *negative z* along $y = 0$, on the other hand, was better but still suggestive that slow terminalization was everywhere continuing.

In the blunt corner of the kite, with the effect sharply accentuating around the extremity at $(-\frac{1}{4}, 0)$, a region was found where protected polymorphisms can occur: here, consequently, if δ is high enough, sex is stable. In other words, following the guaranteed survival of its various alleles, the sexual strain itself can be protected from extinction from pressure of its asexual mutants. In our runs $\delta = 5$ appeared to be just sufficient to give LGMF >2.

The point $y = -\frac{1}{4}$, $z = 0$ corresponds to what might be called a "flat-top, flat-bottom" fitness pattern for the loci, an example being:

$$\begin{bmatrix} 1/r & 1/r & 1 \\ 1/r & 1 & r \\ 1 & r & r \end{bmatrix}$$

where r as before is some fitness value > 1. Since $\delta = 5$ corresponds to $r = e^{\delta} = 42.52$, the lowest fecundity capable of stabilizing sex in this random environment model is about 85.

Can the model really achieve what, at first reading of the literature of selection in fluctuating environments (Gillespie, 1973; review in Felsenstein, 1976), seems to have been shown impossible? The seeming contradiction depends on the fact that Gillespie summarized a sufficient condition for polymorphism but not a necessary one (see Felsenstein, 1976). The polymorphism generated by this system is "unprotected" in the sense that it has a vanishing tendency to preserve itself at extreme gene frequencies, and this property was the matter of concern in Gillespie's proof. However, small as it may become, an overall centralizing tendency exists as long as the gene frequency is not zero or 1. When with the present model at $y = -\frac{1}{4}$, $z = 0$, we temporarily focus on one locus and treat the other as if merely contributing to "variability" in fitness within each of the three genotypes, it turns out that overdominance in heterozygote geometric mean fitness actually holds for every combination of gene frequencies (varying both q and Q, between 0 and 1) and of linkage disequilibrium. That this is true in the framework of assumptions reasonable for our model (random mating, equal frequency of the four environments, neither locus already fixed and at least four of the nine genotypes present) is proved in the Appendix.

A less rigorous but perhaps useful intuitive approach to the working of this model may also be outlined as follows. The fitness matrix oriented as before, at the same time that it tends greatly to increase the frequency of the favored double homozygote (bottom right), tends also to create linkage disequilibrium in favor of the homozygotes on the non-principal diagonal (top right and bottom right). While by chance one environment is repeating itself, the increasingly common homozygote is also the most highly fit, so that very high mean fitnesses are attained. But obviously this cannot continue if polymorphism is to be preserved, and if the environment completely *reverses* (so as to favor the opposite-corner genotype), the common genotypes are then extremely unfit, and previous gains to the LGMF product are offset. But the direction of the linkage disequilibrium means that if, instead of reversing, the environment *turns* (i.e., favors top right or bottom left after a run on top left or bottom right), there tend to be substantial numbers of homozygotes and heterozygotes able to express moderate or high fitness. The amount of ''turning'' in a random sequence is evidently enough for this effect to achieve results of the kind needed: the same line of thought, however, obviously extends greater hopes as regards what may be found with models where cyclical tendencies are built in and cause turning at a suitable rate. One simple case already tried, for example, had the factor that switches selection for A versus a subject to random change only every fifth generation while the factor switching for B versus b was subject to random change every fourth: it was then found that $r = 9$ was enough to give advantage to sex. This would correspond to a fecundity of 18. Of course this schedule does not give a cycle, but it does provide for many more turns than reversals and also for many short runs of the same environment. Special kinds of cycles can probably lower the requisite fecundity still further; and, as already indicated, biotic inteerractions in nature may supply cyclical pressures rather freely—Baltensweiler (1970), for example, documents one example.

Turning back from this preview to limitations of the present model, the reason why other authors attached importance to there being more than negligible centripetal tendency from selection at extreme gene frequencies is that a polymorphism is likely to be lost by drift if extreme frequencies are reached, and here it has to be admitted that the model described with $r = 42.5$ and random equiprobable environments gives a very concave distribution (Figure 22–2) and quite frequently visits gene frequencies so extreme (e.g., 10^{-7}) that in any reasonable population an allele would be lost. In the case just mentioned with $r = 9$ similar extremes were visited. Considerations that oppose this tendency for fixation however are that (a) extremes for an allele tend to occur when frequencies at the other locus are in the mid-range and here the tendency to recover is stronger, and (b) weak density-dependent effects and also recurrent mutation could, in nature, provide for potential buffering or recovery at extremes. Altogether the need for polymorphism protection at the extremes seems overemphasized in the literature and may have caused neglect of otherwise plausible models.

How plausible is the specific fitness pattern suggested? So far variants of the general matrix have not been much explored although it has been confirmed that the seemingly even more artificial condition $y < -.25$ on $z = 0$ permits stability of sex at much lower values of δ.

Jointly the ''flat top'' and ''flat bottom'' condition as it stands does not suggest any easy genetical or ecological interpretation. Equality of the three higher fitnesses could be subject to a claim similar to one sometimes brought in for the common occurrence of dominance: if having three out of four alleles ''right'' for a current environment permits full fecundity (say), then having all four right can gain no additional advantage. But this cannot be applied to equality of the three low fitnesses. If we let the low-corner fitness sink to $1/r^2$ (or completely to zero) it is obvious that all four doubly homozygous asexual strains are at once rendered inviable compared to the rest. Perhaps this is not unreasonable: apomictic

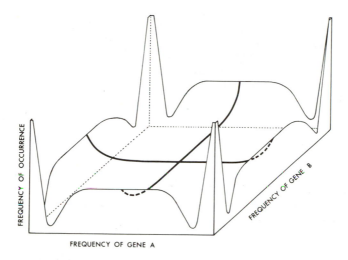

Figure 22–2.   Roughly sketched form of the ultimate distribution of gene frequencies at two un-linked loci when each serves as epistatic modifier of multiplicative interaction at the other, so as to produce the "flat-top, flat-bottom" pattern described in the text. Environment is fluctuating at random (i.e., no gene-frequency dependence) among four states, these each favoring a particular corner of the diagram, i.e. favoring an "ab", "aB", "Ab", or "AB" allele combination.

strains are often claimed to be highly heterozygous. It will be of interest to see how the distribution and the conditions for sex change in these circumstances, and also perhaps in various others that will leave the doubly heterozygous asexual strain as the *only* possible contender against sex. However, a hint that with or without such modification the "flat top" condition in our model at least could correspond to a relevant feature of the real world comes from various studies of the so-called "gene-for-gene" interactions that often hold between the genetic polymorphisms of parasites and of their hosts (Day, 1974; Barr, 1975). It is very commonly reported that resistance to a given strain of parasite is dominant. Be-cause the genetic tests were often made by first selecting for the trait that would be advanta-geous to the host (in the given context) and then backcrossing, and because reference to modifiers or an element of polygenicity often occurs in the reports as well, it seems possible that, seen in terms of our model, the experimental procedure is unintentionally selecting only the high side of the fitness matrix for examination; along this side, of course, our ma-trix shows dominance as found. But if the "polygene" or "modifier" effects are indeed accountable to another locus of equal importance, as suggested here, we have to confess to complete ignorance as to the realities of selection with which that other locus might be con-cerned.

A weakness in the above tentative view is that for variants of the *parasite* it is more often the apparently less advantageous avirulent type that appears to be dominant. But per-haps neither artificial selection in the maintenance of parasite cultures nor natural selection of wild variants is easily able to press virulence to its extreme, this being caused, in each case, by the difficulty of "maintaining the culture."

Involvement of these gene-for-gene systems would, as already argued, greatly im-prove the situation for sex because they must bring at least some element of gene frequency dependence into environmental changes. Once this or another source of autocorrelation of environment is brought in, a wide variety of other forms of the matrix, including, it is to be hoped, forms that are much more realistic, may prove successful.

What has been shown is that at least for one special pattern of epistasis such dependence or auto correlation is not strictly necessary: the sequence of environments can be random. This suggests that climatic variability, for example, could after all be contributing substantially towards the maintenance of sex, even though on general evidence it seems very unlikely to be the sole agent. Because one recent study found very high correlations between prevalence of enzyme polymorphisms and climatic variability, leaving apparently not too much polymorphism in need of explanation by anything else (Bryant, 1974), extension of the model in a way that would help climate to play a part might seem an almost necessary step to secure its survival. However, while climate may be very important generally for polymorphism, Bryant's analysis did not exclude the possibility of other agencies, possibly biotic ones, being important for at least a few polymorphisms. While principal factors in his factor analysis of polymorphisms generally regressed on climatic variability very well, the same regression for second factors was usually weak and there were always some loci that loaded very heavily on second factors while light on the first. Perhaps these second factors were concerned with the kind of hostile biotic forces that have been the main focus of the present discussion. Of course, complete independence of climate would not be expected; if the biotic emphasis in the problem of sex is right, climatic fluctuation is still certain to play some part in the detail of how an array of co-antagonist species keep constantly on the move.

CONCLUSIONS

Compared to parthenogenetic offspring, sexual offspring transmit genes of a mother diluted by one half. Yet the record of the living world shows that in most circumstances females "prefer" sexual offspring. In some cases it is known also that females prefer some mates to others; and that they do so on some sort of eugenic grounds is plausible. In spite of these indications and the ramification of sex-dependent phenomena throughout biology—e.g., diploid genetics—we still do not know what sex is for.

In the field of social behavior such lack of understanding leaves large gaps in genetical kinship theory. For example, benefits of outbreeding versus inbreeding underpin breeding structure and breeding stucture itself determines, through kinship considerations, major trends of social behavior. Again, if benefits of sex are immediate and substantial, there is a missing factor based on outbreeding that ought to be included in assessments of reproductive value.

Circumstantial evidence accumulates to suggest that complexity of the biotic environment is particularly supportive to sex. This paper has furthered such evidence by examples and study of possible mechanisms. Mechanisms with cyclical interactions among species are highly promising. In our attempt to clear ground of possible non-cyclical, although fluctuating, selection, we find simple models where even random environmental sequences give sex short-term stability against parthenoform competition, and that succeed in this (a) without high fecundities, (b) without sibling competition, (c) without involvement of more than one locus, (d) without overdominance in the fitness pattern manifested in any single generation. However, in these models (c) and (d) could not be achieved together, and both the one-locus and two-locus successful cases had certain grave and seemingly ineradicable artificial features. Hence, former theoretical emphasis on recombination as intrinsic to the function of sex was upheld by the results: at least two loci and two at least partially independent agencies of selection appear to be necessary for a reasonable model. As a whole the results suggest that cycles of selection and/or selection responsive to the dynamics of the species themselves (as in interspecies interaction) may be crucial, especially in the cases hitherto treated as the most puzzling (low fecundity organisms with no paternal care). It is suggested that pure random fluctuating selection may play a supportive role that is secondary to effects of cycling selection. Further work in progress (not reported in this paper) shows that indeed conditions (a), (b), and (d) can be retained under much more natural patterns of dominance and epistasis when forms of environmental cyclicity are added.

It seems justified to conclude the seemingly rather non-social theme of theoretical biology reported here by the suggestion that to understand social behavior at a deeper level evolutionary behaviorists may soon need to pay closer attention to transgenerational patterns in the major forces of selection on their organisms; in such patterns eventually may be found reasons why one species tolerates or prefers incest, why one has lower fecundity, more parental care, and why one has males that are more showy, less industrious, and yet more preferred.

APPENDIX

We assume two loci each with two alleles (a, A and b, B), and an environment that has four equally probable states labelled "ab," "aB," "Ab," and "AB". Labels designate the type of double homozygote favored in each state and indicate the orientation of the fixed fitness matrix. This matrix is shown below for the "aB" state:

	bb	bB	BB	
aa	1	r	r	
aA	r^{-1}	1	r	
AA	r^{-1}	r^{-1}	1	(1)

(Form for "AB" state is shown in text.)

Given (a) random mating, (b) loci A and B not completely linked, and (c) $r > 1$, it is required to prove that occurrence of the four environments in random sequence establishes polymorphism for both loci.

From symmetry of environment and of the matrix it is obviously sufficient to prove this for one of the two loci. We proceed, therefore, to show that the LGMFs for the three genotypes at locus A fulfill a condition of overdominance in geometric mean fitness, treating locus B as a modifier.

Let p, q, P, Q denote frequencies of alleles a, A, b, B ($p + q = 1$ and $P + Q = 1$) and let D denote "linkage disequilibrium," implying that the frequencies of the four chromosome types ab, aB, Ab, and AB are $pP + D$, $pQ - D$, $qP - D$ and $qQ + D$. Under random mating the state of the population is then completely determined by the three parameters q, Q, and D. If polymorphism and a steady state distribution over q, Q, and D is attained, then any small region in the neighborhood of a specified (q, Q, D) will be visited by the population repeatedly, albeit with very varying frequency according to location. With one quarter of these visits an "ab" environment will follow, with one quarter an "aB" environment and so on: hence for the very long-term assessment of the geometric mean performances of aa, aA, and AA we can group visits in fours that cover instances of all four environments, and hence see that for each genotype at the A locus the quartic root of the product of the four different mean fitness performances in each environment will evaluate the long-term contribution of that genotype (Gillespie, 1973).

Let $\widetilde{W}_0$, $\widetilde{W}_1$, and $\widetilde{W}_2$, denote LGMFs of aa, aA, and AA in this sense (the tilde used for a GM over the four environments; period in the subscript used to denote AMs within each environment and within A-locus genotype taken over three genotype conditions at the B locus). Then our argument states that $\widetilde{W}_0$, $< \widetilde{W}_1 > \widetilde{W}_2$ for all (q, Q, D) will be a sufficient condition for polymorphism and for existence of an asymptotic distribution as assumed.

We proceed to prove that this condition holds for q and Q in closed interval 0 to 1 with D at any feasible value in closed interval $-\frac{1}{4}$ to $\frac{1}{4}$.

From the frequencies of the four chromosome types and random mating the distribution prior to selection of B genotypes within each A genotype is easily determined to be as follows:

	bb:	bB:	BB	
aa:	P_0^2	$2P_0Q_0$	Q_0^2	/1
aA:	P_0P_2	$P_0Q_2 + Q_0P_2$	Q_0Q_2	/1
AA:	P_2^2	$2P_2Q_2$	Q_2^2	/1	(2)

where $P_0 = P + D/p$, $Q_0 = Q - D/p$, $P_2 = P - D/q$ and $Q_2 = P + D/q$. When D is such that one of these four frequencies is zero while the rest are positive, then D is at maximum or minimum of its range for the (q, Q) in question (however, at the one point $q = Q = .5$ either both P_0 and Q_2 or P_2 and Q_0 reach zero together at the extreme of D). We may take as typifying the form of (2) at an extreme of D the case where $Q \leqslant p$ and D is at its minimum, $D = -qQ$, which gives $Q_2 = 0$, $P_2 = 1$:

$$\begin{bmatrix} P_0^2 & 2P_0Q_0 & Q_0^2 \\ P_0 & Q_0 & 0 \\ 1 & 0 & 0 \end{bmatrix} \tag{3}$$

Other extreme forms, i.e., for other (q, Q) and/or D_{max} rather than D_{min}, always have (i) "convergence" to a unit in some corner of the matrix, (ii) either P_0 and Q_0 or P_2 and Q_2 placed so as to be either right- or left-adjusted in the middle row, and (iii) the remaining row filled by a distribution that can be considered as that "Hardy-Weinberg" that derives from frequencies recorded in the middle row. When $D = 0$, $Q_0 = Q_2 = Q$ and all rows are "Hardy-Weinberg" and identical.

Turning to fitnesses, imagining (1) rotated to its four positions, it is seen that for the middle row (aA) only two equiprobable patterns occur. Hence, the LGMF of Aa, W_1, is particularly simple. For $D = -qQ$ for example, enabling (3) to be used, producing frequencies with fitnesses and adding to obtain AMs, then producing again and taking square root to obtain the GM, we have

$$\widetilde{W}_1\,(D = -qQ) = \sqrt{(P_0 r^{-1} + Q_0)(P_0 r + Q_0)} \tag{4}$$

By like procedure for $D = 0$ we have

$$\widetilde{W}_1\,(D = 0) = \sqrt{(P_0^2 r^{-1} + 2P_0Q_0 + Q_0^2 r)(P_0^2 r + 2P_0Q_0 + Q_0^2 r^{-1})}$$

Multiplying first factor by r^1 and second by r, so as to form perfect squares, we find

$$\widetilde{W}_1\,(D = 0) = (P_0 r^{-1} + Q_0)(P_0 r + Q_0) = \{\widetilde{W}_1\,(D = -qQ)\}^2$$

$$= P_0^2 + P_0Q_0(r + r^{-1}) + Q_0^2 \tag{5}$$

For $r > 1$ we have $r + r^{-1} > 2$ and hence $\widetilde{W}_1(D = 0) > \widetilde{W}_1\,(D = -qQ) > 1$, except that when $Q_0 = 0$ or 1 both LGMFs are unity. With the general form of the mid-row as in (2) and treating Q_0 as constant and Q_2 as a variable reflecting D it is easily shown $\widetilde{W}_1(D = 0)$ is a maximum of a wholly upward-convex function. Hence (4), which applies both for D_{min} and

D_{max} (with Q_0 fixed), gives a minimum for the LGMF of the heterozygote. If it can be shown that even this minimum exceeds $\widetilde{W}_0.\,(Q_0)$, for all Q_0 then $\widetilde{W}_1. > \widetilde{W}_0.$ will be proven for all Q_0 and Q_2.

The distribution of B genotypes within the genotype aa may be combined with fitnesses of B genotypes in all four environments to give the following formula for the LGMF of aa analogous to (4):

$$\widetilde{W}_0. = \left\{ \begin{array}{l} (P_0^2 r^{-1} + 2P_0Q_0 r^{-1} + Q_0^2) \\ \times (P_0^2 + 2P_0Q_0 r + Q_0^2 r) \\ \times (P_0^2 r + 2P_0Q_0 r + Q_0^2) \\ \times (P_0^2 + 2P_0Q_0 r^{-1} + Q_0^2 r^{-1}) \end{array} \right\}^{1/4}$$

With some effort this can be reduced to the form:

$$\widetilde{W}_0.^4 = 1 + 2(1 - P_0Q_0)P_0Q_0 Z + (2 + P_0Q_0)P_0^3 Q_0^3 Z^2 \tag{6}$$

where $Z = r + r^1 - 2$.

From (5) we find in similar notation:

$$\{\widetilde{W}_1. (D = -qQ)\}^4 = (1 + P_0Q_0 Z)^2$$

$$= 1 + 2P_0Q_0 Z + P_0^2 Q_0^2 Z^2 \tag{7}$$

From $r > 1$ we have $r + r^1 > 2$, so that $Z > 0$; and we also have $0 < (1 - P_0Q_0) \leq 1$ and $0 \leq (2 + P_0Q_0)P_0Q_0 < 1$. Hence Z and Z^2 are positive and for each the coefficient in (6) is smaller than in (7), so that $\{\widetilde{W}_1. (D = -qQ)\}^4 > \widetilde{W}_0.^4$. Quartic roots of these are unequal the same way. As already explained it follows from this generally that $\widetilde{W}_1. > \widetilde{W}_0.$.

The inequality $\widetilde{W}_1. > \widetilde{W}_2.$ can be obtained by exactly the same argument except that at the start Q_2 is fixed while D is varied such that Q_0 passes from zero to one: this argument, in effect, explores the entire feasible space of (q, Q, D) a second time. Finally, of course, the whole argument can be repeated to demonstrate overdominance in the LGMFs and consequent polymorphism at the B locus.

We have not yet tried very hard to extend the foregoing proof to the more general matrix given (in log form) in the text; but preliminary points about work in this direction seem worth making. Firstly, there is a large region within our kite where polymorphism will not be obtained. When the function $\widetilde{W}_1. (D = 0)$ lies wholly below the function $\widetilde{W}_0. (Q_0)$, then the required overdominance cannot occur: it appears that this may apply to the whole region $y > 0$. Secondly, our proof as given identifies merely a sufficient condition for polymorphism, not a necessary one, and it is obvious that there must exist a variety of related fitness matrices that give polymorphism, but have $\widetilde{W}_1. (D = -qQ) < \widetilde{W}_0.$. In spite of such relation, it is easy to image that $\widetilde{W}_1. > \widetilde{W}_0.$ could hold overall if, for example, the more extreme values of D are rarely visited. For such cases other criteria, perhaps based on behaviors at low gene frequencies, need to be developed.

REFERENCES

Aoki, Shigeyuki. 1977. *Colophina clematis* (Homoptera, Pemphigidae), an aphid species with "soldiers." *Kontyu* 45(2): 276–282.

————, S. Yamane, and M. Kiuchi. 1977. On the biters of *Astegopteryx styracicola* (Homoptera, Aphidoidea). *Kontyu* 45(4): 563–570.

Askew, R. R. 1971. *Parasitic Insects*. Heinemann, London. 316p.

Auslander, D. J. Guckenheimer, and G. Oster. 1978. Random evolutionarily stable strategies. *Theor. Popul. Biol.* (13): 276–293.

Baltensweiler, W. 1970. The relevance of changes in the composition of larch bud moth populations for the dynamics of its numbers. *Proc. Adv. Study Inst. Dynamics Numbers Popul.* (Oosterbeck, 1970) 208–219.

Barr, A. R. 1975. Evidence for the genetical control of invertebrate immunity and its field significance. In K. Maramorosch and R. E. Shope [ed.] *Invertebrate Immunity Mechanisms of Invertebrate Vector-Parasite Relations*. Academic Press.

Bryant, E. H. 1974. On the adaptive significance of enzyme polymorphisms in relation to environmental variability. *Am. Nat.* 108: 1–16.

Charlesworth, B. 1976. Recombination modification in a fluctuating environment. *Genetics* 83: 181–195.

Clarke, B. 1976. The ecological genetics of host-parasite relationships. In A. E. R. Taylor and R. Muller [ed.] *Genetic Aspects of Host-Parasite Relationships*. Blackwell, London.

Crow, J. F., and M. Kimura. 1965. Evolution in sexual and asexual populations. *Am. Nat.* 99: 439–450.

————, and M. Kimura. 1969. Evolution in sexual and asexual populations. *Am. Nat.* 193: 89–91.

————, and M. Kimura. 1970. *Introduction to Population Genetics Theory*. Harper and Row, New York.

Cuellar, O. 1977. Animal parthenogenesis. *Science* 197: 837–843.

Day, P. R. 1974. *Genetics of Host-Parasite Interaction*. W. H. Freeman, San Francisco. 238p.

Dolinger, P. M., P. R. Ehrlich, W. L. Fitch, and D. E. Breedlove. 1973. Alkaloid and predation patterns in Colorado lupine populations. *Oecologia* (Berl) 13: 191–204.

Dunn, J. A., and D. P. H. Kempton. 1972. Resistance to attack by *Brericoryne brassicae* among plants of Brussels sprouts. *Ann. appl. Biol.* 72: 1–11.

Edmunds, G. F., Jr., and D. N. Alstad. 1978. Coevolution in insect herbivores and conifers. *Science* 199: 941–945.

Elton, C. S. 1966. *The Pattern of Animal Communities*. Methuen, London.

Eshel, I. 1977. On the founder effect and the evolution of altruistic traits: An ecogenetical approach. *Theor. Popul. Biol.* 11: 410–424.

————, and M. W. Feldman. 1970. On the evolutionary effect of recombination. *Theor. Popul. Biol.* 1: 88–100.

Felsenstein, J. 1974. The evolutionary advantage of recombination. *Genetics* 78: 737–756.

————1976. The theoretical population genetics of variable selection and migration. *A. Rev. Genet.* 10: 253–280.

Ghiselin, M. T. 1975. *The Economy of Nature and the Evolution of Sex*. University of California Press, Berkeley.

Gilbert, L. E. 1976. Postmating female odor in *Heliconius* butterflies: A male-contributed antiaphrodisiac. *Science* 193: 419–420.

Gillespie, J. 1973. Polymorphism in random environments. *Theor. Popul. Biol.* 4: 193–195.

Glesener, R. R., and D. Tilman. 1978. Sexuality and the components of environmental uncertainty: Clues from geographical parthenogenesis in terrestrial animals. *Am. Nat.* 112: 659–673.

Hamilton, W. D. 1978a. Wingless and fighting males in fig wasps and other insects. In M. S. Blum and N. A. Blum [ed.] *Reproductive Competition and Selection in Insects*. Academic Press, New York.

————1978b. Evolution and diversity under bark. In L. A. Mound and N. Waloff [ed.] *Diversity of Insect Faunas*. Royal Entomological Society of London, Symposium 9. Blackwell, London.

Hassell, M., and C. Huffaker. 1969. Regulatory processes and population cyclicity in laboratory populations of *Anagasta kühniella* (Zeller) (Lepidoptera: Phycitidae). III. The development of population models. *Res. Popul. Ecol.* 11: 186–210.

Hubbell, T. H., and R. M. Norton. 1978. The systematics and biology of the cave-crickets of the North American tribe Hadenoecini (Orthoptera Saltatoria: Ensifera: Rhaphidophoridae: Dolichopodinae). *Mis. Pubs. Mus. Zool. Univ. Mich.* 156: 1–124.

Jaenike, J. 1978. An hypothesis to account for the maintenance of sex within populations. *Evol. Theory* 3: 191–194.

Karlin, S. 1973. Sex and infinity: A mathematical analysis of the advantages and disadvantages of recombination. In M. S. Bartlett and R. W. Hiorns [ed.] *The Mathematical Theory of the Dy-*

namics of Biological Populations. Academic Press, London.

Levin, D. A. 1975. Pest pressure and recombination systems in plants. *Am. Nat.* 109: 437–451.

May, R. M. 1974. Biological populations with nonoverlapping generations: Stable points, stable cycles and chaos. *Science* 186: 645–647.

Maynard Smith, J. 1968. Evolution in sexual and asexual population. *Am. Nat.* 102: 469–473.

———1971. What use is sex? *J. Theor. Biol.* 30: 319–335.

———1976. A short-term advantage for sex and recombination. *J. Theor. Biol.* 63: 245–258.

———1978. *The Evolution of Sex*. Cambridge University Press, Cambridge.

Mitter, C., and D. Futuyma. 1977. Parthenogenesis in the fall cankerworm, *Alsophila pometoria* (Lepidoptera, Geometridae). *Entomologia exp. & appl.* 21: 192–198.

Olson, D. C., and D. Pimental. 1974. Evolution of resistance in a host population to an attacking parasite. *Environ. Entom.* 3: 621–624.

Richards, C. S. 1975. Genetics of the host-parasite relationship between *Biomphalaria glabrata* and *Schistosoma mansoni*. In A. E. R. Taylor and R. Muller [ed.] *Genetic Aspects of Host-Parasite Relationships*. Blackwell, London.

Rutter, J. M., M. R. Burrows, R. Sellwood, and R. A. Gibbons. 1975. A genetic basis for resistance to enteric disease caused by *E. coli*. *Nature, Lond.* 257: 135–136.

Thompson, V. 1976. Does sex accelerate evolution? *Evol. Theory* 1: 131–156.

Treisman, M. 1976. The evolution of sexual reproduction: A model which assumes individual selection. *J. Theor. Biol.* 60: 421–431.

Trivers, R. L. 1976. Sexual selection and resource-accruing abilities in *Anolis garmani*. *Evolution* (Lancaster, Pa.) 30: 253–269.

White, M. J. D. 1973. *Animal Cytology and Evolution*, 3rd ed. Cambridge University Press, Cambridge.

Williams, G. C. 1975. *Sex and Evolution*. Princeton University Press, Princeton, New Jersey.

———, and J. B. Mitton. 1973. Why reproduce sexually? *J. Theor. Biol.* 39: 545–554.

23.

Genome Parliaments and Sex with the Red Queen

John Hartung

INTRODUCTION

The recent burst in nucleotide sequencing has revealed a level of order in genes that lends new credence to an old idea—the structure-rate hypothesis. Order at the nucleotide level implies order at higher levels and this provides a reasonable basis for speculation about gene-gene relationships, units of selection, the selective value of sex, and the parameters for selfish and altruistic behavior.

THE STRUCTURE-RATE HYPOTHESIS

In 1957 H. A. Itano speculated that genes may be endogenously regulated by their fine structure. More precisely (from his 1965 elaboration): "The existence of more than one adaptor sRNA with different coding specificities for the same amino acid [tRNA species] provides a basis for a difference in the process of assembly of identical polypeptides." The idea was picked up by Ames and Hartman (1963) and was succinctly recapitulated in a review article by G. S. Stent in 1964:

> Because of the probable degeneracy of the genetic code, some of the 20 standard amino acids are represented by more than one kind of nucleotide codon, and hence are cognate to more than one species of transfer RNA. If the intracellular availabilities of different transfer RNA species cognate to the same amino acid are widely different, corresponding to "major" and "minor" representations of that amino acid, then the rate of synthesis of a polypeptide . . . depends on the relative occurrence of major and minor coding representations in the [DNA] message.

This *regulation hypothesis* turns on the "degeneracy" of the genetic code — that redundancy and wobble cause 20 elementary instructions to be given by 61 different nucleotide triplets, some of which give that instruction in a manner that uses the same decoding mechanism (same tRNA) as another triplet. That is, we seem to have a code in which many words have the same meaning — some by virtue of being straightforward synonyms and some because they are translated consistently even though the translation seems a bit loose.

The distinction between degeneracy that results from redundancy and "two-fold degeneracy" that results from redundancy with wobble can be illustrated by examining the messenger RNA triplets that call for arginine: AGA, AGG, CGU, CGC, CGA and CGG. Six possible distinct tRNAs, after having been attached to a molecule of arginine by an aminoacylating enzyme that is specific to that tRNA's anticodon (apparently no degeneracy there), can transfer that molecule of arginine on to a growing polypeptide chain at a ribosome. If the first 2 nucleotides of a codon are the same and the third is either A or G, they can both use the tRNA whose anticodon complements the first two nucleotides and has U in the third position (G→U wobble). This means that the arginine codon AGG can utilize a tRNA with a UCC anticodon or a UCU anticodon. The ability of this UCU tRNA to transfer arginine to 2 different messages (AGA and AGG) results from the fact that the nucleotides in the third position of the codon-anticodon connection can wobble (Crick, 1966). Accordingly, CGG can bind with the anticodon GCC (non-wobble) or the anticodon GCU (G → U wobble). Similarly, if the first two nucleotides of a codon are the same and the third is U or C, they can both use the tRNA whose anticodon complements the first two nucleotides and has G in the third position (U → G wobble). This allows the codon CGU to bind with anticodon GCA or GCG. However, U → U, U → C, C → A, C → U, and C → C pairing is (would be) too spatially confined to wobble in the third position and such codon-anticodon interactions are not compatible. Also, of course, because there cannot be first or second position wobble (at least, there can no longer be any — see Barricelli 1977 on the evolution of wobble), a codon cannot bring in its amino acid by using a tRNA that does not complement these two nucleotides; e.g., AGA and CGA cannot call in arginine from the same tRNA.

In short, for the arginine case, there are 27 ways in which DNA (through mRNA) can call for arginine and *not* be able to incorporate it from an available, aminoacylated arginine tRNA: i.e., within the arginine set of codon-anticodon combinations, AGA → UCC, AGA → GCU, AGA → GCG, AGA → GCC, CGU → UCU, CGU → UCC, → CGU → GCU, CGU → GCC, AGA → GCA, AGG → GCU, AGG → GCG, AGG → GCC, → AGG → GCA, CGA → UCU, CGA → UCC, CGA → GCG, CGA → GCC, CGA → GCA, → CGC → UCU, CGC → UCC, CGC → GCU, CGC → GCC, CGC → GCA, CGG → UCU, → CGG → UCC, CGG → CCG, and CGG → GCA are not compatible. There are three codon-anticodon combinations that will work with a wobble and six that work in a straightforward (triple complement) manner. This story becomes more complicated if one considers species of tRNA whose anticodon has been enzymatically modified in a manner that increases its ability to wobble: e.g., A (adenine) in the third position can be converted to I (inosine) allowing wobble with A, C, or U. Also there are *subspecies* of tRNA (same anticodon with some differences in internal sequences) that can be the product of different tRNA-coding DNA segments or the product of post-transcriptional modification (see Altwegg and Kublï 1979 for an example of the latter). Further complications can be left aside without losing the point that translation of the message at the ribosome is a more complicated process, involving a more variable host of actors, than is transcription of mRNA from DNA. The point to be focused on is that of all the possible combinations between a codon and a tRNA that has the amino acid called for by that codon, most will not work because of codon-anticodon incompatibility.

The question at hand is whether this is a system in which the noise is louder than the message or a system in which apparent sloppiness (redundant, degenerate, synonymous codons) is actually the stuff of mechanical subtlety. If it were the case that some codons could be easily misread and thereby specify any one of several amino acids, it would be clear that protein production is a somewhat haphazard process. Since the case is, instead, that each codon specifies only one amino acid while most amino acids have several such specifiers, and that most of those codons depend on the availability of different tRNAs to complete their mission, different codons for the same amino acid may be decoded at different rates. Explicitly, the structure-rate hypothesis is that redundancy and wobble can slow the rate of protein synthesis by causing two kinds of ''congestion'' at the ribosome: redundancy by affecting the demand for particular species or subspecies of tRNA; wobble by affecting the rate at which wobbling tRNA brings its amino acid into position (Fitch, 1976; Topal & Fresco, 1976; Mitra *et al.*, 1977). The relative abundance of different species and subspecies of tRNA will depend on the frequency and activity of repetitive sequences coding for different tRNAs, and on the tRNA requirements of all genes being simultaneously translated on all other ribosomes. The question is whether this logistical situation is functional.

Two things have happened to the structure-rate hypothesis. First, in 1961 Jacob and Monod proposed the whole DNA → messenger RNA → 3-unit codon system that characterizes transcription and translation. In the same paper they put forth the first version of their ideas on the effector→ repressor→ operator operon system for the regulation of what were called inducible and repressible enzymes. The rapid accumulation of experimental evidence regarding the first part of the Jacob and Monod paper allowed Stent to write only three years later that, "Today, 'messenger RNA' is a household word of molecular biology" (1964). The operon model had a longer developmental history and required more refinement but it has managed to occupy center stage ever since as the means by which genes regulate their own activity. There is, of course, nothing mutually exclusive about the operon model and the structure-rate hypothesis—they can both operate simultaneously or independently without working at cross purposes. However, an inverse relationship seems to have existed between the amount of attention paid to the on-off effect of the operon model and the rate-determining effect of the structure-rate hypothesis i.e., the *stop-go* regulator as distinct from the accelerate-decelerate regulator. The second problem to plague the structure-rate hypothesis (unlike the operon model) was a lack of evidence suggesting either its validity or invalidity. Before the recent development of rapid sequencing techniques (e.g., Sanger & Coulson, 1975; Maxam & Gilbert, 1977) few codon sequences were known. The best was one of 420 codons from the MS2 virus. As Watson notes in the third edition of *Molecular Biology of the Gene* (1976), if alternate codons for the same amino acid affect translation rates, we would expect to see some bias in their representation. The MS2 results were discouraging: "While some codons are used somewhat more often than their alternatives, in almost every case there is no reason to ascribe such bias other than to chance."

Now the structure-rate hypothesis is being revived. Two areas of research are primarily responsible—one is a spate of recent papers on the rate-limiting effects of scarce tRNA species,[1] the other is the data flowing in as a result of rapid nucleotide sequencing techniques.[2] When the number of known codons for MS2 went from 420 to 1,068, pattern became evident (Fiers et al., 1975). As put by Berger (1977), "the analysis of MS2 mRNA clearly points out that natural selection has acted as an editor of the genetic message for substitutions which leave the protein product intact"—and so it seems to be in almost every case where a substantial sequence has been determined. The complete sequences for rabbit and human β -globin have been determined. They are analyzed and compared in an article by Kaftos et al. (1977), who find that

> synonymous codons are used quite nonrandomly, and similarly in both β -globin mRNAs. This implies selection of the nucleotides occupying the silent substitution sites. There are 54 possible codons corresponding to amino acids abundant enough in β -globin to permit statistical evaluation of possible preferential codon use. Of these, 16 are strongly favored, 8 are more or less avoided, 18 are not used at all, and 12 are indifferent, i.e., they are not used at a frequency significantly different from that of their synonyms. The preferential codon usage in β -globin mRNA is positively correlated with the relative abundance of the respective isoacceptor tRNAs in rabbit reticulocytes.[3]

[1]Gilbert and Anderson, 1970; Hilse and Rudloff, 1975; Ilan and Ilan, 1975; Sharma et al., 1975; Smith, 1975; Geddes-Dwyer and Cameron, 1976; Lerman et al., 1976; Mukerjee and Goldfeder, 1976; Sharma, Beezley and Borek, 1976; Sharma, Beezley and Roberts, 1976; Westerberg et al., 1976, Holmes et al., 1977; Palatnik et al., 1977; von der Haar and Cramer, 1978.

[2]E.g., Fiers et al., 1975; Fiers et al., 1976; Baralle, 1977; Chang et al., 1977; Efstradiadis et al., 1977; Marotta et al., 1977; Proudfoot, 1977; Sanger et al., 1977; Seeberg et al., 1977; Shine et al., 1977, Ullrich et al., 1977; Air et al., 1978; Fiers et al., 1978; Godson et al., 1978; McReynolds et al., 1978; Reddy et al., 1978; Nakanishi et al., 1979; Bernard et al., 1978; Hamlyn et al., 1978; Heindell et al., 1978; Rogers, 1979; Schaffner et al., 1978; Fiddes and Goodman, 1979; van Ooyen, van den Berg, Mantei, and Weissmann, 1979.

[3]Ever on the alert for a challenge to "non-Darwinian evolution" (King and Jukes, 1969), Jukes and King (1979) have published an analysis of nucleotide sequence data that they see as showing Kafatos et al.'s rate regulation argument to be "unconvincing." Two major points are made: (1) the neutrality of silent nucleotide substitutions (nucleotide changes that do not change the amino acid sequence) is inferred from the fact "that in three of the four summarised examples, code-altering single-base changes

GENES IN GENOMES

Mounting evidence is making it difficult to deny that something is going on, not just beneath the electrophoretic level, but beneath the amino acid level as well. However, those who have serious doubts about the degree to which selection has determined whole traits (Lewontin, 1979) (let alone whole genes—Lewontin, 1974) can be expected to resist conceding adaptive significance to the particular form of a gene as opposed to other possible forms that would leave it coding for the exact same string of amino acids. Indeed, a controversy is brewing over the degree to which each genome in each cell can adapt to whatever tRNA requirements its particular protein synthesis schedule calls for, and therefore the degree to which the manner in which those proteins are called for (the tRNA specificities) can regulate the rate at which different products are made. Garel and others (Garel, 1974; Garel, 1976; Garel et al., 1976) have shown that differentiated cells with identical genomes generate different proportions of tRNA species according to differences in protein synthesis activity. However, a false opposition is set up when differential production of the tRNA species is held up as an ''alternate hypothesis'' (Kafatos et al., 1977) to the structure-rate hypothesis. That is, it is entirely possible that while cells do differentially produce different tRNAs (it is difficult to imagine how they could do otherwise in a differentiated organism), the degree to which they can adjust their tRNA populations and the alacrity with which they can do so are not unlimited. If that is the case, the particular tRNA demands of different cells and different genes within a cell will affect rates of synthesis. If, in fact, tRNA of all varieties were so metabolically cheap and easy to make that no appreciable shortage of any particular species or subspecies would be likely to arise, then why do we find such skewed distributions of synonymous codons? Also,. if cells are capable of keeping all tRNAs readily available, what is to be made of evidence that the elusive phenomena of differentiation draw heavily on tRNA as an induction-repression initiator while changes in the amount of repetitive sequence DNA (amplification-deamplification—Strom and Dorfman, 1976) act as a differentiating mechanism that operates by manipulating within-cell tRNA supply/demand ratios?[4]

A population geneticist might speculate that nonrandom codon utilization is the result of within-gene random walk (cf. King and Jukes, 1969). If this were so, one would expect identical alleles at a locus (meaning alleles that code for the exact same protein without necessarily being identical nucleotide for nucleotide) across individuals and identical alleles within homozygous individuals to have, more often than not, walked in different directions. Nucleotide sequencing data to date indicate that this is not the case.

Details of how the fine structure of genes influences genome function remain to be elucidated—perhaps master regulatory genes determine different rates of tRNA species and subspecies production, perhaps repetitive sequences determine tRNA availability (see Davidson and Britten, 1979; Moore, Constantini, Posakony, Davidson and Britten, 1980),

---

are 1.8–3.0 times as likely to be rejected as are silent changes.'' (i.e., silent substitutions are more prevalent); and (2) ''It seems highly improbable that closely related mammals would have different requirements for mRNA structure and tRNA usage for the same protein.''

Two peculiarities should be noted: (1) the structure-rate hypothesis (from Itano on) depends on a skew in the distribution of *types* of silent substitutions (creating the disparity between the tRNA's called for and the tRNA's available)—given such a skew, the relative number of silent vs. code-altering changes is beside the point; and (2) what seems ''highly improbable,'' in this context, is in the eye of the beholder—presumably, there is a functional relationship between what goes on at the molecular level and speciation itself (though Kimura (1979) seems to doubt even this assumption).

[4]Yang and Comb 1968; Tonoue et al. 1969; Sueoka and Kano-Sueoka, 1970; DeWitt 1971; Elska et al., 1971; Smith and McNamara 1971; Lewis and Ames 1972; Littauer and Inouye 1973; White et al. 1973; Denis et al., 1975; Ilan and Ilan, 1975; Denes and Nagy, 1976; Renart and Sebastian, 1976; Palatnik et al., 1977; Klee et al., 1978; Watanabe and Saneyoshi, 1978. For additional tRNA-regulation hypotheses see also Altman, 1978; Celis and Smith, 1979; and Cortese, 1979. For evidence of an interactive effect from mRNA to tRNA to rate of translation, see Bossi and Roth, 1980.

and perhaps the recently discovered intervening sequences have some effect (Crick, 1979) (they, too, are subject to skewed silent substitutions and synonymous codon distributions— Kafatos et al., 1977—and to considerable polymorphism—Jeffreys, 1979)—but these are matters whose resolution can be left to the future without obscuring the significance of what is already known. Meanwhile, it seems reasonable to question the assumptions of non-functionality, randomness, neutrality, and noise that characterize neoclassical theory.

GENOMES IN POPULATIONS

Theoretical population genetics has been profoundly influenced by the argument that available genetic polymorphism is too great to be the result of selection for heterozygote advantage, and that, therefore, most of this variation must be neutral or very close to it (e.g., Hubby and Lewontin, 1966; cf. Racine and Langley, 1980). Perhaps there is order at the nucleotide level that is not apparent at the electrophoretic level, and perhaps the selective value of a particular variant is derived in reference to the particular genome that it is part of rather than in reference to other alleles in the population. That is, if genomes are coordinated for their overall tRNA requirements, a particular allele may be quite fit in an individual genome without having any particular relative fitness in the population at large. If allele *A* causes individual *A* to have higher fitness than would allele *B*, while allele *B* causes individual *B* to have higher fitness than would *A*, etc., then different alleles can have different selective values according to their within-genome environments as well as their extra-genome environments, and several alleles can be maintained at the locus as a result of selection for compatibility with alleles at independent loci. This sort of ''fit'' would not generate gene frequency change, but such alleles should not be considered neutral in the sense of being interchangeable across individuals. Admittedly, the importance of order at this level depends on the question one is asking; however, it is always of some importance to avoid pretending that genes behave as randomly as the molecules of a perfect gas. [5]

This brings up the question of the glaring absence of linkage disequilibria; i.e., why, if genomes are such coordinated units, do we not see more linkage? The answer is that linkage disequilibrium is strong evidence that two alleles at different loci enhance each other's se-

---

[5] I do not mean to ignore or belittle a hundred years of evidence regarding the veracity of Mendelian genetics. That is, the sense in which genes behave randomly for purposes of Hardy-Weinberg equilibrium (that formalization of the realization that if nothing happens nothing changes) does not apply here.

By way of explanation, the best I can do is offer an analogy: imagine a man who investigates the forces that determine which side of a fair coin will come up on a single flip. He may postulate hypotheses that involve the angle at which the coin leaves the thumb, the force with which it is flipped, the air currents that play on the coin, and other recurrent variables. Like the craps shooter who meticulously arranges his dice and throws them in a stylized manner, the coin flipper's hypotheses may be useless. However, he is right to assume that the outcome of each flip is determined, in its entirety, by a determinable set of forces. If a mathematician told him that his study was born of ignorance, that coin flipping is a random process, and that the number of ''heads'' will approach $1/2$ as the number of flips increases, the coin flipper should not be dissuaded.

If this analogy were put to a population geneticist, he might argue that the mathematician would have been wrong to discourage the coin flipper, that it is fine to investigate the causes that bring about a particular elementary event on a single trial, but that the mathematician would have been right to realize that causation at this level does not affect the distribution of outcomes and is thereby not relevant to his own concerns. This would be correct—and if the evolution of living matter did not go beyond the analogy of flipping coins or throwing dice, it would be correct in an important way.

However, if, over a long period of time, we could see that a pair of continuously thrown dice produced a distribution that strayed from the predicted distribution, we would say the dice were loaded. If the apparent skewed distribution changed its skew, we would say that the load had changed. If new numbers appeared on some dice sides while other numbers disappeared, and if the number of sides on a die changed, we would suspect that the dice were alive. At this point, if we wanted to understand the distribution of outcomes, we would do well to monitor the forces that determine the result of a single trial.

lective value, and a lack of linkage is not evidence for anything. That is, if the relationship between genes is more complicated than a straightforward association between two alleles, linkage disequilibrium would not be apparent. One can easily imagine (though it quickly becomes impossible to model mathematically) allele *A* and *B* being associated in the presence of *C, D,* or *E* but not in the presence of *F, G,* or *H,* or, in the presence of *I* with *J* but not *I* alone, and so on. As soon as the number of alleles becomes as large and as intimately related as the genes in a genome, one would expect them to have more subtle relationships than 1 x 1 association.

If a gene's tRNA requirements influence the rate at which its protein is assembled, heterozygote advantage (hybrid vigor) may derive simply from being diploid and having, at as many potentially heterozygous loci as possible (non-fixed loci), more than one way to code for a product—and inbreeding depression may be the result of being exactly homozygous (nucleotide for nucleotide) across many loci (without reference to the nature of the protein coded for—cf. Seger, 1976, 1979). That is, inbreeding depression in diploids may be the result of losing the fundamental advantage of being diploid more than the result of being homozygous for deleterious mutations (see Packer, 1979).

UNITS OF SELECTION

Questions about the appropriate unit of selection might be clarified by consideration of within-genome relationships. If one makes a scheme of some of the possible combinations of effects that a trait might simultaneously have on the gene or genes that cause it, a social individual having a trait, and the group of which s/he is a member (Table 23–1), only trait C requires group selection. Just as Williams (1966) advocates parsimony with regard to arguments that apply to any unit of selection higher than the individual, so it might be parsimonious to avoid going below the level of the individual.

If one is to advocate the gene or ''replicator unit'' (Dawkins, 1978) as the unit of selection (or, lower yet, the codon), then one is considering cases where the gene spreads at some cost to individuals that carry it (trait D, Table 23–1) or at a rate faster than the rest of the non-linked genes in the genome (otherwise, one might as well stick with individual selection). For example, if an allele occurring in an individual who would normally have 8 offspring caused that individual to have only 6 offspring, but managed to get itself into all six of them (by, say, meiotic drive) instead of the expected 3, it could spread. A similar spread could be effected by skewing investment in offspring (or other kin) according to the presence of a particular allele rather than the overall degree of relatedness. Blick (1977) has modeled the spread of a truly selfish gene for parent-offspring conflict (cf. Trivers, 1974; Hartung, 1977), adding the caveat: ''the interest of this mutant is contrary to the interests of all other non-linked genes, and hence, selection for genes which repress such selfish mutants might

Table 23–1.   Traits A and B are evolvable by individual selection; C by group selection over individual selection; and D by gene selection over individual selection. These last two are logically straightforward but biologically dubious and seem of little evolutionary consequence. E requires divine intervention.

Effect on reproductive success of

		gene(s)	individual	group
	A	+	+	+
	B	+	+	−
Trait	C	+/0	−	+
	D	+	−	−/0
	E	−	−	−

be expected." It seems to me to be nearly as unlikely that a gene can spread at some cost to the genomes it operates in as to suppose that a particular codon can replace its synonyms within a gene at some cost to the spread of the gene. Or, as put in Lewontin's caveat (1974, p. 318) "The fitness at a single locus ripped from its interactive context is about as relevant to real problems of evolutionary genetics as the study of the psychology of individuals isolated from their social context is to an understanding of man's sociopolitical evolution." Of course, gene selection (over individual) is a logical construct and has been empirically demonstrated in the laboratory and in nature (Crow, 1979). The question is not whether it can happen but whether it can happen for an evolutionarily significant amount of time.

If a gene's tRNA requirements can affect its rate of synthesis, then each gene has some epistatic effect on every gene in a genome. Such functional interdependence and the presence of phenomena like repair enzymes that comb strands of DNA correcting point mutations suggest logical and empirical support for the evolution of Leigh's "parliament of the genes" (1977). At a more apparent level, one wonders how genes in genomes could produce such highly coordinated individuals if their selfish interests were not constrained by mutual interests. By way of analogy, one can imagine 10 businessmen entering a joint venture—if each one had the power to eliminate any partner caught taking more than his share of the profits, the group would behave cooperatively even though each member were motivated solely by individual profit. In short, Dawkins' (1978) effort to disabuse several authors of thinking in individual selection terms should raise the question of just how selfish a gene can be—or how much selfishness it can actually get away with, and for how long.[6]

[6]Doolittle and Sapienza and Orgel and Crick (1980) have applied Dawkins' notion of The Selfish Gene (1976) to "nonspecific" DNA (most of the DNA in eukaryotes) and allied this, via "non-phenotypic selection", with the neoclassicist's concept of "genetic junk". In the author's words, "If there are ways in which mutation can increase the probability of survival within cells *without effect* on organismal phenotype, then sequences whose only 'function' is self-preservation will inevitably arise and be maintained . . . (italics added)" (Doolittle and Sapienza, 1980). Orgel and Crick note that 'selfish DNA' must be "a slight burden to the cell that contains it", and Doolittle and Sapienza relax the stipulation of no phenotypic effect to include any effect which is not "sufficiently negative". So, just as selfish individuals can evolve to the detriment of their social group, so selfish DNA can evolve at some cost to its genome counterparts. Doolittle and Sapienza strongly emphasize (7 times in 2 pages) that this explanation for nonspecific DNA is so parsimonious and satisfactory that "no other explanation for its existence is necessary."

The argument that selection operating at the organism level is too slow to keep up with selfish DNA is persuasive. Orgel and Crick suggest "the study of these processes will clearly require a new type of population genetics." But the population genetics appropriate to units selected at the level of nonspecific DNA may already be at hand—its formulation was begun by Wynne-Edwards (1965) and it continues today (e.g. Wilson, 1980). Group selection can cause the evolution of "altruism" and the elimination of "selfishness" if selfish groups go extinct faster than altruistic groups arise—the problem is practical rather than logical. The key asymmetry that makes classical group selection impractical can be stated simply, though somewhat crudely, if the necessary anthropomorphisms are tolerated: *if an altruistic group is "contaminated" by a selfish migrant or a selfish mutant, that group converts from altruistic to selfish. The reverse does not hold—selfish groups are immune to invasion by altruists.* Accordingly, extreme and unrealistic assumptions must be made about rates of group extinction, group generation, migration and/or mutation if group selection is to work for groups composed of individual organisms (Maynard Smith, 1976). However, if the frame of reference is shifted down one level such that individual genes and snippets of nonspecific DNA are thought of as "individuals" while single cells or organisms are thought of as discrete "groups" of such individuals, then the feasibility of the assumptions required for group selection changes drastically.

That is, subcellular replicators, whether they be organelles like mitochondria or independently replicating nuclear DNA, have sufficiently high extinction rates and low enough migration rates to be group selected. When the individual organism is the group, one "group" extinction occurs for every gamete that fails to initiate a successfully reproducing organism and, with the exception of that gamete, migration requires viral transmission from one individual organism to the germ line of another. For most sexual reproducers, literally millions of such groups go extinct for each new group formed. The question is whether that new group, formed by 2 out of millions of gametes, had a higher probability of being formed because those gametes contained fewer selfish "individuals" than their competitors. For example, imagine a typical mammalian zygote. The egg came from one of nearly a million oocytes that

If one thinks of the genes in a genome as a group[6], then individual selection is a viable form of "group" selection—having low (zero) migration rate, short group life span relative to individual member life span, and small group size relative to mutation rate per replication (cf. Maynard/Smith, 1976). Hamilton's (1964) measure of inclusive fitness is a form of group selection only in this rather twisted sense of individual selection as "group" selection. Thereby, inclusive fitness might be more appropriately considered an extension of individual selection rather than a different level of selection. George Wald (1967) addressed the issue rather persuasively (before it was recognized) in a 1966 paper on "vicarious selection":

> The germ plasm as the bearer of heredity and ultimately therefore of evolution, ordinarily takes no part in the struggle for existence. Indeed, it is elaborately protected from all the eventualities that compose that struggle. It is represented in that struggle by the soma, another body of cells that engages in competition for survival; and the germ plasm endures or fails depending upon how effectively the soma has represented it. Clearly there is no great gap in principle between this dependence of the germ plasm upon its own soma in the struggle for survival and extending that dependence to another soma. . . .

Darwin (1859) seems also to have had the basic idea:

> I will not here enter on these several cases, but will confine myself to one special difficulty, which at first appeared to me insuperable, and actually fatal to my whole theory. I allude to the neuters or sterile females in insect-communities: for these neuters often differ widely in instinct and in structure from both the males and fertile females, and yet, from being sterile, they cannot propagate their kind. . . . This difficulty, though appearing insuperable, is lessened, or as I believe, disappears, when it is remembered that selection may be applied to the family, as well as to the individual. . .

developed in the first trimester of fetal life. Most of its competing oocytes (others in the same female fetus) died before the female was born. Of those that survived to sexual maturity, only 1 out of 10 to 100 thousand will become a zygote. The sperm do not have such a long period of "suspended meiosis", but there are generally several hundred million per ejaculate and there may be several ejaculations per conception. Approximately one in a billion sperm make it through the female tract (see text under "Sex and Selection") and go on to penetrate the vitelline layer of an egg. In the analogy of natural selection to a sieve, the gamete attrition rate that characterizes fertilization suggests a very fine mesh. The "selfish DNA" proponents argue that the cost to the cell is very small. The question becomes whether such DNA can account for a significant portion of the genome and simultaneously entail a negligible cost.

In short, just as Wynne-Edwards and others have tried to apply group selection where it does not work (individual organisms), so Doolittle and Sapienza and Orgel and Crick and, I think, Dawkins, have not recognized group selection's potential applicability to sub-individual units of selection. If these units are group selected, one would expect endosymbiosis to far outweigh endoparasitism, and it would be reasonable to expect the evolution of repair mechanisms that lead to selfish DNA 'individuals'. Additionally, when endoparasitism does occur in the germ line, it could be expected to represent a condition analogous to cancer in the soma rather than the ongoing evolution of independently replicating DNA.

Finally, Doolittle and Sapienza warn that "The search for other explanations [for nonspecific DNA] may prove, if not intellectually sterile, ultimately futile." We all must contend with the prospect of ultimate futility. However, concern for the pending intellectual sterility of those who "rationalize in neo-Darwinian terms" might be more appropriately extended in the other direction. As has been emphasized by Clutton-Brock and Harvey; "No better object lesson is needed than Tinbergen's (1964) description of his undergraduate days: 'In the post-Darwinian era, a reaction against uncritical acceptance of the selection theory set in, which reached its climax in the great days of Comparative Anatomy, but which still affects many physiologically inclined biologists. It was a reaction against making uncritical guesses about the survival value, the function, of life processes and structures. This reaction, of course healthy in itself, did not (as one might expect) result in an attempt to improve methods of studying survival value; rather it deteriorated into lack of interest in the problem—one of the most deplorable things that can happen to a science.' " (Tinbergen, from Clutton-Brock and Harvey, 1979).

SEX AND SELECTION

The points made here depend upon a rather vitalistic view of the nature of genes in genomes and, thereby, of genes in populations. This can be seen to increase the debt on the sex question. Maynard Smith (1971, 1978), G. C. Williams (1975), M. T. Ghiselin (1974), and others have pondered what seems to be the most pressing question in evolutionary biology (perhaps not the most important question, but somehow the most pressing): why reproduce sexually? Fortunately, they have also answered the question with regard to many forms of sexuality and various reproduction rates and capacities. Unfortunately, long-lived, obligate-sex, low-fecundity females who do not get the benefit of appreciable male help in rearing offspring are still a paradox. For an individual female of this type, who happens to be at the high end of the fitness distribution (Emlen, 1973), reproducing sexually seems like being dealt a pat-hand straight flush in 5-card draw poker and drawing (throwing) 3 cards.

Without being so presumptuous (or ambitious) as to review this complicated controversy, I would like to make two points that seem to bear on the efficacy of sex: first, on the assumption of randomness with regard to gamete formation and recombination; second, on what Maynard Smith has so eloquently called the malady of population geneticists: an obsession with the equilibrium state (1978).

Two general correlates of low fecundity are internal fertilization and extraordinary sperm-to-egg ratios per conception (typically several hundred million sperm per egg per conception). In an article *"Gamete Redundancy—Wastage or Selection?"* Cohen (1975) points out that in addition to a plenitude of mechanical obstacles that must be overcome by sperm between ejaculation and conception, the female immune system treats sperm like an infection. Cohen asks why, if sperm count is a male adaptation to competition (Parker, 1970) in a hostile environment (likened, at one point, to a mine field), some males do not take

> the alternative solution of producing a bigger, better sperm instead of simply *more* sperms—better at crawling up female tracts, perhaps with a pair of antennae on the front to find its way. All mammals do, however, produce millions of tiny sperms; it seems to me that some organisms might have taken the other fitness route possible under the above explanations, so that instead of three millilitres of fluid with 350,000,000 "cells" in it, a man might produce an organism resembling a large planarian and exquisitely designed to find the egg.

Along the line of pressing questions, one might ask why internally fertilized eggs are such elaborate structures (Epel, 1977; Gwatkin, 1977). What selection pressures could produce the fantastic ritual that goes on when so many sperm beat their heads against the vitelline layer of an egg until the microvilli around a single sperm extend to interdigitate around that sperm's head and draw it through the plasma membrane, thereby initiating a chain reaction and the release of charged ions that so change the plasma membrane as to make it henceforth impermeable? That seems like a lot of song and dance for a random result. Might it not be less presumptuous to suspect that this process is a low-fecundity female's adaptation to being K-selected? That is, instead of producing prodigious numbers of zygotes, as in Williams' (1975) elm-oyster model, perhaps low-fecundity organisms represent an improvement on the high fecundity system—a sort of pre-lottery in which all the investment that would otherwise go into both losing and winning tickets goes only to likely winners. But how could the egg judge the potential phenotypes that would result from different sperm; i.e., by what criteria and mechanism could this ultimate female choice be effected? One need not anthropomorphize eggs to see that compatibility with *self* is tested by the female immune response before any sperms even reach the egg. Although self-compatibility is not a speculation about the eventual phenotype of a zygote, it could suffice as a means of vastly reducing the potential range of phenotypes in a selective manner, thereby precluding most of the need for expensive post-zygotic testing. With regard to mechanisms, *Genetics of the Cell Surface* (Bodmer, 1977) leaves one impressed with the amount of information that a cell can advertise on its membrane, and, concomitantly, the amount of information that can be read and analyzed by another cell. Presumably, cells' abilities along these lines are even greater than we have thus far been able to decipher and appreciate. That haploid sperm cells can produce proteins that will advertise their individual characteristics either on their surface or in the acrosome appears increasingly likely (see Yanagisawa et al., 1974, 1974a; Monesi et al., 1978; Geremia et al., 1978). If an individual's immune system can identify microbes that are being constantly selected for their ability to evade detection, is it too fantastic to suspect that eggs have developed an ability to "read" sperm? In short, low-fecundity ($<1,000$ offspring/female—Williams, 1975), internally fertilizing species may fit (with a variation on the theme) the elm-oyster model (high fecundity). The numbers are there (in terms of potential zygotes—sperms/egg), we know that the mechanisms are available in another context (the immune system), and certainly the effect on reproductive success would be substantial. If internal fertilization does not result in random gamete combination, it is no wonder that selection in low-fecundity animals is difficult to detect in nature—we can only examine a highly selected subset of the zygotes that could have been formed (for a process analogous to prezygotic selection in angiosperms, see Mulcahy, 1979). In terms of presenting a challenge to our understanding of selection, the evolution of species with low fecundity and long generations presents an even greater paradox than sexual reproduction. The concomitant evolution of increasingly proficient systems of selection would seem a necessity for such species, and the evolution of such systems may account for the observation (often cited as evidence by neutralists— see, e.g., Kimura 1979) that rates of change at the molecular level seem to be nearly the same for short and long life-span species.

THE RED QUEEN

> . . . so long as a country remains physically unchanged, the numbers of its animal population cannot materially increase. If one species does so, some others requiring the same kind of food must diminish in proportion . . . those species which from some defect of power or organization are the least capable of counteracting the vicissitudes of food supply, etc., must diminish in numbers, and, in extreme cases, become altogether extinct.
>
> —A. R. Wallace, 1858

The second point relevant to the efficacy of sexual reproduction can be introduced with a semi-idealized example. Glander (1979) has described the dynamic relationship that exists between trees and leaf-eating monkeys. Trees that lack effective toxins are frequently devastated (stripped of all their leaves) by voracious troops of howlers whose available food sources are limited by the array of antitoxins they can produce. In this system, a powerful selective advantage can accrue to a monkey with a new antitoxin or to a tree with a new toxin. If one ranks forms of sexuality by the degree to which they can cause deviation from Hardy-Weinberg equilibrium without jeopardizing reproduction rates, then obligate, high sperm/egg ratio, internally fertilized, diploid sex with high variance in male reproductive success (sex wth sexual selection) must rank at the top. If, among the large bands of roving males who are excluded from the species' basic social unit (groups of related females and their young) one male has shown himself to be superior in male-male competition, his superiority is more likely to be the result of an ability to better utilize food resources than the result of superior (or additional) genes for aggression. Accordingly, females will maximize (sufficicize?) their reproductive success (*rs*) by mating with this male. Anthropomorphizing a bit, the parliament of a female's genes should incur the cost of sexual reproduction if obtaining the association of the gene for that new antitoxin is the best long-term strategy for the majority. Extending such a strategy may lead to a female preference for genetically new males (see Ehrman, 1972; Watanabe and Kawanishi, 1979).

What is being hypothesized is that degrees of sexuality are a response to degrees of evolutionary dynamic—i.e., a response to the degree to which an organism is in circular (spiral?) competition or the degree to which it is in the situation described to Alice by the Red Queen: "Now here, you see, it takes all the running you can do, to keep in the same place." (Carroll, 1871 from Van Valen, 1973). The more dynamic an organism's circumstance, the more it applies selective pressure on the organisms it depends on for its own rs, and/or the more it is pressured by other organisms—a potentially self-perpetuating escalation of selective pressures. Put conversely, the more symbiotic or neutral an organism's effect on its own environment (the degree to which it does not devastate its own way of making a living and/or is not devastated), the less sexual it needs to be—e.g. (in order), bees, aphids, ferns (see Chapman et al., 1979 for 'sex' in ferns). Evolutionary dynamic may most commonly be the result of predator-prey relationships across trophic levels, but could also be the result of within-species social competition.

According to this view, sex with high male investment (low variance in male rs) would be a secondary response to increasingly stable (non-dynamic) environmental circumstances (as opposed to reverting to asexuality) in K-selected organisms. Perhaps the high frequency of monogamy in birds indicates that fundamental avian adaptations have left birds in a less dynamic evolutionary circumstance than mammals; e.g., superior ability to locomote may lower the amount of selective pressure that birds put on their food sources. As noted by Wallace (1858) in reference to *Ectopistes migratorius*, "The bird is capable of a very rapid and long-continued flight, so that it can pass without fatigue over the whole of the district it inhabits, and as soon as the supply of food begins to fail in one place is able to discover a fresh feeding-ground." That is, if moving to a new food source is metabolically cheaper (than it would be for a land mammal), then birds would be less likely to crop a resource below its ability to recover (see Prager and Wilson, 1975, for molecular evidence that birds have evolved more slowly than mammals).

Van Valen's (1973) view of evolution as a zero-sum game (the Red Queen Hypothesis) has impressed Maynard Smith (1978) as an "attractive" and "persuasive" hypothesis that seems the best candidate for justifying sex in "an environment in which qualitatively new challenges are forever arising." However, the objection is raised (Maynard Smith, 1976; 1978) that "This zero-sum assumption must be obeyed exactly"—i.e., that an advance by one species must be exactly balanced by deterioration of the environment for other species. It might be useful to bring the argument down to the level of competition between individuals within a species (cf., Williams, 1978) and assume a relative zero-sum game. That is, in a sexual species, an individual's rs is always balanced relative to the population's mean rs, whether the population is stable ($\overline{rs} = 2$), increasing, or decreasing—i.e., individuals above the mean must be exactly offset by individuals below the mean within each sex. The beauty of sex is that two games can go on simultaneously—a high-stakes, long-odds game (males) and a low-stakes, short-odds game (females) with regard to $F_i\,rs$ (i.e., high across sex difference in within-sex variance—cf. Hartung, 1976). In this sense, low-investing males are a breeding experiment that benefits females—a proving ground from which females can cull winning genes and, through egg selection, incorporate them in a compatible combination.

As Williams (1975) and Maynard Smith (1978) have pointed out, a parthenogenetic female with average rs who produces parthenogenetic daughters who produce parthenogenetic daughters who . . . in a sexual populaton will reproduce at twice the rate of her (ex-) conspecifics (*ceteris paribus*).[7] This would be analogous to an invasion by a new species

[7]The sex question is an inspiring and heuristic one, but should not, I think, be taken too seriously re the actual adaptive value of sex. It is as if Newton put the question "why does the apple fall?" to a panel of distinguished colleagues and, in order to get them to take the question seriously, put forth reasons why it should not be expected to fall. Concluding that sex is maladaptive would be analogous to having some

occupying the same niche (Alexander and Borgia, 1978). That invasion would instantly supply the sort of dynamic that would confer a strong selective advantage upon a sexual reproducer who has a gene that gives her a relative economic advantage over the asexual line. The difference between the asexual line and the sexual line in this case is that the advantageous gene can spread quickly (given high sexual selection) among the sexual reproducers, while the spread of any response in the asexual line is severely constrained. In this sense, the selective pressures that initiate obligate sexuality are the ones that make it self-perpetuating and immune to invasion from within. With regard to the requirement that "qualitatively new challenges" be forever arising, those challenges may not arise with sufficient frequency to cause sexual reproduction to be to the advantage of an individual female of a given generation and yet that frequency can be enough to cause an advantage to a female who does not pass on the option of asexual reproduction to her daughters and/or granddaughters. This would soon lead to species-wide obligate sexuality as a result of individual inclusive fitness strategies in which the kin group is a line of descendants.

Within the recent climate of viewing sexual reproduction as something for which excuses must be found and in which non-working (non-parenting) males are seen as a drag on the system, there is a tendency to think of females as parasitized individuals who have lower mean rs than would be the case under parthenogenesis and lower variance in within-sex rs than do males. The latter is certainly true (often dramatically so) in reference to F_1 rs, but with any constant male rs variance across generations, the female variance must increase successively with reference to successive generations. That is, every male at the high end of the fitness distribution contributes to his female parent's F_2 rs. Accordingly, while that female may have been near the mean for number of offspring, she will be at the high end of the higher variance fitness curve for number of grandoffspring. This will necessarily follow whether the additive heritability of fitness is large or non-existent.[8] If, as speculated by Maynard Smith (1971), the additive heritability of fitness is not zero (as would be the case

panel members elaborate the reasons why Newton's apple should not fall and conclude that falling is the result of a temporary mechanical mistake that persists for some pernicious reason—and that when the world straightens itself out, apples will stop falling.

[8]*Heritability* has two senses—one is a static (in time) measure of the degree to which variance in a trait is caused by variance in genes (Hartung, 1980), the other is the degree to which a trait "breeds true" across generations. When considering the heritability of any trait other than fitness, there can be little disparity between these two senses of heritability, and so the distinction is not of practical importance. However, if the trait under consideration is fitness (reproductive success) and one is asking about the static heritability of fitness, this will be different from the degree to which the variance breeds true. Differences in fitness across individuals for a set block of time may be largely caused by differences in genes, but the descendents of an individual at the high end of the fitness distribution may (probably will) have lower relative fitness even though differences in fitness remain the result of differences in genes—i.e., the heritability of fitness can remain high while the trait fails to breed true. This occurs because fitness is the ultimate product of first-order traits that spread according to their contribution to fitness. As a first-order trait with high heritability spreads, it does not lose heritability even though the variance for that trait decreases as the genes responsible near fixation. However, as the variance in that trait decreases and the *relative* fitness of bearers of that trait decreases, the degree to which fitness breeds true diminishes because heritable differences that result in fitness differences become the result of other traits that have higher variance.

Williams (1975) points out that in a constant environment sexually reproduced genotypes are "sysyphean" in the sense that recombination breaks up the most fit genotypes. Fitness is sisyphean in the sense that as an advantageous trait spreads, the relative advantage it confers decreases. This is different from regression toward the mean in the sense that if the population could expand infinitely, the mean would appear to advance, thus eventually swallowing a fitness which was once relatively high. Since populations do not expand infinitely, fitness appears to regress to the mean—and what actually happens is evolution.

Sexually reproducing organisms can be thought of as more immediately sisyphean (and thereby faster evolving) in the sense that the rapid spread of advantageous traits (see text) allowed by recombination causes the mean to "advance" faster.

This view contrasts with Lewontin's statement (1970) that: "the rapidity of response to selection depends upon the heritability of differences in fitness between units. The heritability [of fitness] is highest in units where no internal adjustment or reassortment is possible since such units will pass on to

in the leaf-eating monkey example, until the gene for the new antitoxin lost all heritability by reaching fixation), variance in $F_2, F_3, F_4 \ldots$ female rs can increase enormously (a necessary adjunct to male variance that is in need of formal modeling). This post-F_1 increase in female variance is why high-status females in economically stratified human societies (mothers) gain as much or more than high-status males (fathers) by preferentially skewing investment toward sons (Hartung, 1976). That is, a male can dramatically increase his own rs through multiple mating and/or by enhancing his son's ability to obtain multiple mates. A female, on the other hand, only has the latter option. Accordingly, one would expect family conflict over the expenditure of resources that could increase either a father's rs *or* a son's rs through extra females (other than the mother), with mother and son generally siding against father—perhaps the foundation of what Freud interpreted as an Oedipal attraction.

There has been some discussion of whether females should choose for male parental investment (*PI*) or genes (Trivers 1972, e.g., Borgia, 1979). If one sticks to R. L. Trivers' original definition of *PI* as a cost function (1972; e.g. Hartung & Ellison, 1977), a female should choose the male who will give her the *least* paternal *PI* per unit of benefit (per unit decrement to her own *PI*/offspring) whenever there is any heritability of fitness. That is, a male who can increase a female's rs by x offspring at only a small cost to his own total rs (low *PI*) is preferable to a male for whom conferring the same benefit represents substantial cost to himself. If fitness has no heritability, then a female should choose only for F_1 benefit conferred, with no regard for the concomitant cost (*PI*) to her mate. *Least male Parental Investment/unit benefit* is a useful formulation because it collapses the genes vs. work[9] dilemma—whichever combination results in greatest F_2 (or subsequent) female rs should be chosen.

If variance in male rs is high and fitness has some heritability across generations, one might expect females mating with high rs males to skew their F_1 sex ratio toward males. For example, the females that mate with the male carrying the new gene for the new antitoxin (back to the leaf-eating monkey example) would vastly increase their F_2 and subsequent rs if they skewed their F_1 sex ratio toward males. This would be the most effective means of increasing a female's rs until such time as the genes responsible for the relative advantage became so widespread that they only conferred an absolute advantage (loss of fitness—through the looking glass[10]). Of course, if genes conferring an advantage were X-linked, or if the species is sex-reversed (higher female variance than male variance), the stipulated females should skew their F_1 sex ratio toward females.

The connection between tRNA and genome self-compatibility, female choice at the sperm level, and female choice at the male level is that the latter allows a female to obtain

their descendent units an unchanged set of information.'' These two uses of ''the heritability of fitness'' are each correct in one sense of the heritability of fitness, but their conflation can result in the conclusion that general evolution (''response to selection'') will occur more rapidly in asexual organisms.

In short, there are two ways that fitness can fail to breed true. First, when traits that confer fitness are few and slight in their effects—i.e. when their variants are neutral or near neutral. Second, when the traits that confer fitness are many and strong in their effects—i.e. when the fitness conferred by a variant of one trait is swamped by the effect of dozens, if not hundreds, of variants of other traits. If one observes the lack of heritability of fitness that characterizes most species, it seems fair to argue that this may result from either extreme situation. Accordingly, the argument between ''pan-selectionists'' and ''pan-neutralists'', which has become passé to many biologists, should be reheated. That is, concluding that the truth lies in the middle ground requires more justification than the assent of conventional wisdom.

[9]''Work is meant to indicate a contribution of effort that reduces the female's *PI*/offspring *without reference to the amount of male Parental Investment (cost to worker's other reproductive success) that work represents*. Again, the less male *PI* the work costs per unit reduction of female *PI*/offspring (benefit), the more valuable it will be—given any heritability of fitness (even efficiency of working and willingness to work could have heritability.

[10]If advantageous genes are carried by only a small percentage of the available males but that percentage is sufficient to inseminate all the females (high polygyny), the heritability of fitness based on those genes can rapidly disappear (see footnote #2).

the genes that allow her descendants to obtain the genes that allow her descendants to obtain the genes . . . at the high end of the fitness distribution,[11] while sperm choice allows her to choose from millions of different combinations, that combination that contains those genes in a manner that results in a self-compatible zygote.

Still, up to half of the alleles at heterozygous loci, and that percent at homozygous loci that do not recombine with their homologue, incur a cost when an individual reproduces sexually. The fixed genes, however, are not at risk. They remain at >99 per cent whether reproduced sexually or asexually. Fixed genes are not usually considered in such analyses because they are out of the competition by virtue of being sure winners (as long as the species or breeding group survives). However, each fixed gene is subject to invasion by new mutants at its locus, and any such genes that resisted zygote formation with gametes containing new mutants would retain their status (one can envision the evolution of a sort of "old boy" network). From the fixed gene's point of view, the benefit of reproducing sexually could be twofold: (1) the quick shunting of new mutants at "fixed" loci (not possible in asexual reproduction—see Shields, 1979) and (2) recombination with beneficial alleles at other loci (beneficial to the genome at large re the organism's evolutionary dynamic—see preceding discussion). This latter advantage indirectly ensures the status of the fixed gene (at no cost) as a byproduct of the enhancement that accrues to its breeding group from the spread of a beneficial allele—i.e., if the group responds sufficiently rapidly in that "environment in which qualitatively new challenges are forever arising" (Maynard Smith, 1978), the absolute number of individuals will not get so low as to cause a significant probability that individuals with mutations at "fixed" loci will combine gametes and start an "invasion." In this sense, sexual reproduction may be the result of a sort of "majority tyranny" exercised by that part of the genome that benefits—i.e. (1) the fixed genes, (2) the genes at homozygous loci that recombine with their homologue, and (3) the genes at heterozygous loci that make it into the zygote-forming gametes and/or are made up for in the gamete from the other genome (the sexual partner's gamete).

This sort of genome parliament would resist change in its fixed portion and thereby require discrete, major genomic alterations to effect speciation. That may partially account for the punctuated nature of change in the fossil record (Eldredge and Gould, 1972).

The degree to which this genome parliament applies is the degree to which the parameters for selfishness and altruism should be amended. Under the standard assumptions (considering only the non-fixed genes or a single allele) an individual should behave selfishly toward an unrelated conspecific without regard for the cost to the victim's rs. Taking the fixed genes and the non-fixed genes that are alike in state (genes held in common as a result of their frequency in the population) into consideration, an individual should behave selfishly toward an unrelated conspecific only until the costs inflicted equal the benefits multiplied by the reciprocal of that proportion of the genomes held in common. For example, if two unrelated conspecifics held half their genomes in common,[12] individual Y would only behave selfishly toward individual X until X's costs were greater than twice Y's benefits (in units of rs). If they were full sibs, Y would behave selfishly toward X only until X's costs were 1.33 times Y's benefits. Similarly, for altruistic behavior between unrelated conspe-

---

[11]This is distinct from Fisher's runaway sexual selection (1930) in that it spreads genes that cause organisms to better fit (in Darwin's original sense) their environment in some practical way—as opposed to genes whose value is a product of arbitrary popularity with females (fad genes).

[12]Re percentages of genes held in common by conspecifics, or even nonconspecifics: "King and Wilson (1975) estimate that man and chimpanzee share 99 per cent of their *genetic material;* they also estimate that the races of man are 50 times closer than are man and chimpanzee. Individuals whom sociobiologists consider unrelated share, in fact, more than 99 per cent of their *genes*." (Washburn, 1978, p. 415: italics added).

King and Wilson and others have used the latest lab techniques to line up long strings of transcribed DNA (or mRNA) from different individuals and different species to see, on a nucleotide for nucleotide basis, how similar they are. Their findings are of unquestionable validity and the implications they have drawn are the most exciting development in systematics since Linnaeus. However, the

cifics, an individual should behave altruistically whenever the costs are less than the benefit times the reciprocal of the proportion of the genes that are fixed and alike in state. This could be an additional reason for the apparent decrease in competition that seems to accompany high levels of population-wide homozygosity (see Seger, 1976; 1979; Sherman, 1979).

One would expect this effect of the total genome held in common (as opposed to only that portion in common by descent) to fluctuate inversely with the size of the breeding population. These less stark parameters for selfishness and altruism may account for the apparent discrepancy between what is usually observed and what would be predicted by a straightforward application of the Hamilton figures (Hamilton, 1964; see Daniels, 1979). Of course, the Hamilton parameters are the only ones that apply to the spread of an allele, (see also, Williams and Williams, 1957), but to presume an organism will behave according to those parameters is to equate the reproductive interests of the organism with the reproductive interests of a single allele.

CONCLUDING REMARKS

According to the neoclassical view as propounded by Lewontin (1974, pp. 197–99)

> many mutations are subject to natural selection, but these are almost exclusively deleterious and are removed from the population. . . . when natural selection occurs it is almost always purifying . . . there is a class of subliminal mutations which are irrelevant to adaptation and natural selection. . . . They are "genetic junk," revealed by the superior technology of the laboratory but redundant physiologically. . . . The theory does not deny adaptive evolution but only [sic] that the vast quantity of molecular variation within populations and, consequently, much of the molecular evolution among species, has anything to do with that adaptive process.

In short, there is a lot of noise within every gene, and most alleles are just noise. With its impressive (if not intimidating) quantitative refinements, the theory we are left with convincingly accounts for evolutionary stability and non-adaptative change. However, this kinematic[13] study of genes in populations cannot account for the evolution of such empirically verifiable phenomena as ferns, flowers, frogs, dogs, people, etc.—i.e., although neoclassicism is not so incautious as to deny adaptive evolution, it does make it seem unlikely (cf. Mayr, 1967).

This is a bit like an argument over the time of day between a man with a watch and a man with a sundial. The man with the watch can display and explain the precision and intricacy of the instrument with which he investigates the question; he can even demonstrate

statement that *99 per cent of the genetic material is identical* is quite distinct from the statement that *99 per cent of the genes are identical*.

For example, β-chain hemoglobin has 146 amino acids coded by 438 nucleotides—one gene. The difference between normal hemoglobin and sickle hemoglobin results from a change of one nucleotide in one codon which causes a substitution of one amino acid in the chain. Nucleotide for nucleotide these two strings of DNA are identical over 99.9 per cent of their length. For taxonomic purposes this indicates a very close relationship—a single point mutation separates the two. However, it is not valid to conclude that $<.01$ per cent difference leaves little for selection to affect.

Another way to clarify the distinction is to point out that it is logically possible for two genomes to be identical across 99 per cent of their DNA without having a single identical gene. In fact, chimpanzees and humans have "many" identical genes, but the functional percentage is anybody's guess and can not be inferred from the per cent of identical genetic material. (A. C. Wilson (pers comm)—"we expect most human genes to differ from their chimpanzee counterparts. A small fraction of the genes will be identical. The identical genes are likely to be shorter than average."

[13]Lewontin (1979) has described population genetics as "kinematic," which Webster defines as *a branch of dynamics that deals with aspects of motion apart from considerations of mass and force*.

empirically the accuracy with which it measures any interval. Regrettably, the man with the sundial can only agree that the watch is marvelous and hope that its owner will set it by the sun. Though critical of neoclassical theory, Lewontin asserts that it cannot be challenged "by pointing to the elephant's trunk and the camel's hump" (1974). I can only disagree and suggest that he has missed the point. The challenge is over adequacy, not accuracy, and those who wish to learn about evolution by studying its results should not be discouraged by those who, having studied the kinematics of genetic change, claim that we go too far because they have not yet modeled the means by which those results have come to be. Also, with regard to the voluminous evidence demonstrating that genes generally do behave as randomly as is generally stipulated by assumption, it should be borne in mind that it is as wrong to ascribe to the members of sets the properties of their sets as it is to ascribe to sets the properties of their members (cf. Lewontin, 1977). That is, nothing is gained if an ability to see the forest for the trees entails losing sight of the trees.

The sort of natural selection processes hypothesized in this paper are awkwardly vitalistic. Certainly they cannot be operative according to the strictures assumed by some neoclassicists. However, unless we start thinking in terms of evolved systems that can vastly increase the power of selection, we will be stuck with the embarrassment of accounting for genuinely awesome forms of life as the produce of a nearly forceless, if not feckless, evolutionary process—a process that could never explain "how the innumerable species inhabiting this world have been modified, so as to acquire that perfection of structure and coadaptation which most justly excites our admiration" (Darwin 1859).

ACKNOWLEDGEMENTS

I thank R. D. Alexander, P. T. Ellison, P. H. Harvey, D. B. Hrdy, S. B. Hrdy, W. Shields, D. W. E. Smith, R. L. Trivers, I. B. DeVore and G. C. Williams for encouragement, patience and suggestions.

REFERENCES

Air, G. M., Coulson, A. R., Fiddes, J. C., Friedmann, T., Hutchison, C. A. III, Sanger, F., Slocombe, P. M., and Smith, A. J. H. 1978. Nucleotide sequence of the F protein coding region of bacteriophage ϕX174 and the amino acid sequence of its product. *J. Mol. Biol.* 125,

Alexander, R. D., and Borgia, G. 1978. Group selection, altruism, and the levels of organization of life. *Ann. Rev. Ecol. Syst.* 9:449.

Altman, S. 1978. *Transfer RNA*. S. Altman (ed.), MIT Press, Cambridge.

Altwegg, M., and Kubli, E. 1979. The nucleotide sequence of phenylalanine tRNA of *Drosophila melanogaster:* four isoacceptors with one basic sequence. *Nucleic Acids Research,* 7(1)93.

Ames, B. N., and Hartman, P. E. 1963. The histidine operon. *Cold Spring Harbor Symp. Quant. Biol.* 28,349.

Baralle, F. E. 1977. Complete nucleotide sequences of 5' noncoding region of human α- and β -globin mRNA. *Cell* 12, 1085.

Barricelli, N. A. 1977. On the origin and evolution of the genetic code. 1. Wobbling and its potential significance. *J. theor. Biol.* 67, 85.

Berger, E. M. 1977. Are synonymous mutations adaptively neutral? *Am. Nat.* 111 (979), 606.

Bernard, O., Hozumi, N. and Tonegawa, S. 1978. Sequences of mouse light chain genes before and after somatic changes. *Cell* 15, 1133.

Blick, J. 1977. Selection for traits which lower individual reproduction. *J. theor. Biol.* 67 (3), 597.

Bodmer, W. F. (ed) 1977. Genetics of the cell surface. *Proc. R. Soc. Lond.* B. 202,1.

Borgia, G. 1979. Sexual Selection and the Evolution of Mating Systems. In *Sexual Selection and Reproductive Competition in Insects.* M. and N. Blum (eds.), NY: Academic Press.

Bossi, L. and Roth, J. R. 1980. The influence of codon context on genetic code translation. *Nature*. 286, 123.

Carroll, L. 1871. *Through the Looking-Glass, and What Alice Found There*. Macmillan, London.

Celis, J. E., and Smith, J. D. (eds.) 1979. *Nonsense Mutations and tRNA Suppressors*. Academic Press, London.

Chang, J. C., Temple, G. F., Poon, R., Jeumannl, K. H., and Kan, Y. W. 1977. The nucleotide sequence of the untranslated 5' regions of human α- and β -globin mRNAs. *P.N.A.S. USA*, 74(11) 5145.

Chapman, R. H., Klekowski, E. J., and Selander, R. K. 1979. Homoeologous heterozygosity and recombination in the fern *Pteridium aquilinum*. *Science*, 204, p. 1207.

Clutton–Brock, T. H. and Harvey, P. H. 1979. Comparison and adaptation. *Proc. R. Soc. Lond.* 8, 205, 547.

Cohen, J. 1975. Gamete redundancy—wastage or selection? In: *Gamete Competition in Plants and Animals*. D. L. Mulcahy (ed), North-Holland, Amsterdam.

Cortese, R. 1979. Role of transfer RNA in regulation. In *Biological Regulation and Development, Vol. I*. R. F. Goldberger (ed.). Plenum Press, New York.

Crick, F. H. C. 1966. Codon-anticodon pairing: the wobble hypothesis. *J. Mol. Biol.*, 19, 548.

Crick, F. H. C. 1979. Split genes and RNA splicing. *Science* 204, 264.

Crow, J. F. 1979. Genes that violate Mendel's rules. *Sci. Am.*, February 1979.

Daniels, R. A. 1979. Nest guard replacement in the antarctic fish *Harpagifer bispinis:* possible altruistic behavior. *Science* 205, 831.

Darwin, C. 1859. *On the Origin of Species*. Murray, London. pp. 3., 236, 237.

Davidson, E. H., and Britten, R. H. 1979. Regulation of gene expression: possible role of repetitive sequences. *Science* 204, p. 1052.

Dawkins, R. 1976. *The Selfish Gene*. Oxford University Press.

Dawkins, R. 1978. Replicator selection and the extended phenotype *Z. Tierpsychol.*, 47, 61.

Denes, G., and Nagy, J. 1976. Allosteric enzyme-tRNA complexes as regulators of transcription of translation. *Acta microbiol. Acad. Sci. Hung.* 23, 171.

Denis, H., Mazabraud, A., and Wegnez, M. 1975. Biochemical research on oogenesis. Comparison between transfer RNAs from somatic cells and from oocytes in *Xenopus laevis*. *Eur. J. Biochem.* 58, 43.

DeWitt, W. 1971. Differences in methionyl- and arginyl- tRNA's of larval and adult bullfrogs. *Biochem. Biophys. Res. Commun.* 42, 266.

Doolittle, W. F. and Sapienza, C. 1980. Selfish genes, the phenotype paradigm and genome evolution. *Nature* 284, 601.

Efstratiadis, A., Kafatos, F. C., and Maniatis, T. 1977. The primary structure of rabbit β -globin mRNA as determined from cloned DNA. *Cell* 10, 571.

Ehrman, L. 1972. Genetics and sexual selection. In *Sexual Selection and the Descent of Man*. B. Campbell (ed.). Aldine, Chicago.

Eldredge, N., and Gould, S. J. 1972. Punctuated equilibria: an alternative to phyletic gradualism. In *Models in Paleobiology*, T. J. M. Schopf (ed.). Freeman, Cooper & Co., San Francisco.

Elka, A., Matsuka, G., Matiash, U., Nasarenko, I., and Semenova, N. 1971. tRNA and aminoacyl-tRNA synthetases during differentiation and various functional states of the mammary gland. *Biochem. Biophys. Acta* 247, 230.

Emlen, J. M. 1973. *Ecology: An Evolutionary Approach*. Reading, Mass., Addison–Wesley.

Epel, D. 1977. The program of fertilization. *Sci. Am.* November.

Fiddes, J. C., and Goodman, H. M. 1979. Isolation, cloning, and sequence analysis of the cDNA for the A-subunit of human chorionic gonadotropin. *Nature* 281:351, 356.

Fiers, W., Contreras, R., Duerinck, F., Haegeman, G., Merregaert, J., Min Jou, W., Raeymakers, A., Volckaert, G., and Ysebaert, M. 1975. A-protein gene of bacteriophage MS2. *Nature* 256, 273.

Fiers, W., Contreras, R., Duerinck, F., Haegeman, G., Iserentant, D., Merregaert, J., Min Jou, W., Molemans, F., Raeymakers, A., Vanden Berghe, A., Volckaert, G., and Ysebaert, M., 1976 Complete nucleotide sequence of bacteriophage MS2 RNA: primary secondary structure of the replicase gene. *Nature* 260, 500.

Fiers, W., Contreras, R., Haegeman, G., Rogiers, R., Van de Voorde, A., Van Heuverswyn, H., Van Herreweghe, J., Volckaert, G., and Ysebaert, M. 1978. Complete nucleotide sequence of SV40 DNA. *Nature* 273, 113.

Fisher, R. A. 1930. *The Genetical Theory of Natural Selection*. Oxford University Press. Oxford.

Fitch, W. M. 1976. Is there selection against wobble in codon-anticodon pairing? *Science* 194, 1173.

Garel, J. P. 1974. Functional adaptation of tRNA population. *J. theor. Biol.* 43, 211.

_____., Hentzen, D., Schlegel, M., and Dirheimer, G. 1976. Structural studies on RNA from *Bombyx mori* L. *Biochimie,* 58, 1089.

_____. 1976. Quantitative adaptation of isoacceptor tRNAs to mRNA codons of alanine, glycine and serine. *Nature* 260, 805.

Geddes-Dwyer, V., and Cameron, D. A. 1976. Influence of exogenous tRNA on growth of transplantable ^{32}P-induced osteosarcomata. *Br. J. Cancer* 33, 600.

Geremia, R., d'Agostino, A., Monesi, V. 1978. Biochemical evidence of haploid gene activity in spermatogenesis of the mouse. *Exp. Cell Res.* 111(1)23.

Ghiselin, M. T. 1974. *The Economy of Nature and the Evolution of Sex.* Univ. of California Press.

Gilbert, J. M., and Anderson, W. F. 1970. Cell-free hemoglobin synthesis II. Characteristics of the transfer ribonucleic acid-dependent assay system. *J. Biol. Chem.* 245, 2342.

Glander, K. E. 1979. Howling monkey feeding behavior and plant secondary compounds: a study of strategies. In *The Ecology of Arboreal Folivores,* G. F. Montgomery (ed.), Smithsonian Inst. Press, Washington. Also, Leaves and leaf-eating primates. paper delivered at annual meeting of The American Anthropological Association, Houston, December 1977.

Godson, G. N., Barrell, B. G., Staden, R., and Fiddes, J. C. 1978. Nucleotide sequence of bacteriophage G4 DNA. *Nature* 276, 236.

Gwatkin, R. B. L. 1977. *Fertilization Mechanisms in Man and Mammals.* Plenum, New York.

von der Haar, F., and Cramer, F. 1978. Valyl- and phenylalanyl-tRNA synthetase from baker's yeast: recognition of transfer RNA results from a multistep process, as indicated by inhibition of aminoacylation with modified transfer RNA. *Biochemistry* 17(21), 4509.

Hamilton, W. D. 1964. The genetical evolution of social behaviour. I and II. *J. theor. Biol.* 7, 1.

Hamlyn, P. H., Brownlee, G. G., Cheng, C.-C., Gait, M. J., and Milstein, C. 1978. Complete sequence of constant and 3' noncoding regions of an immunoglobulin mRNA using the dideoxynucleotide method of RNA sequencing. *Cell,* 15, 1067.

Hartung, J. 1976. On natural selection and the inheritance of wealth. *Curr. Anthrop.* 17(4), 607.

_____. 1977. An implication about human mating systems. *J. theor. Biol.* 66, 737. See also, Parent-Offspring Conflict: a retraction, *in press,* J. theor. Biol.

_____. 1980. On the geneticness of traits: beyond $h^2 = V_g/V_p$. *Curr. Anthrop.* 21(1)130.

_____. and Ellison, P. 1977. A eugenic effect of medical care. *Social Biology* 21(3), 192.

Heindell, H. C., Liu, A., Paddock, G. V., Studnicka, G. M., and Salser, W. 1978. The primary sequence of rabbit alpha-globin mRNA. *Cell* 15, 43.

Hilse, K., and Rudloff, E. 1975. Glutamine cognate codons in rabbit haemoglobin mRNAs. *FEBS letters* 60(2), 380.

Holmes, W. M., Goldman, E., Miner, T. A., and Hatfield, G. W. 1977. Differential utilization of leucyl-tRNAs by *Escherichia coli*. *P.N.A.S. USA* 74(4), 1393.

Hubby, J. L., and Lewontin, R. C. 1966. A molecular approach to the study of genic heterozygosity in natural populations. *Genetics* 54, 577.

Ilan, J., and Ilan, J. 1975. Regulation of messenger RNA translation during insect development. *Curr. Top. Dev. Biol.* 9,89.

Itano, H. A. 1957. The human hemoglobins: their properties and genetic control. *Adv. Protein Chem.* 12, 215

_____. 1965. The synthesis and structure of normal and abnormal hemoglobins. In *Abnormal Hemoglobins in Africa.* J. H. P. Jonxis (ed.). Blackwell, Oxford. (p. 12.)

Jacob, F. and Monod, J. 1961. Genetic regulatory mechanisms in the synthesis of proteins. *J. Mol. Biol.* 3, 318.

Jeffreys, A. J. 1979. DNA sequence variants in the $^G\gamma-$, $^A\gamma-$, $\delta-$ and $\beta-$ globin genes in man. *Cell* 18, 1.

Jukes, T. H., and King, J. L. 1979. Evolutionary nucleotide replacements in DNA. *Nature* 281: 605, 606.

Kafatos, F. C., Efstratiadis, A., Forget, B. G., and Weissman, S. M. 1977. Molecular evolution of human and rabbit β -globin mRNAs. *P.N.A.S. USA* 74(12)5618.

Kimura, M. 1979. The neutral theory of molecular evolution. *Sci. Am.* November.

King, J. L. and Jukes, T. H. 1969. Non-Darwinian evolution: random fixation of selectively neutral mutations. *Science* 164:788.

King, M. C. and Wilson, A. C. 1975. Evolution at two levels in humans and chimpanzees. *Science* 188, 107.

Klee, H. J., Dipietro, D., Fournier, M. J., and Fischer, M. S. 1978. Characterization of transfer RNA from liver of the developing amphibian, *Rana catesbeiana*. *J. Biol. Chem.* 253(22), 807.

Leigh, E. G. 1977. How does selection reconcile individual advantage with the good of the group? *P.N.A.S. USA* 74(10), 4542.

Lerman, M. I., Pilipenko, N. N., Ugarova, T. Y., Sokolova, E. S., Vinnizky, L. I., and Phishkova, Z. P. 1976. The limiting effect of transfer RNA's on the rate of protein synthesis in cell extracts of rapidly growing tumors. *Cancer Research* 36. 2995.

Lewis, J. A., and Ames, B. N. 1972. Histidine regulation in *Salmonella typhimurium*. XI. The percentage of transfer RNA His charged in vivo and its relation to the repression of the histidine operon. *J. Mol. Biol.* 66, 131.

Lewontin, R. C. 1970. The units of selection. *Ann. Rev. Ecol. Syst.* 1, 1.

———. 1974. *The Genetic Basis of Evolutionary Change*. Columbia University Press, New York.

———. 1977. Caricature of Darwinism (review of *The Selfish Gene*, R. Dawkins). *Nature* 266, 283.

———. 1979. Sociobiology as an adaptationist program. *Behavioral Science*, 24, 5.

Littauer, U. Z., and Inouye, H. 1973. Regulation of tRNA. *Annu. Rev. Biochem.* 42, 439.

Marotta, C. A., Wilson, J. T., Forget, B. G. and Weissman, S. M. 1977. Human β -globin messenger RNA. *J. Biol. Chem.* 252 (14), 5040.

Maxam, A. M., and Gilbert, W. 1977. A new method for sequencing DNA. *Proc. Natl. Acad. Sci. USA* 74(2), 560.

Maynard Smith, J. 1971. What use is sex? *J. theor. Biol. 30, 139.*

———. 1976. A comment on the red queen. *Am. Nat.* 110 (973), 325.

Maynard Smith, J. (1978) The Evolution of Sex. Cambridge University Press, London. 1976. Group selection. *Quarterly Rev. Biol.* 51, 277.

Mayr, E. 1967. Evolutionary challenges to the mathematical interpretation of evolution. In: *Mathematical Challenges to the neo-Darwinian Interpretation of Evolution*. Moorhead, P. S. and Kaplan, M. M. (eds.), Wistar Institute Press, Philadelphia, p. 47.

McReynolds, L., O'Malley, B. W., Nisbit, A. D., Fothergill, J. E., Givol, D., Fields, S., Robertson, M., and Brownlee, G. G. 1978. Sequence of chicken ovalbumin mRNA. *Nature* 273, 723.

Mitra, S. K., Lustig, F., Akesson, B., Lagerkvist, U., and Strid, L. 1977. Codon-anticodon recognition in the valine codon family. *J. Biol. Chem.* 252, 471.

Monesi, V., Geremia, R., D'Agostino, A., and Boitani, C. 1978. Biochemistry of male germ cell differentiation in mammals: RNA synthesis in meiotic and post meiotic cells. *Curr. Top. Dev. Biol.* 12, 11.

Moore, G. P., Costantini, F. D., Posakony, J. W., Davidson, E. H. and Britten, R. J. 1980. Evolutionary conservation of repetitive sequence expression in sea urchin egg RNA's. *Science* 208, 1046.

Mukerjee, H., and Goldfeder, A. 1976. Transfer RNA species in tumors of different growth rates. *Cancer Research* 36, 3330.

Mulcahy, D. L. 1979. The rise of angiosperms: a genecological factor. *Science* 206, 20.

Nakanishi, S., Inoue, A., Kita, T., Nakamura, M., Chang, A., Yi, C., Cohen, S. N., and Numa, S. 1979. Nucleotide sequence of cloned cDNA for bovine corticotropin-β -lipotropin precursor, *Nature* 278, 423.

Orgel, L. E. and Crick, F. H. C. 1980. Selfish DNA: the ultimate parasite. *Nature* 284, 604.

Packer, C. 1979. Inter-troop transfer and inbreeding avoidance in *Papio anubis, Anim. Behav.* 27, 1.

Palatnik, C. M., Katz, E. R., and Brenner, M. 1977. Isolation and characterization of transfer RNAs from *Dictyostelium disoideum* during growth and development. *J. Biol. Chem.* 252, 694.

Parker, G. A. 1970. Sperm competition and its evolutionary consequences in the insects. *Biol. Revs.* 45, 525.

Prager, E. M. and Wilson, A. C. 1975. Slow evolutionary loss of the potential for interspecific hybridization in birds. A manifestation of slow regulatory evolution. *P.N.A.S. USA* 71, 200.

Proudfoot, N. J. 1977. Complete 3′ noncoding region sequences of rabbit and human β -globin messenger RNAs. *Cell* 10, 559.

Racine, R. R. and Langley, C. H. 1980. Genetic heterozygosity in a natural population of *Mus musculus* assessed using two-dimensional electrophoresis. *Nature* 283, 855.

Reddy, V. B., Thimmappaya, B., Dhar, R., Subramanian, K. N., Zain, B. S., Pan, J., Ghosh, P. K., Celma, M. L., and Weissman, S. M. 1978. The genome of simian virus 40. *Science* 200, 494.

Renart, J., and Sebastian, J. 1976. Characterization and levels of the RNA polymerases during the embryogenesis of *Artemia salina*. *Cell Diff.* 5, 97.

Rogers, J., Clarke, P., and Salser, W. 1979. Sequence analysis of cloned cDNA encoding part of an immunoglobulin heavy chain. *Nucleic Acids Research* 6(10), 3305.

Sanger, R., and Coulson, A. R. 1975. A rapid method for determining sequences in DNA by primed synthesis with DNA polymerase. *J. Mol. Biol.* 94 (3), 441.

_____, Air, G. M., Barell, B. G., Brown, N. L., Coulson, A. R., Fiddes, J. C., Hutchison, C. A. III, Slocombe, P. M. and Smith, M. 1977. Nucleotide sequence of Bacteriophage X174 DNA. *Nature* 265, 687.

Schaffner, W., Kunz, G., Daetwyler, H., Telford, J., Smith, H. O., and Birnstiel, M. L. 1978. Genes and spacers of cloned sea urchin histone DNA analyzed by sequencing, *Cell* 14, 655.

Seeburg, P. H., Shine, J., Martial, J. A., Baxter, J. D., and Goodman, H. M. 1977. Nucleotide sequence and amplification in bacteria of structural gene for rat growth hormone. *Nature* 270, 486.

Seger, J. 1976. Evolution of responses to relative homozygosity. *Nature* 262, 578.

Seger, V. 1979. Inbreeding recombination and the chromosome number of insects. Unpublished manuscript.

Sharma, O. K., Mays, L. L., and Borek, E. 1975. Functional differences in protein synthesis between rat liver tRNA and tRNA from Novikoff Hepatoma, *Biochemistry* 15(19), 4313.

_____, Beezley, D. N., Borek, E. 1976. Modulation of the synthesis in vitro of a hormone-induced protein by transfer RNA. *Nature* 262, 62.

_____, Beezley, D. N., and Roberts, W. K. 1976. Limitation of reticulocyte transfer RNA in the translation of heterologous messenger RNAs. *Biochemistry* 15(19), 4313.

Sherman, P. W. 1980. Insect chromosome numbers and eusociality. *Am. Nat.* 113, 925.

Shields, W. 1979. Philopatry, inbreeding, and the adaptive advantages of sex. Ph.D. dissertation, Ohio State University.

Shine, J., Seeburg, P. H., Martial, J. A., Baxter, J. D., and Goodman, H. M. 1977. Construction and analysis of recombinant DNA for human chorionic somatomammotropin. *Nature* 270, 494.

Smith, D. W. E., and McNamara, A. L. 1971. Specialization of rabbit reticulocyte transfer RNA content for hemoglobin synthesis. *Science* 171, 577.

Smith, D. W. E. 1975. Reticulocyte transfer RNA and hemoglobin synthesis. *Science* 190, 529. See also *Science* 193, 429 (1976).

Stent, G. S. 1964. The operon: on its third anniversary. *Science* 144, 816 (p. 818).

Strom, C. M. and Dorfman, A. 1976. Amplification of moderately repetitive DNA sequences during chick cartilage differentiation. *P.N.A.S. USA* 73(10), 3428.

Sueoka, N., and Kano-Sueoka, T. 1960. Transfer RNA and cell differentiation. *Prog. Nucleic Acid. Res. Mol. Biol.* 10, 23.

Tonoue, T., Eaton, J., and Frieden, E. 1969. Changes in leucyl-tRNA during spontaneous and induced metamorphosis of bullfrog tadpoles. *Biochem. Biophys. Res. Commun.* 36, 81.

Topal, M. D., and Fresco, J. R. 1976. Base pairing and fidelity in codon-anticodon interaction. *Nature* 263, 289.

Trivers, R. L. 1974. Parent-offspring conflict. *Am. Zool.* 14, 249.

_____. 1972. Parental investment and sexual selection. In *Sexual Selection and the Descent of Man*. B. Campbell (ed.) Aldine, Chicago.

Ullrich, A., Shine, J., Chirgwin, J., Pictet, R., Tischer, E., Rutter, W. J., and Goodman, H. M. 1977. Rat insulin genes: construction of plasmids containing the coding sequences. *Science* 16. 1313.

van Ooyen, A., van den Berg, J., Mantei, N., and Weissmann, C. 1979. Comparison of total sequence of a cloned rabbit β-globin gene and its flanking regions with a homologous mouse sequence. *Science* 206: 337–344.

Van Valen, L. 1973. A new evolutionary law. *Evolutionary Theory*. 1,1.

Wald, G. 1967. The problems of vicarious selection. In: *Mathematical Challenges to the Neo-Darwinian Interpretation of Evolution*. Moorhead, P. S. and Kaplan, M. M. (eds.), Wistar Inst. Press, Philadelphia. p. 59.

Wallace, A. R. 1858. On the tendency of varieties to depart indefinitely from the original type. J. Linn. Soc. *(Zool.)* 3:45.

Washburn, S. L. 1978. Human behavior and the behavior of other animals. *Am. Psychol.* 33, 405.

Watanabe, T. K., and Kawanishi, M. 1979. Mating preference and the direction of evolution in *Drosophila. Science,* 205, 906.

_____., and Saneyoshi, M. 1978. The changes of tRNA^{Arg} content and arginyl-tRNA synthetase activity in developing salmon testes during spermatogenesis. *Nucleic Acids Res.,* special publication #5, s44.

Watson, J. 1976. *Molecular Biology of the Gene,* 3rd ed., W. A. Benjamin, Inc. Reading, Massachusetts.

Westerberg, U., Bolcsfolui, G. and Eliasson, E. 1976. Control of transfer RNA synthesis in the presence of inhibitors of protein synthesis. *Biochim. et Biophys. Acta* 447, 203.

White, B. N., Tener, G. M., Holden, J., and Suzuki, D. T. 1973. Activity of transfer RNA modifying enzyme during the development of *Drosophila* and its relationship to the Su(s) locus. *J. Mol. Biol.* 74, 635.

Williams, G. C. 1978. Mysteries of sex and recombination. *Quart. Rev. Bio.* 53, 287.

———. 1975. *Sex and Evolution*. Princeton University Press. Princeton.

———. 1966. *Adaptation and Natural Selection*. Princeton University Press.

Williams, G. C. and Williams, D. C. 1957. Natural selection of individually harmful social adaptations among sibs with special reference to social insects. *Evolution* 11, 32.

Wilson, D. S. 1980. *The Natural Selection of Populations and Communities*. Benjamin/Cummings, Menlo Park, California.

Wynne-Edwards, V. C. 1962. *Animal Dispersion in Relation to Social Behaviour*. Oliver and Boyd, Edinburgh.

Yanagisawa, K., Bennett, D., Boyse, E. A., Dunn, L. C., and Dimeo, A. 1974. Serological identification of sperm antigens specified by lethal t-alleles in the mouse. *Immunogenetics* 1, 57.

———, Pollard, D. R., Bennett, D., Dunn, L. C., and Boyse, E. A. 1974. Transmission ratio distortion at the T-locus: serological identification of two sperm populations in t-heterozygotes. *Immunogenetics* 1, 91.

Yang, S. S., and Comb, D. G. 1968. Distribution of multiple forms of lysyl transfer RNA during early embryogenesis of sea urchin, *Lytechinus variegatus*. *J. Mol. Biol.* 31, 139.

VII

Humans

24

Abuse and Neglect of Children in Evolutionary Perspective

Martin Daly & Margo I. Wilson

Children have been abused and neglected throughout history and in a variety of cultures (Thomas, 1972; Langer, 1974; Dickemann, 1975; Straus, Gelles and Steinmetz, 1979). Only since Kempe et al. (1962) described diagnostic features of the ''battered-child syndrome,'' however, has discussion of the problem burgeoned. Most writers have favored socio-economic, psychopathological, and developmental factors as explanations for mistreatment of children (Gil, 1970; Helfer and Kempe, 1976; Martin, 1976; Parke and Collmer, 1975; NIMH, 1977). While these are all important factors, an evolutionary perspective may provide a more encompassing view of circumstances exacerbating the risk of abuse and neglect and of the ultimate rationale for variations in parental solicitude and negligence.

ADAPTIVE VARIATION IN PARENTAL NURTURE

Parental nurture is a crucial component of reproductive effort and is as much subject to optimization by natural selection as clutch size or any other flexible aspect of reproductive strategy (Williams, 1966; Trivers, 1972, 1974; Barash, 1976a). Nurturant behavior on the part of individual parents is furthermore likely to vary adaptively. Parental solicitude is neither dispensed indiscriminately to all conspecific young (e.g., Hrdy, 1976) nor is it invariant over the reproductive lifetime nor even over the course of a single reproductive episode. If parental inclinations are indeed adaptively variable, one may expect them to be mitigated by circumstances that predict either a reduced probability of inclusive fitness payoffs or intolerable costs of the parental effort.

The first circumstance under which parental care might adaptively be terminated (or at least reduced) is that of doubtful parenthood. Several authors have discussed the relevance of paternity confidence to the evolution of a male parental role (Alexander, 1974; Barash, 1976b; Kurland and Gaulin, 1979): where they cannot reliably identify their own offspring, males are unlikely to contribute parentally. Mistaken maternity is less a risk in internally fertilizing animals including mammals; accurate identification of one's own young is assured by individualized bonding of mother and young at birth (Hersher, Moore, and Richmond, 1958; Klopfer, 1970, 1971). Subsequently, maternal solicitude is likely to be highly discriminative. A goat nursing her own infant may simultaneously reject a strange kid's approaches. What is more, parental solicitude appears to be discriminating or not according to whether natural circumstances are such that parents are likely to be exposed to unrelated young and are therefore at risk of misdirecting their care (Alexander, 1974; Hoogland and Sherman, 1976). For example, individual recognition of eggs and chicks is well developed in guillemots that breed in dense aggregations and is absent in related species with dispersed nest sites (e.g., Birkhead, 1978). Furthermore, such parental discrimination commonly develops at precisely that stage of the young's developing mobility when mixups become a possibility. Female flying squirrels, for example, will accept artificially introduced alien pups up to 40 days postpartum, at which age young become capable of leaving the tree-hole nest; after that age, strange juveniles are attacked (Muul, 1970).

Even when one's offspring can be reliably identified, their prospects of growing up and breeding successfully may sometimes be so poor that a parent's best course of action is to abandon the reproductive enterprise. This might be because of an inadequate resource base or some deficiency in the offspring. Purple martins abandon nests infested with parasites (Camin and Moss, 1970) and bank swallows eject cracked eggs from the nest (Hoogland and Sherman, 1976). Where parental resources are limiting, parents may cull their broods to match their capabilities or terminate a reproductive episode altogether to await a more propitious opportunity. The decision to cut one's losses in this way should occur as early in the reproductive process as feasible; when a large proportion of the requisite parental investment for the raising of an offspring has been expended and relatively little more is required, parents should tolerate greater risks before abandoning dependent young (Barash, 1975).

Insofar as the abuse and neglect of human children result from a failure of parental inclinations, the above considerations suggest that they should prove particularly likely under circumstances in which adults are called upon to play parent to children not their own, in which the mother-infant attachment process is absent or disrupted (Klaus and Kennell, 1976), or in which parental capacities and resources are overtaxed.

HOUSEHOLD COMPOSITION

Parental solicitude should be correlated with true biological parenthood. The ultimate rationale for such a correlation is selection against squandering parental resources on non-kin. Relevant proximate factors include discriminative mother-infant bonding and whatever experiences promote paternity confidence. It follows that parent substitutes may not easily develop genuine parental affection for their wards. A study of stepparents in Cleveland, Ohio, for example, found that only 53 per cent of stepfathers and 25 per cent of stepmothers could claim to have "parental feelings" toward their stepchildren (Duberman, 1975). Such considerations suggest that the risk of child abuse should be examined as a function of household composition.

Table 24–1 presents a breakdown of four samples of physical abuse cases according to household composition. In all samples, only about half of the abused children lived in households containing both natural parents and a large proportion, ranging from 24.8 per cent (U.S.A.) to 41.2 per cent (New Zealand) lived with one or more parent substitutes.

Ideally, these proportions should be compared to proportions of such households in the population-at-large to arrive at estimates of risk according to household type, but direct information on the living arrangements of children in the population-at-large is not available for any of the countries in Table 24–1. Indirect information indicates that many more than half of all children live in two-natural-parent households in each of the three countries. For the United States in 1976, the census bureau has estimated the prevalence of mother-only and father-only households (U.S. Bureau of the Census, 1977a) and we have estimated the prevalence of two-natural-parent and stepparent households in order to arrive at the abuse and neglect incidence estimates of Figure 24–1.

According to the U.S. Bureau of the Census (1977a), 80.0 per cent of all children lived with "two parents" in 1976. This category includes stepparents, for whom we used the estimate of 10 per cent made by Glick (1976). For age-group-specific estimates, we then assume that the relative increase by age of proportions of children living with stepparents has not changed since 1967, for which year living arrangements of children were estimated from sample data by Sweet (1974). The resulting estimates of proportion of children living with one natural parent and one stepparent were: 0–2 years old, 2.1 per cent; 3–5, 5.7 per cent; 6–9, 9.9 per cent; 10–12, 12.5 per cent; 14–17, 14.7 per cent. Estimates for the category "both natural parents" were then obtained by subtracting stepparent estimates from "two-parent" figures, to give 0–2 years old, 80.9 per cent; 3–5, 74.8 per cent; 6–9, 70.5 per cent; 10–13, 66.8 per cent; 14–17, 63.8 per cent. Glick's (1976) estimate of 10 per cent considers all children born between first and second marriage (8 per cent of all children of women in intact second marriages) stepchildren regardless of paternity. Furthermore, Glick estimated the proportion of children in maternal remarriages who are step-children, and used the same figure for paternal remarriages. Both of these factors contribute to overestimation of stepparent incidence in the population. Imprecision in the estimate also derives from Glick's having estimated the proportion of children living with one or more remarried parents in 1975 by extrapolating from 1970 data, and from our application of his estimate another year later. Despite potential biasing factors, we consider our estimates to be conservative in the following sense: we are unlikely to have underestimated the incidence of stepparent households in the population at large and hence are unlikely to have overestimated the incidence of abuse and neglect in such households. Data presented by the U.S. Bureau of the Census (1977b) support this contention of conservatism: In June 1975, 14.3 per cent of children aged 14 to 17 lived "with father and mother" where one or both parents was remarried. This figure, which includes offspring conceived after the remarriage, constitutes an upper limit on the proportion in stepparent households, while the figure which we have estimated independently is 14.7 per cent. In computing the incidences in Figure 24–1, children living with two adoptive parents were included in the both-natural-parents category, because such families are indistinguishable in census information; they comprised only 0.7 per cent of abuse and neglect cases in this category. Households containing one natural parent and one adoptive parent were treated as stepparent households. Households containing one natural parent and a paramour were treated as single-parent households because such households are so classified in census information. These paramour households are of necessity included in the single-parent category, although it would be preferable to include them in the stepparent category. These paramour-households contributed only 2.9 per cent of single-parent-household abuse and neglect cases; if included in the stepparent category, they would augment the total number of cases in that category by 10.7 per cent.

The abuse and neglect data analyzed constituted the complete set of validated cases reported to the American Humane Association, Englewood, Colorado, in 1976 from the 28 states and 3 territories (then comprising 44.6 per cent of the total U.S. population [U.S.

Table 24–1.   Distribution of child abuse victims according to household composition.

Household Composition	Per Cent of All Validated Abuse Cases			
	U.S.A. 1976	England 1975	England 1976	New Zealand 1967
Both natural parents	46.1	52.5	52.0	50.2
Natural mother only	25.2	18.5	17.4	8.2
Natural mother and father substitute	18.5	20.1	22.1	8.2
Natural father only	3.9	3.1	2.5	0.4
Natural father and mother substitute	4.0	2.7	4.6	11.4
Adoptive parents	0.8			4.7
Foster parents	0.5	{3.1	1.4}	5.1
Other	1.0			11.8
No. of Cases	26,779	556	638	255

SOURCES: U.S.A.: present study; England: Creighton and Owtram, 1977, Creighton, 1978; New Zealand: Fergusson, Fleming, and O'Neill, 1972.

Bureau of the Census, 1978a]) that were then full participants in a national program for reporting standard information on all cases of suspected abuse or neglect. The age breakdown in Figure 24–1 was dictated by available data for the population-at-large. The percentages of abuse and neglect cases in each age category are as follows: 0–2 years old, 20.0 per cent; 3–5, 18.1 per cent; 6–9, 23.3 per cent; 10–13, 21.3 per cent, 14–17, 17.2 per cent.

We present the data in terms of household composition rather than perpetrator for several reasons. While stepparents are relatively frequent perpetrators of abuse, so to a lesser extent are natural parents with stepparent spouses. The labelled ''perpetrator'' is not necessarily the instigator, and moreover, one party may assume responsibility to protect another. In the case of neglect, identification of a single perpetrator seems inappropriate. For these reasons, household composition is the more reliable datum.

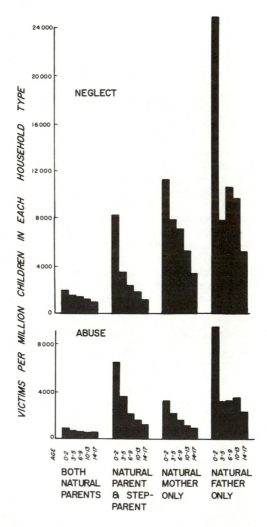

Figure 24–1.   Incidence of validated cases of neglect ($N = 64, 544$) and abuse ($N = 26, 304$) of children in U.S.A. for 1976 according to household composition and age of victim.

Figure 24–1 indicates that the incidence of both abuse and neglect varies dramatically as a function of household composition. Risk is seriously elevated in households other than those containing both natural parents. Father-only is much the riskiest situation, especially with the youngest children. Although biparental care appears to be a fundamental human attribute, men are nowhere the primary caretakers of infants. Men participate directly in infant care in some but by no means all societies (Stephens, 1963), and in America, men make various contributions as material providers, protectors, educators, and the like, but less often bathe, clothe, and feed children (Benson, 1968; Parke and Sawin, 1976; Stafford, Backman and Dibona, 1977). The data in Figure 24–1 suggest that men left alone with infants are not very well prepared—emotionally or otherwise—to care for them adequately.

The data in Figure 24–1 also indicate that abuse differs from neglect in the pattern of relative incidences. In the case of abuse, stepparent households rank second in risk, well above mother-only, whereas this order is reversed in the case of neglect. The implication that stepparent households are relatively fertile ground for abuse is supported by the data in Table 24–2, comparing two samples of injured children in New Zealand. 19.6 per cent of severe child-abuse victims lived in a home containing a stepparent in contrast to 9.3 per cent of a comparison group of children whose injuries were investigated on suspicion of similar abuse, but were concluded to be possibly or probably accidental on medical and circumstantial evidence.

Available information does not permit accurate comparisons of stepfather and stepmother households. In the United States, total cases of abuse in 1976 were 4.6 times as frequent in the former (Table 24–1). Incidences may be similar, however, since children generally go with the mother upon the dissolution of marriage and are therefore likelier to acquire a stepfather than a stepmother. How *much* likelier is unknown. Estimates of this ratio for the population-at-large below 4.6 would imply a higher risk of abuse with stepfathers; estimates above 4.6 would imply a higher risk with stepmothers. Data for teen-aged children in Washington in 1953, Ohio in 1960, and North Carolina in 1960 (Bowerman and Irish, 1962) yield ratios of 3.2, 3.8, and 4.8, respectively. It cannot at present be concluded that one type of step-household is riskier than the other. Stepmother households are notably frequent in New Zealand abuse cases (Table 24–1).

A further analysis of abuse and neglect data, which circumvents the problems involved in estimating incidences, underscores the special nature of the risks faced by children in stepparent households. For each of seven household composition types, the percentage of all validated cases (abuse and/or neglect) that involved abuse are presented in Table 24–3. Only the three household compositions indicated by boldface type include an adult unrelated to the victim. In each of these three the proportion of cases involving abuse is significantly higher than in each of the other four household compositions in which resident adults are biological kin of the victim ($p < .0001$ by Chi-square test for each comparison). That stepparent households (and perhaps adoptive and foster parent households as well) are relatively fertile ground for physical abuse may reflect nepotistic selectivity of parental solicitude.

Table 24–2.   Abuse versus accidental injury in relation to presence of a stepparent (New Zealand, 1967)

	Presence of Stepparent in Household	
	Yes	No
Validated abuse cases	50 (19.6%)	205 (80.4%)
Injuries not validated as abuse (presumed accidental)	10 (9.3%)	98 (90.7%)

SOURCE: Fergusson et al., 1972. Chi-square (1*df*) = 5.22, *p* <0.05

Table 24–3.   Abuse cases as a percentage of total validated cases in each of seven household composition types (United States, 1976).

Household Composition	Total Cases (abuse and/or neglect)	Abuse Cases as % of total cases
Two natural parents	35,860	34.4
Natural mother only	31,824	21.2
Natural mother and father substitute	9,137	54.2
Natural father only	3,437	30.4
Natural father and mother substitute	1,786	59.1
Adoptive or foster parents	616	59.7
Other relatives	904	30.9

SOURCE: Present Study.

PARENTAL RESOURCES

As we noted above, neglect and abuse differ in their relative incidences in stepparent and mother-only households (Figure 24–1). Whereas an unrelated parent substitute seems particularly relevant to the risk of abuse, the lone-parent circumstance seems particularly relevant to the risk of neglect. It is hardly surprising that lone parents are often neglectful: they are likely to be short of time and of a partner's assistance, and they are likely (especially in the case of lone mothers) to be poor (U.S. Bureau of the Census, 1978b).

That poor financial resources are particulary germane to the risk of neglect is indicated by the data in Figure 24–2. Poverty is clearly relevant to the risk of both abuse and neglect (Gil, 1970; Kadushin, 1974; Smith, Hanson and Noble, 1974; NIMH, 1977) but is especially relevant to the risk of neglect. Median family income for abuse-only cases was $6,885 and for neglect-only cases $4,249 (American Humane Association, 1978), while for all families with children in the population-at-large, median income was $15,388 (U.S. Bureau of the Census, 1978b). In validated case reports to the American Humane Association, "insufficient income" was cited as a factor in 48.0 per cent of neglect-only cases, in 47.4 per cent of neglect-and-abuse cases, and in only 25.2 per cent of abuse-only cases (American Humane Association 1978; see also Giovannoni and Billingsley, 1970).

Housing is another element of the parental resource situation that proves especially relevant to neglect. In validated case reports to the American Humane Association, "inadequate housing" was cited as a factor in 26.2 per cent of neglect-only cases, in 26.5 per cent of neglect-and-abuse cases, and in only 9.2 per cent of abuse-only cases (American Humane Association, 1978).

CHARACTERISTICS OF THE CHILD

From the view of parental solicitude as adaptively variable, one might also anticipate that offspring with a variety of imperfections predictive of poor prospects for survival or reproduction would be likely victims of parental neglect and abuse. There is evidence that this is indeed the case, though the interpretation of the evidence is not always straightforward.

A number of studies indicate a relatively high incidence of abuse of mentally retarded children (Sandgrund, Gaines, and Green, 1974; Morse, Sahler, and Friedman, 1970; Martin et al., 1974) and emotionally disturbed children (Morse et al., 1970; American Humane Association, 1978). Perhaps mentally defective children are disproportionately victimized, but this interpretation must be suspect since the symptoms may in many cases be consequences rather than causes of parental maltreatment (see e.g., Sandgrund, Gaines and Green, 1974; Oliver, 1975) or even consequences of prenatal abuse of the mother (Gelles, 1975).

That the defect in fact antedates abuse is clearer in cases of such congenital handicaps as spina bifida, fibrocystic disease, talipes, cleft palate, and Down's syndrome. Table 24–4 summarizes data from several studies indicating that congenitally handicapped children are at relatively high risk.

When defective children are institutionalized, there is a substantial probability that they will be abandoned. A 1976 census study indicated that there were then more than 16,000 institutionalized children in the United States who were never visited by their families. A total of about 30,000, some 22 per cent of all the institutionalized children, were visited only once a year or less (U.S. Bureau of the Census, 1978c).

Though a mitigation of parental feeling toward defectives is an expected consequence of selection against investment in inviable and/or infertile young, it is not necessarily the case that parental feeling is directly inhibited by overt signs of abnormality. Parental abuse and neglect of the handicapped may instead be mediated by interference with the mother-infant attachment process, whether as a result of perinatal separation for medical purposes or of inability of the defective child to interact with the mother normally. In fact, considerable evidence supports this mediational hypothesis as will be discussed further. However, there is also some evidence that certain defects in the newborn are likely to evoke immediate shock and rejection in parents (Roskies, 1972; Fletcher, 1974; Drotar et al., 1975; Irvin,

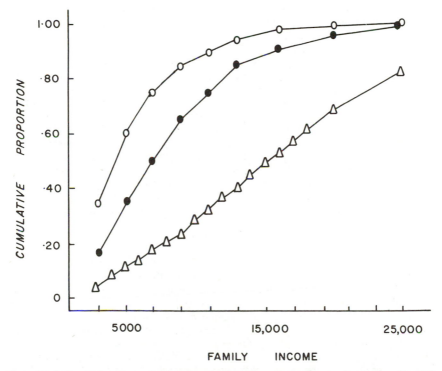

Figure 24–2. Family income as cumulative proportions for neglect-only cases (○—○, N = 10, 477), abuse-only cases (●—●, N = 7, 184) (for all cases where family income was reported), and for all families with children in the population at large (△—△, N = 31, 435, 000).

Table 24–4.   Abuse of children with congenital physical abnormalities.

| Abused Sample | | Control Sample | | | |
Per cent with Congenital Physical Abnormality	N	Per cent with Congenital Physical Abnormality	N	Comments	Source
26%	42			Severe abuse or gross neglect. Australia.	Birrell and Birrell, 1968.
7.5%	134	1.8%	population-at-large	Hospitalized abuse cases. England.	Smith and Hanson, 1974.
18%	28			Severe abuse cases. England.	Holman and Kanwar, 1975.
60%	10	21%	245	All children in both samples premature (birth weight <2500g).U.S.A.	Hunter et al., 1978.
$1.4\%_1$	13,182	$0.7\%_3$	65,500,000	Abuse cases$_1$, neglect cases$_2$, population-at-large$_3$. U.S.A. 1976.	American Humane Association, 1978; Snapper and Ohms, 1977.
$1.5\%_2$	24,426				

Kennell, and Klaus, 1976). Case descriptions of such initial parental reactions suggest that such children might often be abandoned posthaste in social circumstances different from the modern hospital setting. Indeed, defective children have routinely been killed at birth in many human societies (Dickemann, 1975).

Despite these initial negative emotions, parents often develop extremely strong parental affection for handicapped children, and where they do not, it is commonly the case that the infant was prolongedly separated from the mother at or soon after birth. Evidence is mounting that even relatively brief imposition of mother-infant separation (indeed no more than is "routine" in many hospitals) can have long-lasting negative effects on maternal behavior and affection (Klaus & Kennell, 1976; Lozoff et al., 1977). A particularly suggestive result is that of Lynch (1975) who found that 40 per cent of a sample of severely abused children had been separated from their mothers during the first 48 hours after birth compared to just 6 per cent of their non-abused siblings. The duration of such separation is likely to be longer in the case of handicapped children (Sugarman 1977; Irvin et al., 1976) and this factor alone may explain their relatively high risk of subsequent mistreatment.

Another type of child for whom prolonged postpartum separation from the mother is likely is the prematurely born. Numerous studies have shown that premature (body weight at birth <2500 g) children stand at high risk of abuse and neglect (Fomufod, Sinkford, and Louy, 1975; Smith and Hanson, 1974; Martin et al., 1974; Klein and Stern, 1971, Simons et al., 1966; NSPCC, 1975; Hunter et al., 1978; Creighton and Owtram, 1977). Presumably this elevated risk results from the separation though it should be noted that a relatively high proportion of premature infants may be congenitally handicapped (see e.g., Hunter et al., 1978) or otherwise sickly (Kennell and Klaus, 1976).

All of the studies in the preceding paragraph are correlational in nature, so that apparent effects of mother-infant separation might be the result of other correlated characteristics. More direct evidence for the relevance of postpartum separation to maternal attachment and behavior comes from experimental studies with random assignment of mothers to groups differing in contact time with their infants (Klaus and Kennell, 1976; Hales et al., 1977; Lozoff et al., 1977). Only one of these experimental hospital studies has used a large enough number of mothers to detect subsequent differential mistreatment of young. In that study, O'Connor et al. (1977) assigned low-income primiparous women to one of two groups: a "hospital routine" group in which mothers held and fed their children for 20 minutes at 4-hour intervals for the first two days after birth, and a "rooming-in" group in which an additional 6 hours of contact on each of the two days was allowed. In follow-up studies in the second year, 9 of 143 "hospital routine" children were categorized as victims of abuse, neglect, abandonment, or non-organic failure to thrive, compared to 0 of 134 "rooming-in" children. This constitutes a highly significant ($P = .0023$, Fisher Exact Test) reduction in the risk of parental mistreatment as a result of just 12 extra hours of contact in the first two days after birth.

The mother-infant attachment process that is disrupted by neonatal separation is not merely a matter of proximity but involves complex, rather stereotyped behavioral interactions between the two. If given her infant immediately after delivery, the mother typically orients so that the two are "en face" and gazes intently. Within the first few hours after birth the infant exhibits precocious responses including eye contact (visual attentiveness and following) and attentiveness to human speech sounds (Lozoff et al., 1977; Sugarman, 1977; Klaus and Kennell, 1976; Kennell, Voos and Klaus, 1976; Klaus, Trause, and Kennell, 1975). After having had the close physical contact with their infants over the first few days, mothers report developing a feeling that the child is special and wonderful; mothers deprived of this postpartum interaction frequently report feeling emotionally detached from the child (Kennell, Trause, and Klaus, 1975). Defective infants may be incapable of participating normally in these postnatal interactions that evidently facilitate maternal attachment. Blind babies, for example, cannot track their mothers' eye movements nor do they smile and laugh in response to facial cues; one consequence of this is that their mothers may resort to more vigorous tactile interactions to elicit smiles and laughter (Fraiberg, 1974). A mother who does not recognize her infant's blindness may become frustrated and convinced that her baby does not love her, a situation that may in some cases lead rather directly to abuse (e.g., Ounsted, Oppenheimer, and Lindsay, 1974). Other defects and sickliness can interfere with the attachment process by various effects, including direct alteration of the infant's responsiveness and indirect interference by reducing contact as a result of the mother's apprehensiveness about the baby's fragility (Parke and Collmer, 1975; Kennell and Klaus, 1976; Sugarman, 1977). Congenital defects may thus disrupt mother-infant attachment (and presumably elevate the risk of subsequent abuse or neglect) in a variety of ways, without the mother necessarily responding directly to overt indicants of poor infant quality *per se*.

Little is known about the nature of father-infant attachment. Men witnessing the birth of their children reportedly experience powerful emotions descriptively similar to those of the mothers (Greenberg and Morris, 1974). This and other postpartum experiences with one's child may influence the future development of the father-child relationship (Parke and Sawin, 1976; Parke and O'Leary, 1975; Kennell, Voos and Klaus, 1976). Whether this paternal responsiveness can reasonably be considered to have been specifically selected for can, at present, only be speculated upon; cross-cultural examination of adult male-infant interactions, perhaps with special emphasis upon hunter-gatherers, would be of interest. Cognitive factors distinct from the father-child interaction must be relevant to a man's confidence about his paternity, and so are overt resemblances between the child and himself. We would anticipate that such factors should powerfully influence paternal solicitude, but these issues have yet to be investigated systematically.

CONCLUSION

Parental feeling or solicitude is an adaptively variable motivational system that is normally sensitive to (a) specific attachment experiences that are naturally correlated with both biological parenthood and offspring quality, and (b) indicants of parental capacity to rear the young, especially the resource situation. Where parental feeling is weakened by inadequacies in these requisites, it is not surprising that the likelihood of children being physically abused or neglected increases.

ACKNOWLEDGMENTS

We thank P. C. Glick, J. A. Sweet and S. J. Weghorst for discussions, the American Humane Association for use of their data, and the Harry Frank Guggenheim Foundation for research support.

REFERENCES

Alexander, R. D. 1974. The evolution of social behavior. *Ann. Rev. Ecol. Syst.* 5: 325–383.

American Humane Association. 1978. National analysis of official child neglect and abuse reporting. American Humane Assoc., Englewood, Colorado.

Barash, D. P. 1975. Evolutionary aspects of parental behavior: the distraction behavior of the alpine accentor, *Prunella collaris. Wilson Bull.* 87: 367-373.

———. 1976a. Some evolutionary aspects of parental behavior in animals and man. *Amer. J. Psychol.* 89: 195–217.

———. 1976b. Male response to apparent female adultery in the mountain bluebird (*Sialia currucoides*): an evolutionary interpretation. *Amer. Nat.* 110: 1097–1101.

Benson, L. 1968. *Fatherhood: A Sociological Perspective.* Random House, New York.

Birkhead, T. R. 1978. Behavioural adaptations to high density nesting in the common guillemot *Uria aalge. Anim. Behav.* 26: 321–331.

Birrell, R. G., and J. H. W. Birrell. 1968. The maltreatment syndrome in children: a hospital survey. *Med. J. Australia* 2: 1023–1029.

Bowerman, C. E., and D. P. Irish. 1962. Some relationships of stepchildren to their parents. *J. Marr. Fam. Living* 24: 113–121.

Camin, J. H., and W. W. Moss. 1970. Nest parasitism, productivity, and clutch size in purple martins. *Science.* 168: 1000–1002.

Creighton, S. J., and P. J. Owtram. 1977. Child victims of physical abuse. A report on the findings of NSPCC special units' registers. National Society for the Prevention of Cruelty to Children, London.

———. 1978. Personal communication.

Dickemann, M. 1975. Demographic consequences of infanticide in man. *Ann. Rev. Ecol. Syst.* 6: 107–137.

Drotar, D., A. Baskiewicz, N. Irvin, J. Kennell, and M. Klaus. 1975. The adaptation of parents to the birth of an infant with a congenital malformation: a hypothetical model. *Pediat.* 56: 710–717.

Duberman, L. 1975. *The Reconstituted Family: A Study of Remarried Couples and Their Children.* Nelson-Hall, Chicago.

Fergusson, D. M., J. Fleming, and D. P. O'Neill. 1972. Child abuse in New Zealand. Gov't. of New Zealand printer, Wellington.

Fletcher, J. 1974. Attitudes toward defective newborns. *Hastings Center Studies* 2(1): 21–32.

Fomufod, A., S. Sinkford, and V. Louy. 1975. Mother-child separation at birth: a contributing factor in child abuse. *Lancet* 2: 549–550.

Fraiberg, S. 1974. Blind infants and their mothers: an examination of the sign system, p. 215–232. In M. L. Lewis and L. A. Rosenblum (ed.) *The Effect of the Infant on Its Caretaker.* John Wiley & Sons, New York.

Gelles, R. J. 1975. Violence and pregnancy: a note on the extent of the problem and needed services. *Fam. Coord.* 24: 81–86.

Gil, D. 1970. *Violence Against Children: Physical Child Abuse in the United States.* Harvard Univ. press. Cambridge, Mass.

Giovannoni, J. M., and A. Billingsley. 1970. Child neglect among the poor: a study of parental adequacy in families of three ethnic groups. *Child Welfare* 49: 196–204.

Glick, P. C. 1976. Living arrangements of children and young adults. *J. Comp. Fam. Stud.* 7: 321–333.

Greenberg, M., and N. Morris. 1974. Engrossment: the newborn's impact upon the father. *Amer. J. Orthopsychiat.* 44: 520–531.

Hales, D. J., B. Lozoff, R. Sosa, and J. H. Kennell. 1977. Defining the limits of the maternal sensitive period. *Dev. Med. Child Neurol.* 19: 454–461.

Helfer, R. E., and C. H. Kempe (eds). 1976. *Child Abuse and Neglect. The Family and the Community.* Ballinger, Cambridge, Mass.

Hersher, L., A. U. Moore, and J. B. Richmond. 1958. Effect of post partum separation of mother and kid on maternal care in the domestic goat. *Science* 128: 1342–1343.

Holman, R. R., and S. Kanwar. 1975. Early life of the "battered child." *Archs. Dis. Childh.* 50: 78–80.

Hoogland, J. L., and P. W. Sherman. 1976. Advantages and disadvantages of bank swallow *(Riparia riparia)* coloniality. *Ecol. Monog.* 46: 33–58.

Hrdy, S. B. 1976. Care and exploitation of nonhuman primate infants by conspecifics other than the mother. *Adv. Study. Behav.* 6: 101–158.

Hunter, R. S., N. Kilstrom, E. N. Kraybill, and F. Loda. 1978. Antecedents of child abuse and neglect in premature infants: a prospective study in a newborn intensive care unit. *Pediat.* 61: 629–635.

Irvin, N. A., J. H. Kennell, and M. H. Klaus. 1976. Caring for parents of an infant with a congenital malformation, p. 167–208. In M. H. Klaus and J. H. Kennell (ed.) *Maternal-Infant Bonding.* C. V. Mosby, St. Louis.

Kadushin, A. 1974. *Child Welfare Services.* Macmillan, New York.

Kempe, C. H., F. N. Silverman, B. F. Steele, W. Droegemueller, and H. K. Silver. 1962. The battered-child syndrome. *J. Amer. Med. Assoc.* 181: 105–112.

Kennell, J. H., and M. H. Klaus. 1976. Caring for parents of a premature or sick infant, p. 99–156. In M. H. Klaus and J. H. Kennell (ed.) *Maternal-Infant Bonding.* C. V. Mosby, St. Louis.

———, M. A. Trause, and M. H. Klaus. 1975. Evidence for a sensitive period in the human mother, p. 87–101. In *CIBA Foundation Symposium 33.* Elsevier-Excerpta medica-North Holland, Amsterdam.

———, D. Voos and M. H. Klaus. 1976. Parent-infant bonding, p. 25–55. In R. E. Helfer and C. H. Kempe (ed.) *Child Abuse and Neglect. The Family and the Community.* Ballinger, Cambridge, Mass.

Klaus, M. H., and J. H. Kennell (ed.) 1976. *Maternal-Infant Bonding.* C. V. Mosby, St. Louis.

———, M. A. Trause, and J. H. Kennell. 1975. Does human maternal behaviour after delivery show a characteristic pattern? p. 69–85. In *CIBA Foundation Symp. 33.* Elsevier-Excerpta medica-North Holland, Amsterdam.

Klein, M., and L. Stern. 1971. Low birth weight and the battered child syndrome. *Amer. J. Dis. Children* 122: 15–18.

Klopfer, P. H. 1970. Discrimination of young in galagos. *Folia primat.* 13: 137–143.

———. 1971. Mother love: what turns it on? *Amer. Sci.* 49: 404–407.

Kurland, J. A., and S. J. C. Gaulin. 1979. Aspects of sexual selection. I. Parental certainty and reproductive effort. Unpublished manuscript.

Langer, W. 1974. Infanticide: a historical survey. *Hist. Childhood Quart.* 1: 353–365.

Lozoff, B., G. M. Brittenham, M. A. Trause, J. H. Kennell, and M. H. Klaus. 1977. The mother-newborn relationship; limits of adaptability. *J. Pediat.* 91: 1–12.

Lynch, M. A. 1975. Ill-health and child abuse. *Lancet* 2: 317–319.

Martin, H. P. (ed.). 1976. *The Abused Child: a Multidisciplinary Approach to Developmental Issues and Treatment.* Ballinger, Cambridge, Mass.

———, P. Beezley, E. F. Conway, and C. H. Kempe. 1974. The development of abused children. Part I. A review of the literature. Part II. Physical, neurologic, and intellectual outcome. *Adv. Pediat.* 21: 25–73.

Morse, C. W., O. J. Z. Sahler, and S. B. Friedman. 1970. A three-year follow-up study of abused and neglected children. *Amer. J. Dis. Children* 120: 439–446.

Muul, I. 1970. Intra- and inter-familial behaviour of *Glaucomys volans* (Rodentia) following parturition. *Anim. Behav.* 18: 20–25.

National Institute of Mental Health. 1977. Child abuse and neglect programs: practice and theory. U.S. dept. Health, Education & Welfare, Public Health Service. Alcohol, Drug Abuse and Mental

Health Administration, Washington, D.C.

National Society for the Prevention of Cruelty to Children. 1975. Registers of suspected non-accidental injury. A report on registers maintained in Leeds and Manchester by NSPCC special units. NSPCC, London.

O'Connor, S. M., P. M. Vietze, J. B. Hopkins, and W. A. Altemeier. 1977. Post-partum extended maternal-infant contact: subsequent mothering and child health. *Pediat. Res.* 11: 380.

Oliver, J. E. 1975. Microcephaly following baby battering and shaking. *Brit. Med. J.* 2: 262–264.

Ounsted, C., R. Oppenheimer and J. Lindsay. 1974. Aspects of bonding failure: the psychopathology and psychotherapeutic treatment of families of battered children. *Devel. Med. Child Neurol.* 16: 447–456.

Parke, R. D., and C. W. Collmer. 1975. Child abuse: an interdisciplinary analysis, p. 509–590. In E. M. Hetherington (ed.) *Review of Child Development,* vol. 5 Univ. of Chicago Press, Chicago.

———, and S. E. O'Leary. 1975. Family interaction in the newborn period: some findings, some observations, and some unresolved issues, p. 653–663. In K. Riegel and J. Meacham (ed.) *The Developing Individual in a Changing World.* vol. 2. *Social and Environmental Issues.* Morton, The Hague.

———, and D. B. Sawin. 1976. The father's role in infancy: a re-evaluation. *Fam. Coord.* 25: 365–371.

Roskies, E. 1972. *Abnormality and Normality: The Mothering of Thalidomide Children.* Cornell Univ. Press, Ithaca.

Sandgrund, A., R. Gaines, and A. Green. 1974. Child abuse and mental retardation: a problem of cause and effect. *Amer. J. Ment. Defic.* 79: 327–330.

Simons, B., E. F. Downs, M. M. Hurster, and M. Archer. 1966. Child abuse: epidemiological study of medically reported cases. *N.Y. State J. Med.* 66: 2783–2788.

Smith, S. M., and R. Hanson. 1974. 134 battered children: a medical and psychological study. *Brit. Med. J.* 3: 666–670.

———, R. Hanson, and S. Noble. 1974. Social aspects of the battered baby syndrome. *Brit. J. Psychiat.* 125: 568–582.

Snapper, K. J., and J. S. Ohms. 1977. *The status of children.* U.S. dept. Health, Education, & Welfare, Washington, D.C.

Stafford, R., E. Backman, and P. Dibona. 1977. The division of labor among cohabiting and married couples. *J. Marr. Fam.* 39: 43–57.

Stephens, W. N. 1963. *The Family in Cross-Cultural Perspective.* Holt, Rinehart & Winston, New York.

Straus, M. A., R. J. Gelles, and S. K. Steinmetz. 1979. *Behind Closed Doors: Violence in the American Family.* Doubleday/Anchor, New York.

Sugarman, M. 1977. Paranatal influences on maternal-infant attachment. *Amer. J. Orthopsychiat.* 47: 407–421.

Sweet, J. A. 1974. The family living arrangements of children. Univ. Wisconsin Center for Demography and Ecology Working Paper 74–28. Univ. Wisconsin Center for Demography and Ecology, Madison.

Thomas, M. P. 1972. Child abuse and neglect. Part I: Historical overview, legal matrix, and social perspectives. *North Carolina Law Rev.* 50: 293–349.

Trivers, R. L. 1972. Parental investment and sexual selection, p. 136–179. In B. Campbell (ed.) *Sexual Selection and the Descent of Man 1871–1971.* Aldine, Chicago.

———. 1974. Parent-offspring conflict. *Amer. Zool.* 14: 249–264.

U.S. Bureau of the Census, 1977a. Marital status and living arrangements: March 1976. *Current Population Reports P-20,* No. 306. U.S. Gov't. Printing Office, Washington, D.C.

———. 1977b. Marriage, widowhood, and remarriage by family characteristics: June 1975. *Current Population Reports P-20,* No. 312. U.S. Gov't. Printing Office, Washington, D.C.

———. 1978a. Population estimates and projections. *Current Population Reports P-25,* No. 727. U.S. Gov't. Printing Office, Washington, D.C.

———. 1978b. Money income in 1976 of families and persons in the United States. *Current Population Reports P-60,* No. 114. U.S. Gov't Printing Office, Washington, D.C.

———. 1978c. 1976 survey of institutionalized persons: a study of persons receiving long-term care. *Current Population Reports. Special Studies Series P-23,* No. 69. U.S. Gov't Printing Office, Washington, D.C.

Williams, G. C. 1966. *Adaptation and Natural Selection.* Princeton Univ. Press, Princeton.

25

Paternal Confidence and Dowry Competition: A Biocultural Analysis of Purdah

Mildred Dickemann

INTRODUCTION

Why is there such interest in the sexuality of women rather than men? (Yalman, 1963).

In the end, the question must be asked, Why? Why the emphasis on the bodily modesty of women, their seclusion, their chastity, their sexuality, their punishment, their protection, and their control? In short, why the modesty code? (Antoun, 1968).

The question is asked by anthropologists Nur Yalman, in an article "On the Purity of Women in the Castes of Ceylon and Malabar," and Richard Antoun, in an article "On the Modesty of Women in Arab Muslim Villages." Answers offered, both before and since, by social scientists, historians, religious authorities, journalists, travelers, and feminists form an enormous and diverse corpus of materials. I add to it here to present an analysis from the perspective of social biology, which I believe sheds light on some central aspects of the seclusion of women. After a brief description of the forms of female claustration and veiling, I review previous explanations and then propose an explanation in terms of the theory of mating systems. Finally, I will comment on the adequacy of this sociobiological approach to the problem. (A review of some of the historical data is attached as an appendix.)

If women are secluded, veiled, protected, defended, controlled, we must look in explanation either to some value, some valued attribute, possessed by all women, or else to some attribute acquired by claustrated women alone. Claustration either protects a preexisting feminine quality, or it at once creates and maintains such a quality. The latter assumption is the obvious, if unstated, premise from which most explanations proceed: since not all women are so enclosed, both across societies and within societies, therefore the value of individual women varies. Second, admittedly or not, previous investigators are influenced by the testimony of practitioners, from authors of sacred dogma to village informants, and native testimony is overwhelmingly to the effect that what is being protected and controlled is female premarital chastity and marital fidelity. The "attribute" is one that any individual woman may or may not possess, but *only* women may possess. Once we articulate this generally unstated distinction, we note that the socially defined "attribute" of premarital *virginity* and marital *fidelity* is, in reproductive and physiological fact, not a unitary attribute at all. If veiling covers both these preparous and parous states, we must assume that female "purity" is a symbolic and social code, standing for some unitary phenomenon lying behind these states or dependent upon them as well as for the means by which that phenomenon is produced.

These initial remarks may seem belabored to those who have anticipated my conclusion. I make them to demonstrate the value of close attention to unstated aspects of meaning for anthropologists concerned with unraveling function and to show that such attention may often reveal biological content. Read as metaphor for the facts and strategies of human reproduction, traditional and religious justifications for human behaviors make surprising good sense. In hindsight it is odd that, perhaps with some psychoanalytic exceptions, these metaphoric communications have gone so long unread. There is clearly an opportunity here for sustained analysis both of customary speech forms and of other symbolic communications, offering another evidence of the validity of biological perspectives on human behavior.

A GENERAL DEFINITION OF CLAUSTRATION AND VEILING

The claustration of women consists of their concealment, beginning at or before puberty, in areas easily controlled by their natal or affinal kin, to prevent contact with males who are potential sexual partners, whether strangers or relatives. The *se*clusion of women is in fact the *ex*clusion of men. It must be emphasized, however, that the kin who enforce and maintain claustration are both *female* and male, and that women themselves voluntarily seek seclusion. The human socialization process makes claustration far more a matter of values than of force, values shared by the overwhelming majority of both sexes in the contexts in which it occurs.

Intersexual dining and socializing between adults are tabued, with exceptions in some cases for certain categories of kin, and public religion, especially in its most formal, prestigious aspects, is restricted to men. This segregation encourages the construction of architectural devices from the simplest of curtains or screens to the most elaborate of walled courtyards and recessed women's apartments; it may involve special modes of transportation in enclosed vehicles or palankeens, and the guarding of the women's quarters by nightwatchmen, eunuchs, elderly male, or female servants. Slaves, servants, or male members of the kingroup may take over public chores such as marketing or watercarrying, elsewhere assumed by women.

Seclusion is generally accompanied by forms of veiling, which covers, in increasing intensity, the nape of the neck, the hair and top of the head, the forehead, the chin, the face, and finally the whole body from top to toe, the greatest degree of covering being assumed in public and in the presence of certain categories of males. Veils or other stigma of claustration may be prohibited to women of outcaste status, such as slaves, prostitutes, or professional entertainers. Thus the *Koran* (Surah 34:59, M. M. Pickthall trans., my italics): "O prophet! Tell thy wives and thy daughters and the women of the believers to draw their cloaks close round them (when they go abroad). That will be better, *that so they may be recognized and not annoyed*" (cf. de Vaux, 1967). One function of the veil, then, is to state publically that a male or males assume responsibility for the woman's reputation, a statement made in less claustrating cultures by other symbols such as the wedding ring.

Extreme forms of claustration result in an ideal of womanhood as unseen and unheard, reflected in strikingly parallel linguistic devices. In Japanese, another's wife is *okusan, okusama,* literally, interior or secluded (honorific), while *oku* is the interior apartments where she ideally dwells (Bacon, 1902: 254; Nelson, 1974). In Arabic, the triliteral *hrm,* gives *hurma,* respectable woman or wife, *haram,* wife, sacred or sanctuary; *harīm,* the women's quarters or its occupants; and *harām,* sacred, sin, sacrally prohibited (Antoun, 1968). The Nambudiri Brahmins of South India refer to another's wife as *antarjanam,* interior being (Mencher and Goldberg, 1967; Yalman, 1963): presumably independent evolution of a metonomy has occurred, avoiding direct reference to the woman and emphasizing her ideal condition. Again, these examples (vide Cooper [1915]: 122; Kahn, 1972: 34–7; Sorabji, 1908: 97; Urquhart, 1927: 30) suggest the value to sociobiologists of comparative linguistic analyses.

As well as being inculcated through socialization, claustration is supported by customary and formal legal sanctions: penalties for the loss of virginity may be inability to find a husband, rejection by the suitor, or even murder of the girl or her violator by her kinsmen; adulterous wives may suffer similar penalties. Murder of the violated woman or her violator is generally treated with less severity in law than are other homicides, and often with approval in fact. This is the "crime of honor," a concept recognized throughout the Mediterranean basin (Antoun, 1968; Peristiany, ed. 1966; Pitt-Rivers, ed. 1963). In claustrating societies, the notions of "honor" and "shame" have as their core social meanings the defense of, and the loss of sexual morality of the family's women. Each becomes, in Antoun's phrase, a "governing attribute" of one sex:

> Although it would be an exaggeration to say that modesty is an exclusive attribute of the female and honor is an exclusive attribute of the male, the idioms translating these concepts into the uses of every day life cluster around the female on the one hand and the male on the other. . . . the woman, particularly the wife and mother, represents the family in its aspects as a moral corporation through her reputation for modesty. The man preserves his honor, in great part, by protecting the modesty of the woman (Antoun, 1968).

And, as Arabic *'ard* means both "honor" and "woman,"

> the height of immodesty, and thereby the greatest loss of honor, comes with the exposure of that which, above all, must remain protected and hidden, the pudenda. The symbolic unity of honor and modesty in the female genitalia is expressed by the fact that one of the worst insults one man can hurl at another is the phrase "your mother's genitals *(kus immak)*" (Antoun, 1968).

Out of this opposition of male and female sexual roles emerges an extreme duality in the conception of male and female character and in the positive and negative aspects of feminine character as well. Men are assertive, strong, rational, capable of self-control, especially sexual control; women are vulnerable, weak, emotional, uncontrolled, and unreliable, especially sexually. Hence women threaten men as seducers, destroyers of masculine honor, so are typified and deified as temptresses, witches, evil goddesses. Yet as mothers preserving family modesty and honor, they are adored as well: the two Marys are products of a long tradition of at least moderate claustration and concern for feminine sexual purity, with equivalents in other claustrating societies.

It is significant that claustration, where it occurs at all, is always assumed at least by puberty, and that the moment of greatest ritual veiling is the wedding, while young girls and post-menopausal women may enjoy less severe concealment. (Widows, though, where remarriage is discouraged, may symbolize their chastity by rather intense veiling.) Wherever they occur, claustration and veiling are also prestige matters: the higher the socioeconomic status of the family, the greater the intensity of the practice, both as regards degrees of seclusion and of veiling and as regards their duration extending from the centerpoint of puberty toward the termini of birth and death. Women's modesty and the investment of energy into its maintenance become marks of family pride, major indices of public reputation. One example will suffice:

> There is a saying [in Northern India] that you can tell the degree of a family's aristocracy by the height of the windows in the home. The higher the rank, the smaller and higher are the windows and the more secluded the women. An ordinary lady may walk in the garden and hear the birds sing and see the flowers. The higher grade lady may only look at them from her windows, and if she is a very great lady indeed, this even is forbidden her, as the windows are high up near the ceiling, merely slits in the wall for the lighting and ventilation of the room (Cooper [1915]: 121).

In those same societies in which we find intense claustration at the top of the social hierarchy, we are likely to find other expressions of concern for female chastity and fidelity at middle levels, namely, clitoridectomy and infibulation, and virginity tests such as the inspection and display of nuptial sheets. The overlap is not total, as these energetically less expensive forms have a wider distribution beyond the bounds of claustrating societies. Similarly correlated with claustration are the practice of early, often pre-pubertal betrothal and marriage, most common in the upper classes in most cases, and the transfer of wealth (dowry) from the bride's to the groom's family as the major marriage exchange, again an upper class form which is replaced by bride exchange, bride service, and bride price in lower strata. In examining claustration and veiling as here defined, we are focussing upon one end of a continuum of human concern for female sexual morality, milder in many societies but perhaps non-existent in none.

SOME PREVIOUS VIEWS OF THE MATTER

The preceding discussion will serve as a very generalized sketch of the central features of claustration. What explanations have been offered for it? Religious codes mandating the practice often contain both historical and functional explanations. Understandably, adherents of a religion assume the date of promulgation of their sacred laws as the origin of the practice, as most Muslims assume that purdah was created by the Prophet. Religious traditions may be justified not only by the divinity of their commands but by origin tales as well, as the *Koran* is accompanied by folk traditions (Hadith), expressing in personalistic terms the motivations of the ''inventor.'' Masculine sexual jealousy is a common component of such origin tales. An equally common theme is the fear of stranger males, especially conquerors. In North India, where the most intense Indian forms of claustration occurred, the folk explanation commonly repeated by travelers, journalists, and even some anthropologists is that claustration either appeared or became widespread at the time of the Muslim conquest to protect wives and daughters of high status from rape and kidnap. Two embarrassing North Indian customs may be simultaneously justified: since ''Islam forbids abduction of married women as slaves or concubines,'' so child marriage became common, but because Muslims then broke the law and began to abduct married women, therefore claustration was resorted to (Hauswirth, 1932: 64–5, cf. Cormack, 1953: 67). The recurrent themes of folk explanation are obviously not irrelevant to a biological analysis. They appear in even clearer form in some functional explanations provided by sacred dogma itself:

> *Men are in charge of women,* because Allah hath made the one of them to excel the other, and *because they spend of their property (for the support of women).* So good women are the obedient, guarding in secret that which Allah hath guarded (*Koran,* Surah 4:34; M. M. Pickthall, trans., my italics).

Here is an overt recognition of the relation between masculine control over female sexuality and male investment of effort in offspring: an aspect of the phenomenon that has previously gone unnoticed by social scientists, so far as I can discover.

Other modern, secular explanations have been proposed besides those derived from folklore. Unilinear cultural evolutionist theory, deriving ultimately from Morgan and his contemporaries, is by no means out of fashion. Engels, rejecting religious explanations, saw the development of the modern family as part of the ''world historical defeat of the female sex'' (1942: 51). The transition from group marriage and matriarchy to polygynous and monogamous forms retained sexual freedom for men but denied it to women. This theory of early matriarchy and feminine devolution is popular in current feminist writing: it is the product of overgeneralization from scanty signs of early feminine authority, such as the occasional queen, confusion of the queen's role as regent for her infant son with independent power, and the overextension of royal statuses to other classes. (For examples and discussion see Lacey, 1968: 194–216; Pomeroy, 1975: 35ff. on Greece, especially Sparta and Crete; Grimal [1965] on Pharaonic Egypt; Pharr, 1977 but Sansom, 1936: 28–9 on Japan). Yet, to dismiss this evolutionary view entirely is also an oversimplification. If early matriarchy is mythical, still there is historical evidence for an increase in the intensity of claustration over time, corollary to significant declines in female control over property and legal and inheritance rights and to an increase in patrilineality, patrilocality, and unigeniture in the pre-industrial agrarian states of the Islamic Near East, South Asia, and the Far East. Unjustified is the projection backward from early patriliny to a nonexistent matriarchal stage, as is the assumption that this historical change in the social relations of the sexes represents an inevitable unidirectional evolutionary process. In any case, unilineal evolutionary "theories" are not theories at all, but merely descriptive generalizations providing no causal explanation for the presumed progression through time.

Economic explanations focus on the status-grading of claustration as an example of "conspicuous" (or inconspicuous?) "consumption," yet fail to specify why these behaviors should be chosen for status display. Diffusionists, likewise, avoid functional explanation, appealing to some inevitable process of borrowing. Their works have, however, the virtue of revealing the antiquity and the extensive distribution of the practice. One classic psychosocial analysis is Murphy's (1964) discussion of the masculine face-veiling of the Sagaran Tuareg. I will not explore that case here, but note in passing that Tuareg males, though veiled, are never claustrated, and that Tuareg women engage in moderate status-graded veiling. Murphy's Tuareg do call our attention to the universal ethological substrate of veiling, the tendency of both sexes to cover the mouth and face in contexts of modesty, humility, and shame, even of intense emotion. There seems a parallel tendency to cover the head as a symbol of subordinacy. Although Leach (1958) has called attention to the magic of hair, I know of no general ethological analysis of these universal and probably genetic bases out of which the specific forms of veiling everywhere arise. Why, after all, should female sexuality be associated with the head and face?

The approaches to the problem summarized above are non-comparable, referring as they do to different aspects of the practice, its origin, and its local forms. It should be noted that none of them provides a causal hypothesis for the repeated appearance of this phenomenon in human history, in what must be to some degree independent historical contexts. It is, however, in the specifically functional analyses of social anthropologists that we see the social scientist grappling most directly with the sexual content of the custom emphasized above. I comment briefly on two classic analyses, those of Yalman (1963) and Antoun (1968), from which I have already quoted.

Yalman sought to explain not claustration and veiling but some South Indian female puberty ceremonies and the associated obsession with feminine sexual purity. He sees the concern for female sexuality as a means of maintaining caste purity in a context of hypergynous marriage systems. A few quotations will represent his views:

> Thus the sexuality of men receives a generous *carte blanche*. But it always matters what the women do: (a) They may have sexual relations with superior and "pure" men. No harm comes to them in terms of purity. (b) They may have children from "pure" men; or from men of their own caste.
> But, if they engage in sexual relations with men lower than themselves, then they get "internally" polluted. Moreover, they bear "polluted" children.
> . . . It is clear that these rules of hypergamy are directly associated with systems in which membership in the group is acquired through both parents, but where the purity of the group is protected through women. . . . Hence, even though caste membership derives through both parents, there is a built-in asymmetry in all these systems.
> . . . . We are now in a position to understand the overwhelming interest in the sexuality of women rather than men. It is through women (and not men) that the "purity" of the caste-community is ensured and preserved. It is mainly through the women of the group (for the men may be of higher castes) that blood and purity is perpetuated (Yalman, 1963: 42–3).

Yet this analysis fails to explain *why* purity is linked to hypergyny, let alone why hypergyny, with its peculiar inconsistency in approved male and female marriage patterns, exists. Further, Yalman's limitation of his analysis to caste societies denies its general applicability. As he concludes, ''I certainly do not claim that customs concerning female purity must always be traced to caste. . . . There may be many reasons why certain societies single out the purity of women for attention.'' Yet, given this admission of inadequacy, there are some important perceptions in his analysis. These are the recognition that, in some way, paternity is involved, that female purity concerns are linked to hypergyny, and that there is a covert system of ''inheritance of purity'' operating through females even in societies whose formal descent systems are patrilineal. All of these are important components of a sociobiological analysis of claustration and its concomitant, female modesty.

In attempting to analyze Middle Eastern female sexual modesty, Antoun (1968) is no more definitive. He appeals to the interaction between Redfieldian ''great'' and ''little'' traditions (an essentially diffusionist position) and to the force of sacred dogma, confessing uncertainty regarding the historical origins of Near Eastern claustration. Reviewing a variety of local village cases in which ideals of feminine purity are in conflict with other social norms, he identifies the differing commitments to the ideal on the part of differing social statuses and of the two sexes. Ultimately, he rejects the concern for blood paternity as an explanatory factor, because he feels the Islamic legal code, with its recognition of fictional paternity, offers contrary evidence. He retreats finally to the ''logic of the beliefs themselves,'' that is, a historical justification of normative behaviors on the basis of pre-existing ideology regarding the attributes of men and women.

Like Yalman, Antoun points to the correlation of claustration and the ideology of feminine purity with other cultural traits: patriliny, child betrothal, and so forth. Neither list of correlates warrants repetition here, as each is based on a single cultural region, hence is in large part demonstrably false. Antoun's conclusion is as pessimistic as Yalman's. He confesses to having examined ''various historical, psychological, and structural explanations for the persistence of the modesty code. . . . No single explanation was regarded as satisfactory.''(For another critique of Antoun and Yalman, and a review of other theories, see Jacobson [1970]: 200–226.)

I have dwelt this long on previous views not merely to emphasize the weaknesses of social scientific approaches but to highlight two central qualities of their failure. Both of these authors are at pains to resolve apparent conflicts between behavior, ideology, and law. Thus, in the Near East, religion speaks clearly of paternity concerns, yet the law allows loopholes for adoption; observed social events appear to be products of a complex mixture of economic, political, and ideological motives, compromising stated principles. The analysts are likewise unable to choose between theories of origin and theories of maintenance, between ultimate and proximal causes. What is at issue here is the assignment of priorities to events in generating explanatory theories, the weighting of the significance of specific events on some basis other than mere frequency. In short, what is absent is a general theoretical framework that discriminates ultimate (phylogenetic) from proximate (ontogenetic) aspects, which is expressed in probabilistic terms, and which recognizes multiple causation.

Secondly, it is clear that these authors, like others venturing into the same area, find themselves continually confronted with the matter of sexuality. Yet each author ultimately rejects the facts of reproduction as analytically central and retreats in defeat. Again, what is lacking is a theoretical framework that makes sense of the obsession with female sexuality. It is precisely these capacities Darwinian theory offers.

The elemental puzzle for all commentators is indeed even more paradoxical than either Yalman or Antoun expresses. It is not just that there is ''such interest in the sexuality of women rather than men'' that confuses. It is that *female* sexuality and sexual purity, *not male,* is a concern of *men,* and indeed it is so in systems characterized by an overriding emphasis on masculine superiority, masculine authority and control, masculine alliance, inheritance, and descent. This is the core paradox that only a theory of mating systems can unravel, illuminating at once the confusion of the anthropologist and the certainties of the *Koran.*

PROBABILITY OF PATERNITY AND DOWRY COMPETITION: A HYPOTHESIS

I have noted that folk and religious traditions about claustration often appear to refer to paternity concerns and that anthropologists likewise have repeatedly found themselves considering paternity as a possible source of the practice. I turn now to the biological literature on "confidence of paternity" or more accurately, probability of paternity, to make sense of the human phenomenon.

Concern for paternity is a consequence of the greater uncertainty of parenthood that males experience especially when fertilization occurs within the female body, while females do not experience such doubt. In these situations, specific mechanisms may evolve as a result of intrasexual competition to increase the inseminating male's probability of paternity, guaranteeing that the energy invested in searching and courtship was not wasted. A variety of such mechanisms occurs in vertebrates and invertebrates, including pre- and post-copulatory guarding of the female, attempts to determine her "virginity" prior to copulation, methods, either behavioral or pheromonic, of inducing receptivity or estrus in the female to increase the likelihood of fertilization, postcopulatory blocks or plugs to prevent inseminations by subsequent males, and finally, behavioral or pheromonic means of aborting or destroying a preexisting zygote or infant of the female that was sired by another male. These devices occur in organisms as diverse as flies and grasshoppers, ducks and doves, mice and langur monkeys (for a review of the literature see Dickemann [1978a]). Before suggesting how this body of data may relate to the human species, I call attention to some general attributes of human mating systems, that will suggest what kinds of probability of paternity mechanisms we might expect in our species and in what contexts (for theory of mating systems, see Campbell, ed., 1972; Emlen and Oring, 1977; Orians, 1969; Wilson, 1975: 314–335).

As in other mammals, human males compete for access to females, experiencing greater variance in reproductive success than the latter. Their lesser physiological investment in sperm production should mean that they are facultatively polygynous. Reliance on internal fertilization results in masculine uncertainty of parenthood. In addition, low efficiency of sperm utilization, low sperm viability, and random mixing of ejaculates in the inseminated female all result in low probability of conception both for each insemination and for each male (Bailey[1977]; Nag, 1972). Hence multiple matings are advantageous to the male whether or not he has sole access to the female.

These considerations are aggravated by the design of the human ovulatory cycle: an absence of seasonality, general asynchrony of females, and the recurrence of ovulation at relatively short intervals make guarding of the female between cycles immensely more rewarding to the male who has the capacity to do so than mere sperm competition through repeated copulations. In addition, long pre- and postnatal female parental effort, especially where lactation may extend up to three years or more and the investment of all this effort in only a single offspring at a time must intensify competition between males not only for access to but for control over females, especially those in pre-conception status. Both the value of each offspring and the level of female investment are high: therefore, the ratio of benefit to cost is high. Almost four years of maternal effort (not including subsequent socialization) may be gained by a single male for his own offspring if he can pay whatever costs are involved in controlling (herding) the female for a month. We should anticipate, then, both pre- and postcopulatory guarding of females to increase probability of paternity through the exclusion of other males and probability of fertilization through repeated copulations.

The degree of investment of energy in confidence of paternity devices should be correlated with the degree to which mating is promiscuous or "bonded." Bonding means fundamentally the intention or existence of male parental care, and human matings are often characterized by significant amounts of male parental care. This effort is more variable than that of the female, being dependent upon the ecological opportunities and consequent social structure of the specific breeding unit. Nevertheless, some paternal contribution, some specifically economic investment is universal in human societies, although it is not universal as regards individual reproducing males. We should expect, then, that Trivers' 1972 prediction would hold for humans: *ceteris paribus,* males who invest more heavily in their offspring should show greater concern for paternal confidence. Trivers restricted his prediction to monogamous males. But this is an artifact of the association between monogamy and paternal care in those species from which he induced his generalization. The human species teaches us that monogamy and paternal care are by no means necessarily associated.

If the above is true, then all human males should show some desire to control the fidelity of their mates even during casual liaisons, and this concern should increase in intensity and duration as the male's investment in his offspring (direct and indirect) increases. I do not review the data for the first assertion here, but I believe it can be shown to be reasonable: sexual jealousy is probably universal in human males, and attempts to control female sexual fidelity are by no means absent from even those societies and subcultures that involve a good deal of female promiscuity and short-term sexual liaisons (see Dickemann [1978]). They are, however, milder than the forms we are considering here.

The importance of male parental care depends upon another and more distinctive human attribute that plays a role in defining the character of confidence of paternity mechanisms, and that is the nature of the human breeding unit, a subject of much sociological disputation and confusion. Whether we call it a "domestic group," a "family," or whatever, the human unit is characterized by extreme variability in size and structure, that is, a capacity to expand into extended corporations usually associated with territory and based on ties of inclusive fitness or to contract to the minimal mother-infant pair. Where they are feasible, nepotistic extensions of the parenting unit enormously increase the capacity for energy investment in care of the young. It is their existence that makes possible the unusual simultaneous occurrence of intense male parental care and high levels of polygyny in some human groups.

But we may go much further than this. The precise cultural definitions of group membership and expected degrees of kin investment of which our species is capable (i.e., kinship systems) make possible cooperation in much more than merely the care and socialization of the young. Human kin groups may take over the competitive searching and courtship roles of the mating pair: they *breed* their members as they breed their cows and camels. It should not surprise us to find that this ready-made organization would also assume responsibility for the control of paternal probability for members in whom they have nepotistic interest. These transfers of function are, I would guess, unique attributes of the human species and seem to me to be striking testimonials to the significance of inclusive fitness in our species.

The basic motivation for the formation of such groups seems to be the necessity to control and defend the means of production in competition against other breeding units. If such a competitive context is sufficient for the evolution of kin altruism in the care of the young, another requirement must prevail in order for polygyny to evolve simultaneously with extended parental care, since polygyny, in a species with a sex ratio near 50:50, must depend on some significant distortion of reproductive access. Biological theory tells us (Orians, 1969; Verner and Willson, 1966; Wilson, 1975; 327 ff.) that polygyny will occur where differences in resource access of males (or their families) are sufficient that a female gains more from association with an already-mated male than from association with an unmated male in a less reproductively advantageous environment. Extreme variance in masculine access to those environmental resources necessary for reproductive success is, of course, the hallmark of pre-industrial stratified human societies. As competition produces increasing differences between families in access to and control over the primary means of production, variance in male *RS* increases by extensions at both ends of the spectrum: while the rich get richer and more politically powerful, poorer males are excluded partially or totally from breeding, not only through the negative survival effects of poverty per se but through higher rates of mortality from warfare and homicide and through incarceration, exile, and castration. Thus the increasing intensity of social stratification increases the benefit to a female of matings with high-status males, that is, hypergyny. The excess of the *totality* of females over the number of *high-status* males, in a pyramidally stratified society, makes harem polygyny possible (cf. Trivers and Willard, 1973; Alexander, 1974). And since kin groups, as we have seen, have already developed kin-inclusive forms of childcare, it is natural that their inclusive fitness interests, in a situation of intense competition for high-status mates, should produce hypergynous competition between families that control the courtship and mating of their sisters and daughters.

This may seem a long digression from claustration. Yet it is precisely those societies with the greatest extremes between rich and poor, in which court and palace enjoy unimagined luxury while the masses live on a level always close to starvation, in which large numbers of beggars, outcasts, floater males, and celibates exist at the bottom while intense polygyny in the form of secondary wives, concubines, and harems occurs at the top that the most extreme forms of claustration, veiling, and incapacitation of women occur. And, as was noted, it is at the top that these forms of control are most intense.

It may at first appear senseless, to those familiar with the female supply networks that existed in these societies, that families should compete for matings of their women with high-status males. In all these claustrating societies, elaborate and often institutionalized systems evolved for the capture of women in warfare, the kidnapping and sale of wives and infants of the very poor, and their transmission through trade networks into the harems of the wealthy and the brothels that served them. This apparent contradiction is resolved by attention to the forms of mating involved. High-status men enjoyed not only promiscuous mating (many kings or lords, for example, having legal access to all subordinate women in their domains) but harem concubinage, while simultaneously holding several secondary wives and a single primary wife. These statuses are clearly distinguished in the linguistic and legal taxonomies of the cultures: the essential difference is the degree of paternal effort promised or given. Thus it is not at all irrational that families, insofar as they were able, should compete to place their daughters in association with upper-level males, regardless of the flood of other females filling their harems. What these families strove for was not merely sexual access to the preferred male's genes but the commitment of significant paternal care to the female and her offspring, including ultimately bequeathal of goods and political preferment to her descendants, which the preferred statuses of concubine and wife denote. For the very poor, placement of a daughter in the king's harem would surely increase her chances of survival and reproductive success over her peers who remained at the lowest levels of society; even she, like her sister in the brothel, might if fortunate find herself chosen as favorite and elevated to the status of preferred concubine or of wife, and her son, in consequence, polygynously powerful. But for the wealthy family, the goal was acceptance of their daughter as a stable primary or secondary consort whose probability of reproductive success was far greater.

Before demonstrating how this competition operated in cultural terms, I would like to underline some of the biologically peculiar, but nevertheless predictable, consequences of this intense mating competition in a stratified context. In a society with high male mortality and reproductive variance, parents should regard the bearing and rearing of boys as a high-risk, high-benefit strategy, and the rearing of girls as of lower risk but lower gain (cf. Trivers, 1972; Hartung, 1976). Female offspring give more reliability of genetic survival but less competitive advantage. However, this proposition presumes that offspring of both sexes operate within the same ecological context, i.e., under the same environmental determinants of mortality and reproduction. But where socioeconomic conditions of the offspring differ, then the relative value of each sex differs: thus in the hypergynous context under discussion, the proposition is reversed. With a hypergynous mating, a female off-spring may convert her own physiologically lower *RS* into the higher *RS* of sons (grandsons of her strategy-designing parents). Further, the hypergynous female's advantage includes the probability that her own female offspring may make further hypergynous matings into a yet higher *RS* stratum. Thus, the rearing of females becomes a long-term rather than a short-term strategy (dependent upon the human cognitive capacity for long-range planning). But it is a high risk, as well as a high-benefit strategy, since the social pyramid has fewer and fewer grooms at the top, and the hypergynous society many suppliant brides. Indeed it is in these situations that the risk may outweigh any possible benefit, and large numbers of fe-males remain celibate or are removed by infanticide in the topmost strata (Alexander, 1974; Dickemann, 1979a).

The obverse of this biologically peculiar but predictable situation is that the competi-tion for high-status grooms, associated with scarce reproductive resources, defines those grooms as the scarce, valuable sex, hence courted rather than courting, more selective than their mates (cf. Trivers, 1972: 153; Dawkins, 1976: 177–8). Desirable high-status grooms, or more exactly their kin groups, can now exact specific requirements from the suppliant family in exchange for the proffered bride. And they do exact a high price, in addition to her physical attractiveness, good health, and intelligence.

This brings us to the specific cultural form of this contest for grooms, and to the final ingredient in this analysis of claustration. The most visible and most widely discussed of these exactions is the dowry, defined here as any net economic benefit to the groom and his family transmitted in exchange from the bride's family. Dowry competition is the human, social structural, expression of the Verner-Willson-Orians effect in a context of regular kin altruism. At a minimum, in the lowest (land-associated) levels engaged in hypergynous competition or in less intensely stratified societies, dowry consists of a trousseau, a tangible piece of capital investment in the future household, materials, and machinery of lifelong worth for the mated pair and their young. The more wealthy may greatly enlarge the trous-seau to include extensive furniture, clothing, heirlooms and jewelry, slave girls, and ser-vants. It is the trousseau that is displayed in procession to the groom's residence, informing the community at large of the economic status of the bride's kin-group. At higher levels, dowry will include a monetary payment, often very large, and sometimes livestock and land as well. Whole provinces with their attached dependents, as we know, were the dow-ries of queens. In addition, in situations of intense competition, the dowry is accompanied by lifelong obligations of support and repetitive gift-giving from the bride's to the groom's family.

This is not the place for an extended analysis of dowry systems. Let me assert however that underneath the often deceptive folk terminologies and the frequent lack of accord be-tween legal systems and customary behavior, I am convinced that it can be demonstrated that in all these societies there was a gradual transition from the net payment of bridewealth in the lowest classes, where the poor paid to acquire reproductively more valuable females, through transitional forms of exchange of equal value, to the payment of dowry or groom-wealth at the top, where, as we have seen, association with higher-status grooms was bought. What this suggests is that, if the data could be obtained, a quantitative expression of the relation between the economics of marriage exchange and the probable relative *RS* of each sex at each level of society could be made.

If the desirable groom exacts a monetary price, he exacts as well something less tangi-ble if no less public. In exchange for the promise of paternal investment of the resources of his higher-status household in the bride and her future offspring, his breeding unit demands a guarantee of high probability of paternity, insofar as it can be assured by the bride's kin. This, I believe, is a component of dowry competition heretofore neglected by most anthro-pologists. We can now understand why the most intense symbolic statement of female chastity-fidelity, one that persists even in societies and families that have little claim to the genuine article, is the bridal veil: a symbolic *bona fides,* true or deceitful, made at the moment of transfer of the woman from her own family to the groom's. We can understand as well the masculine obsession with feminine virginity, apparently characteristic of all stratified societies, seemingly so irrationally focussed on such an infinitesimal number of copulations. And most importantly, we can now see why claustration and veiling are universally status-graded. The higher the groom's status, the greater the degree of paternal investment of effort into his offspring, the greater the groom's demand for probability of paternity, the greater the competition between bridal families to demonstrate and assure confidence of paternity to future grooms.

Of what does this assurance consist? Of a good deal more than virginity at marriage, as will be seen. But first, let me propose that tests of virginity are not 100 per cent reliable, either because of variations in the morphology of the hymen, or its possible non-sexual rupture, or the kin-altruistic machinations of experienced ladies in the bride's kingroup. Consequently these tests are relied upon only by those, in the middle strata of the society, for whom cost-benefit ratios do not warrant any very great energetic investment in confidence of paternity. Where the investment is warranted, much more reliable methods, namely claustration, veiling, and incapacitation, are preferred.

These forms at once control the woman's freedom to engage in sexual activity of her own choosing and at the same time hide her from the gaze and even knowledge of any males who might be tempted to seek or to force copulations with her. I have not attempted here to unravel the difficult puzzle of the relative contributions of these two sources of danger in the evolution of claustration. On the one hand, ideological emphasis on female sexuality would lead one to suspect that women are largely at fault. So would the incapacitation of footbinding. But this may be partly masculine projection. I think it is important to recall that the societies we are examining were characterized not only by arbitrary sexual rights of lords and rulers but by large numbers of masculine floaters and promiscuous semi-floaters, beggars, bandits, outlaws, kidnappers, militia, and resentful slaves and serfs. "Out of sight, out of mind" was probably a sensible proposition for a high-status family in such a society.

I noted intially that the concept of feminine purity conflates premarital chastity and lifelong marital fidelity. To insure the latter, a woman must be more than guarded, she must be socialized to value feminine modesty, to submit to the goals and demands of her future husband and his kin, to maintain the honor of his family, and finally to socialize her own daughters into the ideology of female purity. This is what the public reputation of the bride's family and the formal symbolic displays are intended to attest. Hence a covert, but critical element in dowry competition is a competition to produce and make credible the ability to produce women of modesty. Thus it is that in the highest status groups, girls enter claustration long before menarche, and women continue in it long after menopause. Thus the dual definition of family honor that we have noted in these societies; for men, honor is the capacity and willingness to defend and to enforce the purity of their female kin, which allows them to achieve reproductively successful matings for their daughters and sisters; for women, it is the possession of that which is defended, chastity and fidelity, sexual morality itself. The core of a family's honor is its ability to produce such women.

Again, let me point to some peculiarities of this situation. The emphasis on competition in the mating of females means that in these largely patrilineal groups, kin-inclusive fitness based on genetic relationships to daughters and sisters may be equally or more important to males than their own direct fitness. This is understandable in societies with high masculine mortalities, but it warns us that the overt forms of kinship and inheritance may be misleading as guides to reproductive strategies. (This is, of course, what Yalman was suggesting.) Concomitantly, we are analyzing societies in which masculine upward mobility, achieved through economic or political means, is rare and impermanent. Through dowry competition, the major means of upward mobility, and hence the major upward gene flow, is achieved by women, a point which I believe has gone unnoticed till now. Is there another such peculiar species, in which groups of genetic relatives engage, through manipulation of their females, in confidence-of-paternity competition?

SUMMARY AND CONCLUSIONS

I want to be clear that this very general theory of claustration has not explained many of the specifics of the practice as it appears in various times and places. I have not dealt with the local and regional variations nor the varying degrees to which the practice obtrudes downward into the lower classes. Nor have I dealt with the variation in forms that may be correlated with differing systems of exogamy and endogamy (for India, see Jacobson [1970]: 187–199, 482–498, 508–531). Nor such unusual phenomena as the masculine veiling of the Tuareg nor the husband-wife avoidance that seems inevitably to evolve in conditions of intense claustration. Nor have I attempted here to elaborate in ecological terms exactly why some societies have evolved intense claustration and others only milder forms nor the fate of these practices in industrial societies though I believe that biologists familiar with the literature on mating systems and especially polygyny can read some of that between the lines.

Nevertheless, this analysis does explain the universal features of the phenomenon, both behavioral and ideological: the conjunction of virginity and fidelity, the double standard and the dual code of honor, and the status-grading of the intensity of claustration, while illuminating some previously unidentified aspects of dowry competition. This hypothesis may have even more functional significance for our attempt to develop a theory of human biology if, as I believe, we have here a case of direct economic acquisition of reproductive success. In general, the ethnographic sources that I have used give very little indication that the dowry-producing family gains any reciprocal benefit from its time and energy investment, in the form of economic or political favors. Indeed, in the most extreme cases, as in Northern India, the subordinacy of the bride-giving family and the one-way, upward flow of economic value, are strongly emphasized. If this is so, then the transaction we have been analyzing cannot be reduced to purely economic or political terms. I have proposed that the bride's family, in exchange for dowry gifts and other economic obligations and for its guarantee of paternal confidence to the groom, *is purchasing increased probable RS,* for itself (inclusively), for its daughter and most directly for her as-yet unborn sons. We have here a clear case of the necessity, in Marvin Harris' [1975] words, to conjoin, in our analyses of human behavior, the ''mode of reproduction'' with the ''mode of production,'' in short, to attend to Darwinian theory.

Darwinian theory does, I think I have shown, allow us to answer the initial question: ''Why is there such interest in the sexuality of women rather than men?'' ''Why the emphasis on the bodily modesty of women, their seclusion, their chastity, their sexuality . . . their protection, and their control?'' As the *Koran* had already told us, ''Men are in charge of women . . . because they spend of their property for the support of women. So good women are the obedient, guarding in secret that which Allah hath guarded.''

Appendix A: A NOTE ON FOOTBINDING

Footbinding, which was invented sometime from the late Tang to early Sung Dynasty, spread during the subsequent Sung and Yüan and had become general by the Ming Dynasty (1368–1644 A.D.). While some more psychologically oriented authors, van Gulik (1974) among them, deny its function as a claustrating device, focussing only on the erotic and esthetic connotations that it acquired, most social scientists and many Chinese authors are explicit that it was a means of restricting movement. Thus Lang (1946: 45–6) asserts: ''Whatever the origin, the purpose was clear. Bound feet kept women at home, made them safer, less movable property. . . . *Nu Erh Ching*, one of the numerous books about virtuous women, is . . . explicit: 'Feet are bound, not to make them beautiful as a curved bow, but to restrain the women when they go outdoors.''' The intensity of footbinding varied both by region and by status, in precisely the same manner as do other forms of claustration. The very wealthy woman strove for a foot so small that "the longest walk she would take was from one room to the next, and she was obliged to sit down after walking a few steps on her marble floors. I have seen those whose feet were but two inches long upon the sole . . . . Only the very rich can afford to be so helpless as such feet render their possessor, and there are not many who are very rich'' (Fielde, 1887: 30). When moving short distances, these women leaned on a cane or a servant or were carried on the backs of natural-footed female slaves. Middle-class women were able to walk four or five miles a day (Fielde, 1887: 30). Among the poor, there was greater variation, both in the presence or absence of binding and its degree. The urban poor were more likely to be bound-footed than rural women, as is true of other forms of claustration as well. Perhaps most village women were large-footed, many of them merely wrapping their feet tightly to resemble the true deformation when going to town or festival or during their wedding ceremonies. Others began footbinding later than the higher-status woman, thus producing a larger, though nevertheless deformed foot. In the north of China, however, rural women had bound feet sufficiently crippled that it was necessary for them to do agricultural labor on their knees (Davin, 1975; Nevius, 1869: 201–3).

The practice was variable in regard to prostitutes and courtesans, though it seems that a bound-footed courtesan was more desirable (Fielde, 1887: 31; Lang, 1946: 45–6; Nevius, 1869: 201–3). Slaves generally were natural-footed, as were Hakka women, and the out-caste "beggar" women of Kiangsu and Anhui were expressly forbidden to engage in the practice (Ch'ü, 1965: 130). By Ch'ing Dynasty, footbinding had reached its greatest extent and intensity: one Chinese historian referred to the period as "the age of small feet fools" (Ropp, 1976: 5–6). In spite of the fact that footbinding focuses upon the opposite end of the human body than that involved in veiling, these parallels with other forms of control, both in evolution and in distribution, lead to the conclusion that it is a claustrating device. It appears less unique if placed in the context of other attempts to incapacitate through the modification of feminine shoes, such as the high geta of the Japanese courtesan or the high heel of the incapacitated modern Western woman.

Appendix B: BRIEF OVERVIEW OF OLD WORLD CLAUSTRATION, INCAPACITATION, AND VEILING

While there is no space here for a thorough presentation of the distribution and evolution of these customs, a brief review of some of the historical data may give some sense of the descriptive data involved. Some degree of control and claustration of women appears almost with the appearance of civilization, though it is difficult to determine its precise nature. Although many authorities agree that women's legal and political status was higher during the Old Babylonian period than subsequently (Batto, 1974; Harris, 1966; Oppenheim, 1964: 77), nevertheless, harems and concubinage existed, at least for kings, in addition to the queen and secondary wives (Batto, 1974). Batto believes he may have discovered, in analysis of documents from Mari, the earliest reference to veiling (Batto, 1974: 39). This society shows other familiar aspects of the pattern: legal documents reveal demand for virginity and virginity tests, at marriage: the Code of Hammurapi imposed the death penalty for a girl who was unchaste while still in her father's house. Dowry competition also existed among the wealthy: excess daughters of kings, nobles and the upper merchant class were sent with dowry and other financial support into religious establishments as lifelong celibates (Batto, 1974; Harris, 1964). By middle Assyrian times, there is clear record of veiling in legal documents that required that wives and daughters of free men cover their heads when outside, but prohibited prostitutes, temple slaves, and servants from doing so. The first certain record of eunuchs employed to guard harems appears here (Oppenheim, 1964: 104). But nothing is known of the life of women of lower status, other than their appearance as slaves in private households, as harem servants, and as serfs and weavers attached to temple and palace. Some were war captives, but others were sold into slavery as wives and children of debtors or famine victims (Batto, 1974: 28; Crawford, 1973; Oppenheim, 1964: 75–6, 96–7, 107). Other scattered evidence of veiling can be found in later periods: a study of surviving art would uncover more. Thus, the Kouyunjik reliefs of Sennacherib (705–681 B.C.) depicting the flight of Luli from Phoenician Tyre, show women with heads completely covered except for the face (Harden, 1963: 124, 132, Plate 50). Biblical veiling is something of a conundrum too. Women traveled with their faces uncovered, but Rebecca veiled herself on first meeting her betrothed (Genesis 24: 65) and both the veil and latticed windows appear in Canticles (2:9, 5:7). But emphasis on female virginity is clear: the nuptial cloth was used as legal evidence and the unchaste bride was stoned to death (Deuteronomy 22: 13–21). Whatever the situation at this time, veiling became common in post-biblical Judaism as the Mishnah (ca. 200 A.D.) describes Persian and Arabic women veiling during the Sabbath.

I have mentioned the latticed window: architectural history can yield important clues to claustration. By Biblical times, both styles of claustrating architecture are present: the second storey with narrow or latticed windows, the common Phoenician (Harden, 1963: 132, Pl. 61) and Biblical (Judges 5:28; 2 Kings 9:30) form, and the walled or interior courtyard, probably represented by an early house model from Babylonian Mari (Mallowan, 1965: 85).

I do not review Egyptian materials here, but Vercoutter's [1965] careful analysis suggests that its reputation for matriliny and feminine freedom may be undeserved. Greek history also seems to involve increasing claustration from Mycenean to Classical times, though there are great difficulties in the interpretation of Homeric and non-Athenian materials. Pomeroy (1975: 35–42) maintains that the legal codes of Sparta, Cretan Gortyn, and Athens reveal a chronological decline in the legal status of women. Homeric epics depict women as modest, chaste, traveling in public with escorts, apparently unveiled. Many secondary wives and concubines appear and female slaves captured in war (Lacey, 1968: 39–47; Pomeroy, 1975: 18–31). Classical Athenian forms, after the seventh century B.C., are clearer though there is still much dispute about details. The respectable Athenian woman was moderately veiled. A head veil, *xalyptra*, was rarely worn, instead a fold of the outer garment (*himation*) was brought over the head, and if occasion demanded, across the face, thus producing a favorite gesture of classical sculptors, the raised hand with drapery of the modest girl. Respectable women seem to have kept head hair covered in public, in contrast to courtesans and slaves, though in less formal context only the nape of the neck might be veiled. But high-status women rarely left their homes: when they did they might be escorted by a servant carrying a parasol, but they relied on slaves to run errands, carry water and do other external chores and were excluded from most public events except religious festivals, almost certainly from the theater and games. The upper-status ideal was that the free woman be seen only by closely related men; the women's quarters (*gynecea*) consisted of rooms either at the rear of the house or in the upper storey. Wealthy country landowners might have walled gardens. Older women had some slight increase in freedom, but only the poor were seen regularly outside the house, in retail trade, small manufactures, going to wetnurse, and in the country doing agricultural labor (de Vaux, 1967; Lacey, 1968: 138, 168–171, 175; Pomeroy, 1975: 78 ff., 238; Seltman, 1957: 94, 97). Polygyny occurred, but large harems do not seem to have been common nor were eunuchs used. Prostitution was of all grades from street prostitution to the well-known *hetaira* (Licht, 1969: 296ff.). These women were foreigners, slaves, girls too poor to marry, or the illegitimate offspring of slave girls and their owners. The rest of the pattern is familiar: dowry competition was intense in the upper classes, virginity highly valued and adultery severely punished, and the ideological definition of woman as merely vessel for her husband's seed, dependent upon father, brother and sons was predictably present (Flaceliere, 1962: 101–61; Lacey, 1968 passim; Levy, 1963; Pomeroy, 1975 passim). Aristotle himself recognized a correlation between claustration and political structure: "A magistracy which controls the boys or the women . . . is suited to an aristocracy rather than to a democracy; for how can the magistrates prevent the wives of the poor from going out of doors? Neither is it an oligarchical office; for the wives of the oligarchs are too fine to be controlled" (*Politica*, Book 4 Chap. 15: 1229–30).

Improvement in female freedom is said to have occurred during the Hellenistic period, but I have not reviewed the literature on this or on Roman and Byzantine periods. By Christian times, the face veil had been adopted by Jews, Christians, and Arabs at least in some communities in Greece, Yemen, and elsewhere. Arabs employed a veil covering all but the eyes, and their women traveled in covered camel-borne litters (de Vaux, 1967).

The evolution of Islamic claustration and veiling is again a matter of dispute among scholars, conservative religious scholars tending to regard them as unchanged since the time of the Prophet, and modernizing scholars in favor of relaxation proposing that extreme forms are not truly Islamic but developed or diffused at a later date. However, the evidence reviewed above and the *Koran* itself make clear that veiling was a common practice of respectable women (cf. von Grunebaum, 1954: 174). The less severe claustration of early Islam may merely reflect the middle rather than upper-class origins of the sect; however, women were originally educated, prayed in the mosque with men and had some public authority. Nor is there any clear early evidence for the totally concealing modern *burka*. Harem claustration appeared with the first Ummayyad Caliphs (Walid II, 473–4 A.D.) as did eunuch guards, apparently copied from Byzantium (Hitti, 1953: 228–9; Khan, 1972: 31). Some authorities maintain complete claustration of respectable women had developed by the time of Harun al-Rashid (786–809 A.D.) (Levy, 1957: 127; von Grunebaum, 1954: 175). Al-Mutawakkil (847–861 A.D.) decreed complete segregation of the sexes at public ceremonies. By the 900s, women had been excluded from most mosques (Levy, 1957: 125–131). Learning, like singing and dancing, became appropriate only to concubines and courtesans (Hitti, 1953: 342). Hitti (1953: 333) dates full claustration a littler later, in the tenth century. The influence of Byzantium and Persia, the latter especially at the Abbasid court, is noted by most authorities. By the mid-thirteenth century, in any case, claustration was entrenched and intense: Islamic scholars debated whether female hands and feet could be seen in public, while veiling, at least in Persia, was forbidden to slaves and other women of low status (de Vaux, 1967; Khan, 1972: 26–34; von Grunebaum, 1954: 155–56, 174–5; Yarshater, 1967). (Khan supports his reconstruction with architectural evidence, but more can be done here.)

Other aspects of the pattern are more or less clear. Patrilineal emphasis in inheritance had developed by the middle Abbasids (Khan, 1972: 50, footnote); by the eighteenth and nineteenth centuries women of middle and upper status regularly sacrificed their inheritance rights, guaranteed them by the *Koran*, to their brothers (Levy, 1957: 244–46; Rosenfeld, 1958, 1960; Yarshater, 1967). I believe it can be shown that dowry competition evolved in the upper strata, again in contradiction to Koranic marriage rules (Cooper [1915]: 34; Fernea, 1976: 130–31; Jacobson, 1973: 217–18; Patai [1956]: 274–5; Smock and Youssef, 1977); at least some upper-class elites practiced child betrothal and marriage (Churchill, 1967).

There was, however, much variation over this vast region: Egypt is reported to have been less restrictive until the fifteenth century (Smock and Youssef, 1977); Persia until the sixteenth–seventeeth centuries (Yarshater, 1967); and Lebanon was reported to be less limiting until modern times (Patai, [1956]: 222–23). Jennings (1973, 1975), in a study of Anatolian Ottoman legal records, emphasizes the difficulty of generalizing from women's degree of claustration to their legal status. The reverse is also true: we do not know what the association of these various measures is. Some of these reports may be special pleading or the product of difficulties in making comparative judgments. Some may be the product of uneven attention to social class variation in each locale and especially inadequate attention to the upper classes. Nevertheless, there does seem to be a general consensus that claustration increased in severity from the Abbasids down to the eighteenth or nineteenth century.

One other continuity may be mentioned, that is, the growth of slavery on a scale far exceeding that of the Greeks: prevalent since Babylonian times, it had evolved into a large trading operation by the Ummayyad Dynasty. A prince might regularly hold about a thousand slaves in his retinue; a private in the army might have from one to ten as servants. Slave routes supplying slave girls and eunuchs led from southern Europe, India and Africa; poor Muslims sold their children into slavery although this was forbidden by Islam. This superabundance increased under the late Ummayyads and early Abbasids, and several Caliphs were themselves sons of slave concubines. The Abbasid Harun al-Rashid (786–809 A.D.) had 7,000 eunuchs in his service: Al-Muktadir (908-932 A.D.) had 11,000 mostly Greeks and Sudanese. Of concubines, Al-Mutawwakil, (847–851 A.D.) is reputed to have had 4,000; other figures for harems range from 200 to 6,000 women (Hitti, 1953: 303, 341–43; Kahn, 1972: 38–9; Lane 1973: 183–86, 194; Levy, 1957: 76, 81ff.). It seems clear that levels of concubinage and slavery far exceeded those of Athenian Greece.

Received doctrine has it that "It was the Mohammedans who brought the 'purdah' system, or the seclusion of women, into India. Before the invasion of these warlike people the women of India went about freely" (Cooper [1915]: 102). The greater intensity and universality of claustration in the North of India than in the South conveniently accords with the greater impact of Islam. Yet even in recent centuries it is not evident that Muslims secluded their women more than others. Indeed, North Indian Muslims blamed the Rajput nobility for carrying the practice to greater extremes than did any Muslims (Rothfeld [n.d.]: 26, 86–7). These quarrels have little relation to historical reality.

The *Rig Veda* may depict men and unmarried women in free association, but the *Arthashastra* of the Mauryan Period (322–183 B.C.) records closely guarded harems, illegal entry into which was punished by burning alive, while rules and fines controlled women who left their houses without their husbands' permissions. Even if reduced to poverty, formerly upper-class women moved outside at dawn and dusk to avoid being seen. Polygyny, dowry, brideprice, and wife capture are all mentioned in the *Rig Veda*, before 900 B.C., as are dancing girls and slave girls (Basham, 1967: 119, 169, 174); during the same period, the first accounts of *satidaha* or widow immolation appear. Referred to in both the *Ramayana* and the *Mahabharata*, it became more common after the Period of Invasions (ca. 1–200 A.D.) (Basham, 1967: 188–90); Hauswirth, 1932: 50–61; Narain, 1967).

By about 1 A.D., women along with "Sudras and servants" had been forbidden to hear or to study the Vedas and were restricted to lesser literature, kitchen gods, husband worship, and the Tantric sects (paralleling the local saint worship of Islamic women). Failure to marry one's daughter before her puberty became a grave sin for the father, divorce became impossible for upper-class women, and woman's subservience to male kinsmen was clearly defined (Basham, 1967: 174; Hauswirth, 1932: 23–34). Polygyny had become the rule for those who could afford it; slave girls and prostitution are frequently referred to, a slave trade having been established with the Roman Empire (Basham, 1967: 154, 174–5).

There is controversy regarding the covering of women during these early periods because of ambiguities of art and the omissions of literature. Sculpture at Bharhut and Sanchi (second–first centuries B.C.) shows "wealthy ladies, naked to the waist, lean[ing] from their balconies to watch processions. . . ." "In some literary sources there are references to married women wearing veils, but there is no evidence that these were normally more than head coverings . . ."; "early Arab travellers remarked that queens were often to be seen in Hindu courts without veils," and in some sources respectable women attended temples and festivals without escorts. Nevertheless, "the ancient Indian attitude to women was . . . ambivalent. She was at once a goddess and a slave, a saint and a strumpet" (Basham, 1967: 180–83, 214). Again, architectural developments are suggestive: after the Gupta Period, flat roofs on which the family slept appear. Windows and balconies appear very early but are not covered with lattice until the Medieval Period (Basham, 1967: 204).

By Medieval times (after 540 A.D.), hypergynous dowry marriage had become the rule in upper and middle classes; Derrett (1964) believes upper-class female infanticide probably began during this period as a result of dowry competition. Widow remarriage, even for virgins, was prohibited; legal and inheritance rights of women steadily declined (Basham, 1967: 147–49; 187–88).

Prostitution is referred to from ancient times, and by the Middle Ages, an elaborate courtesan role, comparable to that of the Greek hetaira, had evolved, requiring training in literature, arts, and sports. In addition to his own harem of wives and concubines, the king retained salaried prostitutes for his own and his courtiers' use. State brothels were established and devadasis or temple prostitutes were legally recognized, some temples having hundreds on their staffs (Basham, 1967: 180, 184–87, 387; Derrett, 1964). Slavery, temporary and permanent, was a part of Indian life from Vedic times, and by the date of the *Arthashastra* included war captives who were not ransomed and those sold into slavery for debt or crime. The Laws of Manu permitted the sale of one's children only during dire emergency. Slave trade with the Roman Empire began at least by the early centuries A.D.; foreigners are reported selling their children to Hindus during the Medieval Period, and the slave trade continued into recent times in both directions, with Indian pilgrims to Mecca transporting children for sale (Basham, 1967: 137, 164; Derrett, 1964; Levy, 1957: 81ff.).

As elsewhere, Indian claustration seems to be correlated with polygyny, dowry competition, and class stratificaton. It is instructive that none of the polyandrous societies of India claustrate their women to the degree that their polygynous neighbors do. If these Indian events can be dismissed as the product of a long series of contacts with Greeks, Persians, Scythians, Kushans, Huns, and other even more mysterious invaders from the Middle Eastern regions, the famous South Indian case of the Nanbudiri Brahmins is less easy to attribute to diffusion and appears to authorities to be independently evolved. A landed aristocracy of Kerala, in a political system comparable to feudal Europe, the Nambudiris claustrated both married and celibate women in separate apartments; even wedding festivals were observed from behind screens. Although they went with breasts uncovered at home, women left the house covered "with a long piece of cloth, leaving only the head and feet exposed. One end of the cloth is so held up in the hand which holds also the . . . umbrella" (Yalman, 1963, quoting Iyer, 1912) as to hide her face. She was preceded by a Nayar maidservant who called out to disperse people from her path. Women left their homes, in any case, only to visit temples or for occasional social visits: they rarely visited natal villages after marriage. The unchaste woman was stripped of her umbrella and covering cloth and outcasted (Yalman, 1963). The context of this claustration and veiling was predictable: strong emphasis on patrilineal inheritance and patrilocality, intense dowry competition, and the only regular primogeniture reported from South India. Only the first son could marry; subsequent sons formed liaisons with women of lower-ranking castes or remained celibate. Excess Nambudiri women remained celibate all or most of their lives (Mencher, 1966a, 1966b; Mencher and Goldberg, 1967; Jacobson, 1973: 528–31).

Data relevant to the history of Chinese claustration have been synthesized by van Gulik (1974). Both he and Ropp (1976) present a picture of increasing intensity. As far back as Former Chou Dynasty (1500–771 B.C.), women of royalty and nobility were segregated in their own apartments, served meals separately, and observed festivals from behind screens. Young girls were also secluded; virginity was a prerequisite for principal wife. Polygyny already involved formal distinctions between primary and secondary wives and concubines. The latter were supervised by court ladies; an upper-class or noble bride brought concubines with her as part of her dowry, a custom continuing down to modern times. Apparently commoners did not yet participate in these customs, however (van Gulik, 1974: 11–21).

By Later Chou Dynasty (770–222 B.C.) a literature of female obedience had begun to appear: female chastity and the complete separation of the sexes were enjoined; the "three obediences" of a woman to father, husband, son were idealized. Respectable married women traveled in covered chariot, going out only to visit tombs and temples. Ideally they saw their husbands only at mealtimes and in bed although they might be present behind screens while their husbands entertained guests. Music, dancing, and literacy were abandoned by respectable women, and the professional female musician developed. Such women were sent by the wealthy as gifts and bribes to princes, judges, and other officials to add to their harems. Eunuchs supervised the king's harem. Common prostitution also developed: public brothels and tea houses were a response to the appearance of a mercantile class, which often bought its concubines from them (Kiang, 1935: 224–7; van Gulik, 1974: 29–106).

During Chin or Former Han Dynasty (221 B.C.–24 A.D.) women wore a shoulder shawl and covered their heads when outside the home (van Gulik, 1974: 64). Sometime between Tang and Sung Dynasties (908–1279 A.D.), footbinding was invented, becoming general by the Ming Dynasty. The role of footbinding as a form of claustration is reviewed in Appendix A. From Sung Dynasty onward, modesty required a high collar concealing the neck and a gown that disguised the shape of the female body (Cooper [1915] :223).

By Tang Dynasty (618–907 A.D.), a "full hetaira complex" of educated courtesans, playing important roles in literature and politics, had evolved. Palace agents recruited concubines and servants, while military brothels served lower-ranking officials and officers. One source mentions 3,000 women in the Palace harem. An increase in brothels and wine shops was accompanied by traffic in kidnapping and sale of girls; numerous poor women became prostitutes when outcasted or condemned as criminals or the relatives of criminals or when taken captive in war (van Gulik, 1974: 108, 206).

By Yüan Dynasty (1279–1367 A.D.), the ideology of seclusion and separation of women was intense: heavy religious penalties were believed to result from touching a woman, entering her quarters, debauching a married woman, a virgin, or nun. Divorce was disgraceful as was the remarriage of widows. During the Ming Dynasty (1369–1644 A.D.), the first Westerners entering China reported the absence of middle or upper-class women on the streets, except for the very elderly; nor were they seen by visitors to their homes. Travelling was in enclosed chairs. Homes of the wealthy had the familiar courtyard pattern, with separate rooms for each wife and her offspring. In the upper classes, early betrothal was the rule (Cooper [1915]: 212 ff.; van Gulik, 1974: 246–9, 265). With government approval monuments might be erected to virtuous widows who remained chaste; the greatest virtue was to commit suicide. Female infanticide was intense, as was the slave trade, especially in females (Dickemann, 1979a, Ropp, 1976). Although dowry competition is not reflected in my historical sources, it may be inferred, as it was intense in recent times. Polygyny continued to be popular; many officials and merchants in the nineteenth century and early twentieth centuries had from two to ten wives (Cooper, [1915]: 230, 242–4; Dickemann, 1978).

An evolutionary process is less clear in my Japanese sources. Patriliny, polygyny, and slavery are reported from the first two centuries A.D.; by the 600s, after the introduction of Buddhism, daughters of the nobility entered nunneries, hypergyny occurred in the upper classes, while slavery, banditry, and piracy were widespread (Sansom, 1936: 1–98). By Heian period (782–1068 A.D.) polygyny was common in the upper class; the empress, secondary wives, and concubines of the Emperor were housed in a "forbidden interior" of the palace, with the residences of ladies-in-waiting nearby (Sansom, 1936: 191). The Confucian ideology of yin-yang, of the three obediences and husband worship had been adopted: the upper-class woman was lodged inside a "twilight world" that Morris compares to Islamic purdah, hidden by screens and interior apartments from all men except her father and husband, travelling only in covered carriages. "Ghosts and women had best remain invisible," remarks a contemporary lady. However, women were still at this period able to inherit and own property, and virginity was expected only for principal wives. Yet dowry competition and child betrothal were already characteristic of the upper classes. Professional courtesans appeared during this period, but their social role was as yet unimportant (Morris, 1969: 211 ff.). Private, public, and temple slaves originated in war captives, criminals, and the sale of women and children of the poor (Fréderic, 1972: 115–17; Sansom, 1936: 214–15). Degrees of claustration and veiling in later periods are not entirely clear. Sansom (1936: 294) illustrates a picture of Kyoto ladies out-of-doors, after a Kamakura scroll, in which the hair but not the face is covered; one covers the side of her face in the Grecian gesture of modesty, with her garment in her raised hand. Fréderic (1972: 82) describes the wide hat with gauze veil worn outside the house by feminine nobility in the twelfth century. All sources agree, however, that women's status declined during the thirteenth and four-teenth centuries: as unigeniture became common, their property rights declined, divorce became the husband's prerogative, and widow chastity was idealized. The Emperor's daughters, who could not find marriage partners of sufficient status, entered nunneries; many samurai women spent their lives as celibate servants to the nobility. The term "oku-san" for wife dates from the Muromachi Period (1382–1573). By Tokugawa times, men had legal right to kill adulterous wives (Akroyd, 1959; Asakawa, 1955; Bacon, 1902; Brown, 1966; Fréderic, 1972: 47–48; Sansom, 1936, 354–56). Nevertheless, among middle-class and rural women claustration seems never to have assumed the intensity that it did in China, India, or the Middle East (Akroyd, 1959; Bacon, 1902; Koyama et al., 1967; Pharr, 1977). If medieval Japan was more claustrating than medieval Europe, it seems to fall closer to that feudal nation than to the other societies reviewed.

Finally, a word on Europe itself. If Medieval European women, especially in the North, moved about more publicly and with less veiling, even in the middle and upper classes, the ideal of feminine modesty was still present. Covering of the head except for the face with the wimple or a corner of the cloak or shawl, and even some chin covering were common; according to Higounet [1966] usual in France in the twelfth century, and even the face veil was not unusual though it was often gauzy (see illustrations throughout Grimal, ed. [1966], v. 2). In Southern Europe, in Greece, Italy, and especially Portugal and Spain, extreme claustration was usual among elites, persisting down to modern times and being carried to the New World. These are precisely those areas of Europe in which concubinage, slavery, and the Mediterranean slave trade network were most elaborate and enduring, in which patrilineal emphasis in residence and inheritance, the double standard and the crime of honor most accord with our previous definition. In Spain, face veiling in some public contexts persisted down to the eighteenth century (Pescatello, 1976: 20–47, 144–50, 168–73). Throughout Europe, we know that dowry competition and early betrothal charac-terized the upper classes, and the ideology of woman as weak and sexually unreliable is familiar. Still, the greater economic independence of North European women and their greater ability to control and inherit property are consonant with their lesser claustration than in the South (vide Dickemann, 1979b).

This cursory survey, while extremely uneven, does suggest possibilities for compara-tive analysis. If we view societies as points on a scale of intensity in claustration, we note a number of other coordinated variables. Besides the closely linked and expectable hy-pergyny and dowry competition, patrilocal-patrilineal emphasis in residence and inheri-tance, intensity of polygyny, extent of prostitution, concubinage and female slavery, extent of masculine involvement in banditry, vagrancy and criminality all seem to be involved. Even such apparently unrelated phenomena as evolution of the hetaira role, elite male ho-mosexuality and male prostitution, the public restaurant, and the theater are in some way part of this complex. Some of the ecological precursors are explored elsewhere (Dickemann [1978b]); it is likely, however, that a single continuum will ultimately prove to be too simple a model to explain all of the historical variation reflected here.

ACKNOWLEDGEMENTS

This paper was made possible by a grant from the Harry Frank Guggenheim Founda-tion, for which I am very grateful. Thanks especially to John Hartung for advice, encouragement, and assistance with sources, to S. Parker and L. Tiger for encouragement, to P. Brucker, D. Jacobson, and R. Trivers for assistance with sources and to M. Rebhan for editorial advice and support. Responsibility for my errors is my own.

REFERENCES

Akroyd, Joyce. 1959. Women in feudal Japan. Transactions, *Asiatic Society of Japan*, 3rd. ser., no.7 (November): 31–68.

Alexander, Richard. 1974. The evolution of social behavior. *Ann. Rev. Ecol. System*. v. 5: 325–83.

Antoun, Richard T. 1968. On the modesty of women in Arab Muslim villages: a study in the accommodation of traditions. *Amer. Anthropol*. v. 70 no. 4 (August 1968): 671–97.

Aristotle. 1941. "Politica," trans. B. Jowett. In McKern, R., ed. *The Basic Works of Aristotle*, pp. 1113–1316. New York: Random House.

Asakawa, Kan-ichi, ed. and trans. 1955. *The Documents of Iriki*. 2nd ed. Tokyo: Japan Society for the Promotion of Science.

Bacon, Alice M. 1902. *Japanese Girls and Women*. Rev. and enl. ed. Boston: Houghton, Mifflin.

Bailey, Robert C. [1977]. Variations in the human live-birth sex ratio. [ms.]

Basham, A. L. 1967. *The Wonder That Was India: A Survey of the History and Culture of the Indian Sub-continent Before the Coming of the Muslims*. 3rd rev. ed. London: Sidgwick and Jackson.

Batto, Bernard F. 1974. *Studies on the Women at Mari*. Baltimore: Johns Hopkins University Press.

Brown, Keith. 1966. Dōzoku and the ideology of descent in rural Japan. *Amer. anthropol*. v. 68 no. 5 (Oct. 1966): 1129–51.

Campbell, Bernard, ed. 1972. *Sexual Selection and the Descent of Man 1871–1971*. Chicago: Aldine.

Ch'ü, T'ung-tsu. 1965. *Law and Society in Traditional China*. Paris: Mouton.

Cooper, Elizabeth [1915]. *The Harem and the Purdah: Studies of Oriental Women*. New York: Century Co.

Cormack, Margaret. 1953. *The Hindu Woman*. New York: Teachers College, Columbia University Press.

Crawford, H.E.W. 1973. Mesopotamia's invisible exports in the third millennium B.C. *World Archaeol*. v. 5 no. 2 (Oct. 1973): 232–41.

Davin, Delia. 1975. Women in the countryside of China. In Wolf, M. and Witke, R., eds. *Women in Chinese Society*, pp. 243–73. Stanford: Stanford University Press.

Dawkins, Richard. 1976. *The Selfish Gene*. New York: Oxford University Press.

de Vaux, Roland. 1967. Sur le voile des femmes dans l'Orient ancien: a propos d'un bas-relief de Palmyre. *Bible et Orient*, pp. 407–23. Paris Éditions du Cerf.

Derrett, J. Duncan. 1964. Law and the social order in India before the Muhammadan conquests. *J. Econ. Soc. Hist. Orient*. v. 7 pt. 1 (April 1964): 73–120.

Dickemann, Mildred. 1979a. Female infanticide and the reproductive strategies of stratified human societies: a preliminary model. In Chagnon, N.A. and Irons, W., eds. *Evolutionary Biology and Human Social Behavior: an Anthropological Perspective*. North Scituate, Mass.: Duxbury Press.

———[1978]. Confidence of paternity mechanisms in the human species.

———1979. The ecology of mating systems in hypergynous dowry societies. *Social Science Information*. v. 18 no.2:163–195.

Emlen, Stephen T., and Oring, L. W. 1977. Ecology, sexual selection, and the evolution of mating systems. *Science* v 197 (15 July 1977): 215–23.

Engels, Frederick. 1942. *The Origin of the Family, Private Property and the State in the Light of the Researches of Lewis H. Morgan*. [n.t.] (Trans. of the 4th ed., 1891). New York: International Publishers.

Fernea, Elizabeth W. 1976. *A Street in Marrakech*. Garden City, New York: Doubleday, Anchor Books.

Fielde, Adele M. 1887. *Pagoda Shadows: Studies from Life in China*. London: T. Ogilvie Smith.

Flaceliere, Robert. 1962. *Love in Ancient Greece*. Trans. J. Cleugh. New York: Crown.

Fréderic, Louis. 1972. *Daily Life in Japan at the Time of the Samurai, 1185–1603*. Trans. E. M. Lowe. London: Geo. Allen and Unwin.

Grimal, Pierre, ed. [1965–66]. *Histoire mondiale de la femme*. v. 1: Prehistoire et antiquité; v. 2: *L'Occident, des Celtes a la Renassance*. Paris: Nouvelle Librairie de France.

Harden, Donald. 1963. *The Phoenicians*. Rev. ed. London: Thames and Hudson.

Harris, Marvin [1975]. Mode of production and mode of reproduction. Paper presented at an A.A.A.S. Symposium on Mode of Production, New York, 1975.

Harris, Rivkah. 1964. The nadîtu-woman. In Adams, R. M., ed. *Studies presented to A. Leo Oppenheim*, pp. 106–35. Chicago: Oriental Institute of the University of Chicago.

———. 1966. Review of Histoire mondiale de la femme. Prehistoire et antiquité, sous la direction de Pierre Grimal. *J. Econ. Soc. Hist. Orient*, v. 9, pt.3 (December 1966): 308–9.

Hartung, John. 1976. On natural selection and the inheritance of wealth. *Curr. Anthropol*. v. 17, no. 4 (Dec. 1976): 607–22.

Hauswirth, Frieda. 1932. *Purdah: the Status of Indian Women*. London: Kegan Paul, Trench, Trubner.

Higounet, Arlette [1966]. La femme du Moyen Age en France dans la vie politique, economique et sociale. In Grimal, P. ed. *Histoire mondiale de la femme*. v. 2. pp. 135–84. Paris: Nouvelle Librairie de France.

Hitti, Philip K. 1953. *History of the Arabs: From the Earliest Times to the Present*. London: MacMillan.

Jacobson, Dorothy A. 1973. *Hidden Faces: Hindu and Muslim Purdah in a Central Indian Village*. (Ph.D. Diss., Columbia University, 1970). Ann Arbor: University Microfilms International, 2 vols. No. 73–116,209.

Jennings, Ronald C. 1973. Loans and credit in early 17th century Ottoman judicial records: the Sharia court of Anatolian Kayseri. *J. Econ. Soc. Hist. Orient*. v. 16, pts. 2–3 (Dec. 1973): 168–216.

———. 1975. Women in early 17th century Ottoman judicial records—the Sharia court of Anatolian Kayseri, *J. Econ. Soc. Hist. Orient*. v. 18, pt. 1 (Jan. 1975): 53–114.

Khan, Mazhar ul Haq. 1972. *Purdah and Polygamy: a study in the Social Pathology of the Muslim Society*. Peshawar: Nashiran-e-Ilm-o-Taraqiyet.

Kiang, Kang-hu. 1935. *Chinese Civilization: an Introduction to Sinology*. Shanghai: Chung Hwa Book.

Koyama, Takashi, Nakamura, H., and Hiramatsu, M. 1967. Japan. In Patai, R. ed. *Women in the Modern World*, pp. 290–314. New York: Free Press.

Lacey, W. K. 1968. *The Family in Classical Greece*. London: Thames and Hudson.

Lane, Edward W. 1973. *An Account of the Manners and Customs of the Modern Egyptians*, 5th ed., E. S. Poole, ed. (published 1860.) New York: Dover.

Lang, Olga. 1946. *Chinese Family and Society*. New Haven: Yale University Press.

Leach, Edmund R. 1958. Magical hair. *J. Royal Anthropol. Inst*. v. 88, pt. 2 (July-Dec. 1958): 147–64.

Levy, Harry L. 1963. Inheritance and dowry in classical Athens. In Pitt-Rivers, J.ed. *Mediterranean Countrymen: Essays in the Social Anthropology of the Mediterranean*, pp. 137–43. Paris: Mouton.

Levy, Reuben. 1957. *The Social Structure of Islam*. Cambridge: Cambridge University Press.

Licht, Hans [Paul Brandt]. 1969. *Sexual Life in Ancient Greece*. Trans. J. H. Freese. London: Panther Books.

Mallowan, M. E. L. 1965. *Early Mesopotamia and Iran*. London: Thames and Hudson.

Mencher, Joan P. 1966a. Kerala and Madras: a comparative study of ecology and social structure. *Ethnology* v. 5, no. 2 (April 1966): 135–71.

———. 1966. Namboodiri Brahmins: an analysis of a traditional elite in Kerala. *J. Asian African Stud*. v. 1, no. 3 (July 1966): 183–96.

Mencher, Joan P., and Goldberg, H. 1967. Kinship and marriage regulations among the Namboodiri Brahmins of Kerala. *Man* N.S., v. 2, no. 1 (Mar. 1967): 87–106.

Morris, Ivan. 1969. *The World of the Shining Prince: Court Life in Ancient Japan*. Baltimore, Md.: Penguin Books.

Murphy, Robert F. 1964. Social distance and the veil. *Amer. Anthropol*. v. 66, no. 6, pt. 1 (Dec. 1964): 1257–74.

Nag, Moni. 1972. Sex, culture and human fertility: India and the United States. *Curr. Anthropol*. v. 13, no. 2 (April 1972); 231–37.

Narain, Vatsala. 1967. India. In Patai, R., ed. *Women in the Modern World*, pp. 21–41. New York: Free Press.

Nelson, Andrew N. 1974. *The Modern Reader's Japanese-English Character Dictionary*. 2nd rev.ed. Rutland, Vt.: Charles E. Tuttle.

Nevius, John L. 1869. *China and the Chinese: a general description of the country and its inhabitants*. ... New York: Harper and Bros.

Oppenheim, A. Leo. 1964. *Ancient Mesopotamia: Portrait of a Dead Civilization*. Chicago: University of Chicago Press.

Orians, Gordon H. 1969. On the evolution of mating systems in birds and mammals. *Amer. Natural.* v. 103, no. 934 (Nov.–Dec. 1969): 589–603.

Patai, Raphel, ed. [1956]. *The Republic of Lebanon*. Vol. 1. (HRAF-46 Patai-6). New Haven: Human Relations Area Files.

Peristiany, J. G., ed. 1966. *Honour and Shame: the Values of Mediterranean Society:* Chicago: University of Chicago Press.

Pescatello, Ann M. 1976. *Power and Pawn: the Female in Iberian Families, Societies, and Cultures*. Westport, Conn.: Greenwood Press.

Pharr, Susan J. 1977. Japan: historical and contemporary perspectives. In Giele, J. Z., and Smock. A. C. eds. *Women: Roles and Status in Eight Countries*, 217–255. New York: Wiley.

Pickthall, Mohammed M., ed. and trans. 1953. *The Meaning of the Glorious Koran, an Explanatory Translation*, New York: New American Library.

Pitt-Rivers, Julian, ed. 1963. *Mediterranean Countrymen: Essays in the Social Anthropology of the Mediterranean*. Paris: Mouton.

Pomeroy, Sarah B. 1975. *Goddesses, Whores, Wives, and Slaves: Women in Classical Antiquity*. New York: Schocken.

Ropp, Paul S. 1976. The seeds of change, reflections on the condition of women in the early and mid-Ch'ing. *Signs.* v. 2, no. 1 (Autumn 1976); 5–34.

Rosenfeld, Henry. 1958. Processes of structural change within the Arab village extended family. *Amer. Anthropol.* v. 60, no. 6, pt. 1 (Dec. 1958): 1127–39.

——. 1960. On determinants of the status of Arab village women. *Man* v. 60 (May 1960): 66–70.

Rothfeld, Otto [n.d.]. *Women of India*. London: Simpkin, Marshall Hamilton, Kent.

Sansom, George B. 1936. *Japan, a Short Cultural History*. New York: D. Appleton Century.

Seltman, Charles. 1957. *Women in Antiquity*. 2nd ed., rev. London: Pan.

Smock, Audrey C., and Youssef, N. H. 1977. Egypt: from seclusion to limited participation. In Giele, J. Z., and Smock, A. C., eds. *Women: Roles and Status in Eight Countries*, pp. 33–79. New York: Wiley.

Sorabji, Cornelia. 1908. *Between the Twilights: Being Studies of Indian Women by One of Themselves*. London: Harper and Bros.

Trivers, Robert L. 1972. Parental investment and sexual selection. In Campbell, B., ed. *Sexual Selection and the Descent of Man, 1871–1971*, Chicago: Aldine. pp. 136–79.

——, and Willard, D. C. 1973, Natural selection of parental ability to vary the sex ratio of offspring. *Science.* v. 179 (5 Jan. 1973): 90-92.

Urquhart, Margaret M. 1927. *Women of Bengal: a Study of the Hindu Pardanasins of Calcutta*. 3rd. ed. Calcutta: Association Press (Y.M.C.A.).

van Gulik, Robert H. 1974. *Sexual Life in Ancient China; a Preliminary Survey of Chinese Sex and Society From ca. 1500 B.C. till 1644 A.D.* Leiden: E. J. Brill.

Vercoutter, Jean [1965]. La femme en Egypte ancienne. In Grimal, P., ed. *Histoire mondiale de la femme*. v. 1: Prehistoire et antiquité, pp. 61–152. Paris: Nouvelle Librairie de France.

Verner, Jared, and Willson, M. F. 1966. The influence of habits on mating systems of North American passerine birds. *Ecology.* v. 47, no. 1 (Winter 1966): 143–47.

von Grunebaum, Gustave E. 1954, *Medieval Islam*. 2nd ed., Chicago: University of Chicago Press.

Wilson, Edward O. 1975. *Sociobiology: The New Synthesis*. Cambridge Mass.: The Belknap Press of Harvard University.

Yalman, Nur. 1963. On the purity of women in the castes of Ceylon and Malabar. *J. Roy. Anthropol. Soc.* v. 93, pt. 1 (Jan–June 1963): 25–58.

Yarshater, Latifeh. 1967. Iran. In Patai, R., ed. *Women in the Modern World*, pp. 61–73. New York: Free Press.

26.

Uterine vs. Agnatic Kinship Variability and Associated Cousin Marriage Preferences: An Evolutionary Biological Analysis

Mark Flinn

Neglect of biological factors — doubtless related to a fine reaction against naive forms of biological determinism — has been a serious mistake in the strategy of social science. (Marion J. Levy Jr., 1963: ix)

Extrafamilial conflicts and coincidences of genetic interest may often have become significant influences on behavioral evolution, partly as extensions or ramifications from a substantial parent-offspring bond, because strong familial bonds provide a basis for subsequent recognition of different classes of relatives. For this and other reasons, an evolutionary theory of familial interactions may represent a core item in analyses of complex social systems. (Richard D. Alexander, 1974: 339)

INTRODUCTION

Recent modifications of evolutionary theory (Fisher, 1958; Hamilton, 1964; Williams, 1966) have generated a number of theoretical arguments concerning family and kinship behavior (Orians, 1969; Trivers, 1972, 1974; Alexander, 1974). These developments in biological theory appear to have far-reaching ramifications for the study of human social behavior (Alexander, 1971 – 1979; Fox, 1975; Wilson, 1975; Chagnon and Irons, 1979) although considerable controversy surrounds this issue. Regardless of the outcome, a number of important questions have been raised that are, at this point, very difficult to dismiss without further empirical analysis.

Tests of the new biological theories of family and kinship behavior depend upon knowledge of how genealogical relationships (or more precisely, their proximate cues in social learning) correlate with individual behavior affecting the distribution and flow of reproductive resources. Unfortunately, such data are lacking for most human societies. However, many ethnographies provide extensive descriptions of how kinship affects patterns of inheritance and alliance. These anthropological studies provide a useful data base for comparative cross-cultural analysis of family and kinship behavior from a biological perspective.

Current biological models of family and kinship behavior are largely based on Hamilton's (1964) theory of the evolution of social behavior by kin selection (see also West-Eberhard, 1975). Kin selection theory explains how tendencies to help related individuals survive and reproduce (referred to as ''altruism'') can be adaptive, that is, favored by natural selection. Hamilton proposed that it is adaptive for an individual (the ''altruist'') to assist another individual (the ''recipient'') when $k > 1/r$ (where r equals the coefficient of genetic relatedness between altruist and recipient, and k equals the benefit to the recipient divided by the cost to the altruist of the assistance, in terms of reproductive consequences, i.e., genetic representation in future generations). Kin selection theory suggests an ultimate reason for behavioral tendencies such as assisting a brother during an axe-fight (Chagnon and Bugos, 1979), leaving inheritances to offspring, and other potentially altruistic behav-

439

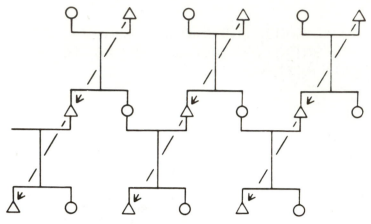

Figure 26–1.   Agnatic flow of altruism. Males dispense benefits to their own putative offspring (arrows represent the flow of altruism among male kin).

ior. Reciprocity, or the exchange of altruism, can also be adaptive (Trivers, 1971) and is likely to be an important consideration among kin (Alexander, 1975) as well as non-kin.

Variability of human kinship behavior and its apparent inconsistencies with genetic relatedness stand as a major challenge to the recent developments in evolutionary biology such as kin selection theory. Sahlins, for example, has asserted that "no system of human kinship relations is organized in accord with the genetic coefficients of relationship as known to sociobiologists" (1976:57). An especially prominent and important aspect of human kinship variability is the occurrence of different patterns of behavior among maternal kin compared to paternal kin—or more precisely, uterine kin compared to agnatic kin (uterine relatives are kin related through female genealogical links; agnatic kin are related through male genealogical links).

In societies with strong agnatic kinship biases', males primarily interact with, dispense altruism to, and receive altruism from kin related through males (e.g., brothers, father's brothers, father's brother's sons, etc.). Females are often relegated to subordinate roles in both their natal and their marital households. Residence after marriage is usually with the husband's kin (see Fig. 26–1).

In societies with uterine kinship biases, individuals (both males and females) primarily interact with, dispense altruism to, and receive altruism from kin related through females (e.g., siblings, mother's brothers. sister's children), sometimes to the extent that fathers rarely interact with or dispense benefits to their own offspring. The male parental role is instead provided to varying degrees by the mother's brother (hereafter referred to as the avunculate or the "mother's brother's phenomenon") (see Fig. 26–2).

Although uterine kinship biases are fairly common throughout the world and are highly significant for both theoretical and pragmatic reasons (e.g., King, 1945; Richards, 1950; Schneider and Gough, 1961; Gonzalez, 1969), there is no widely accepted explanation for their occurrence.

Uterine vs. agnatic kinship variability presents a critical test of a kin selection model of family and kinship behavior, because if no differences exist between uterine and agnatic kin

---

'By agnatic or uterine "kinship bias" I mean a reproductively significant behavior that occurs asymmetrically between uterine and agnatic kin (e.g., altruism (such as inheritances) is preferentially distributed to agnatic kin). This behavioral definition may include many anthropological concepts such as descent practices and residence preferences whose reproductive significance has yet to be documented.

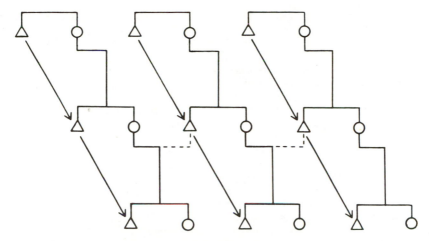

Figure 26–2.   Uterine flow of altruism. Males dispense benefits to sister's offspring. Genealogical links through males may be uncertain—see text. Arrows represent the flow of altruism among male kin.

in the degree of relatedness (r) or the costs and benefits of altruism (k) then uterine or agnatic kinship biases of altruism would clearly be inconsistent with kin selection theory. The prominent parental role of the mother's brother in some societies is a particularly conspicuous anomaly.

AN APPARENT ANOMALY: THE MOTHER'S BROTHER PHENOMENON

In a number of human societies, males tend to behave more altruistically towards their sister's offspring than to their own putative offspring. The male parental role[2] is directed primarily towards uterine nephews and nieces. For example, among the Djuka: "The head of the family is not the father, but the mother's oldest male relative — her brother or her mother's brother. . . . All children belong to their mother's family, and are subject to the authority of her brother or maternal uncle" (Kahn, 1931: 120). Among the Trobrianders, "A child belongs to the clan and village community of its mother, and wealth, as well as social position, are inherited, not from father to son, but from maternal uncle to nephew" (Malinowski, 1961:55). Among the Plateau Tonga, "mother's brother has authority and should be treated with respect. . . . It is also the mother's brother who has the greatest obligation to provide support and assistance" (Colson, 1961:86). And among the Nayar, the mother's brother,

> As their legal guardian he exercised the rights and obligations which normally accrue to the legal father in the higher patrilineal castes of India. He was responsible for his nephews' training in the laws and morality of their caste, in literacy, in agricultural work, and in military skills. Much of this training he often dispensed in

[2]The use of "parental role" here concerns the actual flow of altruism, not just ideology or "sentiments." Although positive sentiments often may be associated with the flow of altruism, the two are not necessarily concomitant. See Ryder and Blackman's (1970) critique of theories relating sentiments and family structure, such as Levi-Strauss (1949), Radcliffe-Brown (1924), and Homans and Schneider (1955).

person either before or after he became karavanan. He was responsible for maintaining the junior men of his taravad and for guarding, and, if possible, augmenting the ancestral property on their behalf. In turn they owed him obedience, loyalty, and submissive respect (Gough, 1961a:348).

Fathers, on the other hand, do not play as important a parental role. Among the Nayar, "an individual man had no legal rights in a particular wife and her children. He did not reside with them, did not eat regularly with them, did not produce with or for them, and he did not customarily distribute goods to his children" (Gough, 1961a:363). In societies in which the avunculate is prominent, fathers are frequently referred to as "outsiders" or "mother's husbands."

The mother's brother–sister's son pattern of altruism appears inconsistent with kin selection theory, for a man is more closely related to his own offspring ($r = 1/2$) than to his sister's offspring ($r = 1/4$ or $1/8$, on average). Moreover, in many societies, this anomalous pattern of mother's brother–sister's son altruism extends to discriminate between uterine and agnatic kin, in general, although the mother's brother is occasionally an important figure in societies with agnatic kinship biases (e.g., patrilineal descent).

Clearly, this apparent anomaly of the mother's brother phenomenon and other uterine kinship biases presents a critical test of the validity of biological theory for human social behavior.

Alexander's Resolution

R. D. Alexander (1974, 1977a) provides a resolution to the paradox of the mother's brother phenomenon, based on the differences in male and female proximate mechanisms for recognizing offspring. Noting that adultery, promiscuity, and/or divorce were reported as relatively frequent in societies with the mother's brother phenomenon, Alexander proposed that uncertainty of paternity might cause a male to be more closely related to his sister's offspring (with whom relatedness was certain) than to his spouse's offspring (who might have been sired by another male). This led him to hypothesize that "lowered confidence of paternity causes a man's sister's offspring to assume increased importance as recipients of nepotistic benefits, and in some cases to exceed spouse's offspring in this regard (hence, the importance of the 'mother's brother' to dependent children in many societies . . .)" (Alexander, 1977a:310). Paternity uncertainty decreases genetic relatedness through putative agnatic kinship links but does not decrease genetic relatedness through uterine kinship links.

A few anthropologists have also suggested that lowered confidence of paternity results in the mother's brother phenomenon. For example, Kahn (1931) describes this relationship among the Djuka:

> The head of the family is not the father, but the mother's oldest male relative — her brother or her mother's brother. *The father is technically unrelated to his children.* As a matter of biological fact, he can never be sure of his paternity, whereas maternity is never in doubt. All children belong to their mother's family, and are subject to the authority of her brother or her maternal uncle. The former is more closely related to them than any other male. (Kahn, 1931: 120)

Rodman provides many insights in his study of family structure among lower socio-economic class Trinidadians:

> The stress upon genealogical relationship is another factor which leads to a child's stronger bond with his mother's kin than with his father's kin. Since the identity of the biological father may well be in doubt, the father's kin as well as the father will be chary about whether the child is related to them:
>
> (Who would have more affection for a child, the mother's or the father's family?) . . . The mother will say, that is my grandchild, but the man's mother, she might

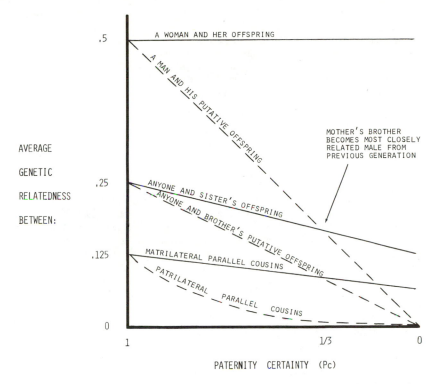

Figure 26–3.   Adapted from Alexander, 1977a:320. The differential effect of paternity certainty on relatedness among uterine vs. agnatic kin. Uterine kin are represented by solid lines; agnatic kin are represented by dashed lines.

> say the child is not my son's own, any man can make a child . . . Some people say they have more love for a sister child than for a brother child. (Why is that?) Because you're certain your sister's child is hers, but [your brother's] . . . can' be certain, may be another boy's. . . . That's why is so important to have only one husband. If married to one and friendin' with another, may not know whose child it is. Woman may say is his child, and maybe he won' own it. (Rodman, 1971:138–139)

Some of the early cultural evolutionists (e.g., Morgan; Bachofen) proposed a progression from an early condition of "primitive promiscuity" to subsequent stages of matriarchal social organization. However, these cultural evolution schemes postulated a historical not an adaptive-functional relationship.

Alexander's resolution is based on a modification of the kin selection equation, $k > 1/r \times Pc$ (where Pc equals paternity certainty[3]). This model predicts that men will be more altruistic towards their sister's offspring than their own offspring when confidence of paternity drops below $1/3$ (Figure 26–3).[4]

[3]For purposes of simplification, paternity certainty and the probability of paternity for a putative father are assumed to be equal, which is the case if the proximate mechanisms for ascertaining probability of paternity are accurate.

[4]Greene (1978) computes the paternity threshold at .268 by assuming that the probability of sibs sharing the same father is equal to the probability of paternity squared (Pc^2). Greene's model assumes only one

Alexander's explanation of the mother's brother phenomenon has subsequently been discussed by Greene (1978), Irons, (1979b) and Kurland (1979). However, as yet no comprehensive empirical analysis of Alexander's resolution has been conducted: Alexander (1974, 1977a) cites a few anecdotal cases (there is no other type of data available on this rather delicate subject) and refers to the *Ethnographic Atlas*; Kurland (1979) cites several anecdotal cases; and Greene gives three (unspecified) cases, and "of these three, there was one in each of the three highest categories of promiscuity" (out of a total of four categories) (Greene, 1978:155).

In order to establish a broader empirical base for this important theoretical issue, I conducted a cross-cultural survey. Some of the data had to be gathered by reading through actual ethnographical accounts because the *Ethnographic Atlas* unfortunately does not contain data useful for a reliable test of Alexander's explanation.[5] About 300 societies were surveyed in the following fashion: 150 societies were chosen randomly from the 565 society version of the *Ethnographic Atlas* (Murdock, 1967). These societies were evaluated for "confidence of paternity" by reading HRAF material encoded under #837 (extramarital sex) and #684 (sex and marital offenses). These societies were then evaluated for "source of altruism" (HRAF codes #428, #590–619), "frequency of conjugal bond dissolution" (#580–589) "relation between confidence of paternity and socio-economic status" (#837, #684), and "relation between cousin marriage and socio-economic status" (#580–589). Societies not in the HRAF were evaluated from original sources where possible and coded by checking material indexed under appropriate categories (e.g., adultery), or by searching through the text. Societies with very little pertinent data were rejected and replaced by a society from the closest available area. The final data for the randomly chosen societies — "marital residence," "alternative marital residence," "cousin marriage preference" (with some modifications), "succession," and "descent" were coded from Coult and Haberstein's (1965) *Cross-tabulations of Murdock's World Ethnographic Sample*.

Next, all societies in Coult and Haberstein's cross-tabulations with an indication of a possible uterine kinship bias (i.e., matrilocal, avunculocal, duolocal, or sorolocal for marital and/or alternative marital residence; matrilineal or duolineal for descent; matrilineal for succession) were evaluated for "confidence of paternity," "source of altruism," and the rest of the above variables. Finally, all societies with asymmetric cousin marriage preferences (e.g., matrilateral cross cousin) were evaluated for all of the above variables. The non-random sample was chosen because uterine kinship biases and asymmetric cousin marriage preferences are not very common, and I wanted to investigate as many societies with these phenomena as possible. Because no significant differences were found between the correlations derived from the random and non-random samples,[6] the data were pooled. All analyses are based on the pooled data.

Because most ethnographic accounts of behavior pertaining to some of the variables considered such as "confidence of paternity," and "source of altruism" are anecdotal and often highly ambiguous, evaluation of these variables is necessarily subjective.[7] Moreover,

father could be in common between sibs (Kurland, 1979, also adopts this model). However, if the same males have certain probabilities of paternity for a group of siblings, then the sum of the probabilities of sibs sharing any one father equal Pc. Actual values of the probability of sibs sharing the same father are likely to be predictable based on proximate mechanisms and lie between Pc and O.

[5]Textor's (1967) massive compilation of cross-cultural correlations contains some useful information, such as correlations between premarital sexual activity and some uterine kinship biases (e.g., matrilineal descent), as do Murdock, 1964; Goethals, 1971; Ford, 1945; Ford and Beach, 1951; and Broude and Green, 1976.

[6]All statistical tests reported in this paper were significant for the random and non-random samples separately with the exception of the analysis of variance effects of conjugal dissolution on source of altruism after the effects of confidence of paternity (Footnote[11]).

[7]It is unfortunate that tests of Alexander's resolution must rely on such low-quality data. The only paternity exclusion studies of primitive populations that I know of are on the Yanomamo (Neel and Weiss, 1978) and the !Kung Bushmen. Pc is about .9 for the Yanomamo. Field studies have yet to examine the

the vast array of ethnographic accounts are of variable quality (Flower's problem), have non-universal methodologies, and are occasionally contradictory. Consequently, conclusions drawn from these data must be regarded as tentative, even though it is unlikely that there is any introduced bias in the data favoring validation of the hypotheses tested.

The following procedures were used to detect any such bias: First, the random and non-random samples were compared. As noted above, the correlations obtained from the two samples were not significantly different. Second, because time limitations only allowed about one hour to evaluate each society (I opted for quantity), this potential source of error was checked by comparison with data gathered by more extensive re-analysis (about three hours per society) for 20 societies. The data were 92 per cent consistent (for 20 societies, 101 out of 110 bits of information were the same). Third, repeatability was checked by independent re-analysis of 20 societies by another researcher (Laura Betzig), and the data were not significantly different. In fact, the data were remarkably similar: no coding was different by more than one value, and 47 of 60 codes were the same.[8] Fourth, the data were analyzed for time effects, and none was found (those societies analyzed first were not evaluated differently from those analyzed last). Finally, the large sample size distributed over all of the continental areas, and the analysis of within society variability as well as between society variability, has presumably minimized the effect of diffusion (Galton's problem).[9]

The following are brief examples of the type of anecdotal descriptions used to evaluate confidence of paternity: Among the Truk, "Extramarital affairs are practically universal" (Schneider, 1961:213). Among the Ashanti, "The high incidence of adultery among women . . . is no new thing, as the elaborate scale of adultery damages, which forms part of the traditional legal code, shows" (Fortes, 1950:275). Among the Dobu , "fidelity is very, very rare. Typically his wife will commit adultery with a village 'brother,' he with a village 'sister.'" (Fortune, 1963:277). Among the Nayar, "It is not certain how many husbands a women might have at one time; various writers of the fifteenth to eighteenth centuries mention between three and twelve" as well as receiving "occasional fleeting visits" (Gough, 1961a:358). Thus the adage "no Nayar knows his father" (ibid:364).[10]

The data indicate a strong correlation between behavior that probably generates low confidence of paternity (e.g. adultery, promiscuity, separate residence of mates) and uterine biases in the flow of altruism, such as the mother's brother phenomenon (Table 26–1).

Although cross-cultural data show a fairly convincing correlation between paternity uncertainty and the mother's brother phenomenon, a better test of the biological model would evaluate data on individual behavioral variability. Unfortunately, such data have not been systematically gathered; however, there are occasional anecdotal references. For instance, among the Nayar, "A man is said to have been especially fond of a child whom he knew with reasonable certainty to be his own" (Gough, 1961a:364).

Alexander's explanation of the mother's brother phenomenon is consistent with cross-cultural data on both inter- and intrasocietal variability. However, several aspects of the mother's brother phenomenon remain problematical. First, confidence of paternity is probably not less than $1/3$ in some of the societies in which the mother's brother phenomenon is prevalent (Table 26–1). Alexander suggests that the mother's brother phenomenon can

relationship between the paternity certainty of individuals and their altruistic behavior.

[8]Time limitations allowed only the evaluation of the three major codes: confidence of paternity, source of altruism, and frequency of conjugal dissolution. Two of the twenty societies compared are not in the sample.

[9]I opted for large sample size rather than a controlled sample (cf. Naroll and Cohen, 1970).

[10]Confidence of paternity in these societies was coded as follows (based on the previously described procedure): Truk — moderate; Ashanti — moderate; Dobu — low; Nayar — very low (see appendix). The subjective categories of confidence of paternity were roughly assigned the following hypothetical values of Pc: very low $Pc < 1/3$; low $1/3 < Pc < 2/3$; moderate $2/3 < Pc < 4/5$; high $4/5 < Pc < 1$; very high $Pc > .95$.

Table 26–1.   Confidence of paternity (Pc) and the source of altruism.

CONFIDENCE OF PATERNITY

			VERY LOW	LOW	MODERATE	HIGH	VERY HIGH	ROW TOTAL	
S	AGNATIC BIAS	FATHER AND AGNATIC KIN	0	0	2	27	21	50	(COUNT)
O U R	↑		0.0	0.0	0.7	9.4	7.3	17.4	(% TOTAL)
C E	BALANCED	MIXED- FATHER MAJOR	0	2	22	104	17	145	
			0.0	0.7	7.6	36.1	5.9	50.3	
O F		MIXED	1	8	30	16	3	58	
			0.3	2.8	10.4	5.6	1.0	20.1	
A L T		MIXED- MOTHER'S BROTHER MAJOR	0	3	26	2	0	31	
R U			0.0	1.0	9.0	0.7	0.0	10.7	
I S	UTERINE BIAS	MOTHER'S BROTHER AND UTERINE KIN	2	2	0	0	0	4	
M			0.7	0.7	0.0	0.0	0.0	1.4	
		COLUMN TOTAL	3	15	80	149	41	288	
			1.0	5.2	27.8	51.7	14.2	100.0	

$\chi^2 = 261.00 \quad 16_{df} \quad P < 0.0001$

GAMMA = -0.78918

(ALL STATISTICS WERE COMPUTED USING THE SPSS PROGRAM AT THE PENNSYLVANIA STATE UNIVERSITY COMPUTER FACILITIES)

adaptively occur even if $Pc > \frac{1}{3}$, especially if the males involved are:

> (1) young and childless brothers, (2) brothers estranged from other wives, (3) unusually wealthy or powerful brothers, or (4) brothers who are for other reasons unlikely to be successful with their own offspring . . . Prominence of the avunculate obviously does not require that a man's sister's offspring average a closer relationship to him than his spouse's offspring (1977a:323–324).

However, no empirical analysis of the relationship of these factors to altruistic behavior has been conducted. Second, conjugal ties in societies with uterine kinship biases are notoriously fragile — among the Nayar "marriage was the slenderest of ties" (Gough, 1961a:357), among the Cewa, "marriage ties sit loose" (Richards, 1950:233). The adaptive significance of this correlation has not been examined. Third, the environmental (social and physical) conditions influencing confidence of paternity and hence family structure have not been examined. The following section addresses these issues respectively.

Extensions and Modifications of Alexander's Resolution

In most societies with the mother's brother phenomenon, although confidence of paternity is relatively low, it is probably not low enough to cause a man's sister's children to be more closely related to him than his own putative offspring (i.e., $Pc > \frac{1}{3}$). For instance, among the Mayombe, where the mother's brother phenomenon is fairly pronounced,

> Marriage amongst the Mayombe is described as a system by which a man acquires sex access to a woman, and certain clearly defined rights to her services and those of her adolescent children, in return for a substantial payment in money or goods. The Mayombe husband never acquires full authority over his wife or children, as we shall see, but the marriage payment enables him to remove his bride to his own

> village immediately on marriage; his sex rights over her are exclusive, and payments as damages for adultery are heavy. In the old days, in fact, adultery was a crime punishable by death. (Richards, 1950:215)

It may be however, as Murdock notes, that sanctions against adultery are ''sometimes more honored in the breach than in the observance'' (1949:265). But for some societies, accounts of behavior also suggest that the paternity certainty threshold is likely to be exceeded ($Pc > \frac{1}{3}$). Here, then, the occurrence of the mother's brother phenomenon again seems contradictory to biological theory. Several factors are particularly apposite: pressure from kin, high frequency of divorce, and competition among agnates.

Pressure From Uterine Kin

In many of the societies with the mother's brother phenomenon, males appear to be coerced into behavior (e.g., inheritance distribution) that is congruent with the interests of their uterine kin. For example, among the Menangkebau (a matrilineal society), ''A man could not give self-acquired property to his wife or children except with the consent of his lineage'' (Gough, 1961c:589). With any paternity uncertainty, uterine relatives are more closely related on average than agnatic relatives. Although a man might be more closely related, on average, to his own putative offspring than to his sister's (i.e., $Pc > \frac{1}{3}$), with any paternity uncertainty on the part of his brothers ($Pc < 1$), he will be more closely related on average to his sister's children than to his brother's putative children. (Figure 26–3; see also Kurland, 1979). In this circumstance, a man might want his brothers to behave parentally (i.e., dispense altruism) towards their mutual sister's children. He might therefore support, but perhaps not practice, an ideology that prescribes male parental behavior towards sister's children. If paternity certainty is greater than a third, a man's closest relatives, on average, in the next generation are his putative offspring; however, his uterine relatives are more closely related to his sister's offspring if the paternity of his putative offspring is not absolutely certain ($Pc < 1$) (assuming that the man's wife and potential cuckolder are not closely related to the man's uterine kin).

Thus, a conflict between a man and his uterine kin over the distribution of altruism is predicted to develop when paternity certainty is greater than a third, but less than one ($\frac{1}{3} < Pc < 1$). Such conflict is frequently cited among societies with a uterine kinship bias. Among the Ashanti, a woman

> jealously watches her brother to make sure that he discharges the duties of legal guardian faithfully. . . .'' Hence, ''There is often jealousy between a man's sister and his wife because each is thinking of what he can be made to do for her children. That is why they cannot easily live in the same house. Divorce after many years of marriage is common, and is said to be due very often to the conflict between loyalties towards spouse and towards sibling (Fortes, 1950:263, 275).

Even though ''Ashanti say that no man loves his sisters' children as much as his own children'' (ibid:269), pressure from uterine kin apparently influences men to care for, and leave their inheritance to, sister's children.

The strength, or in some respects the ''corporateness'' of the matrilineal kin group appears to have a significant influence on the outcome of this conflict between a man and his uterine kin. Richards (1950) suggests that the corporate nature of the matrilineal kin group may be associated with the pattern of residence. Where related males are localized, the kin group is strengthened. In general, the ''stronger'' the kin group, the more influence it appears to have on male parental behavior.

Predictably, with the breakdown of matrilineal kin groups during modernization, the mother's brother's phenomenon frequently disappears — apparently the result of increased individual mobility, individual acquisition of property, and the cessation of warfare or trading patterns that cause male absenteeism (Gough, 1961e; Fuller, 1976; Fortes, 1950). However, it is difficult to determine the effect of reduced pressure from uterine kin independent of increased confidence of paternity from accounts of modernization in matrilineal societies. Moreover, modernization involving capitalist economies sometimes generates social situations in which the parental role of the father is diminished, for instance, with migratory wage labor (Gonzalez, 1969; see also Blumberg and Garcia, 1977; Goode, 1970, for discussion of modern economic development and family organization).

But there is another way of testing the hypothesis that pressure from uterine kin causes males to direct altruism towards sister's offspring or other uterine kin. If pressure from uterine kin is an important factor controlling male parental behavior, then those aspects of parental altruism that are more easily controlled by kin should be distributed to a man's sister's offspring, whereas those aspects of parental altruism that are more difficult for kin to control should be distributed to a man's putative offspring. In many matrilineal societies, a man typically must give his heritable possessions such as land to his sister's children but is more likely to be involved in the day-to-day care of his own putative offspring (Richards, 1950; Fortes, 1950, 1969). Furthermore, there is often a discrepancy between actual behavior and ideology in this regard. Males in matrilineal societies frequently dispense benefits to their offspring discreetly, so as to avoid conflict with their uterine kin. Malinowski notes that a "strong tendency of surreptitious patrilineal transmission of property and influence" is common in some matrilineal societies (in Fortune, 1963:xxxi).

Conjugal Instability

As noted earlier, conjugal instability is characteristic of societies with the mother's brother phenomenon. The high frequency of "divorce" (i.e., dissolution of the conjugal or mating relationship) may in itself result in lowered confidence of paternity, or be the consequence of infidelity (a common cause of divorce — Murdock, 1949; Stephans, 1963). Hence, the effect of the frequency of divorce on family structure is difficult to evaluate independent of confidence of paternity. Nonetheless, there are some societies in which confidence of paternity appears to be greater than the $1/3$ threshold, but the frequency of divorce is high (i.e., typically an individual will have been divorced three, four, or more times in a lifetime). In such societies, the parental role of the father is usually reduced compared to the parental role of the father in societies with low rates of divorce (Table 26–2). This is especially true if the offspring remain with the mother after separation (there are a few societies with high divorce rates and an agnatic flow of altruism — e.g., the Kanuri, Cohen, 1967 — but in these societies children often stay with their fathers).

Thus, independent of paternity uncertainty, frequency of divorce may be a significant factor influencing male parental behavior.[11] Biological theory suggests the following reasons: First, altruism dispensed by a man to his offspring might be utilized by his offspring's uterine half-siblings (or other relatives of his ex-wife) who are unrelated to him. Among Barbadians, women usually leave their children from prior unions with maternal relatives because "The man will not accept a woman with children because a man does not support another man's child. Should the true father cease to make payments to the mother, as frequently happens, the new boy friend will fear that his money will be used for such support" (Greenfield, 1966:123) Among Black Caribs,

> When a marriage is terminated, children generally stay with the mother or with one of her maternal relatives. Exceptions to this practice may occur if the woman has several other children by another man. In this case, the father may choose to take his child or children and place them with one of his sisters or with his mother rather than contribute money toward their support which might be used by the mother for her other children as well. (Gonzalez, 1969:70)

[11]Analysis of variance effects of conjugal dissolution frequency is significant ($p < .01$) after confidence of paternity effects.

Table 26–2.   Frequency of conjugal dissolution and the source of altruism.

FREQUENCY OF
CONJUGAL DISSOLUTION

SOURCE OF ALTRUISM		LOW	MODERATE	HIGH		
	FATHER AND AGNATIC KIN	38 13.6	9 3.0	2 0.7	50 17.5	(COUNT) (% TOTAL)
	MIXED–FATHER MAJOR	56 20.3	74 25.9	12 4.2	142 49.7	
	MIXED	4 1.4	42 14.7	13 4.5	59 20.6	
	MIXED–MOTHER'S BROTHER MAJOR	0 0.0	17 5.8	14 4.7	31 10.8	
	MOTHER'S BROTHER AND UTERINE KIN	0 0.0	0 0.0	4 1.4	4 1.4	
	COLUMN TOTAL	99 34.6	142 49.7	45 15.7	286 100.0	

$$\chi^2 = 117.15 \quad 8_{df} \quad P < 0.0001$$

$$\text{GAMMA} = 0.75220$$

Men are apparently reluctant to dispense altruism to their putative children when the altruism is likely to be used to benefit another man's children. This effect of divorce is similar to paternity uncertainty, in that a man is uncertain to what extent his altruism actually benefits his offspring (see also Kurland, 1979).

The second reason why frequency of divorce may affect patterns of altruism is the potential impediment to parental behavior caused by the separate residence of father and offspring. If the distance between residences is such that the cost of parental behavior is greatly increased or makes appropriate parental behavior difficult—perhaps because of the lack of knowledge concerning offspring's needs—then coresiding sister's children may become more advantageous recipients of a male's altruism.

In addition, the reluctance or inability of a male to behave parentally towards his putative offspring makes their mother ever more dependent upon her relatives for her children's support. Among the Ashanti,

> A divorced woman or the mother of a love-child feels entitled to lean more on her brother than one who is married. The brother feels the obligation to provide for his sister's children as fully as he does for his own. Though their father is held by custom to be obliged to support them, divorce often makes him less amenable to their claims on the grounds that a wife and children of an existing marriage require prior consideration. A man whose sister's children live with him can more easily be a kind of a father to them, as well as their legal guardian, if his own children are living elsewhere. (Fortes, 1950:272-3)

Competition Among Agnatic Kin

In strongly patrilineal societies, the role of the mother's brother is somewhat different than in matrilineal societies. Although rarely a primary source of altruism, the mother's brother and other uterine kin are often an individual's close and important social allies. This could be in part because of the absence of competition with them. In agnatically biased societies, a man's father's brothers and father's brother's sons may be his closest competitors for political power, mates, economic assets and other reproductive resources (i.e., altruism). The mother's brother can be an important source of assistance to his sister's son in this competition among agnates because he is not directly involved in the competition, and by helping his nephew he is not jeopardizing his son's standing in the competition (because his uterine nephews and his sons are not agnates). Among the Tswana:

> The close proximity in which they [agnatic kin] live, and the rules of patrilineal succession and inheritance, breed jealousies and conflicts that may prove stronger than the ties of mutual dependence.
> One's maternal kinsmen (ba ga etsho mogolo) are not as a rule involved in the situations just described; they generally (although by no means invariably) belong to some other ward. In consequence, perhaps, they are notoriously more affectionate and devoted than agnates. . . . It is to his maternal uncle perhaps more than anyone else that a man looks to for disinterested advice and aid in times of difficulty; and when disputes arise between father and son, or brother and brother, it is often the uncle that reconciles them or with whom the oppressed child or younger brother goes to live if peace cannot be restored. (Schapera, 1950:144–145)

In summary, at least several factors seem to be relevant to variation in male parental behavior and subsequent family structure: confidence of paternity, pressure from kin, frequency of divorce, and competition among kin. I shall now address the question of what environmental conditions influence these factors.

Environmental Determinants

Richards (1950) suggests that environmental conditions that determine the distribution of heritable property are relevant to variation in family structure:

> The presence or absence of inheritable possessions in the form of land, trees, cattle, or money have been correlated with the type of marriage, and the position of the father as against that of the mother's brother. It has also been associated with the corporate nature of a unit like the western Congo matrilineage, as against the dispersed descent groups of the peoples of Northern Rhodesia. (Richards, 1950:251)

There seem to be two potentially opposing effects generated by heritable property. First, Richards notes that heritable possessions may affect bride price, and that higher bride price might strengthen the position of the father relative to the mother's brother (cf. Gluckman, 1950). Second, the density, location, and type of heritable resources may affect the corporateness of the matrilineal kin group. It might be "the shortage of land and the value of the permanent palm-trees that make members of a matrilineage willing to live together in one closely organized group" (Richards, 1950:251). Hence, while increased heritable possessions may strengthen the role of the father, under certain conditions they may also strengthen the corporateness of the matrilineage, which is likely to diminish the role of the father. Because of the lack of comparative data, Richards was unable to provide a definitive solution to this paradox.

Morgan (1870), Tylor (1889), Spencer (1967), and Lowie (1920), among others, championed the relative role of men and women in subsistence as relevant to family structure and kinship organizaton. Where women are the primary providers, they suggested, residence is likely to be matrilocal and kinship matrilineal (Hence the parental role of the mother's brother is strong). Subsequent studies (Murdock, 1949; Aberle, 1961; Gough, 1961b; Driver and Scheussler, 1967) have shown the relationship between subsistence and kinship to be somewhat more complex but still consistent with the earlier hypothesis. Aberle (1961), in an extensive cross-cultural analysis of the environmental conditions associated with matriliny, concludes that "In general, matriliny is associated with horticulture, in the absence of major activities carried on and coordinated by males, of the type of cattle raising or extensive public works. It tends to disappear with plough cultivation and vanishes with industrialization'' (Aberle, 1961:725).

Alexander, from a biological perspective, suggests that environmental conditions that affect confidence of paternity and the importance of inheritance are likely to influence family structure:

> Men would ordinarily gain reproductively from being able to tend their own offspring rather than those of sisters. But under certain conditions — such as when inheritance of resources such as land and cattle is very important, and living conditions, absence as a result of military requirements, or other factors cause lowered confidence of paternity—it is easy to understand how shifts toward prominence of mother's brother, matrilineality, fragility of marriage bonds, and lowered confidence of paternity might go together, in patterns entirely consistent with a Darwinian model of human sociality. (Alexander, 1977a:324)

On the basis of Alexander's hypothesis, environmental conditions that cause low confidence of paternity, concomitant with important heritable resources, should be associated with uterine kin biases. It is useful to consider these conditions separately. Lowered confidence of paternity may result from a number of different environmental conditions that lead to male absenteeism or separate residence of mates, such as warfare (e.g., Nayar: Fuller, 1976; cf. Gough, 1961b), trading (e.g. Menangkebau: Loeb 1934), or migratory wage labor (e.g., Black Caribs: Gonzalez, 1969). Table 26–1 suggests that Alexander is correct in predicting an association between lowered confidence of paternity and uterine kin biases.

However, it is not so clear that Alexander's other condition, ''when inheritance of resources such as land and cattle is very important'' (op. cit.) by itself favors matrilineality and the mother's brother phenomenon (cf. Aberle, 1961; Richards, 1950). To the contrary, in general, cattle and valuable land result in a stronger parental role of the father, and a tendency towards patrilineal kinship. Murdock notes that in regard to family structure and kinship organization,

> Especially important is the development of any form of movable wealth which can be accumulated in quantity by men. With such property, whether it be herds, slaves, money or other valuables, prosperous men can offer a bride price to the parents of girls which will induce them to part with their daughters. The concentration of property in the hands of men specifically facilitates a transition to patrilineal inheritance among peoples who have previously followed the rule of matrilineal inheritance, for men now have the power and the means to make effective their natural preference for transmitting their property to their own sons rather than to their sororal nephews. (Murdock, 1949:206-7)

However, where both valuable heritable resources and low confidence of paternity are concurrent, as Alexander stipulates, matrilineality and a strong mother's brother parental role are usually present, as for example, among the Nayar. The apparent contradiction here results from the conflict between an increased male parental role, and the ''natural preference'' to dispense benefits to one's own offspring, who are more closely related. The critical factors are confidence of paternity and to what degree ''corporateness'' of the kin group is favored by the distribution of resources in the environment (Richards, 1950). As males acquire more heritable resources, their importance to potential heirs (whether own offspring or sister's offspring) increases. Hence, the importance of the mother's brother role increases as heritable resources increase if there is low confidence of paternity or other conditions causing uterine kin to be optimal recipients of altruism. For example, the Ashanti and the Mayombe-Kongo groups have a more prominent role of the mother's brother and more corporate matrilineal kin groups than do the Bemba-Bisa group, who have fewer heritable resources (Richards, 1950) even though confidence of paternity is probably about the same in these societies. Nonetheless, as potential parental benefits increase, the advantage to a male of directing parental benefits to his own offspring, who are more closely related to him than his sister's offspring, also increases.

Family Structure and the Balance of Parental Effort
Between the Sexes

The more potential parental effort (i.e., altruism, e.g., heritable possessions and parental care — see Trivers, 1972; Low, 1978; Hirshfield and Tinkle, 1976; Alexander, 1977a; Borgia, 1978) a male has, the more adaptive it is for him to establish high confidence of paternity and dispense benefits to his own offspring rather than to more distantly related sister's children. The factors influencing male behavior that result in lower confidence of paternity or conjugal instability (e.g., male absenteeism for military service among the Nayar) must therefore be more compelling as potential male parental effort increases. On the other hand, if a male has no potential parental effort, there may be no adaptive reason for him to establish paternity. Davis (1949) notes that the less wealth, reputation, and prestige a man has to pass on, the less concerned he is about transmitting such benefits to his sons. And King suggests that "The maternal family will continue to exist as long as the economic insecurity of men exists" (among lower-class American blacks; King, 1945:103; see also R. T. Smith, 1956; E. Clarke, 1957; M. G. Smith, 1962; Gonzalez, 1969; Blumberg and Garcia, 1977).

In addition, the more parental effort a man has, the more his spouse has to gain — benefits distributed to her offspring — from behavior on her part that leads to high confidence of paternity for her spouse and a stable conjugal relationship (i.e., fidelity). Conversely, as a woman's economic and social position relative to her mate's increases, the importance of her mate's economic and social contribution to her offspring may decrease. This could be the adaptive basis for the association between socio-economic position and family structure noted by many social scientists (see Dickemann's discussion of Purdah, this volume). As the ability of males to reciprocate in the conjugal relationship diminishes, family structure is likely to become increasingly "matrifocal" (and usually, but not necessarily, uterine kin biased — see Gonzalez, 1970). When males have little contribution to make to the family, women may gain from a short-term, multiple-mate strategy (Gonzalez, 1969; Stack, 1975).

There are several other possible reasons why the potential amount of male parental effort may significantly influence family structure. Males with high parental effort (again presumably associated with socio-economic position) may be better able to isolate their wives from potential cuckolders. Among the Nayar, "aristocrats seem often to have exercised the power to monopolize the attentions of their favorite Nayar wives. They were therefore more sure of the paternity of their Nayar sons, upon whom they sometimes conferred military or political offices" (Gough, 1961a:379). Similarly, the ability to provide a large bridewealth may affect post-marital residence (Murdock, 1949; Richards, 1950; Gluckman, 1950; Goody and Tambiah, 1971) and hence confidence of paternity. Males with high parental effort may be influenced more by western values concerning family structure, either because of increased exposure or greater social pressure to conform. High parental effort males may be the most attractive mates; their wives might therefore have little reason to seek outside mates. Occupational differences associated with parental effort may result in differences in confidence of paternity. For example, low status and/or poor males may seek migratory wage labor more frequently than high status and/or wealthy males (Gonzalez, 1969).

Agnatic altruism (e.g., patrilineal inheritance of land) may become increasingly adaptive if males control the distribution of important resources, because resources dispensed to a married sister or her offspring (uterine altruism) are likely to be used by her husband to benefit his kin, who are unrelated to his wife and her kin (Alexander and Borgia, ms.). Agnatic biases may also be adaptive when coalitions of closely related males are very important (e.g., as among the Yanomamo — see Chagnon, 1975, 1979a).

Among the societies surveyed, there is a tendency for high status and/or wealthy males (as defined in the respective ethnographies) to be more likely to direct parental benefits towards their own putative offspring relative to lower status and/or poorer males in the same society. In 89 of 303 societies surveyed, there was evidence suggesting that high socio-economic status males tended to have higher confidence of paternity. In no society did high socio-economic status males appear to have lower confidence of paternity.

In general, both inter- (Murdock, 1949) and intra- (R. T. Smith, 1956; Clarke, 1957; M. Smith, 1962; Gonzalez, 1969) societal variability in family structure with respect to valuable resources — such as land, cattle, or money — confirm the widely posited association between the economic position of males and their parental role (see also Dickemann, this volume). The relative role of males vs. females in resource accrual appears to be an important determinant of the balance of parental effort between the sexes, and hence the male parental role (e.g., see Barth's comparative study of the Fur, 1967; Aberle, 1961; Gough, 1961b).

In summary, environmental conditions probably influence family structure for at least three reasons: First, environmental conditions affect confidence that altruism, such as parental effort, is benefiting appropriate kin, such as offspring. Second, the distribution of resources in the environment may partially determine the balance of power between individual and kin group. And third, the distribution and type of heritable resources in the social and physical environment affect the distribution of parental effort between the sexes as well as among individuals and social classes. As discussed, these reasons are likely to be interrelated.

A FURTHER TEST OF A BIOLOGICAL MODEL: PATTERNS OF ALTRUISM, RESIDENCE, AND MARRIAGE

Lowie (1920) and Linton (1936), following, in part, Morgan, Tylor, and others, postulate a functional association among the transmission of property rights, residence, and kinship organization. In addition, they and other anthropologists have suggested that cousin marriages may be part of this complex. In many respects, this proposed association is germane to a biological model of kinship variability and marriage systems.

Residence: An Adaptive Choice?

Linton (in agreement with many other anthropologists, such as Morgan, 1870; Lowie, 1920; Levi-Strauss, 1949) states that "matrilineal descent is normally linked with matrilocal residence, patrilineal with patrilocal" (1936:169). Murdock (1949:59) provides substantial evidence supporting Linton's hypothesis (see also Aberle, 1961; Gough, 1961bc; Driver and Scheussler, 1967). This hypothesis, in terms of biological theory, suggests a functional association between the flow of altruism, residence, and kinship behavior (see also Chagnon, 1975, 1979ab; Irons, 1979b). If the biological basis for this hypothesis is valid, then the potential altruism an individual is likely to receive in a given location should be a criterion for residence choice. If a male child receives the most altruism from his mother's brother, avunculocal residence is expected if co-residence enhances the benefits derived. If the flow of altruism changes over an individual's life history, then different residences at different life history stages are predicted. For example, if females leave their uterine kin group at marriage to join their husband's uterine kin group, children will at first reside with their mothers upon whom they are probably the most dependent and from whom they are receiving the most altruism during childhood. However, as the children grow up, if male they should return to their uterine kin group, where they may receive inheritance and other benefits from their mother's brother; if female they may be married off and reside in their husband's kin group. This changing pattern of residence is quite common among matrilineal societies (Richards, 1950).

The combination of matrilineal descent and male inheritance poses conflicting interests for residence choice, termed the "matrilineal puzzle" (Richards, 1950). If a man's wife and his uterine kin do not coreside, he must choose between the two. A similar situation exists for a child if his mother does not reside with their mutual uterine kin.

Richards (1950) offers several ethnographic solutions to this dilemma: (1) Women and their children coreside, and men visit back and forth between their uterine households and their wive's households (e.g., Nayar, Hopi). This usually requires close proximity of both residences. (2) Uterine male kin live together, but their sisters and young children live away with their husbands, the male children eventually moving to reside with their mother's brothers and other uterine kin (avunculocal) and the female children moving away to their husband's residence (virilocal) (e.g., Trobriand Islanders). (3) Men reside with their wives and children, but a few men (sometimes based on primogeniture) remain with their sisters to maintain the matrilineage (e.g., Cewa, Yao). (4) Most children coreside with their mothers and fathers, with a few chosen "heirs" returning to their matrilineal community (e.g., Mayombe). Yet another solution is alternate residence between the husband's uterine kin and the wife's uterine kin (e.g., Dobu). Predictably, socio-economic status affects residence choice, as "men of wealth and distinction are able to reverse the usual rules of residence" (Richards, 1950:248), keeping their wives and putative offspring — of whose paternity they are likely to be relatively certain — resident with them. In general, patterns of residence appear to be associated with the flow of altruism,[12] although the direction of causality is difficult to determine.

Table 26–3.   Marital residence and the source of altruism.

PRIMARY MARITAL RESIDENCE

SOURCE OF ALTRUISM		PATRI-LOCAL	BI-LOCAL	NEO-LOCAL	MATRI-LOCAL	AVUNCU-LOCAL	DUO-LOCAL	ROW TOTAL
	FATHER AND AGNATIC KIN	48 / 15.9	3 / 1.0	0 / 0.0	0 / 0.0	0 / 0.0	0 / 0.0	51 (COUNT) / 16.9 (% TOTAL)
	MIXED-FATHER MAJOR	105 / 34.8	9 / 3.0	4 / 1.3	34 / 11.2	0 / 0.0	1 / 0.3	153 / 50.7
	MIXED	20 / 6.6	2 / 0.7	2 / 0.7	36 / 11.9	1 / 0.3	2 / 0.7	63 / 20.9
	MIXED-MOTHER'S BROTHER MAJOR	1 / 0.3	0 / 0.0	0 / 0.0	17 / 5.6	16 / 5.3	1 / 0.3	31 / 10.3
	MOTHER'S BROTHER AND UTERINE KIN	0 / 0.0	0 / 0.0	0 / 0.0	0 / 0.0	2 / 0.7	2 / 0.7	4 / 1.3
	COLUMN TOTAL	51 / 16.9	14 / 4.6	6 / 2.0	83 / 27.5	19 / 6.3	6 / 2.0	302 / 100.0

$\chi^2 = 262.67$ 20_{df} $p < 0.0001$

GAMMA = 0.82424

[12]Because I may have been inadvertently influenced by the pattern of residence while evaluating the flow of altruism, the association between these two variables may be inflated.

The Flow of Altruism and Cousin Marriage Preferences

Perhaps most interesting and strikingly consistent with a biological model of family structure is the effect of residence and the flow of altruism on marriage patterns. In many societies certain kin (e.g., mother's brother's daughter) are preferred[13] marriage partners. In some societies the preferred kin are related in an actual genealogical way; in others the marriage partners need only be classificatory kin.

Several adaptive criteria may exist for the choice of a marriage partner: (1) physical and mental condition (phenotypic fitness, possibly indicative of genotypic fitness); (2) economic and social status (or other indicators of potential parental effort); (3) age (indicative of reproductive potential); (4) genealogical relatedness (both for avoidance of deleterious inbreeding and optimizing potential kinship relations); (5) reciprocity, involving both the exchange of mates (or other resources of reproductive significance, e.g., bride price) and potential alliance considerations; and (6) propinquity, particularly where immobile resources such as land are important and heritable.

If a biological model is appropriate, the above criteria should account for some aspects of the non-random variability of human marriage patterns, such as preferences for certain types of cousin marriages.

There are no systematic differences in physical and mental condition among different kin types, so this criterion certainly offers no ready solution. Economic and social status may, in some hypergamous societies, favor matrilateral cross cousin marriage because mother's brother's daughter is of appropriate status or will otherwise create desirable status affinal bonds (Leach, 1951). Reciprocity is apparently an important factor involved with classificatory MBD or more distant (e.g., MMBDD) cousin marriage rules in societies with complex marriage exchange systems, such as among Australian aboriginal groups (see, e.g., Radcliffe-Brown, 1951). However, demographic factors associated with the respective ages of marriage partners might also favor matrilateral cross-cousin marriage in these societies (Rose, 1960).

The effects of genealogical relatedness and propinquity are probably the most important criteria for testing a biological model. If, as suggested earlier, there is an adaptive functional association between residence and the flow of altruism, then marriage patterns should in some respects be influenced by genealogical relatedness and propinquity.

The effect of genealogical relatedness on marriage choice appears quite complex. It might be adaptive to mate with as distant a relative as possible for avoidance of inbreeding (see Williams, 1975, for discussion of the biological advantages of genetic outbreeding), but this could be in conflict with other factors, such as propinquity and advantageous kinship relations, that favor marriage with a relative. Consolidating kinship ties and sources of altruism by arranging marriages among kin is apparently advantageous in many societies. For example, among the Tswana,

> It is largely because parents wish to find a good wife for their son that they prefer to marry him, if possible, to the daughter of some close relative, with whose conduct and reputation they are themselves well acquainted. Near relatives, informants also argue, are apt to be more tolerant of each other than strangers, and, because of the pre-existing ties, their kin will take greater interest in the welfare of the marriage and try to ensure its success. Such marriages, moreover, bind the two families together even more closely than before and make for increased harmony and cooperation — a factor of much importance in a society where people depend greatly upon their relatives for help in major household activities. (Schapera, 1950:162)

Cousin marrige increases genetic relatedness among generations. If heritable items

---

[13]The use of the term "preferred" here is not meant to involve the preference vs. prescription controversy in structural anthropology. I use the term to signify that certain kin are more desirable marriage partners. "Preference" is expected to be reflected in actual behavior.

such as land or political power have adaptive significance, then individuals may gain from increasing the amount of genetic relatedness with recipients, such as grandoffspring, of heritable items. Hence manipulating the marriages of offspring so as to increase genetic relatedness with grandoffspring who will benefit from heritable possessions might be expected in certain circumstances (see, e.g., Alexander, 1979). However, the potential benefits of increasing relatedness with heirs could be offset by the potential disadvantages of genetic inbreeding. Establishing ties with unrelated individuals by marriage may also frequently be important (Tylor, 1889; Chagnon, 1968). Hence a balance is likely to be struck between factors favoring distant vs. close relatives as mates (Alexander, 1977a).

In some societies there may be a difference between putative parallel cousins (offspring of same-sexed siblings) and cross cousins (offspring of different-sexed siblings) in the degree of genetic relatedness. Alexander (1974, 1977a) points out that with the levirate, sororate, sororal polygyny, or wife sharing by brothers, parallel cousins may frequently be half-siblings. This would not be the case for cross cousins. Consequently, in the presence of the above phenomena, cross cousin marriage is predicted to be preferred over parallel cousin marriage (Alexander, 1974, 1977a). Uni- or bi-lineal marriage exchange coalitions may also favor cross cousin marriage (Chagnon, 1979a; Irons, this volume).

On the basis of the flow of altruism, cousin marriages are predicted where such marriages increase benefits derived from altruism among kin (e.g.: consolidation of land resources and herds among the Kurds, Barth, 1954; residence conflict resolution among the Yao, Richards, 1950; strengthening kinship alliance ties among the Yanomamo, Chagnon, 1979a). Hence, not all societies are expected to have cousin marriage preferences, and not all individuals are expected to have identical interests in regard to how certain marriages might affect the flow of altruism. For example, Alexander (1979) suggests that the sexes might differ in their preferences for type of cousin marriage (each sex preferring marriages that increase relatedness among their kin and potential heirs) and that the balance of power between the sexes influences the outcome.

But if considerations of altruism influence marriage choice (and vice versa), then asymmetric uterine or agnatic altruism should be associated with marriage preferences that are consistent with the respective flow of altruism. From this hypothesis we can make the following simple predictions: where the father's brother (or other agnatic kin) are important sources of altruism, father's brother's daughter marriage will be preferred; where the mother's brother is an important source of altruism, mother's brother's daughter marriage will be preferred; where the father's sister is an important source of altruism, father's sister's daughter marriage will be preferred; where the mother's sister is an important source of altruism, mother's sister's daughter marriage will be preferred; and where there are no consistent differences among these relatives (e.g., societies organized on the basis of bilateral kinship, which tend not to have strong asymmetric kinship biases), asymmetric cousin marriages are predicted not to be preferred.

Of the above cousin marriage preferences, mother's sister's daughter (MZD) and father's sister's daughter (FZD) are predicted where females are the primary sources of post-marital altruism, and a cousin marriage of these types would increase benefits derived from altruism among kin. Females generally are not primary sources of post-marital altruism for their male relatives, because males usually control political power and the distribution of socio-economic resources. Therefore, MZD and FZD marriage preferences are predicted not to occur, based on the simplistic relationship between marriage preferences and the flow of altruism posited here. There is, however, a more complicated circumstance in which father's sister's daughter marriage is predicted on the basis of the flow of altruism (see following).

Conversely, father's brother's daughter (FBD) and mother's brother's daughter (MBD) marriage preferences are predicted where males are the primary sources of post-marital altruism, and a cousin marriage of these types will increase benefits derived from altruism among the respective kin. FBD marriage is predicted to occur in societies with a strong agnatic bias (and the basis for distinguishing between parallel cousins and half siblings)

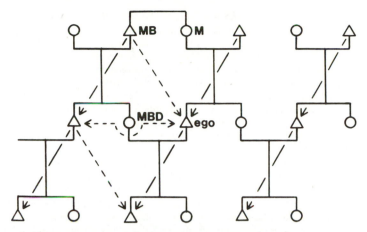

Figure 26–4.   Mother's brother's daughter marriage. Dashed arrows indicate kinship ties and flows of altruism that are likely to be increased by MBD marriage in a society with a balanced or moderate agnatic bias in the flow of altruism among kin (solid arrows).

because it consolidates agnatic kin ties exclusively. MBD marriage is predicted in societies with a moderate agnatic to uterine bias because both uterine and agnatic kin ties are consolidated. I shall now discuss each cousin marriage type separately and examine whether these predictions are consistent with ethographic evidence.

MOTHER'S BROTHER'S DAUGHTER MARRIAGE

Where the mother's brother is an important potential source of altruism and propinquity or the son-in-law relationship is likely to increase the benefits obtained from the mother's brother sufficiently to offset the potential disadvantages of the slight inbreeding ($Fg = 1/16$), then matrilateral cross-cousin marriage could become adaptive. Perhaps more importantly, the interests of the potential marriage partners' kin may also be served by the obligations and reciprocalities that the marriage may establish. Among the Ashanti,

> As has been mentioned, a cross-cousin is regarded as the most satisfactory spouse. At least this is still the view of the older people. Many young men take a different view. They say that a cross-cousin is "too near", almost a sister, and so she is never as attractive as an unrelated girl . . . . But in rural areas there are still many young men who approve of marriage with a mother's brother's daughter (wofa ba) on the grounds that it creates an additional bond with their maternal uncles and that it is a more secure marriage than a match with an unrelated woman. Women often argue in favor of the custom. They say it strengthens their claims on their husbands and their children's claims on both paternal and maternal kin. The older people — parents, mother's brothers, and father's sisters—in whose interests and at whose insistence cross-cousin marriages are arranged* defend the custom on various grounds. The commonest argument is on the grounds of property and wealth.* Cross-cousin marriage most often occurs between the children of full siblings or of uterine first cousins. Such a marriage, it is contended, ensures that a man's daughter and her children derive some benefit from the property he is obliged to leave to his sister's son . . . . (Fortes, 1950:281-2)

Thus, marriage with mother's brother's daughter is evidently preferred in some societies because it can establish favorable kinship relations and increase benefits obtained

*Rattray, 1927.

from mother's brother. This relationship between the flow of altruism and the mother's brother's daughter marriage is represented by Figure 26-4.

Matrilateral cross cousin marriage can also resolve residence conflicts. If post-marital residence is uxorilocal (with wife's family), but a male's most important source of altruism—such as inheritance of land—is mother's brother, then males may find themselves in a dilemma over whether to spend time with their wives in one locale or with their mother's brothers and inherited land in another locale. Marriage with the mother's brother's daughter is one solution to this dilemma: "By the mother's brother's daughter marriage of the Yao the son of one of the married sisters belonging to the sororal family marries the daughter of the manager-brother and therefore contracts what is virtually a viri-local marriage" (Richards, 1950:248).

If older male relatives are the most important sources of altruism after the childhood period, then under certain conditions the mother's brother's daughter marriage could be advantageous in both matrilineal and patrilineal societies. Because a man is closely related to his mother's brother, and likely to receive altruism from him, but is probably not genetically related to his father's sister's husband or his mother's sister's husband, establishing a son-in-law relationship with the mother's brother may be sufficiently advantageous to favor the mother's brother's daughter marriage. Indeed, the giving of the daughter in marriage may itself be altruism.

MBD marriage is not predicted to occur when confidence of paternity is very low because MB may be uncertain of his putative daughter's paternity and unlikely to contract a marriage on the basis of increasing altruism to her. Hence MBD marriage is not predicted in societies with very strong uterine kin biases, except by occasional males (usually of high socio-economic status) that do have high confidence of paternity. Among the Nayar, MBD marriage was "arranged only with the child of an uncle who has had a long and satisfactory marriage relationship" (Gough, 1961a:365). Indeed,

> A karavanan was particularly likely to encourage his nephew to enter marital relations with a daughter of the karavanan's favorite wife. In this case it was felt that the marital interests of uncle and nephew would be harmonized and the nephew might be less likely to accuse the uncle of infidelity to the taravad if he favored his wife and her children (Ibid:365).

Finally, as noted earlier, a man's agnates may be his closest competitors in agnatically biased societies, resulting in the maternal uncle (MB) becoming an important source of altruism. For this and the above reasons, MBD marriage is predicted to be fairly common and occur in societies with moderate agnatic biases as well as societies with uterine biases. This prediction is consistent with cross-cultural data.

Father's Brother's Daughter Marriage

Patrilateral parallel cousin (FBD) marriage is predicted to occur where father's brother is an important source of altruism, and where pooling of inheritance from father and father's brother is advantageous (Barth, 1954: Goody, 1976; Alexander, 1977a). Hence this type of

Table 26-4.   Mother's brother daughter marriage and the source of altruism. See Table 26-8 for summary of cousin marriages and for statistics.

SOURCE OF ALTRUISM

	FATHER AND AGNATIC KIN	MIXED-FATHER MAJOR	MIXED	MIXED-MOTHER'S BROTHER MAJOR	MOTHER'S BROTHER AND UTERINE KIN		
MOTHER'S BROTHER DAUGHTER MARRIAGE	4	35	5	4	1	49	(COUNT)
	8.2	71.4	10.3	8.2	2.0	100.0	(% TOTAL)

marriage is likely to occur in societies that emphasize agnatic kinship. In fact, this type of cousin marriage does occur exclusively in agnatically biased societies, and appears to be a response to considerations of altruism:

> in explaining the relative popularity of marriage with a father's brother's daughter, the Tswana often add that it keeps the bogadi cattle in the same family circle and prevents them from passing into the hands of outsiders. . . . Among nobles, where marriage with the father's brother is actually the most common form of cousin marriage, the dominant factor is certainly not bogadi but status. It is considered highly desirable that the chief's heir and other senior children should marry persons of rank. The motive is not so much ''to keep the blood pure'' as to secure the political advantages attached to union with powerful or influential families. (Schapera, 1950:163)

Father's brother's daughter marriage is preferred in the following societies:[14]

AFGHA	1	1	23	3	1	2	5	1	0	7	2
BAIIN	1	1	23	3	1	2	4	1	0	7	2
BEJAS	1	1	23	1	1	1	5	1	0	7	2
BERAB	1	1	23	1	1	1	5	1	0	7	1
EGYPT	1	1	23	3	1	1	5	1	1	7	1
FOUTA	1	1	23	1	1	1	5	1	0	7	1
HAUSA	1	3	23	3	1	2	4	2	0	7	2
IRANI	1	3	23	3	1	2	5	1	0	7	2
KABAB	1	1	23	1	1	1	5	1	0	7	2
KURDS	1	1	23	1	1	1	5	1	0	7	2
MERIN	1	1	27	3	1	1	5	1	0	7	1
SHAWI	1	1	23		1	1	5	1	0	7	2
TSWANN	1	1	21	3	1	2	5	1	0	7	1
ULADN	1	1	23	1	1	1	5	1	0	7	2

These societies are remarkably similar in many significant respects. For example, they all are patrilocal (#1 in first numeric column), most allow cross cousin marriage symmetrically (#21 and #23 in third column), all are patrilineal (#1 in fifth column) all have father and agnatic kin as the primary source of altruism (#1 and #2 in sixth column, see Table 26–5 below), and high or very high confidence of paternity (#4 and #5 in seventh column). See data key for further description. Some of the similarity among these societies could be accounted for by common religion (Islamic) and subsistence (pastoral).

Because of the high confidence of paternity and the infrequency of marriage to the sister of a brother's wife or sororal polygyny in these societies, the inbreeding coefficient between patrilateral parallel cousins in unlikely to exceed 1/16. Hence, the balance between inbreeding costs and the benefits of consolidating kinship ties and altruism may frequently favor patrilateral parallel cousin marriage in these societies. The association between father's brother's daughter marriage and an agnatically biased flow of altruism is represented in Figure 26–5:

Table 26–5.   Father's brother daughter marriage and the source of altruism.

SOURCE OF ALTRUISM

	FATHER AND AGNATIC KIN	MIXED- FATHER MAJOR	MIXED	MIXED- MOTHER'S BROTHER MAJOR	MOTHER'S BROTHER AND UTERINE KIN		
FATHER'S BROTHER'S DAUGHTER MARRIAGE	11	3	0	0	0	14	(COUNT)
	78.6	21.4	0.0	0.0	0.0	100.0	(% TOTAL)

[14]The abbreviations are those used in the *Ethnographic Atlas*. A sixth letter is occasionally added to further define the group: C = commoners, N = nobles, M = modern, T = traditional.

Father's Sister's Daughter Marriage

Because father's sister is rarely an important source of post-marital altruism, FZD marriage preference was predicted to not occur. However, FZD marriage is preferred in some societies under rather limited circumstances, which present a remarkable verification of some of the hypotheses suggested earlier. As previously discussed, high socio-economic status males tend to have higher confidence of paternity. Consequently, high-status males in societies with uterine kinship biases often dispense benefits to their putative offspring contrary to the uterine flow of altruism. Coresidence of father and offspring is frequently concomitant with this pattern of altruism. However, in societies with uterine kin groups, it is difficult for high-status and/or wealthy males to dispense benefits to their sons and keep them co-resident, because uterine kin are usually adverse to such an arrangement, preferring a male to dispense benefits to sister's offspring instead. Father's sister's daughter marriage can resolve this conflict between a man and his uterine kin, because a man's sister's daughter (and her offspring) are his closest uterine kin of those generations. With FZD marriage, father to son altruism, which uterine kin oppose, becomes mother's brother to sister's daughter and offspring altruism, which uterine kin prefer. Among the Trobrianders,

> A man will ordinarily go to the village of his sub-clan after marriage, where he has a claim to land. His mother's brother will bring pressure to bear upon him if he delays too long in coming, because the matrilineally related group of males is strengthened by each addition, which may be useful in feuds of inter-village disputes. However, because of the high rank of a chief, and particularly the chief of the Tabalu, the uncle will not object if the chief wishes to keep his son in the village with him. The chief grants his son the right to reside in the village, and may also give him priviledges and magic which belong to the sub-clan. The son's right to reside in the community is usually terminated upon the death of the father. His residence right is strengthened if he was married in infancy to his father's sister's daughter. This makes his right to remain in the village even after his father's death almost, but not quite, inalienable. . . . Since the marriage is made in infancy, the members of the father's sub-clan are not worried about the advantages he gives his son since they know that they will get back these privileges in the next generation (Fathauer, 1961:242–245).

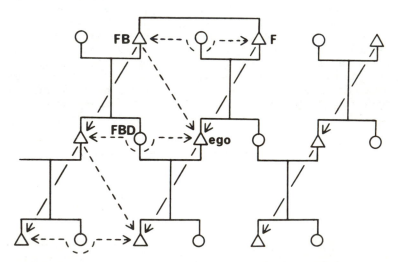

Figure 26–5.   Father's brother's daughter marriage. Dashed arrows indicate kinship ties and flows of altruism that are likely to be increased by FBD marriage in a society with an agnatic bias in the flow of altruism among kin (solid arrows).

Table 26–6.   Father's sister's daughter marriage and the source of altruism.

SOURCE OF ALTRUISM

	FATHER AND AGNATIC KIN	MIXED-FATHER MAJOR	MIXED	MIXED-MOTHER'S BROTHER MAJOR	MOTHER'S BROTHER AND UTERINE KIN		
FATHER'S SISTER'S DAUGHTER MARRIAGE	0	3	5	6	0	14	(COUNT)
	0.0	21.3	35.7	42.6	0.0	100.0	(% TOTAL)

Among the Nayar, mother's brother's daughter marriage was occasionally preferred during traditional times when the mother's brother was a young man's primary source of assistance and inheritance. But as the parental role of the father increased after the cessation of warfare (and presumably increased confidence of paternity), Gough states that: "My data suggest also that deliberately arranged patrilateral cross-cousin marriages may have become more popular in the late nineteenth century, as fathers became instrumental in maintaining and educating their sons" (1961a:366).

Father's sister's daughter marriage is preferred under certain circumstances in the following societies:

```
BIRIF    1  5  13  1  4  2  3  2     1  1
BUSHN    5  4  12  2  3  4  2  3  0  1
CALLI    4  1  11  3  2  2  4  2  1  1
ESPIR    1  1  11     3  3  3  2  0  1
FURES    4  4  12  1  3  3  4           1
HAIDA    5  5  13  2  3  4  3  2  1  1  1
HERER    1  5  13  1  4  2  3  2  0  1
ILAES    1  5  11  2  4  3  3  3     1  1
KERALM   6  1  13  2  3  3  3  2  1  1  2
LOBIS    1  4  13  2  3  3  4  2  1  1
TLING    5  5  12  2  3  4  3  2  1  1  1
TROBR    5  1  11  2  3  4  3  2  1  1  1
YAKOS    1  5  11  3  4  3  4  2  1  1  1
YAOES    4  7  13  2  3  4  3  2     1  1
```

The following are questionable (Maybury-Lewis, 1967; Chagnon, pers. com.) and left out of data analysis:[15]

```
APALA    1  1  11  1  1  2           1
SHERE    1  1  12  1  1  2  4  2     1
```

The TURKS and TIWIS are coded in Coult as preferring patrilateral cross cousin marriage. However, I could find no definite evidence of such a preference in these societies. The TURKS apparently prefer cross cousin marriage symmetrically, and often prefer patrilateral parallel cousin marriage (Stirling, 1965). The TIWIS prefer MBD marriage (Hart and Pilling, 1960).

Societies in which FZD marriage is preferred are consistent in the following respects: Most have low or moderate confidence of paternity and uterine sources of altruism (Table 26–6), and the marriage is usually preferred by high-status individuals in connection with atypical patrilocal residence of the couple (see also Gough, 1961d:621).

The relationship between FZD marriage and the flow of altruism in an uterine-biased society is represented by Figure 26–6:

[15]Among both the APALA and the SHERE, FZD preference was apparently classificatory. Its adaptive significance in these societies could be that it resulted in residence of ego with his patrilineal kin in spite of uxorilocal post-marital residence (see Nimuendaju, 1939, 1942).

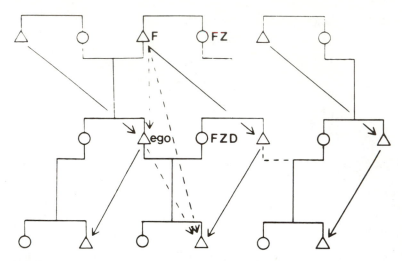

Figure 26–6.   Father's sister's daughter marriage. Dashed arrows indicate kinship ties and flows of altruism that are likely to be increased by FZD marriage in a society with a uterine bias in the flow of altruism among kin (solid arrows).

Mother's Sister's Daughter Marriage

Mother's sister is not a primary source of post-marital altruism in most societies, and her daughters may frequently be ego's half-siblings as a result of sororal polygyny, or at the least ego's most closely related cousins if there is any paternity uncertainty (see Kurland, 1979). Thus the flow of altruism and inbreeding avoidance do not provide conditions for MZD marriage preference. Consistent with this prediction mother's sister's daughter marriage is not preferred in any known society.

Symmetrical Cross Cousin Marriage

Preference for symmetrical cross cousin marriage suggests a general advantage to cousin marriage but no special advantage to marriage with either specific cross cousin type. On the basis of inbreeding avoidance, symmetrical cross cousin marriage is predicted to be preferred where putative parallel cousins could actually be half-siblings. Alexander (1977a) demonstrates a convincing correlation between cross cousin marriage preference and mating practices that could result in parallel cousins being half-siblings: "75 of 79 societies (95 per cent) favoring or prescribing sororal polygyny treat parallel- and cross cousins asymmetrically [i.e., differently], but only 35 of 101 monogamous societies (35 per cent do so (p <0.0001)" (1977a: 327).

On the basis of the flow of altruism, symmetrical cross cousin marriage is predicted to be preferred in societies with no strong asymmetric kinship biases. In Coult and Haberstein's *Cross Tabulations,* only 3 of 204 societies[16] with bilateral kinship have asymmetric cousin marriage preferences, whereas 171 of 204 treat them symmetrically, 114 preferring symmetrical cross cousin marriage, and 47 prohibiting cousin marriage symmetrically (p <.0001). Symmetrical treatment of cousins is not significantly associated with asymmetric flows of altruism.

[16]Excluding the TURKS; see p. 465.

Table 26–7.   Symmetrical cross cousin marriage and the source of altruism.

SOURCE OF ALTRUISM

	FATHER AND AGNATIC KIN	MIXED- FATHER MAJOR	MIXED	MIXED-, MOTHER'S BROTHER MAJOR	MOTHER'S BROTHER AND UTERINE KIN		
SYMMETRICAL CROSS COUSIN MARRIAGE	21	73	33	16	3	146	(COUNT)
	14.3	50.1	22.6	11.0	2.1	100.0	(% TOTAL)

An additional aspect to symmetrical cross cousin marriage occurs when the marriage partner is an actual bilateral cross cousin, i.e., both FBD and MBD, which occurs with sister exchange. The exchange of women among competing coalitions of male kin is often prevalent in societies where there is an absence of valuable resources usable as an indirect exchange commodity, i.e., brideprice, such as money or herd animals. In such societies, the exchange of women between family groups (as in Figure 26–7) is likely to be continued over several generations, possibly resulting in bilateral cross cousin marriage, because families that reciprocated in the past are probably more trustworthy partners for future exchange, especially as kinship ties become closer with additional mate exchanges. Cousin marriages based on reciprocal exchange usually involve rules (often an extended "incest taboo") stipulating who proper marriage partners are, similar to rules concerning other modes of exchange. This could be an important biological reason for the "preferred vs. prescribed" marriage distinction made in anthropology.

Bilateral cross cousin marriage has other important exchange and alliance ramifications (Irons, this volume) with possible reproductive significance (Chagnon, 1979c; Chagnon and Flinn, in prep.). With marriage between actual bilateral cross cousins, kinship ties are consolidated and reinforced in a reciprocal way, and the flow of altruism among kin is intensified symmetrically (Figure 26–7).

Relatedness among affinal relatives increases rapidly with bilateral cross cousin marriage. For example, r between brothers-in-law increases from 0 in the first generation to 1/4 in the second and 3/8 in the third. Hence in-laws not only have ties based on exchange and reciprocity but are closely related as well (see Chagnon, 1979a). However, because bilateral first cousins are related by 1/4 or more on average (same as half sibling), the potential costs of inbreeding are quite high for this type of marriage, and the balance may frequently be tipped in favor of marriage with second or more distant bilateral cross cousins.

Summary of Cousin Marriage Preferences

Human residence and mating-marriage systems are consistently associated with patterns of altruism and appear adaptive for the individuals involved in the choice-making process. Age, physical and mental condition, socio-economic position, and genealogical relatedness are universal considerations in mate choice (Murdock, 1949; Stephans, 1963). Highly supportive of a biological model of marriage choice is the association between cousin marriage preferences and certain patterns of altruism. Matrilateral cross-cousin (MBD) marriage is often associated with mother's brother-sister's son altruism, in both matrilineal and patrilineal societies. Patrilateral parallel cousin (FBD) marriage is exclusively found in societies with strong agnatic kinship biases, such as patrilineal descent and inheritance, and is usually associated with close social and economic ties among brothers and their offspring. Patrilateral cross cousin (FZD) marriage is in most of the societies for which relevant data are available, associated with high-status father-son altruism and atypical patrilocal residence in conflict with a general society preference for uterine kin altruism. Asym-

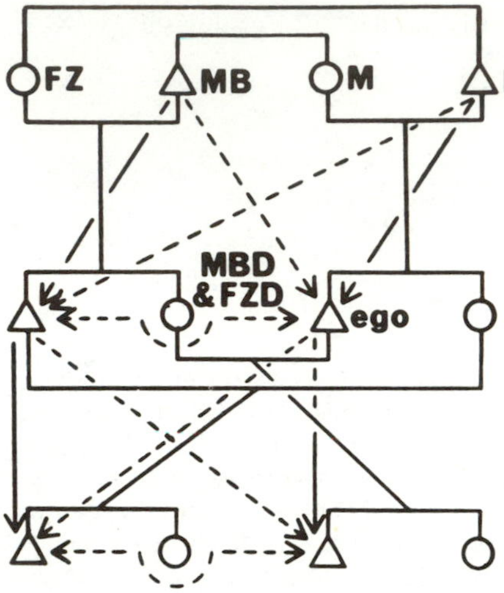

Figure 26–7.   Bilateral cross cousin marriage. Dashed arrows indicate kinship ties and flows of altruism that are likely to be increased by bilateral cross cousin marriage in a society with a balanced or moderate agnatic bias in the flow of altruism among kin (solid arrows).

metric cousin marriage preferences are extremely rare in societies organized on the basis of bilateral kinship (only 3 of 204). These patterns of cousin marriage are also consistent with the avoidance of close inbreeding otherwise possible with certain mating systems (e.g., the avoidance of parallel cousin marriages where sororal polygyny might result in parallel cousins being half-sibs; Alexander, 1974).

Table 26–8 summarizes the association between the flow of altruism and cousin marriage preferences.

Table 26–8.   Cousin marriage preferences and the source of altruism.

COUSIN MARRIAGE PREFERENCE

S O U R C E O F A L T R U I S M		FZD	SYM.	MBD	PROH.	FBD	ROW TOTAL	
	FATHER AND AGNATIC KIN	0	21	4	12	11	48	(COUNT)
		0.0	7.5	1.4	4.3	3.9	17.2	(%TOTAL)
	MIXED– FATHER MAJOR	3	73	35	30	3	144	
		1.1	26.2	12.5	10.7	1.1	51.6	
	MIXED	5	33	5	8	0	52	
		1.8	11.8	1.8	2.9	0.0	18.6	
	MIXED– MOTHER'S BROTHER MAJOR	6	16	4	6	0	31	
		2.1	5.7	1.4	2.1	0.0	11.1	
	MOTHER'S BROTHER AND UTERINE KIN	0	3	1	0	0	4	
		0.0	1.1	0.4	0.0	0.0	1.4	
	COLUMN TOTAL	14	146	49	56	14	279	
		5.0	52.3	17.6	20.1	5.0	100.0	

$\chi^2 = 67.41$ 16_{df} $P < 0.0001$

GAMMA $= -0.37737$

CONCLUDING REMARKS

The biological model of family structure and mating-marriage systems presented here does not rely on genetic differences to account for behavioral differences. Rather, the variability of a few basic factors—confidence of paternity, genetic relatedness, and the distribution of reproductive resources in the physical and social environment—are postulated to explain behavioral differences within the context of individual adaptation.

This type of theoretical approach is nothing new; anthropologists have traditionally proposed adaptive-functional explanations for behavior that closely relates to the environment. For example, the different clothing and shelter used in the arctic as compared to the tropics clearly has adaptive significance as a behavioral response to different environmental conditions and yet requires no genetic differences. Anthropology has long realized the constraints on culture imposed by individual survival. But individual survival is no longer enough. Modern evolutionary theory posits that individuals strive not only to survive, but also to reproduce and increase the survival and reproduction of genetic relatives.

I believe the acceptance of this change in evolutionary theory will revolutionize anthropological theory just as it has biological theory. If we accept the proposition that humans evolved the capacity for culture, and I know of no feasible alternative, then we must face the likelihood that selection has favored propensities to learn information of adaptive significance and behave appropriately, i.e., learning and culture are not random with respect to individual adaptation (see Alexander, 1971, 1977b, this volume). It has been very difficult for social scientists to relate this proposition to the incredible diversity of human social behavior, probably in large part caused by the inadequacies of evolutionary theory in the past.

But evolutionary biology has undergone some highly significant changes in the past decade. No longer are biological explanations tied to genetic determinism. And no longer are they based on the vague and imprecise notion of group adaptation. New theories highly relevant to human sociality with powerful predictive value have been developed, such as kin selection theory and reciprocity theory. I hope I have shown that these new biological theories are germane to the analysis of human social behavior although the anecdotal and often ambiguous nature of the data currently available unfortunately preclude definitive conclusions. Clearly, more research, particularly field research examining individual behavioral variability, is sorely needed to resolve the critical issues generated by the application of modern evolutionary theory to human social behavior.

ACKNOWLEDGEMENTS

I especially wish to thank Dr. Richard D. Alexander, who has constantly provided ideas, inspiration, and criticism. Dr. Alexander suggested some of the hypotheses discussed in this paper to me in 1973 while I was trying to gather information from the HRAF for him and has suggested a great many others since then. I also wish to thank Dr. Napoleon A. Chagnon, Dr. William G. Irons, Dr. Jeffrey Kurland, Eric V. Fredlund, Nancy Berte, other participants in the Darwin dining club seminar at the Pennsylvania State University during 1976 and 1977, Jim Hurd, Dr. Graham Spanier, and Dr. Raymond Hames. Special thanks to Laura Betzig, who performed the tedious task of re-analysis of some of the societies to test for repeatability and provided many helpful criticisms.

APPENDIX

Data key:

col 1-6   society code name from Ethnographic Atlas.   I added an occasional sixth letter to further define the group ("C" for commoners, "M" for modern-19th century, "N" for nobles, and "T" for traditional, pre-western contact).

col 8-11   area code from Ethnographic Atlas.

col 13   primary marital residence;   1=patrilocal,   2=bilateral, 3=neolocal,   4=matrilocal,   5=avunculocal,   6=duolocal, 7=sororolocal

col 15   alternative marital residence (same as above)

col 17   cousin marriage type;   1= FZD, 2= symmetrical cross cousin, 3= MBD, 4= cousin marriage prohibited, 7= FBD

col 18   extent of preference for cousin marriage type;   1,2,3= preferred, 7,9=not preferred or prohibited   (from Ethnographic Atlas)

col 20   succession; 1=patrilineal, 2=matrilineal, 3=non-hereditary, 4=councils, 9=no political authority

col 22   descent;   1=patrilineal,   2=bilateral,   3=matrilineal, 4=duolineal

col 24   sources of altruism: 1=father and agnatic kin primary source; 2=mixed, father major source; 3=mixed, father and mother's brother both important sources; 4=mother's brother and uterine kin major source;   5=mother's brother and uterine kin primary source.

col 26   confidence of paternity;   1=very low,   2=low,   3=moderate, 4=high, 5=very high

col 28   frequency of conjugal bond dissolution; 1=low,   2=moderate, 3=high

col 30   correlation of confidence of paternity with socio-economic status; 0=no difference, 1=higher, 2=lower

col 32   parallel cousin marriage preferred;   1= prohibited or not preferred, 7= patrilateral

col 34   relationship between socio-economic status and cousin marriage; 1=higher socio-economic status individuals prefer closely related cousin (i.e. first or second cousin), 2=no difference on basis of socio-economic status, 3=higher socio-economic individuals prefer more distantly related cousin

ABIPO	SI4	3	3	47	1	2	2	4	3		1	2
ABORS	AR2	1	1	32	3	1	2	4	1		1	1
ACOMA	NT7	4	1	29	2	3	2	3	2		1	
AFGHA	AU1	1	1	72	3	1	1	5	1	0	7	1
AINUS	AB6	2	3	23	1	2	2	4	1	0	1	2
ALACA	SH2	4		23	9	2	2	3	2	0	1	2
ALEUT	NA6	1	4	23	9	2	2	3	2	0	1	2
ALFUR		1	1	32	1	1	2	4	3	0	1	2
ALORE	CF5	1	1	29		2	2	4	3	0	1	2
ALSEA	NR5	1	4	29	3	2	1	4	2		1	2
AMBRY	CO4	1	1	47	4	4	2	4	2	0	1	2
AMHAR	MP5	1	3	49	3	2	1	4	1	1	1	2
ANDAM	AZ2	2	2	29	9	2	2	3	1	0	1	2
APINA	SP3	4	4	29	2	3	4	3	2		1	2
ARAND	CI8	1	1	29	1	4	2	4	2		1	2
ARAUC	SG4	1	1	31	1	1	1	4	1		1	2
ARAWA	SR10	4	4	33	3	4	2	4			1	2
ASHAN	FE12	5	5	33	3	4	4	3	3	1	1	2
AUAES	CM15	6	6	23	1	3	3	3	2		1	2
AYMAR	SF5	1	1	29	9	1	2	4	3	0	1	2
AZAND	FO7	1	3	29	1	1	1	4	1	0	1	2
AZTEC	NU17	1	1	29	1	2	1	5	1	1	1	2
BACAI	SP7	1	1	23	3	2	2	4	2	0	1	1
BALIN	OF7	1	4	72	3	1	2	4	1	1	7	2
BANKS	CO7	6	5	29	3	3	4	2	3	0	1	
BASSA	FF8	1	4	29	1	1	1	4	2	1	1	2
BATAK	CA9	1	4	29	1	1	1	4	1	1	1	2
BEJAS	MR9	1	1	72	1	1	1	5	1	0	7	2
BELLA	NE6	1	4	29	1	1	2				1	
BELUS	OF20	4	4	31	2	3	3	3	2		1	1
BEMBA	FQ5	5	4	21	2	3	4	3	3	1	1	2
BERAB	MW5	1	1	72	1	1	1	5	1	0	7	1
BHILS	AW25	1	1	29	1	1	1	5	1	0	1	2
BIJOG	FB4	4	4	29	2	3	4	3	2	1	1	
BIRIF	FE4	1	5	13	1	4	2	3	2		1	1
BOROR	SP8	4	4	23	2	3	3	3	2	0	1	
BOUGA	ON6	5	2	33	3	3	4	3	3	1	1	1
BUKAS	ON6	2	2	47	2	3	3	4	3	1	1	2
BURME	AP4	4	3	23	3	2	3	5	1	0	1	2
BURUS	AV7	1	1	29		1	2	5	1	0	1	2
BURYA	RW1	1	1	32	1	1	2	4	1	0	1	1
BUSHN	SR8	5	4	12	2	3	4	2	3	0	1	
CADDO	NC5	4	1	47	1	2	2	4	2	0	1	2
CAGAB	SC7	4	4	29		2	2	3	2	0	1	2
CAING	SM3	2	2	23	9	2	3	2	3	0	1	2
CALLI	ST13	4	1	11	3	2	2	4	2		1	
CARAJ	SP9	4	4	23	1	2	2		2		1	
CARIB	SR9	1	4	29	9	2	2	4	2	1	1	2
CARRI	NE7	4	1	21	2	3	3	4	2	0	1	2
CASHI	SQ6	4	4	21		2	2	4	2	0	1	
CAYAP	SO6	2	3	47	1	2	2	4	2	0	1	1
CHAGG	FN4	1	3	47	3	1					1	
CHAMA	AE10	4	1			2	2		2	0	1	
CHAMA	SK14	4	4			3	3	2	2	0	1	

```
CHAMB   FF15  1 5 29  1 4 2 3 2 1 1 2
CHENC   AW51  2 2 33  3 1 2 4 2   1
CHERO   NN8   4 4 29  2 3 4 3 2 0 1 2
CHEYE   NQ8   4 1 49  3 2 2 5 2 0 1 2
CHIBC   SC11  1      2 3 3   2 0 1
CHINE   AF    1 1 23  3 1 1 5 1 0 1 2
CHIRI   NT8   4 4 49  3 2 3 4 2 0 1 2
CHIRI   SF10  1 1     1 2 1       1 2
CHOCT   NN10  4 3 49    3 4 3 2 0 1 2
CHOCW   FP4   5 5 33  2 3 4 3 3 1 1 2
CHORO   SK6   4 4 29    2 3 3 2 1 1
CHUKC   RY2   1 4 23  3 2 2 4 3 0   2
COCHI   NT12  4 3 47  3 3 2 4 2 0 1 2
COORG   AW5   1 1 23  1 1 1 4 1 1 1 2
CREEK   NN11  4 4 47  3 3 3 3 2   1
CREES   NG4   1 4 21  3 2 2     0 1 1
CROWS   NQ10  1 1 29  3 3 3 4 2 0 1 2
CUNAS   SB5   4 4 27  3 2 2 3 2   1
DAGOM   FA40  1 4 23  3 1 2 3 2 1 1 2
DARDS   AV3   1 1 29    1 2 4 1 0 1 2
DELAW   NM7   4 3     2 3 3 2 3 0 1
DERAS   FF19  1 5     1 4 2 3   0 1
DOBUA   CL4   5 4 29  9 3 5 2 3 0 1 2
EASTE   OY2   1 4 29  9 2 2 4 2   1
EGYPT   MR13  1 1 72  3 1 1 5 2 1 7 1
ESPIR   OO11  1 1 11    3 3 3 2 0 1
EYAKS   NA7   5 5 23  2 3 4 4 2   1 2
FOUTA         1 1 72  1 1 1 5 2 0 7 1
FOXES   NP5   2 2 49  1 1 2 4 1 0 1 2
FURES   MQ8   4 4 12  1 3 3 4     1
GAESE   FE6   6 1 33  1 1 2 3 1 1 1 1
GANDA   FK7   1 3 29  3 1 1 4 1 1 1 2
GAROS   AR5   4 1 33  2 3 3 3 2 1 1 1
GILYA   RX2   1 1 31  9 2 2 2 2 0 1 2
GOAJI   SC13  5      23  2 3 3 3 2 0 1 2
GOLDI   RX3   1 1 32    1 1 4 1 1 1 1
GONDS   AW32  1 1 21  1 1 1 4 1 0 1 2
GROSV   NQ13  1 1 49  3 2 1 4 2 1 1 2
GUAHI   SC14  4 4     1 3 3 4 2 0 1
GUANC   MZ4   1      23  2 3 3 4 2 0 1
GUAYM   SB6   4 4     3 3 4 2 0 1
GURES   FF35  5 7 47  9 3 4 3 3 1 1 2
HAIDA   NE9   5 5 13  2 3 4 3 2 1 1 1
HANUN   OA18  4 4 49  9 2 3 3 2 1 1 2
HAUSA   MS13  1 3 72  3 1 2 4 2     7
HEHES   FN9   1 3 33  1 1 2 4 1 1 1 2
HERER   FX12  1 5 13  1 4 2 3 2 0 1
HOPIS   NT9   4 4 47  4 3 4 3 2 1 1 2
HOTTE   FX13  1 1 23  1 1 2 4 1 0 1 2
HURON   NG5   4 4 29  2 3 3 3 2 0 1 2
IBANS   CC6   2 2 23  3 2 2 4 1 0 1 1
IFUGA   OA19  2 2 49  9 2 2 4 2 0 1 2
IFALU   CR21  4 4 29  2 3 3 2 2 1 1 2
ILAES   FQ6   1 5 11  2 4 3 3 3   1 1
```

```
ILIMA   OF9    1  1  33  1  1  2  4  2  1  1  1
INCAS   SE13   1  1  23  1  2  1  5  1  1  1  1
INGAS   FJ13   2  5  47  1  2  1  4  2  0  1  2
IRANI   MA1    1  3  72  3  1  1  5  1  0  7  1
IRISH   ER1    1  3  47  3  2  1  5  1  0  1  2
IROQU   NM9    4  4      2  3  3  3  2  0  1
JEMEZ   NT11   3  2  47  2  3  3     2  0  1  2
JIVAR   SD9    1  4  23  9  1  3  3  2  0  1  2
JUKUN   FF33   4  1  27  1  2  2  4  2  0  1  2
KABAB          1  1  72  1  1  1  5  1  0  7  2
KACHI   AP6    1  1  32  1  1  2  4  1  1  1  1
KADAR   FF34   1  5  49  1  1  2  4  1  1  1  2
KALIN   CA24   4  1  47  1  1  2  4  2  1  1  2
KARAD   OI13   1  1  32     4  2  4  2  0  1  1
KAREN   AP7    4  4  23  1  3  3  5  1  0  1  2
KASKA   ND12   4  4  31  9  3  3  3  3  1  1  2
KAZAK   RQ2    1  1  49  1  1  1  3  1  0  1  2
KEIIS   OH13   1  1  32     4  2  4  2  0  1  2
KERALT  AW11   6  5  33  2  3  5  1  3  1  1  2
KERALM  AW11   6  1  13  2  3  3  3  2  1  1  2
KHASI   AR7    4  4  27  2  3  4  3  3  1  1  1
KIKUY   FL10   1  1  49  4  1  1  5  1  0  1  2
KIOWA   NQ15   1  4  29  3  2  2  5  2  0  1  2
KISSI   FA23   1  1  32  1  1  1  4  2     1  2
KLAMA   NR10   1  1  49  3  2  2  5  2  1  1  2
KONGO   FO21   4  4  23  2  3  4  3  2  0  1  2
KPEES   FF43   1  5  49  1  4  2  4  2  0  1  2
KUBAS   FO23   4  5  47  2  3  4  3  3  1  1
KUNAM   FK12   1      47  4  3  3  4  2  0  1  2
KURDS   MA11   1  1  72  1  1  1  5  1  0  7  2
KURYA   RY4    1  4  29  3  2  2  4  1  0  1  2
KUTCH   ND10   1  4      1  3  3  4  2  0  1
LAKHE   AR8    1  1  31  1  1  2  4  1  1  1  1
LAMBA   FQ8    5  1  33  2  3  4  3  2  1  1  2
LAMET   AM28   1  1  32  1  1  2  4  1  0  1  1
LAPPS   EP4    1  2  27  1  2  1  4  1  0  1  2
LAUFI   CQ6    1  4  21  1  1  2  3  2  1  1  2
LENGU   SK10   4  1      1  2  2           1
LEPCH   AK5    1  1  47  1  1  1  4  1  0  1  2
LESAS          5  1  29  2  3  4  3  3  0  1  2
LOBIS   FA26   1  5  13  2  3  3  4  2  1  1
LOLOS   AE4    1  1  21  1  1  2  3  1  0  1  1
LOVED   FX14   1  1  33  1  1  2  4  1  0  1  2
LOZIS   FQ9    1  4  49  1  2  2  4  2  0  1  2
LUIMB   PP9    1  5  23  2  3  3  3  2  0  1
MAANY   OC9    4  1          3  2  4  2  0  1
MACAS   CG6    4  1  29  1  2  2  4  1
MALAY   AN5    1  3  23  1  2  2  5  1  0
MANDA   NQ17   4  4          3  3  3  3  3
MANGA   OZ9    1  4  47  1  2  2  4  2
MANIH   CZ10   1  4  23  1  2  2  4
MANUS   OM6    1  1  29  1  4  2
MAORI   CZ4    2  2  29  1  2  2
MARGI   FF12   1  5  47  1  1
```

MARQU	OX6	1	3	21	1	2	2	3	3	1	1	2	
MARSH	OR12	4	7	21	9	3	4	2	3	1	1		
MASAI	FI12	1	4	49	4	1	2	5	1	0	1	2	
MATAC	SI7	2	2	29		2	1	4	1		1		
MAYAS	NV4	1	3	32	1	1	1	5	1	1	1	1	
MBUGW	FN16	1	1	29	4	4	2	4	2	0	1	2	
MBUND	FP12	1	5	33	1	4	2	4	1	0	1	1	
MENDE	FC7	1	4	31	1	1	2	4	2	0	1		
MERIN	FY5	1	1	72	3	1	1	5	1	0	7	1	
MESAK	FJ21	5	1	49	2	3	4	3	2		1	2	
MIAOS	AE5	1	1	23		1	2	5	1	0	1	1	
MIKIR	AR10	1	1	31	4	1	2	5	1	0	1	2	
MINAN	CD10	6	6	21	4	3	5	1	3	1	1	2	
MISKI	SA15	4	3	21	3	2	3				1		
MONGO	AH1	1	5	29	1	1	2	4	2	0	1	2	
MONGU	AE9	1	1	23	1	1	1	4	1	0	1	1	
MOSSI	FA28	1	1	47	1	1	1	4	1	1	1	2	
MOTIL	SC10	4	1	21		2	2				1		
MUNDU	SQ13	4	1	21	1	1	3	3	2	0	1		
MURNG	OI17	1	1	31	1	4	2	3	2	0	1	2	
NAKAN	CM16	5	1	21	9	3	4	3	2		1	1	
NAMBI	SP17	1	1	21	3	2	2	4	2	0	1	2	
NATCH	NO8	1	1	47	2	2	1	4	2	0	1		
NAURU	OR13	4	4	21	2	3	4	3	2		1	2	
NAVAH	NT13	4	4	47	2	2	2	4	3	0	1	2	
NDORO	FF49	5	7	21	2	3	5	2	3	0	1	1	
NEWIR	CM10	4	4	29	3	3	3	3	3	0	1	2	
NGONI	FR5	1	4	23	1	2	2	4	2	0	1	1	
NICOB	AZ7	4	1	29	3	2	2	4	1	0	1		
NIKAS	FL14	1	1	23	4	4	2	4	2	0	1	2	
NOOTK	NE11	1	4	47	1	2	2	5	1	0	1	2	
NUERS	FJ22	1	3	49	9	1	1	5	1	0	1	2	
NYAKY	FN17	3	4	47	3	2	2	4	2	0	1	2	
NYANE	FP18	5	5	23	2	3	4	3	2	1	1	2	
OJIBW	NG6	1	4	21	3	1	2	4	3	0	1		
OMAHA	NQ12	4	1	47	3	1	2	4	2	0	1		
ONTON	CT8	4	1	49		4	2	4	1	0	1	2	
PAEZS	SC15	3	3			2	2	4	1	0	1	2	
PALAU	CA36	5	1	49	2	3	4	3	3		1	2	
PANAR	SS21	4	1	33	3	2	2	4	1	0	1	1	
PAPAG	NU28	1	1	47	4	2	2	3	3	0	1	2	
PARES	SP19	4	1		1	2	2	4	2	0	1		
PAWNE	NQ18	4	1	29	1	2	2	4	1	0	1	2	
PENOB	NL4	4	1	29	1	2	2	4	2	0	1	2	
PIROS	SE18	4	4	23	3	2	3	3	2	0	1		
POMOS	NS18	2	2	29	2	2	2				1		
PONAP	CR16	4	5	21	2	3	4	3	3	1	1	2	
PUKAP	OZ11	1	1	47	1	4	2	4	2	0	1		
PUYAL	NR15	1	4	29	3	2	2	4	1	0	1	2	
RENGM	AR13	1	3	31	1	1	2	4	2	1	1	2	
ROSSE	CI5	1	1	29	1	3	2	4	3	0	1	2	
ROTUM	OQ7	4	7	29		3	4	3	3		1		
MCY	RU4	1	1	31		1	2	5	1	0	1		
DA	FN23	1	1	31	1	1	2	5	1	0	1	1	

SANTA	AW41	1	4	29	1	1	2	4	2	0	1	2
SEMAN	AN7	1	1	29	9	2	1	4	3	1	1	2
SERBS	EP6	1	3		4	1	1	5	1	0	1	2
SERER	FA32	1	5	29	2	3	4	4	2	0	1	2
SERIS	NU31	1	1	29		2	1	4	1	0	1	2
SHAST	NS21	1	4	47	1	2	2	4	1	0	1	2
SHAWI	MV8	1	1	72		1	1	5	1	0	7	1
SHERE	SP20	1	1		1	1	2				1	
SHOSH	NR14	4	1	21	3	2	2	4			1	2
SINHA	AW4	1	4	21		1	3	4	3	0	1	2
SINKA	AI1	2	2	49	1	2	1	4	1	0	1	
SIRIO	SF21	4	4	31	1	2	3	2	2	0	1	2
SLAVE	ND14	4	4	29	3	2	3	4	2	1	1	2
SOMAL	MO4	1	1	29	3	1	1	5	3	0	1	2
SUMBA	CF17	1	1	31	1	1	2	4	1	1	1	1
TAGBA	OA37	4	4	27	3	2	3	3	2	1	1	2
TAINO	SV5	1			2	2	3	4			1	
TALAM	SA19	4	4		2	3	3	2	3	0	1	
TALLE	FE11	1	1	29	1	1	2	4	1	0	1	2
TANAI	NA11	1	5	47	1	3	3	3	1	0	1	2
TANAL	FY8	1	1	21	3	1	2	3	2		1	
TANIM	OF19	1	1	33	1	1	2	4	1	0	1	2
TAPIR	SP22	4	4	29		2	2	3	2	1	1	2
TARAH	NV33	3	4	29		2	3	3	3		1	2
TARAS	NU34	1	1	23	1	2	1	4	1	0	1	2
TEHUE	SH3	1	1		1	2	1	4	1		1	
TELUG	AW17	1	1	33	1	1	2	4	1		1	1
TENDA	FA36	1	5	23	2	3	3	3	3	1	1	2
TENET	SO6	4	3	29		3	3	3	2		1	
TENIN	NR18	1	4	47	1	2	2	3	1	1	1	2
TETON	NQ11	1	4	29	3	2	2	4	1	0	1	2
THADO	AR8	1	1	31	1	1	2	5	1	0	1	1
THAIS	AC1	4	4	23	3	2	3	5	1	0	1	2
THONG	FT6	1	5	29	1	1	2	4	2	1	1	2
TIBET	AJ1	1	4	23	3	1	2	5	1	0	1	2
TIKOP	OT11	1	1	29	1	1	2	4	2	1	1	2
TIMBI	SO8	4	4	29	9	3	3	4	2		1	2
TIMUC	NN18	4	4		3	3	3	2			1	
TIVES	FF57	1	5	29	3	1	2	4	1	0	1	2
TIWIS	OI20	1	4	31	3	3	3	2	3	0	1	2
TLING	NA12	5	5	12	2	3	4	3	2	1	1	1
TOBEL	OH12	1	4	29	3	2	2	4			1	
TODAS	AW60	1	1	21	4	4	3	1	3	1	1	2
TOKEL	OZ12	4	1	47	1	2	2	4	2	0	1	2
TOLOW	NR22	1	4	32	3	1	2	4	1	0	1	1
TONGA	OU9	1	4	27	1	2	2	4	2	1	1	2
TORAJ	CG11	4	4	27	3	2	3	4	2		1	2
TROBR	OL6	5	1	11	2	3	4	3	2	1	1	1
TRUKE	CR19	4	7	29	2	3	3	3	2	1	1	2
TRUMA	SP23	1	1	21	1	2	1	4	1	0	1	2
TSWANN	FV6	1	1	72	3	1	2	5	1	0	7	1
TSWANC	FV6	1	3	33	3	1	2	5	1	0	1	1
TUARE	MS23	1	5	21	3	3	3	3	2	1	1	2
TUBAT	NS22	1	1	47	1	2	1	4	1	0	1	2

TU CAN	SQ19	1	1	33		1	2	4	1	0	1	2
TU LLI	PJ21	1	1	29	1	4	2	4	1	0	1	2
TUPIN	SO9	4	1	21	1	2	2	4	2	0	1	2
TU RKM	RM2	1	1	31	1	1	2	5	1	1	1	2
TUR KS	MB1	1	3	21	3	2	2	5	1	1	1	2
TZ ELT	NV9	1	1	32		1	2	4	1	0	1	2
ULADN	MV4	1	1	72	1	1	1	5	1	0	7	2
URU ES	SF24	1	3		9	2	2	4	1		1	
UTEES	NT19	4	4	49	1	2	2	4	2	0	1	2
VANUA	OQ8	1	4	29	1	4	3	2	2	1	1	2
VIE TN	AM11	1	4	23	1	2	2	4	1		1	2
WAL AP	NT14	1	4	23	1	2	2	4	2		1	2
WAR OP	CJ26	1	1	31	9	1	2	4	2		1	
WAS HO	NT20	4	1	49	1	2	2	4	2	0	1	2
WE SAP	NT21	4	1	49	2	3	3	3	2	1	1	2
WICHI	NO10	4	4	29	3	2	2	4	2	0	1	
WI TOT	SC19	1	1	32	1	1	2	3	1	0	1	2
WOGEO	OI27	1	1	27	9	4	2	2	3		1	2
WOLOP	MS30	1	5	21	1	4	2	4	2	1	1	2
WONGA	OI5	1	1	29	1	4	2	4	2	0	1	2
YAGHA	SH6	1	1	49	9	2	2	4			1	2
YAKOS	FF60	1	5	11	3	4	3	4	2	1	1	1
YA KUT	RV2	1	1	23	1	1	1	3	2		1	
YANOA	SQ18	1	1	21	3	1	2	4	2	0	1	1
YAOES	FT7	4	7	13	2	3	4	3	2		1	1
YAP ES	OR22	1	5	29		4	3	3	2	1	1	2
YAR UR	SS19	4	7	21	1	3	2	3	2	1	1	2
YIRYO	OI25	1	1	31	3	1	2	4	2	0	1	2
YOR UB	FF62	1	1	29	1	1	1	4	1		1	2
YUCHI	NN20	3	1		3	3	2	4	2	0	1	
YUNGA	OI26	1	1	21		4	2	4	1		1	1
YUROK	NS31	1	1	49	9	2	2	4	3	1	1	
ZUNIS	NT23	4	4	29	4	3	3				1	

REFERENCES

Aberle, D. 1961. Matrilineal Descent in Cross-cultural Perspective. In *Matrilineal Kinship*, D. Schneider and K. Gough, eds. Berkeley: University of California Press.

Alexander, R. D. 1971. The Search for an Evolutionary Philosophy of Man. *Proc. Royal Society of Victoria*, Melbourne 84:99–120.

———. 1974. The Evolution of Social Behavior. *Ann. Rev. Ecol. Sys.* 5:325–383.

———. 1975. The Search for a General Theory of Behavior. *Behavioral Science* 20:77–100.

———. 1977a. Natural Selection and the Analysis of Human Sociality. In *Changing Scenes in the Natural Sciences*, C. E. Goulden, ed. Academy of Natural Sciences, Special Publication 12:283–337.

———. 1977b. Evolution, Human Behavior, and Determinism. *Proc. Biennial Meeting Phil. Sci. Assoc.* 2:3–21.

———. 1979. *Darwinism and Human Affairs*. Seattle: University of Washington Press.

———. This volume. *Evolution, Culture, and Human Behavior.*

———, and G. Borgia ms.

Barth, F. 1954. Father's Brother's Daughter Marriage in Kurdistan. *Southwestern J. of Anthrop.* 10:164–171.

———. 1967. On the Study of Scoial Change. *American Anthropologist* 69:661–669.

Blumberg, R. I. and M. P. Garcia. 1977. The Political Economy of the Mother-Child family: A Cross-Societal View. In *Beyond the Nuclear Family Model*, L. Lenero-Otero, ed. London: Sage.

Borgia, G. 1978. Sexual Selection of Mating Systems. In: M. F. Blum and N. Blum (eds.), *Sexual Selection and Reproductive Competition in Insects*, pp. 19–80. Academic Press, N.Y.

Broude, G. and S. J. Greene 1976. Cross-Cultural Codes on Twenty Sexual Attitudes and Practices. *Ethnology* 15:409–429.

Chagnon, N. A. 1968. *Yanomamo: The Fierce People*. New York: Holt, Rinehart and Winston.

———. 1975. Genealogy, Solidarity, and Relatedness: Limits to Local Group Size and Patterns of Fissioning in an Expanding Population. *Yearbook of Physical Anthropology* 19:95–110.

———. 1979a. Mate Competition, Favoring Close Kin, and Village Fissioning Among the Yanomamo Indians. In *Evolutionary Biology and Human Social Behavior*, N.Chagnon and W. Irons, eds. N.Scituate, Mass: Duxbury Press.

———. 1979b. Terminological Kinship, Genealogical Relatedness and Village Fissioning Among the Yanomamo Indians. This Volume.

———. 1979c. Kin Selection Theory, Kinship, Marriage, and Inclusive Fitness Among the Yanomamo Indians. In *Sociobiology, Beyond Nature-Nurture*, G.W. Barlow and J. Silverberg, eds. AAAS special symposium 35. Boulder, Col.: Westview Press.

———, and P. Bugos. 1979. Kin Selection and Conflict: An Analysis of a Yanomamo Axe Fight. In *Evolutionary Biology and Human Social Behavior*, N. Chagnon and W. Irons, eds. N. Scituate, Mass.: Duxbury Press.

———and M. V. Flinn. In preparation. Frequencies and Degrees of Cousin Types Among the Yanomamo Indians.

———and W.G. Irons. 1979. Eds. *Evolutionary Biology and Human Social Behavior*. N.Scituate Mass.: Duxbury Press.

Clarke, E. 1957. *My Mother Who Fathered Me*. London: Allen and Unwin.

Cohen, R. 1967. *The Kanuri*. New York: Holt, Rinehart and Winston.

Colson, E. 1961. Plateau Tonga. In *Matrilineal Kinship*, D. Schneider and K. Gough, eds. Berkeley: University of California Press.

Coult, A. and R. Haberstein. 1965. *Cross Tabulations of Murdock's World Ethnographic Sample*. Columbia, Mo.: University of Missouri Press.

Davis, K. 1949. *Human Society*. New York: Macmillan.

Dickemann, M. This volume. Paternal Confidence and Dowry Competition: A Biocultural Analysis of Purdah.

Driver, H. and K. Scheussler. 1967. Correlational Analysis of Murdock's 1957 Ethnographic Sample. *American Anthropologist* 69:332–352.

Fathauer, G. 1961. Trobrianders. In *Matrilineal Kinship*, D. Schneider and K. Gough, eds. Berkeley, University of California Press.

Fisher, R. A. 1958. *The Genetical Theory of Natural Selection* (2nd ed.). New York: Dover.

Ford, C. S. 1945. *A Comparative Study of Reproduction*. Yale publications in Anthropology 32 New Haven, Conn.: Yale University Press.

_____and F.A. Beach. 1951. *Patterns of Sexual Behavior*. New York: Harper and Row.

Fortes, M. 1950 The Ashanti. In *African Systems of Kinship and Marriage*, A.R. Radcliffe-Brown and D. Forde, eds. Oxford: Oxford University Press.

_____. 1969. *Kinship and the Social Order*. Chicago: Aldine.

Fortune, R. F. 1963. *The Sorcerers of Dobu*. Dutton: New York.

Fox, R. 1975. *Biosocial Anthropology*. New York: Halsted.

Fuller, C.J. 1976. *The Nayars Today*. Cambridge: Cambridge University Press.

Gluckman, M. 1950. Kinship and Marriage Among the Lozi of Northern Rhodesia and the Zulu of Natal. In *African Systems of Kinship and Marriage*, A.R. Radcliffe-Brown and D. Forde eds. Oxford: Oxford University Press.

Gonzalez, N. S. de. 1965. The Consanguineal Household and Matrifocality. *American Anthropologist* 67(6):1541–1549.

_____. 1969. *Black Carib Household Structure*. Seattle: University of Washington Press.

_____. 1970. Toward a Definition of Matrifocality. In *Afro-American Anthropology*, N.E. Whitten and J.F. Szwed, eds. New York: Free Press.

Goode, W. J. 1970. *World Revolution and Family Patterns* (2nd edition). New York: the Free Press.

Goody, J. 1976. *Production and Reproduction*. Cambridge: Cambridge University Press.

_____and S.J. Tambiah. 1971. *Bridewealth and Dowry*. Cambridge: Cambridge University Press.

Gough, K. 1961a Central Kerala Nayars. In *Matrilineal Kinship*, D. Schneider and K. Gough, eds. Berkeley: University of California Press.

_____. 1961b. Variation in Residence. In *Matrilineal Kinship*, D. Schneider and K. Gough, eds. Berkeley: University of California Press.

_____. 1961c. Variation in Interpersonal Kinship Relations. In *Matrilineal Kinship*, D. Schneider and K. Gough, eds. Berkeley: University of California Press.

_____. 1961d. Variation in Preferential Marriage Forms. In *Matrilineal Kinship*, D. Schneider and K. Gough, eds. Berkeley: University of California Press.

_____. 1961e. The Modern Disintegration of Matrilineal Descent Groups. In *Matrilineal Kinship*, D. Schneider and K. Gough, eds. Berkeley: University of California Press.

Greene, P. 1978. Promiscuity, Paternity and Culture. *American Ethnologist* 5:151–159.

Greenfield, S. 1966. *English Rustics in Black Skin*. New Haven: College and University Press.

Hamilton, W.D. 1964. The Genetical Evolution of Social Behavior, Parts I and II. *J. of Theor. Biol.* 7:1–52.

Hart, C. W. M. and A. R. Pilling. 1960. *The Tiwi*. New York: Holt, Rinehart and Winston.

Hirschfield, M., and D. Tinkle. 1976. Natural Selection and the Evolution of Parental Effort. In *Proc. Nat. Acad. Sci.* 72:2227–2231.

Homans, G. C., and D. Schneider. 1955. *Marriage, Authority, and Final Causes*. Glencoe: Free Press.

Irons, W. G. 1979a. Investment and Primary Social Dyads. In *Evolutionary Biology and Human Social Behavior*, N. Chagnon and W. Irons, eds. N. Scituate, Mass.: Duxbury Press.

_____. 1979b. Cultural and Biological Success. In *Evolutionary Biology and Human Social Behavior*, N. Chagnon and W. Irons, eds. N. Scituate, Mass.: Duxbury Press.

_____This volume. Why Lineage Exogamy?

Kahn, M. C. 1931. *Djuka: the Bush Negroes of Dutch Guiana*. New York: Viking Press.

King, C. E. 1945. The Negro Maternal Family: A Product of an Economic and Culture System. *Social Forces* 24:100–104.

Kurland, J. 1979. Paternity, Mother's Brother, and Human Sociality. In *Evolutionary Biology and Human Social Behavior*, N. Chagnon and W. Irons, eds. N. Scituate, Mass.: Duxbury Press.

Leach, E. 1951. The Structural Implications of Matrilateral Cross Cousin Marriage. Reprinted in *Rethinking Anthropology* (1961) New York: Humanities Press.

Levi-Strauss, C. 1949. *Les Structures Elementaires de la Parente*. Paris: Plon.

Levy Jr., M. 1963. Preface, *Aspects of the Analysis of Family Structure*. A.J. Coale et al. Princeton, Princeton University Press.

Linton, R. 1936. *The Study of Man*. New York: Appleton-Century-Crofts.

Loeb, E.M. 1934. Patrilineal and Matrilineal Organization in Sumatra. Pt. 2: The Menangkebau. *American Anthropologist* 36:25–56.

Low, B. S. 1978. Environmental Uncertainty and the Parental Strategies of Marsupials and Placentals. *American Naturalist* 112:197–213.

Lowie, R. 1920. *Primitive Society*. New York: Liveright.

Malinowski, B. 1961. Argonauts of the Western Pacific. New York: Dutton.

Maybury-Lewis, D. 1967. *Akwe-Shavante Society*. Oxford: Clarendon.

Morgan, L.H. 1870. Systems of Consanguinity and Affinity of the Human Family. *Smithsonian Contributions to Knowledge XVII* 1–590.

Murdock, G. P. 1949. *Social Structure*. New York: Macmillan

——. 1964. Cultural Correlates of the Regulation of Premarital Sex Behavior. In Process and Pattern in Culture, R.A. Manners, ed. Chicago: Aldine.

——. 1967. *World Enthnographic Sample*. Pittsburgh: University of Pittsburgh Press.

Naroll, R., and R. Cohen. 1970. Eds. *A Handbook of Method in Cultural Anthropology*. Garden City, N.Y.: Natural History Press.

Neel, J., and K. Weiss. 1978. The Genetic Structure of a Tribal Population, The Yanomama Indians. XII Biodemographic Studies. *American Journal of Physical Anthropology* 42:25–52.

Nimuendaju, C. 1939. *The Apinaye*. The Catholic University of American Anthropological Series, no. 8 Washington, D.C.

——. 1942. *The Serente*. F.W. Hodge Publication Fund, Vol. IV Los Angeles.

Orians, G.H. 1969. On the Evolution of Mating Systems in Birds and Mammals. *Amer. Nat.* 103:589–603.

Radcliffe-Brown, A.R. 1924. The Mother's Brother in South Africa. *South African Journal of Science* 21:542-555.

——. 1951. Murngin Social Organization. *American Anthropologist* 53:37–55.

Rattray, R.S. 1927. *Religion and Art in Ashanti*. London: Oxford University Press.

Richards, A.I. 1950. Some Types of Family Structure Amongst the Central Bantu. In *African Systems of Kinship and Marriage,* A.R. Radcliffe-Brown and D. Forde, eds. Pp. 83–120. London: Oxford.

Rodman, H. 1971. *Lower Class Families*. Oxford: London.

Rose, F. G. G. 1960. *Classification of Kin, Age Structure, and Marriage Amongst the Groote Eylandt Aborigines: A Study in Method and a Theory of Australian Kinship*. Berlin: Akademic Verlag.

Ryder, J.W. and M.B. Blackman. 1970. The Avunculate: A Cross-Cultural Critique of Claude Levi-Strauss. *Behavior Science Notes* 5(2):97–115.

Sahlins, M. 1976. *The Use and Abuse of Biology: An Anthropological Critique of Sociobiology*. Ann Arbor: University of Michigan Press.

Schapera, I. 1950. Kinship and Marriage Among the Tswana. In *African Systems of Kinship and Marriage,* A.R. Radcliffe-Brown and D. Forde, eds. Pp. 140–165. London: Oxford.

Schneider, D. 1961. Truk. In *Matrilineal Kinship*, D. Schneider and K. Gough, eds. Pp. 202–233.

——and K. Gough. 1961. Eds. *Matrilineal Kinship*. Berkeley: University of California Press.

Smith, M.G. 1962. *West Indian Family Structure*. Seattle: University of Washington Press.

Smith, R.T. 1956. *The Negro Family in British Guiana*. New York: Humanities Press Inc.

Spencer, H.1967. *The Evolution of Society: Selections from Herbert Spencer's Principles of Sociology*. R. Carneiro, ed. Chicago, University of Chicago Press.

Stack, C. 1975. *All Our Kin*. New York: Harper and Row.

Stephans, W. N. 1963. *The Family in Cross-Cultural Perspective*. New York: Holt, Rinehart and Winston.

Stirling, A. D. 1965. *Turkish Village*. London: Weidenfeld and Nicolsen.

Textor, R. 1967. *A Cross-Cultural Summary*. New Haven: HRAF Press.

Trivers, R. L. 1971. The Evolution of Reciprocal Altruism. *Quart. Rev. Biol.* 46(1):35–57.

——. 1972. Parental Investment and Sexual Selection. In *Sexual Selection and the Descent of Man, 1871–1971,* B.H. Campbell, ed. Pp. 136–179 Chicago: Aldine.

——. 1974. Parent-Offspring Conflict. *American Zoologist* 14:249–264.

Tylor, E.B. 1889. On a Method of Investigating the Development of Institutions; Applied to Laws of Marriage and Descent. *Journal of the Royal Anthropological Institute*. 18:245–269.

West-Eberhard, M. J. 1975. The Evolution of Social Behavior by Kin selection. *Quarterly Review of Biology* 50:1–33.

Williams, G. C. 1966. *Adaptation and Natural Selection*. Princeton: Princeton University Press.

——1975. *Sex and Evolution*. Princeton: Princeton University Press.

27.

Why Lineage Exogamy?

William Irons

    In this paper, I address the question of why in many human societies the incest prohibition and rules of exogamy are extended beyond close kin to all of the members of a lineage of several generations of genealogical depth. I start with the assumption that in the evolution of the human species, as in the evolution of most sexually reproducing animals, natural selection has favored behavioral propensities that lead to a low frequency of close inbreeding (Bischof, 1975; Shepher, 1971; Wolf, 1966, 1968, 1970). Cultural rules prohibiting primary incest, mating with parents, siblings, and children are expressions of, and reinforcers of, this evolved behavioral tendency (Maynard Smith, 1978:142–5; Wilson, 1978).

    I suggest here, however, that the extension of incest prohibitions and rules of exogamy beyond such close kin along lineage lines has a different function, that of assisting males in the mate competition that is necessary for them in a polygynous breeding system. On the surface this may appear unlikely. How does excluding certain related females from the category of potential mates assist males in gaining and keeping wives? The answer suggested here is that the exclusion of certain kinswomen as possible mates is part of a strategy of pooling resources for gaining mates and allies. Those who pool resources are a group of closely related individuals whose solidarity is based on relatedness. The resources they pool are of two varieties: (a) their sisters and daughters who can be given as mates to males outside the group (or can consent to become the mates of outsiders) and (b) their ability to use violence, or the threat of violence, in pursuit of an ally's interests. A group of related males can offer these resources to another similar group in return for reciprocation in kind. When two groups agree to such an arrangement two things are accomplished: (1) a larger number of individuals are united in mutual defense, and (2) most males in each group have a better chance of acquiring a wife than they would have by relying only on the exchange of closer female kin (sisters and daughters) for mates.

    An important element in the exchange tying two such groups together is the promise of future mates including as yet unborn females. The rule of exogamy is a part of this promise. It is, in a sense, a public ideological statement by a group of closely related men that all of their daughters and sisters—not just some but all—will be given to their allies. All one has to do to claim the benefits of such exogamy is to be an ally. At the same time, the rule of exogamy is a statement to the effect that one's allies must give their daughters and sisters to others (most probably one's own group), they cannot keep them within their group as their own mates. In short, it strengthens the promises of future exchange of mates, and of other benefits such as political support, between two groups of closely related males.

    Throughout this paper, I will be using some technical terms from both social anthropology and evolutionary biology, In some cases, different terms drawn from these separate disciplines have very similar meanings. The anthropological term ''solidarity'' and the biological term "altruism" are the most conspicuous examples. In this paper, I relate these two terms by defining solidarity with someone as a high degree of willingness to behave altruistically toward him or her. Following a similar logic, in a relationship of reciprocal altruism, solidarity can be defined as a low probability that cheating will occur. The usage, in my opinion, reflects faithfully the meanings of both technical terms in their respective disciplines.

A THEORETICAL MODEL

The most basic strategy underlying this exchange is that of close kin assisting one another in mate competition. Most human populations throughout most of human evolution appear to have been mildly polygynous (Alexander et. al., 1979). This means that, for males, competition for mates has been a necessary step toward reproductive success. In contrast, females are virtually guaranteed mates, and are concerned only with choosing the more desirable of several possible mates (Trivers, 1972). Human kinship in general appears to be based on reciprocity among close kin (Trivers, 1971). It, therefore, entails altruism, which is based on both genetic relatedness (Hamilton, 1964) and reciprocity (Trivers, 1971). Since the success of close male relatives in mate competition contributes strongly to the inclusive fitness of each individual, it is expectable that reciprocal aid among close kin be directed toward acquiring mates for males.

The assistance given by females to their brothers and fathers who are pursuing mates appears to be based on different things at different stages in their life histories. In societies that have rules of lineage exogamy, it is common for females to be betrothed at an early age, in some cases even before birth (Chagnon, 1979a; Hart and Pilling, 1960). When this occurs parental manipulation (Alexander, 1974) would appear to be an important element in their compliance with the strategies described above. As they mature and become aware of the social arrangements that affect them, they could be expected to try to exert their influence in pursuit of their own inclusive-fitness interests rather than those of brothers or fathers. When this is the case, however, they are still likely to comply with the rule of lineage exogamy and assist brothers and other male kin in mate competition (cf. Hartung, 1976:612). One reason is that the success of male kin in mate competition would increase their own inclusive fitness. A second reason would appear, from the available ethnography (e.g., Chagnon, 1968), to be a form of reciprocal aid between male and female lineage mates in which female lineage members aid male lineage members in mate competition and, in return, the males protect their kinswomen's interests via-a-vis husbands.

For males, participation in this pattern of reciprocity is based on direct gains to their reproductive success, inclusive fitness gains from the success of close male relatives and, while young, to some degree on parental manipulation.

Nuclear Families as Basic Units in Mate Exchange

Assuming that close kin want to assist one another in mate competition and, at the same time, that close kin do not want to mate with one another because of inbreeding depression, the nuclear family would appear to emerge as a unit ready to enter into reciprocal mate exchange with other nuclear families. Each nuclear family has female members that it cannot use as mates for its own males and at the same time, needs mates for its males (cf. Fox, 1967:31–33). Assuming the choice of mates is made by the older members of the group in pursuit of their inclusive fitness interests, the exchange of female members as mates between nuclear families would appear to be a good strategy based on reciprocal altruism. As long as each family had the same number of females of approximately the same age, it should be easy to overcome the threat of cheating, which is the principal barrier to the development of social ties based on reciprocity (Trivers, 1971). Given continual sexual receptivity, concealed time of ovulation (cf. Alexander and Noonan, 1979), and the long period of reproductive potential, the parties to the exchange would confer benefits on one another simultaneously for a long period of years. The chances would be very small that one party could terminate the pattern of exchange at some point in time and enjoy substantial benefits for itself without having paid the cost of reciprocation. If one family were to retrieve its kinswomen from the other, the cheated party could quickly do the same thing before having paid substantial unrewarded costs.

Advantages and Disadvantages of Lineages over Nuclear Families as Exogamous Units

There are, however, several difficulties with this hypothetical exchange. Different nuclear families are not likely to have the same numbers of daughters of the same age. Also assuming that exchanges of mates are acceptable to each party only if the numbers of mates given equals approximately those received, single nuclear families are frequently going to have disadvantageous sex ratios. Any family with many sons and few daughters would have difficulty exchanging its few daughters for the many mates it needed. Those with many daughters and few sons might appear to have an advantage, but this also is untrue given the fact that coalitions of closely related males use violence in mate competition. The optimal brood for any nuclear family wishing to enter into an exchange of mates with another nuclear family would be a large brood containing many males who would be dependable allies in using violence (defensively or offensively) and many daughters to be given in exchange for mates.

Few nuclear families are likely to achieve this ideal. Only a minority can be larger than the average in size. Also the chance of achieving anything near a 50/50 sex ratio is small given the fact that most broods are small. A brood of children is analogous to a very small sample drawn from a very large population that is half male and half female. The small size of the samples makes it unlikely that many of them will have sex ratios close to the 50/50 ratios of the large population from which they are drawn.

Several nuclear families can overcome to some extent both the problem of size and that of sex ratio by pooling their resources. Pooling of resources makes a sex ratio closer to 50/50 more probable by increasing "sample" size. However, such a pooling of resources increases the chances of cheating. Different nuclear families will pay the cost of such an alliance and reap its benefits at different points in time. There are likely to be numerous opportunities for a family that has, at one point in time, enjoyed a higher ratio of benefits to cost than the other members of the alliance to withdraw from the allied group before paying its "fair" share of the cost.

Counterstrategies Against Cheating

Two things can overcome this tendency to cheat by discontinuing the alliance: relatedness (Hamilton, 1964) and the need to preserve a large group of allies in the face of competition. A nuclear family that pools its resources with related families is less likely to be cheated, but, nevertheless, that possibility still exists. Exactly what resources each family has, what groups they exchange with, what threats of violence they must cope with will vary over time and the possibility may still arise that one group can gain by shedding a former ally despite some loss in terms of inclusive fitness owing to the genes shared with that ally.

I suggest that in many human societies in which mate competition is important each nuclear family is faced with the dilemma of gains to be had by pooling its resources for mate acquisition with related families and the danger of being cheated by such pooling arrangements. The basic strategy is to form alliances that have, as far as possible, low risks of cheating, that is, a nuclear family should enter such alliances based on a sharing of resources, but should, in doing so, employ counterstrategies against cheating. Further I offer as a hypothesis that lineage exogamy and reciprocal mate exchange between lineages are the outcomes of two counterstrategies against cheating. The first is that of limiting the pooling to related families. The second is for a group of closely related nuclear families to offer all of their kinswomen to another similar group of families. The promise of a steady and dependable supply of mates in an environment in which mates are hard to come by is a valuable thing if believable. A rule of exogamy does more to make such a promise believable than a preference for exogamy. Once mate exchange is established between lineages a prescription of cross-cousin marriage similarly is part of a promise to give all of a lineage's kinswomen to its allies.

A Different View of the Same Theoretical Model

An alternate way of looking at these strategies is to consider what would be optimal for a pair of brothers who each have sons for whom they wish to acquire mates and also have daughters to exchange for such mates. It is ethnographically realistic to assume that mate choices are initially made by parents for their children. It is reasonable to assume that they can trust each other because of their relatedness and that their resources both in the form of daughters and in the form of the ability to wield violence will be used for mutual benefit in the pursuit of mate acquisition for their respective sons. Assuming each brood has approximately a 50/50 sex ratio, the two brothers might exchange daughters, thus arranging parallel cousin marriages. The problem of mate acquisition would be solved, and the solidarity of the two brothers would be increased by the additional merger of reproductive interests. An alternate strategy is for the two brothers to offer all of their daughters to another group of brothers in exchange for the other group's daughters and a promise of all future daughters in similar exchanges. The second solution fails to strengthen the solidarity between brothers but has the advantage of drawing additional men into the circle of solidary allies (cf. Tylor, 1889; Levi-Strauss, 1949).

I am suggesting here that the combination of marriage ties and promise of future mates can be a basis of solidarity, i.e., a counterstrategy against cheating that is comparable in effectiveness to relatedness. The strength of this tie depends on a shortage of alternate sources of mates, and on the advantage of preserving existing mating ties in a species in which investment by both parents over a long period of time is important to the success of the children. Assuming existing mating ties and promises of future mates do create solidarity, the first strategy noted above has the advantage of increasing the magnitude of solidarity but not the size of the solidary group. Assuming the size of competing groups is large enough to make it advantageous to increase the size of one's own group, the second strategy would be preferable.

Once such an alliance is established in one generation, repeating it in the next generation does not pose the same cost. It is no longer a matter of using daughters to create mating ties with nonkin at the cost of foregoing a chance to use mating ties to strengthen solidarity with kin. When the exchange of mates between two lineages is repeated in the next generation mating ties are strengthening kin ties, albeit not the brother-brother ties (cf. Chagnon and Bugos, 1979). Rather the ties strengthened are between brother and sister in one generation, and between cross-cousins in the next generation.

Thus, it is only in some cases that lineage exogamous marriages entail sacrificing the chance to strengthen existing kin ties in order to create new solidary ties of a different kind. The flexibility to create new ties under some circumstances is, however, useful. For instance, it allows a lineage to seek new allies when it grows much larger than its affinal lineage of previous generations. It also allows small groups of related kin to establish allies in a new location after migrating.

This argument is summarized in Table 27–1.

Table 27–1.   The comparative advantages of lineages and nuclear families as exogamous units.

Lineages	Nuclear Families
(1) Creates larger solidary group	(1) Less chance of being cheated by other members of one's exogamous unit because of higher relatedness of group members
(2) Units exchanging women as mates are more likely to have a sex ratio allowing them to acquire a mate for all their male members by direct exchange	
(3) Greater flexibility in forming new alliances because more women to give	

THE USE OF GAME THEORY MODELS

The above description is an attempt to explain how a rule of lineage exogamy could arise as part of a strategy of reciprocal aid among close kin in mate competition. I stated the model in loose game theory terms *as if* the actors in the societies were acting rationally in response to a limited number of constraints and opportunities posed by a particular social environment and were negotiating a set of social compacts without the encumbrance of pre-existing rules. In fact, individuals are born into ongoing social systems with social compacts inherited from the past. The assumption that I think justifies thinking in game theory terms is that people either attempt to change or to circumvent inherited social compacts that are not congruent with their interests defined in terms of maximizing inclusive fitness (cf. Alexander, 1979 and Irons, 1979b). (This is not meant to imply that an interest in maximizing inclusive fitness is cognized as such. It merely implies that individuals do formulate and strive to fulfill certain aspirations which have the unrecognized effect of increasing their inclusive fitness.) This bending and changing of social rules in pursuit of perceived self interest leads to gradual renegotiations of inherited social compacts. If the relevant constraints and opportunities that define particular strategies as optimal remain stable long enough, the process of renegotiation leads to a social compact corresponding to the one actors would create if faced with these same constraints and opportunities without inherited social arrangements (cf. Fox, 1971).

UNDERLYING ASSUMPTIONS

The model presented here is phrased in terms of responses by the individuals who constitute a local population to their particular environments. (An individual's environment in this discussion includes everything external to the individual that affects his or her inclusive fitness—including conspecifics and their patterns of behavior.) The responses consist of the working out of social compacts that are mutually acceptable given these conditions. Implicit in such a model is the assumption that, given other environmental conditions, other social compacts would be devised. Following is a discussion of the specific environmental states which I hypothesize to be those which make lineage exogamy optimal as a strategy of mate competition.

1.   Primary Incest Avoidance Decreases Inbreeding Depression The entire discussion above began with the assumption that members of the same nuclear family avoid mating with one another because of the cost of inbreeding depression. Avoidance of primary incest appears to be a near universal among human populations.

2.   Marriage is Superior to Extramarital Sex as a Reproductive Strategy This social condition, though perhaps less universal than primary incest avoidance, also appears close to universal in human populations.

3.   Polygyny Makes Females a Limited Resource for Which Males Compete Another assumption is the existence of a polygynous breeding system in which both by synchronous polygyny and by serial monogamy, some males are able to monopolize the reproductive potential of several females. A necessary consequence of this is that other males are excluded from marriage until after a large portion of their potential reproductive years have passed. While females are virtually assured of marriage and mating opportunities throughout their reproductive years, males must expend considerable effort in competition with other males for the opportunity to mate. This is the familiar situation in non-human polygynous breeding systems, the implications of which were explored in Trivers' 1972 paper. In the human case, however, males are assisted in important ways by close relatives in this competition.

4.   Warre Makes Violence, or the Threat of Violence, an Important Element in Mate Competition Another assumption is the condition of warre (Sahlins, 1968), i.e., a condition in which each individual is in a position to use violence in pursuit of his own interest. This is the opposite of the more familiar condition in state societies in which the state monopolizes the legitimate use of violence and imposes peaceful settlements of disputes among individuals. Without this condition or something approximating it, the process of building up networks of male allies stressed above would be less important.

In some cases, this condition may be met in state societies. This would be so whenever a state is ineffective in controlling violence in a certain population, or chooses not to regulate violence in a certain population that falls under its sovereignty.

5. Individual Mate Choices are Limited by the Need for Kin Aid in Mate Competition Another assumption is that because of the importance of assistance from close kin in mate acquisition, an individual does not have full control of his or her mate choices. Rather, the wishes of those whose assistance is necessary for gaining mates must be respected to some degree in order to gain their assistance. Usually initial mate choices are made for an individual by parents and parents' siblings while an individual is very young as noted above. At this point, an individual may have no say in the matter. Later in life, an individual tends to have more control over his or her mate choices, but nevertheless the wishes of certain close kin must still be respected if one is to depend on their aid in the future. This condition appears in fact to be met in all but some social classes of modern industrial societies.

6. The Mate Pool Is Not so Small as to Make Exogamy Impractical In some populations of very low density, the exclusion of certain kinswomen as potential mates may impose too high a cost. If the actual number of individuals of the opposite sex that one encounters in a lifetime is very small, it may be necessary to consider as potential mates all members of the opposite sex other than nuclear family members. This may explain the lack of exogamous lineages among arctic hunters and gatherers. However, the need to cope with other scarcities discussed below may also explain this.

7. Wives Are Most Easily Obtained by Exchanging Women for Women Another crucial assumption is that women who are in shorter supply than male demands are most easily obtained by exchanging a woman for a woman. The familiar situation described in much of the anthropological literature is one in which two men exchange their sisters as wives. Often in reality, sets of parents exchange daughters as sons' wives; that is, the arrangement is made by parents for their offspring. In addition to exchanging women for women, individuals also obtain women by giving political support or a combination of political support and women. Political support in the relevant ethnographic contexts means using violence or the threat of violence in pursuit of another individual's interests. Exchanges of women for women and of political support for women are in effect forms of reciprocity. Extortion and abduction are alternate means also used in these societies to obtain wives that are not based on reciprocity, unless one wishes to use Marshall Sahlins' (1968) extension of the term and call such activities negative reciprocity. (His definition of negative reciprocity as attempting to get something for nothing reflects the fact that those who extort or abduct hope that their victims will be unable to reciprocate.) Extortion and abduction are much more expensive ways of gaining wives than reciprocity, since these means produce enemies, whereas reciprocity produces allies. Thus, the best strategy for all but those who have networks of allies who are especially effective at applying violence is to gain wives by reciprocity and in the process build up networks of allies to defend themselves against others who are tempted to use extortion or abduction.

8. Competition For Other Resources Does Not Dictate the Formation of Other Social Compacts Another assumption is that competition over resources other than mates does not dictate the formation of different patterns of alliance. The above model assumes that competition among males for mates is the only activity relevant to the formation of alliances. In societies in which competition for land or other economic resources becomes prominent, alliance patterns must also adjust to these. If competition for heritable forms of wealth becomes a very important means of achieving reproductive success (cf. Hartung, 1976), exchange of wealth for mates may replace the exchange of mates for mates. Such a change would transform the social system hypothesized above.

The conditions listed above vary in the frequency of their occurrence. The first two—primary incest avoidance and marriage as the most successful reproductive strategy—appear to be near universals. The third and fourth—polygyny and warre—are close to universal in preliterate societies. Condition five—kin control of mate choice—would appear logically to flow from conditions three and four, and seems to be present, as noted above, in almost all pre-industrial societies. Condition six—sufficient population density—appears also to be very widespread. Conditions seven and eight—women exchange and limited competition for other resources—are less universal and deviations from these conditions would appear to account for important transformations of systems of lineage exogamy as discussed below.

THEORETICAL MODELS AND ETHNOGRAPHIC CASES

The above model is stated in deductive terms in order to make its logic as clear as possible. However, the model was constructed with the Yanomamö in mind (Chagnon, 1968, 1974, 1979a). The original thinking was, therefore, more inductive than deductive in character. The Yanomamö appear to be a society in which competition for mates is the primary factor accounting for differences in reproductive success. This accords well with their low population density and the abundance of horticultural land and other resources necessary for subsistence (Chagnon and Hames, 1979). These conditions among the Yanomamö suggest that they may have recently moved into a previously unoccupied niche in the tropical forest and may be experiencing the early stages of rapid population growth that would follow such an event. The logic in this paper differs from that in Chagnon's (1979a) paper not in emphasizing the importance of mate competition, but rather in trying to go beyond his analysis in one way, i.e., in arguing that the creation and maintenance of a rule of lineage exogamy is itself a strategy of mate competition and, further, in arguing that such a strategy will emerge whenever the eight conditions described here are met.

WHY EXTEND LINEAGE TIES

The model given, I suggest, explains the emergence of small local descent groups that are exogamous and that reciprocally exchange mates. As noted, the model was developed with the Yanomamö case in mind. Among that group more distant lineage ties are forgotten or denied (Chagnon, 1968, 1975, 1979a). Chagnon has documented well the tendency of lineages to fission into groups that operate in terms of separate interests as relatedness among members declines over generations. As such groups grow apart their relationship is usually hostile and their status as potential allies in mate competition is in most cases irrelevant. However, for individuals who have no, or few, close kin, the ability to call on lineage ties to more distant kin as a basis for becoming second-class members of their alliance may be valuable. This possibility may account for the theoretical extension of exogamy and other kin obligations to more distant kin who in fact are rarely actively involved in assisting an individual in mate competition. This is based on the assumption that being a second-class member of a group of kin united for mate acquisition is better than the solitary pursuit of mates.

This hypothesis could be verified by demonstrating the following: (a) nuclear families who have close kin use their resources for mate acquisition primarily on behalf of close kin despite the presence of distance lineage-mates and distant lineage-mates of their closest affinal allies; (b) nuclear families that lack close kin beyond the nuclear unit use their resources on behalf of more distant kin and receive assistance in return, but less assistance than would be returned to close kin; (c) nuclear families that have no close kin beyond the nuclear unit and that attempt to pursue a strategy of mate competition without the assistance of distant lineage-mates have less success than those who pool their resources with distant lineage-mates.

If the above explanation for the extension of exogamy to distant lineage-mates is correct, ties to distant lineage-mates should become more important as the probability increases that an individual will be unable in adulthood to call on close lineage-mates for assistance. A low rate of population growth, no population growth, or a declining population would increase this probability. Frequent migration of individuals from one local group to another would do the same. The Yanomomö have a high rate of population growth but also a high occurrence of migration, which might seem to make them intermediate in terms of the occurrence of adults who lack close adult kin. However, the fact that the Yanomamö usually migrate between local groups in clusters of closely related individuals weakens the effect that migration would have on the chances of lacking close kin. It is, therefore, reasonable to suggest that for the Yanomomö there is a low probability of lacking close kin in adulthood compared to most other societies in which lineage exogamy occurs. This may explain the absence among them of ritual and other practices that tend to keep the memory, or theory, of distant lineage ties alive. The above reasoning would suggest that low rates of population growth and high levels of population dispersal (especially migrations by individuals or very small kin groups) would encourage the development of institutions which facilitate the maintenance of distant lineage ties.

It should also be noted in considering the extension of exogamy and incest prohibitions to progressively more distant kin that the quality of reaction to violations of the incest taboo varies as the individuals involved become more distantly related. Although described as the same thing verbally, matings between distantly related members of exogamous lineages draw a less negative reaction than would matings between primary kin (Chagnon, personal communication; Oliver, 1967 [1955]:121). This fact by itself does not provide very strong inferential support for the above hypothesis, but it is consistent with basic assumptions that the extension of the incest prohibition beyond primary kin has a different function than the prohibition of incest with primary kin.

Another condition that may cause lineage ties and the rule of lineage exogamy to be extended beyond small local groups is the need to form larger and larger political units as population becomes denser. This is discussed next, along with other topics, under the heading of competition for other resources.

COMPETITION FOR OTHER RESOURCES: SOME BRIEF OBSERVATIONS ON TRANSFORMATIONS OF THE ABOVE MODEL

Scarcity of other resources as a factor limiting reproduction would lead to additional competition for these other resources as well, and probably as noted to modification of the pattern of alliance and mate exchange hypothesized here. Attempts to account for variations in systems of marriage exchange in terms of the addition of other scarcities affecting reproduction would appear to be the most straightforward way of extending and refining the model presented here.

Food Scarcity Among Some Gatherers and Hunters

The Tiwi may provide an example of a society in which additional scarcities, other than the scarcity of wives, can transform the system of lineage exogamy described above. The Tiwi are a society in which mate competition appears to be important. Here, however, occasional food shortages appear also to limit survival and reproduction (Hart and Pilling, 1960). The best way to cope with this environmental limitation on reproduction is to build households with large numbers of women based on sororal polygyny (Hart and Pilling, 1960). It would be interesting to inquire whether this difference alone can account for the differences in their system of alliance formation and mate competition. Here as a rule all of a woman's daughters are married to the same man. Men use daughters primarily in exchange for their own rather than their sons' wives, and men begin their legitimate reproductive careers much later in life than among the Yanomamö (when their fathers are most probably deceased). Men are launched on their careers of mate acquisition frequently by mothers who use *de facto* rights to remarry widowed daughters to acquire mates for sons (Hart and Pilling, 1960:18–21). This may explain why they have developed exogamous matrilineages rather than patrilineages. The crucial alliance may be between sisters manipulating daughters' marriages on behalf of sons (cf. Hart and Pilling, 1960). Other conditions that may lead to the formation of matrilineages rather than the patrilineages hypothesized above are discussed as follows.

Population Density and Intergroup Conflict

Another factor that under certain conditions may cause lineages to become larger is increasing population density. At the low population densities characteristic of the Yanomamö, arable land exists in far greater supply than potential demand. Under these conditions competition for land does not occur. Warfare between autonomous local groups is a form of mate competition (Chagnon, 1979a) and groups that are unable to defend themselves militarily against larger neighboring groups can use flight and relocation at a safe distance from enemies as a means of defense (cf. Carneiro, 1970; Chagnon, 1968; Irons, 1979a). Under these conditions there is little advantage to forming larger solidary groups other than the pairs of intermarrying local descent groups that form the core of most Yanomamö villages. As groups grow larger and come to contain large numbers of unrelated individuals, internal conflict becomes more common and they fission (Chagnon, 1975). After fissioning, relocation at a safe distance from enemies is common (Chagnon, 1968, 1974,

1975). Where population density becomes too great for such easy and safe relocation from hostile, or potentially hostile, neighboring groups, there is an advantage to forming larger groups for defense (Chagnon, 1974; cf. Carneiro, 1970 and Irons, 1979). A village that cannot move away from a hostile neighboring village has an advantage if it is larger than its neighbors. The advantage of size can outweigh the disadvantage of coresidence with, and reciprocity with, distantly related or unrelated individuals.

Shortages of Arable Land

The advantage to size described above occurs whenever population density restricts the use of relocation as a means of defense. This may occur before agricultural land becomes scarce. Once arable land becomes scarce, however, and there is competition for land, owing to increasing population density, the advantage to size can be expected to increase. It seems a reasonable hypothesis that local descent groups under these circumstances would increase in size by holding together more and more distant kin. The strategies of exogamy and reciprocal exchange between such larger lineages would still appear to be the best means of defense in competition for both mates and territory. Accordingly, exact size of both lineages and politically solidary groups consisting of intermarrying lineages would be determined by a balancing of the advantage of size against the disadvantage of close interaction with less related individuals. Data from many of the groups in the more densely populated areas of highland New Guinea should provide opportunities to test this explanation of increasing lineage size.

Among groups that have very large segmentary lineage systems, lineage ties based on fictive genealogies often extend far beyond the boundaries of the largest exogamous descent groups (e.g., Nuer, Tiv). These distant ties appear to function exclusively for the recruitment of defensive (or offensive) political groups against hostile neighboring groups and to have no relationship to mate competition.

PATRILINY AND MATRILINY

The above discussion suggests that the most basic function of lineage exogamy is to enlarge the number of males who assist one another in mate competition. Each man attempts to increase the number of reliable male allies by exploiting two forms of solidarity, one based on kinship and one based on reciprocal mate exchange. The circle of kin beyond the nuclear family with which a man attempts to build up such a network of allies starts with full siblings. A group of full brothers pool their resources in daughters to acquire mates for all their sons. If they are successful in establishing an alliance with another local descent group, the most advantageous procedure is to repeat the exchange in the next generation. Doing so means holding patrilateral parallel cousins together in an exogamous group that exchanges its females with a similar group. In other words, it creates an exogamous patrilineage. Such a model, however, assumes that a man maintains a high degree of control over his offspring, and a strong interest in investing limited resources in the pursuit of their welfare.

In societies in which the husband-and-wife bond is attenuated by tolerance of extramarital sex and frequent divorce, such control over children and willingness to invest in them may not occur (Alexander, 1974; Greene, 1978; Kurland, 1979). In a society such as this, a man may typically have children by a series of wives, each of whom has children by several other men. Some of the children of each wife, or former wife, are clearly those of other men by other marriages (see especially Kurland, 1979), some are of doubtful paternity because of promiscuity, and others he may be confident are his. Since many of the things a man does to invest in offspring, such as building a house or cultivating a garden with a wife, necessarily are shared by all of the offspring of a wife (see especially Kurland, 1979), this situation dilutes a man's parental investment in wives' children and may make it adaptive to shift much of his investment to sisters' children (Alexander, 1974, 1977). In societies in which the marital bond is attenuated as described above, men typically invest substantially in both wives' and sisters' children. Nevertheless, the ability of a man to treat all of his children as a single brood exchanging daughters for sons' wives, or for close lineage-mates' wives, is limited by such a situation. Wives and their brothers are interested in all of a woman's children and unconcerned about the particular interests of their several putative fathers. Given these conditions, the most logical groups to pool resources for mate competition may be a group of brothers, their sisters and sisters' children. Here the basic units out of which a lineage can be built are groups of half-siblings with the same mother. Given paternity uncertainty, such groups would be more closely related than groups of half-siblings with the same putative father. From the point of the mother, such a group is more profitably treated as a unit for purposes of arranging marriages than are groups of half-siblings with the same father. From a man's point of view, the choice between devoting his effort to arranging marriages for sisters' sons or his own sons may be a difficult one. The balance may be tipped in favor of the former by the fact that brothers, with whom he would be most closely allied, share his interest in sisters' children more than his interest in his own children. Other relatives, such as a man's parents, will also, given the greater certainty of kin ties through females, push his effort in the direction of sisters rather than own children (Alexander, 1977). Thus, even if a man is convinced he can identify a number of children as his own, he may find it impossible to persuade brothers and other close kin to pool their resources with his on behalf of these children. Persuading them to pool resources on behalf of sisters' children, however, may be possible. Forming the latter kind of alliance also does not preclude efforts to help putative sons in the pursuit of mates. This is especially true in view of the fact that sisters' daughters, under a system of intermarrying matrilineages, are potential mates for his putative sons. Thus the mixed strategy of trying to assist both his sisters' sons and his own putative sons may be best served by mobilizing the aid of other relatives where it can be mobilized, on behalf of sisters' sons, while trying as best he can to arrange marriages of sisters' daughters to putative sons.

Given high accuracy of paternity ascertainment and marital stability, however, the preference for building patrilineages should be strong. Not only would a man be more closely related on average to his wife's children than to his sister's children, he should find his brothers as willing to pool resources on behalf of his wife's children as they would be on behalf of sister's children. Given this, for brothers to pool resources on behalf of sons is more satisfactory. Further, males whose fathers were successful reproductively would find their closest allies, full and half brothers with the same father, numerous. Thus, the advantage of size would be greater in the pooling of resources along agnatic lines for the more successful members of the population (Chagnon, 1979b).

DATA THAT COULD FALSIFY THE HYPOTHESIS

The above model suggests three advantages to lineages over nuclear families as units that enter into reciprocal mate exchange: (1) they are larger and more effective as groups wielding violence, (2) they are more likely to have a 50/50 sex ratio, and (3) they have greater flexibility in creating new alliances because they have more women to give. Each of these statements is potentially falsifiable using data of the kind available for the Yanomamö. The first could be falsified by showing that there is no correlation between a man's success in mate competition and the number of lineages and affinal allies he can call on. This may be somewhat difficult to test since ideally one would want a life-history of support from allies rather than a measure of their numbers at one point in time. The second could be falsified by showing that smaller lineage groups have no more difficulty in exchanging women for women as a result of sex ratio deviating from 50/50 than do larger lineage groups. The lineage groups referred to here are not the total membership of a lineage in a particular local group, but rather the number of lineagemates who actually pool resources to aid one another in mate competition. This fact may also make testing somewhat difficult. The implications for data gathering, however, seem clear: (1) detailed quantitative data of the sort available for the Yanomamö provide our best chance for testing this sort of theoretical model; (2) the most appropriate sorts of data are not likely to be gathered by a researcher who does not have the model, or a similar model, in mind.

One might also falsify the model by showing in a cross-cultural study that lineage exogamy and reciprocal mate exchange between lineages do not correlate with the eight conditions outlined above. The greatest difficulty here, apart from finding the correct data on the eight conditions for a large sample of societies, would appear to be assessing the role of competition for scarce resources, other than mates, in creating lineage systems which conform only partially to the above model.

EPILOGUE

This paper should be viewed as a synthesis of Tylor's (1889) theory of exogamy and Darwin's (1871) theory of sexual selection. The task of integrating these theories was made possible by more recent contributions of both an empirical and a theoretical nature. Bateman's (1948) and Trivers' (1972) work has clarified the nature and importance of competition among males for mates. Chagnon's data on the Yanomanö suggested to me that the ultimate cause of competition and need for alliance among many culturally primitive groups has been mate competition (1968, 1974, 1979a). Hamilton's (1964) paper provided an evolutionary explanation for something that Tylor perspicaciously assumed: that kinship produces solidarity. Trivers' (1971) paper clarified the difficulties that plague attempts by human beings to base their sociality on reciprocity, difficulties that seem to me to be a very real part of human social life everywhere. Alexander's (1974) idea about the effect of paternity uncertainty on human sociality provided an explanation for the occasional extension of rules of exogamy along uterine lines.

I hope this essay will serve as an illustration of the fact that the time is now ripe for syntheses of ideas from evolutionary biology and anthropology. Such syntheses can, I believe, begin to provide us with better answers to such basic questions as why lineage exogamy is a widespread institution or why it exists at all.

ACKNOWLEDGEMENTS

R. D. Alexander, N. A. Chagnon, and J. Hartung made helpful suggestions for improving earlier drafts of this paper. I remain solely responsible for its flaws. My exploration of the implications of evolutionary biology for human social behavior, which has occupied much of my attention since 1973, would not have been possible without the support of the Harry Frank Guggenheim Foundation, the National Science Foundation, and the Ford and Rockefeller Foundations' Program on Population Policy. This paper is one product of the broader research effort that they generously supported.

REFERENCES

Alexander, R. D. 1974. The evolution of social behavior. *Annual Review of Ecology and Systematics* 5:325–383.

———. 1977. Natural selection and the analysis of human sociality. In C. E., Goulden, ed., *Changing*

Scenes in the Natural Sciences, 1776–1976. Pp. 283–337. Academy of Natural Sciences, Special Publication 12, Philadelphia, Pennsylvania.

———. 1979. Evolution and culture. In N. A. Chagnon and W. Irons, eds., *Evolutionary Biology and Human Social Behavior: An Anthropological Perspective.* Pp. 39–59. Duxbury Press, N. Scituate, Massachusetts.

———, and John L. Hoogland, Richard D. Howard, Katharine M. Noonan, and Paul W. Sherman. 1979. Sexual dimorphism and breeding systems in pinnipeds, ungulates, primates, and humans. In N. A. Chagnon and W. Irons, eds., *Evolutionary Biology and Human Social Behavior: An Anthropological Perspecive.* Pp. 402–435. Duxbury Press, N. Scituate, Massachusetts.

———, and Katharine M. Noonan. 1979. Concealment of ovulation, parental care, and human social evolution. In N. A. Chagnon and W. Irons, eds., *Evolutionary Biology and Human Social Behavior: An Anthropological Perspective.* Pp. 436–453. Duxbury Press, N. Scituate, Massachusetts.

Bateman, A. J. 1948. Intrasexual selection in *Drosophila. Heredity* 2:349–368.

Bischof, Norbert. 1975. The comparative ethology of incest avoidance. In R. Fox, ed., *Biosocial Anthropology.* Pp. 37–67. Malaby Press, London.

Carneiro, R. L. 1970. A theory of the origin of the state. *Science* 169:733–738.

Chagnon, N. A. 1968a. *Yanomamö: The Fierce People.* Holt, Rinehart and Winston, New York.

———. 1968b. Yanomamö social organization and warfare. In M. Fried, M. Harris, and R. Murphy, eds., *War: The Anthropology of Armed Conflict and Aggression.* Pp. 109–159. Natural History Press, Garden City, N.J.

———1968c. The culture-ecology of shifting (pioneering) cultivation among the Yanomamö Indians. *Proceedings, III International Congress of Anthropological and Ethnological Sciences,* Tokyo 3:249–255. Also pp. 126–142 in D. R. Gross, ed., *Peoples and Cultures of Native South America,* 1973. Natural History Press, Garden City, New Jersey.

———1974. *Studying the Yanomamö.* Holt, Rinehart and Winston, New York.

———1975. Genealogy, solidarity, and relatedness: limits to local group size and patterns of fissioning in an expanding population. *Yearbook of Physical Anthropology* 19:95–110. American Association of Physical Anthropologists, Washington, D.C.

———1979a. Mate competition, favoring close kin and village fissioning among the Yanomamö Indians. In N. A. Chagnon and W. Irons, eds., *Evolutionary Biology and Human Social Behavior: An Anthropological Perspective.* Pp. 86–132. Duxbury Press, N. Scituate, Massachusetts.

———1979b. Is reproductive success equal in egalitarian societies? In N.A. Chagnon and W. Irons, eds., *Evolutionary Biology and Human Social Behavior: An Anthropological Perspective.* Pp. 374–401. Duxbury Press, N. Scituate, Massachusetts.

———In Press. Kin selection theory, kinship, marriage and fitness among the Yanomamö Indians. In G. W. Barlow and J. Silverberg, eds., *Sociobiology: Beyond Nature/Nuture?: Reports, Definitions and Debate.* AAAS Selected Symposium 35. Westview Press, Boulder, Colorado.

———, and P. E. Bugos, Jr. 1979. Kin selection and conflict: an analysis of Yanomamö ax fight. In N. A. Chagnon and W. Irons, eds., *Evolutionary Biology and Human Social Behavior: An Anthropological Perspective.* Pp. 213–238. Duxbury Press, N.Scituate, Massachusetts.

———, and E. V. Fredlund. In Preparation. Genealogical Dimensions of Yanomamö Incest Practices.

———, and R. B. Hames. 1979. Protein Deficiency and Tribal Warfare in Amazonia: New Data. *Science* 203:910–913.

Darwin C. 1871. *The Descent of Man, and Selection in Relation to Sex.* London: John Murray.

Fox, R. 1967. *Kinship and Marriage: An Anthropological Perspective.* Penguin, London.

———. 1971. The Cultural Animal. In J. E. Eisenberg and W. S. Dillon, eds., *Man and Beast: Comparative Social Behavior.* Pp. 273–296. Smithsonian Institution Press, Washington, D.C.

Greene, Penelope J. 1978. Promiscuity, paternity, and culture. *American Ethnologist* 5(1): 151–159.

Hamilton, W. D. 1964. The genetical evolution of social behavior, parts I and II. *Journal of Theoretical Biology* 7:1–52.

Hart, C. W. M., and A. R. Pilling. 1960. *The Tiwi of North Australia.* Holt, Rinehart, and Winston, New York.

Hartung, John. 1976. On natural selection and the inheritance of wealth. *Current Anthropology* 17:607–622.

Irons, W. 1975. The Yomut Turkmen: a study of social organization among a Central Asian Turkic-speaking population. Museum of Anthropology, University of Michigan, Anthropological Paper No. 58, Ann Arbor, Michigan.

———1979a. Political stratification among pastoral nomads. In *Equipe Écologie et Anthropologie des*

Société Pastorales, eds., Pastoral Production and Society. Cambridge University Press and Maison des Sciences de l'Homme, New Rochelle, New York and London.

————1979b. Natural selection, adaptation, and human social behavior. In N.A. Chagnon and W. Irons, eds., *Evolutionary Biology and Human Social Behavior: An Anthropological Perspective.* Pp. 4-39. Duxbury Press, N. Scituate, Massachusetts.

————1979c. Investment and primary social dyads. In N. A. Chagnon and W. Irons, eds., *Evolutionary Biology and Human Social Behavior.* Pp. 181–213. Duxbury Press, N. Scituate, Massachusetts.

Kurland, J. A. 1979. Paternity, mother's brother, and human sociality. In N. A. Chagnon and W. Irons, eds., *Evolutionary Biology and Human Social Behavior: An Anthropological Perspective.* Pp. 145–180. Duxbury Press, N. Scituate, Mass.

Levi-Strauss, C. 1949. *Les Structures élémentaires de la parénte.* Plon, Paris.

Maynard Smith, J. 1978. *The Evolution of Sex.* Cambridge University Press, Cambridge.

Oliver, D. L. 1955. *A Solomon Island Society.* Harvard University Press, Cambridge.

Sahlins, M. D. 1968. On the sociology of primitive exchange. In M. Benton, ed., *The Relevance of Models for Social Anthropology.* Pp. 139–227. Tavistock, London.

Shepher, J. 1971. Self-imposed Incest Avoidance and Exogamy in Second Generation Kibbutz Adults. Ph.D. Thesis, Rutgers University.

Trivers, R. L. 1971. The evolution of reciprocal altruism. *Quarterly Review of Biology* 46(1):35–57.

————. 1972. Parental investment and sexual selection. In B. H. Campbell, ed., *Sexual Selection and the Descent of Man, 1871–1971.* Aldine, Chicago.

Tylor, E. B. 1889. On a method of investigating the development of institutions; applied to laws of marriage and descent. *Journal of the Royal Anthropological Institute* 18:245–256, 261–269.

Wilson, E. O. 1978. *On Human Nature.* Harvard University Press, Cambridge.

Wolf, A. P. 1966. Childhood association, sexual attraction, and the incest taboo: A Chinese case. *American Anthropologist* 68:883–898.

————. 1968. Adopt a daughter-in-law, marry a sister: A Chinese solution to the problem of the incest taboo. *American Anthropologist* 70:864–874.

————. 1970. Childhood association and sexual attraction: a further test of the Westermarck hypothesis. *American Anthropologist* 72:503–515.

28.

Terminological Kinship, Genealogical Relatedness and Village Fissioning among the Yanomamö Indians

Napoleon A. Chagnon

INTRODUCTION

There are many anthropological opinions on the nature and content of human kinship. One extreme view holds that whatever else human kinship is all about, it has nothing to do with biology (Schneider, 1964; 1965). At the other pole is an equally legitimate and very different perspective—that human kinship is the rock-bottom of social amity and emanates from the facts of procreation (Fortes, 1969). While the latter position does not equate human kinship with biological relationships, it comes much closer to acknowledging that kinship has some kind of "natural" content that is not reducible to other phenomena commonly studied by anthropologists—economic relationships, political ties, structural relationships, ritual, etc.

Anthropological views on the purpose or meaning of kinship tend to focus on "functional" relationships, i.e., showing how systems of kinship classification reflect and articulate with other social institutions, economic activities, rules about marriage, rights and duties individuals have vis-a-vis each other, the purpose generally being to document the integration of social parts into a coherent, systematic whole. It would be reasonable to say that until the impact of Hamilton's 1964 paper began to filter into literature that made occasional reference to human kinship as part of a more general class of behavioral phenomena characterizing a large number of non-human societies, anthropologists paid very little attention to the possible evolutionary functions of kinship behavior in humans. The central question that emerges once the legitimacy of an evolutionary perspective on human kinship is admitted is the role of social behavior in individual fitness-maximizing strategies that entail social interactions with other individuals and classes of individuals—and the extent to which relatedness figures in the choices made by individuals among the alternatives immediately available to them. Admitting the possibility that social behavior has evolved functions (Williams, 1966) logically leads to an exploration of any and all phenomena that might have measurable consequences on individual reproductive success and inclusive fitness. The general theory of sexual selection (see review of this theory and the issues it raises in Campbell, 1972) emerges as both a relevant and an important theory for predicting and interpreting social behavior in the kinds of human societies traditionally studied by anthropologists, drawing attention to competition among males for opportunities to mate and the "alliance choices" made by females or by their kin on behalf of them. My own growing suspicion is that sexual selection theory is far more useful in understanding the social behavior of most tribesmen than kin selection theory although the latter contributes appreciably to understanding the overall patterns of behavior.

The following arguments about Yanomamö social behavior will, therefore, consider kinship taxonomy, genealogical relatedness, choice of residence when a village fissions, and choice of individuals with whom one should live after a fission from the vantage of (a) kin selection theory, (b) sexual selection theory and (c) alliance theory. The first section of the paper will explore the relationship between the terminological system of kinship classification used by the Yanomamö to define their social world and the demonstrable genealogical relationships between individuals who are placed into the various kinship categories. The purpose of that exercise is to contest the argument that human kinship has nothing to do with genealogical relatedness (Schneider, 1964; 1965) or that no human society known organizes the calculus of its social relationships in a manner predictable from kin selection theory (Sahlins, 1976). The social behavior I will use to address these arguments is the choices by individuals to remain with or separate from relatives they classify into various kinship categories in a way that is independent of their known genealogical (biological) relatedness to the individuals in those kinship categories.

The second part of the paper discusses village fissioning as a "selfish" process in which coalitions of adult males attempt to establish new villages within which the intensity of mate competition for themselves and their male offspring is reduced by comparison to the conditions in the pre-fission village. To do so, they must surround themselves with as many social allies as possible and remove themselves from as many social competitors as possible. The choices made by individuals regarding their next residence and who they should live with after a fission are considered to reflect inclusive fitness maximizing strategies in the context of mate competition.

Village Fissioning

Since the process of village fissioning will be the basis of both sections of the paper, I will briefly discuss that process as it occurs among the Yanomamö Indians of southern Venezuela.

Population growth occurs at an appreciably high rate among Yanomamö (Chagnon, 1974). The organizational features of the tribe are such that villages cease to grow once a certain size limit is reached and divide into two (or more) independent groups (Chagnon, 1966; 1968a; 1968b; 1968c; 1974; 1975; 1979a; 1979b). The principles of cohesion and village integration are largely derived from (1) the ethic of kinship and its prescriptive altruism, as Fortes aptly phrased it (1969), (2) the rights, obligations and privileges that emanate from reciprocal marriage ties among groups of kin and (3) the charisma of local leaders or "headmen," who invariably come from the largest kinship groups in the village (Chagnon, 1975). Thus, village solidarity and cooperation appear to be largely a function of kinship, marriage, and headmanship, and when these are strained beyond their range of endurance, the village fissions and a disgruntled faction moves away to establish its own political and economic independence. To a large extent, marriages within the new group are endogamous, and the new populations (villages) can be viewed as breeding populations.

The nature of the warfare pattern can inhibit fissioning up to a point, leading to increasingly larger villages, since it is politically unwise to subdivide into two smaller villages more vulnerable to surrounding enemies and allied blocs of enemies. In much of the tribes, fissions occur when villages reach approximately 100 to 150 people. In the region of the tribe discussed here, villages sometimes grow to 250 or 300 people before internal bickering, antagonisms, and clubfights become intolerable and fission occurs (Chagnon, 1974).

I will focus here on one large village, Mishimishimaböwei-teri, hereafter called "Old Village 16." It grew to a very large size before it fissioned. The residents of the village had never been contacted by outsiders until 1968, when I ascended the Mavaca River and found their village several hours' walk east of the headwaters of that river (Chagnon, 1974). At that time the village had just fissioned, the result of a sequence of bitter clubfights over women, and the residents were living temporarily in several somewhat widely separated gardens. The following year, when I revisited them,. they were living in two relatively large villages containing some 250 and 150 inhabitants respectively, a few hours' walk from each other. Thus, the pre-fission size of the village must have been approximately 400 people, very large by Yanomamö standards.

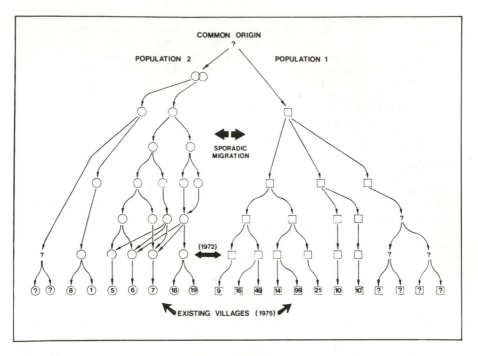

Figure 28–1.   Schematic diagram of village fissioning in two Yanomamö sub-Populations. Villages discussed in text are labeled 09, 16, and 49 (bottom row).

For the next several years individuals and families migrated back and forth between the two villages and, from time to time, sizable factions would split off to form temporary groups of 40 or so people but ultimately would rejoin one or the other village. This is characteristic of the fissioning process in this region of the tribe. I continued to document fluctuations in village size from 1968 through 1972 on an annual basis and returned again in early 1975 when I took the final census in this and a dozen other villages. Between 1971 and 1972 minor changes took place in the composition of the two villages. A major fission, however, occurred between 1972 and 1974: Old Village 16 fissioned into three major factions. One group of 55 individuals had joined the neighboring group, which I have designated as Village 09. Another group formed a new, independent village, 68 of whose 77 members came from old village 16. Most of the others, 127 people, remained behind and are, in my post-1975 publications, designated as Village 16. Another major event occurred between my visits of 1972 and 1974: a respiratory infection killed 60 people, most of them children.

Figure 28–1 gives the schematic relationships of the major population fissions for the population, summarizing graphically the events just described.

RELATEDNESS AND FISSIONING

The process of village fissioning among the Yanomamö separates clusters of more-closely-related individuals from others, i.e., the average relatedness within a village before a fission is lower than the average relatedness in the two (or more) newly-formed fission groups. I have documented this in a number of previous publications (Chagnon, 1975;

1976; 1979a). The measurement of relatedness I have adopted is called F_g, the coefficient of relationship, derived from Wright's (1922) inbreeding coefficient (see Chagnon, 1974; 1975 for more discussion). The calculations are based on genealogical data I collected in the several villages I have been studying since 1964. In essence, I have genealogies for the residents of some dozen villages in this area that range in generational depth from three to seven generations, depending on the age of the individual in question. It is therefore possible to calculate the coefficient of relationship between any individual in my sample and any other individual in the sample, taking them a pair at a time. Procedurally, the genealogy of one individual is generated by a computer program and systematically compared to the genealogy of another specified individual. If they are related, the common ancestor (or ancestors) is identified and the coefficient of relationship is calculated.

With this procedure, each individual in all the villages under study has been systematically and exhaustively compared to all other individuals in the village to calculate an average coefficient of relationship between that individual and all others in the village. Moreover, an average coefficient of relationship for the entire village can likewise be calculated and a precise statement can be made regarding the *amount* of relatedness within a village before and after a fission. I am, therefore, calculating r from genealogies and not from entire knowledge of genomes, and I am using Hamilton's "genes identical by descent" by using the F_g statistic. I agree with Alexander and Borgia (1978) that this is the relevant measure in analyses of kinship and inclusive fitness maximizing studies.

The following data will often provide two values of the F_g statistic. One of them is the average relatedness to *all* individuals compared, basing the average on total number of compared individuals *including unrelated ones*. For example, the F_g ("*r*") value for a full brother is $F_g = 0.5000$. If it were found that a man called three men "brother" in a village and one wanted to get the average relatedness, one would determine by genealogies (through the computer) if all were brothers. If it turned out that only one was a brother and the other two were not related at all, the total value of the F_g for all three would simply be 0.5000, with an average value of $0.5000/3 = 0.1667$. I call this the "F_g ALL" value in the tables below. The second use of the F_g statistic, following this example, would calculate the average for just the *actual brothers*, i.e., those men who are genealogically demonstrable brothers. In this case, there is just one actual brother, so the average value of F_g for the consanguineal relatives would be $0.5000/1 = 0.5000$. This statistic will be called "F_g CON" in the tables and, in general, these values will be higher than the F_g ALL values, since the numerator will usually be smaller—the non-related "brothers" are not counted in the average.

Table 28–1 gives the average coefficients of relationship for the original, pre-fission Old Village 16 and the averages found in the newly-formed villages 09, 16 and 49. It should be obvious that within-group average relatedness is higher in the newly-formed villages than it was in the larger, pre-fission village. This pattern obtains for other fissions I have analyzed (Chagnon, 1974; 1975) and seems to be invariant.

Kinship Terminology Data

In 1971 I collected an exhaustive list of kin terms used by six different people for all 268 residents of Old Village 16. I showed each of the six informants a photograph of each person in the village, whispered his or her name to the informant, and asked "What do you call that person?" The responses were tape recorded and later transcribed. This work was conducted in public amidst delighted groups of on-lookers, whose reactions ranged from blushing to outright side-splitting laughter as names of individuals were recited one after another: the Yanomamö think it outrageously funny and embarrassing to ask people about certain tabooed relatives, such as mothers- or fathers-in-law, and were amused at the good-natured embarrassment of the informants when such names were said aloud in their presence and they were asked to examine photographs of people to whom they owed deference, respect, and avoidance. One positive aspect of working this way was the quickness of the on-looking kibbitzers to ''correct'' an informant if he or she did not respond with the appropriate kinship term. Such ''errors'' usually resulted from the informant focusing on the wrong person in an identification photograph while simultaneously ignoring the whispered name.

The six informants were selected because of their membership in prominent descent groups that comprised the village and for their sex. The purpose was to reveal the differences in usage between males and females on the one hand and between brothers and sisters on the other. The discrepancies in usage thus identified give a rough measure of the degree to which violations of the marriage rules have occurred, violations that cause re-shuffling of kinship usage (Chagnon, 1968a). Four men and two women were selected as informants, all mature adults. Two men and one woman were full siblings to each other; one other man and woman were ''classificatory siblings,'' i.e., parallel second cousins, and the sixth informant was an old but very prominent shaman in the village. The selection of informants was not made with the intention of demonstrating anything about the relationship of kinship usage to questions of biological provenance but to illustrate essentially traditional social anthropological questions and issues. While the six informants chosen were more than enough to adequately accomplish the anthropological demonstration, it is now clear that many more informants of both sexes should have been questioned in the same way to arrive at conclusive tests of some of the hypotheses that derive from kin selection theory. Of particular interest is the apparent difference between males and females with respect to favoring and disfavoring relatives within terminological categories, a difference that unfortunately hinges on the classifications and behavior of just the two women questioned. In 1971 I had not yet heard of kin selection and evolutionary biology, and none of my field research was conducted with tests of biological hypotheses in mind.

The responses to the kinship questions given by the six informants were then published, without modification, in 1974 (Chagnon, 1974: Appendix A). The analysis of kinship usage here is based on that set of data, modified slightly to give a shorter list of kinship

Table 28–1.   Average relatedness among individuals before and after village fission.[1]

Village	Size	No. of Dyadic Comparisons	Av. Cons. Comparisons	Average No. Loops	F_g ALL	F_g CON
Old 16	268	35,511	220	3.73	0.0790	0.0956
			AFTER FISSION:			
New 16	127	16,002	111	4.06	0.0880	0.1001
New 09	55	2,970	52	3.58	0.1345	0.1402
New 49	68	4,556	53	3.58	0.1075	0.3553
Others	18*					
	268					

[1] I have discussed the possibility of testing the differences in the values of the F_g statistics in the newly formed fission villages with Dr. Clifford Clogg, a statistician at the Pennsylvania State University. Because of the interconnectedness of individuals in the genealogies and the way the average values of relatedness were calculated, difficulties in establishing the sampling variances are manifold, and an elaborate statistical attempt would be required to describe levels of significance.

* Includes individuals who died after the 1971 census and before the fission, and several young men who left the village to do bride service in other villages.

Definition of Terms:

Av. Cons. Comparisons: the average number of actual genealogical relatives each individual has in the village.

Av. No. Loops: the average number of ''inbreeding loops,'' i.e., different ways each individual is related to his actual relatives in that village.

F_g ALL and F_g CON: see text for description and meaning of these.

terms: the modifications entailed pooling of some terms that had identical meanings, such as the term *shoriwä* and *heriyä* (brother-in-law, male cross-cousin for male speakers).

The Yanomamö kinship system falls into the category described by anthropologists as "Iroquois" terminology, one of the most commonly found systems of kin classification in the primitive world (Murdock, 1949; 1957). The major characteristics of the Iroquois system are (1) mother (M) and mother's sister (MZ) are called by identical terms and distinguished from father's sister (FZ); (2) father (F) and father's brother (FB) are called by the same term and distinguished from mother's brother (MB); Parallel cousins are distinguished from cross-cousins and equated with siblings, and (4) cross-cousins on both sides are equated. Figure 28–2 gives a paradigmatic summary of the system, a paradigm called an "Egocentric diagram" since all terminological specifications are with reference to some Ego, located in the center of the diagram in Figure 28–2 as the dark triangle (triangle represent males, circles represent females). Later in the paper I will be distinguishing Ego's generation ("own generation") from both ascending and descending generations. Ego's own generation kin in Figure 28–2 are those kin that are classified into the categories numbered e, f, g and h. Ego's ascending generation relatives are those individuals in categories numbered a, b, c and d. All other kinship categories will be descending generation relatives (i, j, k and l). This diagram is a highly simplified summary of the more complex set of terms actually used by the Yanomamö and the reader is directed to Chagnon, 1974, Appendix A for further information. The complexity I refer to has to do with the fact that female Egos (informants) use different terms for relatives; there are terms used only by males for females only, term used only by females for males only, etc.—but all conform to the Iroquois pattern as given in Figure 28–2.

Like all other kinship systems, the terms used in this one are extended outward and applied to more remote kinsmen than those specified in Figure 28–2. That is, the term that includes "mother" also potentially includes a great many other females as well, such as mother's sister, mother's patrilateral parallel cousins, father's other wives, etc. And, like all kinship systems, the terms are applied to unrelated individuals: nobody escapes the kinship system, not even strangers or anthropologists wearing sneakers. It follows, then, that for each specific kinship term used by the Yanomamö there will be a collection of persons called by that term, a collection that includes (1) genealogically-close relatives, (2) genealogically-remote relatives and (3) non-relatives.

A number of additions and comments should be made at this point about kinship systems. The list of kinship terms specified in Figure 28–2 can be broken down into various broad categories. All the terms, as discussed here, can be put into distinct generation levels. Another distinction that can be made has to do with what we call "in-laws" as distinct from "blood relatives." Technically, the Yanomamö have no terms in their entire kinship system that apply exclusively to affines (in-laws): every "affinal" term also applies to some "consanguine" (blood relative). Thus, the term that men use for wife also includes female cross-cousins so that in fact a man's cross-cousins are called by "wife" terms and a rigid

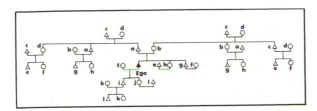

Figure 28–2.   Yanomamö egocentric kinship paradigm (Iroquois pattern). The categories for offspring of Ego's own-generation relatives (not shown on Figure 28–2) would be as follows: offspring of 'e' = 'k', 'l'; offspring of 'f' = 'i', 'j'; offspring of 'g' = 'i', 'j'; offspring of 'h' = 'k', 'l'.

distinction between affinal and consanguineal terms is not appropriate. Still, the Yanomamö make use of the difference between marriageable and unmarriageable people in, for
example, their own generation: cross-cousins are marriageable and parallel cousins are
called by sister-terms and unmarriageable. For sake of analysis I have utilized this distinction in the tables below, using the words "affinal" and "consanguineal" to distinguish
classes of kin on this axis, here reminding the reader that they have a somewhat different
meaning than "in-laws" versus "consanguines" as they might in our own kinship distinctions.

The data on kinship classification just described can be compared to the data on coefficients of relationship derived from the known genealogies of the same people who have
been classified into kinship categories by the six informants. For example, one can examine
the set of individuals an informant calls "brother" and determine how, if at all, the informant is genealogically related to each of men who are called "brother." Moreover, one can
examine the distribution of each informant's "terminological kinsmen" after the fission
and compare average relatedness within each kinship category for those kin who remained
with the speaker and those who fissioned away. Thus, if a man had fifty "sons" in the pre-
fission village, i.e., fifty male individuals that he called by the kinship term into which his
sons fell and the village fissioned, one could determine who of the 50 "sons" distributed
themselves at random with respect to their degree of relatedness to the informant in question. If kinship classifications, genealogical relatedness, and social behavior were independent of each other, one would predict that there would be no significant difference in the
degree of relatedness between the man and his "sons" who stayed with him and the "sons"
that fissioned away. To state it another way, if people favored close kin over distant kin by,
for example, remaining in the same village with them when it fissioned, then one would
predict that the distribution of "sons" would not be random and that the ones who remained
behind would be more closely related to the "father" than the ones who separated. While I
am here using "fathers" and "sons" to illustrate the method that is used, the analysis will
focus primarily on own-generation kin for the six informants, people who would fall into
various categories of cousins (cross and parallel, close and distant) and siblings, people
who would generally be adults because of the ages of the six informants chosen to classify
their kin.

Table 28–2 considers the broadest display of the data on kinship classification and
kinship relatedness as measured by the F_g statistic and will subsequently be broken down
into more refined categories that distinguish female from male classifiers and consanguineal kin from affinal kin. In Table 28–2, the classifications of all six informants (four males,
two females—all adults) are considered. Their classifications have been subdivided into
those terms that are used to refer to individuals in (a) ascending generations (Generation
Level I of Table 28–2), such as the terms for "father," "mother" "grandfather," "grand-
mother," etc., in (b) own-generation (Generation II of Table 28–2), such as terms for
"brother," "sister," "cross-cousin," "husband," etc., and (c) descending generation
(Generation III of Table 28–2), such as the terms for "son," "daughter," "grandson,"
"niece," etc. Because all the informants were mature adults, they have few relatives who
fall in generations superior to their own. An examination of the age/sex pyramid (Figure
28–3) will also reveal that in this population there are very few individuals in older age
categories, so that even relatively young informants would have few ascending generation
relatives. The upper half of the table (F_g ALL) shows that the informants had a total of 27 +
66 = 93 terminological relatives whom they classified by kin terms appropriate for ascending generation. Of these 93 relatives, 27 remained in the same village with the informants who classified them and 66 "fissioned" away from the classifiers. The average
relatedness of the classifiers to the 27 individuals who remained in the village with them
was 0.0307 whereas the average relatedness of the 66 who "fissioned" away was 0.0315.
As the statistical test shows, this distribution of relatives could have occurred at random
with respect to closeness of relationship and therefore the kin-selection hypothesis that

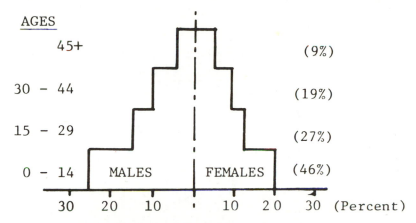

AGES

45+   (9%)

30 – 44   (19%)

15 – 29   (27%)

0 – 14   MALES   FEMALES   (46%)

30   20   10   10   2 0   30   (Percent)

Figure 28–3.   Age/Sex Distributions in Population.

close relatives will remain together and separate from distantly related people does not receive support for this generation of kin classified by these six informants in this particular village. Whether this would be the case had more or younger informants been chosen remains to be documented by further field research.

The data for Generation Levels II and III indicate that the kin-selection hypothesis is confirmed at the 0.05 level of significance for these six informants' classifications of all co-residents and their subsequent choices to remain with closer kin within own-generation and descending generation taxons and to separate from more distantly related kin of the same taxons at village fissioning. Thus, it seems unwarranted to conclude that "no human population organizes the calculus of its social life in terms that are consistent with predictions from kin-selection theory." These data indicate that it is reasonable to expect a research project designed to test this hypothesis to generate data that could give even more convincing evidence in support of kin-selection theory—and these data were not collected with such tests in mind. My suspicion is that such projects are not only likely to add such support, but that it would require relatively little effort to do so.

The second half of Table 28–2 (F_g CON) shows how the six informants behaved toward just those co-residents in Old Village 16 to whom they were demonstrably related when that village fissioned. One might look at this portion of the table as "choices among kin of varying degrees of relatedness" whereas the upper half pertains more to "choices among both kin and non-kin." The pattern in this portion of the table is similar to that found in the upper half. This portion of the table supports the kin-selection hypothesis in a somewhat different way: it shows that of those people who remain with the "classifiers," a higher proportion of them are known kin than those who fission away from the classifiers. For example, in Generation II, the upper half (F_g ALL) of the table indicates that 210 individuals remained with the classifiers; of these, 71 per cent were known relatives (149 of them, from the bottom half of the table) whereas only 43 per cent of the people who fissioned away from the classifiers in Generation II (168/388) were known relatives.

Table 28–3 constitutes a more detailed examination of the same data. It appears that males conform more to the prediction from kin-selection theory than females do—if the six informants in this village are to be taken as the basis of comparison. Males seem to "prefer" close kin more clearly than females do, a tendency that makes more sense in terms of sexual selection theory: males make coalitions with other, closely related males to improve their chances of finding mates for themselves and for their male offspring. The coalitions take the form of "alliances" between clusters of brothers who promise to give their sisters and daughters away to similar clusters of brothers in different lineages. Since it is relatively

Table 28–2. Comparison of relatedness within terminological categories after village 16 fissioned, pooling the classifications of all six informants and separating the classifications by generation (all 268 individuals in Old Village 16 included below).

Generation Level	Individuals Who Remained in Same Village with "Classifiers"		Individuals Who Fissioned Away from "Classifiers"		Descriptive Level of Significance (P)
	Number of Individuals	Average relatedness to classifiers	Number of Individuals	Average relatedness to classifiers	
F_g ALL					
I	27	0.0307	66	0.0315	0.4787
II	210	0.1024	388	0.0472	0.0001
III	335	0.1201	582	0.0671	$P < 0.0001$
F_g CON					
I	7	0.1183	18	0.1154	0.4662
II	149	0.1443	168	0.1090	0.0410
III	275	0.1463	357	0.1094	$P < 0.0001$

Table 28–3.   Comparison of relatedness within terminological categories after village 16 fissioned. Own generation classifications and relatedness only, male versus female informants, consanguineal versus affinal term-types and F_g CON versus F_g ALL. Statistics for the analysis with all children under 10 years of age removed are given in parenthesis.

		Individuals Who Remained in Same Village with "Classifiers"		Individuals Who Fissioned Away from "Classifiers"		
	Type of Kin Terms	Number of Individuals	Average relatedness to classifiers	Number of Individuals	Average relatedness to classifiers	Descriptive Level of Significance (P)
F_g ALL / MALES	CON	48 (42)	0.2656 (0.2946)	127 (93)	0.0640 (0.0790)	$P < 0.00005$ $P <(0.00005)$
	AFF	85 (66)	0.0259 (0.0267)	132 (109)	0.0215 (0.0213)	0.1868 (0.1597)
F_g ALL / FEMALES	CON	38 (28)	0.1320 (0.1384)	69 (57)	0.0788 (0.0932)	0.1020 (0.1947)
	AFF	39 (32)	0.0396 (0.0404)	60 (53)	0.0320 (0.0327)	0.1419 (0.1614)
F_g CON / MALES	CON	44 (39)	0.2900 (0.3173)	52 (39)	0.1562 (0.1883)	0.0050 (0.0127)
	AFF	44 (34)	0.0500 (0.0518)	47 (40)	0.0603 (0.0580)	0.0805 (0.2164)
F_g CON / FEMALES	CON	30 (21)	0.1672 (0.1762)	37 (35)	0.1469 (0.1518)	0.3536 (0.3559)
	AFF	31 (26)	0.0498 (0.0498)	32 (29)	0.0600 (0.0598)	0.0679 (0.0947)

easy for a female to find a spouse and since males cannot find spouses unless they cede sisters and daughters, males must associate themselves with allies and control the reproductive futures of their sisters and their sisters' daughters. Success in this depends on the nature of the alliances with men in other lineages and the extent to which sister-exchange binds the male allies together and enables each to keep their sisters (and sisters' daughters) with them when they fission. Wives in general would go with their *husbands* when the village fissions, but they can go with their *brothers and husbands* only if sister-exchange binds groups of brothers and sisters to other groups of brothers and sisters. Preliminary results of analyses of cross-cousin marriage (which would be the result of systematic sister-exchange over several generations between members of two descent groups) in large descent groups (Chagnon, 1980) suggests that the inclusive fitness of males depends to a high degree on their ability to get their own offspring married off to the offspring of their sisters—which means that they must try to keep sisters with them. The extent to which they are able to do this depends on the prominence of their descent group—the number of social allies they have. Men whose sisters have married into larger descent groups are less likely to be able to keep their sisters with them if their descent group is small and their own wives come from descent groups that fission away from the larger groups.

Sister exchange as an alliance strategy cannot be practiced by all males for demographic reasons and because successful males in larger descent groups manage to acquire more females than they cede. Thus, there will always be some women who are compelled to separate from their brothers and remain with their husbands when a village fissions. One would therefore expect that women would be less likely to be able to remain with close agnatic kin and there would be considerable variation in the extent to which their residence choices are predictable *from kin selection theory alone*. These features of Yanomamö mate competition should be borne in mind in considering the data provided in Table 28–3. I will come back to this in the next section of the paper and examine the differences in *types* of kinsmen males and females have before and after fissioning rather than emphasize just the amount of relatedness as Tables 28–2 and 28–3 do.

Table 28–3 summarizes kinship classification and relatedness data for just the six informants' relatives *in their own generation:* just those individuals who fall into kinship categories like ''cousin'' and ''sibling,'' from the point of view of the six informants, are included in the statistics. As in Table 28–2 relatedness to all co-residents (F_g ALL) is distinguished from relatedness to genealogically demonstrable kin (F_g CON). Female classification and relatedness is separated from male classification and relatedness and, finally, the kinship terms applied to own-generation kin are distinguished into the two above-mentioned categories that reflect ''affinality'' (AFF) and ''consanguineality'' (CON). Figures in parentheses give the statistics when children under the age of 10 years are removed from the data; no apparent differences in the patterns result from removing the children.

A number of points can be made from the data in Table 28–3. First, males remain with those own-generation kin that they place in consanguineal taxons, i.e., siblings and close parallel cousins (of both sexes); this is true for ''all relatives'' (F_g ALL) as well as for genealogically demonstrable relatives (F_g CON). Second, males appear to stay with affinal relatives to a lesser extent (F_g ALL, Males, AFF row of Table 28–3), and if their genealogically related affines (technically, they would be cognatic kin) are examined (F_g CON, Males, AFF row of Table 28–3), it appears that there is a slight tendency for more closely related individuals of these categories to separate. The general pattern is that kin who are classified into ''sibling'' and ''parallel-cousin'' categories tend more often to be known genealogical kin: 92 per cent (44/48) of male informants' relatives in these categories who remain with the informants after fissioning are genealogically demonstrable relatives, compared to only 52 per cent (44/85) of the relatives who are classified into affinal kinship categories (cross-cousins). This suggests that males are better able to keep siblings and closely-related parallel cousins with them than they are able to keep closely-related cross-cousins with them. While this is true as a general pattern, we will see in the next section that individuals in particular villages do not conform to the general pattern: some males are better able to surround themselves with both close agnates and close affines when they fission away from the larger village. A third point is that males tend to have more classificatory affines around them after they fission than the females do: about two-thirds of a male's relatives ($85/133 = 64$ per cent) after fission are classified into affinal terms, whereas only about half ($39/77 = 51$ per cent) of a female's relatives are affines (F_g ALL portions of Table 28–3). The fourth point is that females do not appear to conform to the kin-selection hypothesis that they will remain with close kin and separate from more distant or non-kin. Although the *direction* of the means is correct for F_g ALL for both consanguineal terms and affinal terms, the values are not significant at the 0.05 level. The values for F_g CON are in the predicted direction for consanguineal relatives but in the opposite direction for affinal relatives. It is possible that these results are spurious and caused primarily by the fact that only two female informants were used as classifiers, or perhaps by the choice of particular females as informants. Personal knowledge of these women leads me to suspect that one of them might, if she has not already done so, move from the village she was in in 1974 (on which the statistics are based) to the village that her brothers are now in. This single act would substantially change the statistics in Table 28–3 and make her classifications and associated relatedness patterns conform more closely to that of the male informants. Nevertheless, as of 1974 the distributions are as given above and raise the possibility that females behave very differently from males insofar as kinship classification and relatedness covary when a village fissions. If this is correct, it demands much more investigation than what my own data, collected for a different purpose, can bring to bear on this fascinating question. I suspect that the pattern for females will be similar to that of males only in those cases where females (a) belong to the politically more prominent descent groups and (b) are married to cross-cousins.

Discussion

These data on kinship classification and how it co-varies with genealogical relatedness when a village fissions lend some support to the kin-selection hypothesis that no matter how individuals classify people into kinship categories they favor more closely-related genealogical relatives over less-closely related relatives or non-relatives by remaining with them when a village fissions. The prediction appears to hold for males only at a 0.05 level of statistical significance although the direction of mean-relatedness kinship category is as predicted for females. Removing highly-dependent children (under ten years of age) does not affect this pattern when own-generation kin are considered (nor for descending generation kin, not included in Table 28–2).

The analysis was based on a very limited set of data—the kinship classifications of four adult males and two adult females—and therefore might not be substantiated if a larger set of informants were used, particularly informants drawn from younger age categories and other descent groups. However, I predict that the overall pattern just described and the conclusions I draw will hold when a larger number of informants is used.

The apparent differences between males and females are possibly related to the facts that: (1) males decide if and when a village will fission and they attempt to surround themselves with primary social allies (close agnates and potential wife-givers) and move away from primary social competitors for mates[1] (distantly related agnates in particular, and distantly related kin of all categories in general), and (2) females are able to remain with both husbands *and* brothers only if their marriages reflect long-term reciprocal exchanges between matrimonially-bound descent groups that exchange women. These facts pertain more to the theory of sexual selection than to kin selection, and I will explore them in the following section of the paper.

[1] The useful concepts of ''primary social ally'' and ''primary social competitor'' were developed for analyses such as this by William Irons (1979).

Mate Competition, Sexual Selection and Distribution of Own-Generation Kin Types

Since adult males make the decisions about fissioning and compete among themselves for mates (Chagnon, 1979a) it is reasonable to consider the process of village fissioning in the context of sexual selection theory and examine patterns of kinship between adult males before and after fissioning. This can be done by examining the known genealogical connections between each male and all other males in his own generation and exploring the extent to which particular *types* of kinsmen remain with each other and/or separate from each other. By using known genealogical connections the analysis is independent of kinship classification and not restricted to the six informants as was the case in the first portion of the paper.

I have defined 90 different genealogical specifications for own-generation relatives and exhaustively described how any particular individual is related to any other individual in his/her own genealogical generation. These specifications cover all types of cousins out to third cousin as well as siblings and half-siblings. All individuals in Old Village 16 were exhaustively compared to each other to determine if and how they were related to all others in the village (see Table 28–1 for "number of dyadic comparisons"). In cases where individuals were related in multiple ways, the closest relationship demonstrable was taken to be the diagnostic relationship. The results of this analysis make it possible to discuss *types* of relatives each individual has in the population, i.e., to specify the *structure* of relatedness as well as its "quantity." This dimension of kinship in human societies must be integrated into hypotheses about the evolved functions of kinship, for humans, unlike other animals, do in fact behave according to idealogically defined categories of kinship (Fox, 1979) and not exclusively to amount of relatedness. Thus, in addition to kin-selection theory, both sexual selection theory and alliance theory from social anthropology are germane to the analysis of village fissioning. Combining the three theoretical perspectives, one would make a number of predictions about village fissioning in the context of inclusive-fitness maximizing arguments. First, adult males should be expected to behave in such a way that they would increase the likelihood that their inclusive fitness would be enhanced. This means that they should, at fissioning, attempt to both eliminate mate competitors for themselves and their sons as well as increase the number of potential mates for themselves and their sons. Second, they should attempt to associate themselves with coalitions of males who will aid them in this, close kin who are likely to be altruistic. Third, they should favor particular culturally significant categories of potential allies and not simply track "amount" of relatedness. For example, a second parallel cousin is (given paternity certainty) as closely related as a second cross-cousin, but the former is a potential competitor for mates and the latter a potential wife-giver. One would expect a male to favor the potential wife-giver over the potential competitor, i.e., the culturally-relevant *type* of relationship is more significant than the biological equivalence of the relationship. The extent to which these predictions hold can be explored in a descriptive manner, as the following analysis will show.

Since I will be discussing genealogically demonstrable kinship relatedness, it is important to determine the fraction of the population that falls within the analysis, i.e., the relative proportion of kin versus non-kin by age-category. Figure 28–3 gives the age-sex distribution of Old Village 16. Figure 28–4 gives the distribution by age category of kin that individuals in the four age categories defined have, on the average, in Old Village 16 prior to fission. Curve A shows that for males between the ages of 0 and 14, each is related, on average, to 90 per cent of all other members of the village. For males between the ages 15 and 29, 90 per cent of all co-residents are known kin. The fraction of known kin drops to 75 per cent and 58 per cent respectively for the next two age categories, statistics that are probably as much a function of getting genealogical information on older people as they are a function of the possible fact that there are more "unrelated" people in older age categories. Curve B shows the relative fraction of an individual's relatives that fall within his own genealogical generation. Thus, for a male between the ages of 0 and 14, about 40 per cent of his relatives in Old Village 16 fall within his own generation, i.e., are some sort of cousin or sibling. Future analyses will define similar categories of kin for ascending and descending generation since the possible pool of allies and competitors cross-cuts generations. For the moment I will deal here only with own-generation relatives by age category.

The composition of Old Village 16 or any village can be considered to be the result of fissioning decisions by adult males in previous generations. The distribution of types of own-generation kinsmen for individuals in any age category thus represents the consequences of earlier political decisions that set Village 16 into being, and the accumulated results of marriage and reproduction that took place once the village was established as an independent political entity, i.e., the consequences of relative success by particular individuals in acquiring mates and increasing the size of the village through their reproductive efforts.

Figure 28–5 shows how males in the four age categories (*x*-axis) are surrounded by male kin of various genealogically specified types. Males in Age Category 1 (0–14 years old) have approximately 3 per cent of own-generation relatives as siblings (and half-siblings). This category of own-generation relative increases over time (over the life-cycle) such that by the time a male is over 45 years old (Age Category 4), about 30 per cent of his male co-residents are siblings or half-siblings. The main feature of these data is that, over a male's lifetime, the proportion of relatives that are either siblings or first cousins to him increases whereas the proportion of relatives that are second and third cousins decreases. While differential mortality, age at reproduction, and migration probably account for part of the pattern, a very large fraction of it is probably the result of the decisions made by

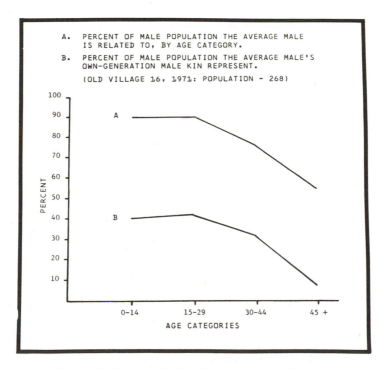

Figure 28–4.   Per cent of male population that the average male is related to by age category and fraction of male relatives that fall within own-generation.

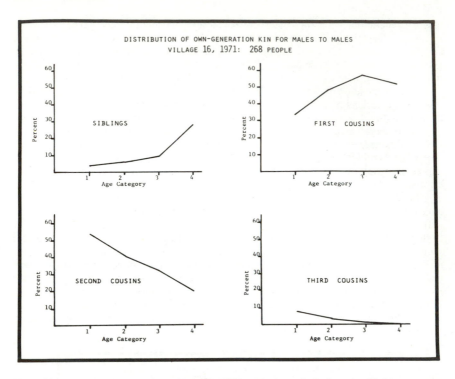

Figure 28–5.   Distribution of male kin in Old Village 16 prior to fissioning, classified from vantage of male Egos. Own-Generation types only.

males in earlier generations to fission away from the previous, larger village. The "mix" of a male's kinsmen changes over time, tending to become more biased in the direction of closer kin.

The composition of a male's kin "mix," if viewed in terms of social allies and competitors, dramatically changes during his life-cycle. Siblings and first cousins include a male's closest potential allies; second and third cousins include his most likely competitors. If we combine siblings and first cousins and define them as "allies," and combine second and third cousins and define them as "competitors," a startling pattern emerges; Figure 28–6 shows this pattern. Since the own-generation relatives of a male fall into the four categories shown on Figure 28–5, the curve labeled "allies" is the reciprocal of the curve labeled "competitors".

If we now take the curve in Figure 28–6 that is labeled "allies" as a baseline, and examine the composition of the three villages that resulted from the fission of Old Village 16 in a similar fashion, it appears that males in some of the villages that were formed after the fission have created for themselves *and their sons* a more desirable mix of allies and competitors than what obtained for them in the larger, pre-fission village. Figure 28–7 compares the composition of the three new villages to the composition of the original village in terms of the mix of siblings and all first cousins. The decisions of the adult males who initiated the fission appear to have led to a set of new villages in which the distribution of potential allies for their sons varies markedly. Thus, young males in Village 49 have a higher proportion of own-generation male kin who fall into the "allies" category than do males from the other two villages (09 and New 16). For all four age categories, it appears

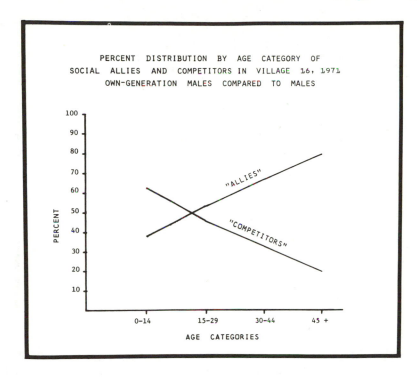

Figure 28–6.   Per cent distribution of "social allies" (siblings and all first cousins) and "social competitors" (all second and third cousins) in Old Village 16 prior to fissioning, males compared to males.

that males in Village 16 have done more poorly in creating a situation for themselves and their sons than have the males in Villages 09 and 49 (note that in Village 09, there are no males above the age 45).

Figure 28–8 removes parallel cousins from the "allies" category and defines allies as the sum of all siblings and cross-cousins only. The result is that members of Village 49 appear to have done better at surrounding themselves with more male allies so defined than members of Villages 09 and 16. Figure 28–9 compares males in the villages to their relative proportions of *female* relatives of their own generation, i.e., sisters whose daughters they potentially control, and female cross-cousins who are potential mates. Again, the members of Village 49 appear to have gained more by fissioning than the two other villages, and the members of New Village 16 appear to have "lost" in the mate competition struggle by comparison.

DISCUSSION

It would appear from the data on distribution of kin *types* defined as allies and competitors that village fissioning results in an unequal distribution of both potential allies and potential mates: not all newly formed villages have the same mating potentials as others

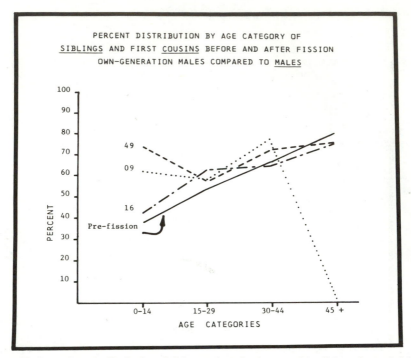

Figure 28–7.   Per cent distribution of siblings and cousins (cross- and parallel cousins pooled) before and after Old Village 16 fissioned. Own-generation males compared to males, showing "mix" of
siblings and cousins in the new villages (09, 14, and 16) after fissioning.

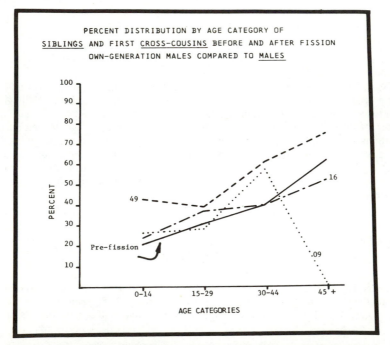

Figure 28–8.   Per cent distribution by age category of male siblings and male cross-cousins (parallel cousins are removed) the average male has in the new villages 09, 16, and 49 relative to other own-
generation male relatives, compared to pre-fission condition.

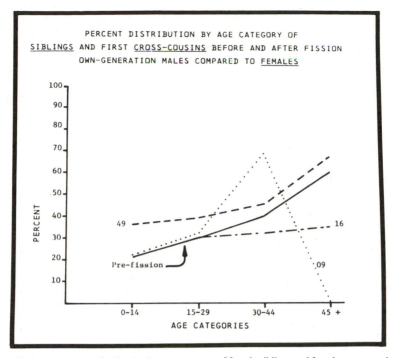

PERCENT DISTRIBUTION BY AGE CATEGORY OF
SIBLINGS AND FIRST CROSS-COUSINS BEFORE AND AFTER FISSION
OWN-GENERATION MALES COMPARED TO FEMALES

Figure 28–9.   Per cent distribution by age category of female siblings and female cross-cousins the average male has in the new villages 09, 16, and 49 relative to other own-generation female relatives, compared to pre-fission condition.

formed as a consequence of fissioning. The tendency for Yanomamö villages to increase their ''dual'' organization (Chagnon, 1979a) after a fission seems to make sense in terms of mate competition, for a village so comprised contains a mix of kin such that a female can remain with her two most significant sources of investment—brothers *and* husbands—and males can more effectively manipulate the reproductive potentials of sisters *and* sisters' daughters to their own inclusive fitness interests: they can increase the likelihood that their sons will find mates (they can marry the daughters of their fathers' sisters) in a competitive milieu where males have difficulty finding mates and must have dependable and numerous male allies to find mates. Dual organizations *do* exist, and they exist because they are adaptive (Levi-Strauss, 1963). The remarkable fact is that there appears to be a consistent strategy on the part of males to achieve a social stituation conducive to their inclusive fitness interests that is in fact dual, not triadic (ibid.). The fact that bilateral cross-cousin marriage systems occur so widely and frequently might have something to do with their efficiency in solving mate competition problems in those societies, like the Yanomamö, where the relative ease in making a living leads to polygyny as a desirable and affordable marriage form for males and, because of this, increases competition among males for available females. While kin selection theory predicts that the males should align themselves with close kin to form successful coalitions, social anthropology theory predicts that those close kin will be selected from particular structural types, and not simply on the basis of closeness of kinship alone.

ACKNOWLEDGEMENTS

I would like to thank the editors of this volume for the helpful critical comments they made on the manuscript in first draft and for suggestions for improving it. The research and writing was generously supported by the Harry Frank Guggenheim Foundation, the National Institute of Mental Health, and the National Science Foundation.

REFERENCES

Alexander, Richard D., and Gerald Borgia. 1978. Group selection, altruism, and the levels of organization of life. *Annual Review of Ecology and Systematics* 9:449–74.

Campbell, Bernard (Ed.). 1972. *Sexual Selection and the Descent of Man, 1871–1971* Chicago, Aldine.

Chagnon, Napoleon A. 1966. *Yanomamö Warfare, Social Organization and Marriage Alliances.* Ph.D. Dissertation, University of Michigan. University Microfilms. Ann Arbor.

———. 1968a. *Yanomamö: The Fierce People.* Holt, Rinehart and Winston. New York.

———. 1968b. Yanomamö Social Organization and Warfare. In *War: The Anthropology of Armed Conflict and Aggression,* M. Fried, M. Harris, and R. Murphy, Eds. pp. 109–59. Garden City: Natural History Press.

———. 1968c. The culture-ecology of shifting (pioneering) cultivation among the Yanomamö Indians. *Proceedings, III International Congress of Anthropological and Ethnological Sciences,* Volume 3, pp. 249–55. Tokyo.

———. 1974. *Studying the Yanomamö.* Holt, Rinehart and Winston. New York.

———. 1975. Genealogy, solidarity and relatedness: limits to local group size and patterns of fissioning in an expanding population. *Yearbook of Physical Anthropology,* 1975, Volume 19, pp. 95–110. American Association of Physical Anthropologists. Washington.

———. 1976. Fission in an Amazonian tribe. *Sciences,* 16:14–18 New York Academy of Sciences. New York.

———. 1979a. Mate competition, favoring close kin, and village fissioning among the Yanomamö Indians. In *Evolutionary Biology and Human Social Behavior: An Anthropological Perspective.* N. A. Chagnon and W. Irons, Eds. pp. 86–132. North Scituate, Mass. Duxbury.

———. 1979b. Is reproductive success equal in egalitarian societies? In *Evolutionary Biology and Human Social Behavior: An Anthropological Perspective.* N. A. Chagnon and W. Irons, Eds. pp. 374-401. North Scituate, Mass. Duxbury.

———. 1980. Kin selection theory, kinship, marriage and fitness among the Yanomamö Indians. In G. Barlow and J. Silverberg, Eds. *Sociobiology: Beyond Nature/Nurture?* AAAS Selected Symposium 35. Westview Press. Boulder, Colorado.

Fortes, Meyer. 1969. *Kinship and the Social Order.* Chicago: Aldine.

Fox, Robin. 1979. Kinship categories as natural categories. In N. A. Chagnon and W. Irons, Eds. *Evolutionary Biology and Human Social Behavior: An Anthropological Perspective.* pp. 132–44. North Scituate, Mass. Duxbury.

Hamilton, William D. 1964. The genetical evolution of social behaviour, Parts I and II. *Journal of Theoretical Biology* 7:1–52.

Irons, William. 1979. Investment and primary social dyads. In N. A. Chagnon and W. Irons, Eds. *Evolutionary Biology and Human Social Behavior: An Anthropological Perspective.* pp. 181–212. North Scituate, Mass. Duxbury.

Levi-Strauss, Claude. 1963. Do dual organizations exist? In C. Levi-Strauss, *Structural Anthropology,* pp. 132–63. New York. Basic Books.

Murdock, George P. 1949. *Social Structure.* New York. Macmillan.

———. 1957. World ethnographic sample. *American Anthropologist,* 59:664–687.

Sahlins, Marshall D. 1976. *The Use and Abuse of Biology: An Anthropological Critique of Sociobiology.* Ann Arbor. University of Michigan Press.

Schneider, David M. 1964. The nature of kinship. *Man,* 217:180–1.

———, 1965. Kinship and biology. In A. J. Coale et al., Eds., *Aspects of the Analysis of Family Structure.* pp. 83–101. Princeton: Princeton University Press.

Williams, George C. 1966. *Adaptation and Natural Selection.* Princeton: Princeton University Press.

Wright, Sewall. 1922. Coefficients of inbreeding and relationship. *American Naturalist,* 56:330–38.

29

Evolution, Culture, and Human Behavior:
Some General Considerations

Richard D. Alexander

Darwin's thoroughness ensured that, after 1859, general theory would remain a central and conscious theme in biology—something that is not always true in all sciences. Even Darwin was unable to cause it to be true universally in biology, as is evidenced by use of the term "evolutionary biology," which implies not only that some people care but that some others do not. On the other hand, even if biologists do care about evolution—and even if they pretty much agree—this does not necessarily mean that they are right. Thus, what some regard as the most important book in evolutionary biology since Fisher (1930) was titled "Adaptation and Natural Selection" but had as its subtitle the phrase "A critique of some current evolutionary thought" (Williams, 1966). If this is not enough, then one has only to recall the screams of outrage and anguish that came mostly from the population of biologists aged over 30 in the wake of Williams' book and that still echo faintly around us now and then.

If general theory has usually been the strength of biology, it has usually been the nemesis of the social sciences. Psychology and sociology have ordinarily been content with their own private view of learning theory as all-encompassing, even though there has been precious little in learning theory to explain either why learning exists or why it takes many of its particular forms, and these shortcomings seem likely to become increasingly important.

Consider anthropology: It is the science closest to evolutionary biology in approach, subject matter, and methods. Indeed, anthropology is the only social science ever much concerned about evolution either as long-term change or as long-term contingency underlying present features. Yet anthropology has always floundered on general theory. Anthropologists have consistently sought general theory, but I think I only echo the vexation of a long succession of its practitioners in saying that they have never found it within their own science.

George Peter Murdock was surely one of the great anthropologists of all time. He wrote plainly, not poetically, and he changed his mind—sometimes rather profoundly. But he was responsible for the development of an enormous cross-indexed file on the behavior of the human species (The Human Relations Area File) that has to be the envy of every biologist who ever fell in love with a group of organisms and set out to monograph all the variations in the life histories and behavior of the different species belonging to that group—something that most of us associated with museums have, in fact, as one of our lifetime goals. Of course, Murdock was tabulating, not what happens in different species but what happens in different cultures within a single species. Nevertheless, his work, more than anything else, established a comparative method (called "cross-cultural analysis" and usually regarded as begun by Tylor, 1889) quite analogous to that used in systematic and evolutionary biology.

The anthropologists, who have filled thousands of pages with every kind of correlation and comparative study they could imagine from Murdock's file and arrived at no particularly earth-shaking conclusions, have decided that there must be something wrong with it. Of course, there is: The data are incomplete and imperfect. Like every repository of so-called information, the file is filled with factual errors, observer bias, misinterpretations, and inappropriate codifications. It may even be worse than most such repositories.

But there has also been something wrong with the efforts to use Murdock's grand file. They never were derived from a useful or even remotely satisfactory general theory. Until very recently, the right questions had simply never been asked.

Murdock, the compiler, must have been thinking in terms of general theory. During most of his career he regarded adaptation in culture as somehow utilitarian to the society as a whole (Murdock, 1949–1967). Society was often the subject of one after another of his explanatory sentences. Society, he said, would have to do this or that for its own good, and society could not afford to ignore this or that. But he was never very specific about this theory nor was he entirely consistent. In retrospect, how could he have been?

But Murdock could change his mind. And in one of his last papers (Murdock, 1972), from an address to the Royal Anthropological Institute of Great Britain and Ireland, he did change his mind, so profoundly that anthropologists have almost totally ignored the paper, which was titled ''Anthropology's Mythology,'' except to cite it occasionally to show how far Murdock went astray (e.g., Sahlins, 1976).

In the 1972 paper Murdock declared that anthropology is suspect *as a science* because no two of its foremost theoreticians can agree on even the most basic issues. He said that he had to conclude that his own approach, across all the years, had been fundamentally wrong; that it now seemed clear to him that society and culture are mere epiphenomena—no more than the products of the collective activities of individuals; and that it is to the behavior of individuals that we must look if we are ever to understand. He said that it is good that anthropology has developed a considerable body of fine ethnographic data, because its efforts at theory will have little part to play in the future science of man.

In all fairness one has to add two caveats. First, Murdock must have known that his own contribution would be recognized as principally not in theory but in making those fine ethnographic data more available. Second, conclusions similar to Murdock's have been approached independently from within anthropology by several investigators; I think particularly of the Europeans, Frederik Barth (1967) and Jeremy Boissevain (1975). But these conclusions are by no means widely accepted. I believe one has to conclude that general theory has simultaneously seemed important and been unattainable within anthropology.

The social sciences lie somewhere between philosophy and evolutionary biology, if the latter is seen as the only natural science with any truly general theories about life. In the broadest sense, philosophers have always theorized about human nature. So, in fact, have ordinary humans. Roger Masters (manuscript) of the department of government at Dartmouth, has traced two major views of human nature through recorded history from the ancient Greeks. They are simple ideas, and they also seem to oppose or contradict one another. One is that we are hedonistic individualists out to serve our own ends and able to cooperate only because we set up social contracts and agree how far we can go in interfering with one another. The other is that we are group altruists, with missions larger than our own selfish ends, here to serve the greater good. I would ask: What ordinary human has not toyed in his mind with the precise riddle posed by these two grand, seemingly contradictory views of himself and his fellows—whether we are selfish individualists or group altruists?

The two ideas are philosophical, and they are also simple theories about human nature—the kinds of theories, it seems, that we are always seeking to explain ourselves. Most social scientists would probably say that they are far too simple, and they would also note wryly that we seem always to be seeking, and too hastily accepting, oversimplified theories about human nature. Yet these two simple, widespread notions are also profound.

Darwin's successful argument, in 1859, that we—as with all organisms—are products of an evolution guided by natural selection, surprisingly did not solve the riddle posed by the ancient Greeks and, as well, by ordinary thoughtful humans. The reason, as we know now, was that Darwin could never answer a crucial question: Survival of the fittest what? Certainly he could not have meant survival of the individual because, of all the units identifiable in the hierarchy of organization of life, the individual is the shortest lived. Moreover, the vast majority of lifetimes are exceedingly short: hardly anyone competes with redwoods and bristlecone pines. Clearly, during the billions of years available to them, individuals have not evolved to survive.

It is possible that Darwin never realized that conflicts of interest could exist at different levels (e.g., between individuals and groups) as well as at the same level (e.g., among individuals), thus posing the question of which among all the levels of organization of life has actually evolved to survive; but I believe that several of his discussions (e.g., of interspecific hybridization, sex ratios, and sterile castes in social insects) indicate an awareness of this problem and at least a vague realization of his inability to solve it (Darwin, 1859, 1871).

Other than individuals, only two candidates for the evolution of survival ability were available to Darwin's senses: phenotypic traits and species (or populations). Both seem to last a long time — at least sometimes. At different times, Darwin talked about each — traits and species—as if they were the units of selection. Genes, of course, were unknown to him. At best he had only a fragment of the picture in regard to where heritable traits come from.

So Darwin did not resolve the ancient question whether humans are selfish individualists or group altruists. In my opinion, however, the two recent arguments from evolutionary biology responsible for this symposium, and recurring throughout it, have solved that problem, and simultaneously they have shown us how to develop the simple, general theory of human nature that we have always sought. The arguments were presaged by Fisher (1930) and Haldane (1932), and developed, respectively, by George C. Williams (1957–1966) and William D. Hamilton (1963–1964) (see also, in particular, Dawkins, 1976–1977; Leigh, 1977; Alexander and Borgia, 1978). They are, first, that only subgenomic genetic units last long enough to have been evolving to survive, and, second, that these units have evolved to survive by helping their copies reproduce wherever those copies may live. That the genes have evolved to survive by *reproducing*, it seems to me, is itself a comment of the deepest significance about the general nature of the environments of life throughout history— namely, that environments predictably change but in unpredictable ways. Biologists are still trying to discover exactly what this means (e.g., Williams, 1975; Maynard Smith, 1978; Leigh, 1978); probably we will not be able to understand sexuality in adaptive terms until the problem is solved.

We are, then, hedonistic or selfish individualists to the extent that such behavior maximizes the survival by reproduction of those copies of our genes residing in our own bodies; and we are group altruists to the extent that this behavior maximizes the survival by reproduction of the copies of our genes residing in the bodies of others. At least this is what we have evolved to be—and to all accounts it is all that we have evolved to be.

It is paramount to realize, however, that—as opposed to what we have evolved to be— what we actually are or become is whatever we can make of ourselves, given our history, and our propensities and talents, which are great, for creating novelty in our environments at rates and of kinds that the process of genetic evolution has no possibility of controlling or keeping up with. Nowadays, we are closer than ever before to being able to become what we wish to be, if for no other reason than because we know about ourselves the things that I have just mentioned. On the other hand I would caution against a too-loose interpretation of this concept by repeating the wry comment of a comic strip character who said, ''Why is it that a human can grow up to be whatever he or she wishes to be, but a caterpillar can only grow up to be a butterfly?''

For the first time in history, then, we are on the brink of formulating a simple and convincing general theory of human nature. With generality and simplicity in its structure, any theory of human nature must inevitably become exceedingly complex in its application. I stress this fact, particularly for those who hold to the strange idea that there cannot, in principle, be a simple theory of human nature—that any effort in that direction is by definition intolerably reductionistic (One has to wonder how they feel about the elegantly simple 122-year old theory that is demonstrably adequate to explain life in general and has no serious challenge—or, indeed, about $E = MC^2$).

So long as we thought of grand conflicts of interest existing only at the level of the social group, they were simple to consider. Now we have driven those conflicts of interest all the way to the level of the genes. As difficult as it is to conceive, each individual human is a product of the cooperation of thousands, or hundreds of thousands, of separate genetic units, each of them with potentially separate and conflicting interests.

Picture a gene that could guide its bearer to assist other gene-bearers solely on the basis of its own presence in those other gene-bearer's genomes—that is, independently of the presence or absence of other genes in its own genome. Multiply that conflict about a hundred thousand times and you know that this is not the kind of nepotism that has led to the genetic cooperation necessary to create a phenotype unitary enough to be called an individual, to think, philosophize, and examine questions like those in this symposium.

The cooperation of the genome—the unity of the phenotype and of the individual—seems to require that, in general, each gene's action serves all of the genes in its genome equally. In helping one's own phenotype (one's self) there is usually no problem. In nepotism it is not quite so simple. Nevertheless, as we know now, there is an obvious and simple way to be nepotistic yet serve all of one's genes equally in terms of their survival by reproduction. It is to treat supposed relatives in a way that takes account only of the probability of each gene of the nepotist's genome residing in the relative's genome; these probabilities are approximately equal for genes inherited by immediate descent (Hamilton, 1964). Given the genetic roulette of meiosis, the simplest way to acomplish this kind of nepotism, when one must deal with different classes of relatives, is to learn socially who your relatives are—to learn to accept or reject that one or another individual is this versus that class of relative, a relative versus no relative at all (Alexander, 1977-1979).

That social learning is, in fact, the general mechanism of the evolution of nepotism, is, I believe, strongly supported by the ease of inducing adoptions of unrelated offspring and other relatives once the appropriate social situation has been created. I doubt that any organism is immune to this manipulation, regardless of whether it is regularly nepotistic toward one, several, or many classes of relatives. The stringency of the necessary situation should be greater in social species in which accidental adoptions are most likely in nature, and greater at those times when accidental adoptions are most likely (Daly and Wilson, 1979, and Alexander, 1979, review evidence supporting this hypothesis). Similarly, recognition of close relatives in genetic outbreeding appears to occur as a result of social experiences, at least in mice and humans (Hill, 1972; Spiro, 1958; Shepfer, 1971; Wolf, 1966, 1968). A further test of the involvement of social learning in nepotism could examine the likelihood and degree of forgetting appropriate responses to relatives after periods of non-interaction.

Earlier I said that we are on the brink of developing a simple general theory of human nature. When I first drafted this manuscript I thought it proper to say that we had already accomplished this goal but now I believe that what remains to be learned is sufficiently important and difficult as to deny my earlier optimism. It is true that we are now able to specify the genetic interests of humans, singly and in groups, much more precisely than ever before—indeed, so much more precisely as perhaps to justify the claim that we are able to do it "for the first time." But human behavior—social interactions and the structures of culture that derive from them as history unfolds—is not a simple consequence of gene action or genetic makeup. The conflicts and confluences of interest expressed by human actions are not precisely those reflected by differing amounts of genetic overlap. Behavior is invariably the outcome of genes plus environments, a fact that is as trite to repeat as it is complex to comprehend. Genes cannot act directly in their own interests. They gave up such possibilities long ago when they evolved to realize their interests through phenotypes, which develop their inclinations and abilities differently in different environments. Even if the genetics of conflict and confluences of interests have been worked out, at least in skeletal form, their actual phenotypic expressions and the reasons for them are not yet similarly understood. We do not yet know how the multiplicity of possible, probable, and actual environments available to humans affects the relationship between their quantifiable genetic interests as individuals, families, and other groups and their actual behavior in relation to those interests. We do not know how to specify the effects of cumulative changes in the cultural environment upon our individual and collective behavior. We have little notion of the way in which the accelerating introduction of novelty into our environment is going to alter our behavioral potentials. I believe that we must draw the connections between genetic interests and phenotypic expressions to a much greater degree before we can argue that a simple general theory of human nature is a fact. In some large part this means that we need to know a great deal more about the nature of learning and how it has functioned, in the past, to maximize the inclusive fitnesses of those showing it. The main reason why we currently have no such understanding is, in my opinion, because learning has never been studied in this context.

A simple illustration of the immensity of the problem of correlating genetic interests and phenotypic expressions is to realize, first, that not all of each person's interests are always conscious, and some may never be conscious. Prior to the advent of an acceptable version of organic evolution, there was no possibility of a conscious knowledge of genetic interests, and prior to the recent refinements of evolutionary theory there was no conscious knowledge of the actual nature and extent of genetic conflicts of interest. Yet, unless we are profoundly in error in the most basic realms of biological science, these interests and conflicts of interest existed and in fact guided human existence throughout all of history. We had no way of knowing that our lifetimes evolved in the interests of effecting the long-term survival of our genes by reproducing them, but we neverthless learn to love and assist our own offspring, and often help other relatives even in the face of powerful resistance and high risk to our own status or well-being. In other words, we *act* as though we know about inclusive fitness. We do not yet know the precise significance of genetic outbreeding, but like nearly all sexual plants and animals we practice it: We do it by learning to avoid in sexual matters those with whom we associate most intimately while prepubertal—and they are typically our closest genetic relatives. But we do not, in nepotism and genetic outbreeding, conduct ourselves precisely according to our genetic interests; to know why we have no alternative but to study the environment and its effects on human development.

Now I think that psychology can at last, with justification, view learning as broad enough, and as having an adequate focus, to represent psychology's own, general, all-encompassing theory. Psychology accomplishes this transition by the simple step of realizing that the forms and expressions of learning have long-term historical as well as short-term contingencies underlying them, that those long-term contingencies involve genetic inclusive-fitness-maximizing, or genetic reproduction via all relatives, and that the central questions of social psychology are to determine how this has come about and what it means for the future.

To be more specific, I assume that some combinations of rates, kinds, timings, and accumulated numbers of social learning experiences determine the nature and intensity of human social interactions. That is nothing new. But it will be new to assume that the determining rates and kinds of social interactions among individuals have varied consistently and regularly with degrees of relatedness in genes identical by immediate descent; yet I think this assumption is necessary. It will be new to realize that the correlations of social experience with genetic relatedness can be an incidental consequence of geographic and social proximity and that such correlations can be imposed indirectly by those whose interests are served by creating them. It will be new to realize that the fragility of the correlation between social and genetic distance in a mobile, fluid society like our own can lead to multiple and complex surrogate social-genetic distance correlations, in the end understandable only from knowledge of long-term historical contingencies. It will be new to recognize that disruption of an individual's chances of establishing a pattern in his or her social interactions that reflects the long-term history of social-genetic contingency correlations may lead to that individual's social alienation, to devastating confusion, to feelings of being orphaned, and perhaps even to suicide or outlandish searches for adoptive surrogates, including the substitute kin networks of intensely religious, political, and other support groups. It will be new to establish connections between loss of the social experience of stable kin groups, or their surrogates, and broad-scale rises of concern with the effects of law and public activities on the so-called disadvantaged in every realm, whose vulnerability can be interpreted by even most individuals as paralleling their own. It will be new to hypothesize that variations in cultural patterns stem from variations in how ecological and other extrinsic events modify the social circumstances in which groups of genetic relatives have found themselves during the history of each separate society. It is new to attempt to explain such things as mother's brother, the asymmetrical treatment of cousins, the cloistering of women, the sizes of villages at fissioning, the abuse and neglect of children, clan exogamy, the distribution of male-biased inheritance, and the acceptance or rejection of harem polygyny as consequences of different patternings of social interactions among relatives that lead to outcomes predictable from inclusive-fitness-maximizing in different ecological circumstances and under different histories of cultural patterns and power distributions (cf. Alexander, 1977–1979; Chagnon, 1981, Chagnon and Irons, 1981; Daly and Wilson, 1981; Dickemann, 1981; Flinn, 1981; Irons, 1981). Yet I believe that these are exactly the kinds of subtheories that must be made operational within the social sciences if we are to proceed in the analysis and understanding of ourselves with the least delay and confusion.

I think it will also be recognized eventually within social and cultural anthropology that the central question there is how the different patterns of culture could have derived from the history of individuals behaving so as to maximize their respective inclusive fitnesses according to the environments of history, and what this means for the future. That, too, will be new.

I would like to talk now about one pattern of culture that seems to have been studied relatively infrequently and haltingly by cultural anthropologists. For the most part this pattern of culture is apparently not well represented across the span of human history, and my guess is that it is entirely missing from much of the human chronology. It has evidently remained unusually inaccessible to anthropologists, for a reason apparently well understood by the cultural anthropologist, Leslie White. White used to tell his classes that for a student of human behavior to discover pattern within his own culture would be like a fish discovering water (N. A. Chagnon, personal communications). The culture of which I speak, and of which our own society is a part, has produced essentially all cultural anthropologists, but it seems to create them in such fashion that they are forced to visit alien cultures in order to fulfill the requirements of their profession.

This culture has several striking features, which I will mention not necessarily in the order of their importance. Along with about half of the 862 cultures of the world listed by Murdock, it not only fails to require marriages between first cousins or at least encourage them, it actually disfavors and often disallows such marriages. Like only about 7 per cent of the cultures of the world its members also do not distinguish the several different kinds of cousins—cross-cousins and parallel-cousins, matrilateral and patrilateral cousins. Despite considerable complexity in the structure of this culture, all of the different kinds of cousins are lumped together, and when they are brought up in conversation everyone is confused.

Nevertheless, cousins more distant than first cousins are often traced and identified carefully, especially when they are quite wealthy, heroic, or renowned for their intellectual or political achievement. In general, children learn who their first cousins are and even some of their first cousins once removed or their second cousins. These relationships are taught to them—in my experience, usually by some female members of the family on that side, or, in the case of truly renowned relatives, even by someone on the other side of the family. In many families some person undertakes to trace the genetic relationships of the family out to extraordinary distances, using his or her own family as the center of the network and tracing in all directions until the evidence disappears or until some relative known to the rest of society or connected to an event known to the rest of society has been identified. The people of this society carry out the same procedures for the animals from which they earn their livings, and they publish and advertise pedigrees for both their animals and themselves.

The third prominent aspect of the culture I am describing, and the first unique one, is that it imposes on its individual members a legal limit of one spouse at a time; like most cultures, it also places barriers of various sorts in the way of changing spouses. Such ''socially imposed'' monogamy (Alexander et al., 1979) is unique not only among human cultures but as well to humans among all animals. In general, the one-spouse rule applies only in the strict, technical sense of the law to the various rough equivalents of headmen in the society, who, as we all know, are often respected, and even admired by some, for gathering, for some purposes, actual harems. Even high-ranking females sometimes acquire virtual harems of males, although, as in the other societies of the world, this behavior is less frequent and likely to be frowned upon more severely than its equivalent among males.

It is not trivial to realize that, under monogamy and with isolated nuclear families, putative cousins are not only treated most symmetrically, but by all counts are also likely to be genetically most symmetrical (Alexander, 1977, 1979). Outbreeding societies with socially imposed monogamy and symmetrical treatment of cousins may have generated independently in several different parts of the planet. In such societies—where the data are available—the amount of sexual dimorphism and the sex ratio at birth are both about the same as those known in societies which permit harem polygyny, distinguish the different kinds of first cousins, and often encourage or require—that is, arrange—cousin marriages (Alexander et al., 1979). At least in regard to one of these two traits both harem-polygynous and socially monogamous cultures differ from the small bands of humans surviving today in the marginal habitats of the Arctic and on the fringes of deserts and neither imposing monogamy on their members nor very often getting around to polygyny. Males in societies with ecologically-imposed monogamy, as with males of apparently all monogamous non-human species, seem to have all they can do in assisting one wife to rear even widely spaced offspring. In these same societies, two men—usually brothers—occasionally combine to help one woman rear their offspring; and in these societies sexual dimorphism also may be slightly lower (Alexander et al., 1979).

It would seem, then, that the peculiar culture exemplified by the society in which we live is a recent derivative from harem-polygynous societies. This hypothesis develops from morphological, physiological, and behavioral comparisons (Alexander, et al. 1979). The alternative is that socially monogamous societies have undergone a more or less similar kind of male-female divergence in selection wherever they have arisen. It is probably relevant that within recorded history many small or not-so-unified polygynous societies have converted to a socially-imposed monogamy, while virtually none has been able to sustain a change in the other direction. Morever, socially monogamous groups tend to be the largest of all human social units, ecologically monogamous the smallest, and we have obviously increased group sizes during history. The small ecologically monogamous societies also differ from the large socially-monogamous ones in numerous other features that I will not discuss here, such as premarital and postpartum sexual behavior, family structure, community size and organization, degree of nomadism, and kinds of agriculture, inheritance, cattle, gods, games, and others (Murdock, 1949, 1967; Goody, 1976; Alexander, 1979).

Socially-monogamous culture spreads by conquest, imposes its rules forcibly on others, and perhaps most remarkably has been able to achieve unprecedented combinations of size and degree of unity without evidence of strong tendencies to fission. Even after fissioning episodes, the daughter units are capable of extraordinary cooperative efforts, when these are important, on a scale without the remotest precedent in all of human history;

and following such cooperative efforts they may, for all practical purposes, remain a single socio-political unit.

At the beginning of this essay I argued that the genes could not be expected to cooperate so completely as to produce the unparalleled illustration of unity that is the individual unless they had worked out a way of getting the phenotype to behave in their individual interests more or less equally; and I suggested that social learning about nepotism could be that mechanism. Once set in motion, the stifling of selfish or outlaw nepotistic gene effects by the rest of the genome is as easy to envision as the stifling of dominance expression in deleterious mutants. One needs only to invoke a combination of Fisher's (1930) theory of dominance modification, P. M. Sheppard's (1969) generalization of Fisher's theory to include the concept of developmental canalization in the face of genetic as well as other environmental insults, and Egbert Leigh's (1971, 1977) concept of the parliament of the genes (See also Alexander and Borgia, 1978). The end result is the maintenance of a unity of interest among the genes, at least for all the time that they are involved in actually producing the phenotype and making it successful. Of course it is possible that there are many as yet poorly understood, knock-down-drag-out intragenomic tussles that take place every time somebody has to go into a polar body and be terminated there, but most "skin-in" biologists have not yet adopted the approach that would have caused them to notice such things.

Now I ask whether events like the initiation and maintenance of socially-imposed monogamy are not, in the end, understandable as extraordinarily complex parallels at the social level to simpler intragenomic mechanisms of cooperativeness. Chagnon (1974, 1979), Neel (1978), and others have described harem polygyny as the most powerful continuing force of differential reproduction in small human societies. Maybe this is an exaggeration, even if it does match what we are learning about nonhumans. But, certainly, polygyny is one of the more powerful forces of differential reproduction, and successful polygyny may be the most potent shift that one individual can effect in its own favor. Socially-imposed monogamy eliminates the possibilitiy of such shifts or creates great risks with their achievement, and this kind of monogamy is part of the systems of laws that unite all of the largest most unified modern nations (Alexander, 1978, 1979).

Of course, from the viewpoints of most individuals, monogamy has virtues other than levelling off differential reproduction and, perhaps, creating unity from the realization among individuals that this has occurred and that this particular battle need not be fought continually at every level. For example, it allows one to transmit inheritance through daughters without the jeopardy that such resources may be diverted by a selfish son-in-law to the children of one of his other wives—and Gerald Borgia and I (ms) have found that, just as this idea predicts, inheritance is in fact most male-biased in nonsororally polygynous societies. Monogamy, from whatever source, also creates bonds between spouses, rooted in their common interest in a brood of offspring, and the history of such common interest; as far as adults are concerned, this bond may otherwise be without parallel in all of human history.

The French structural anthropologist, Claude Levi-Strauss (1969), and others have argued that the arranged cousin marriages of most of the world's middle-sized, polygynous societies are vehicles of alliance formation and maintenance. By definition such marriages would tend to set these alliances between groups of relatives—or clans—of rather small sizes. By an extension of the argument the discouragement of cousin marriages in the huge unified societies of the modern technological world may sometimes have generated as part of a multi-facted discouragement of intense unity at subgroup levels, at the expense of the patriotism of whole-group unity. Emotionally united clans are greeted with hostility in our society unless they are tiny and harmless. Nepotism is almost a bad word. Family means immediate family, or else it too may become a bad word. Subgroups involving recognizable morphological differences, especially when they also involve declarations of first allegiance to one's subgroup rather than patriotism to the whole, have led to the genocidal horrors of history. Organized religion is not permitted to permeate the government unless it includes the clear majority or the unchallenged power structures; and, as I see it, the unity of large societies is most fearsome when there is a coincidence of government and intense religion or some surrogate of religion as we ordinarily think of it.

I have been speaking as if culture is just biological adaptation. Long ago George Gaylord Simpson said exactly that about culture (Simpson, 1964), and he said that the sooner we recognize it the better off we will be. The problem then was that Simpson and his contemporaries were too far from understanding what biological adaptation is (Williams, 1966). Many investigators have suggested that the advent of culture in human history marked the end of biological adaptation—at least in regard to behavior—or, more recently, that the only way we can understand is through complex analyses of the degrees of separateness of the processes of inheritance of culture and inheritance of other aspects of phenotypes, or by abandoning the whole idea that culture changes in adaptive directions.

What is the heart of this puzzling issue? It seems to me that it is not heritability in the usual sense: After all, cultural changes can be more heritable than genes or they can lack any heritability at all, and because they are heritable through learning. they can go back and forth between these two extremes within one generation. There are two real questions in comparing cultural and organic evolution: The first is not how heritable is culture but when is it heritable and when not: Who decides, and why? The second question is: How do the causes of cultural changes relate to the causes of their persistence and the needs of the practitioners? We know that in organic evolution the causes of genetic mutations are independent of the causes of natural selection, and this is what depresses the rates of mutations and also accounts for the inertia of evolutionary change. Cultural evolution differs, because the causes of cultural novelties are not always independent of the needs of individuals and groups. Cultural novelties are born in the mind's eyes of individual entrepeneurs and planning groups: They have functions, as it were, before they are actually expressed. This, and the mode of inheritance of culture (learning), which allows swift reversals, are the reasons why culture tends increasingly to outrace genetic change. Whatever inertia culture possesses will be owing to the endlessly complex compromises, stalemates, and power plays that derive from conflicts of interests at all different levels (Alexander, 1979).

To discover how cultural change departs from genetic interests we must know who institutes cultural changes, and why, who accepts and resists them, and why, and what are the effects of the novelty that descends upon us at rates ever-increasing and wholly unanticipatable by the forces that produce the human capacity for culture and thus indirectly the novelty itself.

It is, of course, difficult to understand how culture can be the outcome of the collective efforts by individuals at genetic reproduction, and the surrogates of such efforts in novel environments. The most difficult of all questions in this regard, I think, is how slow directional changes in culture—those occurring across many generations—could reflect such efforts. Again, I believe that the answer will come from considering how the individuals and subgroups within any society turn the existing pattern of culture to their own ends, given the unbelievably complex networks of competition and conflicts of interest that typify every human social group. I think, especially, that we will need to know a very great deal about how individuals weigh the consequences of different possible actions by themselves in terms of how others might view them; and by different possible actions I mean to include mere expressions of agreement and disagreement, and satisfaction and dissatisfaction, with particular rules or attitudes discernible within the society. Changes like the institution of women's rights or the suppression of injustice toward minorities come about because increasing proportions of the population decide it is in their interest, and the effect snowballs—sometimes only with special pressure—as more and more individuals sense the shift of attitude and recognize the value of going along. And always, I would say, there lies behind the terribly difficult analysis of all such cultural phenomena the simple theory of human history that is developing largely from evolutionary biology—unless someone proves it wrong or comes up with a more reasonable alternative, which I regard as exceedingly unlikely.

Our culture emphasizes the immediate family and the individual's set of relatives, as separate from that of every other individual. When subgroup coalitions are discouraged and each individual's personal collection of relatives is continually identified and set before that individual, freer rein is given, at least incidentally, to the individual's abilities and tendencies to serve his own interests so long as, paradoxically, he does not pursue them by establishing too-powerful kin groups or harems. Cultural anthropologists such as Schneider (1968) and Murdock (1949), the sociologist Talcott Parsons (1954), and others have all remarked on the absence of subgroup unity and the emphasis on the individual in the large societies possessing what I have here and elsewhere called socially imposed monogamy.

There follows, perhaps, the capitalistic encouragement of individual initiative in societies with socially imposed monogamy. Moreover, in these most unified societies we all stand to gain from creativity by individuals—hence, one suspects, copyright and patent laws. And we have used our ingenuity in these societies to form new kinds of coalitions—for example, some called corporations and others called cooperatives—both of these, despite their different connotations to some, securing for their members and their immediate families more resources than others would otherwise allow or see as fair shares. Deprived by group rules of the ability to spread resources amongst their clans for the precise purposes of history, and imbued with the drive and creativity of a relatively unleashed individualism, many have become what might be called obscenely wealthy in the expanding economies characterizing these cultures. And the fortunes tend often to stay together because they have come to involve items like money and shares of stock which, unlike the farms and herds of old, can be inflated in value by extreme subdivision; and these are usually transmitted to the few members of immediate families rather than dispersed to enrich the power of growing clans.

Paradoxically, in this urban world of unprecedented novelty and fluidity, and also unprecedented human cooperativeness and competitiveness, the individuality we induce may also cause us to be unusually susceptible to the human brand of loneliness. I quote the cultural anthropologist, Anthony F. C. Wallace (1961), in a statement utterly consistent with the new evolutionary theory of human nature:

> The humanist—the poet, the novelist, the dramatist, the historian—has tended to approach . . . with a sense of tragedy (or humor) . . . the paradox, so apparent to him, that despite the continuing existence of culture and the group, the individual is always partly alone in his motivation, moving in a charmed circle of feelings and perceptions which he cannot completely share with any other human being. This awareness of the limits of human communication, of the impossibility, despite all the labor of God, Freud, and the Devil, of one man fully understanding another, of the loneliness of existence, is not confined to any cult of writers; it is a pan-human theme.

And so, with our individualized sets of genes and our history of individualized interests, we humans write poetry, philosophize, seek adoption by surrogate kin groups, sometimes commit suicide, and travel on through history trying to decide where we should go from here, given what we seem to have found out about where we have been. A part of that finding out is the knowledge of the depth and nature of our conflicts of interest during history, measurable only by carrying our analyses to the level of the gene.

The other part of the finding out is the realization of the profundity and unpredictability of the consequences of the ever-accelerating introduction of real novelty into our environment. So far as I can see, the two ideas together put the lie to any ordinary meaning of the phrase ''genetically determined'' as applied to human behavior, and they cast much doubt on our ability to prognosticate the so-called ''biological limits'' of human nature or the most appropriate behavior or morality of the future. Surely we can take a lesson from those who naively tried to establish an all-wise eugenics as soon as genes were discovered. If someone argues that we must at all cost maintain the diversity of the gene pool, let him also realize that without tolerance of a diversity of opinions about what ought to be—about moral codes and ethical opinions—gene diversity is an empty facade.

I will end by noting that the eccentric nature of our culture has not been lost on the more ancient and perhaps more properly human cultures that have had the misfortune to co-exist with it. Thus, an Eskimo version of the origin of our peculiar culture goes as follows: An Inuit girl (and I am told that Inuit means human), to the horror of her parents, accepted her father's dog as a mate. When the father realized how she had gotten pregnant he banished her to a small, desolate island where, true to his worst fears, she gave birth not to a single child but to a whole litter. The island was so small and poor that she could not support her half-human half-animal litter, and so she set them afloat in the only available boat, which happened to be a leaky one, hoping that they would somehow arrive at a better fate. According to the Eskimos, the restless, obsessive, ambitious, and boorish nature of the members of the culture deriving from this original litter is a consequence of their having been thoroughly infused with the necessity of bailing frantically and continuously to keep their leaky boat from going down (from Kurelek, 1978).

Maybe there is a better analogy than this one; then, again, maybe there is not.

ACKNOWLEDGMENTS

I thank Richard D. Howard and Donald W. Tinkle for commenting on the manuscript.

REFERENCES

Alexander, R. D. 1977. Natural selection and the analysis of human sociality. In: C. E. Goulden (ed.). *Changing Scenes in the Natural Sciences: 1776–1976*. Bicentennial Symposium Monograph, Phil. Acad. Nat. Sci. Special Publ. 12:283–337.

———. 1978. Natural selection and societal laws. In: T. Engelhardt and D.Callahan (eds.). Vol. III, *Science and the Foundation of Ethics. Morals, Science and Society*. Hastings-on-Hudson, NY: Hastings Center, pp. 249–290.

———. 1979. *Darwinism and Human Affairs*. Seattle: Univ. Wash. Press.

———, and G. Borgia. 1978. Group selection, altruism, and the levels of organization of life. *Ann. Rev. Ecol. Syst.* 9:449–474.

———, J. L. Hoogland, R. D. Howard, K. M. Noonan, P. W. Sherman. 1979. Sexual dimorphisms and breeding systems in pinnipeds, ungulates, primates, and humans. In: N. A. Chagnon and W. G. Irons (eds.). *Evolutionary Biology and Human Social Behavior: An Anthropological Perspective*. North Scituate, Mass.: Duxbury Press, pp. 402-435.

Barth, F. 1967. On the study of social change. *Amer. Anthrop.* 69:661–669.

Boissevain, J. 1975. *Friends of Friends*. NY: St. Martin's Press.

Borgia, G., and R. D. Alexander (ms). Polygyny and patrilineal inheritance.

Chagnon, N. A. 1974. *Studying the Yanomamö: Studies in Anthropological Method*. NY: Holt, Rinehart, and Winston.

———. 1981. Terminological kinship, genealogical relatedness and village fissioning among the Yanomamö Indians. In: R. D. Alexander and D. W. Tinkle (eds.). *Natural Selection and Social Behavior: Recent Research and Theory*. NY: Chiron Press.

Chagnon, N. A., and W. G. Irons. (eds.). 1979. *Evolutionary Biology and Human Social Behavior: An Anthropological Perspective*. North Scituate: Mass.: Duxbury Press.

Daly, M., and M. T. Wilson. 1979. Abuse and neglect of children in evolutionary perspective. In: R. D. Alexander and D. W. Tinkle (eds.). *Natural Selection and Social Behavior: Recent Research and Theory*. NY: Chiron Press.

Darwin, C. 1859. *On the Origin of Species*. A facsimile of the First Edition with an Introduction by Ernst Mayr, published in 1967. Cambridge, Mass.; Harvard Univ. Press, xviii + 502 pp.

———. 1871. *The Descent of Man and Selection in Relation to Sex*. NY: Appleton, Vol. 1, vi + 409 pp. Vol. II, v + 436 pp.

Dawkins, R. 1976. *The Selfish Gene*. NY: Oxford Univ. Press, xi + 224 pp.

———. 1977. Replicator selection and the extended phenotype. *Zeitschr.fur Tierpsychol*. 47:61–76.

Dickemann, M. 1981. Paternal confidence and dowry competition: A biocultural analysis of Purdah. In: R. D. Alexander and D. W. Tinkle (eds.). *Natural Selection and Social Behavior: Recent Research and Theory*. NY: Chiron Press.

Fisher, R. A. 1930. *The Genetical Theory of Natural Selection*. Clarendon Press, Oxford (2nd edition, 1958; NY: Dover, xiv + 291 pp).

Flinn, M. V. 1981. Uterine vs. agnatic kinship variability and associated cousin marriage preferences. In: R. D. Alexander and D. W. Tinkle (eds.). *Natural Selection and Social Behavior: Recent Research and Theory*. NY: Chiron Press.

Goody, J. 1976. *Production and Reproduction: A Comparative Study of the Domestic Domain*. Cambridge Studies in Social Anthropology, 17. Cambridge: Cambridge: Univ. Press.

Haldane, J. B. S. 1932. *The Causes of Evolution*. London: Longmans, Green, and Co. vi + 235 pp.

Hamilton, W. D. 1963. The evolution of altruistic behaviour. *Amer. Nat*. 97:354–356.

———. 1964. The genetical evolution of social behaviour. I, II, *J.Theor. Biol*. 7:1–52.

Irons, W. 1981. Why lineage exogamy?: In: R. D. Alexander and D. W. Tinkle, (eds.). *Natural Selection and Social Behavior: Recent Research and Theory*. NY: Chiron Press.

Kurelek, W. 1978. *The Last of the Arctic*. Toronto: Pagurian Press, Ltd.

Leigh, E. 1971. *Adaptation and Diversity*. San Francisco: Freeman, Cooper, and Co. 288 pp.

———. 1977. How does selection reconcile individual advantage with the good of the group? *Proc. Natl. Acad. Sci*. 74:4542–4546.

Levi-Strauss, C.1969. *The Elementary Structures of Kinship*. Boston: Beacon.

Masters, R. D. (ms). Classical political philosophy and contemporary biology.

Maynard Smith, J. 1978. *The Evolution of Sex*. Cambridge: Cambridge Univ. Press.

Murdock, G. P. 1949. *Social Structure*. NY: Macmillan.

———1967. *Ethnographic Atlas*. Pittsburgh: Univ. Pittsburgh Press.

———1972. Anthropology's mythology. *Proc. Roy. Anthrop. Inst. Great Britain and Ireland for 1971*, pp. 17–24.

Neel, J.V. 1978. The population structure of an Amerindian tribe, the Yanomamö. *Ann. Rev. Genet*. 12:365–413.

Parsons, T. 1954. *Essays in Sociological Theory* (rev. ed.). Glencoe, Ill.: The Free Press.

Sahlins, M. D. 1976. *The Use and Abuse of Biology: An Anthropological Critique of Sociobiology*. Ann Arbor: Univ. Mich. Press.

Schneider, D. M. 1968. *American Kinship: A Cultural Account*. Englewood Cliffs., NY; Prentice Hall.

Shepfer, J. 1971. Self-imposed incest avoidance and exogamy in second-generation kibbutz adults. Ann Arbor. Mich: Xerox Microfilm Publ. No. 72-811.

Simpson, G. G. 1964. *This View of Life*. NY: Harcourt, Brace and World.

Spiro, M. F. 1958. *Children of the Kibbutz*. Cambridge, Mass.: Harvard Univ. Press. xix + 500 pp.

Tylor, E. B. 1889. On a method of investigating the development of institutions; applied to laws of marriage and descent. *J. Roy. Anthropol. Inst*. 18:245–267.

Wallace, A. F. C. 1961. The psychic unity of human groups. In: Kaplan, B. (ed.). 1961. *Studying Personality Cross-Culturally*, NY: Harper and Row, pp.129–163.

Williams, G. C. 1957. Pleiotropy, natural selection, and the evolution of senescence. *Evol*. 11:398–411.

Williams, G. C. 1966. *Adaptation and Natural Selection*. NJ: Princeton Univ. Press. x + 307 pp.

———. 1975. *Sex and evolution*. NJ: Princeton Univ Press, x + 200 pp.

Wolf, A. P. 1966. Childhood association, sexual attraction, and the incest taboo: A Chinese case. *Am. Anthropol*. 68:883–898.

Wolf, A. P. 1968. Adopt a daughter-in-law, marry a sister: A Chinese solution to the problem of incest taboo. *Am. Anthropol*. 70:864–874.

Index